Nuclear Weapon Tests:
Prohibition or Limitation?

sipri

Stockholm International Peace Research Institute

SIPRI is an independent international institute for research into problems of peace and conflict, especially those of arms control and disarmament. It was established in 1966 to commemorate Sweden's 150 years of unbroken peace.

The Institute is financed mainly by the Swedish Parliament. The staff, the Governing Board and the Scientific Council are international.

The Governing Board and Scientific Council are not responsible for the views expressed in the publications of the Institute.

Governing Board

Ambassador Ernst Michanek, Chairman (Sweden)
Egon Bahr (Federal Republic of Germany)
Professor Francesco Calogero (Italy)
Dr Max Jakobson (Finland)
Professor Dr Karlheinz Lohs (German Democratic Republic)
Professor Emma Rothschild (United Kingdom)
Sir Brian Urquhart (United Kingdom)
The Director

Director

Dr Walther Stützle (Federal Republic of Germany)

sipri

Stockholm International Peace Research Institute
Pipers väg 28, S-171 73 Solna, Sweden
Cable: PEACERESEARCH STOCKHOLM
Telephone: 46 8/55 97 00

Nuclear Weapon Tests: Prohibition or Limitation?

Edited by
Jozef Goldblat and David Cox

sipri
Stockholm International Peace Research Institute

CIIPS
Canadian Institute for International Peace and Security

OXFORD UNIVERSITY PRESS
1988

Oxford University Press, Walton Street, Oxford OX2 6DP

Oxford New York Toronto
Delhi Bombay Calcutta Madras Karachi
Petaling Jaya Singapore Hong Kong Tokyo
Nairobi Dar es Salaam Cape Town
Melbourne Auckland

and associated companies in
Beirut Berlin Ibadan Nicosia

Oxford is a trade mark of Oxford University Press

Published in the United States
by Oxford University Press, New York

British Library Cataloguing in Publication Data
Nuclear weapon tests: prohibition or
    limitation?
    1. Nuclear weapons (International law)
    2. Nuclear weapons—testing
    I. Goldblat. Jozef   II. Cox, David
    355.8'25119   JX1974.7
    ISBN 0–19–829120–5

Library of Congress Cataloging in Publication Data
Data available

Set by Wyvern Typesetting Limited
Printed and bound in
Great Britain by Biddles Ltd.,
Guildford and King's Lynn

Contents

Part 2. Overview of nuclear explosions

Part 3. The historical record

Part 4. The question of verification

Chapter X.   Techniques to evade detection of nuclear tests

Part 5. Consequences of the cessation or further limitation of nuclear tests

Chapter XVIII. Political, strategic and psychological effects of a nuclear test ban

Annexes

Foreword

This publication is the product of a study jointly conducted by the Stockholm International Peace Research Institute (SIPRI) and the Canadian Institute for International Peace and Security (CIIPS). It deals with one of the most hotly discussed items on the agenda of international arms control negotiations: nuclear weapon tests. The aim of the publication is to give an analytical review of the complex technical and political issues involved in a possible cessation or limitation of these tests, and to present a wide range of authoritative opinions on this subject.

The comments made by the editors of the book, Mr Jozef Goldblat and Mr David Cox, as well as the conclusions drawn by them, are intended as an informed contribution to the debate among governmental and non-governmental experts, with the view to facilitating the achievement of a meaningful arms control measure. The book may also be useful to those laymen who are concerned about how to control and ultimately stop the nuclear arms race.

Walther Stützle
Director, SIPRI
Stockholm

Geoffrey Pearson
Director, CIIPS
Ottawa

November 1987

Preface

Among the international arms control measures so far agreed or proposed for consideration, constraints on nuclear testing occupy a special place. Apart from the possible health hazards they present, nuclear explosions are the most visible manifestation of the arms race. During the past three decades, therefore, the pressure of public opinion for their cessation has been especially strong. This pressure has brought about certain limitations on testing, but a total test ban—that is, a prohibition of all nuclear weapon explosions for all time—has remained an elusive goal.

The advocates of a comprehensive ban consider it to be the first indispensable step to halting and reversing the nuclear rivalry among the great powers, as well as an essential component in the programme for the prevention of a further spread of nuclear weapons. Others see it as a threat to the system of international security based on nuclear deterrence, and as a measure irrelevant to nuclear weapon proliferation. The arguments for and against the ban have changed over time, and there exists an abundant literature dealing with various facets of the problem. What seems to be lacking is an integrated treatment of its technical and political aspects. It was with the intention of filling this gap that SIPRI and CIIPS embarked on a joint project, inviting contributions from leading physicists, nuclear weapon designers, seismologists, international lawyers, strategic analysts and political scientists, as well as former governmental advisers and arms control negotiators. The papers prepared by these experts were discussed at a symposium convened by the two institutes in October 1986, at Montebello, Canada, and chaired by the undersigned directors of the project.

In addition to the authors, the participants in the Montebello symposium included: Mr William Barton, Chairman of the Board, CIIPS; Mr Bertrand Goldschmidt, former Chairman of the Governing Board of the International Atomic Energy Agency and former French representative on this Board, Paris; Mr George Ignatieff, President, Science for Peace, Toronto; Mr Robert Jeffries, Program Director, Verification and Safeguards, Los Alamos National Laboratory, Los Alamos; Mr Albert Legault, Professor of Political Studies, Université de Laval, Quebec; Mr Robert S. Norris, Senior Research Associate, Natural Resources Defense Council, Washington, DC; and Mr Gregory Vink, US Congress, Office of Technology Assessment, Washington, DC.

The resulting book has been organized into five parts. Part One contains the editors' summary of and comments on the main points made in the remaining four parts, as well as their own conclusions. Part Two is an overview of the problem of nuclear explosions, with particular emphasis on the significance of continued testing for the development of new weapon designs. Part Three provides a historical survey of the negotiations for the cessation or limitation of nuclear tests, as well as an assessment of the test limitation treaties so far concluded. Part Four describes the existing technical capabilities for detecting possible violations of a complete test ban and discusses ways to verify compliance with a ban on all but very-low-yield tests. Part Five reviews the present attitudes of certain states towards nuclear testing and examines the possible military and political consequences of a test ban.

Provided as annexes are: texts of the international agreements containing limitations on nuclear explosions; major official proposals for a comprehensive ban; descriptions of seismological techniques and equipment used in monitoring the tests; and data on nuclear explosions since their inception in 1945.

The editors were assisted by a team which included Jane Boulden, Doina Cioiu, Ragnhild Ferm, Peter Lomas, Marianne Lyons and James Moore.

Connie Wall was director of the publication.

Jozef Goldblat   *David Cox*
SIPRI   CIIPS

Joint project directors and co-editors

Acronyms

ACDA	Arms Control and Disarmament Agency (US)
ACVC	Arms Control Verification Committee
AEC	Atomic Energy Commission (US)
AEDS	Atomic Energy Detection System
CD	Conference on Disarmament
CORRTEX	Continuous Reflectometry for Radius versus Time Experiments
CTB(T)	comprehensive test ban (treaty)
DARPA	Defense Advanced Research Projects Agency (US)
DOD	Department of Defense (US)
DOE	Department of Energy (US)
DSS	deep seismic sounding (technique)
EMP	Electromagnetic pulse
ENDC	Eighteen-Nation Disarmament Committee
FOA	Swedish National Defence Research Institute (Försvarets Forsknings-anstalt)
GSE	Group of Scientific Experts (CD)
GTS	Global Telecommunications System
HE	high explosive
HEDF	High Energy Density Facility
IAEA	International Atomic Energy Agency
ICF	inertial confinement fusion
ICRP	International Commission on Radiological Protection
IHE	insensitive high explosive
IONDS	Integrated Operational Nuclear Detection System
ISC	International Seismological Centre
LASA	Large Aperture Seismic Array
LLNL	Lawrence Livermore National Laboratory
LYTTB(T)	low-yield threshold test ban (treaty)
MOD	Ministry of Defence (UK)
NDS	nuclear (explosion) detection satellite
NORESS	Norwegian Regional Seismic Array
NORSAR	Norwegian Seismic Array
NPT	Non-Proliferation Treaty
NRDC	Natural Resources Defense Council (US)
NSS	national seismic station
NST	Nuclear and Space Talks
NTM	national technical means (of verification)

NTS	Nevada Test Site
NWS	nuclear weapon state
OSI	on-site inspection
PNE	peaceful nuclear explosion
PNET	Peaceful Nuclear Explosions Treaty
PNUTS	Probable Nuclear Underground Test Site
PSAC	President's Science Advisory Committee (US)
PTBT	Partial Test Ban Treaty
SALT	Strategic Arms Limitation Talks
SDI	Strategic Defense Initiative (US)
TSM	test site monitoring (seismic station network)
TTBT	Threshold Test Ban Treaty
USGS	US Geological Survey
VLYTTB(T)	very-low-yield threshold test ban (treaty)
WMO	World Meteorological Organization
WWSSN	World Wide Standardized Seismograph Network

Part 1
Summary and conclusions

Summary and conclusions

Jozef Goldblat and David Cox

I. Introduction

The atomic era began with a test conducted by the United States on 16 July 1945 at Alamogordo, New Mexico. The test confirmed the conclusions reached by a team of scientists that an explosion several orders of magnitude greater than that brought about by conventional explosives was possible. Such an explosion can be produced by an assembly of fissile material exceeding a critical mass. The critical mass is the smallest mass needed for a self-sustaining chain reaction, in which the number of neutrons released from fissile nuclei and absorbed by other fissile nuclei equals the number of neutrons lost by absorption in non-fissile material or by escape from the system. At Alamogordo, for the first time in history, an amount of energy equal to that released by 20 000 tons of the conventional explosive TNT was released by fissioning the nuclei of plutonium in an instantaneous chain reaction. The first US bomb that released energy by splitting the nuclei of uranium was exploded over Hiroshima three weeks later. It had an explosive yield of about 13 kt. In 1949, the Soviet Union ended the US monopoly in the field by exploding its own atomic device. Subsequently, Britain (in 1952), France (1960) and China (1964) joined the 'club' of atomic weapon states.

Even more powerful explosive devices, so-called thermonuclear (or hydrogen) weapons, were developed and successfully tested in the 1950s. These rely on the fusion of light nuclei, such as those of hydrogen isotopes, brought to the extremely high temperatures which are produced by the fission of plutonium or uranium. Even more energy can be released in a fission–fusion–fission process, in which the neutrons generated by fusion are allowed to split the uranium nuclei in a uranium 'blanket' surrounding the weapon. Atomic fission weapons and thermonuclear weapons, including the fission–fusion–fission devices, have all come to be called 'nuclear weapons'.

All explosions which result from the release of a large amount of energy in a confined volume create a rapid increase in the temperature and pressure and consequently convert the surrounding materials into hot, compressed gases which expand, causing a shock wave in the atmosphere, in the ground or in water. Nuclear explosions produce other important effects as well. These are thermal radiation and nuclear radiation, the latter involving harmful rays released both immediately after the explosion and over a longer period of time.

By November 1987, well over 1600 nuclear test explosions of different sizes and varieties had been carried out in different environments by the five nuclear weapon powers mentioned above—the great majority of them by the USA and the USSR. (In addition, one was conducted by India, which, however, maintains that it has no nuclear weapons.) A number of concerns arise in connection with this continuous testing activity, regarding the necessity for explosive tests; the difficulties encountered in the negotiations for a test ban and the value of the treaties they have produced; the problems of verification; the consequences of a possible cessation of tests; and prospects for further test limitations. The following sections address these questions.

II. How necessary was it for the nuclear weapon powers to test a nuclear explosive before building a weapon stockpile?

The first nuclear test explosion was considered indispensable for verification of the feasibility of achieving a large explosion by fission. The material used was plutonium. However, the uranium fission device exploded over Hiroshima, which contained a simpler mechanism, was not tested before being used; such was the scientists' confidence in the correctness of its design. It can, nevertheless, be argued that the use of the bomb was in itself a test. Indeed, the United States possessed no more than two atomic bombs when it decided to employ them in war. Even more essential was the testing of a thermonuclear device, for it is held impossible otherwise to gain confidence in the construction of a fusion bomb. Only after successful tests did the United States start manufacturing nuclear weapons for its stockpile. States which later joined the nuclear 'club' acted similarly.

III. Why were further test explosions needed after nuclear weapons had been developed, manufactured and stockpiled?

New weapon designs

Further testing was required primarily to validate refinements in the design of weapons. It was also necessary to achieve the greatest possible efficiency and economy in the use of fissionable and fusionable materials and, at the same time, make the weapon assembly compatible with the means of delivery, as dictated by current military needs. Thus, while the Hiroshima bomb was designed so as to be compatible with the bomb-bays of the B-29 aircraft, the subsequent proliferation of delivery vehicles called for a variety of weapons of reduced dimensions.

Warheads in the present nuclear arsenals bear little resemblance to the bombs that ushered in the nuclear age. In particular, the development of modern strategic bombers and of strategic missiles equipped with multiple, independently targetable re-entry vehicles (MIRVs) placed a premium on small sizes of nuclear warheads and on optimal yield-to-weight ratios, because one bomber or missile had to accommodate several bombs or re-entry vehicles in addition to guidance systems. Thus new warhead designs became necessary to achieve the desired objectives.

A new weapon design currently requires a testing programme amounting, for the USA, to some 6 explosions or more—depending on the degree of complexity—to 4–5 for the UK, and (according to press reports) to as many as 20 for France, and culminating in a proof test to certify the model for stockpile and deployment. Designs not fully tested through explosions are not deemed reliable. The use of simulation with supercomputers can substitute certain development test explosions, but many weapon designers are sceptical as to the possibility of drastically reducing the number of explosive tests. In any event, at least one explosion of a new or significantly re-designed warhead at or near full yield is generally considered to be indispensable.

It should be added that testing is necessary not only to modernize the first two generations of nuclear weapons—the fission and fusion explosive devices—but also to develop so-called 'third-generation' weapons. These constitute a refinement of the techniques involved in fission/fusion processes for the purpose of achieving special weapon effects for given military missions. For example, the enhanced-radiation weapon has been developed to achieve radiation levels sufficient to incapacitate enemy military forces while minimizing thermal and blast effects as well as radioactive fall-out damaging to civilians and friendly forces. The electromagnetic pulse (EMP), generated by a nuclear detonation, and means of maximizing its effects to damage or disturb electronic devices and disrupt the enemy's command and control capabilities, have also been considered. Another third-generation weapon, the X-ray laser driven by nuclear explosives, is being experimentally tested as one of the possible components of the US Strategic Defense Initiative (SDI) programme. It seeks to maximize X-ray emissions and concentrate the rays in a single beam which can be aimed at a ballistic missile and destroy it in an early phase of its flight. It could also be used to attack space-based elements of a ballistic missile defence system. A great number of nuclear test explosions may be needed for the development of a nuclear-powered X-ray laser.

It is evident that a stop to nuclear testing would also put a stop to the development of essentially new nuclear weapons.

Reliability of the stockpiled weapons

The majority view of nuclear weapon designers, at least in the United States, appears to be that explosive testing is necessary to ensure that weapons which have been deployed or stockpiled continue to be effective. In support of this view, it has been claimed that one-third of US weapon designs introduced into the stockpile after 1958 required such testing for the resolution of reliability problems, and that three-fourths of these problems could not have been discovered and subsequently corrected if nuclear explosive testing had been discontinued. It is likely, however, that the problems that arose were due to design defects rather than to the deterioration of properly constructed weapons. During the period of the test moratorium from 1958 to 1961, some proportion of the newly designed weapons were manufactured and stockpiled without prior testing. It might be added that in certain important cases the defects that were later ascertained related to the yield magnitude rather than to the failure to achieve a nuclear explosion.

It is sometimes asserted, too, that the strict design requirements imposed by the relatively limited payloads of US missiles, and the severe safety and security requirements imposed by US authorities, have necessitated the optimization of weapon designs and thereby increased the possibility of subtle design flaws or susceptibility to unforeseen errors which might emerge only after deployment. US designers assert that Soviet weapons, which are less complex and which are destined for missiles with larger payloads, are considerably less vulnerable to design errors than their US counterparts. They therefore claim that cessation of tests or a moratorium would, for this reason, favour the Soviet Union.

On the basis of experience, one might respond that those weapons which have not been tested at full yield at least once should not be admitted to the stockpile. As regards stockpiled weapons which have been tested, some qualified experts contend that their reliability can be ensured indefinitely without recourse to explosive testing. As far as is known, none of the nuclear weapon states performs much explosive testing for the sole purpose of reliability. Strict adherence to stockpile surveillance programmes, including non-nuclear radiographic, chemical or mechanical testing, may be sufficient. Indeed, meticulous examination of the assembly by visual and electronic means and, if necessary, correction or replacement of faulty components by using materials manufactured in full conformity with the original, proven design specifications, could deal with the ageing problems most frequently encountered in stockpiled weapons. In any case, an explosive test, which destroys the seemingly defective weapon, may not provide confirmation of the diagnosis. Proponents of this standpoint also tend to view with scepticism the suggestion that more 'robust' Soviet designs are less prone to deterioration and point out that physical degradation, such as corrosion, is not related to the size of the weapon and is likely to affect Soviet and US weapons alike. If, however, less sophisticated nuclear warheads appear to be more reliable, they could certainly be designed by US weapon laboratories.

At most, over an extended period of time, a programme to ensure continued reliability might include a replacement, without testing, of certain weapons in the stockpile with newly built weapons of identical design.

Effects and physics tests

Another of the purposes of nuclear testing is to check the effects of an explosion on military equipment. Since warheads of proven design and yield are used for such tests, a secondary purpose, that of confirming the reliability of a given stockpiled weapon design, is simultaneously served. However, considering the impressive number and variety of nuclear explosions carried out so far, it is doubtful whether effects tests alone would constitute a sufficient reason for continued testing. Even less justified, at least from the point of view of arms control, seem to be field explosions to study the complexity of the physics of a nuclear detonation. Such experiments as inertial confinement fusion (ICF) research on the application of thermonuclear energy can be conducted in a contained laboratory setting at extremely low yields. They may have some potential utility for the military, but are not easy to detect and cannot be covered by a test ban treaty anyway.

Security and safety tests

Improved or additional protection of nuclear weapons may require testing, but the testing does not need to be explosive. Should, however, protective devices change the nuclear assembly or its components significantly enough to modify the design of the weapon, explosive testing may prove necessary to check its performance. Whether such far-reaching changes are essential to satisfy security needs is debatable. Many nuclear weapons are deemed already to be adequately protected by the so-called permissive action links permitting the use of weapons only by authorized personnel, as well as by use-denial mechanisms disabling the weapons when their use is attempted by unauthorized persons. Possible improvements of the protective systems would be marginal and could probably be made without affecting weapon design, in so far as they relate chiefly to the mechanical and electrical components of the weapon.

Safety devices on nuclear weapons are intended to prevent inadvertent or accidental explosions. But in this respect, too, considerable advances have been made. Past accidents with nuclear weapons did not result in explosions of nuclear materials. Detonations of the non-nuclear explosive component have, however, taken place, causing the dispersal of radioactive materials. To minimize the risks of such occurrences, weapon designers have in most weapons replaced the conventional explosive serving to initiate the fission or fission–fusion reaction with a so-called insensitive high explosive (IHE) which is less prone to accidental detonation. This replacement has provided an additional reason for explosive testing, because one could not assume with certainty that the IHE would produce exactly the same effect as a conventional explosive. It is arguable whether safety tests will be needed also in the future. In peacetime, safety concerns could be effectively addressed by prohibiting such activities as the routine flights of aircraft carrying nuclear weapons, which present the greatest danger of mishap.

Need to retain the technology base

It is asserted, mainly by the US military, that tests are needed to retain a core of experienced weapon designers, whose accumulated knowledge is indispensable for maintaining confidence in the nuclear stockpile. Without the incentives provided by continued testing, they contend, leading designers would be tempted to move away from nuclear weapon laboratories to other careers—a trend which might prove irreversible for the United States because of its freer job market, but presumably not for the Soviet Union with its different social system. Others suggest that explosive testing does not need to be part of the nuclear laboratory programmes and that, in any event, it would always be possible to offer compensatory research, in which those scientists currently engaged in test explosions could be fully occupied. A staff of knowledgeable individuals who are capable of producing new weapons could thus be retained, should that be judged necessary.

It is clear that modernization of nuclear weapons is the central purpose of testing. There is a controversy as to whether checking the reliability of stockpiled weapons requires explosive testing, but even the proponents of such testing admit that a very small number of explosions would suffice. As regards other reasons, no combination of them would make up a compelling case for the continuation of nuclear detonations.

IV. Why did negotiations for a nuclear test ban begin, and why did they fail?

The idea of stopping all nuclear test explosions grew out of the international concern about nuclear fall-out, especially after the major radiation accident which followed the 1 March 1954 US Bravo test in the Pacific. Thereafter, concerted anti-nuclear movements among scientists and the general public gathered momentum. In addition, in the late 1950s, a number of influential government officials in the USA and the USSR came to regard the test ban as a first step towards more comprehensive discussions on arms control between East and West. On the US side, an additional incentive may have been the belief that unlimited testing by both superpowers could, over time, decrease the strategic lead of the United States over the Soviet Union, primarily in the field of nuclear warhead sophistication. On the Soviet side, the search for the cessation of tests may have been motivated by an apprehension that further testing could widen the technological gap between the two powers to the benefit of the United States. Equally essential was the shared interest of the two powers in stopping or at least dampening the spread of nuclear weapons among nations; in the early days the prime targets of these policies were China, France and West Germany. There were thus both short-term and long-term considerations in negotiating a test ban. From the start, however, the negotiators encountered serious difficulties.

In 1958–62, during the first extended period of negotiation for a comprehensive test ban, verification was a particularly contentious issue. Despite continuous advances in the techniques of checking compliance, it had not proved possible to obtain assurance that all nuclear explosions would be detected with the use of remote instrumentation. Once this was recognized by the negotiating parties, it was judged necessary to provide for on-site inspections on the territory of a state suspected of violation. The number and modalities of such inspections, however, soon became subjects of acrimonious and inconclusive disputes.

Underlying the verification issue was the overriding mutual suspicion between the Soviet Union on the one hand and the United States and the United Kingdom on the other. In this period of the cold war, growing mistrust was undermining the very concept of a comprehensive test ban. From the defence community of the United States came the objection that a test ban would debilitate US nuclear strategy by preventing the development of new weapons, while the Soviet Union could exploit possible loopholes in verification arrangements to clandestinely proceed with weapon modernization. Soviet obstructiveness on the question of 'intrusive' inspections, and the escalation of Soviet military preparedness following the shooting down in 1960 of the US U-2 reconnaissance aircraft over Soviet territory, strengthened the sceptics in their claim that the ban was being sought by Moscow for the sole purpose of arresting Western weapon modernization and consolidating its own position. In spite of repeatedly affirmed intentions to achieve a test ban, neither the United States nor the Soviet Union seemed at that time to be genuinely interested in such a ban. Both sides were conveniently hiding behind the problem of verification: one insisting on measures which were obviously unacceptable, and the other refusing to accept measures which were obviously indispensable.

Nevertheless, the test issue remained on the agenda of international arms control discussions. In 1980, the UK, the USA and the USSR, then engaged in trilateral talks, seemed to be closer to a test ban treaty than ever before. The negotiators were agreed on the following important points. The treaty, initially to be valid for three years, would prohibit any nuclear weapon test explosion in any environment; a moratorium on nuclear explosions for peaceful purposes would be established until acceptable arrangements for conducting them were worked out; the treaty would enter into force upon ratification by 20 signatory governments, including those of the three nuclear weapon powers initiating it; and a conference would be held at an 'appropriate' time to review its operation. A large measure of consensus was reached even on the question of verification, including the possibility of on-site inspection. In 1982, however, at the initiative of the United States, these talks were suspended *sine die*.

In later years, especially since the initiation of the SDI programme, parts of which may require nuclear tests, the United States came to consider a complete ban on nuclear explosions only as a 'long-term' objective and only as a component of a large arms control package. Consequently, the USA has opposed a test ban as a separate measure, regardless of its verifiability, challenged the Soviet contention that a halt to nuclear testing is a necessary step towards diminishing the nuclear threat, and refused to emulate the Soviet Union when it proclaimed in 1985 a unilateral moratorium on nuclear explosions and abstained from all testing for over a year and a half. The negotiations for a comprehensive nuclear test ban have ended in limbo. The long-running controversy over the mandate of a working committee to deal with the subject of tests at the Geneva-based Conference on Disarmament (CD) served simply as a distraction from the fundamental difference between the main partners as to whether cessation of nuclear explosions was at all a desirable measure.

V. What is the value of the test limitation treaties which have been signed?

Thirty years of deliberations and negotiations on a total prohibition of nuclear test explosions have resulted in only partial agreements. The parties thereto may conduct nuclear explosions solely underground, and the yields of the explosions must not exceed the agreed limit.

The 1963 Partial Test Ban Treaty

The multilateral treaty banning nuclear weapon tests in the atmosphere, in outer space and under water, called the Partial (or Limited) Test Ban Treaty (PTBT or LTBT), was signed on 5 August 1963. Its conclusion at that particular time was prompted chiefly by the need to improve US–Soviet relations, which had been severely strained by the 1962 Cuban missile crisis, and to bring about a general relaxation of international tension. The fact that both superpowers had by then already carried out extensive series of tests in the atmosphere and were prepared for testing to be continued underground, reduced the cost of their mutual 'sacrifice'. The Treaty entered into force on 10 October 1963; by 1 January 1987 it had as many as 116 adherents.

It is important to remember that the PTBT was generally considered to be a transitional arrangement: the parties stated their determination to conclude a treaty resulting in the 'permanent banning of all nuclear test explosions'. Underground explosions, whatever their purpose, have not been covered by the Treaty, but they are not allowed if they cause radioactive debris to be present outside the territorial limits of the state under whose jurisdiction or control they are conducted. The pledge concerning the discontinuance of all explosions has not been fulfilled. The US Government's statement of 1982 that it would 'set aside' efforts to negotiate a comprehensive ban on nuclear testing was justifiably regarded by many states as impeding full implementation of the PTBT.

Adherence to the PTBT, though wide, is not universal. Two nuclear weapon powers, France and China, have not joined it. France argued that the Treaty had only limited practical importance, and reaffirmed its intent to proceed with its own nuclear buildup; China criticized the Treaty as not encompassing general disarmament or a ban on underground tests. Both nations eventually gave up atmospheric testing through unilateral statements of renunciation: France in 1975, after a suit had been brought against it by Australia and New Zealand in the International Court of Justice; and China some 10 years later, after a series of protests made by both neighbouring and distant countries against radioactive contamination resulting from Chinese nuclear explosions in the atmosphere. Such a militarily important non-nuclear weapon country as Pakistan, which refuses formally to forgo the acquisition of nuclear weapons, is also missing from the list of parties. But even if Pakistan or another 'nuclear threshold country' decided to cross the threshold to become a nuclear weapon state, it would most probably not do so by detonating a nuclear device in an environment prohibited by such a widely adhered-to treaty as the PTBT and expose itself to international opprobrium. The PTBT appears to have become a norm of behaviour to be observed by parties and non-parties alike.

The PTBT has complicated the development of very high-yield weapons and has made impossible full-scale operational testing of weapons in the environments in which they are meant to be used—notably in the atmosphere. It has also rendered it difficult to measure the effects of the EMP on military and civilian equipment. However, these restrictions have not prevented the USA, the UK and the USSR from satisfying other military requirements. Moreover, by testing underground, they deny important intelligence information to other states about the characteristics of their weapons that could otherwise be gathered from debris produced by atmospheric tests. The rate of testing by the Soviet Union and the United States increased after the PTBT went into force.

The PTBT has helped curb the radioactive pollution of the atmosphere and reduced the health hazards associated with nuclear fall-out. It has thus made an important contribution to the environmental protection regime. In national policies it marked the first major success of the proponents of arms control, who thus managed to overcome the resistance of the proponents of an uncontrolled arms race. In the international arena it became an obstacle to the wider spread of nuclear weapons and paved the way for the 1968 Non-Proliferation Treaty (NPT).

The 1974 Threshold Test Ban Treaty

Talks on a comprehensive test ban resumed after entry into force of the PTBT, but the focus on technical matters precluded systematic discussion of the provisions of a new agreement. The UN General Assembly adopted resolutions deploring or condemning nuclear tests and calling for their complete cessation, but the difficulties encountered gave rise to proposals for a partial approach to a ban on underground nuclear weapon testing. Appeals were made by non-nuclear weapon states for transitional measures of restraint that would suspend testing, or limit or reduce the size and number of tests, pending the entry into force of a comprehensive ban. For a long time, these proposals and appeals were ignored by the main testing powers, the USA and the USSR, until, in the summer of 1974, both countries changed their positions. On 3 July of that year they signed a bilateral treaty on the limitation of underground nuclear weapon tests, which came to be called the Threshold Test Ban Treaty (TTBT).

The scope of the obligations under the TTBT is very limited. The United States and the Soviet Union undertook to 'prohibit, to prevent and not to carry out' any underground nuclear weapon test having a yield which exceeds 150 kt beginning on 31 March 1976. The official justification for setting a distant date for the entry into force of the yield limitation was that considerable time would be needed to make all verification arrangements. A more important reason, however, was that some warheads then under development were planned to have a yield exceeding the agreed limit. Testing, therefore, had to take place before the restrictions became effective. Tests with yields exceeding the threshold were in fact hastily conducted by both the USA and the USSR after the signature of the TTBT and before it was to enter into effect. Although the parties committed themselves to restrict the number of tests to a minimum, neither US nor Soviet testing activities slackened.

Ratification of the TTBT has not taken place because of opposition in the USA to making it formally and legally binding. The parties stated that they would observe the agreed upon limitation during the pre-ratification period. Despite its continuing unratified status, the TTBT has to some extent constrained the development of new high-yield warheads. The yield limitation has also made it difficult for the parties to carry out certain stockpile-sampling, because the existing large thermonuclear weapons cannot be tested at their full yield. (Most strategic nuclear warheads in the superpowers' arsenals have yields in excess of 150 kt.) Moreover, cessation of explosions in the megaton range has had a positive environmental effect: it has further reduced the risks of radioactive venting and of ground disturbance. All this does not alter the fact that the TTBT has hardly contributed to the cessation of the nuclear arms race. The 150-kt yield threshold is too high to be really meaningful: the parties do not experience onerous restraints in continuing their nuclear weapon programmes. Nor does the agreed threshold reflect present verification capabilities: the detection and identification of nuclear explosions of far lower size are possible.

The TTBT was seen by many as a substitute for, rather than a step towards, a comprehensive treaty. It was criticized in both the Conference on Disarmament and the United Nations as inadequate. Unlike the PTBT and other nuclear arms control agreements, it was not welcomed by the UN General Assembly; nor has any international appeal been made for its ratification.

The 1976 Peaceful Nuclear Explosions Treaty

The provisions of the TTBT did not extend to underground nuclear explosions for peaceful purposes. Since such explosions cannot be distinguished, at least from a distance, from explosions serving military ends, the possibility remained that the threshold limitation on weapon tests might be circumvented. The United States and the Soviet Union decided, therefore, to work out a separate agreement, which would contain additional obligations closing this loophole. A treaty on underground nuclear explosions for peaceful purposes, called the Peaceful Nuclear Explosions Treaty (PNET), was signed on 28 May 1976. It regulates the explosions carried out by the USA and the USSR outside their nuclear weapon test sites, as from 31 March 1976, the date valid also for the TTBT.

For many years, peaceful nuclear explosions (PNEs) had been seen as potentially valuable activities for a variety of purposes. In the United States, the so-called Plowshare Programme set out to explore possible uses of PNEs for digging canals or for other industrial ends, such as gas stimulation or oil recovery from otherwise uneconomic deposits. However, progress was slow, given the necessity of systematic tests using both conventional and nuclear explosives, because the need to minimize the risks required careful experimentation. By the mid-1970s, industrial interest in the use of underground nuclear explosions for non-military purposes had waned in the USA, while public concern over possible environmental hazards had increased. These hazards include—in addition to the release of radioactive material—shock wave effects which may occur close to the points of detonation. The programme was terminated in 1977, shortly after the signing of the PNET. It can be concluded that PNEs no longer constitute a motivation for the United States to continue explosive testing, unless circumstances were to change in a manner currently unforeseeable.

By comparison, the Soviet Union has pursued an active PNE programme. Its primary interests seem to have focused on the creation of underground storage facilities, as well as on seismic and geological mapping of Soviet territory. The grandiose Soviet plan for river diversion in Asia, using nuclear explosives, has been stopped, but since Soviet leaders have publicly referred to the economic costs to the USSR resulting from the country's 1985–87 moratorium on nuclear explosions, and since PNEs have been resumed after the expiration of the moratorium, it is reasonable to assume that such activities continue to be considered important in the Soviet Union. It has nevertheless been authoritatively and repeatedly stated that the Soviet Union would be prepared to forgo PNEs if a prohibition on all nuclear explosions were achieved. (The United Kingdom said that it would be prepared to renounce permanently the right to conduct nuclear explosions for peaceful purposes as part of an agreement on a comprehensive test ban.) Projects to use PNEs in countries other than the United States and the Soviet Union have never come to fruition owing to the large economic, environmental and engineering uncertainties involved.

To ensure that explosions declared to be for peaceful purposes should not provide weapon-related benefits not obtainable from limited weapon testing, the parties to the PNET established the same yield threshold for peaceful applications as had been imposed on weapon tests under the TBT, namely 150 kt. The yield restriction applies to individual explosions as distinct from group explosions. The possibility of carrying out individual explosions with a yield greater than 150 kt has been left open for future consideration 'at an appropriate time to be agreed'. A group explosion may exceed the 150-kt limit and reach an aggregate yield as high as 1500 kt (1.5 Mt), if it is carried out in such a way that individual explosions in the group can be identified and their individual yields determined to be no more than 150 kt. Certain peaceful applications of nuclear energy may indeed require many nuclear blasts of varying size. The PNET explicitly provides that they must be consistent with the PTBT, which prohibits any explosion that causes radioactive debris to be present outside the territorial limits of the state conducting the explosion, but it is unlikely that observance of such a limitation could be guaranteed. Development testing of nuclear explosives for peaceful uses would have to be carried out only within the boundaries of the nuclear weapon test sites and would be treated as the testing of a nuclear weapon. It is, moreover, implied in an agreed statement attached to the Treaty that proof would have to be given that the explosion outside a weapon test site was being conducted with a view to serving some practical peaceful ends.

The duration of the PNET was to be the same as that of the TTBT, and the exchange of instruments of ratification of the two treaties was to take place simultaneously. Although the PNET has not been ratified, it is covered by the US-Soviet undertaking to observe the 150-kt yield limitation during the pre-ratification period.

The PNET was an indispensable complement to the TTBT: the latter treaty would be deprived of meaning if peaceful explosions were allowed without restrictions. However, the PNET has not increased the very limited arms control value of the TTBT. By unduly emphasizing the importance of civil applications of nuclear explosives, it may even have had a negative impact on the policy of preventing nuclear weapon proliferation in providing respectability to the arguments of those states that seek to develop a nuclear weapon capability under the guise of an interest in peaceful explosions. Nor has the PNET solved the intractable problem of accommodating peaceful nuclear explosions under a test ban. It is true that some constraints have been provided for in the Treaty to limit the possibility of gaining weapon-related information from the peaceful application of nuclear explosions. This, however, would not prevent testing the performance of a stockpiled warhead or, perhaps more important, some limited testing of a new weapon design. Furthermore, it is clear that with a comprehensive ban on nuclear weapon tests it would be impossible to allow development testing of nuclear explosives for peaceful uses without completely defeating the purpose of the ban. Any nuclear explosive device ostensibly developed for peaceful purposes is inherently capable also of being used as a weapon. Hence, no nuclear explosion could be tolerated under a truly comprehensive ban.

In sum, none of the three nuclear test limitation treaties so far concluded has seriously affected weapon programmes by hindering improvements in nuclear weaponry. Nor have these treaties significantly reinforced the nuclear non-proliferation regime by rendering the development of nuclear weapon capability more difficult for non-nuclear weapon states. Especially flawed are the TTBT and the PNET. Nevertheless, the fact that these treaties have remained unratified for more than a decade has weakened confidence in the arms-control negotiating process. Full operation of these agreements might have facilitated progress towards a comprehensive ban.

VI. How important is verification in achieving a test ban?

The purpose of verification in arms control is to deter secret violations. This presupposes the ability to detect with a reasonably high degree of certainty any evasion that could pose a security risk, and to do so early enough to enable the injured party to mount an adequate response and redress the situation. An equally important role of verification is to demonstrate that activities prohibited by agreements are not taking place and that the parties are fulfilling their obligations. Thus, verification should help generate a climate of international co-operation which is indispensable for progress in arms control. Suspicions of breaches which have not been disproved become a source of discord among the signatories and undermine the validity of the contracted obligations. They also weaken confidence in arms control in general and thereby negatively affect the relations among states. All these considerations apply to a test ban.

VII. How are the existing test limitation treaties verified?

In nuclear test limitation treaties it is necessary for the parties to ensure that test explosions do not take place in the prohibited environments and do not exceed an agreed yield level.

The PTBT

In the case of the PTBT, the nuclear weapon parties were confident that their own means of verification were sufficient to provide an assurance of detection of clandestine explosions in the atmosphere, in outer space or under water. Consequently, no international mechanism was set up to check whether the commitments were being complied with. Indeed, the prohibition on testing in those three environments seems to be largely self-enforceable. Any signatory nuclear weapon nation that decided that it needed to conduct such tests would probably use the escape clause of the treaty and withdraw from it, rather than embark on risky secret testing. Similarly, with regard to the parties' commitment not to encourage other states to carry out nuclear tests in the proscribed environments, one could argue that such an undertaking hardly requires verification. It could not be in the interest of the nuclear weapon powers to help others in obtaining military benefits from tests in these environments.

On the other hand, the absence of an international supervisory body to evaluate events according to some objective criteria makes it very difficult to definitively establish whether, in violation of the PTBT, radioactive substances from an underground nuclear explosion have crossed the national borders of the testing country. In 1984–87 the United States and the Soviet Union formally accused each other of violating the PTBT by allowing radioactive debris from underground tests to vent, but in both instances the charges were denied.

The TTBT

In the TTBT, the 'national technical means' used to verify compliance consist primarily of seismic monitoring. Because seismic signals produced by a given underground explosion vary, yield determination requires knowledge of the environment in which the test has been carried out as well as of previous explosions conducted at the same site. Therefore, to facilitate verification, the USA and the USSR agreed to exchange information necessary to establish a correlation between yields of explosions and the recorded seismic signals. Each party undertakes not to interfere with the means of verification of the other party. This clause can be interpreted as a commitment not to use techniques which might reduce the recorded seismic magnitudes. As a complement to technical verification, the parties undertook to consult with each other and furnish information in response to inquiries. This provision is meant to deal with disputes over explosions that seem to violate the yield restriction.

Soon after the signing of the TTBT, press reports began to appear in the USA to the effect that the Soviet Union had conducted nuclear tests with a yield in excess of the permitted 150-kt threshold. The accusations were later included in an official US list of complaints of Soviet non-compliance with arms control treaties. The USSR countered with similar allegations about US tests. It may well be that some breaches have indeed occurred because, for technical reasons, it is difficult to predict the exact yield of nuclear explosions. This was recognized by the parties themselves when they reached an understanding that one or two 'slight, unintended' breaches per year would not be considered a violation, but would be the subject of consultations at the request of either party. The exchange of data to be carried out simultaneously with the exchange of the instruments of ratification of the TTBT, and complemented with calibration tests to improve each side's assessments of the yields of explosions, has been held up pending ratification of the Treaty. Recent US expert reports suggest that it is precisely the lack of adequate information about the geological features of the Soviet nuclear test sites that has contributed to ambiguous evidence of non-compliance by the Soviet Union.

The PNET

Also under the PNET the parties are to use 'national technical means' of verification and have undertaken to supply each other with relevant information. The amount of information would vary according to yields: the higher the yield, the more extensive the data required. Since in the case of a group explosion it is difficult to determine with distant seismic measuring instruments alone the yield of individual explosions if they occur within a few seconds of each other, observers of the verifying party, properly equipped, are to be given access to the site of the explosion. They would be permitted to check that the local circumstances, including facilities and installations associated with the project, were consistent with the stated peaceful purposes; to examine the validity of the geological and geophysical information provided in accordance with the Treaty; to observe the emplacement of each explosive; to observe the area of the entrance to each emplacement hole until all personnel have been withdrawn from the site; and, finally, to observe the explosions. Mandatory on-site observation is envisaged for a group explosion having an aggregate yield above 150 kt. By mutual agreement, explosions with a planned aggregate yield of between 100 and 150 kt could also be subject to on-site observation when, owing to the special character of the project, the reliability of teleseismic measurement cannot be ensured. Moreover, for any group explosion with a planned yield exceeding 500 kt, the observers would, in addition, have the right to install and operate a local seismic network to help ascertain that no undeclared explosions were taking place along with the announced ones.

So far, no on-site observation of peaceful explosions has been carried out; nor apparently have there been explosions in the category for which the Treaty requires such observation. Besides, it would be difficult to initiate an observation procedure on the basis of an unratified treaty. In any event, peaceful nuclear explosions with yield limitations similar to those set in the TTBT are not likely to produce militarily significant information which is not obtainable through weapon tests permitted under the TTBT. Therefore, the nuclear weapon powers have no incentive to seek such information through allegedly peaceful applications. Although important as a precedent for future arms control measures, the on-site controls—reduced as they are to observing an explosion at a time and place chosen by the host country—are not applicable to a multilateral comprehensive nuclear weapon test ban.

VIII. What are the present capabilities for detecting underground nuclear explosions?

The most dependable way known to detect and identify suspicious underground events is through seismological means.

Geological factors complicate the process of detection, because seismic signals produced by explosions are modified by the geological structures through which they pass. Another difficulty faced by seismologists is the phenomenon of seismic 'noise'—the vibrations in the earth resulting from wind and water wave motion, as well as from industrial activity—from which the discrete events of nuclear explosions and earthquakes must be picked out before they can be distinguished from each other. For these and other reasons, there is no simple correlation between the strength and pattern of the seismic waves as recorded and the energy of a seismic event. There is also a problem of possible evasion, that is, of deliberately engineered measures intended to significantly degrade the effectiveness of a test ban monitoring system. The evasion scenarios include conducting multiple explosions, explosion 'masking' and 'decoupling'.

In the multiple-explosion scenario, deception could be practised by firing a sequence of explosions with increasing yields in order to produce earthquake-like signals. However, if suspicions were aroused, sufficiently detailed seismo-logical examination would show that the signals had not been generated by an earthquake. In another scenario, firing a nuclear explosion shortly after the start of a large earthquake could mask the explosion signal in the tail of the earthquake signal. Such a hide-in-the-earthquake technique could not be undertaken easily: the explosion would have to be conducted only when an earthquake occurred with a magnitude exceeding a given limit and within a given range of the place of testing.

The technique of 'decoupling' seems to be the most likely method of eluding verification. It would consist of conducting an explosion in a large underground cavity (preferably in a salt deposit) so that the explosive energy would be 'decoupled' from, that is, less well transferred to, its geological surroundings. Seismic signals could also be muffled if explosions were conducted in uncon-solidated rock. There is, nevertheless, considerable scepticism as to the probability that the decoupling or muffling techniques would be seriously contemplated by states.

To decouple a nuclear explosion, a stable cavity precisely measured and of suitable shape would be required. Experts doubting the feasibility of effective decoupling argue that these conditions would be very hard to obtain. Moreover, they point out that the extrapolations made to determine the effectiveness of this technique have been based on inadequate or unreliable data, in considerable measure provided by chemical explosions with a yield many times less than that of an average nuclear test. In the event of a sizeable nuclear explosion being decoupled, the reduced seismic signal may still be identifiable as a clandestine nuclear test. Should the cavity collapse, it could leak radiation or cause a surface depression open to detection by radiation and photographic monitoring. In most cases it would also be difficult to pass off the lengthy and elaborate activities connected with decoupling as a conventional mining operation. In other words, attempting to engineer a clandestine test within a cavity while guarding against the risk of detection would be an extremely demanding, expensive and risky procedure. Muffling nuclear explo-sions in loose rock would be even more difficult to achieve, because geological formations suitable for such a technique are not widespread and their locations are presumably known.

At one end of the spectrum, a group of authoritative scientists claim that reliable detection of nuclear explosions can now be obtained down to very low explosive yields. Moreover, owing to the high-frequency seismic waves to which they give rise, the explosions can be clearly distinguished from earth-quakes even at distances of several thousand kilometres. (Explosions put out more energy in high frequency vibrations than do earthquakes of comparable magnitudes.) In addition to the geological data of relevance to test ban verification which have been obtained in recent years, it is now known that high-frequency seismic waves propagate readily across large parts of the Soviet Union, facilitating remote identification of nuclear explosions with yields of only a fraction of a kiloton, at distances exceeding 4000 km, and reducing thereby considerably the chances of evasion. Although the risk of decoupling—a matter of particular concern to the US Administration—cannot be completely dismissed, it is widely acknowledged that a 'decoupled' nuclear explosion of 10-kt yield or above, conducted on Soviet territory, could be identified as a nuclear detonation by a network of seismic stations outside the Soviet Union. With some two dozen seismic stations installed on the territory of nuclear weapon states and equipped with high-frequency seismometers, it would be possible to detect decoupled underground explosions down to or near 1 kt in either the USA or the USSR. The validity of this assessment is now fairly widely accepted.

At the other end of the spectrum, some seismologists take a highly conservative stand, emphasizing the problem of seismic noise. They express the view that, in order to discriminate efficiently between events, verification seismometers would need to be placed at very quiet sites, on land and on the seabed, and that such sites might not be available for technical or political reasons. They further contend that traditional seismological identification techniques are still not fully reliable and that the possibility of evading a test ban should be taken seriously. They suggest that cavity decoupling would provide an effective disguise for a nuclear weapon test. For all these reasons, they believe that the best verification system available today could not persuasively ensure detection of nuclear explosions at the low levels referred to above. Some even mention a figure as high as a few tens of kilotons as the lowest verifiable explosive yield, but they are in the minority.

In between these two extremes, certain seismologists conclude that the present level of seismic knowledge and the presumed effectiveness of cavity decoupling to evade detection allow for near-certain detection of explosions with a yield in the 5–10 kt range.

IX. How could monitoring capabilities be improved to render evasion difficult or impossible?

International system

It is generally accepted that a global seismic system, if properly constructed, would be necessary to verify compliance with a comprehensive ban on underground testing. To establish an optimal level of such verification, Canadian and Swedish seismologists have suggested a three-tier network of seismic stations positioned in key locations. The components of the envisaged system are as follows:

    (*a*) a global network of 50 or more 'primary' stations which, to the degree possible, provide uniform global coverage of seismic events;

    (*b*) networks of 'secondary' stations drawn from national earthquake monitoring networks to provide data on lower-magnitude seismic events occurring on the territories of the participating states; and (*c*) special networks of 'in-country' stations and other arrangements that provide the additional capabilities required to monitor the territories of nuclear weapon states.

To overcome the problems of discriminating between nuclear explosions and earthquakes, instrumentation at seismic stations would have to be standardized at the highest possible level of sophistication and sited in the lowest possible seismic noise environment. The seismic event data to be channelled through the system would have to be reliable and full, their transmission rapid, and their diffusion unrestricted, in order to facilitate their uniform interpretation throughout the world. Multilaterally administered facilities for international data communication and interpretation would be a necessary part of this co-operative seismological effort. An especially sensitive problem would probably be that of the third tier of stations on the territories of nuclear weapon states, for the main purpose of such stations would be to discourage clandestine nuclear explosions. On the whole, however, the scheme as described seems unobjectionable. Its introduction even before the conclusion of a test ban—as recommended by some—would be a highly desirable measure, as it could help interested nations to acquire expertise necessary to eliminate unfounded suspicions of breaches.

In-country stations

In-country seismic monitoring is particularly useful. Stations closer to the source of a seismic event register a fuller range of signals from it and make their interpretation easier. Additionally, seismic noise poses less of a problem. Multiple nuclear detonations meant to simulate an earthquake, or a nuclear explosion detonated in the coda of an earthquake, would be highly unlikely to escape discovery, especially if the in-country seismic stations were linked to a network of stations outside the countries being monitored. Such an arrangement would also permit the detection and identification of decoupled nuclear explosions, as well as the detection of chemical explosions conducted for civil engineering purposes above a certain yield.

Non-seismic means of verification

Supplementary verification capabilities can be provided by monitoring the effects of tests, other than seismic. The most important method of non-seismological remote sensing is satellite photography. Unusual activity—for example, of the kind associated with mining engineering—would be relatively difficult to conceal from military or civilian satellites. It would be possible to concentrate surveillance on existing cavities, sites prepared prior to a test ban, and mining areas which could be converted to test areas. Special satellite- and ground-based stations could be used to monitor for airborne radioactive materials. Given the record of underground tests of which a significant number has released radiation to the surface, the possibility of venting would constitute a dilemma to the potential evader calculating the risk of detection.

On-site inspection

However reliable a test ban verification system might be, the possibility will always remain of unexplained occurrences which the detecting state may wish to investigate: hence the presumed need for on-site inspection. Such inspection would have to consist of interlinked aerial, geophysical and radiological surveys of the area of the suspected nuclear explosion in order to measure ambient radioactivity and temperature anomalies; to discover fresh craters, traces of vehicles, metal artifacts, and so on, connected with a test and preparations for it; and, having identified the location of a suspected underground cavity, to establish whether or not a nuclear explosion has occurred.

On-site inspection does not appear to be particularly useful as a means of checking compliance with a test ban. Visually detectable evidence of breaches would best be detected by satellite photoreconnaissance. The geographical area for conducting on-site inspection might well be very large, while determination of the precise location of the event in question is critical, and the only way to prove that a nuclear explosion had taken place would be to drill and find radioactive samples. For reasons of the expense, time and effort involved, it would be impractical to have more than a very few such inspections in a year. In any event, in most cases, the evidence of a test ban violation collected by on-site inspectors would probably be no better than circumstantial.

For obvious reasons, a violator would not be likely to permit inspection of areas in which clandestine tests had been held, whatever the consequences of his refusal. But a 'threat' of on-site inspection could have a deterrent value: a government contemplating clandestine nuclear testing would certainly have to hesitate before undertaking a politically costly evasion. In this context, the conditions under which on-site inspections would be allowed to take place— that is, whether they would be voluntary or mandatory—are relevant. Co-operation between the parties would be essential for an effective inspection procedure. Withdrawal of co-operation, whatever the justification, including the rejection of inspection in response to a request to investigate a suspicious event, may not necessarily amount to an admission of guilt, but would certainly exacerbate the suspicion.

'Advantages' of cheating

It is not likely that any party would sign a test-ban or a test-limitation treaty with the set purpose of evading its terms. The would-be evader would have to go to extreme lengths to do so successfully, considering that an explosive test is an undertaking of major engineering proportions. If, after a period of time, a party were to find a motivation to resume testing or to shed the limitations, it could always withdraw from the treaty. This is allowed under arms control agreements. However, should there exist an overwhelming interest in cheating and a real possibility of undetectable clandestine nuclear testing in spite of a fully deployed verification system, it would be important to know whether a cheater stood to gain a military advantage.

Under the conditions of a comprehensive test ban, cheating would presumably allow a party to continue its nuclear development at the expense of rivals complying with the ban, or at least to rectify a previously unsuspected serious fault in its weapon stockpile without abrogating its treaty obligations. Under a test limitation treaty the temptation to cheat would be less strong, and the advantage from cheating would depend on the size of the agreed threshold. Thus, for the sake of illustration, if 5 kt were taken as a basis for the minimum fully verifiable yield limit (a threshold many seem to accept today), a programme for the development of certain theatre nuclear weapons would be possible, though it could be restricted by a numerical quota of permitted tests. In addition, some components of existing strategic nuclear weapons could possibly be tested at reduced levels. A lower, 1-kt threshold would, according to the prevailing opinion, prevent militarily significant tests in the sense of denying the development of new weapon designs, even though at sub-kiloton levels some research into as yet undeveloped nuclear weapons would be possible. Clandestine testing of devices with a yield somewhat higher than 1 kt would hardly be expedient; it would carry a great political risk for little military gain.

As regards the development of newly designed strategic weapons, there could be no cheating, because full-yield detonations, generally considered to be necessary to certify such weapons, would be impossible to conceal both under a comprehensive test ban and under a ban on all but low-yield explosions.

X. What are the present attitudes of states towards nuclear testing?

In the field of nuclear testing, as in other fields of nuclear armament, the positions of the United States and the Soviet Union—the states militarily most powerful and, at the same time, the main partners in disarmament talks—are decisive.

The United States

As regards the USA, its official attitude to a test ban has undergone a dramatic change since 1980. At variance with US policies proclaimed during the preceding quarter of a century, President Reagan's Administration views a test ban only in the context of radical arms reductions, maintenance of a credible nuclear deterrent, expanded confidence-building measures and improved verification capabilities. It does not see the ban as a separate measure to be carried into effect in conformity with the obligations accepted under several international agreements. For not only in the PTBT, but also in the NPT, the parties expressed determination to continue negotiations for ending all test explosions of nuclear weapons for all time. Equally, under the TTBT, the parties have undertaken to work towards achieving this goal.

The current attitude of the United States is based on the notion that its security, as well as that of its allies, is best served by nuclear tests. Consequently, technical considerations related to the verifiability of compliance with test bans are of only marginal concern, protestations to the contrary notwithstanding. The continued argument of the inadequacy of verification methods is now viewed by many as a convenient excuse to avoid a complete nuclear test ban. In other words, a test ban would not be acceptable to the present US Administration even with a foolproof guarantee of compliance, as some of its spokesmen have confirmed.

The Soviet Union

The USSR, on the other hand, maintains that halting all testing would diminish the nuclear threat. Reductions in nuclear arsenals alone, without prohibition of tests, would not help in reaching this objective, because continued testing may serve to modernize remaining weapons and to develop more sophisticated ones, including directed-energy devices for defence against ballistic missiles (the focus of Soviet concern because of the US Strategic Defense Initiative). Repeated Soviet proposals for a comprehensive test ban, supported by the lengthy 1985–87 unilateral moratorium on nuclear testing, as well as the expressed willingness to accept far-reaching measures of verification, including mandatory on-site inspection, suggest the seriousness of Soviet purpose.

According to some analysts, the present disagreements between the USA and the USSR on the question of nuclear testing represent the difference between the doctrine of mutual assured destruction, which stresses the deterrent role of nuclear weapons, and counterforce doctrines, which stress the military utility of nuclear weapons, both strategic and tactical.

The United Kingdom, France and China

The UK is pursuing a policy more ambiguous than that of the United States, emphasizing the problem of verifiability of a test ban rather than the military necessity of tests. In practice, however, the official position of the UK does not diverge from the position of the USA, not least because of the former's dependence on US testing facilities and nuclear weapon systems.

France has been consistently hostile to a test ban. This hostility may reflect the more limited technical level of its nuclear programme. Testing is seen by the French authorities as essential for upholding the credibility of their nuclear deterrent, including the need to develop weapon systems with a potential to circumvent SDI-type defences. Any commitment France might enter into regarding tests would be linked with those it would be prepared to undertake regarding the limitation of its nuclear forces. But France would embark on this process only when the USA and the USSR had reduced their nuclear arsenals so as to narrow markedly the gap between those arsenals and the nuclear means possessed by France.

China, too, has for years been opposed to the cessation of tests. Only when the USA and the USSR had taken the lead in ending the testing, improvement and manufacture of nuclear weapons and had reduced their nuclear armaments by 50 per cent would China undertake the commitment to cease the development and manufacture of its nuclear weapons. Some change in China's policy may have been heralded by its recently stated preparedness to participate in discussions of a test ban within the framework of the Conference on Disarmament.

If a complete test ban were to be concluded between the superpowers, it would seem likely that the remaining nuclear weapon states might in time feel compelled by international pressure to stop all testing. In any event, the positions of France and China should not be an impediment to a US–Soviet test ban treaty. For many years to come, no amount of testing by these 'secondary' nuclear weapon powers could have an adverse impact on the security of the superpowers.

Non-nuclear weapon countries

The most outspoken advocates of a test ban are the non-nuclear weapon states, the overwhelming majority of which have joined the NPT and thereby renounced the possession of nuclear explosive devices. At the initiative of these states, successive NPT review conferences have called for the conclusion of a CTB. Participants at the 1985 conference—with the exception of the USA and the UK—deeply regretted that a comprehensive nuclear test ban treaty had not been concluded, and called on the nuclear weapon powers to resume negotiations for the conclusion of such a treaty 'as a matter of the highest priority'.

However, several non-nuclear weapon countries conducting militarily significant nuclear activities—Argentina, Brazil, India, Israel, Pakistan and South Africa—are not party to the NPT and may be expected to resist a test ban which would restrict the development of their nuclear weapon capability or perhaps foreclose altogether their nuclear weapon option. Some of these nuclear threshold countries have taken positions formally favourable to a nuclear test ban under the so-called Six-Nation Peace Initiative (Argentina, Greece, India, Mexico, Sweden and Tanzania). In a document adopted in 1986 in Mexico, the leaders of these countries stated that they were prepared to assist in the seismic monitoring of a moratorium on nuclear weapon tests or of a test ban. However, of the participants in this initiative only Sweden and India had previously been active in the work of the group of seismic experts, established by the Conference on Disarmament and open to all states. Argentina and India claim for themselves the right to conduct nuclear explosions for peaceful purposes, even though it is impossible to develop nuclear explosives which would be capable only of peaceful applications. Neither country has joined the NPT or submitted its nuclear activities to the full-scope safeguards of the International Atomic Energy Agency.

The reluctance of the threshold states to give up their nuclear weapon option has its roots in regional political and military rivalries rather than in the big-power rivalry. None the less, in de-emphasizing the military role of nuclear weapons, a cessation of tests by the present nuclear weapon states could affect the views of the threshold states, though it may not be a sufficient *quid pro quo* for their definitive renunciation of nuclear weapons.

XI. What would be the impact of a comprehensive test ban on the nuclear arms race?

Under a test ban, the present offensive capabilities of the nuclear weapon states would not decline since one need not perform tests to manufacture additional weapons using old designs and since delivery systems would not be affected. But further nuclear weapon development would be rendered largely impossible. Designing and deploying new nuclear weapons without testing would involve too many uncertainties to be resorted to.

In so far as concern about 'technological surprise' drives the arms race, the cessation of tests may remove at least one of the causes of this apprehension by making it unlikely that something completely new, unpredictable and exotic would suddenly emerge in the nuclear field. Thereby, the race for qualitative improvement of nuclear weapons—an important channel of the potentially destabilizing superpower arms competition—would be considerably narrowed. This would make it easier for the nuclear weapon powers to critically assess the excessive levels of the nuclear forces which they already possess.

According to competent sources, a high degree of confidence in the reliability of stockpiled weapons could be maintained under the conditons of a test ban. If, however, it were accepted that the weapons were subject to irremediable deterioration, one would also have to admit that any such deterioration would, to a greater or lesser extent, affect the arsenals of all the nuclear powers party to the ban. The consequent reduced level of confidence in stockpiles would not need to become a matter of concern if US and Soviet nuclear weaponry served only the stated purpose of deterrence of nuclear war. With so many nuclear weapons available, deterrence does not depend on every single weapon functioning exactly as envisaged; there would hardly be a necessity to compensate for a degree of uncertainty. It might be added that confidence that a warhead would detonate is only one factor in the reliability of a weapon, the performance of the missile carrying the warhead being equally if not more important. However, it is conceivable, assuming rational behaviour, that any power would be less likely to launch a first disarming nuclear strike with weapons considered to be of somewhat doubtful reliability: its own weapons might fail, while those of its opponent might not. Nuclear war would be made less likely.

Whereas there is fairly broad consensus on the braking effect of a test ban on the vertical proliferation of nuclear weapons—in particular, on the qualitative improvement of the nuclear arsenals—opinions are widely divergent as regards the impact of a ban on horizontal proliferation, that is, on decisions of the present non-nuclear weapon states whether or not to develop such weapons.

Historically, the widespread opposition to testing has been sustained by a belief that a ban on tests would reduce the chance that additional countries would enter the nuclear arms race, the assumption being that the ban would be universally adhered to. In fact, however, testing would not be indispensable for newcomers to the nuclear club. First-generation fission devices could be produced without testing, and the producer might be confident that the device would actually explode. But the weapon would be highly unsophisticated, of uncertain yield and perhaps also difficult to deliver. It is unlikely that any country would be willing to create a large arsenal of such untested devices. This circumstance would slow down horizontal proliferation. Thermonuclear weapons involve a quantum jump in physical processes over first-generation atomic devices; their development without tests would therefore be out of the question, and their horizontal proliferation would be precluded.

An argument has been put forward in the United States that a cessation of tests by the USA and the USSR, followed by a consequent decline of confidence in their nuclear stockpiles and, thereby, in the reliability of their security guarantees, would compel those dependent upon the superpowers' 'nuclear umbrella' to develop their own, independent nuclear deterrent forces. But the argument appears spurious. There is no sign of pro-nuclear sentiments among the non-nuclear weapon members of the major military alliances. Moreover, a test ban treaty of unlimited duration would no doubt tend to create an international climate in which even non-parties would feel inhibited from engaging in testing, out of fear of being stigmatized as outlaw states. Misgivings that horizontal nuclear weapon proliferation would take place in the aftermath of a test ban are unjustified. On the contrary, a test ban would reinforce the NPT by demonstrating the major powers' awareness of their legal obligation under this Treaty to bring the nuclear arms race to a halt.

XII. What other effects would result from a test ban?

The consequences of a test ban, other than those directly relevant to arms control, are difficult to foresee. Much would depend on the details of the agreement reached and on the spirit in which it was entered into. The view of proponents is that, by relieving psychological stress associated with nuclear weapons, a test ban might create conditions facilitating changes in NATO–Warsaw Pact relations and a return to the era of political détente between the military blocs.

There is strong support for a test ban in many parts of the world. By providing a political signal and a tangible proof that both sides were seriously looking for an alternative to constant tensions accompanied by an unrestricted arms race, it would be a major international event with considerable confidence-building effects.

XIII. Conclusions

At the time of writing—in the summer of 1987—the prospects for achieving a suspension of tests through a multilateral, simultaneous moratorium, or their complete cessation through a single, comprehensive treaty, seem slim. The opposition, coming as it does now from several powerful military and political groups, mainly in the United States, may be difficult to overcome. There seems, however, to be less hostility towards further partial restrictions on testing. In this connection, the question arises as to what kind of restrictions would be more meaningful than those already observed under the PTBT, TTBT and PNET.

The limitations could be both on the rate of testing and on the explosive yield of tests. An effective yield limitation would have to set the threshold low enough to preclude the development of new weapon designs, and a threshold not higher than 1 kt would seem to be suitable for this purpose. Tests with lower yields would not be prohibited. One could even admit a few tests per year with a somewhat higher yield ceiling, if the agreed annual quota and yield were small enough to preclude support for a nuclear weapon development programme. From this point of view, one or two tests with a yield of up to 5 kt, per nuclear country and per year, would not be excessive, but might enable the scaling up of results from such explosions to estimate the effectiveness of certain important components of stockpiled weapons. This would be especially applicable to the fission 'triggers' setting off the fusion reaction in thermonuclear weapons, the reliability of which appears to be of continuing concern. It is clear that over a period of several years, even a minimal quota of tests restricted to a 5-kt yield might be taken advantage of to develop a new design of a small nuclear weapon. But this could probably be achieved only at the expense of the reliability tests and would seem, therefore, to be an acceptable risk.

The freedom to conduct a very limited number of tests with a yield higher than 1 kt but not exceeding 5 kt would not permit significant qualitative improvement of nuclear weapons, but would be of some military usefulness, as described above. It would thus go a long way towards meeting one of the main objections to a comprehensive ban, namely, that the nuclear stockpile would deteriorate and become unreliable, or that the repairs of weapons could not be trusted, without the benefit of testing. Furthermore, the freedom to conduct an unlimited number of tests with a yield of up to 1 kt would preclude a controversy over the military value of sub-kiloton yield explosions and their verifiability. It might also satisfy the need to learn more about the physics and about some effects of nuclear weapons, and thereby dispose of the apprehension voiced by the weapon laboratories that their technical teams would disperse. The risk of a party suddenly breaking out of a very-low-threshold test ban (VLTTB) would be less than in the case of a comprehensive ban.

The verification procedures for a VLTTB could build upon those already accepted under the TTBT and the PNET. In addition to an extensive exchange of data and a few calibration shots to aid in yield estimation, there would be a need for suitably located in-country seismic monitoring stations to reduce the possibility of evasion. All tests would be notified in advance and conducted only at an agreed designated site. In addition, those tests subject to an annual quota would be monitored by outside observers. On-site inspections could be envisaged for suspicious events. Moreover, obligatory international observation of chemical explosions for mining or other engineering purposes, exceeding a specified size, would be provided for at sites where thick low-coupling geological formations are known to exist, or where large underground cavities may exist having a capability to accommodate a decoupled nuclear explosion. Because of the permissiveness to test, there would be fewer 'false alarms' than under a total ban, and the incentive to cheat would not be high.

A test ban is more verifiable than most other arms control measures. But the decision whether or not to go ahead with a treaty would not be made only on verification grounds. It would be essentially a political decision based on governmental calculations of national security and international stability. Arms control benefits would be weighed against the perceived risks of a freeze on the modernization of nuclear weapons.

A VLTTB as sketched out above would of course apply only to the present nuclear weapon powers. It could not be a universal commitment, because most non-nuclear weapon countries have already renounced the very possession of nuclear weapons and consequently also the testing of nuclear explosives. These countries could, however, contribute to the verification procedures. In fact, the greatest possible participation in a world-wide system of seismic monitoring would be indispensable for the viability of a VLTTB.

Arms control cannot remove the motives for possessing arms. But it may stop or slow down the arms race both quantitatively and qualitatively, minimize unwarranted military disparity between states, help save resources needed for peaceful purposes, diminish the dangers to the environment and improve the international political climate.

Arms control measures concerning nuclear testing could help fulfil most of these functions on condition that: they precluded or significantly limited the freedom to develop new weapon designs; reinforced the non-proliferation regime; contained no loopholes facilitating circumvention of the contracted obligations through ostensibly peaceful explosions; provided for reasonable assurance of compliance; and opened the way towards, or complemented, more far-reaching measures, including cuts in nuclear weapon arsenals. A comprehensive test ban would meet these requirements. Failing such a ban, a VLTTB would be a meaningful alternative. However, any partial arrangement should be seen as transitional and contain an explicit unequivocal commitment to achieving a complete prohibition of tests by all states.

Part 2
Overview of nuclear explosions

Chapter I. The purpose of nuclear test explosions

Paper 1

J. Carson Mark

Former Head of the Theoretical Division, Los Alamos National Laboratory, Los Alamos, NM

Abstract

The relationship between weapon development and further testing is discussed. Comments are made concerning the level of confidence which should appertain to the capability of a stockpile of nuclear weapons in the event that further testing should be unavailable. The conclusion reached is that there need be no diminution whatever of 'national security' *vis-à-vis* a major opponent as a result of a mutual forgoing of nuclear tests. Some of the arguments frequently offered in opposition to this view are identified.

I. Introduction

Full-scale nuclear tests are essential to maintaining an advancing weapon programme. At any particular stage, the information sought from a test will depend on the state of advancement of the programme, and this will change as advancement proceeds. For example, a very first test would most probably be for the purpose of confirming that the device one had built would actually produce a nuclear explosion—something giving an energy release 1000 or more times larger, say, than the same weight of chemical explosive would provide. Following that, a range of questions would present themselves. These would include: Could the design be improved to give an even larger yield? or a satisfactory yield using a smaller amount of expensive nuclear material? or from a device of smaller size? or from a device which could be carried by a particular missile? or by a torpedo? and so on. Other questions would relate to the intensity and ranges and effects of the blast waves, the thermal radiation, and the ionizing radiation accompanying the explosion. Having explored some of these questions with pure fission explosives, there would be the question of whether thermonuclear fuels could be used in conjunction with fissile material to reduce costs or sizes or increase yields still further. Again, all these questions, and others as well, would arise in this new context. Since one or more tests are required to explore each of the questions suggested, an extended series of tests would be required if a weapon programme were to follow up on even some fraction of the lines indicated.

However, any test is so expensive and complex, and involves so much time and effort on the part of such a large number of people, that it may be assumed that a test is never conducted except in response to the perceived need for some specific information—or type of information—judged to be of use for improving the weapons on hand, or broadening the understanding of weapon behaviour, or contributing in some currently relevant way to the advancement of the weapon programme. Expensive as a test may be, its cost is a very small fraction of the cost of introducing a new weapon into a stockpile—if one considers the cost of manufacturing the weapons, of setting up a maintenance programme, of preparing carriers and launchers, of training personnel and, perhaps most particularly, of incorporating the new capability into the plans and organization of the defence establishment. Before committing themselves to these major undertakings, those responsible will insist on knowing not only that the new weapon really works but also as much as possible concerning just how it performs.

At the outset it should be made clear that it is not yet possible, except perhaps in the case of interpolation between two quite similar designs for which the performance has already been observed, to calculate the performance of some new design with anything like the high degree of confidence and precision which would be required by those who would have to rely on the actual behaviour. It should also be mentioned that the interpolation between existing designs for which the necessary assurance and precision are already available is not here considered to be 'new', since it would not extend the range of capabilities.

II. US testing experience

Weapon improvements

To exemplify the point that the type of information required of a test will vary with the stage of weapon development, it may be helpful to cite some of the obvious questions encountered in the US experience. The very first test was needed to confirm that an assembly which was supercritical with prompt, unmoderated neutrons would in fact produce an unprecedented energy density and, consequently, a large explosion. This had been expected; but it could not otherwise be ascertained that some unsuspected factor had not been overlooked which might vitiate that expectation. The somewhat secondary matter of the actual size of the energy release was obviously of great interest, since estimates had covered a range of at least a factor of 10, as were also such items as the partition of energy between heat and blast, the propagation of the blast wave in air, the intensity of ionizing radiation, and the movement and distribution of the material in the fireball (including the radioactive weapon debris)—all of which had been estimated in advance but were observed here for the first time. It is no longer necessary for anyone, anywhere, ever to conduct a test to ascertain again that an assembly which is supercritical with prompt, fast neutrons will produce an explosion.

Anyone who can acquire the necessary materials can now construct a device with full assurance that it will produce an explosion, provided he can be certain that his assembly mechanism will result in a supercritical configuration. This he could do by using a gun-type pattern (starting with two mating pieces of fissile material which, when in full contact, without change in shape or density, would form a supercritical unit, and bringing these together sufficiently rapidly); or by using an implosion mechanism to impose some compression on a piece of fissile material which was already nearly critical, provided he had been able to ascertain that the degree of compression which his mechanism would provide would equal or exceed the compression required. These patterns, with essentially guaranteed supercriticality, were the patterns used in 1945. However, just as for the USA, a newcomer, though confident of being able to produce an explosion, would have only a rather rough idea of the yield that might result. This might be satisfactory for some purposes—such as those of a terrorist organization—but would be unlikely to be satisfactory for military purposes. Testing would be necessary to calibrate a yield estimate.

The early designs, with supercriticality guaranteed, were expensive in fissile material—the gun-type obviously requiring more than a critical mass at normal density, and the near-critical implosion type calling for as near a critical mass as one could comfortably build in. In addition, the first designs were ungainly—the assembly mechanisms weighing 2250 kg or so, and, with the outer casings required for handling as a bomb, a weapon weight of about 4500 kg.

The original question of what will happen if one has a supercritical assembly was immediately replaced by a whole spectrum of questions: Will this new design (changed or improved in some way) also produce a supercritical assembly? Can one reduce the size and weight? Can one substitute other materials? Can one use a more effective disposition of materials which, though offering a higher degree of compression, might be more sensitive to perturbations in behaviour? Can one increase the yield from the same investment of fissile material? Can one still obtain an acceptable yield from smaller amounts of fissile material—and so forth? In the years following 1945, many tests were directed to obtaining such information.

Starting in the early 1950s, the range of questions requiring tests to resolve was greatly broadened, and the fact that meaningful information could be obtained only through tests was made more inherently evident by the introduction of thermonuclear fuels. Here, again, the initial question was whether thermonuclear burning would proceed as anticipated under conditions as favourable to that end as could be provided. Once it had been ascertained that it did so, the question shifted to that of whether such burning would also proceed effectively under conditions less favourable for that purpose, but more favourable for practical weapon application. In the case of a pure fission device, a fairly good indication of the state of the materials up to the time an explosion would be expected to occur can be obtained from laboratory experiments using inert (nonfissioning) materials. These indications are unlikely to be good enough to provide a basis for a firm and precise statement concerning the yield, but they can be useful in a comparative way and can provide the basis for a reasonable expectation. In the case of a device employing thermonuclear fuel—whether in a rather small amount to enhance the energy produced by fission (as in the so-called booster), or in a larger amount so that a major fraction of the total energy is provided by thermonuclear reactions (as in the so-called H-bomb)—the yield of the device depends decisively on the efficiency of the thermonuclear burning. Whether this burning would proceed well or poorly depends on the compression of the fuel, on the disposition of the surrounding materials, and on various other factors which may apply at the time the fuel is heated to the point of ignition.

The sort of temperatures needed, or the sort of energy densities required, to initiate a rapid thermonuclear burning—something on the order of 10 million degrees Centigrade, for example—are reached in the course of the explosion of a supercritical fission assembly, but only as it is well on the way to exploding. Consequently, the starting conditions for thermonuclear burning in a device whose behaviour depends essentially completely on the progress of that burning cannot be simulated in the laboratory, but are only realized in the course of a nuclear test. These conditions cannot be directly observed even there; but to some extent it can be inferred from measurements, made in connection with the test, of whether or not the course of events followed the calculated behaviour fairly closely. If the actual behaviour departed from that calculated, it might be possible to draw conclusions as to the reason. Such observations could then suggest corrective changes to be incorporated in some subsequent nuclear test.

Adaptation to weapon carriers

In addition to the considerations already identified—which have mainly had to do with 'improving' weapons in some way or other and with broadening the range of types of weapon available—with the proliferation over the past 20 years or so of special-purpose missiles, there has been a great interest in adapting nuclear devices to the particular features of the carrier and in integrating and optimizing the nose cone–warhead combination. In such cases, the nuclear device is no longer considered as a package to be transported in some carrier—as it was when it was to be employed as a bomb to be dropped from an aircraft—but as an integral component of a weapon system. The desired military characteristics (including size, weight, yield and even shape, possibly—since the nose cone may be intimately associated with the outer layers of the device) are unlikely to be well met by any already existing and tested device. So a new design (and a new test, or tests) will be necessary—at least in the likely event that the integration and optimization studies should suggest that some change might be advantageous in the amount or thickness of a material, or in the disposition of weapon components, or in any other feature which could conceivably affect the assembly and explosion process in a way not already observed and certified as acceptable in a previous test. Many tests have been required in connection with considerations of this sort, and on numerous occasions subsequent tests with modifications or adjustments have been called for to better meet the objectives.

Effects tests

Eighty per cent or more of the tests conducted by the USA (which alone amount to more than half of all nuclear tests ever conducted) were directed at the purposes mentioned above. A relatively modest number of tests have been carried out for other purposes, such as the few tens of tests to study the effects of an explosion occurring underground, or underwater or at high altitude in the atmosphere. Prior to the 1963 Partial Test Ban Treaty, most effects tests were conducted in the atmosphere, but since that time the programme has been continued in underground tunnels. By this means it has been possible to obtain a large part of the information desired, but the particular matter of the properties and effects of the electromagnetic pulse (EMP) cannot be observed under these conditions. No doubt there would have been several tests to obtain more experimental information concerning EMP and its effects, had testing in the atmosphere remained possible. The effects of heat, blast and radiation on various types of structures, on military hardware and, perhaps particularly, on re-entry vehicles or warhead–carrier combination structures have also been studied. In connection with effects tests, a large effort is involved in preparing and instrumenting the targets. Since, in many cases, the objective would be to assess the effects induced, it would usually be important that the target not be utterly destroyed, while still being stressed to the point that some observable effects were imposed. For such a purpose, devices with well-known character-istics would be the obvious choice as sources. These effects tests, then, provide one of the few occasions on which devices which have already been tested are fired again. One can thereby confirm whether the performance is similar to that previously observed.

Safety tests

Another category of tests has had to do with weapons-safety considerations. Safety has to do with provisions to avoid an unintended threat from a nuclear weapon in the course of one's own handling of such devices. Security is concerned with provisions to make it difficult, or impossible, for an unauthorized person to fire a weapon which he might obtain by theft or capture.

With respect to safety, apart from such features as the electrical circuitry for which appropriate provisions to avoid inadvertent operation can be made without nuclear tests, there are two safety measures employed in the USA which may require a nuclear test, or even tests. These are the requirement for 'one-point safety', and the decision to use 'insensitive high explosive' in nuclear devices. The criterion used for one-point safety is that in the event the explosive is detonated at the 'worst' possible single point (as it might if dropped on the ground or if struck by a projectile) the probability of experiencing a nuclear yield larger than 2 kg (HE equivalent) shall not exceed one chance in a million. (Such a criterion was developed to ensure that the range of serious hazards to personnel from nuclear radiation did not exceed the range of hazards from the detonation of the chemical high explosive.) Repeated tests may well be required both to ensure that the safety criterion is met and to confirm the full-scale yield capability of a device which may have had to be modified to meet the safety criterion.

'Insensitive high explosive' (IHE) is a (relatively) new formulation of explosive material which is surprisingly less likely to be detonated by impact than were previously employed explosive mixtures. Although the older explosives were capable of withstanding the jars and jolts encountered in normal handling and transportation and even being dropped from a modest height, there was a high probability that they would detonate on impact if dropped from an aeroplane on to a hard surface. About 30 accidents involving nuclear weapons in aircraft have been reported by the US Department of Defense (DOD) for the period 1950–80, and in about one-quarter of these the high explosive detonated. The matter of primary concern is the possibility of widespread dispersal of radioactive nuclear material—plutonium in particular. Only two accidents—those at Palomares, Spain, in 1966, and at Thule, Greenland, in 1968—resulted in widespread dispersal, but these could have been more serious than they were had they occurred in more densely populated locations.

Since the detonation characteristics of the IHE differ from those of other HE mixtures, nuclear tests are required even for a design which may be retrofitted with the new explosive.

The objective of improving the safety of nuclear weapons is commendable. However, the urgency of the problem is not fully clear. About two-thirds of the incidents listed by the DOD occurred in the 1950s, and since the event at Thule in 1968, no case is listed in which the high explosive detonated. If the DOD list is complete, there could be some question as to whether the problem is of sufficient urgency to stand in the way of arms control objectives.

With respect to security, a number of provisions have been implemented under circumstances for which there was no need for a nuclear test. These include storage in heavily guarded bunkers, the use of protective covers such that attempts to penetrate them would disable necessary components, and the use of coded switches—the so-called PALs. It is possible that provisions which intrude into the nuclear system may be devised and considered, and these might require nuclear tests. However, if new and improved security measures are deemed necessary, they could probably be achieved in such a way as not to require nuclear testing.

Peaceful nuclear explosions

Some (but rather few) US tests were conducted to explore possibilities concerning peaceful applications of nuclear explosions—such as stimulating the production of oil or natural gas. Also, since a nuclear explosion provides an unprecedented source of neutrons and energy at high concentrations, a small number of tests—the so-called 'physics experiments'—were carried out in the past with the main purpose of making use of these unique conditions.

Summary

In summary, from the more than 850 US nuclear tests—and from the 800 or so directed at weapon-programme development—a great number of things have been learned. The range of yields, the sizes and types of devices, economies in the use of fissile material, and other features of practical importance have been enormously advanced. Questions of weapon 'safety' and protection against unauthorized use have been addressed. Beyond this, it has been clearly shown that new weapons having characteristics or capabilities beyond those certified by previous tests will require testing in their own right and in their specific configuration in order to be considered acceptable in the stockpile.

This last point cannot be overemphasized. It comes from the observation that on numerous occasions the observed performance has fallen short of pre-shot predictions, and the fact that some modifications which had been presumed to have little or no effects have in fact been found to have large effects. Although past predictions have not often been seriously poor, they have sometimes been far from good enough. This underlines the comment made a number of times, that a new weapon—or even one that is only partially new—cannot reasonably be considered for stockpiling without being tested.

III. Weapon development without testing

The possibility of continued weapon development without conducting further tests has been commented on quite emphatically for the USA. Similar considerations must apply to any other country that has a varied stockpile of advanced weapons. As mentioned above, a newcomer could provide himself with an assured means of producing a nuclear explosion without the need of a test, provided he restricted himself to an inherently conservative design. In addition, a country having an assortment of fission devices might be able to introduce new models without testing, but that would scarcely broaden its capability. It would not be credible, however, that a country having experience only with some pure fission devices could, without tests, cross the barrier to having devices making use of thermonuclear components on which it could place any reliance at all (unless, of course, it were possible to steal or otherwise acquire a certified design from another country).

In this general connection it may be worth noting—as indicated in the compilation presented in Cochran *et al.*[1]—that, although the USA has conducted something like 800 tests for the purpose of weapon development, fewer than 100 devices have reached the stage of being assigned model numbers, that is, of being officially enrolled as candidates for stockpiling. Some of these were cancelled before ever being put in production, and many have been retired after a number of years in the stockpile. As of 1983, the 25 000 or more units in the US stockpile were composed of only a couple of dozen different devices, and almost half of these were then scheduled for early replacement. Evidently it requires a number of tests before a new model is judged to be advantageous enough to be added to the stockpile. This will apply even more strongly in the case of future additions to the stockpile since these will have to compete favourably with an improved set of devices. In addition, the newer and future models, coming as they do after strenuous efforts to reduce weight, size, cost and so forth, place greater demands than formerly on precision in their fabrication and freedom from extraneous perturbations of their behaviour. They depend more on everything going exactly as planned. To extend a well-established capability requires testing.

IV. Confidence in stockpiled weapons

Whether confidence in the reliability of presently stockpiled weapons can be maintained without continued tests is a complicated question. Many, and widely differing, opinions on this point have been expressed by persons in a position to speak as experts—as also, of course, by many others. A considerable majority claim that confidence would soon be lost. A smaller group (of which the author is a member) believe, and insist, that sufficient confidence is warranted to justify reliance on having an absolutely insufferable capability for retaliation as long as that may be desired. The exact statement of the question is important, and that is: Can confidence in the capability of the presently existing stockpile—without any change in device specifications or any attempts at improvement—be assumed to continue at the present level without conducting further tests?

The author's answer to this question is that it can, provided that a number of obvious—though far from trivial—conditions are fully met. There is, of course, no question but that confidence in the behaviour of the devices in the stockpile must be available as long as nuclear weapons must be relied on to provide an adequate deterrence to the use of nuclear weapons by another party. Some changes in peripheral mechanical and electrical systems could, possibly, be admissible, but absolutely no changes could be allowed which might conceivably affect the assembly behaviour of the nuclear components. There is, of course, a clear possibility of significant chemical changes occurring over time in a weapon assembly: the high explosive is an inherently unstable material which may evolve a variety of gases which could have the effect of changing the crystal structure of the explosive or of interacting with some of the materials in contact with it. Uranium and plutonium are chemically highly reactive materials which might readily interact with gases evolved from the high explosive—or with air or water vapour should they have access. So there could be changes in the behaviour of the explosive, or corrosion of the fissile material itself. The changes (if any) in the efficacy of the explosive could be ascertained by non-nuclear (laboratory) observations, while the fact (if not the effects) of any actual chemical corrosion can be ascertained by a meticulous examination of the materials in the device. Some of those who have commented on the possible deterioration with time of units in the stockpile, and the consequent loss of confidence in their capability, have argued that that would be fine: on the assumption that such effects would apply roughly similarly to weapons in the stockpiles of the USSR and the USA, such deterioration would reduce the risk of either party considering a first strike. In opposition to this it has been argued that, since the USSR has missiles with larger throw-weights, their warheads may be more rugged and hence less subject to deterioration. On this account an asymmetry unfavourable to the USA might develop. There is, of course, no evidence either way. For one thing, the onset of corrosion in particular has little, if anything, to do with throw-weight. That will depend rather on the quality and details of design, on the quality of welds, and on metallurgical details. Similar considerations probably apply to possible faults in electrical circuitry and to possible effects of ageing of high explosives. In addition, it is a thesis of this paper that, with proper procedures, deterioration—if encountered—can be corrected to the extent that confidence in the capability of a stockpile need not erode.

In the USA, at least, a surveillance programme has been in effect for a long time (withdrawing weapons from the stockpile and subjecting them to detailed examination). This process has disclosed indications that one stockpiled weapon (the warhead which at that time was the mainstay of the Polaris weapon system) was defective. (This is quite apart from the instances referred to that some untested designs have not met expectations.) It would have been possible to withdraw the suspect items and remanufacture replacements built to the original specifications, but since this event occurred in an era of active testing, it was possible to substitute a new, improved and tested model to replace the defective version. The author's conclusion from the experience to date is that, by refusing to permit any uncertified variations in design and by insisting on detailed and continuing surveillance measures, no significant departures from previously observed behaviour need be anticipated. It is possible that remanufacture of some existing model might be required, but confidence should continue to be available.

A relevant observation on this point is the following. The present procedure has usually been to construct a prototype of a new model, to test it, and then, providing the performance is acceptable, to manufacture the number desired (whether some hundreds or thousands) to the same specifications as the prototype and put them in the stockpile. As of 1983, about half of the 25 000 units in the US stockpile were more than 20 years old.[2] A considerable fraction of these were at that time scheduled for early replacement; this had nothing to do with any loss of confidence in their capability, but only with the fact that newer and more advantageous models had in the meantime been certified by the testing programme and that the older models were not suitable for the new and improved carrier systems being planned.

As mentioned above, there are different opinions on the continuing availability of confidence than those held by the author. The basis for some of those are specious, and some are based on arguments quite aside from the point. For example, a recent DOD compilation[3] of the reasons for supposing that confidence would no longer be available in the event of a comprehensive test ban (CTB) included the following:

1. *Desired military 'requirements' might stipulate the need for weapons differing from any already certified, and confidence in such weapons would be uncertain.* This is undoubtedly true, but the answer is straightforward; no new military requirements having this effect could be considered without testing. This spectre has nothing to do with the confidence which might be associated with the existing stockpile.

2. *In much the same vein it is said that older designs lack what are now considered essential features for safety and security.* This may be an argument to the effect that new designs would be desirable. Again, it says nothing of the confidence associated with existing designs.

3. *In connection with the possible need to remanufacture a deteriorating model, it is said that materials, fabrication techniques and equipment used for older weapons will not necessarily be available or permissible for health and safety reasons, and that substitutions could affect the operation of the weapon.* The last point is correct, but it seems ridiculous to suppose that a government able to handle plutonium could not arrange to handle beryllium, for example, even if, for health and safety reasons, it were no longer available in commerce. Nevertheless, this line of argument was introduced in 1978 by the (then) directors of the weapon laboratories and has since been taken up by other Administration spokesmen (DOD, etc.).

By far the most searching opinion—that, without a continuing test programme, confidence would be lost—is based on the conviction that it is essential that active designers be on hand to provide informed judgement concerning possible problems. This point is made in the DOD compilation, but it is also strongly advanced by persons who have had an active and distinguished role in weapon design work. In some instances the basic point has been burdened with irrelevancies, such as by arguing that if some modification should be required—as stipulated by military requirements, or by the need of using substitute materials, or by the need of a new weapon to counter some improvement in defence capability on the part of an opponent—then confidence would not be available without the participation of the weapon designers. (It has been pointed out that confidence is not warranted for most changes, even with the participation of designers.) The argument has also on occasion been unfortunately alloyed with the suggestion that possibly the US

Congress or the Administration would falter in its support of an adequate surveillance programme, remanufacturing measure, and so forth. Indeed, in such a case confidence would erode; but for that reason, and not primarily as a consequence of a shortage of designers or tests.

In its pure form the argument is that circumstances could arise, either because of presently unforeseen changes in the weapon itself, or because of the need of a judgement concerning possible sensitivity to parameters not previously considered (presumably temperature or pressure ranges) for which designers would be essential. It goes on to point out that present designers will not always be available, so new designers will have to be in place. It then continues that only by participating in an active testing programme can the necessary skill, experience and sensitivity of the sort of person needed be developed and maintained. Under a CTB, therefore, it states that confidence would be lost.

There would, of course, be changes in the weapon laboratories in the event of an extended CTB. The size of the staff engaged in weapon design and other activities in the weapon programme, and the currency of hand-on-experience with the behaviour of nuclear explosives, would all change. But such changes will not develop suddenly. Their rate and extent will strongly depend on what the laboratories may be directed to do and supported in doing. In fact, the time-scale for major changes within the weapon laboratories would probably not be very different from that of other changes which one might expect to occur under a CTB. There would, for example, be some changes in the views held concerning what was needed for an appropriate deterrence posture—both as regards armament levels deemed adequate for that purpose and as regards deployment policies. Indeed, there has already been considerable discussion of such matters, even in the absence of a CTB.

The argument, or one might better say the insistence, that the changes which might be expected to occur in the laboratories consequent to a CTB would necessarily be detrimental to the national security is largely—if not entirely—associated with the assumption that the present open-ended nuclear arms race will continue to be necessary as a way of life; that only by being confidently able, even under the worst of all possible worst-case analyses, to inflict 'condign punishment', to destroy, and otherwise to foil and out-compete an 'evil empire', can we hope to avoid a fate worse than death. Understandably, many are frightened and bemused by the alarms raised by the military and related laboratory establishments. But for most others a different *modus vivendi* would be preferable.

V. Conclusion

There is no way of knowing the future. Not even weapon designers can provide full confidence and security against all contingencies. We presently have some confidence that, if called upon, our weapons will operate as they did when tested. This is more a consequence of the surveillance programme over the past decades than of repetitive testing. We have so many weapons that our deterrent force does not depend on each one working, and it is most unlikely that each one will find its intended target. We even have enough types of device and types of delivery vehicle that, if a whole type is eliminated, our remaining deterrent force is still awesome. Confidence is available if one wants it. However, if enough people say loudly enough that the sky is falling and confidence will leak away, it will.

Notes and references

[1]   Cochran, T. B., Arkin, W. M. and Hoening, M. M., *Nuclear Weapons Databook* (Ballinger: Cambridge, MA, 1984).
[2]   See note 1.
[3]   *Bulletin of the Atomic Scientists*, Apr. 1986, pp. 11–12.

Paper 2

Donald M. Kerr

Former Director, Los Alamos National Laboratory, Los Alamos, NM

Abstract

The role of nuclear testing in maintaining effective nuclear deterrence has often been misconstrued. Testing is intimately intertwined with the design, engineering and assurance of the nuclear stockpile and is not a separable activity.

I. Introduction

For over three decades, bans or limitations on the testing of nuclear weapons have been one of the most frequently suggested and widely supported forms of nuclear arms control. While testing restraints constitute a highly technical approach to arms control, they have often been advocated as an alternative to political approaches and agreements when this avenue appeared to be closed by political controversy or concern over strategic military problems.

The role testing plays in the development of nuclear weapon systems is often misunderstood or misinterpreted because 'testing' means many things to many people. It is important to recognize that nuclear weapon testing is not product testing and is not operational testing; in fact, it is a process intimately intertwined with the design of nuclear weapon systems. Testing is not an end in itself but the confirmation of a theoretical design. It may also provide the opportunity to explore previously unknown physical regimes or to try new approaches to civil construction using peaceful nuclear explosions.

II. The role of testing in weapon development

The purpose of testing in weapon development is to confirm the calculations which imperfectly represent nature and give some measure of confidence in one's understanding of the physical principles by which these weapons work. Some tests are directed towards engineering purposes, to actually fit a warhead into a new environment. Others are for purposes of safety and security and, in particular, to test the effects of nuclear weapons.

Safety, together with security, has often been a significant concern, particularly for mobile and/or tactical weapons. Concern for weapons that might fall into terrorist hands, and other concerns about the safety of air-carried systems in particular, led to a major effort to improve the robustness of those weapons that are deployed abroad or carried on aircraft: by introducing insensitive explosives that would be immune to detonation, for example, in an aeroplane crash, or safeing systems that would be immune to tampering and which would deny someone the possibility of a nuclear yield if he had possession of such an explosive device.

Those developments could not have been carried out without testing because the changes intruded so far into the nuclear design that they removed the possibility for predicting performance by interpolating between known points.

A further question which must be considered is how much testing is needed for a particular purpose. For very complex, new systems in the past, before the computational capabilities that exist today were available, a new development might necessitate two dozen or more tests. Today it is rather different: with substantial advances in the ability to computationally model the physics, the number of tests is substantially reduced and a few tests suffice to develop certain new designs. It depends on how advanced the new design might be. For instance, a device that was intended to penetrate ice or enter the earth and detonate while underground would have a very complicated test series associated with it because of the intimate association of the structural elements of the weapon with the nuclear components. So there is not a simple answer as to how many tests would be significant if one were to assign a numerical quota.

III. Weapon reliability

The reliability of nuclear weapons is also germane to discussions of nuclear testing. But the real issue is that of confidence in the reliability as assigned to the weapon stockpile, and this has varied over time. There have been past instances where unreliable designs have been put into the stockpile. There have been other instances where weapon systems have been in the stockpile as long as they had a useful military role and have then been retired without change.

Over the past three decades, about one-third of the modern-design weapons put into the stockpile have required post-development modifications, and in three quarters of the instances those modifications were made necessary by information learned through testing. A majority of these problems might not have been suspected without testing. In fact, testing was the way most were discovered and the way changes were confirmed to have restored the reliability of the weapons involved.

Without testing, no weapon with strategic significance and no weapons with new designs could be introduced to the stockpile. Further, without testing, confidence in the existing stockpile would surely diminish.

Arguments might be made, or extrapolations from past experience offered, to justify not testing weapons, but it would over time prove to be a foolish step. A total cessation of nuclear testing entails a corollary decision that new strategic systems in particular are unnecessary for national security.

IV. Can calculations replace testing?

Arguments have been raised that better numerical simulations coupled with laboratory or zero-yield experiments might make possible the development of new systems or the maintenance of present ones. Unfortunately, numerical simulations are only as good as the physical models envisaged, and those models have been demonstrated to be wanting on numerous occasions.

No responsible scientist would claim that he is able to model the physical world with 100 per cent certainty. Hence, science has always advanced using both theoretical and experimental techniques. Today, particularly in the areas of applied science and engineering, theory and experiments are supplemented more and more by 'numerical experiments' that lie somewhat in between. But for real advances in understanding, one can never give up experimental tests, the way to find the truth behind assumptions. That possibility would, of course, be absent in a situation where there was a comprehensive test ban.

V. Consequences of testing restraints

Test restraints such as threshold reductions or numerical quotas provide a different set of questions. With respect to the threshold limitations, strategic weapons with yields much above 50 kt could not be developed as new weapon systems under a threshold limitation of, say, 10 kt or below. Nuclear tests are currently restricted to a yield of 150 kt. Major reductions in this yield level would entail considerable risk to national security. In particular, the following consequences would be expected from currently proposed restrictions to 1-kt or 10-kt levels.

1. A nation would immediately lose its ability to maintain an effective and modern nuclear deterrent force. For the United States, testing for certification of the Trident warhead could not be completed. Design options for the small ICBM (Midgetman) and SRAM II missiles would be restricted, since warheads could not be optimized for them. New programmes such as an earth-penetrating warhead (to attack hardened or deeply buried targets) would be impossible.

2. A nation would immediately lose most of its ability to incorporate modern safety and security features on its existing stockpile. In most cases, such improvements can be incorporated in existing designs only with testing well above the 10-kt level. A 1-kt limit would eliminate any such improvements.

3. A nation would immediately lose much of its ability to evaluate the effects of nuclear weapons on its military systems. Some of these effects tests could be carried out under a 10-kt limit, but very few under a 1-kt limit.

4. Over the next few years, one could expect to see a gradual deterioration in the reliability of the nuclear weapon stockpile. Historically, many reliability problems have been discovered only by means of nuclear tests. Correction of such problems has usually required additional tests, always above 1 kt and often above 10 kt.

5. Over the course of several years, one could expect to lose much of the nuclear design capability, as the best weapon scientists leave for more promis-

ing careers. For the United States, this would eventually make it impossible to respond quickly with a testing programme of its own, if the Soviet Union resumed testing.

6. In the view of the United States, the Soviet Union would not suffer comparable injury to its programmes. The USSR could easily circumvent testing limits by conducting tests in underground cavities or unsaturated soil, making yields appear much lower. In addition, the USSR has always relied more on conventional weapons, on chemical weapons, and on less sophisticated nuclear design technology. Thus, they are less dependent on advanced development and testing than is the United States.

There is, in a sense, a value of testing as a function of yield that is perhaps worth having in mind. At a few hundred tons, there are certain things that can be learned relative to the assembly of the fissile material in the weapon. At a few kilotons, the functioning of the so-called primary or trigger can be effectively investigated, and at a few tens of kilotons, one begins to approach, for certain kinds of weapon designs, the regime where the total functioning of the weapon can be explored. Then, finally, at the full yield, one understands both the thermonuclear and the fissile material behaviour in the weapon system.

The numerical quota issue, on the other hand, goes back to an earlier point. The number of tests required to do something significant is a function of what one is trying to accomplish, and so if one is simply trying to accomplish a certain level of maintenance of confidence or introduce a very small number of new systems per decade, a very few tests per year might be an appropriate way to accomplish that. On the other hand, if one cannot foresee the reasons for which new weapons might be needed, such a limitation would not be appropriate.

Chapter II. The role of laboratory tests

Paper 3

Donald R. Westervelt

Center for National Security Studies, Los Alamos National Laboratory, Los Alamos, NM

Abstract

Laboratory tests play a critical role in the development of nuclear weapons. Both non-nuclear and very-low-yield (sub-explosive) laboratory nuclear tests might be of great importance to 'beginner' states embarking on a nuclear weapon programme. Such tests can be conducted unobservably under a variety of conditions, some of which may resemble 'field tests'. Experiments of this kind are of much less value to established nuclear weapon states, although they can be used to address a very restricted range of issues. The beginner state can unquestionably manufacture reliable nuclear weapons without conducting test explosions of those weapons. For the USA, laboratory tests under any definition cannot effectively replace nuclear weapon test explosions because it has been found that they are inherently incapable of predicting with sufficient confidence the results of nuclear explosive tests.

I. The importance of very-low-yield nuclear tests

What is a nuclear test?

For our purpose, it is useful to distinguish 'nuclear tests' (experiments involving high explosives and small quantities of fissile material, but negligible fission energy release) from 'nuclear explosions' (in which fission energy is significant in controlling the outcome of the experiment) and/or 'nuclear weapon test explosions' (a test explosion involving an object useable as a nuclear weapon). It will be remembered that the 1963 Partial Test Ban Treaty (PTBT) dealt primarily with the last of these categories, extending its prohibitions to the second in order to deal with the question of explosions for peaceful purposes. Since the drafting of the PTBT, many states have declared that nuclear explosive devices having peaceful applications cannot be distinguished from weapons.

There is no generally agreed definition of a nuclear explosion, although a useful one was offered by J. Carson Mark in 1971:[1] an explosion giving at least three orders of magnitude more energy per unit of weight than would be available from high explosives; that is, a specific yield of at least 10^3 kilocalories per gram. Under this working definition, a nuclear explosion might involve a 50-kg object giving about 50 tons of yield, or an object weight around 1 ton producing close to 1 kt. Since the actual fissile material employed in such devices cannot differ by a large factor, being about half a bare critical mass, the second clearly is more efficient, in one sense, as a result of its more massive means of assembly. On the other hand, the smaller device might be considered more suitable as a weapon. Both are within the range of chemical explosions routinely conducted for mining or other purposes.

In both cases, the disassembly, or self-destruction, of the device is driven by the fission energy release, the pressures involved being out of reach of those attainable by conventional high explosives. (The latter point seems to be the most reasonable basis for distinguishing between nuclear and conventional explosions, and it also allows for a distinction between explosions and such prompt-critical devices as Godiva, in which fission energy release is responsible for disassembly, but thermal expansion rather than strong shock generation is the mechanism employed.) In any case, explosions of the kind described here are far less efficient in terms of yield-per-device-pound than those of modern fission weapons; Mark[2] implies that something like 20 kt in 100 lb had been realized in such weapons by 1971.

It will become clear that useful nuclear tests need not involve nuclear explosions, and that significant nuclear explosions might be distinguishable from nuclear weapon test explosions, but only if some attribute of the explosive device precluded any weapon application. The value of tests of each kind, however, depends strongly on the state of technology of the party conducting them.

'Beginner' states

The beginner state seeking an implosion weapon design will be concerned mainly about getting four things right: hydrodynamics (the dynamics of materials in motion), neutronics (which, along with hydrodynamics, determines the criticality behaviour of systems), initiation of the chain reaction at an appropriate time, and estimation of yield. Non-explosive or very-low-yield nuclear tests can be valuable to that state in connection with these problems. These are properly considered laboratory, as opposed to field, tests, although the 'laboratory' may in fact prove to be very similar to the environment in which field tests are conducted. Hydrodynamic experiments with high explosives, even those using completely inert material to substitute for fissile material, are not most conveniently conducted within buildings, although they can be.

Full-scale tests of implosion systems may involve such apparatus as pin-sensors (sea urchin-like assemblies of pin switches that sense the location of a moving surface) or flash X-ray devices (high-power X-ray machines that can take 'snapshots' of materials in motion). Until fissile material is introduced, the objects of such experiments might well be contained in reusable steel vessels, with everything under a concealing shelter, but the next logical step—the introduction of small amounts of fissile material in, say, subcritical multiplying experiments—would introduce risks making continuation of this practice unlikely. For safety reasons, such experiments would more than likely be conducted in an environment strongly resembling that of underground tests, although—hopefully—no nuclear explosion would be involved, much less a nuclear weapon test explosion, and concealment would still be entirely practical.

As a result of these activities, all of which might be unobservable, the clever beginner state should be satisfied that the hydrodynamics of assembly and the neutronics were correct. The timing of initiation will still be a problem contributing to uncertainty in the estimation of nominal yield, but as Mark *et al.*[3] explain, the beginner state will be confident of a nuclear explosion of at least 100 tons or so, with the odds in favour of significantly more yield. This may or may not satisfy the requirements of military authorities, but clearly a great deal will have been accomplished without even a small nuclear explosion, much less an observable field test.

Nuclear weapon powers

The situation as regards nuclear weapon powers is quite different. A nuclear weapon power will long since have covered the ground outlined above. Very-low-yield nuclear tests may still be of value and even of vital importance in connection, say, with safety experiments or other very special goals, but, in general, tests short of nuclear explosions will have little to offer. Low-yield explosions, however, ranging from tons to low kilotons—almost certainly conducted underground for containment reasons and still not intrinsically observable—may serve some essential purposes while failing to serve others. One example of their possible utility is the preservation of important, if incomplete, parts of the weapon design technology base by allowing essential experiments. Another may be reassurance as to the proper functioning of critical components of actual weapons, although recent estimates by Harold Brown and James Schlesinger[4] placed the yields needed for this purpose somewhat higher. A third use might be for development of new small weapon designs, but at the yields in question (well below any having strategic signifi-cance) this would appear important mainly to those concerned about blurring the distinction between nuclear and conventional munitions, a concern that was more often expressed a decade ago than in recent years.

ICF and similar tests

The importance of the Inertially Confined Fusion (ICF) programme to a nuclear weapon state in a test ban environment is uncertain. Attainment of 0.1- to 1-ton fusion yields in the laboratory, essential if ICF experiments are to contribute much technically, lies in the indefinite future. In any case, while a vigorous ICF programme might assist peripherally in efforts to preserve some aspects of a weapon technology base under a CTB, it is inherently incapable of addressing the kinds of problems that experience warns us will occur. Thus ICF can never replace the need for nuclear testing.

Summary

Very-low-yield nuclear tests can be of crucial value to beginner states by satisfying scientific, if not military or political, requirements. They have only limited value to nuclear weapon states unless other testing is prohibited. In that situation, the value of very-low-yield nuclear tests to beginner states as well as to nuclear weapon states lies in the fact that such tests can be of great scientific, if not military or political, value to the former, but limited value to the latter unless other testing is prohibited. In that situation the importance of such tests to nuclear states may be far greater than otherwise, even though they are limited to very narrow objectives.

Furthermore, nuclear tests can be important well below the yield level that is reasonably considered a nuclear explosion, and most of the benefit to beginner states can be acquired with such tests. A continuum exists between nuclear tests at microscopic values of yield (still very valuable to the beginner state for the purposes outlined, but usually of limited value to weapon states), and tests in the low-kiloton range that are still fairly easily concealed. Because of the physics involved, nuclear tests over this whole range are likely to be accomplished in an environment that can tolerate unexpected yield excursions without disaster. This environment may well be available close to home, at least at the lower-yield levels, but it will not be significantly different from that usually associated with 'field tests'. Thus the distinction might be made between nuclear tests, as described here, and nuclear explosions, which in virtually every case must be regarded as nuclear weapon test explosions.

II. Field test requirements for 'beginner' states

Why a field test?

The term 'field test' is here synonymous with the term 'nuclear weapon test explosion'. The implication is that what is being tested at this stage is a weapon, or at least the prototype of one, and that the intent is most probably to confirm yield predictions: 'most probably' because sufficient confidence in weapon performance might already exist at the scientific, if not the military, level as a result of experiments conducted inconspicuously at small yields—laboratory experiments, if the term is flexibly applied—and the motive for a full-scale proof test of a simple fission weapon might well be political. The technical situation will be determined by the scope, sophistication and success of the nuclear tests already conducted. Other factors, such as the amounts of fissile materials available, may enter any decision to do or refrain from a weapon proof test.

The principal uncertainty to be addressed by a weapon test explosion should be that of yield (or of performance in a complete delivery system). The magnitude of the yield uncertainty, as has been explained by Mark *et al.*[5] and Lovins,[6] will depend on the efficiency of the implosion system that has been developed prior to the proof test. If the assembly of the fissile material is very fast, that uncertainty will be relatively small, and this will be known from the earlier nuclear test results. In that event, a proof test might be considered unimportant. If, on the other hand, it is not so fast, the random uncertainty will be larger, and this uncertainty will affect all similar weapons so a proof test is of limited value.

Summary

The technical arguments for a nuclear weapon test explosion in the case of a 'beginner' state are weak at best. Military conservatism and political considerations are likely to prevail in the decision-making process. The beginner state unquestionably could manufacture reliable nuclear weapons without such a test, if 'reliable' is interpreted as permitting some uncertainty in weapon yield. The broader the base of unobservable low-yield nuclear tests the less the uncertainty will be.

William van Cleave correctly described the beginner state situation as follows:

It seems clear that a country could, without testing, develop, and probably produce and stockpile with confidence, warheads that would be regarded as sophisticated by, say, 1950 standards. This might include warheads of different yields, sizes, and delivery requirements. . . . A test programme would be required for the continued development of warheads, if advanced sophistication and versatility are to be obtained, or certainly if a two-stage thermonuclear device were desired. Otherwise, a test of a first-generation nuclear weapon by a Nth country has more political than technical significance.[7]

III.   Laboratory tests to replace underground explosions

The nuclear weapon states and their allies, for better or worse, now rely on nuclear weapons as an essential element of their security policy. While the goals of states, as reflected in their security policies, may differ, the discussion that follows needs only to assume a minimum goal of ensuring continuing international security and stability: the avoidance of nuclear conflict while fundamental values of states are preserved. The nuclear weapon programme of each state will reflect its technical perceptions, based on experience, judgement and internal constraints, of the imperatives imposed by this goal. If these factors differ among states, as they surely do, states may be expected to reach different conclusions regarding their nuclear weapon programmes.

The US policy in this regard has been clearly stated:

A Comprehensive Test Ban (CTB) remains a long-term objective of the United States. As long as the United States and our friends must rely on nuclear weapons to deter aggression, however, some level of nuclear testing will continue to be required. We believe such a ban must be viewed in the context of a time when we do not need to depend on nuclear deterrence to ensure international security and stability and when we have achieved broad, deep, and verifiable arms reductions, substantially improved verification capabilities, expanded confidence-building measures, *and greater balance in conventional forces*.[8] (emphasis added)

In the long term, therefore, US policy defines an international environment in which laboratory tests can effectively replace underground explosions: that is, one permitting a CTB. The nature of this environment is clearly stated. In the interim, whose duration depends on the success of negotiations proceedings in several forums, the maintenance of deterrence and international stability is not compatible, in the US view, with the complete cessation of underground nuclear weapon test explosions. The technical basis for this judgement is explained in the sections below.

Objectives of nuclear weapon programmes

The goal of continued international security and stability is reflected, in the US weapon programme, in several specific objectives. In the view of the present author, these objectives include: (*a*) development of new weapon designs as required by the modernization of the conventional and nuclear forces of potential adversaries, and by other changes; (*b*) development and incorporation into US forces of safety and security improvements; (*c*) assurance of the continued survivability of the US conventional and nuclear forces in a changing threat environment; (*d*) avoidance of technological surprise; (*e*) discovery and correction of major reliability or survivability problems in existing nuclear weapons; and (*f*) maintenance of the weapon-design technology base on which continued confidence in the reliability of the US nuclear deterrent depends.

The role of underground nuclear weapon test explosions in connection with each of these objectives is described below.

Development of new weapon designs

Although reliable nuclear weapons might well be manufactured by a 'beginner' state without weapon test explosions, there is an abundance of expert testimony to the effect that this is no longer possible for an advanced nuclear weapon state, at least not for the United States. That testimony also indicates that the scope for such development is significantly limited by the test restrictions already being observed by the USA, namely the 150-kt threshold of the 1974 Threshold Test Ban Treaty (new weapon designs cannot be deployed without essentially full-yield tests). In the long-term environment defined in the policy statement quoted above, it clearly is assumed that new designs of any explosive yield will no longer be required, an entirely reasonable assumption. Thus, while laboratory tests cannot replace underground explosions for the purpose of weapon development, that purpose itself may—and most hope will—at some point disappear. Until this is achieved, that is, until new requirements cease to exist as a result of the steps cited above, underground tests will be needed for this objective.

It is on this objective of underground testing that most CTB advocates focus their concern. The Threshold Test Ban Treaty (TTBT) reflects an apparent judgement by the parties that the constraint it imposes is not incompatible with the requirements imposed by changing security conditions, provided there is adequate assurance of compliance by all parties. The stated US CTB policy would not seem on its face to preclude eventual further restraints on testing, assuming that verification issues can be resolved, but this clearly is an issue on which views may differ within, as well as among, states.

Improvements in safety and security

Here the requirements of states may differ significantly. It is well known that the United States has imposed very stringent requirements in this area. There must be no nuclear yield as the result of any foreseeable accident or misadventure involving nuclear weapons. Further, the probability of plutonium dispersal in such a situation must be held to an irreducible minimum. US nuclear weapons in stockpile must pose no significant radiation hazard. Finally, US weapons must be as secure as possible from attack or acquisition by terrorist or other hostile forces, and inoperable should they fall into hostile hands.

There is little dissension about the contribution of these policies to security and stability. Their implementation has proceeded steadily over many years, although much work of this kind continues. It is so intimately associated with the design of modern weapons that it is a major factor in determining the US requirements for underground nuclear tests. It is safe to say that laboratory tests cannot adequately serve this need. If the safety and security requirements were less severe, as they may be in some states, this very major reason for nuclear weapon testing would be lessened, but it would disappear only under the stated conditions for a CTB.

Assurance of force survivability

Both nuclear and conventional forces exist in a changing threat environment. Security and stability clearly depend on confidence in their survivability. A wide range of laboratory tests contributes significantly to this objective, but assessment of the ability to survive nuclear threats at present is, in the USA, provided by so-called nuclear vulnerability and lethality tests, in which nuclear explosives are used as sources of energy in various forms that simulate the hostile environments that may be encountered. Virtually all of such tests have revealed weapon or component vulnerabilities where none was expected. As a result of the complexity and very high cost of these relatively low-yield experiments, they are employed only when laboratory simulations cannot suffice, and yet they are a vital component of the US test programme.

The range of effects attainable through ICF in the laboratory may expand at some future time; should this occur, the requirements for nuclear effects tests might diminish, to a limited extent. It is very unlikely, however, that they will disappear entirely until the stated conditions for a CTB have been achieved.

Avoidance of technological surprise

From Greek Fire and the crossbow, through smokeless powder and the machine-gun to atomic weapons, technological surprise has originated in the mind of man. Many technological advances have been regarded, temporarily, as 'making the world unsafe for war', yet wars have continued. Only in the atomic age has war between major powers been averted—an unprecedented condition of international stability whose preservation must reflect a very high goal of states. Few would disagree with the view that technological surprise must not be allowed to erode this stability. In general, what can be conceived in the mind must be explored in the laboratory, but where nuclear weapons are concerned the laboratory, even with the expanded definition used above, may prove insufficient. Paper studies and laboratory experiments may well—and have in the past—led to concerns, for example about existing 'thoroughly tested' weapons, that can be resolved only by additional underground nuclear weapon tests. So long as the conditions for a CTB have not been met, the inability to perform essential tests may well aggravate instability born of such concerns, particularly (but not only, because it is impossible to know what has already been accomplished by a rival) if uncertainty exists about the current actions of others.

It is simplistic to focus on specific, possibly transitory, areas of weapon development on the assumption that if there is no testing there can be no surprises; that if testing is averted, stability automatically will be preserved. This attitude ignores the lessons of history. The mind and the laboratory, as well as the study of what has gone before, may well give results that have grave implications for continued stability and can be resolved only by appropriate tests in the field. When states no longer depend on nuclear deterrence for security and international stability, the avoidance of surprise will recede as a motive for testing, and the products of minds and laboratories, which will still emerge, presumably will be dealt with by other means in an improved political climate.

Discovery and correction of stockpile problems

The issue of stockpile reliability has been somewhat divisive among the US technical and political communities. It has, for example, been asserted that laboratory tests have been sufficient to deal with reliability problems: 'In the past these laboratory techniques have identified a number of reliability problems. *In no case, however, was the discovery of a reliability problem dependent on a nuclear test and in no case would it have been necessary to conduct a nuclear test to remedy the problem.'*[9] (emphasis added)

The laboratory techniques referred to include disassembly of sample weapons, subjecting the components to non-nuclear tests, detonation of the weapons without their nuclear components in place to ensure that the complete assembly operates correctly, and non-explosive tests to determine the effects of deterioration. It is further stated[10] that components with ageing problems revealed by these means can be replaced with newly fabricated ones, using the original design specifications; however, this is a different issue that will be discussed in the following section.

The techniques listed, of course, are used extensively in the continuing US Quality Assurance and Reliability Testing (QA/RT) programme, but as recent testimony has shown,[11] the statement quoted is entirely incorrect as a description of US experience. It is here, perhaps most of all, that the experience of states may differ. To the extent that these factors differ among nuclear weapon states, decisions about the necessity for continued testing can also be expected to do so.

The facts of the matter are as follows. Of all the modern weapon designs placed in stockpile by the United States, that is, weapon designs deployed since about 1958, one-third have required post-deployment nuclear explosive testing for the resolution of reliability problems; of these problems, three-fourths could not have been discovered if nuclear explosive testing had been discontinued. While these facts may not have been publicly articulated in precisely this form until recently, the occurrence of stockpile problems in whose discovery and resolution underground testing have played an essential role has been public knowledge for about a decade.[12]

Given the extraordinary technologies that modern weapon designs· represent, the very reactive nature of some of the materials involved, the changing military and political environments in which the weapons are expected to remain functional over many years, and the severe practical limitations on testing that exist during their development, this fraction is remarkably small. Two-thirds of the designs, including some that have reached stockpile lifetimes greatly in excess of those originally planned, have required no such attention. On the other hand, it is well known that some of the problems that have been discovered and resolved have involved major elements of the deterrent forces.

It is neither necessary nor permissible here to describe in detail the particular US weapon systems that have developed problems, the nature of the problems or the solution adopted, although a number of such examples have been described elsewhere.[13] However, all of these details have long been available within the US classified literature, and they have also been available to the appropriate committees of the US Congress. It is more relevant here to identify some of the technical factors that underlie the facts stated above.

Predominant among those factors are (*a*) the relatively limited payload capabilities of most US strategic delivery systems, compared with those of its principal rival, and (*b*) the extraordinarily severe safety and security requirements imposed by the United States on nuclear weapons of all kinds. US delivery system characteristics such as throw-weight have for the most part remained static since they were first decided in the late 1950s, but the perceived requirements for stable deterrence have not been static in the face of massive deployments and force modernization by the Soviet Union. In addition, pressures towards nearly absolute safety and security have continued throughout this period. These factors, and others, have placed a high premium on the optimization of designs, and they have increased the danger of subtle design error or unexpected design susceptibility to factors initially believed to be unimportant but later discovered (often by nuclear explosive tests) to be vital in an area such as performance, survivability or safety.

It is by now no secret that the large majority of reliability problems discovered in the US stockpile over the years have involved the physical process known as boosting. It is boosting that is mainly responsible for the remarkable 100-fold increase in the efficiency of fission weapons cited by Mark[14] in 1971. The process was described publicly in 1973 by Van Cleave: 'Boosting can increase yields and/or reduce size and weight for similar yields. It involves the injection of fusion materials (gases) into a fission bomb; just the right amounts multiply greatly the supply of neutrons and thus fission the fissile material more efficiently. . . .'[15]

The conclusion that has been forced upon US weapon designers by nuclear test experience is that the design of boosted fission devices is an empirical science. Laboratory experiments of all of the kinds mentioned in the above sections, particularly non-nuclear hydrodynamic experiments with pins or flash radiography, are of inestimable value in assessing a design prior to commitment to an underground nuclear test, but laboratory experiments have been and continue to be incapable of accurately predicting the results of nuclear tests of boosted devices, because conditions for the boosting reaction are established only after considerable fission energy has been released. This is a fact of particular importance when those devices are used as triggers for thermonuclear weapons, where the permissible range of yield may be small.

While the well-known physics problems discovered by testing in the early 1960s[16] have long since been resolved, new problems have arisen requiring resolution, some very recently. No US weapon design is ever approved until every foreseeable failure mode or safety/security concern has been eliminated by laboratory and nuclear testing, but foresight is never perfect, particularly in a changing political and military environment.

It is thus impossible to define away the problem, as has been attempted, by asserting that the weapon designs in which problems have arisen were not thoroughly tested. In each case where a reliability or some other concern has emerged after deployment of a design, it was the judgement of the scientists involved at the time of deployment that all necessary tests had been performed, a judgement based on calculation, *extensive laboratory testing*, nuclear testing believed to be adequate, and the sum of all previous nuclear test experience. Twenty-twenty hindsight is of little value when that collective judgement, very infrequently, proves to be wrong. It has also been suggested that if testing were to cease, the political and military climates would no longer change in ways that might affect confidence in the nuclear deterrent. This is not a tenable thesis; most of the changes in these or other areas that have led to stockpile concerns (reliability, safety, and so on) were essentially independent of nuclear testing by other parties. The crucial issue of designer judgement, which is of the greatest importance here, is discussed in the next section.

Design technology base

The confidence of a state in the reliability of its nuclear weapons ultimately reflects its confidence in the judgement of the scientists responsible for those weapons. That judgement must be exercised frequently by US scientists in their assessment of results of the QA/RT programme. It is also called upon to assess the results of tests, laboratory or nuclear, that relate to deployed weapons, and to evaluate new external conditions that may affect those weapons in some way. It is the integration of theoretical, laboratory, and the whole of past and present nuclear test experience that provides the basis for that judgement, and it is the last of these that provides its ultimate validation. Experience has shown that without validation by nuclear test results, confidence in the judgements made soon begins to wane and, with it, confidence in the reliability of US nuclear weapons.

The opposite effect has also occurred in the past: overconfidence. The 1958–61 moratorium provided well-known examples of this, and also saw the departure from weapon design work of a number of key personnel. Neither a gradual loss of confidence nor the development of overconfidence accompanied by the departure of seasoned design personnel are conducive to long-term stability; both were observed when nuclear explosive tests were suspended for several years.

The question of replacement of doubtful components with newly fabricated ones using the original design specifications is relevant here. This has been done, but more often questions have arisen about the validity of the original specifications, perhaps because of altered circumstances having nothing to do with testing, or because of the results of later tests in the programme. In other cases it has been discovered, as in one case recently, that the test of a device made to exact production specifications, but by slightly different procedures, failed to represent the performance of the production items in a significant way (but only a later confidence test of production hardware disclosed the problem). Designer judgement is critical at every stage of a weapon's lifetime.

It should be noted here that the judgement that a nuclear test is required as a result of QA/RT or other data is rare; in nearly all cases the opposite conclusion is reached, and these are the decisions in which the highest confidence is required. If test experience were to recede from memory, it is unlikely that confidence would long be maintained in designer judgements *not* to test in a particular situation.

Summary

It is precisely the inability of laboratory tests, even laboratory nuclear tests, to predict with confidence the outcome of nuclear test explosions that makes such explosions necessary. The design technology base on which confidence in the reliability of deployed weapons depends cannot be maintained without actual nuclear weapon test data. Laboratory tests will for the foreseeable future not be able to provide a technical substitute for underground nuclear tests. Only when the CTB conditions stated above are met will they be able to do so; not because they can provide the information needed but rather because the need for that information has essentially disappeared.

Notes and references

[1] Mark, J. C., 'Nuclear weapons technology', *Impact of New Technologies on the Arms Race*, eds B. T. Feld, T. Greenwood, G. W. Rathjens and S. Weinberg (MIT Press: Cambridge, MA, 1971), p. 137.

[2] See note 1.

[3] Mark, J. C., Taylor, T., Eyster, E., Maraman, W. and Wechsler, J., *Can Terrorists Build Nuclear Weapons?* Background Paper (International Task Force on Prevention of Nuclear Terrorism: Washington, DC, 1986), p. 11.

[4] Brown, H. and Schlesinger, J., interviews by C. W. Corrdry in '2 former officials say U.S. can afford nuclear-test cuts', *Baltimore Sun*, 26 Aug. 1986, p. 1.

[5] See note 3.

[6] Lovins, A. B., 'Nuclear weapons and power-reactor plutonium', *Nature*, 28 Feb. 1980, pp. 817–23.

[7] Van Cleave, W., 'Nuclear technology and weapons', *Nuclear Proliferation Phase II*, eds R. M. Lawrence and J. Larus (University Press of Kansas: Lawrence, KS, 1973), p. 53.

[8] United States Department of State Bureau of Public Affairs, *US Policy Regarding Limitations on Nuclear Testing*, Special Report No. 150, Aug. 1986, p. 3.

[9] Bethe, H., Bradbury, N., Garwin, R., Keeny, Jr, S. M., Panofsky, W., Rathjens, G., Scoville, Jr, H. and Warnke, P., letter to the Honourable Dante Fascell, 14 May 1985.

[10] Wagner, Jr, R. L., Statement before the United States Senate Committee on Foreign Relations, *Hearing on Nuclear Testing*, 26 June 1986.

[11] See note 10; and Kerr, D. M., Statement before the United States Senate Committee on Foreign Relations, *Hearing on Nuclear Testing*, 19 June 1986.

[12] Westervelt, D. R., 'Candor, compromise, and the comprehensive test ban', *Strategic Review*, no. 4 (fall 1977), pp. 33–44; and Westervelt, D. R., 'Can cold logic replace cold feet?', *Bulletin of the Atomic Scientists*, Feb. 1979, pp. 60–2.

[13] See note 12; and Rosengren, J., *Some Little-Publicized Difficulties with a Nuclear Freeze*, Report RDA-TR-12216-001, 1983; and Cochran, S. B., *Nuclear Testing from a Weapons Scientists' Point of View* (Lawrence Livermore National Laboratory, 4 Aug. 1986), in preparation.

[14] See note 1.

[15] See note 8, p. 67.

[16] See Westervelt, *Bulletin of the Atomic Scientists* (note 12).

Chapter III. Nuclear explosions for peaceful purposes

Paper 4

Iris Y. P. Borg

Lawrence Livermore National Laboratory, Livermore, CA

Abstract

The US Plowshare programme, designed to develop peaceful uses of nuclear explosives, was vigorous from 1957 to 1973 and was of concern during US and Soviet negotiations in that period. In order to accommodate possible future applications, the Peaceful Nuclear Explosions Treaty was signed in 1976. The US programme explored the phenomenology of nuclear explosions and tested their use in industrial applications. Owing to waning industrial interest and public concern over environmental issues, the US programme was terminated in 1977. The Soviet counterpart to the Plowshare programme, which has involved more than 100 experiments, continued until the self-imposed moratorium in 1985. As any peaceful use of nuclear explosives has the potential of furthering weapon research, the USA takes the position that all such experiments would have to be banned in a comprehensive test ban treaty.

I. Introduction

From the start of test ban negotiations between the USA and the USSR in Geneva in 1958 until negotiations reached a stalemate in 1980, the use of peaceful nuclear explosions (PNEs) was at issue. Until 1960 only the USA actively worked for their accommodation in a test ban, but the USSR subsequently became interested as well. In 1957 and 1959 two symposia were held in the USA to discuss the industrial uses of nuclear explosions. In the eyes of most participants the new technology held great promise in unlocking inaccessible resources and in reducing costs associated with large earth-moving projects, such as for canal building. By 1977, after negotiation of the Peaceful Nuclear Explosions Treaty (PNET) the previous year, the USA had abandoned its PNE programme. The last US PNE experiment was conducted in 1973. By this time the USSR was apparently conducting up to nine PNE experiments per year under its programme, which continued until the self-imposed moratorium in 1985.[1] There have to date been approximately 100 presumed Soviet PNE experiments, which must be considered a testimonial to their success and perceived value to the Soviet Union.

In the following sections, the US PNE programme is reviewed together with the reasons for its termination and the impact of treaties concluded during its 20-year existence. Individual US and Soviet experiments were the subject of panel discussions under the aegis of the International Atomic Energy Agency (IAEA), and the reader is referred to these proceedings for technical details.[2] More general information can be found in references 3, 4, 5 and 6.

II. Development of the US PNE programme, 1957–77

Background

The US Atomic Energy Commission (AEC) formally approved the establishment of a programme to investigate non-military uses of nuclear explosives in June 1957. The Commission thus implemented the tacit promise first stated by the framers of the US Atomic Energy Act of 1946 that 'atomic energy is capable of application for peaceful as well as military purposes'. The decision followed informal studies started the previous year at the Lawrence Livermore National Laboratory. Enthusiasm and optimism accompanied the formal establishment of Project Plowshare, a name derived from a passage from the Old Testament: 'And they shall beat their swords into plowshares, and their spears into pruning hooks; nation shall not lift up sword against nation, neither shall they learn war any more'. However, the enthusiasm was tempered by caution since the field of nuclear explosive phenomenology was in its infancy, and it was realized at the outset that full-scale use of nuclear explosives for peaceful purposes would have to be preceded by numerous small-case high-explosive and nuclear experiments with attendant post-shot analysis of their effects.

Research and phenomenology experiments

At the outset of the US Plowshare programme it was realized that, before economically viable projects could be proposed, fundamental questions concerning environmental issues and rock response to large explosions had to be answered. All Plowshare experiments were heavily instrumented and designed to contribute to an understanding of the effects of nuclear explosions and their by-products on the environment. The objectives of the first nuclear Plowshare event were exploratory in nature: the 1961 Gnome test was a multi-purpose underground experiment in a salt formation involving seismic and heat measurements as well as isotope recovery, explosive development and a neutron physics experiment. Of especial importance was the acquisition of information that would validate theoretical calculations on the extent and degree of fracturing of the host rock and the seismic response of surrounding fractured and unfractured rock. By taking advantage of nuclear tests used in weapon development and in the Vela seismic programme, a variety of rock types were investigated. Their response to stress differed significantly and influenced the overall effects, all other things being equal. Post-shot cores were recovered in many of these experiments whereby the migration of radioactivity could be assessed as well as the degree of fracturing as a function of distance from the shot point. Division of radioisotopes between the melt produced and the surrounding rock indicated that the refractory isotopes were encapsulated in the 'melt' (consisting of melted rock and 0.01 per cent device debris) and that the more volatile species were contained within a few cavity radii.

The results did not speak against successful and safe use of nuclear explosions in commercial applications but did indicate areas of special concern. With more experience the calculations were refined and validated, thereby building confidence in the ability to predict effects and ultimately in the technology itself. Nonetheless there remained many untested rock media. For example, there was no experience with water-saturated porous rocks and soils, which was an important area for investigation since formation water had long been recognized as an important determinant in rock response to nuclear explosions.

Excavation

Judged by the number of experiments, it can be seen from table 4.1 that excavation projects were considered to be the most important application of the technology in its first decade of development in the USA. In 1961 the US AEC entered into an agreement with the US Army Corps of Engineers to investigate nuclear excavation as a means of constructing a new sea-level canal through the Central American Isthmus. The 11 high-explosive (HE) and 7 nuclear experiments and the 11 nuclear device development tests reflect the large number of uncertainties, especially those relating to the environment, that attended use of nuclear explosives for this purpose. All excavation experiments were conducted at the Nevada Test Site (NTS) with the exception of two HE tests which were conducted in Montana and south-east Idaho. The early HE experiments were designed to study the relation between crater size, depth of burial and size of the explosive detonated. Distribution of rock and soil displaced by the explosions, ground motion, rate of growth of the dust clouds and air blast effects were studied in detail.

The first nuclear excavation was the small (0.43-kt) experiment conducted in 1962 in basalt. It was followed by the Sedan experiment, which was the largest test conducted in the Plowshare programme, with a nuclear yield of 100 kt. The detonation produced a crater 98 m deep and 366 m in diameter and displaced 5.7 million m^3 of alluvium. Additional tests were conducted to explore cratering mechanisms in hard rock as well as to study dispersion of airborne radionuclides. In 1968 the first nuclear row-charge experiment involving five 1.1-kt charges spaced 46 m apart produced a smooth-walled trench 77 m wide and 20 m deep. Two more experiments were dedicated to excavation by the end of 1970. At that point the final report of the Atlantic–Pacific Interoceanic Canal Commission was published. The Commission was established in 1965 by US

Table 4.1. Plowshare experiments

Purpose	Type of explosive	
	Nuclear	HE[a]
Phenomenology experiments	Rainier 1957[b] Gnome 1961 Hardhat 1962[b] Shoal 1963[b] Handcar 1964[b] Piledriver 1965[b]	Pre-Gnome 1959
Excavation	Danny Boy 1962[b] Sedan 1962 Sulky 1964 Palanquin 1965 Cabriolet 1968 Buggy 1968 Schooner 1968	Toboggan 1960 Stagecoach 1960 Scooter 1960 Buckboard 1960 Rowboat 1961 Pre-Buggy I 1963 Pre-Buggy II 1963 Pre-Schooner I 1964 Dugout 1964 Pre-Schooner II 1965 Pre-Gondola I 1966 Pre-Gondola II 1967 Pre-Gondola III 1968
Underground storage	Salmon 1964[b]	
Oil shale development		Pinot 1960
Gas stimulation	Gasbuggy 1967 Rulison 1969 Rio Blanco 1973	
PNE explosives development	12 experiments 1963–71	
Heavy element production	19 experiments 1962–69	

[a] Pre-1960 HE cratering experiments have been omitted.
[b] Multi-purpose experiments.

Public Law 88–609 to study sites and methods of constructing a sea-level isthmian canal connecting the Atlantic and Pacific oceans. The Commission did not criticize the use of nuclear explosions for other excavation projects but concluded that the water-saturated rock at the Isthmus represented a unique situation which had not yet been fully investigated. In addition, stability of the canal walls produced by the row explosions in the presence of wave action was brought into question.

Development of PNE explosives

Twelve experiments took place in an effort to develop an explosive suitable for use in peaceful applications. The principal focus was development of an explosive that would minimize the amount of radioactivity reaching the biosphere in excavation projects. The approach was to limit the fission yield, and therefore production of fission products, by using a thermonuclear device in which almost all of the energy came from fusion reactions. Products of neutron activation on the surrounding rock and in device materials from high-energy neutrons produced by thermonuclear reactions posed an additional problem. Experiments were carried out to provide neutron shielding for the explosive so as to limit the amount of activation.

Special problems in explosive design arose in connection with gas stimulation. Tritium proved to be the chief radioactive contaminant of gas produced following the early Gasbuggy test. Tritium can be released during detonation of a fusion device, but it also can arise through neutron capture by trace amounts of lithium in the surrounding rock. A special fission explosive was designed and tested (Miniata test) for use on the full-scale gas stimulation experiment conducted in Colorado in 1973.

In view of the ultimate Plowshare objective to provide less costly ways of developing resources, considerable effort was expended to minimize costs associated with emplacement of explosives principally by reduction in the size and diameter of the explosive system. Successful design resulted in a 20-cm multi-device system in a single well bore to depths of 3000 m and which was tolerant of ambient temperatures up to 150°C.

Gas stimulation

Three gas stimulation experiments were conducted under the Plowshare programme. Each was co-sponsored by an industrial firm or consortium that, in addition to contributing to the funding of the project, provided the sites and post-shot reservoir analyses. All three sites were in so-called 'tight gas reservoirs' whose low permeability prohibited conventional production. The Gasbuggy experiment took place in the San Juan Basin, New Mexico; Rulison followed two years later in Colorado; and the final experiment, Rio Blanco, also in Colorado, became in 1973 the last Plowshare experiment in the programme. The first two tests involved explosives in the 30- to 40-kt range. Both provided extensive information on the radioactive contaminants, and the quantity and quality of the gas produced after the tests, which in turn reflected the extent of nuclear fracturing. In both cases post-shot cores and/or calculations based on gas production indicated that fracturing extended out to 70–90 m or roughly three cavity radii. Rulison broke new ground in the developing technology since it was the deepest PNE-application nuclear explosion ever conducted in the USA (at 2568 m).

Spacing of discrete gas-bearing strata at the Rio Blanco site dictated use of three 30-kt nuclear explosives 37–44 m apart in the same emplacement hole. It was expected that after their simultaneous detonation the void space created by each explosive would be connected by fractures, and the released gas would be produced by drilling into the uppermost chimney. Post-shot re-entry into both the lower and upper voids created by the explosions indicated that a vertical connection had not been made.[7] The reasons for the lack of connection remain conjectural; however, it was considered to be more of an inconvenience than a failure to stimulate the gas-rich portions of the geological section. The gas produced from the two re-entry wells consisted of 52–58 per cent CO_2, 10–14 per cent H_2 and 32–34 per cent hydrocarbons. About 7 per cent of the tritium produced was associated with the gas.[8] Negligible amounts of other radio-isotopes were detected.

Unfortunately there had been no testing of the gas reservoir before the Rio Blanco experiment. The amount of gas that was shown to be in place by post-shot testing proved to be considerably less than pre-shot predictions based on general reservoir properties. Analysis of post-shot production data suggested that pre-shot extrapolations used to estimate permeability and to calculate the permeability-height parameter in pre-shot predictive models were over-estimated by factors of six to ten in the three potentially productive strata. Height in this context is the effective thickness of the gas-bearing strata. Pressure buildup after pumping during production tests also suggested that the gas-producing sections were much more limited laterally than had been believed before the experiment. Nonetheless permeability was enhanced twenty-fold to 2.85 cavity radii, or a distance of 57 m. In summary, the disappointing results with respect to gas production have been attributed to poorer than anticipated reservoir properties. A principal participant on the project summed it up with the statement, 'if we had known in 1972 what we know now about this site, the project would not have been executed there'.[9]

Heavy element production

The Plowshare programme endeavoured to develop special nuclear explosives that would test nuclear theories and lead to the production of elements beyond atomic number 100 (fermium) in the intense neutron fluxes developed within the device cores. The ultimate uses envisioned for the isotopes were in diagnostic and therapeutic medicine. Despite numerous experiments (see table 4.1), no mass number greater than 257 was found, and the search was discontinued after 1969.

Underground storage

Production of standing cavities that could be used for underground storage of hydrocarbons or waste material was suggested as a useful application of nuclear explosions. An experiment conducted in the Tatum salt dome in Mississippi in 1964 (Salmon test) demonstrated the concept. Salt is an ideal medium because of its low strength and hence its plasticity at relatively low temperatures and pressures. In contrast to the rubble-filled chimneys and cavities associated with nuclear explosions in brittle rock, the Salmon salt cavity was nearly spherical and devoid of rubble. Almost all of the radioactivity was encapsulated in a salt puddle at the bottom of the cavity. Although the cavity was found to be under partial vacuum when re-entered, its integrity was not tested at high pressure. It subsequently survived detonation of a 0.38-kt explosive within the void space in a decoupling experiment. No further experiments relating specifically to storage were carried out by the USA.

III. Feasibility studies on application of nuclear explosions

The US Government entered into agreements with private companies to undertake in-depth feasibility studies on specific projects (see table 4.2). Many other applications of PNEs were suggested but did not reach the feasibility study stage for lack of an industrial sponsor. Many proposed uses of PNEs, however, have had extensive development in the USSR, for example, oil stimulation and deep seismic sounding.

One of the most detailed feasibility studies was made by the Atlantic–Pacific Interoceanic Canal Commission, mentioned above. Although the Commission concluded that the nuclear technology posed too many uncertainties to be considered a viable option at that time, the final report estimated the savings associated with the use of nuclear explosives to be on the order of $1–2 billion out of total costs of $3–5 billion, depending on the route.

Perhaps in response to the provisions of the 1968 Non-Proliferation Treaty (NPT), two non-nuclear weapon states undertook preliminary feasibility studies. The Kra Canal project in Thailand proposed to link the Gulf of Thailand with the Andaman Sea. The use of 139 explosives ranging from 100 to 1000 kt and totalling 41.35 Mt was envisioned. Although use of nuclear excavation techniques was estimated to save several billion dollars and two to four years in construction time, the Thai Government was uncertain whether

Table 4.2. Plowshare feasibility studies

Excavation	Atlantic–Pacific Interoceanic Canal, 1965–70	
	Kra Canal, Thailand 1975	
	Qattara depression, Egypt 1976	
	Project Carry-all 1963–64	Atkinson, Topeka and Santa Fe Railroad
Oil shale development	Project Bronco 1966–67	CER Geonuclear representing 20 oil companies
Copper ore leaching	Project Sloop 1965–67	Kennecott Copper Corp.
Underground storage	Project Ketch 1965–67	Columbia Gas System Service Corp.
Gas stimulation	Project Dragon Trail 1966–69	CER Geonuclear and Continental Oil Co
	Project Wagon Wheel 1968–70	El Paso Gas Co.
	Project WASP 1969–70	Oil and Gas Futures, Inc.

the nuclear option was practical 'in light of current world perspectives'.[10]

The second proposal was to channel Mediterranean Sea water 54–79 km into the Qattara Depression, Egypt, and to use the difference in elevation to generate hydroelectric power. Numerous surveys and pre-feasibility studies preceded the final study which was described in 1976.[11] It called for use of at least 181 explosives in the 150- to 500-kt range or 439 140-kt explosives. Costs associated with the project were estimated to be $510–820 million depending on the number of explosives. The 1976 PNET ultimately placed a 150-kt ceiling on such detonations, and the proposal did not go any farther.

IV. Termination of the Plowshare programme

The termination of the US programme in 1977 was due to waning industrial interest and mounting public concerns about environmental consequences. These two factors are linked. Every effort was made during the Plowshare years to assess costs associated with commercial application of PNEs and to compare them with costs of conventional development. In the case of virtually inaccessible deeply buried resources, comparisons of this sort cannot be made. Cost estimates in these instances had to be related to the value of the resource recovered. Here the potential industrial sponsors' financial resources and their willingness to risk them were the critical factors. At the same time, public objections in the USA to the use of nuclear explosives because of possible radiation releases and contamination added a new and unknown dimension to cost estimates. Project Rulison had been delayed by a possible injunction against the release and burning of gas produced by the explosion because of the possible presence of radioactivity. The US District Court ruled in Colorado in 1970 that gas releases after the explosion did not present a threat to public health and safety; however, there was no guarantee that similar attempts to stop experiments would not occur in the course of carrying out planned projects. Through a public referendum the state of Colorado went so far as to amend its constitution in 1974, so that detonation of any nuclear explosion in the state had to be approved by the voters.

Technical questions and uncertainties connected to many of the proposed PNE projects remained; however, project scientists believed that they could be dealt with satisfactorily. Excavation presented special environmental risks related to possible radioactive release into the atmosphere which, together with the limitations set by the 1963 Partial Test Ban Treaty (PTBT), led the United States to focus its research efforts on underground detonations starting in about 1968. At that point, 7 nuclear excavation experiments, 11 excavation device development tests, and more than 13 HE excavation experiments had been carried out. This is to be contrasted to only 2 fully contained underground nuclear Plowshare experiments and 2 HE experiments conducted in the same period. In this count, multi-purpose tests with military objectives that contributed to the understanding of explosive phenomenology have been ignored, as have heavy element production experiments. In short, by the time that criticism of the Plowshare concept began to surface, US experience related primarily to shallowly buried explosions associated with excavation and not with development of deeply buried resources, such as oil, oil shale and natural gas. The Rio Blanco experiment, designed to stimulate natural gas production, was a disappointment; however, in the final analyses the technology itself was not called into question but rather the choice of reservoirs with limited potential for resource recovery as experimental sites. The two previous gas stimulation sites had similar characteristics. However, the Gasbuggy and Rulison tests in 'tight' gas sands were aimed more at exploring the use of nuclear explosives in a hydrocarbon environment than in demonstrating that theretofore unavailable gas supplies could be brought to commercial markets.

V. The Soviet PNE programme to 1973

By the end of 1973, the year of the last US Plowshare explosion, the USSR had conducted 39 presumed PNE experiments, as judged by announcements by seismic laboratories such as the Hagfors Observatory of the Swedish National Defence Research Institute (known as FOA) and by the location of the shots away from the normal weapon testing sites.[12] Many of these experiments had been described by the USSR at international conferences and in the literature.[13] There are several detailed reviews of this information,[14] so it will be only briefly summarized here.

In the early years of the Soviet programme the focus was on understanding and developing the technology. Small and large excavation experiments were undertaken in preparation for proposed projects such as diversion of the Pechora River into the Kama River and thence to the Caspian Sea. The largest experiment, called '1004' with an estimated yield of 125 kt,[15] was detonated in a river and produced two lakes. The excavation technology was described as 'proven'; however, as in the case of the US Plowshare programme, excavation did not develop as a viable PNE option. Possibly the Soviet concern over their ability to contain radioactivity from large excavation experiments within their borders led to curtailed development and use. Radioactive debris from the large '1004' excavation experiment and the Pechora-Kova canal experiment in 1971 was detected in northern Europe and elsewhere.[16]

Deeply buried PNEs served to explore their use in breaking up ores in mining applications, and a proposed mineral development project was described whereby a 1.8-kt explosive would break 1 million cubic metres of ore.

A small PNE experiment in a salt dome explored the possibility of creating void space underground for storage purposes. Another larger experiment was followed by an experiment in a gas condensate field that produced storage for 300 000 barrels of condensate. Underground storage was also considered to be a 'proven technology'.

Oil stimulation in two fields using several small explosives in each case was initially described as highly successful. Increased oil production was reported for a 15-year period following the shot in Field A.[17] These experiments broke new ground since they demonstrated not only the technology but also that nuclear explosions could be set off in oil fields without damaging operating wells, pipelines and other facilities. No radioactivity was detected in the oil, according to Soviet observers.[18]

The last of the 'proven technologies' described by Soviet scientists was control of runaway gas wells. In two gas fields, relatively large (30–40 kt) nuclear explosives were able to choke off gas flow from otherwise uncontrollable wells, thereby saving millions of rubles.

VI. The Soviet PNE programme after 1973

In the intervening years since the last IAEA Conference on Peaceful Uses of Nuclear Explosives in 1976, little has been published in the Soviet Union about what apparently has been a large programme with diverse objectives. At the end of 1985 more than 100 explosions outside of the normal weapon testing areas had been recorded and identified as nuclear by one or more governmental agency such as the Swedish National Defence Research Institute, the US Department of Energy (formerly the AEC), and the National Earthquake Information Service of the US Geological Survey. This must be considered a minimum since some of the small experiments described by the USSR early in its programme were not identified as such by these agencies. In addition, it is likely that others have not been detected for various reasons, for example, because of overlapping seismic signals from large earthquakes in other parts of the world.

From the location of Soviet PNEs it can be surmised that there have been two principal uses: creation of underground storage and production of strong sources for deep seismic sounding. Explosions have been recorded in the immediate vicinity of giant gas condensate fields under development at Orenburg, Karachagnak and Astrakhan, south-west of the Ural mountains. Only Orenburg has been specifically identified as a storage site.[19] Construction of nuclear storage facilities here was reported to have been three to five times cheaper than conventional storage, presumably that being surface tanks or storage constructed using standard salt washing techniques to create void space. Salt formations and salt domes present at depth at all three fields are ideal media for production of underground storage volumes by nuclear means. Such caverns proved to be both devoid of fractures and leak-proof, and radiation was not considered to be a hazard.[20] Typically the gas and condensate in these fields have a high sulphur content, and in addition to providing interim storage for the condensate, such facilities could provide storage for sulphurous waste products from nearby processing plants.

In addition to PNEs associated with underground storage near gas condensate fields, a large number of nuclear explosions for unknown purposes have been recorded in the general area north of the Caspian Sea. These were also detonated in salt domes and produced open underground cavities of various undisclosed sizes. There may be a total of 30–40 such cavities if the gas condensate storage facilities are included. The seismic magnitude (m_b) associated with these explosions are in the 5–6 range, suggesting that most of the nuclear explosives were modest in size. They are environments which could be appropriate for decoupled weapon tests that could escape detection. There remains the possibility that some cavities are interconnected vertically or horizontally, or that several detonations at the same location led to enlargement of the first cavity formed, thereby producing larger cavities than suggested by individual yields and which could be appropriate for decoupling if that were desired.

Deep seismic sounding (DSS) is an exploratory technique whereby seismic waves generated from a strong source are recorded at stations distant from the sources. Shallowly buried explosives or vibrators on the surface are normally used to generate the signal. The seismic waves are reflected and refracted at discontinuities in the crust, and analysis of the data enables accurate mapping of geological structure at depth. Nuclear sources are strong enough to reach the mantle of the earth underlying the crust as well.[21] Use of widely spaced nuclear sources, called 'large industrial explosions' by Soviet geophysicists,[22] is a convenient and novel technique to explore inaccessible areas of the USSR that are not amenable to the use of conventional, closely spaced seismic sources. Some measure of this portion of the Soviet PNE programme can be garnered from the coincidence of nuclear explosions along seismic lines described in the Soviet geophysical literature.[23]

The USA is aware of 10 DSS traverses or seismic profiles across the USSR, the last of which occurred in 1984–85. They usually involve four or five nuclear explosions per line, and the data are possibly augmented by the use of smaller, HE explosives. The traverses each span thousands of kilometres. There can be little doubt as to the uniqueness and value of the DSS nuclear programme in producing a back-drop for detailed exploration of shallower geological structure and natural resources.

There is reason to believe that the USSR has in the past decade pursued many of the PNE applications which it termed 'proven technology' in earlier international exchanges. The locations of nuclear explosions reported by seismic laboratories are often in or near oil and gas fields, suggesting that stimulation may have been the objective. Gas stimulation experiments in eastern Siberia are reported to have converted 'non-industrial oil and gas deposits from uneconomic resources into the industrially developable category';[24] however, details have not been given. Similarly, use of nuclear explosives in mining operations and disposal of biologically dangerous industrial waste has been described only cursorily.[25]

In summary, the Soviet PNE programme has been large, multi-faceted, apparently successful and, judging from its size and repeated use of nuclear explosives for particular purposes, of great value to the Soviet economy. General Secretary Gorbachev is on record as having mentioned the economic benefits forgone by instituting the test moratorium in 1985, and the Soviet Ambassador to the UK is quoted to the same effect.[26]

VII. Economic viability of PNEs

The reason for the termination of the PNE programme in the USA did not include the conviction that the proposals were not economically sound. That may have proven to be the case, in view of the unexpected delays and cost overruns that have been associated with development of the nuclear power industry during the past decade in the USA owing to increased public concern. At the time of the termination of the US programme, the Government had not fully worked out details as to how costs associated with the explosive and its development, if it were to be tailored to a specific use, would be shared with its industrial partner. None the less, all cost analyses took into account estimated damage claims associated with seismic effects and safety and radiological monitoring as well as all costs associated with emplacement, firing and post-shot drilling. Table 4.3 gives cost comparisons between conventional and nuclear development.[27]

The best information available as to the total cost of a PNE project was given in the case of gas stimulation in Colorado (the Rio Blanco experiment). Based on three 100-kt explosives per well, the cost per well was estimated at $2.4–3.3 million, in 1976 US dollars.[28]

In the case of the Soviet programme, it can only be surmised that it has been economically profitable. While at the time of the last PNE project the US programme was still in the experimental stage, the Soviet counterpart in the intervening years has progressed far beyond that stage, as judged by the number of PNEs that have been conducted and the repeated use in develop-

Table 4.3. Cost of conventional and nuclear development

	Conventional	PNE
Storage: $ (1970) per barrel		
Leached salt caverns	1.0 – 2.5	
Steel tanks	2.0 – 5.0	
Nuclear cavities		0.77–1.70
Oil shale: $ (1975) per up-graded barrel		
Mining and surface retorting	12	
Nuclear fracturing and in-situ retorting		5
Natural gas: $ (1980) per million cubic feet		
Massive hydraulic fracturing		
High production	0.23–0.63	
Low production	0.43–0.72	
Nuclear fracturing		
High prodution		0.25–0.66
Low production		0.55–0.93
15% discounted cash flow rate of return		

Source: See reference 27.

ment of several types of resources. Thirty-five per cent of the Soviet nuclear tests in 1984, the last full year of testing before the moratorium, were PNEs.[29] Of the 48 PNEs conducted by the USA that were either devoted ('dedicated') to peaceful purposes or 'add-ons' to weapon tests in order better to understand the effects, only 6 were exploded outside of the NTS. By contrast, of the more than 100 Soviet PNE explosions which are known, only a small number were conducted at their usual weapon testing sites. Thus the bulk of the Soviet PNEs were fielded in areas under active resource development. Some idea of the profitability of their oil-stimulation PNEs has been explored from a Western viewpoint using data supplied by Soviet scientists at IAEA exchanges.[30] The rate of return associated with the 'Reservoir A' project is estimated to be 55–60 per cent and the present profit, discounted at 15 per cent, is around 380 per cent. Seven million barrels or 35 per cent more oil was recovered owing to nuclear stimulation at the time of analysis.

VIII. PNEs in emerging nuclear countries

The only country that has recently had an active PNE programme is the USSR; however, several countries which are non-signatories to the NPT have stated that they want to preserve the option of developing all forms of peaceful use of nuclear energy.

In 1974, India detonated a nuclear explosive in the Rajasthan desert which has been repeatedly described by Indian Government officials as an experiment for peaceful purposes. The explosion followed a series of IAEA conferences on the peaceful uses of nuclear explosives in the early 1970s that explored the potential benefits in resource development. The Indian Atomic Energy Department had in 1972 concluded that two minerals—copper and uranium—could be economically extracted using the technology and subsequently undertook geological, hydrological and ecological surveys in order to decide on a specific project. The programme did not proceed although Prime Minister Indira Gandhi maintained in 1980 that the country was committed to the peaceful development of nuclear energy and explosion of nuclear devices if it was in the national interest.[31] As far as is known, India has not detonated another nuclear explosion, although its capability cannot now be doubted.

IX. Impact of the PTBT, NPT, TTBT and PNET

The Partial Test Ban Treaty prohibits detonation of nuclear explosives in the atmosphere, in outer space and under water. The treaty did not deter planned PNE experiments nor discourage feasibility studies involving deep underground burial, such as in storage or gas stimulation applications. Neither did it interfere with excavation experiments. The 100-kt Sedan excavation experiment was carried out before the PTBT at a depth of 194 m, but in the view of US scientists it would in any case not have been considered to be an atmospheric nuclear explosion, despite the fact that rock and debris were ejected hundreds of metres into the air. An additional stipulation of the treaty—that no radioactive debris be allowed 'outside the territorial limits of the state under whose jurisdiction or control the explosion is conducted'—posed no problem to the PNE countries. The terms of the final treaty belied the many PNE issues that had been addressed during the deliberations. By 1960 they [the USSR] seemed to have developed some interest in conducting peaceful explosions themselves and proposed a treaty article that would have permitted such detonations in proportions of one to one for the two sides.[32] They requested the right to inspect Plowshare devices as well. In view of the extensive research that had been and continued to be devoted to developing a tailored device for PNE use, the USA objected.

The Non-Proliferation Treaty stipulated that the nuclear states make available any benefits from peaceful uses of nuclear explosions in order to discourage non-nuclear countries from designing and building nuclear explosives for 'PNE uses'. Its effect was to encourage non-nuclear states such as Thailand and Egypt to consider the nuclear option in solving long-standing development problems and to expect co-operation from the nuclear nations.

Article V of the NPT provides that the benefits from any peaceful applications of nuclear explosions be made available 'under appropriate international observation and through appropriate international procedures'. In 1968 the United Nations General Assembly noted that the IAEA was an appropriate organ to exercise these functions (resolution 2456 (XXIII)). In June 1972, as the first step, the IAEA developed guidelines for international observation of PNEs which would take effect following the signing of an agreement between the country supplying the nuclear services and the country in which the explosion was to be carried out. The observations were designed to assure against violations of Articles I and II of the NPT, or of analogous provisions in other international agreements. As a second step in 1974, the IAEA issued a document outlining procedures for responding to requests for its services in connection with Article V. The procedural guidelines called for the IAEA to review feasibility studies to provide the basis for a decision on whether to proceed with detailed design and implementation. The final study, in addition to dealing with a full range of geological, meteorological, health and safety issues, was to include a detailed evaluation of alternatives to the use of nuclear explosives and a cost-benefit analysis. It also required information on the PNE explosive characteristics. If the project looked feasible and if the state considering the project so desired, the IAEA would invite all PNE supplier states to consider participation. If called upon, the IAEA was willing to provide an independent review of the health and safety aspects of the project in order to reassure concerned nations that economic advantages had not been given precedence. An additional role in the project which was envisaged for the IAEA was as an observer, monitor and reporter.

In 1975 the IAEA set up an ad hoc Advisory Group on Nuclear Explosions for Peaceful Purposes. Its charge was to develop legal instruments and procedures for implementation of Article V. In doing so, it hoped to eliminate any possible excuse for not signing the NPT on the ground that the nuclear states were not living up to Article V commitments. In 1977 the final report recommended the use of the 1974 procedural guidelines and proposed that the IAEA develop a plan for observing, monitoring and reporting on the project.

Failing agreement on a comprehensive test ban treaty, the USA and the USSR began bilateral discussions in 1974 aimed at imposing some restrictions on nuclear testing. The Threshold Test Ban Treaty signed by Nixon and Brezhnev limited underground tests for any purpose to 150 kt. Again, PNEs had been the subject of long deliberation since projects such as the proposed Qattara Depression–Mediterranean Sea canal were jeopardized by such limitations which profoundly affected costs. PNE proposals tended to call for the highest feasible yields since the cost of a nuclear explosive is relatively unaffected by the yield. Also at this juncture, the USSR was more interested than the USA in all aspects of resource development using PNEs. Their early proposals included reversing the flow of major rivers in the USSR that flowed into the Arctic Ocean. To accommodate PNEs the Peaceful Nuclear Explosions Treaty was signed in May 1976. It restated the 150-kt limit, imposed a 1.5-Mt yield on group explosions, and both countries were to have the right to observe multiple PNEs fired by the other.

The Carter Administration did not press for ratification of the TTBT and the PNET and instead decided to negotiate for a comprehensive test ban. In the negotiations that resumed the following year, PNEs continued to be an issue at Soviet insistence. By this time the Plowshare programme in the USA had been terminated. US objections to accommodation of PNEs related to verification issues. In the interim little progress has been made in framing a CTB treaty, and the Soviet programme grew appreciably. Peaceful use or testing of PNE explosives within the limitations set by existing treaties has the potential of providing significant military information to a non-nuclear state. Successful detonation of a PNE in itself could constitute critical information in the absence of a weapon testing programme. Prohibition of such experiments would be required in a comprehensive test ban treaty.

Notes and references

[1] Sands, J. I., Norris, R. S. and Cochran, T. B., *Known Soviet Nuclear Explosions, 1945–1985*, National Resources Defence Council, Inc. Report NWD-86-3, Washington, DC, June 1986, pp. 1–51.

[2] International Atomic Energy Agency, *Peaceful Nuclear Explosions I–V, Proceedings of Technical Panel* (IAEA: Vienna, Austria, 1970, 1971, 1974, 1975 and 1978).

[3] Terman, M. J., 'Nuclear-explosion petroleum-stimulation projects, United States and USSR', *Bulletin of the American Association of Petroleum Geologists*, vol. 57, no. 6 (June 1973), pp. 990–1026.

[4] Toman, J. and Tewes, H. A., 'The potential of Plowshare for resource development', *Nuclear Methods in Mineral Exploration and Production*, ed. J. G. Morse (Elsevier Scientific: Asterdam, 1977), pp. 215–53.

[5] Ballou, L., Nordyke, N. and Werth, G., *A Summary of US PNE Experience*, Lawrence Livermore Laboratory Report UCID-17649, Livermore, CA, Nov. 1977, pp. 1–14.

[6] Crump, J. R., *PNE (Peaceful Nuclear Explosion) Activity Projections for Arms Control*

Planning, GURC Report No. 143 (Gulf Universities Research Consortium: Galveston, TX, Apr. 1975), pp. 1–267.

[7] Toman, J., 'Project Rio Blanco—Part II. Production test data and preliminary analysis of top chimney/cavity', *Peaceful Nuclear Explosions IV, Proceedings of a Technical Committee, Vienna, 1975* (International Atomic Energy Agency: Vienna, 1975), pp. 117–40; and Ballou, L. B., 'Project Rio Blanco—Additional production testing and reservoir analysis', *Peaceful Nuclear Explosions V, Proceedings of a Technical Committee, Vienna, 1976* (International Atomic Energy Agency: Vienna, 1978), pp. 73–95.

[8] Ballou (note 7).

[9] Ballou (note 7).

[10] Srisukh, S., 'Thailand's Kra Canal project', *Peaceful Nuclear Explosions IV, Proceedings of a Technical Committee, Vienna, 1975* (International Atomic Energy Agency: Vienna, 1975), pp. 209–25.

[11] El Shazly, E. M., 'Development of the Qattara Projet, Egypt', *Peaceful Nuclear Explosions V, Proceedings of a Technical Committee, Vienna, 1976* (International Atomic Energy Agency: Vienna, 1978), pp. 97–123.

[12] Note 1.

[13] Note 2.

[14] Note 3; and Nordyke, M. D., 'A review of Soviet data on the peaceful uses of nuclear explosions', *Annals of Nuclear Energy*, vol. 2 (1975), pp. 657–73.

[15] Nordyke (note 14).

[16] Koyama, S., Sotobayanshi, T. and Suzuki, T., 'Highly fractimated nuclear debris resulting from the venting of a Soviet underground nuclear test', *Nature*, vol. 209 (15 Jan. 1966), p. 239; and Kolb, W., 'Tungsten-181 and other short lived fission products in ground level air in North Germany and North Norway', *Nature*, vol. 232 (20 Aug. 1971), p. 552.

[17] Kruglov, A. K., 'Atomic science and technology for the national economy of the country', *Atomic Energy-USSR*, vol. 50, issue 2 (Feb. 1981).

[18] Bakirov, A. A., Bakirov, E. A., Vinogradov, V. N., *et al.*, *Use of Underground Nuclear Explosions in the Oil Producing Industry*, Lawrence Livermore National Laboratory Translation UCRL-TRANS-11958, Livermore, CA, Mar. 1984, pp. 184–5.

[19] Gubarev, V., 'Two steps from the epicenter', *Tecknika Molodezhi*, vol. 12 (Nov.–Dec. 1978), pp. 34–7.

[20] Note 19.

[21] Scheimer, J. F. and Borg, I. Y., 'Deep seismic sounding with nuclear explosives in the Soviet Union', *Science*, vol. 226 (16 Nov. 1984), pp. 787–92.

[22] Yegorkin, A. V., Kun, V. V. and Chernyshchev, N. M., 'Absorption of longitudinal and traverse waves in the crust and upper mantle of the West Siberian Plate and the Siberian Platform', *Izvestiya, Earth Physics*, vol. 17, no. 2 (1981), pp. 105–15.

[23] Note 21.

[24] Note 17.

[25] Note 17.

[26] Jacobsen, C., paper 18, this volume; and Nordyke (note 14).

[27] Note 4, chapter 7.

[28] Rubin, B., Schwartz, L. and Montan, D., *An Analysis of Gas Stimulation Using Nuclear Explosives*, Lawrence Livermore Laboratory Report UCRL-51226, 15 May, 1972, pp. 1–66.

[29] Note 1.

[30] Howard, J. H. and King, J. E., 'Nuclear frac could be feasible for carbonate reservoirs', *Oil and Gas Journal*, no. 81 (12 Dec. 1983), pp. 84–92.

[31] *Washington Post*, 14 Mar. 1980, p. A28.

[32] Seaborg, G. T., *Kennedy, Khruschev and the Test Ban* (University of California Press: Berkeley, 1981), pp. 39–40.

Chapter IV. Environmental effects of underground nuclear explosions

Paper 5

A. C. McEwan

National Radiation Laboratory, Christchurch, New Zealand

Abstract

Underground nuclear explosions give rise to ground disturbance effects which are local to the test site. These include slides, subsidence, ground fractures and minor fault displacements which contribute to aftershocks. Up to 1 per cent of the energy yield may be transmitted away from the site as a seismic wave. Triggering of a major earthquake is not a probable outcome. Radioactive materials produced in explosions are largely incorporated in vitrified rock, although minor venting, particularly of gases and volatiles, may occur at the time of detonation if the depth of emplacement is not sufficient for complete confinement. If ground water is present, leaching of radionuclides allows migration off site at rates dependent on water flow rate and path length and the sorption properties of the geologic strata. No significantly adverse radiological outcomes are seen as a result of leakage from underground test sites.

I. Phenomenological effects

Cavity, fracture and chimney formation

The effects observed when a nuclear device is detonated underground are dependent on such factors as the depth of emplacement, the yield of the device and the nature of the rock medium. In a shallow underground explosion the overburden is blown away to form a crater and there is massive venting of high-pressure gases and vaporized weapon residues formed in the explosion. For a deep underground detonation these effects are essentially fully contained. The surface above the detonation point may be disturbed by the formation of a shallow subsidence crater, by a mound or by compaction of surface layers, and ground tremors may be detected at a distance. No significant venting to the atmosphere occurs, although some of the non-condensable gases present may seep out gradually to the surface. While a considerable number of shallow underground tests have been conducted, particularly to assess the potential for cratering and other civil engineering applications of nuclear explosions, most underground nuclear tests have been in the deep underground category, with depth of burial sufficient to result in no significant venting.

In the conduct of an underground test, a canister containing the nuclear device and instrumentation is lowered to the emplacement depth in a drill hole. The hole is stemmed with cement plugs and gravel and other backfill. The energy of the explosion is released within one microsecond, and in the following few microseconds the emplacement hardware and adjoining rock medium are vaporized and the temperature and pressure in the immediate vicinity of the device are raised to several million degrees and several million atmospheres, respectively. The initial cavity around the detonation point expands spherically with boiling rock vaporizing from its surface, and a strong shock wave expands in all directions at a velocity equal to or greater than the speed of sound in the rock medium. The shock wave crushes and fractures the surrounding rock to a distance several times that of the maximum cavity radius. Once the force of the shock wave falls below the regions of compressional and tensional failure of the rock, it continues as a seismic wave. The cavity size attained is dependent on the yield (varying approximately as the one-third power[1]) as well as on the lithostatic pressure and rock type. As the cavity begins to cool, molten rock and weapon debris material collect and solidify at the bottom of the cavity. With further cooling the gas pressure decreases to the point at which it no longer supports the overburden. Then, commonly, in a matter of seconds to hours, the roof falls in; this is followed by progressive collapse of the overlying rock to form a rock or rubble-filled chimney. The chimney diameter tends to be 10–20 per cent greater than the cavity diameter and to extend upwards to a height of 4 to 6 times the cavity radius[2] (see figure 5.1). If the upper ground layers are too weak to support their own weight, the subsidence proceeds to the surface to form a sink or collapse crater. Tests detonated in alluvium at Yucca Flat in the Nevada Test Site have resulted in hundreds of sinks of varying diameter dotting the landscape.[3]

For an explosion in which the chimney does not reach the earth's surface, the scaled depth of burial, expressed by $d/W^{1/3}$, should be greater than about 100, where d is the depth of burial in metres and W is the yield in kilotons TNT equivalent.[4] The expression for the scaled depth of burial implies that the depth needs to be increased as the third power of the yield to ensure containment. To minimize the possibility of seepage of radioactive gases through the ground to the atmosphere, underground tests have generally been conducted at scaled depths of greater than 125, particularly those of lower yield where depths of burial are relatively small. Scaled depths of burial for a few tests are listed in table 5.1, which includes some of the first underground tests conducted at the Nevada Test Site.[5] For the Blanca test, slight venting was reported.[6]

Seismic and ground shock effects

In a contained deep underground explosion, most of the energy is expended in the formation of the cavity and in the melting, deformation and fracturing of

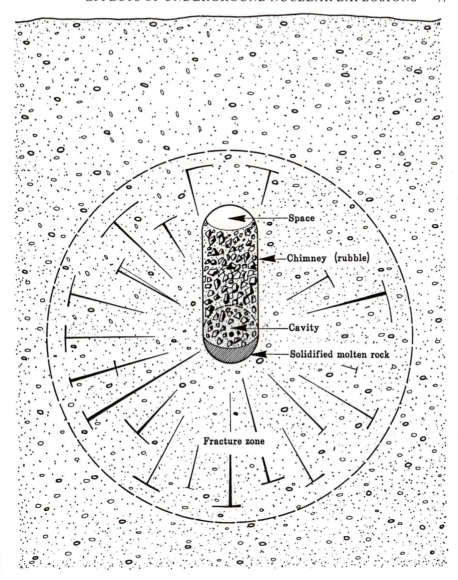

Figure 5.1. The fracture zone and chimney formed after collapse of the cavity in a deep underground nuclear detonation

rock. The energy transmitted as a seismic wave beyond the zone of compressional and tensional deformation may not exceed 1 per cent of the total energy release. The seismic efficiency, which is the fraction of energy that goes into seismic waves, varies between about 0.001 for dry alluvium and 0.01 for hard rocks like granite. Wet alluvium has a higher efficiency than dry by about a factor of 2, while detonation in a large air cavity could reduce the seismic

Photograph courtesy of US Department
of Energy

Figure 5.2. US Air Force helicopters fly DOE radiation-monitoring personnel and photographers over Yucca Flat during tests

Yucca Flat is dotted with more than 200 subsidence craters from underground explosions, which produce cavities. When the cavities collapse, they usually form surface subsidences. The craters vary in diameter and depth, depending on the explosive yield, depth of burial and geology. Dry Yucca Lake is visible in the distance.

efficiency by an order of magnitude.[7] The seismic wave produces a transient elastic displacement of the ground such as is typical of earthquake motion.

Fault displacements, aftershocks and earthquakes

One early concern about underground nuclear explosions was that the shock waves might trigger damaging earthquakes. However, no evidence has arisen which demonstrates that this has occurred, and there is no reason to indicate it to be likely, although nuclear detonations have triggered ground fractures and fault movements. Explosions are generally followed by a train of aftershocks,

Table 5.1. Examples of scaled depths of burial for five tests at the Nevada Test Site

Scaled depth of burial $= \dfrac{DOB}{W^{1/3}}$, where W is yield in kt and depth of burial (DOB) is in metres.

Test	Date	Yield, W (kt)	DOB (m)	Scaled DOB
Rainier	19 Sep. 1957	1.7	241	202
Logan	16 Oct. 1958	5	253	148
Blanca	30 Oct. 1958	19	255	95
Bilby	13 Sep. 1963	235	714	116
Benham	19 Dec. 1968	1 100	1 402	136

many of which are related to slumping associated with cavity collapse and chimney formation. Aftershocks which originate some distance outside the region of formation of the chimney are generally considered to result from small movements along pre-existing fault planes associated with the release of tectonic strain. In a few cases seismic energy released by fault displacement has exceeded that of the triggering explosion.[8] The aftershocks may continue, at a reduced rate, for many days after the chimney has formed.

The 1.1-Mt Benham test was conducted at a depth of 1400 m at the Nevada Test Site in December 1968. Over the next six weeks some hundreds of small to moderate earthquakes were detected, nearly all originating within 12 km of the detonation point. A plot of the focal points of the aftershocks revealed that most of these occurred along a north–south line, which is the general direction of the known faults in the region. Ground displacements also occurred along or near pre-existing fault lines, the maximum vertical displacement observed being about 0.5 m. A rough guide to the production of ground displacement along fault lines, developed from observations at the Nevada Test Site, is that displacements may occur if the distance from surface zero to fault line is less than about 300 $W^{1/3}$ metres, where W is the yield in kt.[9] For a 150-kt detonation, therefore, displacements are not likely to occur in faults at a distance of more than 1600 m.

Concerns that large explosions at the Nevada Test Site could trigger earthquakes as far away as California were raised publicly in 1969. A statistical analysis of the number of earthquakes per month recorded by the Berkeley network showed that no peaks of activity occurred following the known times of the largest explosions. The statistical analysis was in agreement with theoretical calculations that transient strain from underground explosions is not sufficient to trigger fault rupture beyond a limited distance from the detonation point.[10] Another statistical study of earthquake rates in a circular region around the Nevada Test Site compared rates prior to September 1961, when an extensive series of tests commenced, with rates after the high-yield Benham event. There was no significant variation in the earthquake rate.[11]

The focal depths of the aftershocks that have followed deep underground tests in Nevada have ranged from 0 to about 6 km, with most being in the range 1–5 km. Natural earthquakes in the same area occur at considerably greater depths. The two high-yield underground explosions at Amchitka Island in the Aleutians were of particular interest in relation to earthquake stimulation because of the seismically active nature of the region. The Milrow device of about 1.2-Mt yield was detonated on 2 October 1969 at a depth of 1220 m. The Cannikin explosion of 6 November 1971 at a depth of 1790 m had a yield of about 5 Mt. In each case many aftershocks were recorded arising from cavity deterioration and the eventual complete collapse of the cavity at times of 37 and 38 hours post-detonation, respectively. Earth tremors recorded on the following days were all at focal depths of less than about 7 km, whereas essentially all natural earthquakes in the area have hypocentres at depths of greater than about 20 km.[12] The seismic waves from Cannikin, the highest-yield underground detonation, had an amplitude corresponding to magnitude 7.1 (m_b). The final collapse of the cavity in which a crater a few kilometres in diameter was formed produced a magnitude 4.0 shock.[13]

As with naturally occurring earthquakes, ground motion from seismic waves arising from nuclear detonations could cause damage to buildings and other structures. At distances of tens of kilometres from the detonation point for high-yield explosions, a large proportion of the seismic energy appears in ground motion of longer periods. Because high-rise buildings have longer (1–2 second) natural vibration periods than shorter ones, tall buildings tend to exhibit a greater response. High-rise buildings in Las Vegas, more than 160 km from the area where high-yield nuclear tests at the Nevada Test Site have been conducted, have been known to sway in response to ground motions from the tests. Minor non-structural damage such as disturbance of ornamental blocks in one building and a cracked window in another were reported after the Handley event of greater than 1 Mt on 26 March 1970.[14] Mining and construction applications of nuclear explosions where distance separation from populated areas may not be achievable also raise the question of seismic safety. Following the 5.3-kt Salmon shot in 1964 at a depth of 900 m in the Tatum salt dome near Hattiesburg, Mississippi, minor damage to ordinary dwellings led to compensation to building owners amounting to about US $650 000.[15]

Other shock-induced effects

The shock wave radiating from the detonation point of a deep underground explosion, on reaching the surface, causes an upward heave of the ground. This may cause surface rock and soil to separate from the material below, an effect called spalling. The spalled material quickly crashes down again, and the ground surface then returns to approximately the same level as before the explosion. Depending on soil and rock type there may be a slight mound or depression. At the French test site at Mururoa Atoll underground detonations have been carried out in holes drilled into the volcanic rock which underlies the limestone upper layer of the atoll. Shock waves transmitted through the upper limestone levels effect compaction of the upper 70–100 m. This produces a subsidence of perhaps 10 cm per detonation, which is sometimes cumulative with successive nearby explosions. Occasionally a slight recovery is observed. However, an average subsidence of about 1 m has affected parts of the south-western and north-eastern rim of the atoll where extensive testing has been carried out.[16]

Shock waves from underground tests may also induce cliff collapse and slides at island margins similar to those that may be caused by natural earthquakes. Landslides on some of the sea cliffs at Amchitka were reported following the Milrow and Cannikin tests.[17] At Mururoa Atoll submarine slides and slumping have occurred following some tests. A submarine landslide was induced by a test in 1977, and similar smaller slides have been monitored seismically following other tests. The largest slide recorded followed an explosion on 25 July 1979, estimated[18] to have a yield of about 100 kt. The device was detonated at a depth of about 800 m, where the canister had stuck on emplacement, rather than at a design depth of 1000 m. The slide occurred several hours after detonation and involved about 1 million cubic metres of material from the upper and outer part of the reef on the southern margin of the atoll. However, this volume is only a small proportion of the carbonate material forming the slope.[19] The submarine landslide gave rise to a wave which swept over part of the atoll, placing the lives of several technicians at risk. One was seriously injured.

II. Pathways for dispersal of radionuclides in the environment

Production and initial distribution of radionuclides

At the moment of detonation of a nuclear device, an enormous quantity of radioactive products is formed. These radioactive products emit nuclear radiations, principally gamma and beta rays, and arise mostly as a result of the fission process. In addition to fission products, other radionuclides are formed by neutron reactions with the device material. The activity induced in weapon material is highly variable since it is dependent on design and structural characteristics. Another major source of radioactivity in underground explosions results from neutron irradiation of the surrounding rock. However, most of these activation products have a relatively short half-life.

The fission products are initially made up of a mixture of more than 300 nuclides of some 36 elements. Most of these nuclides are radioactive and decay by emission of beta and gamma radiation through up to four or more stages before a stable non-radioactive nucleus is formed. At one minute after a nuclear explosion, the activity of the fission products is about 10^{21} becquerels per kiloton of fission yield.[20] The gamma radiation exposure rate associated with the fission products and weapon material activation products decreases rapidly with time, with roughly a decrease by a factor of 10 for every seven-fold

Table 5.2. Inventory of some fission product and actinide radionuclides arising from underground tests at different times after detonation (PBq per megaton fission yield)

	Half-life	Time after detonation (y)				
		0	10	500	1000	5000
Fission products						
^{90}Sr	28.8	3.8	3.0	2×10^{-5}	—	—
^{99}Tc	2.1×10^5	9×10^{-4}	9×10^{-4}	9×10^{-4}	9×10^{-4}	9×10^{-4}
^{137}Cs	30.2	5.8	4.6	6×10^{-5}	—	—
^{151}Sm	90	7.2×10^{-2}	6.7×10^{-2}	2.1×10^{-2}	3.2×10^{-5}	—
^{154}Eu	16	0.29	0.19	—	—	—
Actinides						
^{237}Np[a]	2.1×10^6	—	2.3×10^{-8}	3.7×10^{-6}	5.4×10^{-6}	6.8×10^{-6}
^{239}Pu	2.4×10^4	4.6×10^{-2}	4.6×10^{-2}	4.6×10^{-2}	4.5×10^{-2}	4.0×10^{-2}
^{240}Pu	6.6×10^3	3.1×10^{-2}	3.1×10^{-2}	3.0×10^{-2}	2.8×10^{-2}	1.8×10^{-2}
^{241}Pu	14.4	1.0	0.62	—	—	—
^{241}Am[a]	433	—	1.3×10^{-2}	1.5×10^{-2}	6.9×10^{-3}	1.1×10^{-5}

[a] Calculated from decay of ^{241}Pu.

increase in time. The rates at 1 week, 1 year and 25 years after the explosion are approximately 2×10^{-3}, 8×10^{-6} and 1×10^{-8} of the value at 1 hour. Table 5.2 lists activities of radionuclides produced in petabecquerels (PBq) per megaton of fission yield based on data obtained from atmospheric testing.[21] The activities of trans-uranic radionuclides can be considered only approximate and for any particular detonation will be dependent upon the device composition.

The greater part of the radioactive material formed in a deep underground explosion condenses with vaporized rock and is incorporated in the vitrified material forming the base and walls of the cavity. The percentage of radioactivity contained in vitrified material has been estimated to be between 75 per cent at one minute after detonation[22] and 99.9 per cent of fission products. Nuclides of elements with boiling points high enough for condensation from the vapour phase by the time of cavity collapse are retained in fused material, while nuclides of volatile elements, or which have volatile precursors, may tend to be relatively depleted in the fused material and be dispersed also in the chimney region. Nuclides in the former category include ^{95}Zr, ^{237}Np and ^{239}Pu. In the latter category are ^{131}I, ^{90}Sr and ^{137}Cs. However, it is known from US experience in Rainier, Hardhat and other tests that radiation exposure rates in collapsed chimneys are relatively low.[23]

A not negligible part of the fission products are rare gases (krypton and xenon) with half-lives of between several seconds and 10.3 years (^{85}Kr). These tend to seep upward through the overburden, and the longer-lived nuclides could be released slowly from the surface. Because of the chemical inertness of the noble gases, the only effect of such a release would be a minor and transient increase in the local gamma background rate. Another gas produced as a result of neutron irradiation of lithium in the rock minerals and in thermonuclear reactions is tritium. On cooling, tritium is rapidly incorporated by replacement of hydrogen in water to form tritiated water. This is dispersed in and will move with local ground water.

Radioactive products formed in underground explosions largely decay radioactively in the detonation cavity where they are formed. However, there may be some loss by venting, slow seepage in the case of non-condensable gases, or leakage. Venting is considered to refer to the loss of radioactivity from the intended geological confinement by gaseous expulsion at the time of detonation. Leakage results from the transport of radioactivity by ground water at any time after condensation of the vitrified material. In considering leakage over long periods of time, account must be taken not only of the inventory of fission and activation products formed at the time of the explosion but also those that may grow in from the decay of precursors in the decay chain.

Venting

One of the central purposes of the 1963 Partial Test Ban Treaty was to reduce or prevent the dispersal of radionuclides in the environment arising from the testing of nuclear weapons. The change to underground from atmospheric testing had the potential for essentially total confinement of the radioactive products formed. This has been borne out in practice in that the deposition of the longer-lived fission products strontium-90 and caesium-137 declined rapidly from the peak years of 1963 in the northern hemisphere and 1964 in the southern hemisphere to much lower levels. With the cessation of atmospheric testing by France in 1974 and China in 1980, deposition levels declined further and in 1985 were the lowest recorded for the period until 1985 over which monitoring has been conducted (see figure 5.3). Values for ^{90}Sr recorded in peak years were about 700 MBq/km^2 in the United Kingdom[24] and 130 MBq/km^2 in New Zealand.[25] Measurements of total beta activities in air provide a more direct indication of the presence of fresh fission products. Total beta activities in air in New Zealand and the Pacific islands included in the National Radiation Laboratory monitoring network have since 1976 remained below limits of detection (0.3 MBq/m^3).[26]

Venting to the atmosphere has, however, occurred for a number of underground tests, other than those associated with Plowshare-type projects, and more minor sub-surface ventings may occur more commonly. The latter may be associated with minor defects in drill hole backfill or in gas blocking measures designed to prevent gaseous and volatile fission products from venting along measurement and other cables lowered to the emplacement depth. Using highly sensitive monitoring equipment, the USA has detected traces of radioactivity from about 100 underground explosions conducted by the USSR. The traces, detected because of the proximity of the test sites to the national border, posed no health risks. In the period 1964–70, 97 underground tests conducted by the USA also resulted in the release of radioactive gases, with, on 31 of these occasions, detectable activity outside the Nevada Test Site.

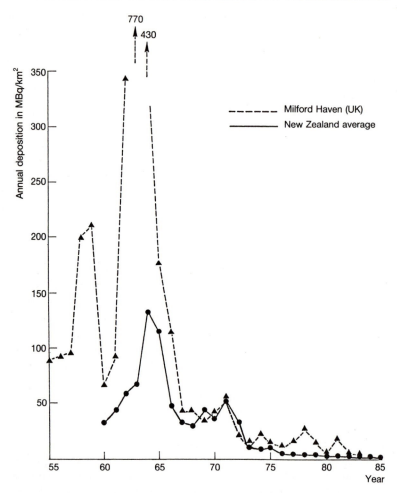

Figure 5.3. Strontium-90 annual deposition in New Zealand and at Milford Haven, UK

The 1958–59 and 1962–63 northern hemisphere and 1964–65 southern hemisphere peaks in annual deposition are due to northern hemisphere atmospheric tests. Beyond 1968 the lesser peaks in annual deposition at Milford Haven are due largely to Chinese northern hemisphere tests and in New Zealand to French southern hemisphere tests.

Three tests since 1970[27] were reported to have released gases. An example of seepage of largely noble gases was the Nash event of 19 January 1967. At 40 miles downwind of the detonation point, the maximum external gamma exposure rate approached 1 mR/h, but there was no radioactivity deposition on the ground. The Pinstripe event of 25 April 1966 was an example of minor venting: at 40 miles downwind, the gamma exposure rate peaked at 8 mR/h; and at 65 miles, deposition of radionuclides on the ground resulted in a peak ^{131}I level in milk of 180 Bq/1.[28] However, this level is more than an order of magnitude below that requiring some intervention in milk use and consumption. In the case of the US Baneberry test on 18 December 1970, radioactivity was detected in Canada, and 600 employees were evacuated from the immediate area of the test site. Half of these had slight radioactive contamination removed by showering. Radioactivity deposition in the immediate downwind vicinity of the release point was sufficient to produce an observable effect on plant growth over the next one to two years.[29]

For the higher-yield Amchitka detonations, containment was effective for all three explosions except for some minor venting of tritium associated with the first and lowest-yield (80-kt) Longshot detonation on 29 October 1965. Tritium levels in ponds near the Longshot ground zero reached a peak concentration of about 500 Bq/l in May 1971.[30] A similar concentration of tritium in sub-surface water was measured at Mururoa Atoll by the South Pacific scientific mission in 1983.[31] The presence of tritium here is suggestive either of venting through or past backfilled drill holes used for placing the nuclear explosive devices, which is known to occur to some limited degree, or to the ground water transport time from the volcanics to the limestones being much shorter than that deduced from the flow rate in undisturbed basalt (around 1m/y) and the assumed distance between the tops of chimneys and the base of the limestones. It may be noted, however, that a 500 Bq/l concentration of tritium in water is a factor of about 11 000 times below the limiting drinking water concentration implied by the International Commission on Radiological Protection (ICRP) annual limit of intake (ALI) for tritium.[32]

Some degree of venting has been associated with a number of near-surface Plowshare and engineering experiments in both the USSR and the USA. These experiments were carried out mostly in the 1960s. The tungsten isotopes ^{181}W and ^{185}W were detected in the air over Europe in December 1968 following the 35-kt Schooner excavation test at the NTS. The traces of radioactivity were of scientific rather than health significance, the activation nuclides being attributed to neutron irradiation of structural materials of the device.[33] Radioactivity from a Soviet explosion in the Urals area on 23 March 1971 was detected in Sweden.[34]

Leakage

Mechanisms

Leakage of radioactive material from an underground testing site may occur if there is ground water present at the emplacement depth at the time of explosion, or if fracturing of rock subsequently allows ground water access to the cavity. If the ground water flow from the area is into the ocean, the potential for uptake of radionuclides by man is likely to be considerably less than if the ground water is subsequently mixed with or forms part of sources that may be used for drinking water supplies or irrigation. This is primarily because of the very great dilution and dispersion provided by the ocean. While transport of radioactive material is dependent on the presence of water, the rate of transport is governed by many factors: the leachability of the radioactive material dispersed in the cavity and chimney and contained in vitrified material, the water flow rate and dissolved mineral content, the sorption properties of the strata through which the water flow occurs, and the length of flow path to the point of emergence. The term 'sorption' is used for all the processes which can lead to retardation of radionuclides by geologic media. These include adsorption, ion exchange, precipitation, colloid filtration and irreversible mineralization. Measurement of radionuclide retardation by rocks and soils for each radionuclide is usually expressed in terms of an empirical sorption equilibrium constant which combines the effects of all processes. The sorption equilibrium constant is the ratio of the ground water velocity to the radionuclide migration velocity.

The migration of radionuclides by ground water transport can be described by a modified diffusion equation for which solutions for several general and particular cases have been determined, including the disposal of high-level water in geologic formations.[35]

In a cavity formed by an underground nuclear explosion to which ground water has access, the concentration of radionuclides will vary with time, with an initial peak concentration relatively soon after water ingress as a result of the more rapid solution of less firmly bound material and the higher rate of leaching associated with the initial elevated temperatures. Thermally driven vertical flows will be generated in the cavity and chimney structure. As cooling proceeds, the rate of transport of radionuclides from the cavity area will become more directly dependent upon the leach rate of the vitrified rock melt. Due to mixing with water flowing into the source area and radioactive decay, the cavity concentration will vary with time for each individual radionuclide.

The leach rate varies with rock type and size, and with pH and temperature. The silicate melts formed by underground explosions in rhyolitic tuff or other silicate rock at the Nevada Test Site are found as discrete bodies of glass at the base of the rubble chimneys and contain most of the radioactivity formed in the explosion.[36] Other types of rock form similar melts, and leachability can be considered to be roughly similar to that of borosilicate glass.[37] There is evidence that leach rates tend to decrease with time. Experiments with buried vitrified waste in Canada indicated a reduction in leach rate by about a factor of 1000 over a 15-year period.

Underground water flow rates may vary from less than 1.5 m/year to more than 1.5 m/day. Hard crystalline rocks, however, tend to have flow rates at the low end of this range, velocities in unfractured rock being normally around 1 m/year.

Estimates of potential radiation doses arising from ground water transport of radionuclides have been made more particularly for postulated high-level waste repositories. These assessments have been based on models of radio-nuclide release by leaching, the migration of the radionuclide in ground water taking account of sorption effects, and their entry into the human environment.

The waste packages have been assumed to be breached by ground water at a minimum of 1000 years after emplacement. Radiation doses have been estimated for hypothetical populations having access to water from aquifers and water supplies entered by contaminated ground water and used for drinking, irrigation and fishing. These studies indicate that neptunium-237 is the radionuclide of dominating radiological significance, as a consequence in part of its relatively poor sorption properties and its high fractional absorption from the gastro-intestinal tract. The contribution to peak annual individual dose from plutonium-239, which has been of more major popular concern, may be less than 10^{-8} times the neptunium-237 dose.[38] The ICRP gastro-intestinal absorption value for neptunium of 0.01[39] which was based on limited available studies, has been questioned, and a recent review in the UK indicates that a value of 0.001 is more appropriate for adults.[40]

Radiological consequence assessments for high-level waste repositories may be applied, with some reservations, to long-lived nuclides formed in deep underground explosions. The application to ^{237}Np is not unreasonable since its precursors (^{241}Am and ^{241}Pu) are both much more strongly sorbed and could be expected to have little migration over the first 1000 years. Calculations by Hill,[41] on the basis of conservatively chosen values of dispersion, ground water velocity, sorption equilibrium constant and leaching rate, and for a 10-km flow path, result in a peak annual dose (effective dose equivalent commitment) from leakage of ^{237}Np of 60 mSv for a high-level waste repository containing 11×10^{14} Bq ^{237}Np at 1000 years after emplacement. The peak annual dose was attained 1×10^4 years after emplacement. Increasing the flow path or reducing the flow rate by factors of 10 both reduced the peak dose rate an order of magnitude.

Leakage from test sites

At the US Nevada Test Site most underground detonations have been carried out at a depth above the permanent water table in tuff or alluvium with a moisture content commonly between 10 and 20 per cent by weight.[42] However, a proportion of tests have been conducted at depths below the water table, and this includes most of the higher-yield detonations. The potential therefore exists for the long-term migration of radionuclides. If a total fission yield available for leaching and water transport at the NTS is of the order of 20 Mt and a water flow path of around 100 km is appropriate, based on the data in table 5.2 the values calculated by Hill for a 0.3 m/d flow rate imply a peak annual radiation dose of around 0.005 mSv from leakage from the site. This value is unlikely to be accurate to within an order of magnitude. The critical input parameters are ground water velocity, sorption equilibrium constant and path length. The value calculated may be compared with the recommended population dose limit of 1 mSv/y,[43] and radiation worker dose limit of 50 mSv/y. Natural background radiation including radon daughters contributes about 2 mSv/y.[44]

For the detonations at Amchitka island, because of the lower fission yield and long-term leakage being into ocean waters, the radiological consequences to hypothetical future residents at Amchitka would be orders of magnitude below that for the NTS. A radiobiological monitoring programme at Amchitka was initiated in 1970 by the University of Washington's Laboratory of Radiation Ecology. This programme was complemented by studies conducted by the US Geological Survey, which were primarily concerned with the measurement of tritium as the most likely indicator of seepage from the underground tests. In the four years following the Cannikin test, extensive studies failed to detect any radionuclides arising from the Cannikin or Milrow events in environmental samples.[45]

Leakage from the French nuclear test site at Mururoa Atoll is also into deep ocean waters. However, measured silica concentrations in the lagoon have indicated that vertical diffusion occurs from the volcanics through the limestones to the lagoon, so that radioactive contaminants would exit largely through the lagoon. Seismic-induced submarine slides have resulted in the removal of some parts of the highly impervious reef front apron, and this could to some extent alter the hydrogeologic pathways to allow oceanic waters to enter and leave the limestones without exiting into the lagoon. This would have the effect of lowering leakage radionuclide concentrations in the lagoon and therefore of lowering the local radiological consequences for a hypothetical resident population.

In the report of the South Pacific countries' scientific mission to Mururoa Atoll,[46] ^{237}Np was identified as having greatest radiological significance for times of greater than 1000 years from the present. On the basis of recently revised estimates,[47] the accumulated yield to the end of 1985 of underground tests conducted at Mururoa is of the order of 1.5 Mt; and even if future testing increased this yield by several times, the lagoon concentration of ^{237}Np would remain several orders of magnitude below an acceptable level for unrestricted food extraction from the lagoon. In the event that the depth of emplacement of a device were inadequate, or the cumulative effect of several adjacent detonations allowed fracturing to extend to the top of the volcanics, an acceleration of fluid movement could occur from the volcanics to the limestones. This might allow the emergence and detection in the shorter term (10–50 years) of longer half-life fission products, particularly strontium-90, which, because of its relatively poor sorption properties is more mobile and potentially of greater radiological significance. However, on the basis of a gross worst case estimate of possible radiological outcome (10 per cent of the total ^{90}Sr inventory released to the lagoon over a period of 30 years), the annual intake of ^{90}Sr and ^{90}Y for a resident at Mururoa deriving all food from local resources and with a predominantly sea food diet would remain below one-hundredth of annual limits of intake for radiation workers. It therefore would appear physically impossible for radionuclide concentrations in sea water to approach levels of radiological concern at Mururoa for the past and projected future rates of underground testing, assuming that the pattern of future testing does not alter significantly. Sea water concentrations around the nearest inhabited islands would be at least three orders of magnitude below that of the lagoon at Mururoa. The widespread South Pacific opposition to and apprehension of the French underground testing programme because of environmental or radiological effects are therefore unfounded.

III. Conclusions

Nuclear tests in the atmosphere gave rise to concerns about the wide dispersal of radionuclides in the environment and the rising radiation dose commitments to human populations. These concerns have been alleviated by conducting tests underground, since this has largely ensured that radioactive products are confined in the immediate vicinity of the point of detonation. While minor venting has occurred for some lower-yield tests, the off-site radiological consequences have been minor or trivial. Subsurface ground water flows at sites used for underground nuclear testing are unlikely to give rise to off-site leakage of radioactive material sufficient to be of significant radiological concern.

The greatest environmental impacts of underground tests result from seismic and local shock wave effects. The latter include ground movements, subsidence, collapse crater formation, cliff falls and submarine slides which may occur within a few kilometres of the detonation points.

Notes and references

[1] The cavity radius, R_c, may be estimated from

$$R_c = \frac{CW^{1/3}}{(\varrho/d)}$$

where R_c is in metres
   C   is a constant for a particular rock medium
   W   is the explosive yield in kilotons TNT equivalent
   ϱ is the average overburden density (g cm^{-3})
   d   is the depth of burst in metres
and α is an exponent determined by the water content of the rock mass at the point of burst.
See Glasstone, S. and Dolan, P. J., *The Effects of Nuclear Weapons*, 3rd edn (US Department of Defense and Energy Research and Development Administration: Washington, DC, 1977), p. 261; and Butkovich, T. R. and Lewis, A. E., *Aids for Estimating Effects of Underground Nuclear Explosions*, Report UCRL 50929, Rev. 1, University of California, 1978, p. 7.
[2] See Glasstone and Dolan (note 1).
[3] Bolt, B. A., *Nuclear Explosions and Earthquakes* (W.H. Freeman and Co: San Francisco, 1976), p. 46.
[4] See Glasstone and Dolan (note 1).
[5] Houser, F. N., 'Application of geology to underground nuclear testing, Nevada Test Site', *Studies of Geology and Hydrology, Memoir 110*, ed. E. B. Eckel (Geological Society of America: Boulder, 1968), p. 23.
[6] See note 3, Appendix A.
[7] See note 3, pp. 38–9.
[8] Dickey, D. D., 'Fault displacement as a result of underground nuclear explosions', Eckel (note 5), pp. 219–31.
[9] See Glasstone and Dolan (note 1), pp. 238–9.
[10] See note 3, p. 207.
[11] See Glasstone and Dolan (note 1), p. 240.
[12] See Glasstone and Dolan (note 1), p. 240.

[13] See note 3, pp. 222–3.

[14] See Glasstone and Dolan (note 1), p. 243.

[15] See note 3, p. 183.

[16] *Report of a New Zealand, Australian, and Papua New Guinea Scientific Mission to Mururoa Atoll* (Ministry of Foreign Affairs: Wellington, 1984), pp. 94–6.

[17] See note 3, p. 223.

[18] Smith, W. D., 'Underground nuclear explosions recorded in Rarotonga: estimation of m_b from T-phase amplitude', *Geophysical Journal of the Royal Astronomical Society* (to be published).

[19] See note 16.

[20] See Glasstone and Dolan (note 1), p. 390.

[21] UNSCEAR, United Nations Scientific Committee on the Effects of Atomic Radiation, *Ionizing Radiation: Sources and Effects, 1982*, Report to the General Assembly (United Nations: New York, 1982).

[22] Borg, I. Y., 'Radioactivity trapped in melt produced by a nuclear explosion', *Nuclear Technology*, vol. 24 (1975), pp. 85–100.

[23] See note 3, p. 190.

[24] *Letcome Laboratory Annual Report 1974* (UK Agricultural Research Council, 1975), p. 97.

[25] *Environmental Radioactivity Annual Report 1984* (National Radiation Laboratory: Christchurch, 1985), p. 3.

[26] See note 25.

[27] *Washington Post*, 8 May 1986, p. 23.

[28] US Atomic Energy Commission, *Environmental Impact Statement: Cannikin* (Atomic Energy Commission: Washington, DC, June 1971).

[29] Rhoads, W. A., in *Selected Environmental Plutonium Research Reports of the NAEG*, NVO-192, vol. 1, ed. M. G. White and P. B. Dunaway (Holmes and Narver Inc., Mercury, NV, June 1978), pp. 127–41.

[30] Held, E. E., Nelson, V. A., Schell, W. R. and Seymour, A. H., *Amchitka Radiobiological Program Progress Report March 1972 to December 1972*, Report NVO-269-19 (University of Washington, Laboratory of Radiation Ecology: Seattle, June 1973), p. 18.

[31] See note 16, p. 122.

[32] International Commission on Radiological Protection, 'Limits for intakes of radionuclides by workers', ICRP Publication 30, Part 1, *Annals of the ICRP*, vol. 2, no. 3/4 (1979), p. 68.

[33] Persson, G., *Radioactive tungsten in the atmosphere following Project Schooner* (Forsvarets Forskningsanstalt: Stockholm, Apr. 1971); Izrael, Y. A., Ter-Saakov, A. A., Malakhov, S. G. *et al.*, 'Tungsten isotopes in fresh radioactive fallout in December 1968', *Atomnaja energija* (*Soviet Atomic Energy*), (Moscow), vol. 30, no. 4 (Apr. 1971), 377–80.

[34] See note 3, p. 85; Kolb, W., 'Tungsten-181 and other short lived fission products in ground level air in North Germany and North Norway', *Nature*, vol. 232 (Aug. 1971), pp. 552–3.

[35] Holly, D. E. and Fenske, P. R., 'Transport of dissolved chemical contaminants in ground water systems', Eckel (note 5), pp. 171–83; Baetsle, L. N.,'Computational methods for the prediction of underground movement of radionuclides', *Nuclear Safety*, vol. 8, no. 6 (Nov.–Dec. 1967), pp. 567–88; Hill, M. D. and Grimwood, P. D., *Preliminary Assessment of the Radiological Protection Aspects of Disposal of High-Level Waste in Geologic Formations*, NRPB R69, National Radiological Protection Board, Harwell, Jan. 1978, p. 25; Ahlstrom, P. E., 'Swedish hard crystalline rock repository', *Concepts and Examples of Safety Analyses for Radioactive Waste Repositories in Continental Geological Formations*, IAEA Safety Series No. 58 (International Atomic Energy Agency: Vienna, 1983), pp. 115–42.

[36] Essington, E. H. and Sharp, J. V. A., 'Some aspects of ground-water solution chemistry, underground nuclear explosion zones, Nevada Test Site', Eckel (note 5), pp. 263–5.

[37] See Kolb (note 34), pp. 21–3.

[38] Costello, J. M., 'Current state of the art in high-level radioactive waste disposal', *Atomic Energy in Australia*, vol. 27 (Jan.–Oct. 1984), pp. 17–41.

[39] International Commission on Radiological Protection, 'Limits for intakes of radionuclides by workers', ICRP Publication 30, Par 2, *Annals of the ICRP*, vol. 4, no. 3/4 (1980), p. 69.

[40] National Radiological Protection Board, *Matabolic and Dosimetric Models for Application to Members of the Public. Recommended Models for the Metabolism of Iodine and Values for the Gut Transfer Fraction of Plutonium, Curium and Neptunium*, NRPB GS3, National Radiological Protection Board, Chilton, Jan. 1984.

[41] Hill, M. D., *Analysis of the Effect of Variations in Parameter Values on the Predicted*

Radiological Consequences of Geologic Disposal of High-Level Waste, NRPB R86, National Radiological Protection Board, Harwell, June 1979.

[42] See note 3, Appendix A.

[43] 'Statement from the ICRP Paris meeting, 1985', *Radiological Protection Bulletin*, no. 65 (July 1985), pp. 5–7.

[44] Note 21, p. 16.

[45] Nelson, V. A. and Seymour, A. H., *Amchitka Radiobiological Program Progress Report January 1975 to December 1975*, Report NVO-269-27 (University of Washington, Laboratory of Radiation Ecology, Seattle, May 1976).

[46] See note 16.

[47] See note 18.

Part 3
The historical record

Chapter V. Survey of past nuclear test ban negotiations

Paper 6

G. Allen Greb

Institute on Global Conflict and Cooperation, University of California, San Diego, La Jolla, CA

Abstract

A CTB has been the most sought after and the most elusive of arms control agreements of the nuclear age. Formal negotiations involving the USA, the USSR and the UK have taken place nearly continuously since 1958, with only partial measures to show as a result (the 1963 PTBT, the 1974 TTBT and the 1976 PNET). Progress has been slow despite strong and long-standing international pressure for a CTB within the United Nations, the Conference on Disarmament and the Non-Proliferation Treaty Review Conferences. Two major problems have hindered negotiations: East–West differences on the issue of verification, and internal bureaucratic opposition centred in the weapon laboratories and the military of both sides. These divisions run so deep that perhaps all that can be expected in the short term is a quota or low-threshold test ban agreement, and only in the context of progress on other arms control measures.

I. Introduction

On 31 October 1958 the USA, the USSR and the UK opened in Geneva the Conference on the Discontinuance of Nuclear Weapon Tests, the first formal round of negotiations on a comprehensive test ban (CTB). On 20 July 1982 President Reagan formally withdrew the USA from negotiations on the same subject. Thus despite over two decades of nearly continuous effort, the major nuclear powers have failed to achieve a CTB. They have, however, concluded a number of partial measures: the Partial Test Ban Treaty (PTBT) of 1963, prohibiting tests in the atmosphere, under water and in outer space; the Threshold Test Ban Treaty (TTBT) of 1974, prohibiting underground tests of more than 150 kt; and the Peaceful Nuclear Explosions Treaty (PNET) of 1976, similarly limiting individual PNEs to no more than 150-kt yield. Why in this long history has some limitation of nuclear tests been possible, while the ultimate objective of a comprehensive ban has proved elusive? This overview of bilateral, trilateral and multilateral negotiations addresses this question.

II. The early years: hope and frustration

The immediate impetus for interest in the issue of a CTB was the series of atmospheric nuclear tests conducted by the USA in 1954 known as Operation Castle. These tests, in particular the 1 March 1954 Bravo shot, which produced a yield of about 15 Mt (over twice that expected), dramatically highlighted the dangers of radioactive fall-out. The fall-out killed a Japanese fisherman and set into motion a world-wide political and scientific protest against nuclear testing. The governments of Great Britain, Japan and India, for example, issued calls for a test suspension. The Indian proposal for a so-called 'standstill agreement' on testing, made by Prime Minister Nehru on 2 April 1954, was the first such initiative of its kind. It became the focus of international attention when the UN Disarmament Commission submitted it for formal consideration on 29 July 1954.[1] Individual scientists, including, as is now known, prominent members of the Soviet scientific community, also rallied to the test ban issue. At least two important international organizations were created: the Campaign for Nuclear Disarmament (CND) and the Pugwash Conferences.[2]

Despite a developing concern about nuclear weapons on the part of President Eisenhower, the USA initially resisted international pressures and rejected the idea of a CTB. Government officials, especially those in the Pentagon and the Atomic Energy Commission (AEC), insisted that the continued development of nuclear weapons was necessary to counter the Soviet threat. Britain, which had joined the 'nuclear club' on 13 October 1952, proposed direct, private US–British discussions on 'test restrictions' in 1956, but this was also rejected by US officials.[3] By contrast, Soviet leaders Khrushchev and Bulganin adopted the test ban as a central item in their extensive arms control agenda in mid-1955, but they offered this proposal as part of a vague and diffuse package of disarmament measures which had no chance of acceptance in the West.

From this initial proposal for a test ban to the beginning of trilateral negotiations in October 1958, a complex set of problems—domestic and alliance politics, questions about nuclear strategy and national security, and general East–West rivalries—stood in the way of serious talks. Widespread public concern over fall-out and the effects of such radioactive by-products as strontium 90, while leading to no real policy formulations, still continued to fuel and push the test ban cause.[4] Both superpowers suggested that nuclear tests be stopped for some finite duration of time, but each conditioned its offers on provisions, in particular regarding verification, that were unacceptable to the other side.

On 31 March 1958 the USSR announced, without prior negotiation with the West, a test suspension if the other nuclear powers agreed to follow suit. The USSR made this proposal following an extensive test series of its own, knowing that the USA planned a similar series. Most certainly, Soviet leaders, in particular the Soviet military, had in mind cutting off further advances in US weaponry, but they also expressed concerns at this time over proliferation or the 'n[th] country' problem, especially the impact that a test ban agreement might have on preventing FR Germany and China from developing nuclear arsenals.[5] Whether disingenuous or not, the test moratorium proposal clearly put the USSR ahead in the international battle for the favour of world opinion.

During this 1955–58 period, the UN became a focal point for international discussion of a CTB. In 1957 the USA and the USSR for the first time debated the major issues of a possible test cessation at the London Disarmament Conference, raising such critical points as the separability of a test ban from other arms control measures, the usefulness of scientific 'experts' for the process, and the ideas of a moratorium and international inspection. The chief Soviet delegate, Ambassador Zorin, paid tribute to outside forces in creating pressure for a CTB. It 'is stirring up feeling throughout the world', Zorin admonished, 'and parliaments, governments and a great many public organizations' regard it as 'a burning political issue'. On this one point, the US representative, Harold Stassen, could agree. The talks, which were then conducted in London, provided an 'opportunity for mutual "education"' on arms control and a 'substantial advance toward negotiations for a formal test-ban agreement'.[6] Subsequent UN General Assembly sessions continued to be both general forums for discussion of a test ban and 'arenas for East–West sparring'.[7]

During this same period, the Eisenhower Administration gradually began to shift its internal views on a CTB. Scientists brought into the White House in the aftermath of the launch of Sputnik—including James Killian of the Massachusetts Institute of Technology, George Kistiakowsky of Harvard University and Isidor I. Rabi of Columbia University—began to counter the strong anti-test ban views of officials and scientists in the AEC and the Pentagon. Organized formally in 1957 as the President's Science Advisory Committee (PSAC), these scientists stressed the value of a test ban, not to prevent fall-out but as an important 'first step' in controlling the arms race. Rabi, for example, at a pivotal PSAC meeting in April 1958, maintained that a 'test ban as such never meant anything per se; only as a step toward something else. Any ban should have a time limitation on it tied to progress in other areas'.[8]

At the same time, the post-Stalin Soviet leadership began to adopt new images of the US–Soviet relationship in the wake of US technological advances. At the 20th Soviet Communist Party Congress in 1956, Premier Khrushchev proclaimed his de-Stalinization campaign and reasserted the foreign policy formula of 'peaceful coexistence', emphasizing the dual tenets of 'struggle *and* cooperation'.[9] Like President Eisenhower, Premier Khrushchev increasingly paid more attention to the danger of nuclear war and demonstrated a willingness, at least in part, to shift away from all-encompassing (and unverifiable) proposals to a focus on specific problems of the US–Soviet arms competition.

Although Eisenhower continued to move cautiously on the test ban issue, a breakthrough came in April 1958 when Secretary of State Dulles drafted and the President agreed to send two letters to Khrushchev calling for technical studies of the question. Eisenhower proposed that a group of scientists from East and West meet to develop a comprehensive plan for monitoring a test ban as a precondition for political talks. Khrushchev, while asserting that such special studies were unnecessary and that control in fact would be 'easy to carry out',[10] none the less agreed to the proposal.

The resulting Conference of Experts met in Geneva for several weeks in the summer of 1958. Scientists from the USA, the USSR, the UK, Canada, France, Czechoslovakia, Poland and Romania took part. By far their most challenging problem was how to detect and identify underground nuclear explosions under any potential CTB regime. After examining this and other questions, the experts concluded in their 21 August 1958 report that it was feasible to set up an effective control system to detect seismic events down to 4.75 magnitude (believed to be equal to a 5-kt explosion). Significantly, the experts also included provisions for on-site inspections (OSIs) of events that could not be identified as earthquakes. The analysis underlying the experts' final report rested on a single datum, the 1957 US test code-named Rainier. It was to prove a shaky base for the proposed edifice of a CTB.

On the basis of the Experts' Conference, Eisenhower announced on 22 August 1958 that the USA was prepared to enter formal political negotiations. He also stated that the USA would stop further testing, unless the USSR tested, for a one-year period. This moratorium would be extended on a year-by-year basis if an agreed control system could be installed and if progress could be made on major arms control agreements. The British Government released a nearly identical statement on the same day.

By this time the UK had again become, as it was during the Manhattan Project, a full partner with the USA in nuclear weapon development, signing an Agreement of Co-operation on 3 July 1958. After World War II, British scientists had initiated a substantial independent research and development programme to develop both peaceful and military applications of the atom. This programme stemmed from the initial post-war US determination to guard atomic secrets and the equal British determination to maintain the status of a first-rank power. In 1947 Prime Minister Attlee created the UK Atomic Energy Authority, a counterpart to the US AEC, and placed William G. Penney, a physicist who had been at the Los Alamos laboratory during the war, in charge of a weapon project. On 13 October 1952 the programme bore fruit with the first successful British nuclear test, followed in 1957 by a test of an H-bomb and in 1958 by the development of the first operational squadron of V-bombers.[11]

The 1958 Agreement of Co-operation (and the later 1962 Nassau Agreement) cemented the renewed Anglo-American partnership in nuclear weapon research. This unique collaboration carried over to the test ban question as well, with President Eisenhower and Prime Minister Macmillan developing Western positions and policies in concert with one another. In general, Macmillan and British public opinion strongly favoured a test ban, and the Prime Minister forcefully put forward this point of view both in public pronouncements and in his consultations with US officials.

Although the Soviet Union objected to the Western linkage of a CTB to other arms control measures, the Conference on the Discontinuance of Nuclear Weapon Tests began on schedule in October 1958 with all three nuclear powers present. Shortly thereafter, the Soviet Union carried out several more nuclear tests but then stopped. A unique product of the personal statemanship of Eisenhower, Macmillan and Khrushchev, the tripartite moratorium would last until September 1961.

The Conference met in almost continuous session until January 1962, but the parties could not convert the informal moratorium into a formal treaty. Moscow initially took the stance that a CTB should be established by treaty, exclusive of any control provisions. US and British negotiators insisted that discussion of verification procedures take place first. The Soviet Union acquiesced, but it soon became apparent that the two sides' ideas about a control mechanism were fundamentally at odds. Washington and London envisaged an international organization, internationally staffed, with decisions made by majority vote. Most important, OSIs could be made whenever a questionable event occurred.

From the Soviet perspective, such an organization could be manipulated by the West for intelligence purposes—what a later Soviet negotiator would call 'legalized espionage'.[12] This position had been staked out early by the USSR when on 5 March 1947 the Soviet representative to the UN Security Council, Andrei Gromyko, asserted that the control body proposed in the US Baruch Plan 'would mean crude interference . . . in the internal affairs and economic life of States'.[13] Moscow therefore in the Conference negotiations sought a verification system that would allow it to retain control of all operations on its own territory. For the West, this simply spelled veto and self-inspection. It was evident that negotiations would be much more difficult than at first anticipated.

Complicating matters was the fact that internal opposition to a CTB remained strong within the Eisenhower Administration. AEC Chairman Lewis Strauss and scientists such as Edward Teller and E. O. Lawrence of the weapon laboratories argued that tests must proceed to develop new weapons, including the 'clean' or neutron bomb. A test cessation, Strauss warned, would be a 'very fateful step' for the USA.[14] Strauss, Teller and other nuclear spokesmen also maintained that verification was not adequate to assure against Soviet cheating. The general assumption on the part of both US and British officials was that the Soviets 'would certainly cheat'.[15] Some later regretted this view, but only in retrospect.[16]

The analysis of new data from underground experiments conducted before the moratorium, the US Hardtack series of October 1958, reinforced the position of CTB doubters. These data led scientists to reinterpret the findings of the Conference of Experts, defining the 4.75-magnitude threshold as equal approximately to 20 rather than 5 kt. In addition, Albert Latter and other scientists at the Rand Corporation developed a new theory about the possible 'decoupling' of explosions, that is, muffling of the seismic signal in large underground cavities. At the Geneva negotiations, the USSR dismissed the new findings, even suggesting that they had been fabricated, and reasserted that all technical issues had been settled by the earlier report.

Problems with the formal Geneva negotiations put serious strains on the informal US–Soviet moratorium. On 28 August 1959 the USSR reaffirmed its intention not to resume tests, but only if the 'Western Powers' did likewise. In September 1959, new AEC Chairman John McCone, who was more favourably disposed to the test ban idea than his predecessor, nevertheless declared that he 'would not continue this type of ban' if negotiations extended beyond 31 October. 'I would think', McCone added, 'that at the end of the year [1959] this policy should be carefully reconsidered'. In fact, on 29 December President Eisenhower, in a short but carefully worded statement, expressed disappointment with the lack of progress at Geneva and announced that 'the voluntary moratorium on testing will expire on December 31', but added that 'we shall not resume . . . tests without announcing our intention in advance of any resumption'.[17]

Despite these myriad problems, the negotiations continued during 1959–60. Each side made concessions, some substantial, and a treaty gradually began to take shape. All parties, for example, agreed in principle to an annual quota of OSIs, although neither side advanced a specific quota number. All were hopeful that the outstanding issues regarding a CTB would be settled at the Big Four Summit Conference to be held in Paris in May 1960. The U-2 incident, however, dashed these hopes and put an end to any expectations that the Eisenhower Administration would achieve a negotiated ban. Eisenhower later described this as the greatest regret of his presidency.

Even without the U-2 episode, it would at best have been problematical to achieve agreement, given the differences between the two sides on the number of OSIs—3–4 on the Soviet side, 20 on the US–British side. In fact, this 'numbers game'[18] came to symbolize the opposing views of the three principals over arms control verification, underscoring the basic East–West conceptual difference about the rights and functions of a control organization.

Those first CTB negotiations were the SALT (Strategic Arms Limitation Talks) of their day; they were seminal for both the future of the test ban and arms control as a whole. The debate had centred almost exclusively on verification (or monitoring), an issue that continues to be dominant in arms control discussions today. Soviet refusal to accept the verification procedures sought by the USA strengthened the belief that the Kremlin was unwilling to accept 'reasonable' control restraints of any kind. Their abrupt and dramatic resumption of testing in 1961 (with a 58-Mt device) reinforced this view and raised the spectre of deliberate Soviet duplicity to close the technological gap with the USA. Despite indications of a shift in Soviet policy away from a moratorium, the Soviet tests, which required long and careful preparation,[19] caught Washington by surprise. They emphasized to the US leadership the difficulty of knowing what the other side *might* be planning in a clandestine way.

The PTBT

President John Kennedy came into office determined to solve the test ban impasse. Kennedy's Administration did not have the obvious internal divisions on this subject that had plagued his predecessor. Moreover, a deep personal bond existed between the US President and Prime Minister Macmillan, who had demonstrated a strong interest in arms control in general and in a CTB in particular since the beginning of his term of office. But several months of meetings with the USSR produced no concrete results. Moscow in effect reintroduced the idea of a veto in any control organ and indicated no desire to compromise.

Apparently, Khrushchev had 'hawks' within his bureaucracy as well who forcefully argued against a CTB after the embarrassing political reverse associated with the 1960 U-2 incident. Under pressure especially from the powerful military élite, the government in quick succession raised the military budget by one-third, deferred a 1960 troop reduction, erected the Berlin Wall, and resumed nuclear testing in September 1961, using the February 1960 test of the first French atomic bomb as the nominal reason. This started an extensive Soviet test series (30 tests in 60 days), including the 58-Mt test, the largest nuclear explosion ever carried out. The internal pressures on Khrushchev were reflected in the Geneva Conference negotiations. According to one US representative, the 'very definite impression was given by the Soviets that they would be content to have the talks break off—though they were not going to take the initiative'.[20] The talks eventually broke off in January 1962.

As one means to reinvigorate arms control discussions, the two superpowers and the UK sponsored the creation of a new international negotiating forum linked to the UN, the Eighteen-Nation Disarmament Committee (ENDC), in 1961. On 4 March 1962 the USA, the UK and the USSR introduced test ban negotiations into this new forum, and on 21 March formed a subcommittee on the test ban. For the first time, non-nuclear and non-aligned states actively engaged in the arms control and disarmament process with the superpowers, bringing new concerns and complications into the debate. But as British Prime Minister Macmillan observed, 'the kind of international circus now proposed gave a certain amount of relief and did little harm'.[21] The ENDC, later changed to the Conference of the Committee on Disarmament (CCD) and now called the Conference on Disarmament (CD), in effect became another focus of international pressure for a CTB.

At the same time, the US Government resoundingly responded to the Soviet test resumption, with over 90 tests of its own by the spring of 1963. It also simplified and reduced its verification requirements for a CTB. But the impasse over OSIs remained. Personal diplomacy again broke the logjam. A letter from Kennedy to Khrushchev (first suggested by Macmillan) proposed that high-level representatives from both sides meet in Moscow to try once again to achieve a treaty. Khrushchev agreed.

A potent underlying factor in this renewal of contact was the Cuban missile crisis of October 1962. Taking both sides to the brink of a nuclear confrontation that neither wanted, the missile crisis represented a major turning point in superpower relations. 'The crisis was a Berlitz course in nuclear communication', one scholar notes. 'The possibility of nuclear war made a deep impression on Kennedy and Khrushchev [and Macmillan], and made both more determined to avoid it in the future.'[22] McGeorge Bundy, national security adviser to the President during the crisis, later commented, 'I think we can be sure that the experience was one that neither the USSR nor the US has wished to repeat. That too is fortunate; great states can learn from shared danger'.[23]

The US intention at Moscow, as expressed by its representative Averell Harriman, was to seek a CTB. But when the US, British and Soviet negotiating teams met in July, the USSR expressed interest only in a partial ban that did not include underground tests. Ironically, the USA had introduced this concept at least three separate times during earlier impasses in negotiations. Eisenhower twice proposed a partial ban as an alternative to a CTB, on 13 April 1959 and again on 11 February 1960. US Ambassador to the ENDC Arthur Dean reintroduced the idea of a 'three environment' ban in August 1962. The development and deployment of reconnaissance satellites made these proposals a more realistic option for the 1960s. As one historian notes, satellites 'made it possible to overcome the perennial sticking point of nuclear negotiations—inspection. They permitted the US to monitor the Soviet Union, and the Soviet Union to keep foreign inspectors from its soil, at one and the same time'.[24]

With the major problem of verification set aside, the parties reached agreement in Moscow in only 10 days. The subsequent US ratification debate over the treaty highlighted a major problem that both had plagued previous negotiations and would continue to undermine future CTB efforts: opposition within the US Government bureaucracy. To ensure the required two-thirds approval by the Senate (a requirement unique to the USA), President Kennedy mounted an extensive public relations campaign at the same time that he made a special effort to gain the support of key internal critics, in particular the Joint Chiefs of Staff. He eventually succeeded, but only after pledging to implement a full range of national security 'safeguards'. These included commitments that a 'vigorous program of underground testing would go forward; that the US would "forthwith" resume atmospheric testing if the Soviets did; that facilities to detect test-ban violations would be improved . . . and that the US would keep its weapons laboratories strong'.[25]

The 1963 PTBT none the less brought to a close a very significant chapter in attempts to ban all nuclear weapon tests. By prohibiting tests in all environments except underground, the treaty met the health and environmental concerns that had precipitated the initial public outcry for a CTB, but it did little to slow actual weapon programmes. The USA (in co-operation with the UK) in fact increased its rate of testing after the PTBT was signed, and the USSR developed its own extensive underground test programme as well.

The NPT

Another hoped-for impact of the PTBT was that it would serve as the impetus for other agreements; this hope was in part realized with the 1968 Non-Proliferation Treaty (NPT). Although US public attention to arms control subsided after the PTBT (with Viet Nam increasingly occupying centre-stage), both the superpower governments began to recognize the problem of horizontal proliferation, or the spread of nuclear weapons to other states. In February 1960 France exploded its first nuclear device and China followed suit just four years later, in October 1964. These were ominous events for the leaders of both the USA and the USSR. A special Committee on Nuclear Proliferation appointed by President Johnson set out US policy in January 1965. The so-called Gilpatric Report (after the committee's chairman, Deputy Defense Secretary Roswell Gilpatric) concluded that 'preventing the further spread of nuclear weapons is clearly in the national interest despite the difficult decisions that will be required'. Significantly, the report noted that the PTBT offered 'a basis on which to take more comprehensive and effective steps' as well as 'the importance of participation by the Soviet Union' in non-proliferation efforts.[26] It called for greater co-operation with the USSR in this area, the negotiation of multilateral agreements on non-proliferation, and the resumption of negotiations on a CTB.

The USA and the USSR brought this issue before the ENDC shortly thereafter and literally pushed the NPT through in 1968. Most of the non-nuclear states viewed the treaty as discriminatory and sought to balance in part their renunciation of nuclear weapons with a superpower promise to negotiate a CTB. The superpowers rejected such an explicit commitment, but did accept as a compromise Article VI of the NPT, calling upon the parties of the Treaty 'to pursue negotiations in good faith on effective measures relating to cessation of the nuclear arms race at an early date and to nuclear disarmament'.[27] The non-nuclear nations took this to mean a CTB, which received specific mention only in the preamble to the NPT. The preamble 'recalled' wording in the 1963 PTBT that expressed the determination of the three original signatories to continue negotiations for the 'discontinuance of all test explosions of nuclear weapons for all time'.[28]

Since then, the CTB has been inextricably tied to the non-proliferation issue in international discussions. The NPT Review Conferences of 1975, 1980 and 1985, for example, all gave high priority to a CTB. Summarizing the views of most of the almost 130 nations which have signed the Treaty, Sigvard Eklund, then Director General of the International Atomic Energy Agency (IAEA), concluded in 1980 that 'the non-proliferation regime can only survive on the tripod of the Non-Proliferation Treaty, effective international safeguards, and a Comprehensive Nuclear Test Ban treaty. The vital third leg is still missing'.[29] Similarly, an influential 1979 UN report to the CD, the Goldblat Report, prepared by four expert consultants, found that a CTB 'could serve as an important measure of non-proliferation of nuclear weapons, both vertical and horizontal'.[30]

More partial measures: the TTBT and the PNET

After 1968, the superpowers shifted their focus from a CTB to limits on defensive and offensive strategic arms. But following the successful negotiation and ratification of the SALT I accords in 1972, these talks also ran into major roadblocks. In 1974, President Nixon and General Secretary Brezhnev faced the prospect of a summit with no new strategic agreement ready for signing. High-level exchanges led to the proposal to negotiate a threshold test ban, which would not require implementing intrusive verification measures. Negotiators (this time only from the USA and the USSR) met in 1974 and finished their work in five weeks, concluding the TTBT in time for the July summit. The Treaty was signed just one month before Nixon resigned because of the Watergate affair. It provided for verification of yield limits by 'national technical means' (NTM) but also provided for the exchange of seismic data to assist in yield determination—the first agreed step in bilateral arms control to go beyond NTM.

The new President, Gerald Ford, 'leaned toward' (as he put it) a CTB, but he did not push this issue with Brezhnev; instead, Ford's primary arms control concern remained the SALT process. 'We had a platter full of other problems and you can only handle so many', he later explained, 'so you start at the top of the ladder. You can only push so many things'.[31] Ford did manage to negotiate with the Soviet Union one bit of unfinished business left over from the TTBT. The TTBT had postponed consideration of the troublesome issue of PNEs, primarily because the Soviet Union had an ongoing, vigorous PNE programme at that time. The two sides agreed to take up the subject in a completely separate negotiation, which began in Moscow in October 1974 and lasted until April 1976. The resulting PNET has a technical content that goes far beyond any other arms control agreement. It provides for extensive data exchange on all PNEs and OSIs for certain group explosions. Under specific and well-defined conditions, designated inspectors would be permitted to bring equipment into the USSR (or the USA) to determine the yield of individual explosions.

Many CTB proponents in the USA, including Democratic candidate for the presidency Jimmy Carter, criticized the TTBT and the PNET for a number of reasons. They claimed that a threshold ban would divert attention from a CTB, and that the threshold was too high to offer any real restraint on weapon development. The PNET, they argued, in effect endorsed PNEs, threatened a CTB and could provide an excuse for potential proliferators to test nuclear weapons. India in fact labelled its 1974 nuclear weapon test as a PNE. In part because of these criticisms and in part because Ford became embroiled in a bitter nomination fight with Reagan, including a sharp challenge from Reagan on Ford's arms control stance, the US Senate failed to act on the ratification of either agreement.

Washington and Moscow none the less have agreed to observe the basic yield restrictions of the TTBT and the PNET, but the verification provisions have not gone into effect. These provisions, however, did break important new ground. Many of the OSI procedures which negotiators painstakingly developed could carry over to a CTB and possibly to other arms control agreements. Moreover, they represented a significant evolution in Soviet thinking about co-operative and intrusive forms of verification.

III. Renewed CTB negotiations, 1977–80

Promptly after taking office, President Carter, who perhaps more than any other President since 1945 was committed to reducing the risks of nuclear war, directed an inter-agency study of the test ban and other arms control issues (PRM-16). At the same time that the Soviet Union sharply rejected Carter's ensuing deep-cut proposal on strategic arms made in Moscow in March 1977, it did accept an invitation to open new talks on a CTB. Potential renewed Soviet interest in a CTB had been foreshadowed a year earlier when Moscow presented a draft treaty to the UN General Assembly that alluded to the possibility of voluntary or challenge OSIs. Full trilateral negotiations—again involving the USA, the USSR and the UK—began in the fall of 1977.

As anticipated, PNEs and verification became the major points of controversy at the new talks. The USA and the UK wanted a ban on all nuclear explosions; the USSR wanted to preserve its PNE programme. As early as 1965 the Gilpatric committee had described PNEs as a major potential 'loophole' in a CTB.[32] In 1977–8 the Western position had hardened and rested on the premise, as a US defence official explained, that 'PNE technology is indistinguishable from that required for weapons tests and that a state undertaking PNE's inevitably derives weapons-related information'.[33] Surprisingly, on 2 November 1977 Brezhnev publicly announced that the USSR would accept a moratorium on PNEs for the duration of a CTB. The Soviet Union also agreed at this time to defer another issue which was key to its national security interests: the adherence of the other nuclear powers, France and China, to any potential CTB.[34] These outcomes early in the tripartite discussions on questions which many thought would be major obstacles seemed to indicate a genuine commitment on the Soviet side to conduct good-faith negotiations.

Soviet general interest in a CTB stemmed from a number of factors. Chief among these was their continued concern about proliferation, which they emphasized at the March 1977 meeting with the US delegation. In addition, the Soviet leadership hoped to check US weapon technology, which had always been superior to that of the USSR. Finally, Brezhnev perhaps hoped to use a CTB to help reinvigorate the US–Soviet arms control process as a whole.

There still remained the verification issue, however. Both before and especially after the signing of the PTBT, the USA learned a great deal about the seismology of underground test detection and substantially increased its technical capabilities in this field. Beginning in 1964, the Defense Department operated through the Air Force Technical Application Center a world-wide network of seismic and intelligence-gathering stations known as the Atomic

Energy Detection System (AEDS). According to 1978 testimony of one official close to the programme, AEDS 'has not been the world's greatest, but it is nonetheless a good, serious system'. The same official reported that AEDS in combination with other 'intelligence means'—Vela satellites, reconnaissance aircraft and geological surveys—have compiled an excellent track record in detecting Soviet test shots.[35] The CCD and SIPRI added important additional independent studies of the verification issue during this period.[36] A detection and identification threshold still existed, however. Verification and OSIs therefore once again constituted a central issue for US negotiators in the 1977–80 round of talks.

The Soviet Union accepted the idea of voluntary or challenge OSIs in 1976. These work as follows: if a seismic event occurs in Country A's territory and the event appears to be ambiguous to Country B—that is, a possible nuclear explosion—Country B can request permission to inspect the region around the event. Country A can then either accept or reject the request. If rejected, Country B might then choose to withdraw from the treaty.

Sweden first introduced the voluntary inspection concept (as well as the idea of seismic data exchanges) at the ENDC during the 1960s. The US Government, initially sceptical about the idea, reassessed its position under President Carter and concluded that challenge OSIs could be as effective a deterrent to cheating as mandatory OSIs, if the rejection of a request could be established as a serious matter. This was a significant political step and, whether intended or not, a response to the Soviet concession on PNEs.

Another verification issue taken up at the Geneva talks (in the context of what was known as the Separate Verification Agreement) was that of establishing permanent national seismic stations (NSSs) within the boundaries of each negotiating nation. In the US view, NSSs would be automatic and tamper-detection proof, thus not requiring foreign personnel on constant attendance. US scientists have in fact developed high-quality, automatic seismic stations and the government has installed five in the USA and Canada. A group of British and Soviet scientists visited the US development programme in July 1979.[37]

In their July 1980 tripartite report to the CD, the major accomplishment of the 1977–80 negotiations, the three parties evidently had made significant progress in implementing verification procedures. As the report summarized:

the verification measures being negotiated—particularly the provisions regarding the International Exchange of Seismic Data, the Committee of Experts, and on-site inspections—break significant new ground in international arms limitation efforts and will give all treaty parties the opportunity to participate in a substantial and constructive way in the process of verifying compliance with the treaty.[38]

Specifically with regard to voluntary OSI procedures, the parties agreed to establish a separate Joint Consultative Commission (in the manner of the SALT Standing Consultative Commission). With regard to NSS, the tripartite report simply states that the parties 'are negotiating' the question.[39] It should be recognized that even consideration of this principle was a significant step forward for the USSR. 'We should try to understand that Soviet acceptance of NSS would be an unprecedented step, which was extraordinarily difficult for a great many Soviet officials to swallow', one senior US negotiator cabled home in November 1978. 'This was psychologically a tremendous step for the Soviets to take'.[40]

Ironically, however, the main sticking point became the actual number and location of NSS on not Soviet but British territory. The chief US negotiator, Herbert York, in fact called this 'the most intractable of the many internal problems faced by the negotiators'.[41] As described by a Soviet political officer, Victor Slipchenko, the issue of whether to accept NSS had been 'touch and go' in the Politburo. 'In the end, approval was reached only on the basis that all three negotiating parties accept an equal number of stations.'[42] This the British proved unwilling to accept. Long-time negotiator Warren Heckrotte believes that this Soviet insistence on equal numbers was designed 'to emphasize—with a vengeance—their view that verification is a political, not technical, matter'.[43]

Even while detailed negotiations on verification and other provisions were under way at Geneva, the Washington bureaucracy that had gone along with the decision to open CTB discussions in PRM-16 began to question the wisdom of concluding a treaty. The fundamental objection, based on assessments by the nuclear weapon laboratories and given bureaucratic clout by the Department of Energy (DOE) and Joint Chiefs of Staff (JCS), related to stockpile reliability. Without tests, the laboratories maintained, confidence in the reliability of the stockpile would inexorably erode. This issue had simmered over the years and, with the possibility of a comprehensive test ban on the doorstep, it became critical.

Laboratory, DOE and JCS representatives expressed their concerns at congressional hearings on the CTB in 1978. In summary, they argued that testing would be needed 'in the long run' to protect against 'stockpile aging', to keep the stockpile 'robust' and to facilitate development of new weapon designs.[44] Under a CTB, the technical expertise necessary for these tasks would be lost through both attrition and the deterioration of skills on the part of those who stayed. Similar domestic opposition emerged in the British camp as well. Scientists in the Ministry of Defence, including chief scientist Victor Macklen, and at the British Atomic Weapons Research Establishment at Aldermaston argued the need for testing to develop their Chevaline programme. Many of these scientists co-operated directly with CTB opponents in the USA. 'It was a microcosm of the situation in Washington with only irrelevant differences in the details', York reports.[45]

Scientific opinion was by no means unanimous on the stockpile reliability question, indicating the essential political nature of any potential CTB. Three prominent members of the US nuclear weapon technical community—Norris Bradbury and J. Carson Mark, formerly of Los Alamos, and Richard Garwin, a noted general consultant on weapon technology—wrote a letter to President Carter at the time of the 1978 hearings disputing the laboratories' position. They argued that the issue of reliability could be dealt with by forgoing changes in existing stockpiles and by remanufacturing or replacing those weapons in which defects appeared. Through these and other measures, the DOE could 'provide continuing assurance for as long as may be desired of the operability of the nuclear weapons stockpile'.[46] Asked by Secretary of Defense Harold Brown to comment on these conflicting scientific views, Ambassador York further complicated matters by making two observations. He agreed with Bradbury, Mark and Garwin that, if their provisions were adopted, 'the weapons in our stockpile will still perform in the future [10–20 years] as they do today'. But in the realm of perceptions, which York regarded as an equally important question, 'it is clear that today's leadership does not have confidence in a stockpile in a hypothetical future in which testing has been banned'. 'The US national security establishment', he added, 'is too high strung and nervous to live contentedly with a CTBT'.[47]

CTB critics also challenged the contention that whatever stockpile degradation took place would affect both sides equally. In their view, because of US–Soviet 'asymmetries' in government and societies and the consequent possibility of clandestine Soviet testing, there would be no guarantee that the reliability of Soviet weapons would erode as that of the US stockpile did. According to DOE spokesman Donald Kerr, later to become director of the Los Alamos National Laboratory, 'a treaty which had zero length would certainly minimize the risks from our weapons [reliability] and development point of view'.[48]

Although internal doubts continued to mount, the Carter Administration remained committed to the negotiations, primarily because of the political gains they offered in checking horizontal proliferation. At the 1978 hearings, Rear Admiral Thomas Davies of the Arms Control and Disarmament Agency (ACDA) and Leslie Gelb of the State Department identified three ways in which a CTB would contribute to US non-proliferation efforts: (a) it would directly bolster the NPT; (b) it would 'inhibit testing by threshold states'; and (c) it would give the USA greater bargaining leverage in general 'nuclear matters'. 'Of course, the CTB is not a panacea', Gelb concluded; 'I cannot quantify exactly how much a CTB would help our proliferation efforts. But I am confident that it will be of substantial benefit'.[49] The British political leadership, under Prime Minister Callaghan, adopted a similar line, although his conservative successor, Prime Minister Thatcher, took a much dimmer view of a CTB from May 1979. Still, Lord Carrington, then Secretary of State for foreign and commonwealth affairs, reported to the UN Association on 24 October 1980 that a CTB 'is important for two reasons: first, it will curb the development of new and more destructive nuclear warheads, thereby curtailing this aspect of competition in strategic weapons; secondly, it will demonstrate our good faith towards those countries which, under the NPT, have formally surrendered the right to develop nuclear weapons'.[50]

Ultimately, the internal opposition to a CTB in the USA and the UK had its effect; overwhelming bureaucratic and political pressure literally consumed the treaty. In 1978 President Carter (made painfully aware of the extent of internal opposition by a visit of the laboratory directors to the Oval Office in June) changed the US position on the duration of a treaty from forever to five and then to three years, with an option to resume tests after the accord lapsed. The DOE and DOE Secretary James Schlesinger favoured an explicit commitment to this option. Interestingly, the chief British negotiator John Edmonds points to this US vacillation on the question of treaty duration (and the underlying internal tensions it reflected) as the most troublesome issue for the USSR at Geneva.[51]

While the CTB controversy raged in Washington's inner circles, Carter's principal arms control item, the SALT II Treaty, ran into its own troubles and delays. The Administration did not need another contentious issue injected into this increasingly difficult strategic arms control debate. Carter's science adviser Frank Press later bluntly commented that the President did not want to 'muck up' SALT with the test ban, although his commitment to the idea never waned.[52] A CTB would have to wait until SALT II was safely out of the way.

The Soviet view of the relationship between a CTB and SALT is more difficult to discern but, according to Carter, he and Gromyko in September 1978 'agreed to conclude the SALT II Treaty first, followed by a CTB agreement'.[53] There is no indication, moreover, that the Soviet Union tried to move matters along in Geneva. SALT II problems, and the Soviet invasion of Afghanistan in December 1979, put to rest any immediate expectation of ratifying SALT and with it any hope of concluding CTB negotiations.

IV. New leaders and the test ban, 1981–86

CTB negotiations recessed in November 1980, just weeks after the US presidential election in which Reagan defeated Carter. They have not resumed. The early Reagan Administration's general antipathy toward arms control extended particularly to the CTB. In July 1982 the President decided not to resume trilateral negotiations until improved verification measures of existing treaties (the TTBT and the PNET) could be achieved. A CTB 'must remain a component of this administration's long term arms control objectives', a Reagan spokesman declared, 'but there are problems to be overcome and these deal essentially with verification'.[54]

Ironically, Soviet positions on the CTB in particular and on arms control in general during the early 1980s remained unclear because of a Soviet problem usually associated with the US political system: rapid turnover in the top leadership. Brezhnev died in 1982, Andropov in 1984, and Chernenko in 1985. This problem appears to be resolving itself under General Secretary Gorbachev, a younger and more vigorous leader who has promised major changes in Soviet domestic and foreign policy. Gorbachev quickly took a number of actions which at the very least have allowed the USSR to capture the public relations high ground with regard to a test ban. Building on an earlier 1983 official statement that the USSR was prepared to resume trilateral negotiations, Gorbachev declared a unilateral moratorium on testing to begin on 6

August 1985 (the 40th anniversary of Hiroshima), later extended three times. At nearly the same time, he opened up Soviet nuclear facilities to IAEA inspection for the first time, although limiting the number of plants to two.[55] Finally, on 5 December 1985, Gorbachev sent a personal letter to Reagan in which he offered the promise of some on-site inspection of Soviet test ranges, which he reiterated in his general 15 January 1986 arms control proposals. As elaborated by Soviet First Deputy Foreign Minister Korniyenko in a speech to the CD on 20 February 1986, the USSR does not 'suggest that verification should be confined to national technical means. It is agreeable to supplementing it with international procedures, including on-site inspection if necesary'.[56]

The same concerns that Moscow has in the past had with both proliferation and US technology persist today. And, like Khrushchev, Gorbachev appears to have a genuine interest in domestic growth and modernization that carries with it at least in the short term a co-equal interest in dampening the expensive military competition with the West. This was reflected, for example, in the proceedings of the 27th Soviet Communist Party Congress of February–March 1986.[57] At the same time, traditional internal forces, such as the Soviet military, continue to exert pressure in the opposite direction. At a recent press conference, Marshal Sergei Akhromeev cautiously sounded an alarm about the Soviet test moratorium. 'We had to accept a certain damage to us', Marshal Akhromeyev commented, 'although for the time being we consider the damage acceptable'.[58] Such statements have obvious propaganda value, but also indicate the presence of a strong internal debate on the subject.

To discover precisely what the Soviet actions and offers mean in practice would require extensive face-to-face negotiations. But in the absence of US willingness to resume formal CTB talks, they have, in the words of Alton Frye, 'put Washington on the defensive internationally'.[59] Or as another commentator says, 'Washington has been reacting to Moscow, dragging its heels, using the old Soviet stonewall tactic just when Moscow has learned the advantage of taking the initiative'.[60] Thus, for example, the 1985 NPT Review Conference in its final communiqué reserved explicit criticism for the USA and the UK with reference to Article VI. As one observer noted, the 'dispute which arose on the subject of nuclear testing almost brought about the collapse of the Conference', but none the less 'the Soviet Union escaped censure'.[61] ACDA Director Kenneth Adelman, responding on behalf of the USA, simply stated that 'we have met, and will continue to meet, our obligations under Article VI'. He cited the resumption of US–Soviet strategic talks and the removal of 1400 tactical nuclear weapons from Europe during 1984–85, following the 1979 withdrawal of 1000 warheads.[62] 'A CTB will not reduce the number of nuclear weapons in the world by one', Adelman added; 'Nor will it, in the near term, make the world any safer'.[63]

Other international groups, both old and new, have added their voices in support of a CTB. As it has since the 1960s, the CD continues to regard a CTB as one of its highest priorities, despite the non-support of four of the five nuclear powers: the USA, the UK, France and China. In their 1980 tripartite report, the USA, the UK and the USSR specifically recognized the CD's role in developing co-operative verification procedures and, based on that work, agreed to establish an international exchange of seismic data if a treaty were achieved.[64] The CD also set up both a working group on verification and compliance and an Ad Hoc Group of Scientific Experts to 'consider international cooperative measures to detect and identify seismic events'. Politically, the so-called non-aligned Group of 21 and the Socialist members of the CD have pressed for a mandate to permit work 'with a view to negotiation of a treaty'.[65] In addition, Sweden introduced a draft treaty in June 1983.

A new international coalition—the non-aligned nations of Argentina, Greece, India, Mexico, Sweden and Tanzania—have been urging the nuclear powers to halt testing (as well as production and deployment) of nuclear weapons since January of 1985. Co-ordinated through the Parliamentarians Global Action (over 600 legislators from 36 countries), the 'Delhi Six' repeated their so-called Five-Continent Peace Initiative, including a call for a test ban, in October 1985, shortly before the Geneva superpower summit, at Ixtapa, Mexico, in August 1986 and again in December 1986, after the Reykjavik summit meeting. In the later versions, the proposals of the six countries reflect the idea that verification should be a concern of all nations, and not simply of the nuclear states. The six offered to help both with 'third party verification' and with the implementation of a comprehensive world-wide verification plan, including OSIs.[66]

In the USA, congressional and public concerns about halting tests began almost immediately after the Reagan Administration tabled consideration of a CTB in July 1982. Several former ACDA directors and chief CTB negotiators criticized the action, as did a number of private organizations such as the Union of Concerned Scientists, the Arms Control Association and the Lawyers Alliance for Nuclear Arms Control. Perhaps more importantly, congressional pressure escalated from an indefinite proposal of 46 senators in December 1985 to begin talks and 'see if we can work something out' to a specific call of the House of Representatives (234–155) in 1986 for a one-year moratorium on US testing if the Soviet Union accepts OSIs. The House measure was offered as part of an unprecedented package of arms control proposals attached to the 1987 Defense Authorization Bill. Congress postponed action on this package, however, in light of the Reagan–Gorbachev Reykjavik meeting.[67]

Congressional sentiment for a test ban apparently meets with US public approval. A Gallup Poll indicated in April 1986 that 56 per cent of Americans agreed that the USA should join the Soviet moratorium while 35 per cent disagreed. Significantly, this support was bipartisan, with 58 per cent of Democrats in favour, 33 per cent opposed; and 51 per cent of Republicans agreed, 43 per cent opposed.[68]

Despite these external and internal pressures, the Reagan Administration remains adamant in its opposition to a moratorium and to reopening CTB negotiations. In response, the Soviet Union announced its intention to resume testing in 1987. 'The USSR is prepared to continue to respect its moratorium', a Soviet statement of 18 December 1986 maintained. 'Yet it will resume nuclear testing after the first nuclear explosion carried out by the United States next year'.[69] Indeed, the USSR resumed testing in February 1987, after a US test was conducted a few weeks earlier.

The major US focus continues to be on verification, which Reagan underscored in several initiatives put forward in response to the Gorbachev overtures: an exchange of US and Soviet seismologists in September 1984, an invitation to the USSR to observe a US test in July 1985, an invitation for technical talks in December 1985, and an offer to share the new CORRTEX verification procedure in March 1986, all of which the Soviet Union rejected.[70] In January 1987 President Reagan submitted the TTBT and the PNET for ratification, requested by both the Senate in 1984 and the House in 1986, but with a controversial proviso calling for new verification provisions before the treaties could go into effect. The Administration added this proviso, which according to one senator makes ratification a 'meaningless exercise', despite growing internal evidence indicating that the yields from past Soviet tests have been overestimated by as much as 20 per cent.[71]

Although the Thatcher Government expressed initial displeasure with the US decision of July 1982, saying that Britain was still committed to a CTB 'of some description',[72] it quickly got in line with Washington. Foreign Secretary Sir Geoffrey Howe asked in March 1986: 'Isn't verification now just an excuse anyhow? The short answer is "no"; it is a very real concern'. Alluding to the possibility of 'covert evasion' and 'vague promises' of OSIs, Howe called on the USSR 'to take up President Reagan's latest offer of discussions and a visit by experts on verification'.[73]

However, US opposition to a CTB goes beyond 'effective' verification. Fundamentally, the Administration does not believe that a CTB is in US national security interests and has resurrected nearly all historical arguments against the CTB to bolster its case. The USA must continue testing, Reagan informed Congress in March 1986, to ensure that 'our weapons are safe, effective, reliable and survivable and [to ensure] our capability to respond to the continued Soviet nuclear arms buildup'.[74] Other officials have highlighted the need to develop new designs for nuclear warheads (including for the Strategic Defense Initiative programme), and indeed the majority of tests conducted are for this purpose.[75] Finally, the Administration has dusted off a little-used argument that a CTB might in fact promote proliferation. Laboratory spokesmen first introduced this idea in the 1970s debate, and some Defense and State Department officials have picked it up nearly verbatim. As stated by the Deputy Assistant Secretary of Defense for Negotiations Policy Douglas J. Feith, 'to the extent that our cessation of testing might raise doubts among some of our friends abroad as to the integrity of the US nuclear umbrella, it might actually stimulate proliferation'.[76] In the final analysis, the Reagan Administration simply does not want to foreclose *any* potential technological option in dealing with the USSR.

While Washington and Moscow continue their propaganda battle over nuclear testing, some positive and surprising developments have taken place. US scientists from the private Natural Resources Defense Council (NRDC) and Soviet scientists from the Academy of Sciences of the USSR agreed in May 1986 to commit the US group to set up and man seismic monitoring stations within the USSR, near the major Soviet test site at Semipalatinsk. The 'unprecedented' agreement, as it has been uniformly described in the US scientific and public press,[77] also called for a reciprocal visit by a Soviet research team. According to Thomas Cochran, senior scientist at the NRDC and the originator of the idea, the 'primary goal is simply to demonstrate that Soviet and American scientists can work together and establish these stations in their respective countries'.[78] The US Government has thus far adopted a hands-off approach to this unique private undertaking, which is co-ordinated on the Soviet side by Yevgeniy Velikhov, the vice-president of the Soviet Academy. In another proposal also generated by informal contacts, the Soviet Union agreed in August 1986 to establish an entire monitoring network inside the USSR if the USA joined in a test moratorium. The NRDC–Soviet Academy arrangement does not, as some claim, demonstrate conclusively the technical feasibility of monitoring Soviet tests; nevertheless, it will provide important new scientific information, and it sets an important political precedent in the context of possible future negotiations.

On an official level, the two sides have resumed discussions on the testing issue. Begun in July 1986 in Geneva, these discussions are not likely to produce significant results. Each side has a different agenda—the USA, for ways to improve verification of existing treaties, and the USSR, for a complete ban on testing—and each regards the discussions as secondary to the main Nuclear and Space Talks. Yet as one US official reported, 'These were serious talks, and the fact that they will resume in the fall is definitely a plus'.[79] The fact that they happened at all is a major surprise to most observers, given the Administration's views on a CTB. Perhaps the last official word on this issue was given by Frank Gaffney of the Defense Department: 'I'm confident that there won't be a halt to testing as long as Ronald Reagan is President'; but he added, 'that is not to say that a future administration won't see things differently'.[80]

V. Conclusion

If the history of test ban negotiations teaches us any one lesson it is perhaps that even if a future President 'sees things differently', and if his Soviet and British counterparts should join him, it will still be very difficult for them to move positively on this highly controversial issue. Two points are fundamental. First, a political judgement is required; there will always remain some element of doubt and ambiguity about technical details. As former British Prime Minister Macmillan eloquently commented in 1973, 'Scientists, who are the poets of the 20th century, seem to be subject to the most conflicting moods'.[81] Technical advances can reduce uncertainties, and have in the past (with regard to verification, for example), but they cannot eliminate them altogether. Decision makers must weigh these technical costs, however small, against the potential political benefits in any consideration of a test ban.

Second, governments are fundamentally divided internally over the CTB issue. In the most obvious case, that of the USA, two former chief negotiators have underscored this problem. According to Paul Warnke, the 'problem isn't just the President. The problem is that there's a whole bureaucracy that's been built up over many, many years that is very much in favor of continuing nuclear weapons tests'.[82] According to Herbert York, 'the Chiefs and the nuclear establishment do, in general, support arms control. They will not, however, willingly endorse or acquiesce in restrictions on the tests [they view as] needed to maintain readiness or to support the kind of modification that is always underway in the military establishment'.[83] Putting the issue in slightly different terms, former PTBT negotiator Franklin Long has said that the President must want a CTB, but that he needs 'enough good advice' to get it.[84] Under such conditions, a CTB seems possible only within a broader arms control framework—what York describes as 'a world in which the great powers are clearly and forcefully moving away from their current dependence on nuclear weapons',[85] or in some diluted form, such as a quota or low-threshold ban.

Notes and references

[1] Jacobson, H. K. and Stein, E., *Diplomats, Scientists and Politicians: The United States and the Nuclear Negotiations* (University of Michigan Press: Ann Arbor, 1966), p. 21; Blacker, C. D. and Duffy, G., *International Arms Control: Issues and Agreements* (Stanford University Press: Stanford, 1984), p. 126.

[2] Included in the group of Soviet scientists was Andrei Sakharov, a leader in Soviet H-bomb development. In 1959, they published a volume expressing their views: *Soviet Scientists and the Danger of Nuclear Testing*. See Salisbury, H. E. (ed.), *Sakharov Speaks* (Alfred A. Knopf: New York, 1974). On Pugwash, see Rotblat, J., *Scientist in Quest for Peace: A History of the Pugwash Conference* (MIT Press: Cambridge, 1972); and Hawkins, H. S., Greb, G. A. and Scilard, G. W., *For a Livable World: Leo Scilard and the Crusade for Nuclear Arms Control*, vol. 3 of *The Collected Works of Leo Scilard* (MIT Press: Cambridge, MA, 1987), pp. 151–237.

[3] Hewlett, R. G. and Schorzman, T. A., *United States Perceptions of the Potential Impact of a Comprehensive Ban Treaty: An Historical Summary*, Study prepared for the Office of International Security Affairs, US Department of Energy (History Associates Incorporated: Rockville, MD, 31 Aug. 1985), pp. 9–10.

[4] Divine, R. A., *Blowing on the Wind: The Nuclear Test Ban Debate, 1954–1960* (Oxford University Press: New York, 1978) provides the most complete account of the fall-out controversy.

[5] Jacobson and Stein (note 1), p. 103.

[6] Zoppo, C. E., *The Issue of Nuclear Test Cessation at the London Disarmament Conference of 1957: A Study in East–West Negotiations*, RAND Report RM-2821-ARPA (Rand Corporation: Santa Monica, Sep. 1961), pp. 21, 24–5, 87; Barton, J. H. and Weiler, L. D., *International Arms Control: Issues and Agreements* (Stanford University Press: Stanford, 1976), pp. 101–2.

[7] Jacobson and Stein (note 1), pp. 100–1, 267–8.

[8] Minutes of PSAC meeting, 8, 9, 10 Apr. 1958, *PSAC Records*, Dwight Eisenhower Papers, Eisenhower Library, Abilene, KS.

[9] Jönsson, C., *Soviet Bargaining Behaviour: The Nuclear Test Ban Case* (Columbia University Press: New York, 1979), pp. 55–7.

[10] US Department of State, *Documents on Disarmament, 1945–1959*, vol. 2 (US Government Printing Office: Washington, DC, 1960), p. 1038.

[11] See Gowing, M., *Independence and Deterrence: Britain and Atomic Energy, 1945–1952*, 2 vols (St Martins Press: New York, 1974); Freedman, L., *Britain and Nuclear Weapons* (Macmillan: London, 1980); Malone, P., *The British Deterrent* (Croom Helm: London, 1984).

[12] Heckrotte, W., 'Soviet Views on Verification', review of Timerbaev, R., *Verification of Arms Limitation and Disarmament*, published in *Bulletin of Atomic Scientists*, vol. 42 (Oct. 1986), pp. 12–15.

[13] *Documents on Disarmament, 1945–1959*, vol. 1, p. 69.

[14] 'Notes by Chairman Lewis L. Strauss, US Atomic Energy Committee, before Subcommittee on Disarmament, US Senate', 17 Apr. 1958, p. 7, in E. O. Lawrence Papers, Bancroft Library, University of California, Berkeley.

[15] Recollection of Harlech, D., 'Hi-tech diplomacy: recollections of the LTBT, 1963', *Test Ban Video History* (Alfred P. Sloan Foundation: New York, 18 Apr. 1984).

[16] See, for example, Seaborg, G., *Kennedy, Khrushchev and the Test Ban* (University of California Press: Berkeley, 1981); 'Seaborg proposal: support a comprehensive test ban', *Chemical and Engineering News* (13 June 1983), pp. 2–3.

[17] *Documents on Disarmament, 1945–1959*, vol. 2 (note 10), pp. 1440–1, 1590–1.

[18] Neild, R. and Ruina, J. P., 'A comprehensive ban on nuclear testing', *Science*, vol. 175 (14 Jan. 1972), p. 141.

[19] Gerald Johnson, who in 1961 was chairman of the Military Liaison Committee in the Department of Defense and heavily involved in the US test programme, later estimated that the Soviet test resumption reflected 'at least two years of secret preparation'. Draft on 'Nuclear Test Moratorium 1958–1961', 13 Sep. 1985, made available to the author.

[20] Heckrotte, W., 'Geneva Trip Report', Lawrence Livermore National Laboratory, 6 Nov. 1961, p. 4. Heckrotte generally characterized that round of negotiations as 'primarily a verbal exercise', and further as a 'caricature of an oriental play with actors, masked, moving ritualistically through the prescribed, ordained intricacies of custom'. 'Trip Report', pp. 2, 6.

[21] Macmillan, H., *At the End of the Day, 1961–1963* (Harper and Row: New York, 1973), p. 143.

[22] Medalia, J. E., 'Problems in formulating and implementing effective arms control policy: the nuclear test ban treaty case', *Stanford Journal of International Studies*, vol. 7 (1972), p. 135.

[23] Bundy, W. M., 'The avoidance of nuclear war since 1945', *The Dangers of Nuclear War*, eds F. Griffiths and J. C. Polanyi (University of Toronto Press: Toronto, 1979), p. 29.

[24] Mandelbaum, M., *The Nuclear Question: The United States and Nuclear Weapons, 1946–1976* (Cambridge University Press: Cambridge, 1979), p. 165. See also Dean, A. H., *Test Ban and Disarmament* (Harper and Row: New York, 1966), p. 58; Jacobson and Stein (note 1), p. 171; Gilpin, R., *American Scientists and Nuclear Weapons Policy* (Princeton University Press: Princeton, 1962), pp. 245–6.

[25] Quoted in Medalia (note 22), p. 149. See also Jacobson and Stein (note 1), pp. 458–64.

[26] Committee on Nuclear Proliferation, *A Report to the President* (The White House: Washington, DC, 21 Jan. 1965), pp. 1, 5–6 (the Gilpatric Report).

[27] ACDA, *Arms Control and Disarmament Agreements: Texts and Histories of Negotiations* (US Arms Control and Disarmament Agency: Washington, DC, 1982), p. 93.

[28] ACDA (note 27), p. 41.

[29] ACDA, Office of Public Affairs, *Special Report: 1980 Review Conference of the Treaty on the Non-Proliferation of Nuclear Weapons*, Nov. 1980, p. 10.

[30] UN Secretary-General, *Report on the Comprehensive Nuclear Test Ban*, CD/86, 16 Apr. 1980, p. 40.

[31] Ford, G. R., *The Vladivostok Negotiations and Other Events*, IGCC Policy Papers, no. 2 (UC IGCC: San Diego, 1986), p. 8.

[32] Gilpatric Report (note 26), p. 20.

[33] *Effects of a Comprehensive Test Ban Treaty on US National Security Interests*, Hearing before the Committee on Armed Services, Intelligence and Military Application of Nuclear Energy Subcommittee, US House, 95th Congress (US Government Printing Office: Washington, DC, 1978), p. 57.

[34] See Edmonds, J., 'Proliferation and test bans', *Armed Peace: The Search for World Security*, ed. J. O. Howe (Macmillan: London, 1984), pp. 77–8.

[35] *Effects of a Comprehensive Test Ban Treaty on US National Security Interests* (note 33), pp. 153–4.

[36] SIPRI, *SIPRI Yearbooks of World Armaments and Disarmament*; records of the CD.

[37] See the special issue of *Energy and Technology Review* (Lawrence Livermore National Laboratory, May 1983) on test ban verification.

[38] *Tripartite Report to the Committee on Disarmament*, CD/130, 30 July 1980, p. 9. Also NPT 1980 Review Conference document, NPT/CONF, II/13, 13 Aug. 1980.

[39] *Tripartite Report* (note 38), p. 10.

[40] Van Atta, D., 'The test ban cables: inside a US–Soviet arms negotiation', *Nation* (19 Dec. 1981), p. 657.

[41] York, H. F., *The Comprehensive Test Ban Negotiations, 1977–1981*, p. 40, draft chapter of memoirs to be published by Harper and Row: New York, 1987.

[42] Van Atta (note 40), p. 658.

[43] Heckrotte (note 12), p. 14.

[44] *Effects of a Comprehensive Test Ban Treaty on US National Security Interests* (note 33), pp. 3–27, 175–6.

[45] York (note 41), p. 59. See also Zuckerman, S., *Nuclear Illusion and Reality* (Viking Press: New York, 1982), pp. 114–18; Owen, D., 'A total test ban', *ADIU Report*, vol. 7 (Mar.–Apr. 1985), who says that British and US laboratory scientists 'worked in cahoots' against a CTB, p. 2.

[46] Bradbury, N. E., Garwin, R. L. and Mark, J. C., communication to President Carter, 15 Aug. 1978. Reproduced in *Effects of a Comprehensive Test Ban Treaty on US National Security Interests*, pp. 181–2.

[47] York, H. F. to H. Brown, 12 Sep. 1978.

[48] *Effects of a Comprehensive Test Ban Treaty on US National Security Interests* (note 33), p. 26.

[49] *Effects of a Comprehensive Test Ban Treaty on US National Security Interests* (note 33), pp. 107–8.

[50] Lord Carrington, 'Arms Control and International Security', Speech before the UN Association, 24 Oct. 1980.

[51] Edmonds (note 34), pp. 78–9, 86–7.

[52] Recollection of Press, F., *Test Ban Treaty Video History* (note 15).

[53] Carter, J., *Keeping Faith: Memoirs of a President* (Bantam: New York, 1982), p. 231.

[54] White House, Office of the Press Secretary, 'Background Briefing on Test Ban Treaty', 20 July 1982, p. 3.

[55] 'Gorbachev extends test ban until Jan. 1', *Current Digest of the Soviet Press*, vol. 38 (17 Sep. 1986), pp. 5–6.

[56] Speech by G. M. Korniyenko, 20 Feb. 1986, 'Nuclear testing and the CTB documentation', *Survival*, vol. 28 (July–Aug. 1986), p. 353.

[57] See *Current Soviet Policies IX: The Documentary Record of the 27th Congress of the Communist Party of the Soviet Union* (Current Digest of the Soviet Press: Columbus, OH, 1986), pp. 33–8; Becker, A., Bialer, S. and Horelick, A.; *Communist Party of the Soviet Union: A Report from the Arlie House Conference* (RAND/UCLA Center for the Study of Soviet International Behaviour: Santa Monica, Dec. 1986), pp. 42–55.

[58] Quoted in Taubman, P., 'Kremlin presses test ban', *International Herald Tribune*, 26 Aug. 1986. See also Herspring, D. R., 'The Soviet military in the aftermath of the 27th Party Congress', *Orbis*, vol. 30 (Summer 1986), pp. 297–315.

[59] Frye, A., 'Nuclear moratorium: a middle path', *Los Angeles Times*, 24 Dec. 1985.

[60] Lewis, F., 'What we do better', *New York Times*, 5 Aug. 1986.

[61] Goldblat, J., 'The Third Review Conference of the Nuclear Non-Proliferation Treaty', *Bulletin of Peace Proposals*, vol. 17 (1986), pp. 13, 17. See also Dunn, L. A., 'Standing up for the NPT', Van Doren, C. N., 'Brighter outlook for NPT regime', and Spector, L. A., 'Unfinished business at the NPT Review', *Arms Control Today*, vol. 15 (Oct. 1985), pp. 6–10.

[62] This refers to the so-called Montebello decision. See 'Nuclear weapons and arms control: documentation', *Survival*, vol. 26 (Jan.–Feb. 1984), pp. 36–7.

[63] IDDS, *Arms Control Reporter*, 602. B. 95.

[64] *Tripartite Report* (note 38), p. 6.

[65] Windass, S. (ed.), *Avoiding Nuclear War: Common Security as a Strategy for the Defence of the West* (Brassey's Defence Publishers: London, 1985), pp. 165–7. The detailed records of the CD are now available on microfilm; 'Committee on Disarmament, 1962–1984: Meetings and Documents' (with a printed guide), University Publications of America, Frederick, MD.

[66] Stockton, W., '6 nations urge halt in nuclear testing', *New York Times*, 8 Aug. 1986; 'An appeal to Reagan and Gorbachev', *New York Times*, 31 Dec. 1986.

[67] 'We Cannot Support President Reagan's Decision on the Comprehensive Test Ban Treaty', Statement from former ACDA Directors and Chief Negotiators, Committee for National Security, Washington, DC, 10 Aug. 1982; Miller, J., 'US confirms a plan to halt talks on a nuclear test ban', *New York Times*, 21 July 1982; Gordon, M. R., 'US aides find hope as Soviet urges test ban', *New*

York Times, 23 Dec. 1985; Coleman, M., 'House urges new talks on atom test ban pact', *Washington Post*, 27 Feb. 1986; Fritz, S., 'House OKs atom test moratorium', *Los Angeles Times*, 9 Aug. 1986.

[68] 'Opinion outlook: views on national security', *National Journal*, vol. 18 (28 June 1986), p. 1625.

[69] Keller, B., 'Soviet rebuffed by US, is planning to renew A-tests', *New York Times*, 19 Dec. 1987.

[70] US State Department, 'Verifying Nuclear Testing Lmitation: Possible US–Soviet Cooperation', *Special Report No. 152* (14 Aug. 1986).

[71] Gordon, M. R., 'CIA evaluating Soviet threat, often is not so grim as Pentagon', *New York Times*, 16 July 1986; Toth, R. C., 'Nuclear test pacts with disputed proviso submitted to Senate', *Los Angeles Times*, 14 Jan. 1987; Fritz, S., 'Senate Democrats unenthusiastic about Byrd's effort to ratify two arms treaties', *Los Angeles Times*, 20 Feb. 1987; Gordon, M. R., 'Reagan plan on verifying nuclear test faulted', *New York Times*, 13 Jan. 1987; Gordon, 'Scientists voice doubts Soviet breached treaty', *New York Times*, 16 Jan. 1987.

[72] 'British displeased at US test-ban decision', *New York Times*, 21 July 1982.

[73] 'Speech by Sir G. Howe, 17 March 1986', Nuclear Testing and the CTB documentation, *Survival*, vol. 28 (July–Aug. 1986), pp. 362–3.

[74] 'Letter from R. Reagan to Sen. R. Dole, 12 March 1986', Nuclear Testing and the CTB documentation, *Survival*, vol. 28 (July–Aug. 1986), p. 356.

[75] Joeck, N. and York, H. F., *Countdown on the Comprehensive Test Ban* (UC IGCC and Ploughshares Fund, Inc.: San Diego, 1986), p. 1.

[76] Feith, D. J., 'Proposal for nuclear test ban failing the test', *Washington Quarterly*, vol. 9 (Spring 1986), pp. 16–17. See also F. C. Ikle testimony, *Effects of a Comprehensive Test Ban Treaty on US National Security Interests*, pp. 136–7.

[77] See, for example, Smith, R. J., 'Soviet, US scientists reach seismic agreement', *Science*, vol. 232 (13 June 1986), p. 1338; Broad, W. J., 'Westerners reach Soviet [Union] to check atom site', *New York Times*, 6 July 1986; Eaton, W. J., 'US scientists to monitor near Soviet A-site', *Los Angeles Times*, 8 July 1986. See also materials available from the NRDC, Washington, DC, including a copy of the original agreement.

[78] Smith (note 77).

[79] Gwertzman, B., 'US–Soviet talks on atom tests end', *New York Times*, 1 Aug. 1986.

[80] 'Underground nuclear weapons testing', *IEEE Spectrum* (Apr. 1986), p. 43.

[81] Macmillan (note 21), p. 177.

[82] 'Briefing on the Comprehensive Test Ban', ACA Media Information Project, 19 Feb. 1986, p. 10.

[83] York (note 41), p. 77.

[84] Recollection of Long, F. A., *Test Ban Treaty Video History* (note 15). See also Smith, R. J., 'Weapons labs influence test ban debate', *Science*, vol. 229 (13 Sept. 1985), pp. 1067–9. Smith concludes that 'given the professional enthusiasm of the lab's employees it is hardly a surprise that the CTB is one experiment they don't wish to try' (p. 1069).

[85] York (note 41), p. 78. One interesting (although very elaborate) formula for implementing such an approach has been offered by Paul Doty, Director Emeritus of the Harvard Center for Science and International Affairs; see Doty, P., 'A nuclear test ban', *Foreign Affairs* (Spring 1987), pp. 750–69.

Chapter VI. The nuclear explosion limitation treaties

Paper 7

Jozef Goldblat
SIPRI

Abstract

Three nuclear test limitation treaties have been signed so far. The parties thereto may conduct nuclear explosions only underground, and the yields of the explosions must not exceed 150 kt. However, these restrictions have not slowed down the race for ever new and more sophisticated types of nuclear weaponry, nor have they contributed to the strengthening of the international nuclear non-proliferation regime. Two of the treaties in question are not yet even formally in force. Their ratification could at least provide verification experience and thereby facilitate progress towards a comprehensive test ban, which is a priority item on the agenda of multilateral arms control endeavours.

I. Introduction

Thirty years of deliberations and negotiations on a total prohibition of nuclear test explosions have resulted in only partial agreements, owing to the divergent strategic interests of the great powers, related to the development of ever new types of nuclear weapons. In 1963 the conduct of nuclear tests in the atmosphere, in outer space and under water was prohibited under a multilateral treaty, but the underground environment was left open for testing. In 1974, under a treaty concluded between the USA and the USSR, a limitation was introduced on the size of US and Soviet underground weapon test explosions, but the agreed threshold was high; and in 1976, in another bilateral treaty, rules were established by the USA and the USSR for conducting underground explosions for peaceful purposes at a time when there was already considerable scepticism, especially in the United States, as to the technical feasibility and economic viability of such explosions. Of these three agreements, moreover, only the first is formally in force. The other two have not yet been ratified, although the parties have undertaken to observe their essential provisions.

In initiating negotiations for a discontinuance of test explosions, the nuclear powers stated that, in addition to their desire to put an end to the contamination of the human environment by radioactive substances, they were guided by the following considerations: the cessation of tests would slow the arms race by imposing restrictions on nuclear weapon developments, check the spread of nuclear weapons to other nations and facilitate progress towards disarmament. It is in the light of these professed goals that the three test-limitation treaties are analysed here—the scope of the contractual obligations and their implementation, as well as the means provided for the verification of compliance.[1] The advantages and shortcomings of each treaty are assessed separately; the concluding section evaluates the existing limitations from the point of view of the requirements for meaningful measures of arms control.[2]

II. The 1963 Partial Test Ban Treaty

The treaty banning nuclear weapon tests in the atmosphere, in outer space and under water, usually referred to as the Partial (or Limited) Test Ban Treaty (PTBT or LTBT), was signed on 5 August 1963. It resulted from talks which had been conducted since the late 1950s, chiefly between the Soviet Union on the one side, and the United Kingdom and the United States on the other. The resolutions adopted by the United Nations General Assembly and the discussions held at the Geneva-based Conference of the Eighteen-Nation Disarmament Committee (ENDC) had stimulated these tripartite exchanges and had given them a semblance of being international multilateral negotiations. (For the text of the PTBT, see annexe 1.)

As confirmed by subsequent events, the conclusion of the PTBT was prompted less by an urge to turn the tide of arms competition than by the need to improve US–Soviet relations, which had been severely strained by the 1962 Cuban missile crisis, and to bring about a general relaxation of international tensions. An additional incentive may have been the desire shared by the USA and the USSR to make it more difficult for France and China to build their own nuclear arsenals. The nuclear testing issue was deemed to be well suited to all these purposes: world opinion was aroused by the risks of radioactive contamination, and public pressure for a test ban was increasing as more evidence on the biological effects of fall-out became available. The fact that both major powers had by then already carried out extensive series of tests in the atmosphere and made certain that testing could be continued underground reduced the cost of their mutual 'sacrifice'.

The Treaty proved to be a popular move. It was well received by most governments and entered into force very quickly—on 10 October 1963.

Scope of the obligations

Compared to other arms control treaties, the PTBT is a very short document, containing only five articles and a preamble; it bears the mark of a transitional arrangement. Indeed, under paragraph 3 of the preamble, the 'original parties'—the UK, the USA and the USSR—pledged themselves to seek to 'achieve the discontinuance of all test explosions of nuclear weapons for all time'. In Article I,1(b), their determination is clearly stated to conclude a treaty resulting in the 'permanent banning of all nuclear test explosions, including all such explosions underground'.

The prohibition under the PTBT covers nuclear weapon test explosions, 'and any' other nuclear explosion in three specified environments—the atmosphere, outer space and under water—at any place under the jurisdiction or control of the parties (Article I,1), without qualification as to the yield. Whether or not experimental micro-explosions in laboratories (in which some states later became engaged) are also prohibited is a moot point.

Whereas the ban on nuclear weapon test explosions is clear, the ban on other nuclear explosions may appear to be somewhat equivocal. As evidenced in the negotiating history, the term 'other' was inserted both to prevent circumvention of the treaty by an explosion of a tested nuclear weapon and to prevent explosions for peaceful purposes in the specified environments, whether tests or otherwise, in view of the difficulty of differentiating between military and peaceful explosions.[3] However, the Treaty is not interpreted as restricting the use of nuclear weapons in armed hostilities.[4] The practice heretofore followed in treaties banning the use of certain weapons or actions has been to state expressly that they apply in time of war.

The phrase 'under its jurisdiction or control' was understood as extending the prohibition to non-self-governing territories administered by states parties, as well as territories under military occupation.

Since there exists no commonly accepted definition of 'atmosphere' and 'outer space' and no agreement on where one ends and the other begins, the two environments are considered, for the purpose of the Treaty, as one continuous environment. Hence the language used: 'in the atmosphere; beyond its limits, including outer-space'. In other words, the ban applies to explosions from the surface of the earth on, into outer space, and there is no area between the atmosphere and outer space which is not covered by the prohibition. (It may be added that the 1967 Outer Space Treaty contains an explicit ban on the testing of any type of weapon on celestial bodies, a ban which has been reiterated and reinforced with regard to the moon in the 1979 Moon Treaty.)

The underwater environment is also understood comprehensively. The enumeration 'territorial waters or high-seas' was not meant to be exhaustive but illustrative; all bodies of water are included in the ban, both inland waters, lakes and rivers, and the seas. High seas were singled out to remove the possibility of an argument being put forward that these parts of the seas were not under the 'jurisdiction or control' of any party, and thus were not covered by the prohibition. In any event, under Article I,2, the parties undertook to refrain from causing nuclear explosions 'anywhere' in the environments described.

Nuclear explosions conducted underground, whatever their purpose, are not covered by the Treaty. However, there is a prohibition on any such explosion causing radioactive debris to be present outside the territorial limits of the state under whose jurisdiction or control the explosion is conducted (Article I,1(b)). This apparently means that an underground explosion which broke the surface of the ground would still be considered as 'underground' as long as it did not produce radioactivity detectable outside the exploding country's boundaries. (In the Russian-language version of the PTBT, the term used for 'debris' is *osadki*, which means deposit or fall-out. Since not all radioactive debris is necessarily deposited on the ground as fall-out, the Russian-language text seems to be less restrictive than the English-language one.)

Radioactive products from underground nuclear explosions may not be completely contained under the earth's surface; they may be released into the atmosphere and pass over national frontiers, whether detected or not. The question which remains unanswered is: What would constitute a violation— any amount, or one that might be considered a dangerous amount of radioactive products? In the latter case the threshold of radiation hazard would have to be defined. In any event, the clause clearly favours large countries, as there is a chance that radioactive material that might vent from an underground test to the surface would not travel beyond their borders. In practice, even that could not be prevented.

The parties to the PTBT also undertook to refrain from 'causing, encouraging, or in any way participating in' the carrying out of nuclear explosions by other nations in the prohibited environments (Article I,2). Of the three terms employed, 'encouraging' is the least definite. If it were to include moral support or economic help indirectly used by the recipient to pay for the cost of nuclear explosions, it might be difficult to prove a breach.

Under the PTBT, assistance in carrying out underground tests was not prohibited if they did not produce the radioactive effects described above. Since 1970, however, with the entry into force of the 1968 Non-Proliferation Treaty (NPT), this kind of assistance has been ruled out with regard to non-nuclear weapon states, because nuclear weapon powers may not assist these states in any way in the manufacture of nuclear weapons or other nuclear explosive devices. But co-operation between nuclear weapon states in the field of underground testing has not been ruled out; they may help each other in developing or improving the techniques for such testing. Thus, the UK carries out nuclear explosions jointly with the United States in Nevada, USA, without breaking its international obligations.

Verification

The PTBT did not set up an international mechanism to check whether the commitments are being complied with. The parties are presumed to monitor compliance with the Treaty unilaterally, using their national technical means of verification. This testifies to the confidence prevailing in nuclear weapon states at the time that these means, which include ordinary intelligence, provided an assurance of detection and identification of clandestine tests in the three environments in question.

Actually, the prohibition on testing in these environments is largely self-enforceable. Any signatory nuclear weapon nation that decided it needed to conduct such tests would probably use the escape clause of the Treaty rather than embark on secret tests; concealment would be extremely difficult, expensive and risky. If any other state party to the Treaty decided to test, it might also prefer to act openly, rather than clandestinely, to demonstrate its capability. Nevertheless, an unidentified low-yield atmospheric nuclear explosion may have taken place in September 1979 in the southern hemisphere, as revealed by the US authorities on the basis of satellite observation. South Africa was accused of being behind this event,[5] with or without Israeli involvement;[6] but it denied having any knowledge of a nuclear explosion occurring in its vicinity, while France, suspected in some newspaper reports of having tested a neutron bomb in the atmosphere, rejected the allegation. The event has not been cleared up. As regards the commitment by the nuclear weapon powers not to provide assistance to other states in carrying out nuclear tests in the prohibited environments, it is possible to argue that such a commitment hardly requires verification; for it could not be in the interest of these powers to help others in obtaining military benefits which they themselves have given up.

On the other hand, the absence of an international supervisory body to evaluate events according to some objective criteria makes it very difficult to definitively establish whether radioactive substances from an underground nuclear explosion have crossed the national borders of the testing country. A regular international exchange of data on atmospheric radioactivity could remove this deficiency. (Such an exchange was proposed by Sweden in 1983 within the framework of procedures to verify a comprehensive test ban.)

Entry into force and amendments

The PTBT entered into force after the deposit of the instruments of ratification by the three original parties—the UK, the USA and the USSR (Article III,3). Any party may propose an amendment to the Treaty, which is to be circulated to all parties (Article II). The amendment must be approved by a majority of the parties to the Treaty, including the original parties.[7] In the subsequent stage of the amending process, when the instruments of ratification are deposited by a majority, including the original parties, the amendment enters into force for *all* parties, that is, also for those who had not supported it. Thus, an amendment adopted by a simple majority can be automatically imposed upon a dissenting minority, provided that this minority does not include an original party.

Owing to the special position accorded them under the Treaty, the three nuclear weapon powers party to the Treaty have reserved the right of veto on any changes. In particular, they have a guarantee that the PTBT will not be extended to underground tests on terms not acceptable to all of them. It is true that upon a request from one-third or more of the parties, which need not necessarily be the original parties, a conference of all the parties must be convened by the depositary governments to consider proposed amendments (Article II,1). But the organization of such a conference would not be an easy task because the Treaty does not specify the time within which the proposals should be circulated or within which the conference should be called, or the place where it should be held. Besides, a nuclear weapon power may refuse to participate in the conference, expressing thereby in advance its opposition to amending the Treaty.

The 1985 and 1986 UN General Assemblies recommended the PTBT parties to take advantage of the provisions of Article II for the sake of converting the PTBT into a comprehensive treaty.[8] The supporters of this recommendation seem to think that the convening of a conference of the parties would put irresistible pressure on the nuclear weapon powers to reach a comprehensive ban. However, considering the present firm opposition of the UK and the USA to stopping all their nuclear weapon tests, such an undertaking is unlikely to succeed. The right of the original parties to block a proposal which is not to their liking cannot be abolished through mere procedural devices. As borne out by the negotiating record, the chief purpose of the amendment procedure, as formulated by the original parties, was to make possible, at the appropriate time, the conduct of peaceful explosions in the environments now prohibited by the PTBT.

The PTBT was opened for participation to all states, without reservation. This constituted progress, as compared to several other multilateral treaties concluded after World War II (including the 1959 Antarctic Treaty). The original parties thereby admitted that, by its very nature, the PTBT ought to have universal application. Nevertheless, for political reasons arising from cold war controversies, it was decided that contacts between the depositary governments and unrecognized political regimes could be kept to an absolute minimum, if not reduced to zero.[9] The issues especially contentious at that time were those relating to the non-recognition of the Republic of China (Taiwan) by the Soviet Union, and of the German Democratic Republic by the United States. To deal with this dilemma, a novel feature was introduced into the realm of international agreements: as distinct from previous treaties, which provided for a single depositary, the PTBT provides for three depositaries— the UK, the USA and the USSR (Article III).

In practice, and in accordance with an oral understanding reached at the final phase of the negotiations, it is enough for a state to deposit its instrument of ratification or accession in any one of the three capitals—London, Moscow or Washington—to become formally committed, and the depositaries do not feel obliged to accept a signature or communication from authorities they do not recognize. In case of the deposit of the instruments of ratification or accession in different capitals and on different dates, it must be presumed that the earliest date is the official date of entry into force of the Treaty for any individual country. The official records of signatories and parties, kept by the depositary governments, differ, but the differences are of no practical significance.[10]

Implementation

The PTBT is of unlimited duration, but each party, 'in exercising its national sovereignty', has the right to withdraw from it if 'extraordinary events, related to the subject matter of this Treaty, have jeopardized the supreme interests of its country' (Article IV). A party would decide for itself whether such events had occurred and would not need to justify its action to any external authority: a simple notice addressed to all other parties to the PTBT three months in advance (as required by the Article) would suffice. This clause was included over initial objections raised by the Soviet Union claiming that a provision for withdrawal was not necessary, because it was its inherent right as a sovereign nation to abrogate any treaty at any time if its national interest required it.

According to the 1969 Vienna Convention on the Law of Treaties, a material breach of a multilateral treaty—that is, a violation of a provision essential to the accomplishment of the object or purpose of the treaty—by one party entitles the other parties, by unanimous agreement, to suspend the operation of the treaty or to terminate it, either in the relations between themselves and the defaulting state, or as between all the parties. The Convention also entitles a party specially affected by the breach to invoke it as a ground for suspending the operation of the treaty in the relations between itself and the defaulting state. If a multilateral treaty is of such a character that a material breach of its provisions by one party radically changes the position of every party with respect to the further performance of its obligations under the treaty, *any* party is entitled to invoke the breach as a ground for suspending the operation of the treaty with respect to itself.[11] An arms control treaty such as the PTBT can be considered as affected by this latter rule. Its material breach would then give any party the right immediately to start or resume nuclear testing in the prohibited environments; Article IV would not restrict that right. The time factor, however, is not of great practical significance because a three-month delay, as required by the withdrawal clause, can hardly be decisive for national security; a party could choose therefore to treat the violation as an 'extraordinary event' in the meaning of Article IV.

What is less well defined is the right to withdraw if 'extraordinary events' *other* than a material breach take place. These events, according to the language of the PTBT, have to be related to the subject-matter of the Treaty. An occurrence of this type could be the conduct of nuclear tests in the prohibited environments by countries which are not party to the Treaty. It could affect primarily those countries which had decided to forgo a nuclear weapon option in the expectation that their potential adversaries would act likewise. But it could hardly jeopardize the 'supreme interests' of the original parties to the PTBT, in view of their overwhelming nuclear superiority over all the other countries, as well as of their retained right to continue testing underground. It is inconceivable that the UK, the USA or the USSR would need to resume testing in the atmosphere in order to redress a possible imbalance created by a nascent nuclear weapon power, be it a party to the

Treaty or not. Indeed, the nuclear tests carried out by China after the conclusion of the PTBT (its first explosion took place a year after the Treaty entered into force) did not provoke withdrawal by the nuclear powers. Nor did continued nuclear testing in the atmosphere by France, another non-signatory of the PTBT, bring about the abrogation of the Treaty.

A multilateral treaty such as the PTBT may, on the other hand, be suspended at the outbreak of a war. This would normally apply only as between the belligerents.

It is possible that the great flexibility retained by the main nuclear weapon powers on the question of withdrawal from the PTBT was related to their uncertainty as to whether atmospheric tests could then be entirely renounced without unacceptably restricting further nuclear weapon developments.[12] If this is so, an exact definition of 'extraordinary events' that would justify withdrawal could not have been in their interest. It is known, for example, that in ratifying the PTBT the USA decided to maintain a high state of readiness to test in the environments prohibited by the Treaty, particularly in the atmosphere.[13] With the passage of time, however, it has become increasingly unlikely that any nuclear power would break away from the Treaty on some flimsy pretext in order to restore its freedom to test in all environments.

By 1 January 1987, as many as 116 states had adhered to the PTBT. (For the list of parties, see annexe 1.)

The record of compliance with the Treaty is generally considered to be good; there has been no charge of a significant breach by any party. In most incidents, in which radioactive substances released from underground explosions spread outside the territory of the testing states party to the PTBT, the USA and the USSR preferred to treat such sporadic venting as no more than a 'technical' breach. Only in 1984–85 did the two powers formally accuse each other of violating the PTBT because of the venting of radioactive debris from underground tests.[14]

The pledge given by the UK, the USA and the USSR to seek the discontinuance of all test explosions of nuclear weapons has not been fulfilled. In particular, the US Government statement of 1982 that it would 'set aside' efforts to negotiate a comprehensive ban on nuclear testing,[15] because it saw such a ban as only a long-term objective, and as part of a large arms control package rather than as a separate measure to be carried into effect in conformity with the previously undertaken obligations, was regarded by many UN members as impeding 'full implementation' of the PTBT.[16]

Adherence to the PTBT, though wide, is not universal. Two nuclear weapon powers, France and China, have not joined it. In declining to sign, France argued that the Treaty had only limited practical importance, and reaffirmed its intent to proceed with its own nuclear buildup; China called the Treaty a 'fraud', because it did not encompass general disarmament or a ban on underground tests. Nevertheless, both nations have eventually given up atmospheric testing through unilateral statements of renunciation: France in 1975, after a suit had been brought against it by Australia and New Zealand in the International Court of Justice;[17] and some 10 years later, China, after a series of protests made by both neighbouring and distant countries (and possibly also by the Chinese people themselves) against radioactive contamination caused by Chinese nuclear explosions in the atmosphere. Such a militarily important non-nuclear weapon country as Pakistan which refuses formally to forgo the acquisition of nuclear weapons is also missing from the list of parties. But even if this or another non-nuclear weapon country decided to cross the threshold to become a nuclear weapon state, it would probably not do so by detonating a nuclear device in an environment prohibited by such a widely adhered-to treaty as the PTBT, and expose itself to an international opprobrium. For the PTBT appears to have become a norm of behaviour, to be observed by parties and non-parties alike.

Assessment of the PTBT

The PTBT has complicated the development of very high-yield weapons and has made impossible full-scale operational testing (including the measurement of certain effects) of weapons already developed in the environments in which they are meant to be used. However, these restrictions have not prevented the USA, the UK and the USSR from satisfying most of their military requirements, since they can test underground and, at the same time, deny important intelligence information to others about the characteristics of the explosions (and thus of the weapons) that can be gathered from atmospheric tests. The rate of testing by the Soviet Union and the United States has increased considerably since the PTBT went into force: over 900 nuclear explosions were carried out by these two countries taken together, from 5 August 1963 to 1 July 1987, that is, almost twice as many as between 1945 and 1963. (For full nuclear explosion statistics, see annexe 4.)

Nevertheless, the PTBT has helped curb the radioactive pollution of the atmosphere and reduce the health hazards associated with nuclear fall-out. It has thus made an important contribution to the environmental protection regime. In national policies it marked the first major success of the proponents of arms control who managed to overcome the resistance of the proponents of an uncontrolled arms race. In international policies it became an obstacle to the wider spread of nuclear weapons and paved the way for the 1968 Non-Proliferation Treaty (NPT). Moreover, the determination of the original parties to seek to end all tests, as stated in the PTBT, has been used as one of the main arguments in favour of a comprehensive test ban.

III. The 1974 Threshold Test Ban Treaty

Talks on a comprehensive test ban resumed after the entry into force of the PTBT, but consideration of technical matters often replaced rather than contributed to a systematic discussion of the provisions of a new agreement.

The UN General Assembly adopted resolutions deploring or condemning nuclear testing and calling for its cessation, but the difficulties encountered gave rise to proposals for a partial approach to a ban on underground testing. Appeals were also made, mainly in the UN General Assembly, for transitional measures of restraint that would suspend nuclear weapon testing, or limit or reduce the size and number of nuclear weapon tests, pending the entry into force of a comprehensive ban. These proposals and appeals were ignored by the main testing powers. The USA asserted that a partial approach would not remove the obstacles to resolving the problem of adequate verification, while the USSR insisted on dealing with the testing problem as a whole and contended that a quota commitment or the establishment of a threshold magnitude for tests would not put a stop to the building of nuclear arsenals.[18] However, in the summer of 1974 both countries retreated from their positions, and on 3 July of the same year they signed a treaty on the limitation of underground nuclear weapon tests, which came to be called the Threshold Test Ban Treaty (TTBT). This Treaty has not yet entered into force. (For the text of the TTBT, and the Protocol to it, see annexe 1.)

Scope of the obligations

Instead of establishing a threshold magnitude for seismic disturbances caused by explosions, as had been suggested in the past, the USA and the USSR chose to set a limit on the amount of energy to be released by the permitted explosions, that is, on their explosive yield. Thus, under the TTBT, the parties undertook to 'prohibit, to prevent and not to carry out' any underground nuclear weapon test having a yield which exceeds 150 kilotons at any place under their jurisdiction or control, beginning 31 March 1976 (Article I,1).

The following questions arise in connection with this obligation: How much have the two powers given up by deciding to limit their weapon explosions to a 150-kt yield? And why did they set the date of effective limitation of explosion yields 21 months ahead of the signing of the Treaty?

To answer the first question, it is necessary to estimate the yields of explosions carried out by the USA and the USSR after the conclusion in 1963 of the PTBT, especially those conducted during the years immediately preceding the signing in 1974 of the TTBT, and relate them to the 150-kt threshold agreed upon. The task is complicated, because many explosions were not announced by the testing states and, when they were announced, the yield was either given in very approximate terms or not indicated at all.[19] Nevertheless, some computations were made by Swedish seismologists for the period 1969–73 on the basis of generally available seismic data.[20] For calibration purposes, the study used the yields officially declared by the USA for 12 underground nuclear explosions conducted in previous years at the Nevada Test Site, and the yields published in the USSR for two large chemical explosions and two peaceful nuclear explosions.

It appeared from these calculations that, for the period examined, most of the US and Soviet explosions had been below 150 kt. Since already at that time attention was devoted to developing nuclear warheads for smaller, tactical weapons, or for strategic weapons with a yield lower than that specified in the TTBT, it might be concluded that the restriction accepted under the Treaty did not interfere with the nuclear weapon development plans of either of the two signatory states.

As to the distant date set for the entry into force of the yield limitation, the official justification was that considerable time was needed to make all verification arrangements. A more important reason, however, was that some warheads then under development were planned to have a yield exceeding the agreed limit. Their testing had, therefore, to take place before the restrictions became effective. Tests with yields exceeding the threshold were in fact hastily conducted by both the USA and the USSR in the period from July 1974, when the TTBT was signed, to the end of March 1976, when it was to enter into effect.

In addition to the limit placed on the size of underground nuclear weapon tests, each party to the TTBT committed itself, under Article I,2, to restrict the number of tests to a minimum. However, the term 'minimum' lends itself to different interpretations. In 1976 some high US officials argued that the concept of minimum testing did not imply a reduction in the number of tests, and that the relevant treaty provision reflected only an intention to keep the test programme to the minimum national security needs. Be that as it may, US and Soviet nuclear testing activities, measured in numbers of explosions, showed no sign of diminishing (see annexe 4).

Verification

The TTBT stipulates that each party will use the 'national technical means' of verification at its disposal to provide assurance of compliance with the provisions of the Treaty (Article II).

National technical means to verify a test ban consist primarily of seismic monitoring, satellite observation or electronic eavesdropping. Seismic monitoring is the most useful method, especially when not only the occurrence of a test but also its size are to be established. In verifying a comprehensive test ban, all one would need to ascertain is whether a nuclear explosion had taken place, whatever its size, while in a threshold treaty the aim of verification is twofold: to determine whether a seismic event had a strength exceeding an agreed yield limit and, if so, whether it was an explosion or an earthquake. It should be noted that the latter problem is relatively easy to solve as existing seismic equipment can distinguish nuclear explosions, especially those with high yields, from naturally occurring phenomena. It is more difficult to satisfy oneself that the explosive yield has not exceeded the permissible limit because seismic signals produced by an underground explosion of a given strength vary, depending on a number of factors. Yield determination requires knowledge of the environment in which the test has been carried out, as well as of the explosions previously performed at the same site.

Accordingly, in a Protocol which forms an integral part of the TTBT, the USA and the USSR agreed to exchange information necessary to establish a correlation between given yields of explosions at the specified sites and the seismic signals produced. The data to be provided comprise: (a) the geographic co-ordinates of the boundaries of each test site and of the boundaries of the geophysically distinct testing areas therein; (b) information on the geology of the testing areas of the sites—the rock characteristics of geological formations and the basic physical properties of the rock, that is, density, seismic velocity, water saturation, porosity and depth of water table; (c) the geographic co-ordinates of underground nuclear weapon tests, after they have been conducted; and (d) yield, date, time, depth and co-ordinates for two nuclear weapon tests for calibration purposes from each geophysically distinct testing area where underground nuclear weapon tests have been and are to be conducted, the yield of such explosions being as near as possible to the limit defined in the Treaty and not less than one-tenth of that limit.

If calibration tests were carried out at the usual test sites (Nevada in the USA, and Semipalatinsk and Novaya Zemlya in the USSR), the data obtained might make it possible to determine with a high degree of reliability the yields of tests previously conducted at these sites. Information hitherto treated as classified by both powers could thereby become generally available. But the parties are allowed under the Treaty to use other sites for testing. The Protocol provides that in the case of testing areas where data are not available on two tests for calibration purposes, 'the data pertaining to one such test shall be exchanged, if available, and the data pertaining to the second test shall be exchanged as soon as possible after a second test having a yield in the above-mentioned range'. (There is no requirement to conduct tests solely for calibration purposes.) The parties are entitled to specify a new test site or testing area after the entry into force of the Treaty, but information on the geographic co-ordinates and geology should be transmitted to the other party prior to using that site or area. The data needed for calibration purposes should also be transmitted in advance, if available; if they are not available, they should be transmitted as soon as possible after they have been obtained by the transmitting party.

Each party undertakes not to interfere with the national technical means of verification of the other party (Article II,2). This clause can be interpreted, inter alia, as a commitment not to use techniques which may reduce the recordable seismic magnitudes. Moreover, the USA and the USSR have obliged themselves in the Protocol to the TTBT to conduct all nuclear weapon tests solely within specified testing areas.

As a complement to technical verification, the parties undertook to consult with each other, make inquiries and furnish information in response to such inquiries (Article II,3). This provision is meant to deal with disputes over explosions that may seem to violate the yield restriction.

Implementation

The TTBT was to remain in force for a period of five years, if not replaced earlier by an agreement, to be negotiated by the parties, on the cessation of all underground nuclear weapon tests. If such an agreement were not achieved, the Treaty could be extended for successive five-year periods, unless either party notified the other of its termination no later than six months prior to the expiration of the Treaty. Before the expiration of this period the parties might hold consultations to consider the situation relevant to the substance of the Treaty and to introduce amendments to its text (Article V,1). A possibility was provided for withdrawing from the Treaty at any time on six months' notice, again, if 'extraordinary events' had jeopardized the supreme interests of either of the parties (Article V,2). The notice should include a statement of the events but, as distinct from the multilateral arms control agreements signed in recent years, there is no obligation to notify the UN Security Council of the withdrawal.

Ratification of the TTBT has been postponed because of the US Administration's opposition to making it formally and legally binding. However, the parties stated that they would observe the agreed limitation during the pre-ratification period. As a matter of fact, since neither party has indicated an intention not to ratify the Treaty, both are obligated under international law to refrain from acts which would defeat its object and purpose.[21] Soon after the signing of the TTBT, press reports began to appear in the USA accusing the Soviet Union of conducting nuclear tests with a yield in excess of the 150-kt threshold. This accusation was eventually included in a 1984 official US list of complaints of Soviet non-compliance with bilateral and multilateral arms control treaties.[22] The rule generally accepted in international law with regard to bilateral treaties is that a material breach by one party allows the other party to declare the treaty void. Nevertheless, the US Government continued to abide by the threshold limitation, admitting that the evidence gathered on alleged Soviet violations was ambiguous and that no definitive conclusion could be reached. The USSR countered with similar allegations about US tests without reneging on its own pledges.

Suspicions of breaches may have arisen because predicting the exact yield of nuclear weapon tests is associated with technical uncertainties. This was recognized by the parties themselves when they reached an understanding that one or two 'slight, unintended' breaches per year would not be considered a violation, but would be the subject of consultations at the request of either party.[23] Moreover, the extensive exchange of data, to be carried out simultaneously with the exchange of the instruments of ratification of the TTBT, and complemented with calibration tests to improve each side's assessments of the yields of explosions (based primarily on measurements derived from its own seismic instruments), has been held up pending ratification of the Treaty. (The parties have presumably not afforded each other, 'on the basis of reciprocity', the opportunity to familiarize themselves with these data before the exchange of instruments of ratification, as contemplated in point 2 of the Protocol.) In any event, recent US expert reports suggest that it is the lack of adequate information about the geological features of the Soviet nuclear test sites that may have led to ambiguous evidence of non-compliance.

In April 1986 it was announced that the US Government had revised its procedure for estimating the yields of Soviet underground nuclear tests.[24] Authoritative US seismologists argue that, when the correct methodology is followed and the correct formula is used for converting the sizes of seismic waves generated by explosions into yields, it should become evident that the Soviet Union has not violated the 150-kt limit of the TTBT, and that both the USSR and the USA have often tested near that limit since the Treaty became effective.[25]

The Soviet Union has repeatedly stated its readiness to ratify the TTBT, though after the unilateral suspension of its underground testing the USSR emphasized its preference for the conclusion of a comprehensive ban, bypassing the TTBT. On the other hand, the United States, which in signing the Treaty expressed full confidence that it would be able to recognize violations owing to the data-exchange provision, now claims that the verification clauses are insufficient. To tighten these clauses so as to ensure that the 150-kt threshold was actually being observed, the US Government proposed mutual visits of Soviet and US experts to the respective test sites to measure on the spot the yield of explosions and establish a basis for the verification of 'effective limits' on underground nuclear testing.[26] It argued that such measurements would validate the data supplied by the other side.

The Soviet Government rejected the US Government's proposal, but in the summer of 1986 the Soviet Academy of Sciences and the Natural Resources Defense Council (NRDC), a private US environmental group, concluded an agreement on the basis of which scientists from both countries installed US-manufactured seismometric equipment near the principal Soviet testing site in the area of Semipalatinsk (Kazakhstan);[27] identical monitoring stations were set up in the USA to monitor US tests at the Nevada Test Site.[28] This agreement, originally valid for one year, was subsequently extended until August 1988 with the provision that the seismometric equipment would be moved further away from the Soviet test site. Since July 1986, the US and Soviet governments have been engaged in discussions known as the Nuclear Testing Experts Meetings. The parties to the TTBT, as under the PTBT, are committed to continuing negotiations 'with a view towards achieving a solution to the problem of the cessation of all underground nuclear weapon tests' (Article I,3).

Assessment of the TTBT

Despite its unratified status, the TTBT has to some extent constrained the development of new high-yield warheads by the USA and the USSR. (Britain also committed itself to abide by the provisions of the Treaty, even though it is not a signatory.)[29] The yield limitation has made it difficult for the parties to carry out certain stockpile-sampling, because the existing large thermonuclear weapons cannot be tested at their full yield. Cessation of explosions in the megaton range has also had a positive environmental effect: it has further reduced the risks of radioactive venting and of ground disturbances. Furthermore, the Treaty requirement for an exchange of detailed information concerning sites and yields of nuclear explosions must be regarded as a step towards greater international openness, as well as progress in the field of treaty verification.

All this does not alter the fact that the TTBT has not contributed to the cessation of the nuclear arms race. The 150-kt yield threshold is too high to be really meaningful; the parties do not experience onerous restraints in continuing their nuclear weapon programmes.[30] In any event, for many years now, the trend has been to improve the effectiveness of nuclear weapon systems by increasing the accuracy of missiles rather than by increasing the yield of warheads. Nor does the agreed threshold reflect present verification capabilities: it is generally recognized that detection and identification of nuclear explosions of much lower size are possible. The TTBT is a poor example of restraint for those who might be planning to start building nuclear weapons themselves.

One has the impression that the idea of a threshold treaty was hastily conceived for purposes only very loosely related to arms control considerations (the negotiations lasted no more than some two months). The TTBT seems to have served chiefly the public relations needs of the parties by giving the appearance of progress in arms control when it was politically expedient to do so, and as a cover-up for the inability of the leaders of the two great powers to reach, at their meeting in June 1974, a considerably more important agreement on strategic offensive arms limitations. It was certainly also motivated by a desire to pre-empt the charge expected to be voiced at the approaching first NPT Review Conference, that the nuclear weapon powers were not fulfilling their disarmament pledges under the NPT.

However, the TTBT was seen by many as an alternative to, rather than a step towards, a comprehensive treaty as envisaged by the NPT. It was criticized in both the Conference on Disarmament and the United Nations as inadequate. Unlike the PTBT or other nuclear arms control agreements, it was not welcomed by the UN General Assembly; nor was there any international appeal made for its ratification.

IV. The 1976 Peaceful Nuclear Explosions Treaty

The provisions of the TTBT did not extend to underground nuclear explosions for peaceful purposes. Since such explosions cannot be distinguished, at least from a distance, from explosions serving military ends, the possibility remained of circumventing the threshold limitation on weapon tests. Moreover, the information to be exchanged under the TTBT is not meant for establishing the yield of explosions conducted in areas where peaceful applications would take place, namely outside the designated weapon test sites. It was therefore decided, in accordance with Article III of the TTBT, to work out a separate agreement with additional obligations closing the loopholes.

The Peaceful Nuclear Explosions Treaty (PNET) was signed on 28 May 1976, as a result of about 18 months of negotiations. Together with a Protocol and an Agreed Statement, it regulates the explosions carried out by the USA and the USSR outside their nuclear weapon test sites, as from 31 March 1976 (the date valid also for the TTBT). The Treaty has not yet entered into force. (For the texts of the PNET, the Protocol to it and the Agreed Statement, see annexe 1.)

Scope of the obligations

To ensure that underground explosions declared to be for peaceful purposes should not provide weapon-related benefits not obtainable from limited weapon testing, the parties had no other choice than to establish the same yield threshold for peaceful applications as had been imposed on weapon tests under the TTBT, namely, 150 kt (Article III,2(a)). A higher threshold would have allowed circumvention of the TTBT, while a lower one would have made it difficult to plan most of the applications then envisaged.

The yield restriction applies to individual explosions as distinct from group explosions (see below). Nevertheless, the possibility of carrying out individual explosions with a yield greater than 150 kt has been left open for future consideration 'at an appropriate time to be agreed' (Article III,3). The Soviet Union considered this provision to be of 'fundamental' importance, because 'it does not make the limit set to the yield of nuclear explosions for peaceful purposes dependent on that of nuclear weapon test explosions'.[31] However, a threshold for peaceful explosions could not be raised without affecting the threshold for weapon tests. Indeed, the US interpretation of the provision in question is that any change in the yield threshold for peaceful nuclear explosions would require an amendment of the Treaty, and that such amendment would have to be ratified.

Different PNET rules govern a 'group explosion', defined as two or more individual explosions for which 'the time interval between successive individual explosions does not exceed five seconds and for which the emplacement points of all explosives can be interconnected by straight line segments, each of which joins two emplacement points and each of which does not exceed 40 kilometres' (Article II(c)). A group explosion may exceed the 150-kt limit and reach an aggregate yield as high as 1500 kt (1.5 Mt) if it is carried out in such a way that individual explosions in the group can be identified and their individual yields determined to be no more than 150 kt. Certain peaceful applications of nuclear energy, such as large-scale excavation projects, may indeed require many nuclear blasts of varying size, but the PNET explicitly provides that they must be consistent with the PTBT, which prohibits any explosion that causes radioactive debris to be present outside the territorial limits of the state conducting the explosion. It is unlikely that such a limitation could be complied with.

The Agreed Statement accompanying the PNET specifies that development testing of nuclear explosives is not considered a 'peaceful application'. Such testing would have to be carried out only within the boundaries of nuclear weapon test sites and would be treated as the testing of a nuclear weapon, even if it were intended to develop a device for subsequent peaceful uses. Moreover, if test facilities, instrumentation or procedures related only to the testing of nuclear weapons or their effects were associated with an explosion carried out under the terms of the PNET, then such an explosion would not constitute a 'peaceful application'. However, a demarcation line between testing and application may, in some cases, be difficult to draw; for example, an attempted application which had not succeeded could be construed as a development test rather than a peaceful use. The Agreed Statement implies that proof would have to be given that the explosion outside a weapon test site was being conducted with a view to serving some practical peaceful ends.

It is noteworthy that the PNET also applies to US and Soviet peaceful nuclear explosions that might be conducted on the territories of third states in conformity with Article V of the NPT. This means that, irrespective of the international regime to be established for such explosions under Article V of the NPT, and unless the explosion services are provided by a nuclear power other than the USA and the USSR, the yield limits, as well as verification procedures required in Article VII of the PNET, would have to be observed.

Verification

In checking compliance with the PNET the parties are to use national technical means of verification (Article IV, 1(a)). They have also undertaken to supply each other with information which would include, among other things: the purpose, the location, the date and the aggregate yield of the planned explosion; the number of explosives, the planned yield of each explosive and its location relative to other explosives in a group; the depth of emplacement of each explosive, as well as the time intervals between individual explosions in a group explosion; a description of specific technological features of the project, of which the explosion is a part; and a description of the geological and geophysical characteristics of the site of each explosion which could influence determination of the yield. The amount of information would vary according to yields: the higher the yields, the more extensive the data that would be required. For each explosion, the party conducting it would have to inform the other party, not later than two days before the explosion, of the planned time of detonation of each explosive with a precision of one second. Not later than 90 days after each explosion, the party which had conducted it would have to supply the other party with the information about the actual time of the explosion and its yield, as well as a confirmation of other data provided before the explosion, including an explanation of any changes and corrections based on the results of the explosion (Protocol, Article II).

It is difficult to determine with distant seismic measuring instruments alone the yield of individual explosions if they occur within a few seconds of each other. If, therefore, a group explosion has an aggregate yield above 150 kt, it could include an individual blast exceeding the threshold limit. To prevent this from happening, observers of the verifying party (or 'designated personnel', as they are called in the Protocol) are to be given access to the site of the explosion. They would be permitted to check that the local circumstances, including facilities and installations associated with the project, are consistent with the stated peaceful purposes; to examine the validity of the geological and geophysical information provided in accordance with the Protocol; to observe the emplacement of each explosive; to observe the area of the entrance to each emplacement hole from the time of emplacement of each explosive until all personnel had been withdrawn from the site for the detonation of the explosion; and, finally, to observe the explosions (Protocol, Articles II and III).

The main function of the observers would be to measure the yield of each individual explosion in the group with the use of special equipment (Protocol, Article IV, 1–5). If the verifying side chooses to use its own equipment rather than that provided by the party carrying out the explosion, an elaborate procedure is to be followed to ensure that there has been no abuse and that the observers have not acquired unwarranted information. Thus, there would be two identical sets of instruments; the side conducting the explosion would choose one set for actual use by the verifying side, while the other set could be examined (Protocol, Article IV,6). Acquisition of photographs would be permitted only under specified conditions (there is a list of acceptable subjects for photographs) and only with cameras having built-in rapid developing capability, so that the pictures could be immediately inspected (Protocol, Article III,5).

For any group explosion with a planned aggregate yield exceeding 500 kt, the observers would, in addition, install and operate a local seismic network to help to ascertain that no undeclared explosions were taking place along with the announced ones (Protocol, Article IV,7).

On-site observation is envisaged also for some explosions with a planned aggregate yield of between 100 and 150 kt, when, owing to the special character of the project, the reliability of teleseismic measurement cannot be ensured. It would not be mandatory, as with explosions exceeding 150 kt, and the need for it would have to be mutually agreed between the parties.

The Protocol to the PNET contains detailed provisions regulating the number of observers, the geographical extent of their access, the duration of their stay in the areas concerned, their equipment and their immunities (as stipulated in the 1961 Vienna Convention on Diplomatic Relations).

A Joint Consultative Commission is to be established to discuss mainly questions of compliance (Article V).

Implementation

The duration of the PNET was to be the same as that of the TTBT, and the exchange of instruments of ratification of the two treaties was to take place simultaneously (Articles VIII and IX). Although the PNET has not been ratified, it is covered by the US–Soviet undertaking to observe the 150-kt yield limitation. The close interrelationship of the two treaties, or rather the subordination of the PNET to the TTBT, is emphasized by the clause excluding the possibility to terminate the PNET while the TTBT remains in force, but allowing withdrawal from the former at any time upon the termination of the latter (Article VIII).

Article VI envisages US–Soviet co-operation, on the basis of 'reciprocity', in areas related to underground nuclear explosions for peaceful purposes. This clause was already a dead letter at the time of signing: after some 40 tests the USA was about to terminate its peaceful nuclear explosions programme, having failed to establish applications which would be technically feasible as well as economically viable, and which would be publicly acceptable. (By 1978, the so-called Plowshare programme had disappeared from the US federal budget.) Only the USSR continued to pursue such a programme (it has so far conducted over 100 explosions outside its established weapon testing sites). However, in the course of British–US–Soviet tripartite talks in the late 1970s, the Soviet Union declared that it was prepared to suspend nuclear explosions for peaceful purposes, and has recently given to understand that it would be ready to forgo them altogether if a treaty were concluded prohibiting nuclear weapon explosions in all environments. In 1986 the USSR halted its river-diversion projects, which would have required the use of nuclear explosives.

No on-site observation of Soviet peaceful explosions has been carried out; none seems to have been in the category of explosions for which the Treaty requires such observation. Besides, it would be difficult to initiate an observation procedure on the basis of an unratified treaty. In any event, peaceful nuclear explosions with yield limitations similar to those set in the TTBT are not likely to produce militarily significant information not otherwise obtainable through weapon tests permitted under the TTBT. The nuclear weapon powers have, therefore, no incentive to seek such information through allegedly peaceful applications. The extremely elaborate methods of verification enshrined in the Treaty appear gratuitous.

Assessment of the PNET

The PNET must be seen as an indispensable complement to the TTBT. The TTBT would be deprived of meaning if peaceful explosions were allowed without restrictions. However, the PNET has not increased the very limited arms control value of the TTBT. It may even have had a negative impact on the policy of preventing nuclear weapon proliferation by providing respectability to the arguments of those states that seek to develop a nuclear weapon capability under the guise of an interest in peaceful explosions.

A positive feature of the PNET, beyond its necessity as an adjunct to the TTBT, relates to the acceptance of on-site observation of certain peaceful nuclear explosions. Although occasions for inviting observers would probably present themselves very rarely, if ever, it is the breakthrough in the great powers' approach, notably that of the Soviet Union, to the problem of verification that was noteworthy as a precedent for other arms control measures. Indeed, the revised Soviet draft treaty on the 'complete and general prohibition of nuclear weapon tests'—submitted to the UN General Assembly on 22 November 1976, that is, only a few months after the signing of the PNET—provided for on-site inspection,[32] and the possibility of conducting such inspection has subsequently been spelled out in all the test ban proposals discussed by the nuclear weapon powers. Recently, the Soviet Union announced that it would also accept on-site inspections to verify a moratorium on testing, if the United States did as well.

However, the PNET control methods, geared solely to the two powers, are hardly applicable to a multilateral and comprehensive nuclear weapon test ban. Peaceful nuclear explosions by the PNET signatories are to be notified in advance, and the verifying side would doubtless be less interested in the nature of these explosions than in checking that the threshold yield set for weapon tests is not exceeded. The checking is to be carried out by seismic means on the basis of information provided by the party conducting the notified explosion and, in specified circumstances, with the help of designated observers present at the site of the explosion. But, under a multilateral and comprehensive ban on nuclear weapon testing, breaches may occur outside the known testing sites, that is, in areas for which no geological information and calibration data are available. On-the-spot verification, if found necessary, would thus mean inspecting the area of a suspected event, instead of observing an explosion at a time and place chosen by the host country; the functions of inspectors searching for evidence of violation would differ considerably from the tasks of observers as specified in the PNET.

Nor does the PNET solve the intractable problem of accommodating peaceful nuclear explosions under a comprehensive ban. It is true that the Protocol to the PNET provides for some constraints to limit the possibility of gaining weapon-related information from the peaceful application of nuclear explosions. For example, it imposes a minimum depth requirement on explosive emplacement in order to minimize information useful to the military on blast and electromagnetic effects produced by the explosion. It does not, however, prevent testing the performance of a stockpiled warhead or, what might be more important, some limited testing of a new weapon design. The observers are expressly forbidden to have or seek access by physical, visual or technical means to the interior of the canister containing the explosive, to documentary or other information descriptive of the design of the explosive or to equipment for control and firing of the explosive (Protocol, Article V,5).

But even the most intrusive inspection regime could not deny all weapon-related benefits to a state carrying out peaceful nuclear explosions. Furthermore, with a comprehensive ban on nuclear weapon tests, it would be impossible to allow development testing of nuclear explosives for peaceful uses, as distinct from peaceful applications of the explosions, without completely defeating the purpose of the ban. In other words, no nuclear explosion could be tolerated under a truly comprehensive ban.

V. Conclusions

A treaty limiting nuclear weapon testing can have a real arms control value to the extent that it: (a) significantly reduces the freedom of the parties to develop new weapon designs, and thereby makes a direct mitigating impact on the arms race; (b) reinforces the nuclear non-proliferation regime by rendering it more difficult for non-nuclear weapon states to develop a nuclear weapon capability; (c) provides reasonable assurance of compliance through verification measures adapted to the scope of the undertakings; (d) contains no loopholes facilitating circumvention of the basic obligations; and (e) constitutes a concrete step towards a total prohibition of nuclear explosions and includes a binding legal commitment to this end.

None of the three nuclear test limitation treaties so far concluded has met all of these requirements. In particular, none has affected the nuclear weapon programmes by hindering improvements in weaponry.

Especially flawed are the bilateral US–Soviet TTBT and the PNET. The yield threshold set by these treaties is so high (10–12 times higher than the yield of the Hiroshima bomb) that the parties have forsaken practically nothing. Their formal commitment to negotiate and achieve more far-reaching measures has proved to be too vague to compensate for the weakness of the main provisions of the treaties. Moreover, by unduly emphasizing the importance of civil applications of nuclear explosive devices which are indistinguishable from nuclear weapons, the PNET may have rendered a disservice to the cause of non-proliferation.

Nevertheless, the fact that the TTBT and the PNET have remained unratified for more than a decade is regrettable; it has undermined confidence in the arms control negotiating process. Full operation of these agreements could provide ample verification experience and facilitate further limitations on the yield and perhaps also on the frequency of nuclear explosions. Prospects for bringing about such measures opened up towards the end of 1986. In the course of the US–Soviet October 1986 summit meeting at Reykjavik, the United States said that it was prepared—upon achieving 'adequate verification' of the TTBT and the PNET and upon ratification of these treaties—to embark on negotiations for further testing limitations 'in association with nuclear-weapon reductions'.[33] Also, the Soviet Union expressed its willingness to initiate a negotiating process in order to consider 'the questions of thresholds, the yield of nuclear explosions, the number of nuclear explosions a year, and the fate of the 1974 and 1976 treaties'.[34] The Soviet Government reiterated this offer in its statement of 18 December 1986, regarding possible termination of its unilateral nuclear test moratorium.[35]

Short of a comprehensive ban, meaningful restraints on tests are certainly better for the cause of arms control than unrestrained testing. An 'all-or-nothing' position has never been helpful in arms control negotiations.

Notes and references

[1] The analysis of the treaties is based on the interpretations given by the parties and the author's own interpretations, as well as on other legal opinions.

[2] Regional bans on nuclear testing—in the Antarctic under the 1959 Antarctic Treaty, in Latin America under the 1967 Treaty of Tlatelolco, and in the South Pacific under the 1985 Treaty of Rarotonga—are not discussed in this paper. For an analysis of the first two treaties, see Goldblat, J., SIPRI, *Agreements for Arms Control: A Critical Survey* (Taylor & Francis: London, 1982), pp. 60–8; for an analysis of the third treaty, see *SIPRI Yearbook 1986*, pp. 499–508 and 520–1. Relevant excerpts from all the three treaties can be found in annexe 1.

[3] The basis for the Moscow negotiations leading to the PTBT was a draft treaty tabled at the Geneva Disarmament Conference, on 27 August 1962, by the delegations of the UK and the USA. Article I of the draft prohibited nuclear weapon tests. Peaceful purpose explosions were dealt with in Article II: they were permitted but were to be subjected to controls. In the course of the negotiations with the USSR, draft Article II was dropped altogether.

[4] A question was asked during the hearings before the US Senate Committee on Foreign Relations, in August 1963, whether nuclear weapon explosions carried out not for the sake of experiment, but with hostile inter*, are also prohibited. The opinion formulated by a legal adviser to the US Government was that the text of the Treaty and its internal construction provide grounds for answering the question in the negative. Even before the PTBT was signed, President Kennedy, in his speech of 26 July 1963, stated that the Treaty 'will not restrict their ‹nuclear weapons› use in time of war'. Also Chairman Khrushchev said in Berlin, on 2 July 1963, that an agreement on the ending of nuclear tests 'cannot avert or even substantially weaken the danger of thermonuclear war'.

[5] *South Africa's Plan and Capability in Nuclear Field*, Report of the Secretary-General, UN General Assembly document A/35/402, 9 Sep. 1980.

[6] Pry, P., *Israel's Nuclear Arsenal* (Westview Press: Boulder, CO, 1984).

[7] In this respect, the rights of the original parties (the UK, the USA and the USSR) exceed even those provided for the great powers in the UN Charter (Article 108). The permanent members of the Security Council do not have a veto in the first stage of the amending process, when the Charter amendment has to be adopted by a vote of two-thirds of the members of the General Assembly. They can prevent the coming into force of an amendment only at the ratification stage, namely by refraining from ratifying.

[8] The 1985 recommendation, contained in UN General Assembly resolution 40/80B, was adopted by a vote of 121 to 3 (the UK and the USA, which are parties to the PTBT, and France, which is not), with 24 abstentions. The 1986 recommendation, contained in UN General Assembly resolution 41/46B, was adopted by a vote of 127 to 3, with 21 absenting. Those voting against were the same as in 1985.

[9] In fact, since recognition cannot be gained automatically and is primarily a matter of the intent of the recognizing state, a depositary could have dealings with a non-recognized political regime, within the framework of multilateral treaties, without thereby recognizing it.

[10] This cumbersome procedure of dealing with three depositaries was applied in a few subsequent arms control agreements, but is now losing its *raison d'être*; the simpler procedure of designating one depositary is being restored.

[11] According to the 1969 Vienna Convention, these rules do not apply to provisions relating to the protection of the human person contained in treaties of a humanitarian character, in particular to provisions prohibiting any form of reprisals against persons protected by such treaties (Article 60).

[12] In subsequent arms control agreements the withdrawal clause was somewhat tightened: a notice of withdrawal is to be given both to other parties and to the UN Security Council, and it should contain a statement of the extraordinary events the withdrawing party regards as having jeopardized its supreme interests. But the margin for arbitrary action has not been significantly narrowed.

[13] *US Congressional Record*, Vol. 109, Part 12, pp. 16790–1.

[14] *Pravda*, 30 Jan. 1984; *US Department of State Bulletin*, April 1985.

[15] *New York Times*, 21 July 1982.

[16] Conference on Disarmament document CD/642.

[17] On 22 June 1973, the ICJ indicated, *inter alia*, that the French Government 'should avoid nuclear tests causing the deposit of radioactive fall-out' on the territory of other countries. UN document A/RES/3077(XXVIII).

[18] Disarmament Conference documents CCD/PV.530, CCD/PV.536 and CCD/336; United Nations documents A/8401/Add. 1, A/C.1/PV.1829, A/C.1/PV.1830, A/C.1/PV.1841, A/C.1/PV.1847.

[19] In this connection it will be noted that by resolution 41/59 N the 1986 UN General Assembly called upon the states concerned to provide within one week of each nuclear explosion the following information and make it available to all other states: the date and time of the explosion; the location of the explosion and depth; the geological characteristics of the site of the explosion; and the estimated yield of the explosion. The Assembly expressed its conviction that such data would supplement and contribute to the improvement of independent monitoring capabilities and thereby facilitate the early conclusion of a verifiable comprehensive nuclear-test-ban treaty. Only France voted against the resolution.

[20] Conference on Disarmament document CCD/438.

[21] The 1969 Vienna Convention on the Law of Treaties, Article 18.

[22] US Information Service, Document Foreign Policy EUR-114, 23 Jan. 1984.

[23] *Arms Control and Disarmament Agreements: Texts and Histories of Negotiations*, 1982 edition, US Arms Control and Disarmament Agency.

[24] *New York Times*, 2 Apr. 1986.

[25] Testimony by Lynn R. Sykes, Professor of Geological Sciences, before the Subcommittee on Arms Control, International Security and Science of the Committee of Foreign Affairs, US House of Representatives, 8 May 1985, and before the Committee on Foreign Relations, US Senate, 26 June 1986, Washington, DC.

[26] Conference on Disarmament document CD/PV.290.

[27] Conference on Disarmament document CD/PV.372.

[28] *New York Times*, 6 July 1986; and *New Scientist*, 24 July 1986.

[29] Conference on Disarmament document CCD/PV.641.

[30] According to General E. B. Giller, deputy assistant administrator of ERDA, the TTBT does not interfere with US strategic weapon requirements. He said: 'Under the . . . 150-kiloton limit, the US can still develop advanced penetrators as well as improved strategic and tactical warheads designed for lower collateral damage.' (*Air Force Magazine*, July 1976)

[31] Zheleznov, R., 'Nuclear explosions for peaceful purposes', *International Affairs*, no. 8 (1976), Moscow.

[32] UN document A/C.1/31/9.

[33] Statement by the Director of the US Army Control and Disarmament Agency in the First Committee of the UN General Assembly on 20 October 1986.

[34] Statement by the Soviet Deputy Foreign Minister in the First Committee of the UN General Assembly on 14 October 1986.

[35] *Pravda*, 19 Dec. 1986.

Part 4
The question of verification

Chapter VII. Present capabilities for the detection and identification of seismic events

Paper 8*

Lynn R. Sykes

Columbia University, Palisades, NY

Abstract

A comprehensive test ban treaty or a low-yield threshold treaty is verifiable with high confidence down to explosions of very small size, approximately 1 kt, provided that US seismic monitoring stations are operated within the USSR and vice versa, that the treaty language deals with the identification of chemical explosions above a certain size, especially in areas of known or potential salt domes, and that a vigorous monitoring effort is carried out. Either treaty would dramatically curtail the testing and development of third-generation atomic weapons. There is now near scientific unanimity on the methodology of estimating the sizes or yields of Soviet underground weapon tests. When this methodology is employed, it is evident that the USSR has not violated the 150-kt limit of the Threshold Test Ban Treaty. Both the USSR and the USA have tested repeatedly near the limit of that Treaty since 1976. It is in the US national interest that the USSR not test very large nuclear weapons and thence emplace either more or higher-yield weapons of lighter weight on their large intercontinental ballistic missiles.

I. Introduction

A comprehensive test ban treaty is verifiable with high confidence down to explosions of very small size. I and a number of my colleagues conclude that reliable identification can be obtained down to explosions of about 1 kt with a combination of seismic listening posts within the Soviet Union and other national technical means such as satellite photography. Recent advances in seismological methods such as the use of high-frequency waves, the greater variety of methods that can now be used to characterize seismic sources and the

* This paper contains edited excerpts from *Nuclear Testing Issues*, Hearings before the Committee on Foreign Relations, United States Senate, 99th Congress, 2nd session, May 8, June 19 and 26, 1986 (Government Printing Office: Washington, DC, 1986); appendix 8B is taken from testimony on 8 May 1985.

use of digital data ensure that a comprehensive test ban treaty will be even easier to monitor than was thought only a few years ago.

A comprehensive treaty or a low-yield threshold treaty would dramatically curtail the testing and development of the so-called third generation of new atomic weapons, including the X-ray laser for the Strategic Defense Initiative, which will use a nuclear explosion as its source of energy. The main impediments to a comprehensive treaty or a low-yield threshold treaty are, in fact, neither scientific nor technical but rest on the assumption that the security of the United States is best enhanced by the continued testing and development of new atomic weapons into the indefinite future. Verification of an eventual comprehensive or a low-yield threshold treaty will require a determined and vigorous monitoring effort by the United States.

II. Recent scientific advances in the verification of nuclear testing

More accurate estimates of yields of Soviet explosions

A great deal of work has been completed in the past few years that bears upon the correct methodology for estimating yields of Soviet nuclear explosions. Yields of explosions at the main Central Asian test site of the USSR have now been calibrated using: (a) seismic surface waves, (b) a high-frequency seismic surface wave called Lg, (c) a Soviet peaceful explosion at that test site that produced a crater of known size (for which the USSR has also released the yield), (d) estimates of seismic attenuation of P-waves beneath the Central Asian and Nevada test sites using the fall-off of the spectrum of seismic waves, (e) a calibration using seismic stations in areas known to be similar geophysically to the Central Asian site, and (f) more indirect estimates based on the known speed of seismic waves and other known geophysical parameters of the Central Asian and other test sites. In addition, it is now possible to remove from surface waves a contaminating effect called tectonic release such that surface waves can now be used for accurate estimates of yield.

Each of the above methods indicates that the Central Asian test site can be quite accurately calibrated in terms of yield. The Defense Advanced Research Projects Agency (DARPA) and the Air Force Technical Applications Center have had committees of seismologists advise them on these matters for many years. Panels of both agencies have submitted classified reports on yield estimations for Soviet explosions and have made specific recommendations on methodology and calibration.

Recent advances in identifying very small underground nuclear tests

The United States has conducted an extensive programme to improve the detection and identification of nuclear tests since 1959. It has spent about half a billion dollars in this endeavour; more than a billion dollars has been spent world-wide. Seismic methods for identifying underground testing have improved greatly during that period not only as a result of funds specifically for test ban work but also as a result of the more than three to four billion dollars that has been spent annually by the petroleum and mineral industries and by various government agencies on acquiring seismic data and improving seismic methods.

In the past few years it has been recognized that high-frequency seismic waves propagate readily across large parts of the Soviet Union. This represents an important advance in the US capability to verify a CTBT. A great deal of seismological data have been obtained in Europe and Asia, including large parts of the Soviet Union, for studies of the crust of the earth and for exploration for petroleum and minerals. Those data are very good for frequencies from about 1 to about 10 Hertz (cycles per second). In addition, high-frequency data have been analysed for several of the seismic arrays operated by the United Kingdom and from several of the sophisticated stations operated by the Department of Energy as a test of instruments that could be deployed in the Soviet Union under a test ban treaty. Those data generally indicate good propagation of high-frequency waves from small explosions in continental areas of older geology. A high percentage of the USSR consists of older geological terrains.

Extensive data from small explosions and earthquakes in several parts of the Soviet Union have been collected by the Norwegian Seismic Array (NORSAR) and by a new high-frequency array in that country (NORESS). Soviet underground explosions with yields of only a fraction of a kiloton have been detected reliably at distances as great as 2600 miles (4160 km) by that new array. US seismic listening posts within the USSR, as agreed to in the test ban negotiations from 1977 to 1980, if they are equipped for high-frequency capability, would allow greater areas of the Soviet Union to be monitored and at closer distances.

High-frequency seismic waves offer not only the possibility of detecting very small underground explosions that would not have been detected by standard techniques but also the opportunity to combat attempts to evade or cheat on a comprehensive treaty. High-frequency waves will help to reduce the two cheating possibilities that worry the USA the most: the so-called hide-in-earthquake and big-hole scenarios.

The hide-in-earthquake idea involves the detonation of a small underground explosion soon after the occurrence of a large earthquake such that its signals will be masked or obscured by those of the larger event. I believe that high-frequency seismic monitoring will effectively eliminate the possibility that the hide-in-earthquake scenario could be used for clandestine testing. Figure 8.1 shows a dramatic example of the use of this technique. The upper seismogram shows a recording in Norway with conventional low frequencies. It and the lower figure show the arrival of waves from a large earthquake in the eastern part of the Soviet Union at 30 seconds on the horizontal axis. The lower

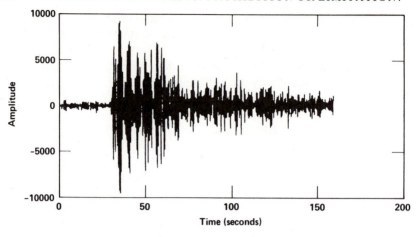

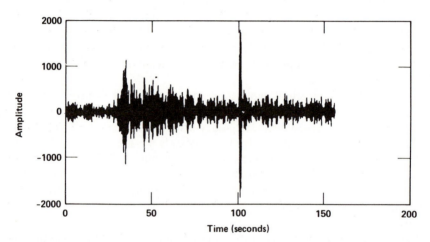

Figure 8.1. Example of recordings made by the Norwegian Seismic Array of a large earthquake followed by a very small underground nuclear explosion at the eastern Kazakhstan Test Site, USSR

The upper record is made with standard band of frequencies between 1.2 and 3.2 Hz. The lower trace, which clearly shows a large, high-frequency signal from a small underground explosion, is made with a passband of 3.2–5.2 Hz.

recording utilizes somewhat higher-frequency waves. It shows a very large high-frequency arrival soon after 100 seconds. That second event, which is not evident on the upper record, was an explosion of less than 1 kt at the Central Asian test site of the USSR. The very small explosion produced the largest high-frequency seismic waves even though it was much smaller than the preceding earthquake. This example also demonstrates the pronounced differences in the excitation of seismic waves of various frequencies by earthquakes and explosions—a factor that can be utilized for identifying sources as being explosions or earthquakes.

Most of those specialists who have worked on seismic verification are in agreement that the detonation of small explosions in very large underground cavities represents the most significant evasion possibility and the one that sets the lower limit to US identification capabilities. High-frequency seismic waves are not reduced as much in amplitude, that is, they are not muffled as much, as the lower-frequency waves that are routinely used for monitoring.

The United States detonated a very small (0.38-kt) underground explosion code-named STERLING in a salt dome in Mississippi in 1966 to test the decoupling theory. The seismic data collected from that experiment as well as theoretical calculations indicate that the amount of muffling is about a factor of 10 less important at higher frequencies, that is, at 15 to 30 Hz, compared to that at lower frequencies commonly used for monitoring.

Several US federal officials emphasized the potential promise of high-frequency signal detection. I believe that reality lies somewhere between the technique being merely one of interesting, but unproven, potential and one that has been fully perfected. While exciting new work is in progress on this topic, the existing results from the high-frequency array in Norway are dramatic. That array must be described as an existing capability. It alone permits monitoring of the western third of the USSR down to a very low level such that even small decoupled explosions would be clearly detected.

During the past five years the field of seismic verification has undergone a major revolution in data recording and analysis. The use of digital data, which was pioneered by the petroleum industry for oil and gas exploration, permits seismic waves of a wider frequency range and a much greater range in sizes to be recorded reliably. The revolution in high-frequency seismic waves probably would not have been possible without digital recording. Our knowledge of the earthquake and explosion sources has advanced to the point at which various 'wiggles' on a seismic record can be analysed and matched by theoretical calculations. This has allowed us to make much more effective use of the major differences that exist in the fundamental character of earthquakes and underground explosions and to utilize those differences for positive identification of an event as either an explosion or earthquake.

For several years the US Department of Energy has operated a network of seismic stations called the Regional Seismic Test Network. Those stations record seismic data in a way that insures that no tampering with the equipment or data has occurred. The data are transmitted for rapid analysis by satellite. That network has provided not only an important test of equipment that could be used in the Soviet Union to monitor a test ban treaty but also valuable data for continued work on improved verification. The network has provided important digital data in the high-frequency range mentioned above.

The Soviet Union recently agreed to allow US seismologists to operate seismic monitoring equipment near their main test site in Central Asia. Such instruments could provide valuable additional information on high-frequency wave propagation. As long as the Soviet moratorium on testing continued, equipment of that type could be used to ascertain that very small tests were, in fact, not being conducted at that testing area.

Soon after the Soviet Union announced its testing moratorium, some statements were made in the United States that the USSR had conducted a particularly large number of tests prior to that announcement. None of our data nor that provided by the National Defence Research Institute (FOA) of Sweden support those contentions. The seismic arrays operated in Sweden and Norway are capable of detecting Soviet weapon tests in hard rock down to a fraction of 1 kt. We tabulated nine Soviet explosions in 1985 compared to 21–31 in each of the preceding seven years. In 1985, 16 announced explosions were detonated in the United States (one of which was a British test conducted in Nevada).

III. Capabilities for monitoring a comprehensive test ban treaty

Table 1 lists my estimates of the threshold for reliable identification of Soviet underground nuclear explosions. An important point here is that US seismic monitoring stations in the USSR, as was agreed to in principle when the test ban talks went into recess in 1980, would permit verification down to explosions of smaller size than would be possible solely with networks located external to the USSR. Hence, obtaining a good internal capability should be a major goal of the United States in test ban negotiations. This would permit smaller earthquakes and explosions to be identified with confidence.

Two evasion possibilities are described: detonation in low-coupling materials and explosions in large underground cavities in salt domes. In both cases the detonation in large underground cavities, the so-called big-hole evasion scenario, is the most limiting: 10 kt for an external network alone and

Table 8.1. Thresholds in kilotons for reliable identification of underground nuclear explosions using seismic networks external and internal to the USSR

	External net alone	Internal plus external net
1. Hard rock or below water table (no evasion attempts, fully coupled)	1 kt	0.1 kt
2. Detonation in low coupling material: dry, porous alluvium	1–2 kt[a]	1 kt
3. Detonation in large underground cavity in salt dome	10 kt[b]	about 1 kt

[a] Limited by maximum thickness of unsaturated alluvium in the USSR.
[b] Limited by maximum sizes of large underground cavities that can be constructed clandestinely and maintained without collapse.

about 1 kt for an internal network. Recent estimates for the latter scenario by credible experts range from 1 to 5 kt.

IV. Soviet compliance with the TTBT

Over the past few years various officials of the US Government have stated that the Soviet Union either has violated or is likely to have violated the Threshold Test Ban Treaty (TTBT) by testing above its 150-kt limit. On 2 April 1986 the *New York Times* announced that the US Government had officially revised its procedure for estimating the yields of Soviet underground atomic tests. The revisions in methodology reported in the *New York Times* are very similar to those that I advocated in testimony before two committees of the US House of Representatives on 8 May and 20 November 1985 and that I and a number of other seismologists have advocated for 10 to 15 years. The change in methodology reported in the *New York Times* would lead to about a 30 per cent reduction in the calculated yields of Soviet underground explosions.

The range of opinions among experts on this matter, in fact, is now not very great, with the possible exception of a few officials and former officials of the Defense Advanced Research Projects Agency (DARPA). Officials and seismological experts at the Lawrence Livermore National Laboratory have expressed views about Soviet compliance with the TTBT that are almost identical to my conclusion. In testimony before the Subcommittee on Strategic and Theater Nuclear Forces of the Committee on Armed Services of the US Senate on 14 March 1985, Dr Batzel, the Director of Livermore, stated: 'Based on our assessment of the relationship between yields and seismic magnitudes of the Soviet test sites and the pattern of Soviet testing, we have concluded that the Soviets appear to be observing a yield limit. A best estimate of this yield limit is consistent with TTBT compliance.' I find that statement to be very important since Livermore has a very strong group of seismologists who work on test ban verification, several of whom developed a position of yield estimation in the late 1970s, before that subject became as politicized as it has become in the past several years. The former Director of the Los Alamos National Laboratory, Dr Donald Kerr, has given more equivocal testimony on Soviet compliance on the TTBT. Nevertheless, it is well known in the seismological community that both the competence and the number of seismological experts working on yield estimation are strong for Livermore and quite poor for Los Alamos.

It is important to ask why the US Government has taken so long to institute a correct methodology for estimating yields of Soviet explosions when a number of scientists who have worked in this area for more than 20 years have repeatedly stated that the United States is seriously overestimating the yields of Soviet underground tests. While recent studies have strengthened conclusions about the correct methodology, the answer was, in fact, available 15 years ago. It might be wondered if seismologists were of varying opinions about methodology or if they are to be faulted for coming up with an incorrect procedure. I must report that neither of those possibilities is correct. In fact, a few seismologists in DARPA and a number of other persons who are not experts on yield estimation managed to thwart attempts to arrive at a correct methodology for more than a decade.

While there is now near scientific unanimity on the correct methodology for estimating yields, several officials of the US Government continue to insist that the Soviet Union is likely to have violated the TTBT. In a letter of 9 June 1986 to Dr Hugh DeWitt of the Lawrence Livermore National Laboratory, Mr M. Eimer, the Assistant Director of the US Arms Control and Disarmament Agency (ACDA), reiterates that view (see appendix 8A). He mentions that statements by competent seismologists brought to the attention of those in the Administration were not ignored, that spirited debate occurred during the preparation of drafts of compliance reports to the Congress, and that no policy considerations were introduced during the preparation of the analytical reports. Whether or not policy considerations, in fact, entered into their deliberations, it is clear to me that their findings are not in accord with those of most seismological experts on yield estimation. ACDA, the agency charged with the preparation of compliance reports, does not have one single person on its staff who is an expert on seismic estimates of yield, the main and most accurate method of ascertaining compliance with the TTBT.

Mr Eimer states that the government's finding about likely violations of the TTBT is not based solely on seismological data but on the full scope of data and analyses available to the Arms Control Verification Committee. Dr Robert Barker of ACDA stated repeatedly in hearings about House Joint Resolution 3 in 1985 that non-seismological data were also an important factor in concluding that the USSR had likely violated the TTBT.

Dr Ralph W. Alewine, III, Director of the Geophysical Sciences Division of DARPA, who was a member of the recent panel of the Defense Intelligence Agency (DIA) that reviewed these matters, briefed the Committee on Seismology of the US National Academy of Sciences about test ban issues at their meeting on 4 and 5 November 1985. In the draft minutes of that meeting he is quoted as stating: 'The Defense Intelligence Agency studied this and reported that seismology was more reliable than other methods [for the estimation of yields of USSR tests].' Thus, the case for ignoring the seismological evidence and giving great weight to non-seismic factors seems to have vanished.

In a letter of 16 December 1985 to Representative Beverly Byron, Chairman of the Special Panel on Arms Control and Disarmament of the House Committee on Armed Services, Dr Alewine of DARPA stated: 'Dr Sykes' assertion that seismic yield estimates of Soviet underground nuclear explosions can be made with a precision of 30% is overly optimistic about many of the aspects of this problem.' Nevertheless, at the above-mentioned meeting of the National Academy of Sciences he also stated that there are now probably three ways for calculating yield, and that this can reduce the error of yield determinations by about a factor of 1.73. It is now widely acknowledged that yields of

Soviet explosions can, in fact, be calculated from three different types of seismic waves; (a) short-period P-waves; (b) long-period surface waves (which are not nearly as sensitive to local variations in geological properties as are P-waves), and (c) a short-period seismic surface wave called Lg.

The US Government has argued that the accuracy of yield determinations for Soviet weapon tests is so poor that on-site monitoring of the main Soviet test site in Central Asia by US equipment is required to ensure verification of the TTBT. That view could only be sustained, however, as long as it could be maintained that uncertainties in yield estimation were about a factor of 2 or so. Alewine's statement that the uncertainty can be reduced by a factor of about 1.73 leads to even better accuracy than I have indicated. Throughout the long course of debates about yields of Soviet tests, I have heard no statements that an accuracy better than 30 per cent would be required to verify the TTBT.

During the House Committee on Foreign Affairs hearing on House Joint Resolution 3 on 8 May 1985, Dr Kerr of Los Alamos was asked: 'assuming just for the purposes of discussion that Dr Sykes is correct in saying that there is 30-per cent variance here, do you believe that a test at 195 kilotons in comparison to a test of a device with a yield of 150 kilotons would give the Soviet Union any potentially military significant advantages which we would not have if we would yield to the treaty and didn't test over 150 kilotons . . . .'. Dr Kerr answered: 'Fortunately I don't have to deal with the "if so" because I don't think the difference between 195 and 150 would be militarily significant. The sort of thing I think would be, is if the Soviet Union, for example, could test at a level like 300 kilotons.'

Thus, while additional verification data may well be useful, the accuracy of present yield estimates is much better than the factor of 2 or greater that Dr Kerr states would be an explosion of military significance in excess of 150 kt.

I have used surface waves and P-waves to make independent estimates of the yields of the eight largest Soviet explosions detonated since the TTBT took effect in 1976. A given seismological estimate always has a certain uncertainty associated with it, the 30 per cent figure (one standard deviation for surface wave estimates) I mentioned above. Thus, if the USSR were to test eight explosions of the same size, we would expect some of the calculated numbers by a given technique to be above the actual yield and some to be below it. For a few Soviet tests, the yields that I calculated from P-waves alone are slightly larger than 150 kt. However, the yield estimates from surface waves for those explosions are somewhat smaller than 150 kt. Thus, when results from these two methods are averaged, the calculated yields are, in fact, very close to 150 kt. Methodology now exists for calculating yields of Soviet tests from surface waves as well as from body waves.

Hence, with the recognition that the USSR has not tested weapons significantly above the 150-kt limit of the TTBT and that yields can be determined with an accuracy much better than a factor of 2, there do not appear to be any verification requirements that would preclude ratification of the TTBT by the US Senate.

V. Disadvantages to US security interests if the TTBT and SALT II do not continue in force

In examining Soviet compliance with the TTBT we discovered that Soviet practice is to test repeatedly weapons of a few specific sizes. We have re-examined the yields of the largest weapons tested underground by the USSR using the same rationale mentioned in the *New York Times* article of 2 April 1986. The time period 1970 to the start of the TTBT in 1976 is crucial since nuclear weapons of high yield probably were being tested, which were deployed in the late 1970s on various versions of large Soviet land-based missiles—the SS-17, -18 and -19.

Figure 8.2 shows a histogram of sizes of the largest Soviet explosions tested from 1964 to 1975 at the Arctic test site. There are a number of prominent peaks in the histogram, of which 500 kt is the largest. We obtained very consistent estimates of yields by using two different types of seismic waves. We deduced that 500 kt is the yield of the weapon or weapons that were emplaced

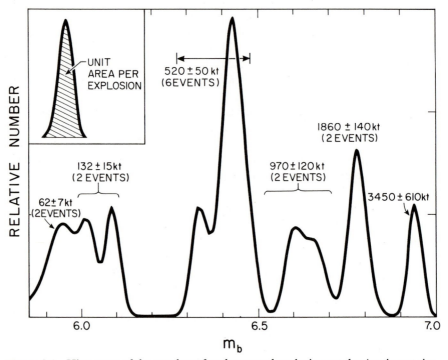

Figure 8.2. Histogram of the number of underground explosions at the Arctic test site, USSR, in Novaya Zemlya from 1964 to 1975 as a function of size (the seismic parameter m_b). Stated yields are averages of estimates made from body and surface waves. Note very prominent peak near 500 kilotons which is identified as the full-yield testing of weapons for the SS-17, -18 and -19. [From Sykes and Wiggins, *Proceedings of the National Academy of Sciences*, vol. 87, Jan. 1986.]

on MIRVed versions of those intercontinental missiles. Our estimates are among the lowest that have been published or given in congressional testimony for those systems.

One aspect of the downward revision in calculated yields that was reported in the *New York Times* is that the yields of those large Soviet explosions at their Arctic test site prior to 1976 have been overestimated. Those overestimations have been used to portray the USSR as having more powerful weapons than the United States. Another result that comes out of this re-analysis is that the nuclear weapons on those Soviet systems have a lower yield-to-weight ratio compared to those of comparable US systems that were deployed about the same time; that is, Soviet weapons are heavier and not as technically advanced. The same thing appears to be true for Soviet submarine-launched ballistic missiles with multiple warheads.

It should be realized that the TTBT has had an important constraint on the Soviet development of large nuclear weapons. A pronounced minimum in Soviet testing can be seen in figure 8.2 for explosions of yields between 150 and 500 kt. Thus, it seems clear that prior to at least 1976 the USSR did not develop nuclear weapons with yields in that range. Since the autumn of 1975 they have not tested weapons with yields significantly in excess of 150 kt. In his House testimony of 8 May 1985, Dr Kerr stated: '. . . it's our belief that one can reasonably safely extrapolate in yield by about a factor of two.' From Kerr's testimony we can conclude that the USSR could not have tested near 150 kt and developed a weapon much larger than 300 kt with high confidence. SALT II and the TTBT have thus prevented the Soviet Union from taking full advantage of the heavier throw-weight of their large intercontinental missiles. Thus, it is certainly not in the interest of the United States to have the Soviet Union test lighter-weight weapons of say 500, 1000 or 2000 kt to full yield. SALT II has limited the number of missiles the USSR can deploy; the TTBT has prevented them from developing lighter-weight weapons with yields much in excess of 150 kt.

Thus, it is in the US national interest that the present threshold be reduced considerably to prevent the USSR from catching up with the USA in the development of new warheads, particularly those of lighter weight.

Appendix 8A. Letter to Hugh E. DeWitt, Lawrence Livermore National Laboratory

UNITED STATES ARMS CONTROL AND DISARMAMENT AGENCY

June 9, 1986

Dear Mr DeWitt:

Ambassador Adelman has asked that I respond to your May 22, 1986 letter commenting on the discussion and debate at Stanford on May 15.

*   *   *

In three Reports to the Congress, which were mandated by law, the President stated that the US Government found that the Soviet nuclear testing activities for a number of tests constitute a likely violation of legal obligation under the Threshold Test Ban Treaty of 1974.

No statements by competent seismologists brought to the attention of those within the Administration responsible for the preparation of the analytical reports that are the foundation of the President's findings on Soviet noncompliance were ignored. No policy considerations were introduced during the preparation of the analytical reports and no one with access to the classified reports has so charged publicly or privately.

As co-chairman of the Arms Control Verification Committee (ACVC) Analysis Group (the NSC committee charged by Presidential Directive with responsibility for analysis of compliance issues), I directed the analysis and the preparation of the draft study on TTBT compliance.

For the initial Report to the Congress in 1984, DOE was assigned responsibility for the first draft. Technical representatives of all appropriate agencies participated in the spirited debates that occurred during the preparation of drafts, or if they so chose, commented on the drafts during the clearance process. The Working Group's final draft was discussed and endorsed in a meeting chaired by the President's Assistant for National Security Affairs with ACVC principals and other officials above the level of Assistant Secretary in attendance.

While there were some differences among agencies on how the proposed findings should be worded, the contents of the analysis represented a consensus. That consensus report was considered at a meeting of the National Security Council chaired by the President and, subsequently, a finding was issued by Presidential Directive (NSDD).

*   *   *

With regard to the charge of distortion, let me simply say that you are wrong and that you do the ACVC Working Group, the ACVC principals, the NSC, and the President a disservice with such an unfounded charge.

With regard to your second charge that important seismological opinions were disregarded or improperly discounted, I do not know of any substantiated view that came before the Committee or its Working Group that was not properly considered.

*   *   *

It was evident during the entire process of analysis that no single class of data available to the US could definitively settle the question of Soviet compliance/noncompliance. The central value yield, coupled with a range of uncertainty, was one of the classes of data carefully considered.

In considering what weight should be given to yield estimates based on seismological measurements, the Working Group availed itself of the full spectrum of published documents and consulted with those they considered appropriate. However, the analytical components of the report forwarded to the President and, in its SECRET version, to the Congress is the product of the ACVC and entirely the responsibility of that Committee.

It is clear from your note that you believe that the findings were not based on sound analysis because the work was distorted by 'policy' consideration and personal biases and because there is a body of opinion that disagrees with the findings. That body of opinion, which you apparently rely on, holds that neither a finding of compliance nor noncompliance is justified by the data (seismological data?).

One of the most fundamental precepts of analysis is that conclusions should be consistent with all the evidence. Those who claim that seismically determined yields, with all their uncertainties, should be the sole basis of assessing Soviet compliance/noncompliance with the TTBT violate that most fundamental of scientific principles.

The President's finding that it is likely that the Soviets violated that TTBT was not based solely on seismologically determined central value yields but on the full scope of data and analyses available to the ACVC. No data or analyses have come to that Committee's attention which would suggest weakening the President's findings.

Sincerely,
M. Eimer
Assistant Director, ACDA

Appendix 8B. Weapons of various sizes that had been tested by Spring 1985

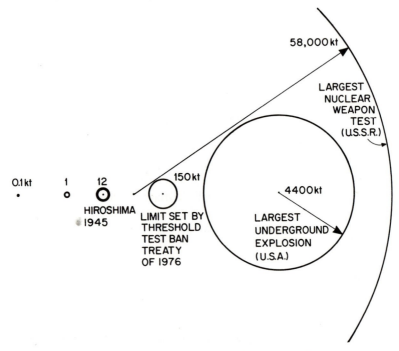

Note: Kt is the yield in kilotons. The energy release of the largest underground explosion (about 5000 kt) is equivalent to that of all the munitions expended in World War II. With US monitoring posts in the USSR, a comprehensive test ban or a low-yield threshold treaty could be verified for explosions of about 1 kt or larger. That size is much smaller than weapons emplaced on strategic systems today (about 40–9000 kt) or the weapons that opened the atomic age in 1945.

Paper 9

Dennis C. Fakley

Former Deputy Leader of the UK Delegation to the tripartite CTB negotiations

Abstract

A treaty banning all nuclear tests will become possible only if there are adequate technical means of verifying compliance. To date, monitoring the underground environment has posed the most difficult problem. Seismic methods offer the best hope of supplying the required verification capabilities. This paper assesses, in terms of detection and identification performance, how nearly current technologies meet the need and examines the prospects for improvements. Views are also given on the reasons for the wide divergence between assessments of seismic verification capabilities by various authorities.

I. Introduction

An effective system for verifying a ban on underground nuclear testing must, first, provide an adequate probability of detecting seismic signals generated by underground explosions, against the ambient background of seismic noise; and, second, allow these signals to be identified so that they can be distinguished from those produced by other human activities and by earthquakes. A further requirement is that the system must be capable of determining the epicentres of seismic events and preferably also their origin times and magnitudes.

This paper summarizes the present state of seismic verification technology and offers an assessment of its adequacy for comprehensive test ban (CTB) treaty purposes. It also indicates some of the possibilities for improving seismic verification performance.

The assessment indicates that seismic technology is not yet good enough for monitoring adequately a ban on underground testing and it differs markedly from other assessments, which support the conclusion that verification is no longer a significant problem. An explanation of why different views can emerge from essentially the same data is suggested in the final section.

II. Seismic detection

Seismic signals have to be detected against an ambient background of noise, originating partly in the neighbourhood of the detection station (owing to such random influences as wind, industrial and domestic activities, and thermal stresses), and partly from remote sources, especially the oceans. With a global network of optimized arrays of seismometers, preferably installed in bore-holes, located at sites where the station ambient noise levels in the short-period wave-band (centred on about 1 Hz) are about equal to that at the quietest known sites, it should be theoretically possible to achieve an effective teleseismic detection threshold equivalent to a body- (or P-) wave magnitude, m_b, of about 3.5.

Such a network does not exist today and it may be unattainable, because the very quiet sites required, both on land and on the seabed throughout the world, may not exist or may be unavailable for political reasons. Data from existing teleseismic stations provide a detection threshold of about $m_b = 4$ for some areas of the northern hemisphere, of about 4.5 for the rest of this hemisphere, and of about 5 for most of the southern hemisphere. Without too large an effort, it should be practicable to lower these thresholds to, perhaps, 4 for the north and somewhat higher for the south. As discussed in a later section, it is likely to be more profitable to seek improvements in this verification perform-ance through the development and use of regional stations rather than through a more elaborate teleseismic network.

The noise level for long-period surface waves is also of importance (see section III). At teleseismic ranges, the surface-wave magnitude, M_s, of a signal needs to be at or above about 3 before it equals or exceeds the noise. For an underground explosion, a teleseismic magnitude, M_s, of 3 corresponds approx-imately to a body-wave magnitude, m_b, of 5, which is significantly higher than most of the body-wave detection thresholds given above. The estimate of the teleseismic surface-wave detection threshold assumes the absence of interfer-ing surface waves from any prior large earthquake, which are present for about 10 per cent of the time.

As would be expected, the signal-to-noise ratio for an event of given magnitude is larger at regional (<3000 km) than at teleseismic (>3000 km) distances. The decay in the strength of long-period surface waves with increas-ing regional distance is slow and regular, but the strength of the first arriving short-period P-wave decreases rapidly with distance in the first 500 to 1000 km. As a result, while the surface wave from an event may be clearly detectable at regional distances, the first arriving P-wave may be below noise level. For these events, it is not possible to apply the most powerful identification criteria, which depend on the availability of data on first short-period arrivals. Although the first arrivals may be undetectable, later short-period phases may well be above the noise level; as yet, however, data from these later arriving phases do not provide sufficient short-period information for identification purposes. The identification problem would be exacerbated by any attempt to 'muffle' explosion signals (see section IV).

Interest has recently grown in the potential of seismic high frequencies, at both regional and teleseismic distances, for underground test ban verification. This has come about from the recognition that earlier estimates of the anelastic attenuation of frequencies in the 5–50 Hz band were badly in error. A re-assessment of the value of high frequencies indicates that they may, in some circumstances, provide a detection threshold as good as, if not better than, that presently available at the more conventional short periods (at about 1 second). It is, however, not yet possible to be sure of this; much more data are required before a firm conclusion can be reached. High frequencies may also prove to be useful for reducing the scope for evasion (see section IV).

III. Seismic identification

In a verification context, a detection system, without an effective identification capability, would be worse than valueless. Currently, it is estimated that there are, on a global basis, some 8500 earthquakes on average every year at a body-wave magnitude of 4 or above. A monitoring network would have to be capable of identifying all but a handful of these signals as of natural, that is of non-explosive, origin, if confidence in compliance with a treaty were not to be speedily and fatally undermined.

Over the past 30 years, attempts have been made to develop seismic means whereby earthquakes can be reliably distinguished from explosions. Initially, three discriminants were proposed, namely location, depth of focus and first motion.

Location

If a seismic signal were measured to originate at sea, it would be reasonable to assume that it had a natural origin, unless hydroacoustic signals indicated that an underwater explosion had occurred. The accuracy with which the epicentre of a seismic disturbance can be determined is dependent on how many seismic stations make a good detection of the disturbance, their azimuthal distribution around the source and the nature of the transmission paths from the source to the stations. Assessments have indicated that, with a reasonable global teleseismic network, a disturbance calculated (with 95 per cent confidence) to have originated, say, 25 or more kilometres from land should be classified as an earthquake. However, the underwater and seabed technologies developed in recent years may cast doubt on this conclusion because it may no longer be valid to rule out the possibility of staging an explosion beneath the seabed. Before leaving the subject of location, it should be noted that epicentre determinations would also be needed for on-site inspection purposes.

Depth of focus

If the depth of focus (in other words, the distance below the earth's surface) of a disturbance could confidently be established to be greater than, say, 10 km, it would be reasonable to conclude that it had a natural cause. Therefore, a focal depth determination could be a useful discriminant in that it would eliminate all but shallow earthquake signals from further examination. Attempts to determine the depths of disturbances of low magnitude solely from travel-times have yielded results with such inaccuracies that it is only safe to conclude that the actual depth exceeds 10 km when the best estimate from measured travel-times exceeds about 50 km. In theory, depth can be calculated from the difference between the arrival-times, at teleseismic distances, of P-waves and their reflections from the earth's surface; but these differences are small and, for low-magnitude events, are often difficult to measure in the presence of reverberations, conversions between the various phases in the seismic wave-train, reflections and scattering close to the source. There is some possibility of improving depth determination for areas which can be calibrated using earth-quake signals with clearly identifiable surface-reflected phases, but it is not yet known how widely this calibration procedure could be applied. The use of regional data should allow depth determinations to be refined, particularly for disturbances within the crust, but it is too early to estimate the improvements that could be achieved.

P-wave first motion

An underground explosion is, in simple theory, a shallow-focus, radially symmetric source of elastic wave energy and should generate an outward pressure in all directions; consequently, the first motion of the P-wave at all seismic stations distant from the source should be outwards and, thus, invari-ably be upwards. On the other hand, an earthquake can be considered to result from a movement of one rock mass relative to another along a fault plane and, accordingly, to constitute a non-symmetrical source, producing outward first motions along some azimuths and inward first motions along others. In other words, an earthquake should produce an upward ground motion at some distant seismic stations and a downward motion at others. It was proposed nearly 30 years ago that, if the first motion from an underground disturbance at one or more stations were downwards, that disturbance could safely be classified as an earthquake and could be excluded from further consideration. The problem with the 'first motion' discriminant is that, for low-magnitude signals, it is frequently difficult, if not impossible, to determine with confidence the direction of first motion; and there are instances where well-recorded explosions have given apparently clear negative first motions. In general, therefore, first motion is no longer considered to provide a reliable discriminant.

Complexity and spectral discriminants

It is to be expected that the spectrum of a seismic signal from an explosion, which generates a very sharp pulse of energy, should differ substantially from that from an earthquake, which releases its energy over a much longer period. Accordingly, at one time it was considered that only an earthquake could generate a complex seismic waveform at distant stations and that all complex waveforms could, therefore, be disregarded when assessing CTB compliance.

However, as a larger number of explosion waveforms became available, it was found that explosions could, contrary to expectation, also produce complex waveforms. This undermined confidence in the complexity criterion. There is, as yet, no widely accepted explanation of the mechanism whereby some explosions produce complex seismograms; if one could be found, it might then be possible to modify the complexity criterion so that it became useful.

More recently, it has been claimed that the spectra of earthquake signals fall off more steeply with increasing frequency than do the spectra of explosions. If this were true, it would be possible to process an incoming seismic signal through a filter which passed only high frequencies so that, for earthquakes, no signals above background noise would be recorded, whereas, for explosions of adequate magnitude, signals would be detected. In other words, the system would act purely as an explosion detector and would be insensitive to earthquakes. Available data on earthquake and explosion spectra do not support this claim; they show that the high-frequency tails of spectra for both earthquakes and explosions fall off at a rate of between the inverse square and the inverse fourth power of the frequency; sometimes the fall-off is steeper for earthquake signals, sometimes it is steeper for explosions, and sometimes the fall-off for both is about equal.

The m_b:M_s criterion

Although the spectral discriminants described in the preceding paragraphs are not especially useful other than for larger-magnitude events, the discrimination procedure which uses the spectral ratios between P-waves of about 1-second period and Rayleigh-waves of about 20-second period is so important that it deserves separate discussion; it is better known as the m_b:M_s criterion. This criterion derives from the observation that an explosion, with a given value of m_b, generates lower-amplitude surface waves (and, hence, has a lower M_s) than do earthquakes of the same body-wave magnitude. Evidence, first published in the early 1960s, confirmed this observation and numerous later studies have validated the criterion derived from it. If the values of m_b and M_s for a large number of explosions and earthquakes are plotted on Cartesian coordinates, it is found that almost all, if not all, the points representing explosions fall above a positively sloping straight line and that almost all, if not all, the points representing earthquakes fall beneath this line. Explosions and earthquakes form two almost wholly separate populations, and the best dividing straight line between them can be determined empirically. When a disturbance of unknown origin is detected, if its m_b and M_s values are plotted on the m_b:M_s diagram, the disturbance can be classified as an explosion if it falls above the line and as an earthquake if it falls below.

It is obvious that the m_b:M_s criterion can be applied only if values of the P-wave and the Rayleigh-wave magnitudes are available and, as stated above, Rayleigh-waves from disturbances producing signals near the P-wave detection threshold at teleseismic ranges are lost in the background noise; and other surface-wave signals could be lost in the coda of prior earthquakes. These remarks apply particularly to explosion surface-wave signals simply because they are relatively weaker than earthquake surface-wave signals. This limitation could be reduced if regional stations were available to make Rayleigh-wave measurements from explosions at or near m_b 4. It would not, however, be satisfactory to assume that the absence of a Rayleigh-wave at teleseismic distances for an m_b 4 disturbance implied that an explosion had occurred.

It is also obvious that the measurements of m_b and M_s must be reasonably accurate. Experience indicates that, for identification, the output signal-to-noise ratios at the receiving stations for both P- and Rayleigh-waves should be about half a magnitude greater than that required for simple detection.

There are examples of a failure of the m_b:M_s criterion to identify earthquakes correctly; they have occurred mostly in south-central USSR and Tibet. They normally exhibit comparatively simple short-period P-wave seismograms with between one and three pulses and little else; the pulses could be due to the P-wave and its surface reflections from a depth of focus of about 25 km. Where the available seismic records have been adequate, modelling has indicated that this is indeed the case. However, relevant data are scarce, so it is not known how widely and how frequently earthquakes defeating the m_b:M_s criterion occur and, hence, whether they would undermine confidence in any proposed CTB verification system.

While the m_b:M_s criterion undoubtedly works efficiently for larger earthquakes and for the larger explosions at known nuclear test sites, the crucial question, which is as yet unanswered, is whether or not it remains valid down to the smallest magnitudes of CTB interest and for all regions. Some theoretical and observational evidence suggests that there is a convergence of earthquake and explosion populations at the lower magnitudes with an overlap at the lowest detectable magnitudes. Until there is a better understanding of the physics of the generation and transmission of seismic waves by explosions and earthquakes, it will not be possible to assess fully how widely the m_b:M_s criterion can be applied.

Identification at regional distances

It was pointed out above that signal/noise ratios at quiet sites are higher at regional than at teleseismic distances (because the amplitudes of the ground motions are that much larger); hence, there should be potential for reducing the detection threshold below that achievable at long range. Such a reduced threshold would, however, be of CTB verification value only if it were accompanied by an improved identification capability. Much effort has been put into the search for ways in which the later short-period phases at regional ranges—see section II—could be used to produce identification criteria, but so far none has been found. Detections at regional ranges do, however, improve the accuracy of depth-of-focus determinations and, as has been noted, allow the application of the m_b:M_s criterion at lower magnitudes.

IV. Yield/magnitude relationships and evasion scenarios

The discussion so far has been expressed in terms of seismic magnitudes but, for CTB assessment purposes, it is necessary to translate magnitudes into equivalent explosive yields. Only then can a view be taken about the adequacy of available verification technology. It has been established that the relationship between yield Y and m_b for fully tamped underground explosions conducted in hard or water-saturated rock has the form:

$$\log_{10} Y = Am_b - B$$

where A is a constant of about unity, and B is a constant of about 4 for regions of low attenuation. Accordingly, a magnitude of m_b 4 for low-attenuation regions can be equated with a yield of 1 kt. For the US Nevada Test Site (NTS), where attenuation is not low, B is about 3.7 and m_b 4 equates to about 2 kt.

The above formula applies only if the explosion is fully tamped, that is, is close-coupled to the surrounding environment, and if this surrounding medium is hard or water-saturated rock. If the medium is a soft, dry rock, for example dry alluvium, then the efficiency with which the explosive energy, provided it remains fully contained, is converted into seismic waves is reduced by a factor of about 10; in other words, for these conditions, a magnitude of 4 would equate to a yield of 10–20 kt. Limitations on the thicknesses of strata of soft, dry rock in the world probably mean that, in order to satisfy the condition of complete containment, explosive yields would have to be restricted to about 10 kt to obtain a decoupling factor of about 10.

The yield/magnitude relationship has been determined empirically largely from data from Western underground tests carried out at relatively few locations, principally at the US NTS, and at depths deemed to be just sufficient to ensure complete containment. NTS is in an earthquake zone and in a region with a highly attenuating upper mantle. Whether the relationship remains valid for aseismic regions, for upper mantles markedly different from that at NTS, and for deeply buried explosions are open questions at the moment; they will not be resolved unless authentic data from other regions and for other containment conditions become available.

The above yield/magnitude relationship could be deliberately invalidated by detonating an explosion in an underground cavity, so that the explosive energy would be less well transferred to the surrounding medium. Theory and some limited experiments indicate that, provided the cavity is sufficiently large and stable, a decoupling factor of about 100 could be achieved at frequencies of about 1 Hz. For example, a fully decoupled 10-kt explosion would generate seismic signals about 100 times smaller than the same explosion close-coupled in hard, dry rock and, if seismically detected, the application of the above formula would lead to a yield estimate of only 100 tons. There is some evidence that the efficiency of decoupling decreases with increasing frequency and that a CTB verification system should include regional high-frequency stations to deter or detect attempts to evade treaty obligations by the use of decoupling cavities. This might allay security concerns over decoupling if some means were found of discriminating between regional high-frequency decoupled-explosion signals and the many other signals of equal or larger magnitude that would be detected by regional stations. These other signals would include those generated by large chemical explosions. There is no prospect of differentiating between nuclear and chemical explosions by seismic means and, therefore, if highly sensitive regional stations form part of a CTB verification system, special non-seismic arrangements would be required to ensure that the seismic detection of chemical explosions did not destroy confidence in verification.

As the experimental validation of decoupling theory in the West has been limited to chemical explosives tests of up to 1000 kg and a nuclear explosives test of 380 tons, it is not possible to be certain that decoupling would be as effective at yields of greater importance in the CTB context, that is, in the 1- to, say, 30-kt range, but there is no doubt that firing an explosion in a cavity would reduce the seismic output.

There is a debate about the practicability of constructing a sufficiently large and stable cavity to decouple fully an explosion with a yield of up to a few tens of kilotons. To do so by conventional mining engineering methods would certainly be formidable, but there are the possibilities of using cavities already created by nuclear explosions or of using solution-mining methods to produce cavities in salt formations.

Decoupling is by far the most important evasion scenario that has been considered in the seismic verification context. It has, however, also been suggested that an explosion could, by design, be masked by a nearby earthquake or that a series of explosions could be so arranged that the resulting seismic signals would mimic those of a large earthquake sufficiently closely that they would not give rise to a suspicion of a test ban violation. While neither of these two evasion scenarios can be completely rejected, there are practical reasons why they would be unattractive to a would-be treaty violator, who would be unlikely to consider them unless an alternative means of satisfying a vital testing requirement was not available.

V. An overall assessment of current seismic verification technology

Before a nuclear weapon state (NWS) could consider accepting a ban on underground testing, it would need to assure itself that no party would be able to cheat and accrue some military or security advantage without running a significant risk of being found out. This leads, at least in the case of the Western NWSs, to the requirement for technical means of verification.

For security reasons, Western NWSs have not disclosed their assessment of the minimum nuclear yield which could have a military or security significance. It is, however, widely assumed by the proponents of a CTB that a verification system that gave a reasonable probability of revealing treaty non-compliance at or above a 1-kt level would be satisfactory. This level would be on the high side if it were thought necessary to allow some margin for unforeseen developments in nuclear weapon design technology, but it is the level assumed for the remainder of this paper.

If extrapolations from existing seismic data are valid, it appears reasonable to assume that it would be possible to instal and operate a global seismic network of short- and long-period seismographs capable of detecting and identifying close-coupled tests, conducted in hard or water-saturated rock, at or above about 1 kt, *provided* the global teleseismic network is supplemented by regional stations with long-period seismographs to detect, primarily for identification purposes, those surface-waves inaccessible at teleseismic distances. In theory, this threshold would rise to about 10 kt for tests conducted in dry, soft rock and to 100 kt for fully decoupled tests; but, in practice, it is unlikely that evasive testing at these levels would be feasible, either because of the non-availability of adequate dry, soft rock testing sites or because of the engineering problems of creating sufficiently large, stable underground cavities. In coming to an overall conclusion on the actual verification capability which could be achieved, it is necessary to take into account the uncertainties in the global applicability of existing seismic data, the loss in performance inevitably associated with an operational seismic network (when compared with results obtained on a research and development basis) and the possibilities of evasion. Taking these factors into consideration, it is concluded that the seismic verification system envisaged here would not do better than give high confidence that testing above a few tens of kilotons was not taking place. It is not possible to be more precise but it is clear that a verification performance down to 1 kt could not yet be provided. In the present state of knowledge, it is further concluded that the verification effectiveness of the envisaged system would not be enhanced by the installation of high-frequency regional stations, because it is not yet possible to identify the sources of regional high-frequency signals.

VI. The potential for seismic verification improvements

There seems little likelihood that further major improvements can be made in teleseismic verification performance, on which much effort has been expended over the past three decades. An exception might lie in the investigation of the potential of long-distance high-frequency—10 to 50 Hz—detection. With this possible exception, it appears more profitable to seek capability enhancements through developments in regional verification, even though the identification problems appear to be formidable. The most important requirement is, perhaps, for a means of countering the decoupling evasion scenario sketched in section IV. At the moment, high frequencies seem to offer the best seismic prospects but, again, identification appears to be the prime difficulty.

The acceptability of a CTB verification system to governments depends in part on their confidence that it would operate in accordance with expectation. The history of CTB seismic verification from the mid-1950s onwards is littered with examples of performance assessments which proved to be inaccurate as the seismic data base expanded, and this has sapped confidence. It could be restored by accumulating more data to establish whether or not the assumptions and extrapolations underlying present-day assessments are valid; this task deserves high priority.

VII. Differences in CTB verification assessments

The capability assessment outlined above differs significantly from some others, which indicate that seismic technology is already sufficiently competent for CTB verification purposes. And these differences emerge from analyses of essentially the same basic data. It might be instructive to enquire why this should be so.

Assessors of the effectiveness of seismic verification capabilities can be classed as optimists and pessimists. For the optimists, it would seem reasonable to assume that some observation favourable to the efficiency of CTB verification would be applicable worldwide, even though it had been obtained under restricted conditions; and they would include the result in their assessment. On the other hand, the pessimists would not find the same result convincing without proof that it had global application and they would, at least for the present, discount it.

Perhaps more importantly, views on the adequacy of seismic verification are influenced by the extent to which it is seen that a CTB could have serious security implications. In general, those with direct responsibilities for national security adopt a more cautious approach in the knowledge that the penalties for error could be severe. Thus, they require a higher verification performance and greater assurance that it is achievable under all conditions of relevance to their security interests. They are also less willing to assume that all CTB parties would comply with treaty obligations if the verification system had potentially exploitable weaknesses, such as an inability to counter evasion scenarios.

There is, however, probably general agreement on the need for a verification system in which all parties to a treaty could have confidence. Without such confidence, a treaty would serve as a continuing source of contention between the parties, exacerbating rather than easing political tensions.

Chapter VIII. International seismological verification

Paper 10

Peter W. Basham

Geological Survey of Canada, Ottawa, Canada

Ola Dahlman

National Defence Research Institute, Stockholm, Sweden

Abstract

Since the onset of underground nuclear testing in the mid-1950s, it has been recognized that seismological monitoring will provide the principal means of verifying compliance with a ban on underground testing. The Conference on Disarmament Group of Scientific Experts defined a conceptual global system that can be used as a foundation for a three-tiered international verification system tailored to meet pre-defined political requirements. The global network (tier 1) would provide the international framework and a reasonably uniform global capability. National networks providing data on lower-magnitude seismic events (tier 2) would lower the threshold on all territories occupied by participants. Special seismograph installations and other arrangements (tier 3) would be designed to meet the requirements that some countries may have for monitoring the territories of nuclear weapon states. Once designed, there should be no political opposition to the early operation of elements of this system to gain experience with a principal task of seismological verification: the elimination of unfounded suspicions about naturally occurring earthquakes.

I. Introduction

Seismology is an international science. Significant earthquake zones follow the large-scale tectonic features of the earth that are seldom confined by political boundaries between states. Observational and theoretical studies of earthquakes require data collected from seismograph stations up to 10 000 km away. Seismological studies of the internal structure and properties of the earth, using seismic waves that have propagated through the earth, require seismic data collected on a global basis. Seismological monitoring of a ban on underground nuclear explosions similarly requires seismic data collected and shared on a global basis. The international, co-operative, seismological effort required to monitor an underground test ban treaty is the subject of this paper.

A distinction is made here between *international*, *seismological* means and other means of monitoring compliance with a test ban. For the Partial Test Ban Treaty, only 'national technical means' (NTM) of verification are used to provide assurance of compliance with the provisions. National technical means of verification are those means at the disposal of a particular state that do not require specific assistance from a state being monitored. NTM were also specified in the SALT Agreement, and the parties undertook not to use deliberate concealment measures which impede verification by national technical means.

For monitoring a treaty banning underground testing, NTM can include non-seismological techniques such as reconnaissance satellites and intelligence methods (see paper 13). Covert seismograph facilities also exist, but their extent and capabilities have not been disclosed, so the means provided by these systems are not discussed in this paper. On-site inspection in the underground test ban case, an issue that has been much discussed over the years, would be a separately agreed part of the treaty. This is considered complementary to seismological monitoring and is also treated separately elsewhere (see papers 14 and 15).

Section II provides a brief historical background to the development of ideas for international seismological verification, and then a description of the conceptual framework for international seismic data exchange that has been developed by the Conference on Disarmament Group of Scientific Experts. This is followed by a description of an international seismological verification system that the authors believe would meet pre-defined political requirements, and finally, by a discussion of the implementation of such system.

II. Historical background

The years 1958–77 saw an uneven pace of developments in seismological verification. The five years prior to the 1963 Partial Test Ban Treaty (PTBT) were ones of extensive discussion and negotiation. Significant national programme developments accompanied by some international efforts took place during 1962–76. In 1976 an international forum was found for systematic seismological discussions in the Conference of the Committee on Disarmament (CCD). A year later the USSR, the UK and the USA began negotiations on a comprehensive test ban treaty (CTBT).

Geneva experts, 1958–59

The first fully contained underground nuclear explosion (Rainer, 1.7 kt) was detonated at the Nevada Test Site on 19 September 1957. The seismic data from Rainer (detected by about 50 seismograph stations from distances of up to 3000 km) and from previous partially contained tests led to the conclusion that seismological means provided the only reliable long-range means of monitoring compliance with a treaty banning underground nuclear weapon tests.

Seismologists were therefore included in the technical delegations of the 'Conference of Experts to study the methods of detecting violations of a possible agreement on the suspension of nuclear tests'[1] that met in Geneva in July 1958. On the basis of seismological information then available, the experts initially agreed (in August 1958) that underground nuclear explosions in the range 1–5 kt could be detected and identified if seismograph facilities were established in 170 land-based control posts, with options for on-site inspection of ambiguous events. It was believed that the control posts would be spaced at 1000-km intervals in seismic areas, and at 1700-km intervals in aseismic areas.

The technical report of the Conference of Experts was considered further at a political conference,[2] with a subcommittee of experts, held in Geneva in November–December 1959, to work out a treaty to control nuclear weapon testing, while the negotiating parties maintained a moratorium on nuclear testing. In the intervening period the Western side had had second thoughts on the 1958 conclusions. They had received additional seismic data from fully contained Nevada Test Site explosions in October 1958 and new evidence that the seismic energy from nuclear explosions would be decoupled by detonation in large cavities. The seismological discussions did not lead to agreement on a verification system. There was lack of agreement on the seismic magnitude of the Rainier explosion, and therefore on the number of earthquakes per year that would have equivalent magnitudes; on the value of the methods for discriminating earthquakes from underground explosions; and on the effect of decoupling.

Although the seismologists did not agree in 1959, the political conference continued until 1961. There was an agreement in principle in March 1960 to a treaty providing for a magnitude 4.75 threshold on underground testing, a moratorium on tests below that level, and a joint programme of research on detection and identification of underground explosions. But these efforts came to an end with the collapse of the Eisenhower–Khrushchev summit meeting and the resumption of testing.[3] The final impasse with respect to a ban on underground testing was on the number of on-site inspections required, the USSR proposing two or three and the USA seven per year. Instead of a comprehensive agreement, the parties agreed in 1963 on a partial solution by signing the PTBT banning tests in the atmosphere, in outer space and under water.

The 1958 Geneva meeting produced the first suggestion for an international seismograph network for monitoring a CTB, and the only commonly agreed network concept until 20 years later. Meanwhile, a number of national research programmes in seismic verification began.

Development of national programmes

The UK and the USA began research and development (R&D) programmes immediately after the Geneva experts' discussions. The experts had recommended that the 170 seismic control stations be arrays with 10 seismometers distributed over an aperture of about 3 km and connected to a central recorder. Because of the small aperture, the signals could be simply summed, and it was hoped that the noise would be suppressed. With the knowledge available at that time, it was assumed that the stations should be as close as possible to the seismic events being monitored. It was planned, for example, that 24 stations should be in North America and Greenland and 40 in Eurasia.

The UK experimented first with a 9-km aperture array installed in Wyoming, 1000 km from the site of the planned Gnome underground nuclear explosion in New Mexico (3.1 kt, December 1961). The analysis demonstrated that weak signals could be enhanced by an array at this distance, but the most important results came from explosions at greater distances. The Wyoming array clearly observed signals from underground explosions detonated by the USSR in eastern Kazakhstan and by France in the Sahara. These recordings focused attention on the fact that, at least for stations in the western USA, the amplitude of short-period P-waves observed at distances around 3000–10 000 km is about the same as at 500 km.[4] The UK therefore switched its efforts to this 'teleseismic' distance range, re-designed its arrays to have 20 seismometers with an aperture of 25 km, for better signal-to-noise improvement at large distances, and installed four such arrays in Scotland, Canada, Australia and India in the early 1960s, which are still in operation today.

The USA drew on the results of the Berkner Panel's report—'The Need for Fundamental Research in Seismology', published in 1959—to embark on a major programme to improve seismic detection and identification. The principal vehicle was the Department of Defense Vela Uniform programme, which funded seismological R&D for the next 25 years[5] and still continues today.

Among the many contributions to general seismology by the Vela Uniform programme, those of relevance to the development of international means of seismic monitoring include:

1. The installation of the first fully integrated global seismograph network, the 'World Wide Standardized Seismograph Network' (WWSSN) with 125 stations in 60 countries, which was completed in 1967.

2. The testing of prototypes of the arrays suggested by the Geneva experts with the construction of five arrays of different geometries in the United States. The USA also developed and tested the concept of large seismic arrays in attempts to achieve maximum detection capability in the teleseismic range. The Large Aperture Seismic Array (LASA) in Montana had 625 seismometers distributed over an aperture of 200 km. LASA failed to come up to expectations and was closed in 1978.

3. More recently, development and installation of improved digital, broadband and borehole seismometers, some of which are replacing WWSSN stations on a global basis and some of which are employing satellite data communications to central data centres.

National programmes in seismological verification were also developed in other countries. The British array at Yellowknife, Northwest Territories, Canada, became the nucleus of the Canadian research programme on seismic event detection and discrimination. Sweden developed a similar programme based on the Hagfors array. Norway developed the teleseismic NORSAR array and, more recently, a small-aperture, high-frequency array, NORESS, tuned to local and regional events. Programmes of various types were also initiated in the Federal Republic of Germany, France and Australia.

Research attention focused on teleseismic means until the late 1970s, when renewed interest in local and regional seismic means was brought about by the trilateral (USSR, UK, USA) CTB negotiations, which included consideration of 'in-country' stations; that is, special stations in nuclear weapon states, the numbers and types of which would be arranged as part of the treaty (see also paper 11).

International efforts

The next meeting of seismic experts from East and West[6] took place in Tällberg, Sweden, in 1968, at the invitation of SIPRI. The participants at this meeting had a large number of new seismological results available for con- sideration, and focused their attention on the issue of identification of seismic events. Although there were disagreements at the meeting and differing interpretations of the conclusions afterwards, the group did agree on a number of statements concerning underground explosion identification capabilities.[7] Most of the new results had come from the recently completed WWSSN, Long Range Seismic Measurements[8] and Canadian seismograph network, the British arrays and the Soviet network.

Since 1958 there had been no other formal suggestions for a global network of stations that would be administered jointly for the specific purpose of providing seismic data for monitoring compliance with a CTB. However, in order to assess existing seismograph facilities and the verification capabilities they might provide, in 1969 Canada sponsored a resolution at the UN General Assembly asking member countries to submit information on the seismograph stations on their territories, from which they would be prepared to supply data on the basis of guaranteed availability. Seventy-five countries responded to a questionnaire circulated by the Secretary-General, 45 reporting information on seismograph stations and 22 indicating that no stations were in operation. Eight Socialist countries replied by indicating that they preferred to retain a bilateral and voluntary form of seismological data exchange and included no information on seismograph stations. Conceptual global networks based on the UN returns were studied for their potential seismic event detection and identification capabilities[9] but, because of the lack of information on Socialist countries' stations, the results were not representative of the capabilities on their territory.

What these studies lacked in 1958 (Geneva experts), 1968 (SIPRI experts) and 1969 (UN resolution) was a clearly defined conceptual and administrative framework that would make the appropriate seismic data available to interested participants in a timely manner. Defining these arrangements in detail became the principal task of the CCD Group of Scientific Experts.

III. The 1978 CCD global system

CCD Group of Scientific Experts

The Conference of the Committee on Disarmament (CCD)[10] was very active in discussions of a CTB and seismological means of verification during the period 1969–76. Informal meetings of the CCD with seismological experts present took place in 1971, 1973 and 1976. These informal meetings provided an opportunity to air various national views, but not for systematic discussions of international seismological verification. Nevertheless, the opportunity was taken to table numerous national working papers, most of which dealt with studies of discrimination between earthquakes and underground nuclear explosions.

A more appropriate forum and a mandate for the seismologists was suggested by Sweden in the spring of 1976.[11] In July 1976, the CCD established the Ad Hoc Group of Scientific Experts to Consider International Cooperative Measures to Detect and Identify Seismic Events, hereafter referred to as 'GSE' (Group of Scientific Experts).

The GSE was open to government-appointed experts from all member countries of the CCD, and by invitation to experts from non-member countries. Currently (1986), under the CD there is participation in the GSE by experts from 28 countries,[12] not all of whom attend regularly. The countries represented are most of those that have reasonably strong national seismology programmes, although not all have national programmes in seismological verification. Both Africa and South America are underrepresented, and only Egypt and Peru, respectively, have sent experts. The GSE meets twice a year for two-week meetings in Geneva.

The GSE began its work in the same time-frame that the trilateral parties began negotiations on a treaty banning underground nuclear weapon tests. Thus, the GSE began with a sense of urgency, as the trilateral discussions could have relatively quickly resulted in a treaty that referred to an international seismological monitoring system. The GSE took less than two years (until March 1978) to complete its first report to the CCD,[13] which defined the basic framework of a global system, and another year (until July 1979) to elaborate on some of the technical details.[14]

In 1980 the trilateral parties adjourned their negotiations, stating that considerable progress had been made[15] but not agreeing on a treaty. In recent years, the GSE has undertaken a number of seismic data-exchange experiments, and there have been important national and co-operative investigations

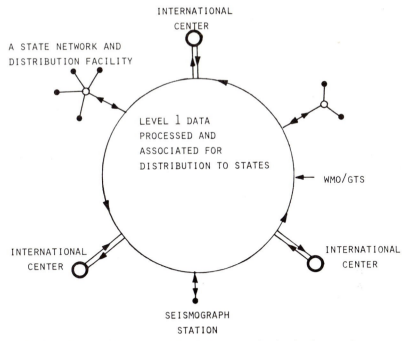

INTERNATIONAL
CENTER

A STATE NETWORK AND
DISTRIBUTION FACILITY

LEVEL 1 DATA
PROCESSED AND
ASSOCIATED FOR
DISTRIBUTION TO STATES

WMO/GTS

INTERNATIONAL
CENTER

INTERNATIONAL
CENTER

SEISMOGRAPH
STATION

Figure 10.1. Schematic diagram of the international seismic data exchange system described by the GSE in its first report (CCD/558), 1978

The GSE used the term 'Level I' data to describe parameter data.

of relevance. The third and fourth GSE reports were submitted to the CD in March 1984 and August 1986.[16]

When it began its work in 1976, the GSE was constrained by the seismograph network, data communications and computing technology of the day. The basic framework for the global system defined in its report[17] is shown in figure 10.1. The system had three basic technical components: (*a*) participating seismograph stations; (*b*) an international data communications facility; and (*c*) international data centres. These three components and other functions of the system are described briefly below.

Seismograph stations

The global network would consist of one or more national seismograph stations offered by each of the treaty parties and operated to agreed international standards. Additional stations on non-party territory and possibly on the ocean bottom could be arranged in national and bilateral programmes. It was assumed that countries with large territories (e.g., the USSR, Canada and the USA) would offer the number of stations commensurate with their size. It was recognized that it would be necessary to allow any country wishing to do so to

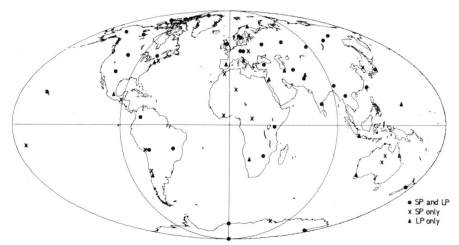

Figure 10.2. A global seismograph network described by the GSE in its first report, in 1978, as an example of stations that might be selected for the global system

'SP' refers to short-period seismographs and 'LP' to long-period seismographs. In a modern digital network, 'broad-band' seismographs would serve the functions of both the SP and LP seismographs.

participate by offering at least one station. For geographical regions with many small countries (e.g., Europe), this would produce more stations than would otherwise be necessary. It was also recognized that, when restricted to teleseismic determinations, a relatively small number of well-distributed sensitive stations could provide global detection and location capabilities that are as good as those provided by a large number of less sensitive stations. The network was usually described as containing 50 or more high-quality stations. One of the hypothetical networks (hypothetical because, although most of the stations existed, not all contained appropriate seismograph instrumentation) considered by the GSE in its first report in 1978 is shown in figure 10.2.

Parameter data derived at stations

The operators at each station were to derive parameters (which the GSE called 'Level I' data) from the recordings of all detected events. These parameters were to be of two basic types: (*a*) arrival times and amplitudes of the principal seismic phases that would enable the international data centres to locate and assign magnitudes to the seismic events; and (*b*) 'identification' parameters to provide a rough characterization of the observed signals. The latter parameters were intended to characterize sufficiently the recorded signals so that a participant with an interest in seismic events from the location in question could form a preliminary impression of the nature of the events; that is, earthquakes or potentially suspicious event.

Waveform data

If a participant is interested in pursuing further the nature of a seismic event appearing in a bulletin, a request would be made for waveform data (i.e., the original recordings which the GSE in its early work called 'Level II' data) to one or more of the participating stations. What a participant does with such data is its own business, and how it acts on any evidence that it might find concerning a possible nuclear explosion would be a national political decision.

Although there were no formal limits, it was anticipated (in 1978) that such requests might be expected a few times per month, and the data could be dispatched by airmail as magnetic tape copies of digital data or photocopies of original paper recordings. Even though it was agreed that continuous recordings would be made, it was implicit that such requests for waveform data would be keyed to seismic events that appeared in a data centre bulletin, or at least to parameter reports indicating that a station had detected an event.

Parameter data communications

Early in the work of the GSE it was recognized that the only then existing telecommunications system that reached essentially every country of the world was the World Meteorological Organization's Global Telecommunications System (WMO/GTS). This system is employed by the World Weather Watch to exchange meteorological data. It is also used for other types of environmental data and has been used for about 10 years by a dozen countries to send seismic data to international earthquake location agencies. After consultation with the WMO, the GTS was specified as the principal telecommunications system for sending parameter data to international data centres, as shown in figure 10.1. In 1983 the GSE received formal permission from the WMO to use the GTS for parameter data communications on a regular basis.

Although there are high-speed, high-capacity circuits between, and computer switching in, some of the nodes of the GTS, many parts of the system are telex-based and many have manual switching. The GSE conducted a technical test over a two-month period in late 1984, during which 75 seismograph stations in 37 countries contributed seismic parameter (Level I) data for processing at three experimental international data centres in Moscow, Stockholm and Washington. This test showed that, even after extensive preparation, the overall efficiency of the GTS in successfully transmitting parameter data to experimental data centres was 83 per cent.[18] However, the efficiency varied markedly among regions: it was 95 per cent for Europe, North America and Australia combined; and 40 per cent for Asia, South America, the Pacific region and Africa combined. Monitoring of the GTS by the WMO itself has shown that the overall global availability of meteorological data remains at about 75 per cent.

Many participants in the GSE believed that the purpose of the system was too important to envisage even 1 per cent of the data being lost in transmission.

These participants attempted, without success until recently, to turn the attention of the GSE to other forms of modern data communications.

International data centres

The principal role of a data centre would be to receive the data from stations, use them to compute the times, locations and magnitudes of seismic events, and distribute seismic event bulletins to participants. These procedures would be undertaken under a strict time schedule: for example, a preliminary event bulletin computed from data available within 5 days, and a final event bulletin within 10 days.

The GSE has proposed that there be more than one standardized international data centre established for the global network. The USSR, the USA, Sweden and Australia have stated that they would plan to operate such data centres. The first three of these countries developed temporary data centres that operated during the GSE data-exchange experiment in 1984; the Australian data centre is currently under development. It is considered highly desirable, for purposes of generating trust, that the data centres be sufficiently similar in computers, algorithms and procedures that they would produce essentially identical seismic event bulletins on the basis of the same input parameter data.

An opening to the future system

The issue of waveform exchange has produced considerable debate in the GSE during the past few years. With the advances in digital seismographs, data communications and computing power, it was felt that much greater use could be made of the raw waveform data in the global system. In particular it was believed that: (a) the availability of waveform data at the data centres would significantly improve the seismic event bulletins; and (b) much more extensive waveform requests should be anticipated.

During these years the USSR would not agree to any modifications of the parameter-based system described above. On 22 July 1986 their position changed with a statement in the CD:

We consider that the operative transmission of level two (waveform) data from stations to the centres and the processing at the international centres will allow a significant increase in the effectiveness of this international system of exchange for the purposes of verification of compliance with a treaty on the complete prohibition of nuclear tests by all participants. We specifically propose that the *Ad hoc* Group of Scientific Experts should start to develop a system of prompt transmission of Level 2 seismic data which would serve as a basis for international seismic verification of the prohibition of nuclear weapon tests. That data would be promptly transmitted from seismic stations participating in the global network using satellite communication channels for processing at the international data centres. There would also be automatic data exchange between those centres, using especially allocated communication channels.[19]

This statement has had a considerable impact on the work of the GSE, although it has just begun to consider its implications. In the following section the authors present their view of the global system that they believe should emerge from further detailed work by the GSE. Much of the framework of the 1978 global system can be retained, but there are a number of important aspects, in addition to the waveform exchange, that must be addressed before the system will be acceptable to all participants.

IV. An international seismological verification system

Political requirements

The verification system adopted under a comprehensive test ban has three purposes: (*a*) to deter the parties to a treaty from conducting clandestine activities; (*b*) to provide confidence that the parties to a treaty observe their treaty obligations; and (*c*) to counteract unfounded suspicions about seismic events caused by natural phenomena. Thus the verification system must be regarded from two different aspects: that of the monitoring side and that of the potential evader.

From the monitoring side the system is assessed in terms of what can be observed with a high degree of confidence. It has usually been assumed that a very high level of confidence in detecting and identifying every violation would be required. Providing confidence that other parties observe their treaty obligations could, in the view of some countries, require that the seismological verification system have a very high capacity to detect, locate and identify seismic events.

A potential evader must, on the other hand, consider what clandestine tests could be carried out without being detected. It is reasonable to assume that a potential evader is not prepared to accept any substantial risk of being detected. Experience has shown that as the seismic events get smaller the ability to discriminate between earthquakes and underground explosions drops from near certainty to near zero. However, a seismological system that has a 90 per cent probability of detecting and identifying events of a certain size might still detect and identify events smaller than one-third of that size with a 10 per cent probability. Such a system would therefore have a deterrence capability at considerably lower thresholds than is usually contemplated when assessing seismological verification systems.

Different countries may have different verification requirements, but each country has a right to satisfy its verification needs and, as a party to the treaty, a duty to contribute to the overall verification of the treaty. These rights and duties must be reflected in the structure of the global system.

The counteracting of unfounded suspicions about naturally occurring earthquakes is a most important function of the verification system. While such a system is often viewed as one that will identify clandestine explosions, it is one that will also confidently identify earthquakes as such. If the system generates a significant number of false alarms on earthquakes, the confidence in the verification system and in the treaty itself will rapidly deteriorate.

The capabilities of the various system components are discussed below, but the authors have avoided drawing any conclusions on the verification capabilities of the overall system: first, because these must be negotiated in advance of final development based on the various political requirements (in principle, a seismological system can be developed to meet any political requirements); and second, because the actual capabilities of the system will not be known until it has been put into operation and tested.

A three-tiered verification system

The GSE has worked for 10 years on the concept of an international teleseismic monitoring system. This system has adopted many of the functions performed by existing international earthquake-location agencies, albeit with more rapid reporting schemes, presumably better seismic event detection capabilities in some portions of the globe and additional provision for access to waveform data from participating stations. This system, alone, may not meet international seismological verification requirements. It is, for example, inferior to national earthquake-monitoring systems covering the territories of potential participants. The requirements that some countries may have for low-threshold monitoring on the territories of nuclear weapon states have not been clearly defined, but additional arrangements might be needed to meet these requirements.

These shortcomings suggest that the international system actually be three-tiered with the following network components: (*a*) a global network of 50 or more 'primary' stations which, to the degree possible, provide uniform global coverage of seismic events; (*b*) networks of 'secondary' stations drawn from national earthquake-monitoring networks to provide lower-magnitude capabilities on the territories of participants; and (*c*) special networks of 'in-country' stations and other arrangements that provide the additional capabilities required on the territories of nuclear weapon states.

Global teleseismic system (tier 1)

The structure and functioning of the global network (tier 1) can be much as described by the GSE, but with the following important refinements:

1. The participating primary stations must be as standardized as possible.
2. These stations must transmit waveform time segments to international data centres for every detected event.
3. The communications systems for parameter and waveform data must be very efficient.
4. Procedures must be established for the processing of waveform data at data centres, and to permit requests for any time segments of waveforms from any participating stations.

Each of these refinements is treated in more detail below, but first, the capabilities of the teleseismic system are briefly addressed.

One recent study[20] has shown that a hypothetical 50-station global network could have a detection and location threshold at about magnitude 3.5 in western Europe, about 3.7–3.8 in North America and Asia, and about 4.2 in the southern hemisphere. To put these seismic magnitudes into perspective, there are approximately 8000 earthquakes of magnitude 4.0 or greater on the globe each year; and empirical evidence from active seismic zones has shown that for each decrease in magnitude by one unit the number of earthquakes increases by a factor of about 10 (i.e., 80 000 per year at magnitude 3.0 or greater). Magnitude 4.0 is also the approximate seismic magnitude of an underground nuclear explosion of 1 kt whose detonation is fully contained in hard rock.

For events in the seismic bulletins for which there will be no other data from the tier 2 and tier 3 systems, the data from the teleseismic system will be the only international data available for verification purposes. A large fraction of these events will be located in oceanic areas that are usually excluded from consideration as potential clandestine test sites. Others will be located on portions of land masses not occupied by participants in the international system. As a teleseismic system has been under consideration for many years, there have been numerous studies of its earthquake/explosion discrimination capacity.[21] For these events, discrimination will have to rely on these data and methods.

With the new impetus to consider extensive use of waveform data in the global system, the GSE will embark on design specification and experiments for a new system. Here the refinements of the 1978 system that should be considered for a modern tier 1 global system are briefly noted.

Station standards. The performance of the seismograph stations determines the capability of the overall global system. Siting in the lowest possible seismic noise environment is essential to maximize detection capabilities. A homogeneous network of standardized stations would greatly facilitate the interpretation, exchange and processing of data. A detailed technical description of such a station has been given in a West German CD working paper.[22] The GSE must agree on the technical specifications of what might be called 'CD monitoring stations', and prototype stations should then be developed and tested.

Array stations can make a significant contribution to seismic event location processing at data centres by giving provisional location information. Medium-aperture (25-km) arrays are valuable for teleseismic events, small-aperture (3-km), high-frequency arrays are valuable also for local and regional events. Not all stations in the tier 1 global network need to be arrays, but these should be well distributed around the globe. One of the options of a CD station should therefore be an array station. The Norwegian NORESS array has produced valuable experience on which to base a prototype.

Data reporting. Waveform time segments will be transmitted to the data centres for every detected event. These waveform segments would be of unfiltered data (filtered data would usually be used for detection processing at the station) and include a noise segment preceding the arrival time and a sufficient time segment following the arrival to include all additional crustal phases (from waves propagating through the shallow regions of the earth) for local and regional events, or all possible depth phases (reflections from the earth's surface above the source) for deep teleseismic events. The waveforms would be accompanied by parameter reports of the arrival times and amplitudes of the principal seismic phases. Array stations would also report their location estimates.

These data are required for event location processing at the data centres. During event processing, particularly on the smaller events, there will be a requirement for further dialogue with the stations. For example, it will be necessary for the centres to be able to request confirmation of a non-detection at a station.

Additional important data recorded by the stations for teleseismic events are the lower-frequency surface waves that follow the first arrival by several tens of minutes. It remains to be discussed by the GSE whether waveform segments that include the surface waves would be routinely transmitted.

All waveforms contributed by primary stations would be available to participants on request to a data centre. There will be other cases in which a participant may be interested in additional specific time segments of a station's recordings—for example, to confirm a non-detection of a weak event, or to study other seismic waves that follow the first arrival.

Data communications. Among the advances in technology since the mid-1970s, the one that can have the greatest impact on the global system is data communications. Real-time satellite data telemetry is currently employed or planned for a number of seismological applications. For example, geostationary satellites are used for the Regional Seismic Test Network, a five-station prototype of an 'in-country' network currently operated by the USA in North America, and for data transmission from the NORESS array in Norway to the USA. Polar-orbiting satellites are used for retrieval of data from automatic seismograph stations operated by the Institut de Physique du Globe (France). Satellite telemetry is planned for the Global Telemetered Seismic Network being installed by the US Geological Survey with stations in Africa and South America, and for transmission from the Yellowknife array to a processing centre in Ottawa, Canada.

Thus there is much experience with satellite telemetry of seismic data that the GSE can draw upon to upgrade communications facilities for the global system. Effective use can also be made of the international packet-switched data systems that connect various computer equipment to public telephone/data networks with internationally agreed standards to provide almost error-free, high data-transfer rates at low cost. Packet-switched data networks currently reach about 70 countries. The WMO has indicated to the GSE that it has upgraded, or shortly will be upgrading, a number of its GTS communications circuits, and has offered these for more extensive data communications in the global system.

Data centre processing. In international earthquake-location agencies, such as the International Seismological Centre in the UK, approximately 50 per cent of the data reported by stations, after processing, remains unassociated with any located seismic events. The data centres of the global verification system must improve significantly on this performance. This will be aided by the national reporting described below for tier 2, and by the presence of globally well-distributed arrays, but there will also be a significant benefit from the access to waveforms at the data centres.

Computer processing of reported parameter data with automatic association algorithms works well for the larger seismic events detected by many stations. However, facilities at a data centre to display and analyse waveforms will significantly improve an analyst's ability to associate data and locate the smaller events. Access to all waveforms for an event being processed also enables the analyst to more confidently identify depth phases and compute accurate depth below the earth's surface.

This routine access to waveform data at data centres will be a new departure in international seismic-event processing. To make it as effective as it must be for a seismological verification system will require a substantial amount of research and experimentation. The potential exists to determine routinely more source parameters than the common ones of location and magnitude— for example, the orientation of the geological fault and the tectonic stress that caused an earthquake. One of the principal tasks facing the GSE is to devise the procedures that can be applied uniformly at all data centres.

National reporting of lower-magnitude events (tier 2)

The basic problem with the global teleseismic system becomes apparent from a look at national and regional earthquake monitoring programmes. Within most reasonably seismically active countries there are national seismograph networks intended to monitor local earthquakes down to the magnitude levels appropriate to improving understanding of the local earthquake processes. To the knowledge of the present authors, all national agencies responsible for monitoring local seismicity make such information freely available to interested outside agencies. In most countries these national programmes will be far superior in detection and location capabilities to the coverage of the same regions by the global teleseismic system.

For example, Canada monitors its national seismicity with a network of more than 100 seismograph stations. These stations provide sufficient data to detect and locate earthquakes down to magnitude 3.5 or less, anywhere on Canadian territory. In the more industrialized parts of the country, sufficient stations are installed to locate all earthquakes down to magnitude 2.5.

Given the purpose of the verification system, it would be highly appropriate that participating countries take responsibilities within the system to report as accurately and completely as possible on relevant seismic events on their territories. The authors would go so far as to say that this should be an obligation of a participant in the verification system. Therefore procedures are required that will divert appropriate information from the national monitoring programmes into the international system. Such procedures have not yet been discussed by the GSE, and they will have implications for national earthquake monitoring programmes. The following guidelines are suggested for these discussions.

The 'trigger' for national reporting on a seismic event would be a detection at a primary station of an event that is believed to fall within the participant's national territory. An attempt would be made to gather sufficient data on the event from the national network in order to report occurrence time, location and magnitude, along with the primary station data, to the data centres. The magnitude threshold down to which the events are locatable will certainly vary for different portions of national territory (as noted above for Canadian territory), and will also vary among countries according to the installed capabilities of the national networks. Nevertheless, the result would be a global system that has a detection and location threshold close to that of the national networks of participants.

The amount of further processing of these events undertaken by the data centres would depend on the amount and type of additional data available to them. Events on the margins of participants' territories would usually bene-fit from further processing. It would be unlikely, however, that the data centres could significantly improve on the location and magnitude parameters of an event, reported by a local agency, that occurred inside its national network.

Such events will in many cases be detected by primary stations in one or more adjacent countries, particularly in a region of small countries like Europe. A rapid location estimate or an established procedure for consultation could determine in whose territory the event falls. However, the system would certainly not be harmed if location and magnitude information for such events were reported by more than one national agency.

In the report to the data centres, the participant would identify the national stations contributing the additional information. It would be understood that waveform data would be available from these additional national stations on request, but the data would not necessarily be in the same standardized form as that available from the primary station.

What does this second tier add to the verification capacity of the global system? The most important effect will be one of confidence building, with a significant reduction of the number of seismic events on participants' territories that will have unassociated data reported to the data centres. The key discriminant will be focal depth, to establish as earthquakes seismic events occurring at depths that are greater than it is practical to drill for a nuclear test.

Some national networks are very successful at estimating focal depth. Analysis of data from the seismograph network in Sweden, with distances of about 100 km between stations, has shown that it is possible to determine depths of local earthquakes to low magnitudes with an accuracy of about 3 km. This is not possible in the remote regions of Canada with a station spacing of about 400 km, but even higher accuracies are achieved in one seismic zone with station spacing of about 30 km. How well this will work with the networks of other participants remains to be determined, and is the principal reason why the authors suggest that the tier 1 and tier 2 systems be put into operation in the near future to gain experience with 'earthquake identification'.

Special stations and arrangements in nuclear weapon states (tier 3)

The above suggestion of a second tier of national reporting of seismic events in a country's territory would apply to all participating countries. The trilateral negotiations of 1977–80 established a precedent for additional measures to facilitate verification:

The treaty will also contain a provision permitting any two or more treaty parties, because of special concerns or circumstances, to agree by mutual consent upon additional measures to facilitate verification of compliance with the treaty. The three negotiating parties have agreed that it is necessary to develop such additional measures for themselves in connection with the treaty under negotiation . . . the three parties are negotiating an exchange of supplemental seismic data. This would involve the installation and use by the three parties of high-quality national seismic stations of agreed characteristics.[23]

Additional measures of various types could be agreed by any two or more parties, including non-nuclear weapon states, but we will address only the question of special arrangements (tier 3) in the nuclear weapon states.

Most of the discussion and technical assessment of this question have concerned the requirement of the USA to operate special stations on Soviet territory to improve verification (see Hannon, this volume). Special arrangements might fall into three general categories: (*a*) special stations or networks that would monitor sites of previous weapon tests or peaceful nuclear explosions to guard against decoupled explosions in cavities generated by pre-treaty explosions; (*b*) special stations or networks that would provide low-threshold monitoring in geological regions of low-coupling media or potential cavity excavation; and (*c*) the posting of observer or inspection teams at sites of large chemical explosions which, seismologically, cannot be distinguished from nuclear explosions. The countries in the 'Five-Continent Initiative' (see below) have suggested early implementation of some of these arrangements.

It is not clear from the above quotation whether it was agreed that the data from the in-country seismograph stations would be made generally available to all the treaty parties participating in the international monitoring system. The wording seems to imply that these arrangements would be restricted to the three negotiating parties.

The Federal Republic of Germany, among the non-nuclear weapon states, has recently made a clear statement of its views on the data from these in-country stations:

Data exchanged or collected among nuclear weapon states would be made available to non-nuclear weapon states. . . . Nuclear weapon states might look upon the in-country stations combined with their own national technical means as a verification system independent of the global system. . . . It is essential that an international verification system of the highest quality is available to all parties to a Nuclear Test Ban Treaty.[24]

The present authors support this position. The following section discusses implementation, but in doing so the authors recognize a distinction between the tier 1 and 2 international system and the tier 3 special arrangements. An international body like the GSE can define specifications for, and propose implementation of, tiers 1 and 2; final specifications for tier 3 will be part of the final negotiations for a test ban.

V. Implementation of the global system

A dilemma concerning implementation of the international verification system is that, on the one hand, it may be understood that only the parties to the treaty will have the right to decide on the details of the global system they wish to have in place to assist the processes of verification. But there can be no parties until there is a treaty. On the other hand, the eventual parties may want the global system to be in place the moment the treaty enters into force, but they recognize that considerable time will be required to negotiate elements and bring the system to a fully operational status.

Both the Federal Republic of Germany[25] and Australia[26] have suggested in recent CD working papers that the global system devised by the GSE be put into operation in the near future. FR Germany concludes that 'while efforts to agree on a CTB continue, an increasingly sophisticated seismic verification system would mature to meet the verification requirements of all parties concerned, so as to be fully operational at the time of the conclusion of a CTBT'.

In a separate Five-Continent Initiative, six countries have offered their assistance with the early implementation of systems for verification of a test ban.[27] These countries have offered to install portable seismic equipment to monitor the Nevada, Semipalatinsk and Novaya Zemlya test sites for one year during a mutual USSR–USA moratorium on testing. They have also offered to post observers at 20–30 national stations in each of the USSR and the USA to 'internationalize' these stations to verify that the instruments are properly operated and that all information obtained is reported without omission. They have also offered to establish procedures for, and take part in, inspections of large chemical explosions.

The six countries have offered their co-operation with the USSR and the USA in developing permanent verification facilities at test sites and optimum networks of national stations. These would be components of the tier 2 and 3 systems described above.

The principal reason for early implementation of tiers 1 and 2 is to develop the essential experience with earthquake identification required for efficient verification. The earthquake zones of the globe have been well defined on the basis of decades of monitoring global seismicity. On many of the continental land masses the detailed three-dimensional distribution and dominant faulting mechanisms of the seismicity have been defined by efficient national networks and other geophysical and geological studies. However, these global and national programmes have not had the purpose of proving that all of the seismic events are earthquakes and not underground nuclear explosions.

There should be no significant political opposition to the early implementation of the tier 1 and 2 global systems specifically for this purpose. The data from these systems are aimed at and must be capable of identifying earthquakes, and only early implementation of these systems will provide the experience that will be required under a treaty.

VI. Conclusions

The technology exists to develop an international seismological verification system to monitor compliance with a ban on underground nuclear explosions. Using a combination of global, national and special arrangements, the system can be designed to meet any specified political requirements.

The system would be based on an international exchange of seismic data using modern technology and operated to internationally agreed standards. The monitoring of the territories of countries that choose not to take part in the international system will have to rely on seismological data acquired from outside those territories. Parties to the treaty that take part in the system will have an obligation to provide data from their national networks to supplement the global capabilities with information on lower-magnitude seismic events. Special stations would be installed and other arrangements made to provide the low-threshold capabilities that may be required in nuclear weapon states. The global and national systems would be designed primarily to maximize the counteracting of unfounded suspicions about naturally occurring earthquakes. The special stations and arrangements would deter clandestine activities and provide confidence that parties observe treaty obligations.

Figure 10.3 shows a schematic diagram of the earth's land areas that would be monitored by the three combinations: tier 1, only, through three tiers.

It is essential that the Conference on Disarmament, through its Group of Scientific Experts, rigorously pursue the detailed technical specifications of the global system, bringing to bear all recent advances in seismograph systems, data communications and computing technology. Once designed, there should be no political opposition to putting elements of the global system into operation to gain experience with a principal task of seismological verification—the identification of earthquakes as such.

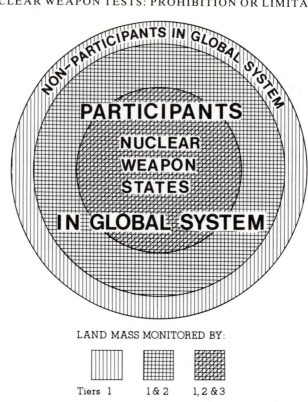

LAND MASS MONITORED BY:

Tiers   1   1 & 2   1, 2 & 3

Figure 10.3. Proportional land areas of the earth occupied by nuclear weapon states (area of inner circle), by potential participants in the global seismic verification system (area of second circle), and by potential non-participants in the global system (area of outer annulus)

The nuclear weapon states (30 per cent of land mass) will be monitored by tiers 1, 2 and 3; territory of participants, including nuclear weapon states (70 per cent), by tiers 1 and 2; and territory of non-participants (30 per cent) by tier 1.

Notes and references

[1] At the 1958 Geneva experts meeting there were representatives from the USA, the UK, France and Canada from the West; and from the USSR, Czechoslovakia, Poland and Romania from the East.

[2] The 1959 political conference was attended by the then nuclear weapon states: the USSR, the UK and the USA.

[3] Romney, C. F., 'VELA overview: the early years of the seismic research program', *The VELA Program: A Twenty-five Year Review of Basic Research*, ed. A. U. Kerr (Defence Advanced Research Projects Agency: Washington, DC, 1985), pp. 38–65.

[4] Douglas, A., 'Seismic source identification: a review of past and present research efforts', *Identification of Seismic Sources—Earthquake or Underground Explosion*, eds. E. S. Husebye and S. Mykkeltveit (D. Reidel: Dordrecht, 1981), pp. 1–48.

[5] Kerr, A. U. (ed.), *The VELA Program: A Twenty-five Year Review of Basic Research* (Defence Advanced Research Projects Agency: Washington, DC, 1985).

[6] Canada, Czechoslovakia, France, India, Japan, Romania, Sweden, the USSR, the UK and the USA.

[7] Davies, D. (ed.), SIPRI, *Seismic Methods of Monitoring Underground Explosions*, Stockholm Papers No. 2 (Stockholm International Peace Research Institute: Stockholm, 1969).

[8] The LRSM network was a portable network of temporary stations deployed by the USA, principally in North America, to record underground tests at the Nevada Test Site.

[9] Basham, P. W., and Whitman, K., 'Seismological detection and identification of underground nuclear explosions', *Publications Earth Physics Branch*, vol. 41 (Earth Physics Branch: Ottawa, 1971), pp. 145–82.

[10] The CCD was expanded from the ENDC in 1969 and subsequently further expanded and changed its name to the Committee on Disarmament (CD, 1979) and to the Conference on Disarmament (CD, 1984).

[11] CCD/482: Sweden, Working paper on co-operative international measures to monitor a CTB (Conference of the Committee on Disarmament), 26 Mar. 1976; and CCD/495: Sweden, Terms of reference for a group of scientific governmental experts to consider international co-operative measures to detect and identify seismic events (Conference of the Committee on Disarmament), 24 June 1976.

[12] Australia, Austria, Belgium, Bulgaria, Canada, China, Czechoslovakia, Denmark, Egypt, Finland, German Democratic Republic, Federal Republic of Germany, Hungary, India, Indonesia, Iran, Italy, Japan, the Netherlands, New Zealand, Norway, Peru, Poland, Sweden, Turkey, the UK, the USA and the USSR.

[13] CCD/558: First Report of the Ad Hoc Group of Scientific Experts to Consider International Co-operative Measures to Detect and Identify Seismic Events (Conference of the Committee on Disarmament), 7 Mar. 1978.

[14] CD/43: Second Report of the Ad Hoc Group of Scientific Experts to Consider International Co-operative Measures to Detect and Identify Seismic Events (Committee on Disarmament, 25 July 1979).

[15] CD/130: (USSR, UK, USA) Tripartite Report to the Committee on Disarmament, (Committee on Disarmament, July, 1980).

[16] CD/448: Third Report of the Ad Hoc Group of Scientific Experts to Consider International Co-operative Measures to Detect and Identify Seismic Events (Conference on Disarmament), 9 Mar. 1984; and CD/720: Report to the Conference on Disarmament on the Group of Scientific Experts' Technical Test (GSETT) 1984: Fourth Report of the Ad Hoc Group of Scientific Experts to Consider International Co-operative Measures to Detect and Identify Seismic Events (Conference on Disarmament), 31 July 1986, 52 pp.

[17] See note 13.

[18] CD/720 (note 16).

[19] Statement by USSR Ambassador V. L. Issraelyan to the Conference on Disarmament, CD/PV 372, 22 July 1986.

[20] Harjes, H.-P., 'Global seismic network assessment for teleseismic detection of underground nuclear explosions: I. Model calculations for different amplitude-attenuation curves', *Journal of Geophysics*, vol. 57 (1985), pp. 1–13.

[21] Blandford, R. R., 'Seismic event discrimination', *Bulletin of the Seismological Society of America*, vol. 72 (1982), pp. S-69–S-87; CD/624: Federal Republic of Germany, A system Design for the gradual Improvement of seismic Monitoring and Verification capabilities for a comprehensive Nuclear Test Ban (Conference on Disarmament), 25 July 1985; Marshall, P. D., and Douglas, A., 'Earthquake or explosion: teleseismic monitoring: where are we now?', in Kerr (note 5), pp. 633–57; Fakley, D. C. (paper 9, this volume); and note 4.

[22] CD/624 (note 21).

[23] See note 15.

[24] CD/624 (note 21).

[25] CD/612: Federal Republic of Germany, A proposal for the establishment and progressive improvement of an international seismic monitoring and verification system relating to a comprehensive nuclear test ban (Conference on Disarmament), July 1985.

[26] CD/717: Australia, Proposal for the immediate establishment of a global seismic network as part of a monitoring and verification system for the future comprehensive nuclear test ban, Conference on Disarmament, 18 July 1986.

[27] Document issued at the Mexico summit on verification measures, 7 Aug. 1986, by Argentina, Greece, India, Mexico, Sweden and Tanzania, reproduced in CD/723, 15 Aug. 1986.

Chapter IX. In-country seismic stations for monitoring nuclear test bans

Paper 11

Willard J. Hannon, Jr

Lawrence Livermore National Laboratory, Livermore, CA

Abstract

In-country seismic systems are elements of most proposals for monitoring a CTB. These systems consist of data acquisition and processing hardware and operational procedures for site selection, data analysis and reporting. The proximity of the stations to potential evasion sites allows the use of multiple seismic waves at each station to detect and identify evasion attempts. Even with extensive in-country systems, earthquakes with explosion-like properties and chemical explosions will produce significant numbers of false alarms. In-country systems have also been proposed to prevent clandestine, off-site testing and to estimate yields for a low-yield threshold test ban. Verified constraints on the source environment, validated calibration procedures, on-site inspections and the application of new techniques are required if the yield estimation properties of networks are to be of significant value. Evaluation of the acceptability of specific systems is difficult given the broad spectrum of values of the decision makers ·and the uncertainties in the estimates of capability. Decision analysis is a possible approach to addressing this difficulty.

I. Introduction

An in-country seismic monitoring system is widely recognized as necessary to obtain an acceptable level of verification for a comprehensive test ban (CTB).[1] However, even with such a system, some violations could go unrecognized. This fact has led to the consideration of a low-yield threshold test ban (LYTTB) as a possible alternative.[2] Some of the proposals for an LYTTB have included the use of in-country monitoring as part of the verification measures.

This paper discusses the value of in-country monitoring systems. It begins with a description of the generic elements of such systems. The verification functions to be performed by the systems are described, and technical performance measures are discussed for both CTB and LYTTB monitoring. The paper concludes with a discussion of the decisions that must be made to evaluate the acceptability of the system. The results obtained from using decision analysis to determine the value of specific in-country systems for CTB monitoring provide an example of a possible approach to structuring the compliance evaluation process.

II. The verification process

For the purposes of the present discussion, an in-country seismic monitoring system is that part of the verification process in which seismic and geological data are collected from locations within the country to be monitored, the data are analysed, and the results of the analyses are reported to those assessing all of the technical, military and political information necessary to evaluate compliance and initiate appropriate responses. The deployment and operation of such a system involve a number of interrelated functions (see table 11.1).[3]

Table 11.1. Functions necessary to deploy and operate an in-country seismic monitoring system

1. Determine the properties of an acceptable system
2. Negotiate:
> Prepare proposal
> Analyse counter-proposals
> Develop responses
3. Exchange and assess pre-installation data:
> Prepare geological data package to be handed over
> Analyse geological data package received
4. Deploy equipment:
> By the country doing the monitoring:
>> Obtain information about sites
>> Select sites
>> Select instrumentation for each site
>> Install and check out equipment
> By the country being monitored:
>> Determine acceptability of sites
>> Monitor installation
>> Participate in check out
5. Carry out monitoring functions both as monitor and as one being monitored:
> Carry out start-up procedures (e.g., calibrate network, characterize site and path)
> Compare actual conditions with estimates
> Seek changes if mismatch
> Operate and maintain equipment
> Archive equipment status and seismic data
> Process data
> Characterize properties of the signals/sources
> Discriminate nuclear explosions from earthquakes and chemical explosions
6. Co-ordinate with other technical elements:
> National technical means
7. Report results to decision makers:
> Events detected
> Locations
> Estimate of source type
> Uncertainties
> Rank unidentified events
8. Attempt to resolve ambiguous events in both countries:
> On-site inspections

Each party to a CTB simultaneously monitors and is monitored by the other parties; the table identifies functions to be carried out by the host nation as well as by the monitoring nations. These functions include site selection, start-up and reporting procedures, as well as the more traditional data-gathering and analysis efforts associated with monitoring systems. These additional functions are important elements of the system and are worthy of considerably more attention than they have received in the public discussions to date.

The technology of in-country seismic systems

In-country seismic systems proposed for reciprocal monitoring of a CTB treaty involving the United States and the Soviet Union involve networks of from 5 to 25–30 seismic stations located at sites within each of the countries.[4] The proposed distances between adjacent stations range from fewer than 1000 km[5] to more than 2000 km.[6] The general areas in which the stations are to be sited would be selected on the basis of the seismicity of the surrounding regions, estimates of the propagation characteristics of the seismic waves, and proximity to other features that could be exploited for evasion (e.g., regions of dry porous material as well as regions in which salt or hard rock exist with properties such that cavities could be constructed and used to decouple the energy of the explosion from the surrounding earth). Within the general areas, specific sites would be selected to maximize the signal-to-noise ratios for seismic waves originating in areas of particular interest.

The instrumentation proposed for such sites ranges from relatively standard seismic stations[7] to state-of-the-art systems involving seismometers with high-frequency response (30+/−15 Hz) deployed in boreholes to reduce surface noise and/or arrays of more conventional seismometers.[8] The sites would cover areas ranging from less than 1 km^2 to several tens of square kilometres. The smaller sites would contain instruments installed in a single borehole and the associated equipment on the surface needed to power the station, digitize the data and transmit the digital data to remote data centres. The larger sites would be needed for small arrays of 15–30 seismometers together with a central facility for collecting and transmitting the data from the individual sensors.

Recent proposals to enhance the monitoring capabilities of the single-borehole sites by using high frequencies depend on exploiting potential improvements in signal-to-noise properties and discrimination between some explosions and some earthquakes at these frequencies.[9] The extent of the contribution of such high-frequency methods is currently being examined. They may be particularly useful to counter evasion schemes based on cavity decoupling (i.e., muffling the signal from an explosion by detonating it in a cavity).

The advantages of arrays are obtained by combining the data recorded by the individual sensors in various ways to form composite data streams with improved signal-to-noise characteristics for signals from specified directions. Achieving the improvement requires that the signals be coherent over the dimensions of the array and that the noise be incoherent, or have a different direction of approach, velocity or spectral content than the signal. Since arrays offer the promise of being able to identify the speed of the seismic waves and their direction of approach, the location of the source can be estimated and some properties of the source can be estimated by a single array. Finally, processing the array data may partition the signals from two sources that are close together in space and time. This feature is important when attempting to counter the evasion strategies that involve detonating a clandestine explosion immediately after a nearby earthquake or chemical explosion.

Future networks may contain both types of station. The mix that will be used will depend on the eventual determination of the relative performance of each type in specific environments and against specific evasion scenarios. Both technologies can be installed at a single site. The use of arrays of high-frequency sensors, as opposed to an array of conventional seismometers collocated with a high-frequency borehole element, is being examined. However, the basic information about signal and noise coherence at high frequencies needed to evaluate such an installation is currently incomplete.

Functions of an in-country monitoring system

The data acquisition and analysis elements of both external and in-country seismic systems must be capable of carrying out a number of specific functions if their performance is to be considered acceptable for monitoring a CTBT. The functions include: (a) detecting the seismic waves generated by militarily significant, clandestine nuclear explosions conducted by an intelligent evader; (b) associating the seismic waves recorded at multiple stations and the multiple seismic waves recorded at a single station with a common source located at a specific location; (c) recording and measuring those properties of the signal that can be used to characterize the strength and characteristics (e.g., pattern of energy radiation and frequency content) of the source: and (d) using the measured properties to discriminate between clandestine nuclear explosions and other events, for example, chemical explosions, rock-bursts and earthquakes.

The heterogeneity of the earth, the variability of the natural and man-made sources, and the ingenuity of the potential evader will introduce uncertainty into the monitor's ability to detect, locate and identify any given event. This uncertainty then becomes part of the monitor's compliance evaluation process. Evaluation techniques such as decision analysis are applicable to the process.[10] Similar uncertainties affect the potential evader's ability to carry out successful evasion. However, the evader's uncertainties are fewer than those of the monitor. The evader can calibrate the in-country monitoring system and systematically select operating conditions that favour evasion because the host country will know the present and past properties of the data from the in-country stations under a variety of conditions.

Even if an event is detected, the combination of the technical uncertainties and the decision criteria determined by the value judgements of the monitor may not allow the monitor to be highly confident that the event is not a clandestine nuclear explosion. In these cases, the information from the in-country system can be used to target other national technical means (e.g., satellites) and to help select locations for on-site inspections. Evidence from all means will be combined to form a final evaluation of the unidentified source.

Monitoring advantages of in-country stations

Networks of in-country stations offer some significant monitoring advantages because of the proximity of some of the stations to the sources. The stations at regional distances from a source (i.e., distances of less than 2000 km) record multiple seismic waves which, in general, have larger amplitudes and higher frequency content than the seismic waves from the same source recorded by stations at teleseismic distances (i.e., distances greater than 2000 km); see figure 11.1.

The multiplicity of waves results from the variety of paths that energy can follow as it travels in the earth's crust and upper mantle from the source to the monitoring stations. The energy recorded at the station as a particular seismic wave follows a path that left the source at a specific angle. If the individual waves recorded at regional stations can be identified, then, in effect, they provide different windows into the pattern of energy emitted by the source. These different views of the source offer the possibility of improved discrimination among source types. This is a topic of active research.[11]

The larger amplitudes and increased frequency content of the regional seismic waves reflect the reduced effect of attenuation and the presence of scattering over the shorter, shallower paths. The effects vary from path to path, and the causes of the variations on the observations are topics of current research. Also, because the noise tends to decrease with increasing frequency in the 1- to 50-Hz range, the signal-to-noise ratio could increase at high frequencies even if the high-frequency propagation is less efficient than claimed. The extent of the contribution of high-frequency waves to verification will also depend on the variability of the high-frequency content of the sources. This, too, is a topic of current research. However, when combined with external stations, even lower-frequency in-country seismic systems will provide improved detection and discrimination in all geologic environments.

III. CTB evasion techniques

In-country stations are valuable for monitoring a CTB because of their ability to counter specific evasion techniques, reduce the number of large unidentified events and deter evasion. Three evasion techniques have been extensively discussed in the literature: (a) simulating earthquake waveforms by detonating multiple explosions appropriately distributed in time and space; (b) hiding the signals from a clandestine explosion in the signals of an earthquake; and (c)

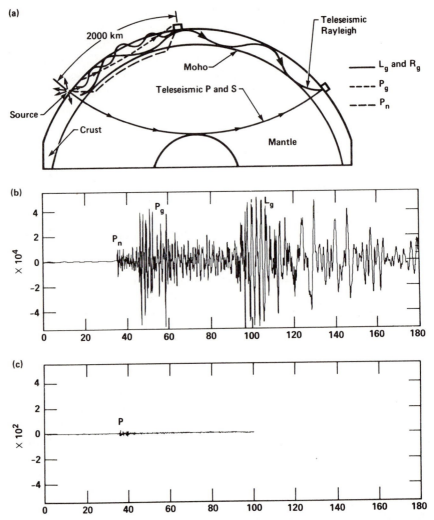

Figure 11.1. *Panel (a).* Regional seismic waves (recorded at distances of less than 2000 km) follow a variety of paths in the crust and mantle of the earth. They exhibit larger amplitudes and higher frequencies than teleseismic waves. *Panel (b).* A regional seismic record from a well-coupled nuclear explosion at the Nevada Test Site measured at Elko, Nevada (distance: 400 km). The multiple bursts of energy are each associated with a distinct path. In general, the earlier arrivals are associated with the deeper paths in the heterogeneous crust and upper mantle. *Panel (c).* A teleseismic record for the same event from a high-quality array station located in Norway (distance: 7935 km). Smaller amplitudes and fewer waves diminish the usefulness of such signals for small events.

reducing the signals from a clandestine explosion by detonating it in dry, porous material or in a cavity. In each case teleseismic stations are of limited benefit in detecting and/or identifying the clandestine explosions.[12]

The in-country systems are able to effectively counter the multiple explosion scenario by comparing the pattern of arrival times, relative amplitudes and frequency content of the multiple regional waves recorded by the network with the patterns expected from earthquakes in the same region. For example, the spatial and temporal distribuion of the explosions may be able to mimic the sequence and properties of waves from a shallow earthquake in some directions and at some distances but not others. The sampling of the wave field provided by the in-country network will detect these variations. Furthermore, the broader frequency range recorded by the in-country network provides a means to discriminate between the relatively uniform frequencies generated by the individual explosions representing specific waves and the characteristic frequencies of the waves they are intended to mimic.

These same properties of the network allow the in-country stations to effectively counter the hide-in-earthquake scenario. The differences between the relatively low-frequency content of a large teleseismic earthquake and the higher frequencies of an explosion, even at teleseismic distances, allow comparatively straightforward separation of the two signals by filtering the records. Figure 11.2 illustrates the separation which is possible using signals from an explosion which, by chance, were recorded during the arrival of signals from a distant earthquake.[13] Regional earthquakes and nearby explosions pose a more difficult problem both to the evader and to the monitor. The evader has to wait until an earthquake occurs near the explosion site and then determine the location and ultimate magnitude of the earthquake in a relatively short time. These time and location constraints are significantly reinforced by the proximity of the in-country stations. Including arrays in the network enhances the ability of even a single site to carry out the spatial resolution of two sources. These increased limitations on the allowable separation between the explosion and the earthquake restrict the opportunities to exploit large, but infrequent, earthquakes that could overwhelm the recording at key stations. If the waves from both sources are recorded (i.e., the earthquake does not saturate the recording system), then the use of frequencies above even 5–10 Hz will allow separation of the signals from the two sources. Improvements in earthquake prediction, earthquake triggering or the exploitation of earthquake swarms or aftershock sequences could make this scenario more attractive to the potential evader. However, the evader's logistical problems would still be great, and the in-country stations significantly increase the probability that the evasion will be detected.

In large measure, the in-country network necessary to acceptably monitor a CTBT is determined by the third evasion method—decoupling—in which the explosion is detonated in dry, porous material or in a large cavity, reducing the seismic signals transmitted into the earth. Figure 11.3 illustrates the reduction in seismic magnitude that occurs as a result of decoupling. It also shows the

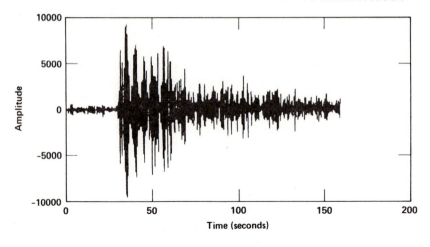

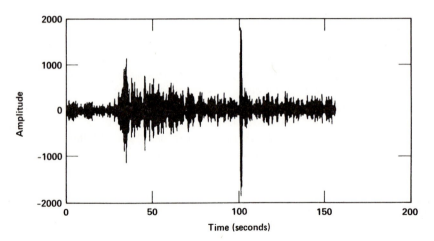

Figure 11.2. Differences in frequency content can be used to detect explosions in the coda of an earthquake

Panel (a) shows a Norwegian recording of the signal from an earthquake in Kamchatka together with the signal from an explosion at Semipalatinsk (see reference 13). The explosions signal at about t=100 s is not readily identified on this record (pass band 1.2–3.2 Hz). *Panel (b)* shows the same signal processed with a filter that emphasizes frequencies of 3.2–5.2 Hz. The signal from the explosion at about t=100 s is readily discernible.

detection performance of some representative monitoring networks with operating characteristics similar to those proposed by the CCD (see reference 4). The figure shows that a 1-kt, fully decoupled explosion is equivalent to a seismic event with a magnitude near 2, and that a similar explosion occurring in dry porous material would have a magnitude in the low threes. Although

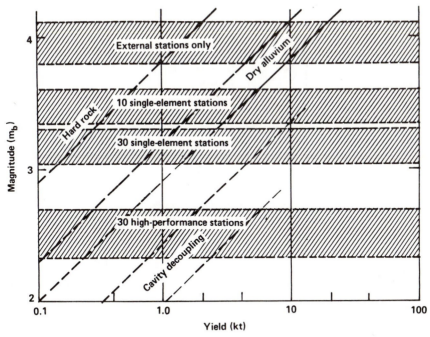

Figure 11.3. Magnitude–yield relationships from Nevada Test Site explosions and estimated detection thresholds for in-country networks deployed in the Soviet Union (90 per cent confidence of detecting four or more waves) are shown for representative media and networks, respectively

The broken lines indicate that, although explosions of less than 1–5 kt have been detonated in all three environments, the data on the precise magnitude–yield relationships are lacking or subject to significant uncertainty. Note that in areas that are older and more stable than the Nevada Test Site, the magnitudes of the same explosion could be several tenths of a unit higher. The predicted detection capabilities are based upon network performance characteristics similar to those proposed by the CCD (reference 4).

explosions with yields of less than 1–5 kt have been fired in all three underground coupling environments, the magnitude–yield relationships at these levels are uncertain. Thus, the curves are shown as dashed lines for yields of less than a few kilotons. Estimates of the detection capability of world-wide networks[14] indicate that decoupled explosions with such small magnitudes would, in effect, be invisible. Current analyses[15] estimate that, in order to monitor an area the size of the Soviet Union, at least 25–30 high-performance in-country stations are required to detect a 1-kt event decoupled in a cavity. These stations will achieve signal-to-noise characteristics that are better than those observed at conventional seismic stations by summing signals from multiple sensors and recording in different fequency ranges. Fewer stations could detect 1-kt explosions fired in dry, porous material (see figure 11.4).[16]

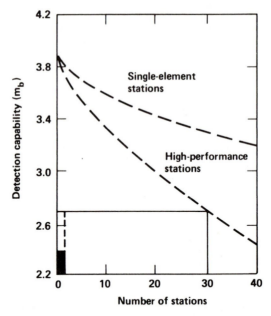

Figure 11.4. The estimated detection capability of an in-country network varies as a function of the number and type of stations deployed

The calculations shown require a 90 per cent probability of detecting four or more waves. The performance characteristics are based upon properties similar to those attributed to international networks (see CCD, reference 4). Significantly improved performance characteristics may be possible using improved operational techniques and the properties of carefully selected sites. Uncertainties of several tenths of a magnitude unit are possible because the signal and noise properties in the Soviet Union are unknown. The small box at the left shows the upper range of the estimate for a 1-kt explosion decoupled in a cavity. The broken line shows the values that might be observed in an older, more stable region. Note that approximately 30 high-performance stations (arrays or possibly high-frequency stations) appear to be required to detect 1 kt with high confidence.

The efficiency of the discrimination process at these low levels is a topic of current research.[17] If networks operating near their detection threshold are able to identify 96 per cent of the earthquakes recorded,[18] then, given the estimates of the number of shallow earthquakes in the Soviet Union each year as a function of magnitude,[19] the annual number of unidentified earthquakes at each magnitude level is as shown in table 11.2. Even given such optimistic discrimination performance, a network whose detection threshold approaches magnitude 2 could have as many as 100 or more unidentified earthquakes per year that could not be distinguished from explosions.

In addition, the many chemical explosions greater than 20 tons conducted each year will pose significant discrimination problems. Since at present they cannot be distinguished from nuclear explosions, they are potential sources of

Table 11.2. Approximate number of unidentified events per year from high-performance seismic systems monitoring the Soviet Union

Detection threshold m_b	No. of earthquakes in Soviet Union per year m_b	Approx. no. of unidentified earthquakes per year[a] m_b
4.0	100–300	0–10
3.5	270–800	10–30
3.0	700–2 000	20–60
2.5	1 800–5 300	60–200
2.0	4 600–14 000	100–400

[a] Assumes that 4 per cent of the earthquakes within 0.5 magnitude units of the detection threshold will not be identified.

false alarms as well as possible masks for clandestine nuclear explosions. It may be possible to address the compliance issues raised by chemical explosions greater than several hundred tons through inspection measures similar to those described in the unratified 1976 Peaceful Nuclear Explosions Treaty (PNET). However, the smaller explosions, whose seismic signals are similar to those from a 1-kt decoupled nuclear explosion, are too numerous to handle by such measures. Therefore, unless very efficient discrimination measures are found for such events, they will be a continuing source of concern as long as cavity decoupling is considered to be a viable evasion scheme.

IV. LYTTB evasion techniques

In-country networks will be needed for monitoring an LYTTB (which would allow nuclear explosions with yields less than the threshold at designated sites) if the threshold is low enough. The networks could perform three functions: (*a*) yield estimation for the explosions at the permitted sites, (*b*) monitoring for clandestine explosions conducted away from the permitted sites, and (*c*) acquisition of data which could be used to evaluate and develop monitoring capabilities for lower thresholds or a CTB. In the first function, the characterization of the size of the source provides the required monitoring function. In the second function, the monitoring functions are qualitatively similar to those proposed for a CTB. However, the monitoring requirements may be relaxed somewhat because evasion will almost certainly involve yields greater than those from detonations at the designated test sites. The third function establishes confidence that further reductions can be acceptably monitored. This may require that the monitoring measures installed at any given level be more stringent than the monitoring requirements necessary for that level.

Figure 11.3 shows that explosions with yields of about 5–10 kt detonated in hard rock and well-coupled to their surroundings will be detected with good signal-to-noise ratios by external networks. Assuming that validated magnitude–yield relationships have been determined for the site to be monitored through the use of calibration events, such external networks should be able to estimate the yields of such events with accuracies similar to but less than those achievable at higher yields. In-country stations could improve the accuracy of the yield estimates by providing an independent yield estimate which could be combined with teleseismic estimates to improve accuracy.

However, 5- to 10-kt explosions can also be detonated in dry, porous material or partially decoupled in cavities. If suitable on-site inspection measures were instituted, these situations could be identified so that the possibility of systematic errors could be reduced. Even if such situations were recognized, the signal-to-noise ratio for these partially decoupled events would be lowered, and the accuracy of the yield estimates made by external stations would be significantly degraded. In addition, the uncertainty would increase because of the increased variability in coupling that is possible in such media and because of the effects of variation in depth of burial and proximity to the water table on the waveforms currently used to estimate yields.

A network of in-country stations surrounding the test site would improve the accuracy of the yield estimates of partially decoupled events in the 5- to 10-kt range. Regional seismic waves such as Lg which propagate in the crust of the earth[20] (see figure 11.1) are the bases for the improvement. Such methods are still being researched and appear to depend somewhat on the properties of the source and receiver. The network would have to be calibrated by a series of explosions whose yields and source regions were validated. New explosions would have to be detonated near the calibration events, and on-site inspections would be necessary to ensure that the materials in the source region were similar for the calibration events and the new events whose yields are to be estimated. Even with such measures, the same increased uncertainties due to variations in depth of burial and material heterogeneity would exist.

For thresholds lower than a few kilotons, systematic uncertainties in both the teleseismic and the in-country measurements could result from these same factors. Given these uncertainties, it could be difficult to distinguish between explosions at the threshold and explosions three to four times larger with high confidence and a low false alarm rate. Thus, without strictly limiting the explosions to well-characterized, constrained environments and verifying that these conditions were met, even in-country stations may not provide sufficiently accurate yield estimates for LYTTBs with thresholds lower than a few kilotons. However, in-country stations deployed for yield estimation under such an LYTTB would gain experience for off-site monitoring in the vicinity of the test site that would be of limited value under a CTBT.

In-country stations will play an important role in detecting and identifying clandestine explosions conducted at locations other than the test sites permitted under an LYTTBT. Partial decoupling of explosions with yields of less than 10 kt could produce signals which would not be identified by an international external network.[21] Thus some in-country stations would be required to identify such explosions. For a 1-kt threshold, the in-country network required to prevent significant off-site testing would be nearly equivalent to that necessary to monitor a CTB.

The above discussion has not addressed the monitoring issues raised by permitting peaceful nuclear explosions in conjunction with an LYTTB. Almost every aspect of yield estimation is more difficult for such explosions because of a lack of calibration. It may be possible to employ yield estimation techniques using the speed of shock waves measured near the source,[22] but the accuracy of such techniques at low yields is uncertain. Such measures should be introduced at yields less than the threshold of the associated LYTTB. In-country systems could play a useful role in monitoring such explosions by providing a rough yield estimate. When combined with the deployment of a local seismic network as in the protocol of the PNE Treaty, they could also help to limit the opportunities for conducting simultaneous clandestine weapon tests at nearby locations.

V. What is acceptable verification?

To discuss the value of in-country seismic systems for the overall verification effort, one must consider the qualities required for acceptable verification. (Here, the adjective 'acceptable' is used rather than the more common qualifiers 'adequate' and 'effective'[23] to emphasize the role that value judgements play in an evaluation process whose fundamental measurements are subject to uncertainty.) Three qualities have been mentioned, either explicitly or implicitly, for evaluating verification:[24] (*a*) militarily significant violations must be recognized in time to mount an appropriate response; (*b*) the false alarm rate must be low enough to maintain the monitor's confidence and not degrade the potential evader's incentive to comply; and (*c*) the system's capability, when combined with the evader's perceptions of the costs of being caught versus the benefits of successful clandestine testing, should deter evasion attempts.

Translating these elements into operational measures of success requires a combination of military, technical and political judgements. From a practical viewpoint, one of the most important judgements in many current discussions is the definition of a militarily significant violation. Forming this judgement involves estimating the immediate and long-term impacts of a test ban and of the potential asymmetry introduced by evasion on such diverse but interrelated elements as stockpile reliability, preservation of infrastructure, ability to respond to developments in the non-nuclear capabilities of the weapon systems, survivability and safety. These impacts must be identified by the military community and evaluated by the decision makers in the broader context of both relative and absolute national security.

In order to evaluate deterrence, the value system of the potential evader must be estimated. The potential evader presumably attaches some cost to an unsuccessful attempt at evasion and some benefit to a successful one. These and related values (e.g., that attached to acknowledged compliance and to compliance in the presence of false alarms) may vary with time. Given such estimates of value and assessments of the efficiency of the monitoring systems, expected costs and benefits can be determined and deterrence can be estimated. Informal evaluations of this type have been invoked to argue, for example, that a 30 per cent probability of being caught is sufficient to deter evasion attempts.[25] Such judgements have significant impacts on the acceptability of a given in-country monitoring system.

Many other factors affect the acceptability of an in-country monitoring system. Intrusiveness, cost and negotiability are also factors that have to be considered from both the monitor's and the potential evader's viewpoints. The whole evaluation must take place in the context of the decision makers' views of national security and the threat posed by the nation to be monitored.

Techniques such as decision analysis allow a structured approach to decision making in complex situations which involve both uncertainties in the technical measures and a variety of value judgements. This approach has been applied in the USA at the Lawrence Livermore National Laboratory to CTBT verification,[26] and preliminary results have been obtained for a number of cases. For example, figure 11.5 compares the relative value of using external monitoring, a network of 10 relatively standard in-country stations and a network of 30 high-performance in-country installations for a case in which cavity decoupling is a viable evasion method and a case in which it is not. The difference in the relative values of the network of high-performance stations *vis-à-vis* the

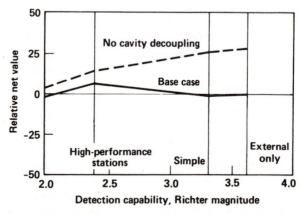

Figure 11.5. The value of different networks depends on the evasion threat

The base case corresponds to 30 high-performance in-country stations or 10 simple stations or external stations operating in an environment where decoupling is feasible. In this case, the 30 high-performance stations have the highest net value. If one assumes that decoupling is not feasible, the NTM system is the most attractive because it can detect all the militarily significant tests at no extra cost. Many assumptions are made in these estimates. The impact of these assumptions can be examined using the decision-analysis framework.

network of simple stations between the two cases is the result of a choice of values that penalizes the high-performance stations for unnecessarily detecting small events (many of which remain unidentified) if cavity decoupling is not a viable option. This figure represents the results of a number of estimates of technical performance and of value judgements. The decision-analysis framework treats these as input values that can be chosen by the decision maker. As such, the framework allows parameter studies that identify critical elements in the decision process, and allows the structured comparison of the implications of different value systems. A similar structured analysis of the issues associated with LYTTBs has been initiated at the Lawrence Livermore National Laboratory.

VI. Conclusions

In-country seismic monitoring systems are composed of data acquisition and data processing hardware as well as procedures to select sites, calibrate the performance of the system in a new environment, operate the system, and report the results in a form useful to the decision makers.

The value of these systems for monitoring a CTB is derived from their ability to counter evasion scenarios such as those using multiple explosions to mimic the signals from an earthquake, hiding the signals from a clandestine explosion in the signals from an earthquake or a chemical explosion, and reducing the signals from an explosion by detonating it in dry, porous media or in a cavity. The decoupling evasion methods pose the greatest challenge, forcing the monitoring system to detect and identify events down to magnitudes of near 2. The presence of high-performance in-country stations (small arrays and/or single high-frequency sensors) allows the recording of multiple seismic waves with relatively large amplitudes and high frequencies. In addition, the distribution of the in-country stations allows the wavefield to be sampled at a variety of distances and directions. The interlocking information provided by these observations allows multiple assessments of the source properties. These multiple assessments provide the basis for identifying differences between the evasion attempts and other seismic sources.

Even with networks consisting of 25–30 such high-performance stations, some events whose signals are equivalent to a 1-kt nuclear explosion detonated in a cavity will not be detected. Evasion attempts that are detected may not be identified against a background of thousands of small earthquakes. Unidentified earthquakes, of which there could be 100 or more, will give rise to false alarms. Chemical explosions will pose severe discrimination problems.

Monitoring an LYTTB requires that the yields of explosions at permitted test sites be estimated with high accuracy, and that clandestine explosions executed away from these sites be detected and identified. Fulfilling this latter requirement for thresholds lower than a few kilotons is made difficult by the background of earthquakes and chemical explosions in which the signals from the clandestine event would reside. For LYTTBs with thresholds near 1 kt, the off-site monitoring requirements would be similar to those needed to monitor a CTB.

Yield estimates from calibrated in-country stations, when combined with calibrated teleseismic yield estimates, should improve accuracy for yield estimates in the 5- to 10-kt range. However, systematic variations in the seismic signals can be introduced by variations in depth and emplacement material. The accuracy of the combined estimates will decrease for LYTTBs with thresholds lower than 5–10 kt without extensive calibration, limitations on the testing environments supported by on-site inspections, and the validation of new techniques using regional seismic waves such as Lg.

The presence of uncertainty in the monitoring capability raises the question of what constitutes acceptable verification. Ultimately this is a value judgement which encompasses a wide range of factors, including the military significance of successful evasion, the impact of false alarms, the potential evader's value system and many other factors covering a wide range of military, political and economic issues. The technical results—with their attendant uncertainties—and the value systems of the decision makers—with their differing priorities—can be combined using techniques such as decision analysis. The structuring produced by the use of such techniques allows the identification of important elements in the compliance evaluation process and the evaluation of the effects of differing or changing viewpoints. Such techniques have been applied to analyse the value of in-country systems to CTB monitoring.

Notes and references

[1] Report of the Geneva Conference of Experts (1 July–21 Aug. 1958) in *Geneva Conference of the Discontinuance of Nuclear Weapons Tests, History and Analysis of Negotiations*, US Department of State Publication 7258, *Disarmament Series* 4, 1961, pp. 15–18; Hannon, W. J., 'Seismic verification of a comprehensive test ban', *Science*, vol. 227 (Jan. 1985), pp. 251–57; Evernden, J. F., Archambeau, C. B. and Cranswick, E., 'An evaluation of seismic decoupling and underground nuclear test monitoring using high-frequency seismic data', *Reviews of Geophysics*, vol. 24, no. 2 (May 1986), pp. 143–215.

[2] Kidder, R. E., 'Militarily significant nuclear explosive yields', F.A.S. Public Interest Report, *Journal of the Federation of American Scientists*, vol. 38, no. 7 (Sep. 1985), pp. 1–3; Brown, H., *Thinking About National Security* (Westview Press: Boulder, 1983), p. 191; Scowcroft, B., Deutch, J. M. and Woolsey, J. R., 'Nukes: continue the tests', *Washington Post*, 29 June 1986, p. C7; Sykes, L. and Evernden, J., 'The verification of a comprehensive nuclear test ban', *Scientific American*, vol. 247, no. 4 (Oct. 1982), pp. 47–55.

[3] Younker, L., Hannon, J., Springer, D., Al-Ayat, R., Judd, B., Morris, P. and Sandling, J., 'Evaluation framework for comprehensive test ban treaty seismic verification systems', Lawrence Livermore National Laboratory, Livermore, CA, Rept. UCID–20423, Apr. 1985.

[4] Conference of the Committee on Disarmament, 'Report to the Conference of the Committee on Disarmament of the ad hoc group of scientific experts to consider international co-operative measures to detect and to identify seismic events', CCD/558, Mar. 1958, Appendix II; Hannon and Evernden (note 1).

[5] Hannon and Evernden (note 1).

[6] CCD (note 4).

[7] Sykes (note 2) and CCD (note 4).

[8] Hannon and Evernden (note 1).

[9] Hannon and Evernden (note 1).

[10] Younker *et al.* (note 3).

[11] McLaughlin, K. L., 'Evaluation of small events using the Pearce focal plane algorithm',

Teledyne Geotech Alexandria Laboratories, Alexandria, VA, Rept. no. TGAL 85–11a, Nov. 1985, pp. 1–7.

[12] Evernden, J. F., 'Study of seismological evasion. Part I. General discussion of various evasion schemes', *Bulletin of the Seismological Society of America*, vol. 66, no. 1 (Feb. 1976), pp. 245–80; and 'Part II. Evaluation of evasion possibilities using microseismic noise', pp. 281–324.

[13] Ringdal, F., 'Teleseismic detection at high frequencies using NORSAR data', NORSAR Royal Norwegian Council for Scientific and Industrial Research, Kjeller, Norway, Scientific Rept. 1/84–85, Nov. 1984, pp. 54–62.

[14] CCD (note 4).

[15] Hannon and Evernden (note 1).

[16] Hannon (note 1). Note that such material is not believed to be very widespread in the USSR, although knowledge of Soviet geology is limited outside of the USSR.

[17] Taylor, S. R., Denny, M. D. and Vergino, E. S., 'Regional M_b:M_s discrimination of NTS explosions and Western United States earthquakes: A progress report', Lawrence Livermore National Laboratory, Livermore, CA, Rept. UCID–20642, Jan. 1986; Pomeroy, P. W., Best, W. J. and McEvilly, T. V., 'Test ban verification with regional data—a review', *Bulletin of the Seismological Society of America*, vol. 72, no. 6B (Dec. 1982), pp. S89–S130.

[18] Taylor (note 17).

[19] Gorbunova, I. V., 'Strong earthquakes on USSR territory', in *Earthquakes in the USSR in 1973*, eds I. V. Gorbunova, N. V. Kondorskaya and N. V. Shebalin (Nauka: Moscow, 1983), pp. 4–17.

[20] Nuttli, O., 'Yield estimates of Nevada Test Site explosions obtained from seismic Lg', *Journal of Geophysical Research*, vol. 91, no. B2 (Feb. 1986), pp. 2137–51.

[21] CCD (note 4).

[22] Heusinkveld, M., 'Analysis of shock wave arrival time from underground explosions', *Journal of Geophysical Research*, vol. 87, no. B3 (Mar. 1982), pp. 1891–98.

[23] Scribner, R. A., Ralston, T. J. and Metz, W. D., *The Verification Challenge* (Birkhauser: Boston, 1985), p. 19.

[24] Martin, J. J., 'Remarks on a review of current progress and problems in seismic verification', *Progress and Problems in Seismic Verification Research*, Defense Advanced Research Projects Agency: Arlington, VA, Rept. T10 73–3, 1973, p. 24; Brown, H., 'Statement by Secretary of Defense Brown to the Senate Committee on Foreign Relations: Verification of the Salt II Treaty, July 18, 1979', in *Documents on Disarmament, 1979* (United States Arms Control and Disarmament Agency: Washington, DC, 1982), pp. 439–88.

[25] Sykes (note 2).

[26] Younker *et al.* (note 3); Strait, R. S. and Sicherman, A., 'Comprehensive test ban treaty seismic verification decision analysis computer model, vol. I & II', Lawrence Livermore National Laboratory, Livermore, CA, Rept. UCID–20704, Mar. 1986; Judd, B. R. and Younker, L. W., 'Decision analysis: evaluating verification options', *Energy and Technology Review*, Lawrence Livermore National Laboratory, Livermore, CA, Rept. UCRL–5200–86–8, Aug. 1986.

Chapter X. Techniques to evade detection of nuclear tests

Paper 12

Jeremy K. Leggett

Royal School of Mines, Imperial College of Science and Technology, London, UK

Abstract

Cavity decoupling in salt deposits would offer a comprehensive test ban treaty or low-yield threshold test ban treaty signatory-state contemplating evasion the most favourable chance of escaping discovery by a verifier state. However, provided certain intrusive monitoring conditions had been negotiated by the verifier at the time the treaty was drawn up, the potential evader could be made to face a daunting seismological gauntlet. He would also face operational, geological and geographical constraints which have often been underplayed in the debate over CTBT verifiability in the past. Assessing the sum of both seismological and non-seismological constraints, parties to a LYTTB with a limit of 1 kt could deter all potential evasion strategies. Were a state to contemplate evasion under a CTBT, there would be a chance of success below about 1 kt, but—given adequate intrusive verification measures—not a guarantee. Current testing practices reveal limited military significance in testing at such low levels. Confidence-building measures are available which could build confidence in the long-term viability of a CTBT or LYTTBT during the early years of its tenure.

I. Introduction

Scientists agree that there must be a size of nuclear blast below which detection and identification would be unlikely without stringently intrusive verification measures. This size varies in published opinion from several tens of kilotons[1] to below 1 kt.[2] Accordingly, a commonly accepted definition of adequate verification—and the one used in this paper—is as follows: 'that which would reduce to an acceptable level the risk that clandestine test programmes of military significance could be conducted'.[3] In this approach, then, there are three critical parameters which would need to be quantified by a government before it decides whether or not to sign a comprehensive test ban treaty (CTBT) or a low-yield threshold test ban treaty (LYTTBT): (*a*) the 'acceptable level' of risk, (*b*), the level of 'military significance', and (*c*) the extent of technical surveillance necessary to guarantee meeting the particular definition of 'adequate verification' which results.

Accordingly, definitions are needed in any analysis of the feasibility of evasion. Following the principle adopted in past CTB negotiations, this paper takes the 'acceptable level' of certainty as being something less than 100 per cent. A series of tests is needed to develop a new warhead. If the principal aim of a CTBT or LYTTBT is to prevent the development of new warheads, then the 'acceptable level' of certainty can be well under 100 per cent. If the principal aim is to stop the development of new generations of strategic warheads, specifically, then current testing practices show that the level of 'military significance' is in excess of 5–10 kt.[4] In this analysis, the term 'militarily significant' is used to describe tests with yields in excess of 1–2 kt.

Clearly, the debate over verifiability of a CTBT or an LYTTBT must draw on a wide range of scientific, technological, political and military disciplines. This analysis emphasizes those general aspects of geoscience which apply to the evasion strategy most commonly proposed as the main threat to the verifier state: cavity decoupling.

II. Evasion by cavity decoupling

For more than a quarter of a century the possibility that nuclear explosions could be conducted in an underground chamber, so as to dampen the shock waves produced, has dominated the debate over verifiability of a CTB and impeded progress towards a test ban. At the pessimistic end of opinion, scientists in the British Ministry of Defence venture that 'it is . . . not possible to estimate precisely how large an explosion could be effectively decoupled, but the decoupling of several tens of kilotons cannot be ruled out'.[5] At the optimistic end, scientists daunted by the problems posed in constructing a cavity big enough, stable enough, deep enough, quiet enough—and secret enough—have argued that the strategy is untenable. Dr J. C. Mark has gone so far as to venture that 'it could be that the big hole was originally designed for the purpose of containing the CTB, and that may well end up being its only use'.[6]

A specialist symposium, attended by weapon laboratory and independent academic scientists, was convened by the Lawrence Livermore National Laboratory (LLNL) for the US Department of Energy (DOE) in July 1985 to consider the problem.[7] The proceedings of that meeting offer the latest views of both optimists and pessimists. The editor, LLNL scientist Dr D. Larson, offered the following assessment in his introduction: 'seismologists in general agree that a well coupled explosion in hard rock of 0.1 kt or greater could be reliably detected with a monitoring network of 15 array stations located within the borders of the testing nation and an unlimited number outside these borders. But on the same basis a device of 5 to 10 kt could be detonated in a large hard rock cavity and avoid detection, assuming cavity decoupling factors of 50–100'. The Director of LLNL, Dr R. Batzel, was asked in a congressional hearing what level the Soviet Union could hope to cheat at, assuming that there were *no* foreign or international seismic stations inside its territory. He replied: 'with cavity decoupling, the Soviets could test up to 10 kt with low probability of detection. . . . However, it is important to note that it would be an extremely difficult engineering feat to construct cavities large enough to decouple explosives much larger than 10 kt'.[8]

Theory and practice

In 1961, Latter *et al.* published theoretical calculations indicating that detonation of a bomb in a suitable cavity could make a yield of more than 300 kt give a seismic signal of magnitude apparently equivalent to 1 kt.[9] Their calculations were based on simple elasticity theory, plus ground particle-motion results obtained from a 1.7-kt blast in solid rock. They called for a programme of experimentation to check that their results were viable in nature.

When a bomb is detonated in hard rock, the immediately surrounding medium will behave in an inelastic fashion; that is, it will flow plastically, crack and deform in a non-linear way. The distance over which this happens depends on the yield and the strength of the medium: as the stresses imposed by the propagating shock decay to a certain 'critical stress' level—which will depend on the medium characteristics and the depth—elastic propagation will begin. This is the normal situation when a nuclear test takes place. Such an explosion is termed 'tamped' or 'coupled'. The zone of inelastic behaviour around the blast ensures that seismic energy is propagated as high-amplitude waves, away from the source.

However, if the bomb is placed in a cavern just large enough for the critical stress to occur on the walls, the rock medium around the source will behave only in an elastic fashion. Much less seismic energy will be transmitted, in much-lower-amplitude waves. Such an explosion is referred to as 'fully decoupled'. If the cavity is not big enough for this effect, the walls will respond inelastically. However, the radius of the zone of inelastic behaviour will none the less be reduced, and such an explosion is termed 'partially decoupled'. The degree of dampening created is known as the 'decoupling factor'.

The size of hole necessary for full decoupling is, according to Latter and his colleagues, generally defined as follows:
$$V = 3 \times 10^5 W_{kt}/p_{kb} \text{ ft}$$
where W_{kt} is the yield in kilotons and p_{kb} is the maximum permissible pressure, in kilobars, exerted on the cavity walls. The pressure must be limited if inelastic effects—both plasticity and cracking—are to be avoided. Cracking would provide a severe limiting factor because most rocks possess zero strength in tension. Latter *et al.* assumed that this requirement would be met, provided that the explosion pressure did not greatly exceed the overburden pressure (i.e., the outward push of the blast versus the downward push of the overlying rocks).

Assuming that an average explosion pressure of 150 atmospheres could be contained, they calculated that a cavity 180 feet (55 m) in diameter would be needed to fully decouple a 1.7-kt blast. Extrapolating from these equations, full decoupling of a 10-kt explosion would require a cavity about 225 feet (69 m) in diameter.[10]

There were other conditions which added uncertainty to the applicability of the theory in nature. First, their calculations had been based on an assumed spherical cavity, and Latter *et al.* conceded that '. . . it may be necessary for practical reasons, to use a nonspherical hole . . .'. (They were presumably referring to mining engineering difficulties.) They made it clear that more work would be needed on the theory if that were the case, although they suggested that a major-to-minor radius ratio of 3 or 4 would be acceptable, and that in certain conditions a nonspherical hole might reduce the distant seismic signal still further. Second, they were unsure of the effect of the pressure pulse caused by the nuclear explosion. Even if over-decoupled in a spherical hole 260 feet (79 m) in diameter, a 1.7-kt explosion will exert a pressure pulse of around 1 kt for a few milliseconds. This might cause inelasticity. To overcome this, Latter *et al.* argued that partially evacuating the cavity, or partially replacing the air within by hydrogen, would be necessary. This, they suggested, would have the requisite effect of reducing or eliminating the pressure spike. However, it would have a side-effect which would further complicate the operation: exacerbation of vaporization pressure, caused by hot gas, to levels where recoil shock magnitude was appreciable. To dampen this, additional material, such as foil, would have to be introduced to the hole to soak up energy and lower the temperature.

A limited number of experimental studies have been carried out since the cavity decoupling scheme was first outlined. These studies, and further theoretical studies which have in the interim been published, are treated in chronological order.

In January 1959 two sets of experiments with chemical explosives demonstrated cavity decoupling. The first project, code-named Orpheus, used complex arrays of small chemical explosive to simulate a step pressure on the walls of a cavity. Decoupling factors of only 10–30 were reported for the early results.[11] Two days later, eight high-explosive (HE) shots (up to 2000 lbs or 900 kg) were fired in two cavities (12- and 30-foot, or 4- and 9-m diameters) in a Louisiana salt mine during project COWBOY. Nine tamped shots were carried out for comparison. A decoupling factor of up to 100 (for 450 kg in the 9-m cavity) was obtained.[12]

In the published accounts of both projects, the uncertainties involved in comparing HE results to nuclear explosions thousands of times more powerful were emphasized. (Nuclear explosions have a lower mass-to-yield ratio, and do not produce as large a spike as chemical explosions do. Moreover, their very high temperatures involve changes in the ratio of the specific heats of air—a significant parameter in the original calculations of Latter *et al.*) None the less, Herbst *et al.*[13] believed that the COWBOY results would scale to a decoupling value of 300 for a Rainier-type nuclear explosion (1.7 kt detonated in tuff), as predicted by Latter *et al.*, and Marshall believed that later experiments in the Orpheus project indicated that, if pressure on the cavity wall had been kept to a value less than the lithostatic pressure, the nuclear-equivalent factor would have been between 120 and 150.[14]

Murphey[15] deployed velocity gauges around the COWBOY source to determine particle velocity versus time on the cavity wall. In their original calculations, Latter *et al.* assumed that the energy of a blast is distributed uniformly over the cavity volume when giving its step-function pressure on the wall. Murphey, pointing out that this was an oversimplification since short-duration pressure pulses would occur, stressed the need for measuring close-in particle motion. He was only partially successful in his attempt to do this, observing that adequate measure of motion near the cavities was difficult to obtain at the low levels of HE charges used in the COWBOY project. He did not feel able to scale his limited data to very large chemical explosions, much less to nuclear explosions, concluding that, 'experimental proof of the degree of decoupling that could be obtained from nuclear explosions can be obtained only from nuclear explosions'.[16]

Further relevant calculations were published by Patterson[17] in 1966. In the interim, two nuclear explosions had been detonated in salt domes: the 5-kt SALMON event at 823 m depth in Mississippi during October 1964, and the 3.1-kt GNOME event at 1200 ft (360 m) depth in New Mexico during 1961. SALMON created a cavity roughly 112 ft (34 m) in diameter (20 000 m^3 volume), and GNOME a chamber 160–170 ft (48 m) wide by 60–80 ft (18–24 m) deep. Patterson used the Latter equations, modified to include the effect of the first reflected shock on the cavity wall, to calculate seismic displacement potentials for decoupled sources. He then compared them with the measured close-in displacement potentials for SALMON and GNOME. He obtained close-in decoupling ratios (for salt) of 200 and 350, respectively. His assumptions included spherical symmetry, and a static pressure inside the cavity equal to one-half the overburden.

The first and only known test of decoupling using a nuclear explosive source was the STERLING explosion, on 3 December 1966, in the cavity created by SALMON. The plan initially was to try to decouple a 5-kt blast, but the SALMON cavity proved to be too small. (The two explosions were part of Project Dribble, in which the detonation of two 100-ton sources had also been planned. These had to be postponed indefinitely because of 'technical difficulties in drill-hole construction'.[18]) The principal objectives were to determine to what extent a cavity shot in salt would be decoupled as a function of frequency, to compare theory with experiment, and to determine the feasibility of re-using a cavity produced by a nuclear detonation.

Average decoupling for STERLING data compared with SALMON data was about 70 for 1–3 Hz energy, and lower at higher frequencies. Calculations suggested that at least in part the lower-than-expected result was a product of inelastic response caused by weakening of the cavity walls during the

SALMON blast,[19] but the results clearly showed that the natural world was more complex than the theoretical.

The high-frequency drop-off in the decoupling factor was in broad accord with a theoretical model for an explosion source published by Sharpe in 1942.[20] Much is made of this phenomenon in the field of forensic seismology—a point which is dealt with in a later section.

In the 1970s there was a noticeable hiatus in experimental attempts to verify the theoretical basis for cavity decoupling. Considering the strategic import- ance of the issue, this is from all standpoints regrettable. High cost, the political problems associated with exploding nuclear bombs in civilian areas, and the lack of salt deposits at the Nevada Test Site (NTS) may be responsible.

Attention has recently focused on the two facets of the theory which Latter *et al.* left as areas of particular uncertainty: the shape of the cavity, and the exact effects of the pressure pulse. Glenn[21] has presented theoretical calculations of the effect of non-spherical cavities whose walls are not uniformly loaded by the explosive source. Though shear waves will be generated as a result of this asymmetry, he did not find that cavity shape alone (i.e., without release of tectonic stress) could make an explosion look like an earthquake.[22] However, he proposed that amplitude, frequency content and azimuthal pattern of the seismic energy radiated 'may be highly modified, to make detection or discrimination difficult in particular directions and in particular cases', with the important proviso that 'it must be pointed out that the cavity size necessary for maintaining the walls in an elastic range for a source energy of several kilotons may be so large that the span of the upper surface of the spherical cavity may be unstable from an engineering point of view'.[23]

In the DOE symposium proceedings, Martinelli provides a review of 'enhanced' decoupling experiments, in which—as originally proposed by Latter and his colleagues—heat sink materials such as graphite were used as a means of absorbing energy so as to augment the decoupling effect. Theoretical considerations had given rise to the prediction that a cubic metre of graphite coke or similar material would provide as much decoupling as 20 m^3 of air-filled space. But when this was tried in practice, in an experiment at NTS code- named Diamond Mine, the results showed decoupling at a factor of two less than expected, leading the editor of the symposium volume to conclude that 'the results were marginal and advances in techniques of fully absorbing the energy are needed to make enhanced decoupling useful'.[24]

In conclusion, empirical observations indicate that—from the point of view of physics alone—the cavity decoupling evasion strategy poses less of a problem than was believed to be the case in 1961. First, the maximum factor by which the low-frequency seismic signal has been reduced by cavity decoupling is about three times less than that which was initially believed possible: a decoupling factor of 60–70 as opposed to 200.[25] Second, observation indicates that seismic decoupling at high frequencies is about 20 times less efficient than at low frequencies, and theory predicts that at the highest recordable frequencies the decoupling factor can be reduced to as little as 3.[26]

The gathering of experts at the DOE symposium apparently reached no clear consensus on the threat posed by cavity decoupling. The DOE representative stated at the outset of the symposium that the objective was to 'develop a consensus of experiments and studies necessary to provide a confident under-standing of the relevant phenomena related to cavity decoupling'. J. Horgan, who in April 1986 wrote the most detailed publicly available account yet of activities at the NTS, volunteered that the Defense Nuclear Agency had sponsored a series of cavity shots within hemispherical chambers 30 to 60 ft (9–18 m) in diameter, and that 'far bigger shots may be in the works, for testing more than just ground shock'.[27] Should results from these tests be published, they will undoubtedly help discussion, for empirical data are clearly too few where cavity decoupling is concerned.

Feasibility

Large cavities can and have been constructed deep underground, and in some areas occur naturally. Cavities have been built in both crystalline rocks (igneous intrusives and metamorphic rocks) and in sedimentary rocks, particu-larly salt.

Natural caverns

The US Geological Survey's Branch of Military Geology has conducted a survey of opportunities for cavern utilization in the Soviet Union. J. Rachlin, a geologist involved in this work, reported at the DOE symposium that large caves are of limited suitability because they are generally shallow (150 m), have very irregular shapes, and contain underground streams and lakes.[28]

Crystalline rocks

Rachlin argues that caverns suitable for cavity decoupling can in theory be constructed in granite, though with difficulty. He presents a map showing outcrops of granite and other crystalline igneous and metamorphic rocks, covering 5–10 per cent of the total surface area of the Soviet Union.

Three questions arise: (a) Could a cavern large enough and stable enough for a militarily significant blast be built? (b) Could it be re-used? and (c) Could the engineering works involved in its construction be screened, or disguised, from arousing suspicion if they came to the attention of photoreconnaissance satellites?

Note that the cost of a 90-m diameter hemisphere for the NTS in 1978 was about $50 million. At today's prices, a full cavern would cost considerably more. At such prices, the potential evader would clearly have to weigh the economics of a clandestine testing programme against the likely military benefits—especially if one accepts the analysis that a series of tests is needed to develop a new warhead.

Were a reusable facility to be feasible, this question may not arise. However, consulting engineers who have studied the problem stress that, for this to be the case, rock reinforcement would be necessary: galleries would have to be installed and grouted annular tendons deployed from them.[29] Even then, the uncertainties involved in the response of the cavern to nuclear explosions would be appreciable. The evader would be uncertain not only of his decoupling factor, but also of the risk of cavity collapse and cratering. He would be mindful of the Midas Myth test in Nevada, which cratered unexpectedly and disastrously above a tiny collapsed cavern at a depth of 1400 ft (427 m).[30]

Surveillance by satellites would be an additional unknown factor. Large engineering works would have to be in place for a period of many months. L. Sykes has pointed out that, in crystalline rock, a volume of material the size of the largest Egyptian pyramid would have to moved to excavate a cavern large enough to fully decouple an 8-kt blast.[31] Others have argued that spoil, and construction work, could be hidden in existing mining complexes, or linked to new construction projects (e.g., hydroelectric schemes) as part of which large underground chambers were being excavated. However, simple geological considerations indicate that conditions associated with mineralization—especially patterns of faulting—imply a country rock state unsuitable for construction of cavities up to 50 m or more in diameter.

Reviewing the mining methods typically available, and the associated conditions of support, the consulting engineers at the LLNL–DOE symposium concluded that the use of mines in crystalline rock is largely precluded as a means for forming large cavities.[32] Large construction schemes not in areas of mineralization and/or faulting could be targeted for particularly close surveillance by photoreconnaissance satellites.

These arguments, combined, make even the pessimists in the debate over CTB/LYTTBT verifiability doubtful of the potential for clandestine testing in crystalline rock.

Sedimentary rock

Researchers in the CTB verifiability debate have unanimously concluded that it is salt which poses the most serious threat to the verifier fearful of duplicity, and the most favourable—or least unfavourable—prospect for a potential evader. However, large underground excavations are routinely carried out in strata other than salt, for example, in the course of hydroelectric schemes.

In considering the suitability of such media for constructing chambers large enough and stable enough in which to explode nuclear bombs, practitioners in the verifiability debate seem to have been largely persuaded that the likelihood of this being feasible at test levels of likely military significance is extremely low. A number of factors, such as the general heterogeneities associated with bedding, the generally poor consolidation of younger strata, and the jointed nature of older strata, conspire to offer manifold uncertainties for decoupling in sedimentary rocks such as conglomerate, sandstone and shale.

Despite the emphasis on salt in the literature, however, verifiers under a CTB or LYTTB would not be able completely to disregard the relatively undeformed sedimentary basins in a potential evader-state during the course of their surveillance effort.

Salt deposits

Salt is a sedimentary rock formed in ancient seas by the evaporation of seawater. This process is taking place today in the Red Sea and the Dead Sea. Where it took place in the past, salt is preserved in the strata in two modes: in bedded deposits, intercalated with other evaporitic strata and normal sedimentary rocks, or as structures which geologists term 'salt domes'. Being less dense than normal rock, salt is capable of forming itself into mobile bodies— sometimes miles across—capable of forcing their way up towards the surface through other strata. The growth of these salt domes, or diapirs, takes place at rates which would normally be unobservable during a human lifespan. In some areas salt domes have broken the surface as hills of solid salt. Salt domes arise from particularly thick beds of salt at depth, which have been rendered gravitationally unstable by the buildup of thick overburden.

Salt has long been mined as feedstock and for the chemical industry. Since the 1920s salt cavities have been used for the underground storage of liquids, and since the mid-1960s they have been used for compressed natural gas.[33] Salt can be mined both conventionally and by solution methods. The US Strategic Petroleum Reserve Program has involved the solution mining of caverns with a storage capacity of 10 million barrels, or 1.6 million m^3.[34] Soviet publications show that, in the USSR, solution mining has produced caverns 10–100 m in diameter and 20 000–1 million m^3 in volume.[35] Examples of well-studied storage caverns in Europe are the shallow (358 m) facility run by British Gas at Billingham, the deeper (1800 m) facility at Hornsea[36] and deeper facilities in France at Manosque (1600 m, and 70–80 m in diameter)[37] and Tersanne (1400 m).[38]

Nuclear explosions can also be used to make caverns in salt. The SALMON and GNOME events in the USA are discussed above. The Soviet Union has employed nuclear explosions to make storage caverns of up to about 50 000 m^3 near gas condensate fields, at Orenburg on the Ural River and Astrakhan on the Caspian Sea. These blasts, of which there have been 10 since 1971, generated body waves of magnitude 5.2–5.6 (according to records from seismic observatories in Sweden, Britain and the United States), indicating yields of around 15 kt. Information subsequently released by the USSR shows that the detonations took place in bedded salt at depths of more than 1 km.[39] The Soviet Union has made use of underground nuclear explosions for a variety of industry-related purposes and has in the past conducted numerous nuclear explosions in areas away from the normal nuclear weapon test sites. I. Borg reports that 30–40 cavities may have been created by explosions in an area of particularly common salt domes north of the Caspian Sea.[40]

Much interest has focused on cavities in salt because of the potential for storage of high-level nuclear waste. Although no such storage facilities have been utilized, it is clear that much of the available research data has been generated as a result of the drive to assess the feasibility of such storage. Particularly valuable information is to be found in the volumes produced after various international symposia on salt organized by the Salt Institute.[41]

Despite intensive research, it is clear that many of the parameters bearing on the stability of caverns in salt are still only imperfectly understood.[42] French engineers have commented, for example, that 'it is often still impossible to know the value of all parameters which have an influence on the stability of an underground structure'.[43] Characteristics of a particular salt deposit which need to be taken into account during mining are the impurities present in the sediment, its water and gas content, its state of in-situ stress, its corrosive properties in contact with steel and concrete, and its mechanical properties. Salt is a weak rock, and its capacity to flow is almost without parallel in rock engineering.[44]

Such considerations may not be of overriding importance where the objective is to create, for example, an underground gas storage facility, but to the planners of a clandestine nuclear testing programme they would pose obstacles. The full list of factors which would have to be taken into account are best considered in the context of the operational requirements which would pertain during cavity decoupling. Much can be learnt from examples of problems which crop up during normal salt mining operations.

Operational and local geological constraints

Large cavities can be constructed—and currently exist—at depths of up to 2 km or more in salt. Whether or not cavities could be used in a clandestine programme of nuclear bomb testing, however, would depend on the answers a potential evader came up with to five critical questions: (a) Could the cavern be made the right shape? (b) What is the depth range at which stable caverns suitable for conducting tests can be built? (c) Could existing chambers be modified and, if not, how long would it take to make a suitable cavern? (d) How difficult would it be to access the cavern and to disguise the surface workings from reconnaissance satellites? (e) What would be the effects on the cavern of a nuclear detonation or series of detonations?

Shape. The more uniform the shape of the cavern, the fewer the difficulties which arise in modelling the effect of the blast. In the case of a clandestine weapon-effects test, the potential evader would need to mine a long horizontal cylinder capable of being grouted to the requisite, exact shape for a horizontal, contained shot.

Solution mining involves using a series of tubes to pump water into the salt and extract brine from the resulting cavern. Industry experience shows that, for a given cavity size, the produced brine saturation is inversely related to the circulation rate, and that the development of a given cavity shape depends on a combination of circulation rate, and the position of the injection point (end of the tube or tubes used for pumping water into the cavity) and the extraction point (end of the tube/s used for drawing brine out).[45] Temperature, salt surface inclination, roughness and impurities in the salt also affect the developing shape.

In practice most solution-mined cavities end up as pear-shaped. The engineer is able to deploy routinely down-hole sonic caliper tools to monitor cavity shape as it develops and allow adjustment of injection/extraction parameters accordingly. The engineer also has at his/her disposal a wealth of numerical simulation models which have been developed since 1974.[47] Despite this, production of a cavity to the kind of symmetry specifications necessary to eliminate shape-related uncertainties from the decoupling calculation verges on the impossible. Creating simple spherical cavities is a problem, in particular because of the difficulties involved in controlling the shape of the floor.

In the case of taper shapes for weapon-effects tests, hydrofracturing from directional boreholes might, with some difficulty, allow development of a carrot shape, accurate to metres as opposed to centimetres. But weapon-effects tunnels at the NTS are 300 m long; it would be virtually impossible to solution-mine such structures in salt.

Depth. The evader's cavern would need to be constructed not so shallow as to risk surface effects after the blast, and not so deep as to cause uncontrollable plasticity in the cavern walls. Both during and after leaching, a number of types of mechanical instability can arise in the salt around a cavern.[48] These are subsurface and (rarely) surface subsidence, closure, local fracture and block flow, and deep fracturing. Failures of leached caverns as a result of these phenomena are rare under normal circumstances, but the potential evader would be extrapolating to highly unnatural physical conditions in the case of nuclear explosions.

Subsidence usually occurs during the development stage, and shallow sites present the greatest risk. Salt undergoes a general transition from bulk elastic behaviour to bulk plastic behaviour with increasing depth. In non-technical language, the greater the depth the greater the propensity of salt to flow. The depth at which the elastic/plastic transformation takes place is variable, being dependent on temperature, time, state of stress and composition of the salt. One advantage is that caverns behaving plastically at depth can 'self-heal'—a major reason for the attention focused on salt in the nuclear waste-disposal business. However, a disadvantage is that caverns will 'close', that is, their walls will converge, reducing the cavity volume. This does not happen overnight, but it is normal for solution-mined salt storage caverns to undergo an initial 5–10 per cent closure during the first year or so following completion; and in certain cases closures of 40–70 per cent have been observed.[49]

Recently, a research team from Utrecht, the Netherlands, has investigated the physical effects of brine in natural rock salt. They discovered that brine-bearing samples show marked weakening relative to dried samples when slowly subjected to strains. Natural-rock salt always contains some brine, the amount of which can vary. Accordingly, the Utrecht team concluded that substantial doubt attaches to the validity of presently accepted creep laws for predicting the long-term flow behaviour of salt in nature.[50] In the mind of a potential CTB evader, such results pose a further area of uncertainty.

Stress is also an important factor in the 'flowability' question. In this respect, salt domes are a particular problem. Their intrusive nature gives rise to residual stresses which are variable and difficult to predict. This is important because regions of high stress, whether induced by the cavern itself or arising from ambient stress field inhomogeneities, can cause fracturing and block flow, giving rise to local failure of the cavity walls and roof.[51] This is more common at shallow depths, where the salt is more prone to brittle behaviour, but it can also occur at depth.

Deep fracturing involves a condition similar to hydrofracturing and arises where caverns are pressured. Instances are known from gas storage reservoirs and waste disposal wells, and Hardy reports that 'in some cases the final result of such an instability has been of a rather large scale; for example, horizontal strata displacements cutting off active oil wells, and triggering of earthquakes'.[52] An evader intent on subjecting a cavity to a large nuclear explosion would evidently have some highly unpredictable phenomena to contend with.

It is also important to bear in mind that solution-mined caverns are brine-filled during development and are commonly full of pressurized gas once in use as storage facilities. The brine is able to 'carry' through its own hydrostatic pressure a considerable proportion of the overburden, or lithostatic, pressure (i.e., the weight of the overlying rocks bearing down on the roof). This is an important contribution to cavern stability.[53] Experience with air-filled caverns is small, and since a cavern usable for nuclear testing would have to be air-filled for long periods both before and after a test, the evader would have to be sure of the rock mechanics parameters.

The experience of practitioners is instructive in considering the extent to which they would be able to do this. The editor of the proceedings of the Fourth International Salt Symposium made the following observation on the state-of-the-art in the rock mechanism of salt in 1974: 'Clearly there is considerable controversy between those who feel that sufficient approximations can now be made using sophisticated down-hole and inplace measurements in mines and those who see past mine failures and the high variability in rock formations as evidence of some wishful thinking about present capabilities. It would appear . . . that the facts may not be as hard as the positions . . . .'.[54] A decade later, studies such as those of Serata and Cundey,[55] and Fischer[56] using an expanded database, finite element analysis and computer simulations, make it clear that modelling of rock behaviour in salt is still fraught with difficulties. Practical experiences bear this out. For example, borehole calliper measurements through time in Louisiana salt domes have demonstrated surprisingly variable closure rates at depth.[57]

Time to build. Construction of a suitable cavern would take a matter of months, providing an existing cavern could not be modified. The evader would have to consider how likely his activities might come to the attention of the verifier in this period, and he might have to be mindful of the concessions (if he had made any) on challenge inspections.

The rate at which the evader could progress would depend on his assessment of the requirements for shape control of the final cavity. Industry objectives are different from objectives the evader would have: a solution mine for the chemical industry is developed slowly over many years so as to optimize brine recovery. Even for a cavern designed specially with storage in mind, the process is a protracted one. For its deep cavity at Tersanne, Gaz de France began leaching operations in 1968, with scheduled completion in 1985 (17 years). To develop large cavities in the shortest time, high circulation rates are required.

Experience shows that multi-well leaching, which might conceptually offer better leaching rates, is in practice inadequate.[58] Podio and Saberian have presented a numerical model for optimizing solution mining. For several different extraction techniques, they calculate the time needed to produce a cavern capable of holding 1 million barrels of oil, using a variety of different circulation conditions. Such a cavern would be equivalent to a vertical cylinder some 300 m high and about 75 m across, variously tapering according to the conditions under which it was mined. The shortest period in which it could, in theory, be hollowed out is 174 days.[59]

Access and surface workings. The evader would have to enter the cavern with his warhead and diagnostic equipment in secret. A common assumption when cavity decoupling is discussed is that the extent of surface workings during solution mining would be such as not to arouse suspicion. This may be true. The well-head of a typical solution mining operation looks like many a pumping station. The evader would be able to argue, even if challenged, that he has launched another chemicals or underground storage operation. However, another common assumption is that, once the cavern is complete, it would be a relatively simple matter to emplace a bomb and test it.

This argument requires greater circumspection. Even a conventional testing operation involves an appreciable engineering operation, and over a period of weeks rather than days.[60] In the case of a solution-mined cavity, the evader would find himself faced with a brine-filled cavern at great depth. Disposal of the brine might prove disguisable or might not. Even if it were, it is extremely doubtful that the evader would be able to use the cavern fruitfully after simply pumping it out—especially if he held ambitions of creating a reusable facility, and felt the need to inspect wall conditions, or to be absolutely sure of his stemming (hole-filling) operation. He would in all probability have to mine access to the cavern in a conventional way before deciding whether or not to test in it. Here he would be running a more serious gauntlet in terms of satellite surveillance.

Other factors which must be borne in mind are the size of the rack and related equipment, such as cables, which are needed in order to optimize information derived from a test. J. Carson Mark has observed that clandestine testing of an entirely new warhead, one sufficiently ahead of its time to offer a military advantage sufficiently great to justify the risk of testing it in the first place, would probably require even more elaborate an operation at the testing ground than is the case at present.[61]

How great a risk would there be of arousing suspicions in the verifier? This is difficult for a civilian scientist to judge, but it is instructive to consider events at the time of one of the extensions of the Soviet testing moratorium of 1985–87. On 18 March 1986, with one of the Soviet deadlines about to expire unreciprocated by the USA, anonymous officials in the Pentagon revealed that the USSR was about to resume nuclear testing. The reason offered was that surveillance satellites had recorded the excavation of holes and tunnels and the deployment of wires on the testing ground at Semipalatinsk.[62]

Since the launch of the KH-9 (Big Bird) satellite in 1971, the USA has had at least a 20-cm ground resolution capability over the USSR.[63] With the KH-12 satellite, due to be put into space on an upcoming shuttle mission,[64] the resolution may be less than 10 cm.[65]

Effects of detonation. Detonation effects fall into two categories: (*a*) the shock waves introduced into the ground at the time of the blast, and (*b*) post-explosion effects. The first, seismological category will be set aside for the moment. It is undoubtedly the more important: but the emphasis which is placed on it in the verification debate often means that the second category—post-explosion effects which could come to the attention of the verifier, such as release of radiation or surface collapse—receives too little attention. Such potential effects in fact constitute a risk which would have to be carefully considered by the evader.

Of course the conditions pertaining on the walls of a cavern at the time of a nuclear explosion have been the subject of some detailed theoretical modelling[66] since they are vital to prediction of the seismic response and the structural response of the wallrock. Such studies assume that salt is a homogeneous, isotropic medium (and most assume that the cavity is perfectly spherical). In nature, however, salt is highly heterogeneous, being basically an aggregate of crystals which can be bound in different ways and which form a rock much afflicted by imperfections of the structure: voids (pore space), cracks, inclusions of water and gas, weaknesses arising at flawed crystal boundaries and as a result of allochthonous sedimentary particles, and the like. Bedded salt is particularly heterogeneous and can consist of salt crystals more or less embedded in weak marl. There is a risk even in simple gas-storage caverns of the stored material penetrating into the microscopic salt interstices and significantly affecting the stability of the cavern.[67] Accordingly, actual industry experience with the stability of gas-storage caverns would need to be sought by the evader when weighing his prospects.

The Soviet Union has ample such experience. Based on it, a potential Soviet evader may or may not be encouraged. British experience suggests that he might not be. For example, a study by Potts and others involving a major programme of in-situ instrument tests in a shallow gas-storage cavern in Cheshire salt showed that, during the rapid withdrawal of gas from the cavern, the thermal stresses can be of a magnitude theoretically sufficient to fracture the salt.[68]

The question of whether fracturing could be avoided would be critical during a cavity decoupling attempt with respect to the stemming operation. In solution-mined caverns the most critical point is the casing seat of the final cemented casing string and the cement sheath beneath it, which isolates the cavern from zones of porosity and permeability in normal strata above the salt. Any pressure from within the cavity must not exceed the downward pressure exerted by the rocks above, otherwise the overburden may be lifted (i.e., fractured) and the cavity rendered useless. In cavity decoupling such a situation would lead to leakage of radiation on a large scale. Industry estimates commonly assume that fracture will take place at pressures equal to or above 1.0 lbs/ft of overburden over salt domes and somewhat less over bedded salt sections (where in-situ stresses are different).[69] If it is difficult in practice to gauge the effects of changing pressures in a gas storage cavern, it may prove difficult to proceed with confidence from theory to predict the effects of the changing pressures which would arise from a nuclear explosion in a cavern.

Another potentially dangerous parameter for the evader would be the gas content of the salt. Kelsall and Nelson provided in 1983 previously unpublished data on gas problems in mines in salt domes in the Gulf of Mexico.[70] They reported that gas, commonly methane, is found in intragranular bubbles and intergranular cracks, and 'occurs to some degree in the majority (if not all) of the Gulf region mines and is frequently encountered in holes in the salt drilled in other domes'. They further observe that, 'In some domes gas occurs in large quantities and is a hazard to mining unless proper precautions are taken'. They add that outbursts (cavities created by gas explosions) have been observed in several mines, the extent of the outburst cavity increasing with depth. (They quote data from mines ranging from 90 to 470 metres deep.)

All the characteristics of salt and salt deposits which cause them to behave in a non-isotropic manner also cause uncertainties in predicting both cavern stability and the amount of seismic energy coupled into the wallrock. In their seminal paper on cavity decoupling, Latter *et al.* did not address in detail either the rock mechanisms of salt or the problems that might arise during attempts at cavity decoupling in shallow sites. Realizing the likely need to attempt the strategy at depth, they wrote a follow-up paper (also in 1961) which sought to assess the influence of plastic flow at depth (during the construction of cavities) on the final decoupling achieved. They concluded that the decoupling factor would not be significantly decreased, provided that the pressure in the hole is small enough. Assumptions made during their calculations were spherical symmetry for the cavern and hydrostatic stress in the medium prior to the existence of the hole: the former is virtually impossible to obtain, and the latter does not apply for salt domes.

With these assumptions, it seems doubtful whether an evader would be willing to base his assessment of the feasibility of cavity decoupling on theoretical calculations alone. However, a verifier would have to bear in mind the possibility that a potential evader had already accrued secret experimental experiences at the time a CTB was signed. This is particularly so in a country the size of the Soviet Union. Were that so, there is a possibility that some measure of encouragement might have been obtained by the potential evader. This prospect suggests that, under a CTB or LYTTB, collaborative experiments on cavity decoupling would be an attractive component in a package of confidence-building measures.

Regional geological constraints

The Soviet Union is richly endowed with salt deposits. Three particularly large areas are located north of the Caspian Sea, in Siberia north-west of Lake Baikal, and on the Arctic coast around Nordvik. This fact may encourage evasion attempts. A possible discouragement, however, is the fact that all three regions are in stable geological locations: ambient seismicity is low, which reduces the chance of the verifier—provided that his network of seismometers is sufficiently extensive—dismissing a small shock as an earthquake.[71]

Alewine has calculated that areas of bedded salt and salt domes suitable for cavity decoupling cover more than 2.9 million km^2 of the Soviet Union: some 13 per cent of the country.[72] He estimates that over 80 per cent of the known salt areas in the Soviet Union contain salt formations which are thick enough for cavities of 50 000 m^3—large enough in theory to fully decouple 1 kt—and that about 25 per cent contain salt deposits thick enough to hold caverns of 500 000 m^3—big enough in theory to fully decouple nuclear explosions of at least 10 kt. (The yields quoted by Alewine assume that the same theoretical conditions assumed by Latter *et al.* in 1961 are realizable in practice.) About half the area suitable for very large cavities is located in the Caspian Sea lowlands; others are scattered between the Afghan border and the Arctic coast.

Other scientists believe that the potential area for cavity building is smaller than this. Sykes argues that Alewine has included in his estimates areas of thin as well as thick salt.[73]

Data on the occurrence of salt in the Soviet Union can be found on the map and in the statistics available in the *Handbook of World Salt Resources*,[74] and in maps prepared by the US Geological Survey (USGS) Branch of Military Geology[75] and by the Lawrence Livermore National Laboratory.[76] Interestingly, none of the three maps compares well in fine detail. There is evidently considerable scope for a detailed study of the salt deposits of the Soviet Union. This should ideally include not only the extent of their outcrop, and likely thickness, but also a consideration of their composition and stratal characters. Much can be done remotely, using geological data obtained by the civilian Thematic Mapper (LANDSAT) and SPOT satellites. Such data is openly available.

A point particularly in need of being included in the equation is the likely character of bedded salt in the different areas. Considerable complexities can arise for cavern construction and stability, as a result of sedimentary hetero-geneity in bedded salt. The USGS map shows that bedded salt comprises more than two-thirds of the total salt subcrop of the Soviet Union.

Geographical constraints

A common assumption in the debate over verifiability is that, since the Soviet Union is a vast country (more than 22 million km²), candidate sites for attempting cavity decoupling are legion. This is another argument which may require greater circumspection. The process of testing nuclear warheads is complex, and even routine underground tests require large engineering sup-port facilities.[77] Much of the Soviet Union would be immensely difficult of access for the purposes of running a clandestine testing programme as a consequence of simple human geography. No proper trunk road runs all the way across the USSR, the total length of hard-topped roads (about 750 000 km) is less than that in Britain (a country one-ninetieth of its size), and only two railways—one yet to enter service—cross the country from west to east.[78] Furthermore, the pattern of urban settlement is highly concentrated, resem-bling a stretched triangle with its wide base west of the Urals and a thin tapering apex reaching east into Siberia along the lines of communication to Omsk, Novosibirsk and Novokuznetsk. Rarely are Soviet ICBMs deployed far from these lines of communication. The more-used of the Soviet testing sites, at Semipalatinsk, is also on them.

The geographic difficulties facing a potential Soviet evader should not be over-emphasized: the second currently used test site, for example, is on the remote island of Novaya Zemlya in the Arctic Ocean. However, neither should they be ignored. It seems improbable that a complex site for clandestine nuclear testing could be too far from good channels of communication. Knowing also that areas of thick salt and certain sedimentary basins would be the likely sites for any attempt at cavity decoupling, the verifier could con-centrate (though not necessarily confine) his photoreconnaissance effort accordingly.

Seismological constraints

The discipline of seismology is at the heart of the debate over whether or not a ban on nuclear testing can be confidently verified. It is covered in detail elsewhere in this volume; since this paper is intended to draw attention to facets of the verifiability debate other than the seismological, what follows is only a brief synopsis of the main arguments presented by seismologists.

Were the USSR to test a device of 1 kt in hard rock, the chances of successfully evading detection would be negligible. There is general agreement on this, for two reasons. First, there are significant differences between the type of shock waves generated by earthquakes and explosions. Second, shock waves from 1-kt tests (or earthquakes of equivalent energy release) register above-normal seismic noise levels far enough from their origin to ensure that at least some stations in a monitoring grid would pick them up and discriminate the contrasts in the signals. Sykes and Evernden argued in 1982 that with 15 stations in the Soviet Union, the largest blast which would have a 30 per cent chance of evading detection would have a yield of only 0.5 kt.[79]

This leaves us with cavity decoupling, which has been the nub of the verification debate for many years. In the early 1980s the only counter to cavity decoupling lay in the knowledge that the evader would face enormous logistic problems in staging a test (more particularly, a series of tests) and in the deterrence factor of photoreconnaissance satellites looking for signs of the run-up to the clandestine test or tests, and 'challenge' inspections to chase up suspicious undiscriminated seismic events. Indeed, in 1980 significant progress had been made towards negotiating a CTBT under these assumptions. But over the past few years a new factor has emerged. As outlined in an earlier section, empirical data from the STERLING explosion showed that the decoupling factor drops off at the higher-frequency end of the spectrum in which seismic energy is transmitted. This relationship has long been predicted in theory,[18] but was thought to be of no value for monitoring, because the energy would be too quickly attenuated and the signals would be difficult to detect above background noise levels. However, recent studies show that this early assumption is incorrect: there is in fact considerable advantage to be gained in monitoring at higher frequencies than has been conventional at seismograph stations.[81]

Evernden et al. recently presented an exhaustive assessment of this technique.[82] Using a wealth of data they argue as follows: (a) that the theoretical basis for predicting the (differing) spectral properties of compressional (P-) waves from tamped and decoupled explosions is actually observed, thereby allowing the use of theory when assessing the detection capability of seismic monitoring networks; (b) that high-frequency P-wave signals (i.e., up to at least 30 Hz) propagate nearly as efficiently as those of 1 Hz within much of the earth: and, most importantly, especially so in areas of old, stable, continental crust such as those which underlie much of the Soviet Union; (c) that there are many suitable 'quiet' monitoring sites within continents, where high-frequency noise levels are very low in relation to average ambient noise levels at 1 Hz; (d) that the high-frequency (30 Hz) P-wave amplitude levels for large earthquakes are no higher—and generally far lower—than those generated by fully decoupled 1- to 2-kt explosions; and (e) that at high frequencies the P- and S-waves from small seismic events are still usable for discrimination of the different types of energy source (small explosions and earthquakes).

This analysis leads Evernden et al. to conclude that 25 simple monitoring stations inside the USSR, and 15 similar stations in the surrounding countries, would be capable of multi-station detection at high signal-to-noise ratios of fully decoupled 1-kt explosions located at all the sites of potential cavity decoupling.

It is not the purpose of this paper to review the entire body of supporting evidence, but some of the most encouraging results from existing facilities are worthy of mention.

The Norwegian Regional Seismic Array System (NORESS) was designed by the Sandia Laboratories and deployed north of Oslo, Norway, in the summer of 1984 at an installation cost of $1 million. Its 25 seismometers, arranged in concentric circles across a 3-km diameter, give much-improved signal-to-noise ratios relative to conventional stations.[83] Early reports show that before the Soviet testing moratorium it detected sub-kiloton tests from the Soviet Semipalatinsk test site, more than 4000 km away,[84] and has a detection threshold of M_b 2 to 2.5 for events occurring up to 1500 km away:[85] equivalent to a few tens of tons of explosive yield well-coupled over the western one-quarter of the Soviet Union.[86] The identification threshold (at which the verifier could be sure of discriminating the majority of shocks as explosions or earthquakes) would be somewhat higher than this, but still well below the level at which tests of military significance could be conducted in a tamped environment.

NORSAR, a related array run jointly by Norwegian and US scientists near Oslo, also detected minuscule tests—down to 500 tons (0.5 kt)—at Semipalatinsk.[87] Scaling experiments had earlier suggested that explosions of mere hundreds of tons would be detectable above noise level by NORSAR, even if fully decoupled.[88] NORSAR offers a 90 per cent probability of detecting seismic events of body wave magnitude 4.0 (equivalent to 1 kt in hard rock) over a 3000- to 10 000-km range.[89]

Elsewhere, encouraging results have been provided by monitors in both the USA and the USSR. A detector of high-frequency signals at Lajitas, Texas, detected a 5-ton chemical explosion at Kirkland Air Force Base, some 725 km away. Herrin concluded that this result meant that the instrument 'might be expected to detect automatically the signal from a fully decoupled nuclear explosion of 0.2 kt yield at a distance of 1000 km'.[90]

In the USSR, seismologists operating independently of the US Government, in collaboration with the Soviet Academy of Sciences, installed three monitoring stations around the Soviet test site at Semipalatinsk in Kazakhstan. These have recorded regional quarry blasts at high signal-to-noise ratios at distances of more than 300 km. The signals contain substantial energy of up to and above 20 Hz.[91] This important research programme is continuing, with high-quality borehole seismometers due to be installed in early 1987.

Range of assessments

What are the current estimates for the resolving power of this technique? 'Optimists' believe that 15–25 stations inside the Soviet Union would monitor decoupled blasts with an adequate level of confidence down to about 1 kt. This assertion has been made in numerous scientific publications and testimonies to Congress.[92] Leading the academic seismologists who argue for optimism are Professor L. Sykes of the Lamont-Doherty Geological Observatory of Columbia University, a Fellow of the US Academy of Sciences, and Dr Jack Evernden of the US Geological Survey. Sykes, in a November testimony to a House of Representatives Special Panel on Arms Control and Disarmament, offered the view that 'the lower limit of reliable identification can be reduced to about 1 kiloton with a combination of seismic listening posts within the USSR and other national technical means such as satellite photography'.[93] In a testimony to the US House of Representatives Foreign Affairs Committee in April 1986, Evernden argued that 'a network composed of 25 or so simple (non-array) properly placed stations within the USSR augmented by a set of similar stations surrounding the USSR could successfully monitor compliance with a 1 kiloton threshold test ban treaty, even if such explosions were placed in large decoupled cavities'.[94]

Is this view widely supported outside the weapon laboratories? It seems so. The Director of the US Arms Control Association, Hon. Spurgeon Keeny, Jr, said on 19 February 1986 that the view that a test ban can be adequately verified to protect US security interests, and with existing technology, is 'the view that I believe is held by most independent scientists'.[95]

The boundary between the optimists and pessimists in the United States is not sharply defined. Hannon has referred to the evidence that use can be made of high frequencies as 'tentative'.[96] Bache has argued that tens, and probably hundreds, of suspicious events per year would crop up at seismic energy levels equivalent to 1 kt decoupled.[97] Batzel's recent testimonies to Congress, which have stressed that, in his opinion, a CTB is not in the interests of the United States, have none the less not strongly advanced verification as a reason why a CTBT is not advisable. Detecting a fully decoupled clandestine test is only viewed as a problem at the Livermore Laboratory, evidently, in that, 'we estimate that it would require more than 30 high quality in-country arrays or equivalent single stations in the USSR at sites with high signal-to-noise ratios to detect signals from decoupled explosions, or equivalent size earthquakes, with yield of about 1 kiloton, with a 90 per cent degree of confidence'. Although the requirements for discrimination mean that 'the 90 per cent confidence for identification may include events that are 2 or 3 times as large as the detection threshold',[98] this appraisal suggests that the gap between the optimists and pessimists is bridgeable.

In Britain the 'pessimists' are far more pessimistic than their counterparts in the USA. In the UK Ministry of Defence (MOD) technical position paper CD/ 610,[99] no opinions are expressed as to numbers of stations required. Since that paper was presented to the CD in July 1985, there has been no follow-up. The technical content of the paper has been criticized by Sykes[100] and Leggett.[101]

III. Other strategies for evasion

Evasion by dry-alluvium muffling

There is another way to dampen the amplitude of the seismic waves generated by an underground explosion, apart from cavity decoupling: to detonate the bomb in dry alluvium. Explosions in the dry alluvial deposits of Nevada dampen the body magnitude by about a factor of 10, because so much of the source energy is dissipated by pore collapse in the alluvium.[102] However, a number of studies have suggested that there are no geological formations capable of doing this in the USSR.[103] In the US National Academy of Sciences publication *Nuclear Arms Control*, it is argued that the thickness of suitable deposits in the Soviet Union is unsuitable for testing above 1 kt.[104]

Evasion by earthquake masking

Potential treaty violators could conceivably contemplate hiding their clandestine tests in the coda (tail) of a large earthquake. The operational difficulties of this strategy would be substantial: holding the test in instant readiness, probably for a period of years, awaiting the occurrence of a sufficiently large earthquake sufficiently close to the test site. Furthermore, the evader would still face the problem of the richer component of high-frequency energy generated by the explosion.

A small nuclear test at the Soviet Semipalatinsk site was held soon after a large earthquake occurred elsewhere in the Soviet Union. The signals from the bomb arrived at the NORSAR array 30 seconds after the first wave from the earthquake, and though the signals were drowned in the record from the 1.2–3.2 Hz passband, they were clearly visible in the record from the 3.2–5.2 Hz passband.[105]

No hope is held out for successful execution of a clandestine test in this way, even by those prone to caution in their assessments of verifiability. For similar reasons the additional strategy of multiple-shot masking can be discounted. Even a series of closely staggered blasts could not, combined, produce a release of energy which might be confused with an earthquake.

Evasion in space

Batzel has testified to Congress that, in his opinion, the United States cannot rely on the Soviet Union not pursuing extraterrestrial means of clandestinely testing nuclear weapons. On 18 September 1985 he said: 'we believe that it would be possible for the Soviets to launch a rocket, say under the guise of a deep-space probe, that could carry a number of nuclear explosives and a diagnostic package. The tests could be carried out behind the sun'.[106] This argument has been described as belonging to the realms of 'wild fantasy'.[107]

It is true that the Soviet Union has had a remarkably successful space programme, largely as a result of developing tried-and-tested principles of rocketry rather than relying on new, higher-risk ventures such as the space shuttle. Their rate of space launches far exceeds that of the United States. Data from experiments in space could, in principle, be telemetered back to earth. However, considerations such as the difficulty of transferring the involved logistics of a militarily worthwhile nuclear test[108] to deep space, the cost, and the risk of having telemetry intercepted, add up to make this a most unlikely avenue for efforts at evasion of a CTB. Dr Batzel and his colleagues should go further and offer proof that evasion by this means is feasible at realistic cost. If they succeed, a simple political remedy is available in requiring some degree of primitive inspection for the very few deep-space probes sent out each decade.

IV. Conclusions

In this summary of conclusions it is assumed that previously agreed conditions of CTB verification apply, *viz.* internal, tamper-proof monitors, and on-site inspections on a 'challenge' basis. From the technical standpoint alone, it is concluded that a potential evader would be deterred from realistic expectations of successfully conducting a clandestine nuclear test of militarily worthwhile size. Other standpoints—political, economic and geographic—would play a significant role in further deterring an evader.

There are six categories of reason for this conclusion.

1. The deterrence value of seismology for tests in hard rock is essentially proven, offers no reasonable chance of success for the hide-in-earthquake strategy, and is—at the very least—highly daunting for the evasion strategy of cavity decoupling. The potential evader would have to contend with:

i. the knowledge that explosions of much less than 1 kt in the Soviet Union have been distinguished clearly more than 4000 km from their source; and

ii. the knowledge that at high seismic frequencies the dampening effect of a decoupled explosion drops off appreciably, and that highly promising results have been obtained from high-frequency monitoring stations: HF energy from very small explosions has a demonstrated capability to transmit efficiently, and be clearly recorded above background noise, over long distances.

2. An evader would face discouraging uncertainties over the degree of decoupling he could anticipate from a nuclear explosion of worthwhile size, even were he to succeed in constructing, or modifying from present purposes, a suitable cavern. Factors he would need to weigh include:

i. the length of time involved in preparing a solution-mined cavity—a minimum of hundreds of days, probably well over a year—all the while liable to having the operation questioned as result of photoreconnaissance;

ii. the fact that, to access the cavern for testing purposes, conventionally mined adits would be required—much increasing the chances of attracting the unwelcome attention of the verifier;

iii. the involved nature of the operations necessary for carrying out a test of military worth, and the differences between these operations and those normally used in salt mining or underground storage—another parameter in the photoreconnaissance gauntlet;

iv. the fact that experimental results have never matched theory, and have in any case invariably been conducted with chemical explosives—which generate an explosion that differs from that of nuclear explosives—and at yields of thousands of times less than that of an average nuclear test. The one small experiment with a nuclear source was at too low a level (380 tons) to offer reliable extrapolation to higher yields, and in any case gave a decoupling factor of 70 at low frequencies—less than the factor of 200 thought to be obtainable from theory—and even less at high frequencies;

v. the fact that a spherical shape (which reduces uncertainties in calculating the decoupling factor) cannot be produced with available solution-mining technology;

vi. the fact that salt, within diapirs (intrusive bodies of salt which have forced their way up into younger strata) and bedded salt deposits (particularly), is heterogeneous in terms of its physical and chemical characteristics, making it difficult to predict cavern stability—especially with respect to the degree of plasticity at depth; and

vii. the fact that most Soviet salt areas are in regions of low ambient seismic activity; the verifier would certainly wish to concentrate his internal monitors round sedimentary basins with thick salt, and any small seismic event which was not clearly an earthquake would be treated with the utmost suspicion.

3. After a cavity blast of worthwhile size, quite apart from the seismic response, the evader would be uncertain of the response of the cavity itself. There would be a risk of leakage through inadequate stemming, or collapse as a result of miscalculated factors such as residual stresses locked up in the salt (especially in diapirs) or inclusions of gas and brine, both of which would produce potentially detectable effects at the surface.

Apart from the technical considerations, the evader would also weigh military, economic and political factors. The technical factors in this debate cannot be viewed in isolation when making an assessment of feasibility. The more important conclusions are the following:

4. Bleak though his prospects are of success even below 1 kt, the evader would have to consider attempting a clandestine testing programme at well over that level to achieve militarily useful information, according to levels of testing which are deemed to be important today and testimonies of ex-weapon designers. There is a widespread belief among qualified physicists that fission triggers for new strategic warheads could not be tested at levels much below 10 kt. From the evader's point of view, no tests for novel devices—such as the nuclear-pumped X-ray laser—could be contemplated: tests for that device have been close to the Threshold Test Ban Treaty level of 150 kt.

5. The evader would be aware that, even if he were successful with a clandestine testing programme and produced a new warhead, he would be a long way from bringing it successfully to deployment. In the testing of delivery systems, an evader might give a verifier strong clues that a warhead was being developed clandestinely. New missiles invariably require new warheads: delivery-system testing is relatively easy to monitor. Production of a new warhead poses the problems of discovery by the communications monitoring of the verifier's intelligence agencies, or by high-level defections.

6. The evader would in all probability be deterred by knowledge of the political backlash of a detected violation. This would result in two undesirable

stresses: an enforced resurgence of draining defence expenditure as the arms race stepped up again, and an increase in the quarters from which he was threatened with nuclear weapons. This would undoubtedly arise as additional nations, despairing of cynicism of the nuclear weapon states with respect to Non-Proliferation Treaty promises, joined the nuclear weapon club.

In summary, the seismological points alone would certainly deter attempts at testing at a level of 1 kt or more and would present grave risks of detection even below that level. Although each of the additional points might not stand alone as a cast-iron reason for deterrence, their sum represents an insuperable additional gauntlet. Furthermore, were the evader-verifier relationship to err on the side of accommodation during the early years of a CTBT, confidence-building measures could be employed to ensure withdrawal of all intentions of evasion from a later, possibly more military-minded, government.[109]

Notes and references

[1] UK Foreign and Commonwealth Office, *Seismic Monitoring for a Comprehensive Nuclear Test Ban*, United Nations Conference on Disarmament document CD/610, 9 July 1985. (Also reprinted in *Modern Geology*, vol. 10, no. 4 (1986), pp. 277–92.)

[2] Evernden, J. F., Archambeau, C. B. and Cranswick, E. 'An evaluation of seismic decoupling and underground nuclear test monitoring using high-frequency seismic data', *Reviews of Geophysics*, vol. 24, no. 2 (1986), pp. 143–215.

[3] 'Statement by the United States Representative (Martin) to the Conference of the Committee on Disarmament: Comprehensive Test Ban, August 24, 1972', in *Documents on Disarmament, United States Arms Control and Disarmament Agency*, p. 589.

[4] Kidder, R. E., 'Militarily significant nuclear explosive yields', *Journal of the Federation of American Scientists*, vol. 38, no. 2 (Sep. 1985).

[5] See note 1.

[6] Mark, J. C., 'Implications of a comprehensive test ban for a stockpile of nuclear weapons', *Nuclear Strategy and World Security*, eds. J. Rotblat and S. Hellman (Macmillan: London, 1985), pp. 60–9.

[7] Larson, D. B. (ed.), *Proceedings of the Department of Energy Sponsored Cavity Decoupling Workshop*, Pajarop Dunes California (Department of Energy: Washington, DC, 29–31 July 1985).

[8] *To Authorize Appropriations for the Department of Energy for National Security Programs for Fiscal Year 1986 and Fiscal Year 1987, and for other Purposes*, Hearing on S. 911 before the Committee on Armed Services, US Senate, 99th Congress (US Government Printing Office: Washington, DC, 14 Mar. 1985), pp. 158–74.

[9] Latter, A. L., Martinelli, E. A., Mathews, J. and McMilan, W. G., 'A method of concealing underground nuclear explosions', *Journal of Geophysical Research*, vol. 66, no. 3 (Mar. 1961), pp. 943–6.

[10] Evernden, J. F., 'Selected comments on the decoupling conference', in note 7.

[11] Marshall, P. D., 'Project Orpheus', in note 7.

[12] Herbst, R. F., Werthe, G. C. and Springer, D. L., 'Use of large cavities to reduce seismic waves from underground explosions', *Journal of Geophysical Research*, vol. 66, no. 3 (Mar. 1961), pp. 959–78.

[13] See note 12.

[14] See note 11.

[15] Murphey, B. F., 'Particle motions near explosions in halite', *Journal of Geophysical Research*, vol. 66, no. 3 (Mar. 1961), pp. 947–57.

[16] See note 15.

[17] Patterson, D. W., 'Nuclear decoupling, full and partial', *Journal of Geophysical Research*, vol. 71, no. 14 (July 1966), pp. 3427–36.

[18] Springer, D., Denny, M., Healy, J. and Mickey, W., 'The Sterling experiment: decoupling of

seismic waved by a shot-generated cavity', *Journal of Geophysical Research*, vol. 73, no. 18 (Sep. 1968), pp. 5995–6011.

[19] Healy, J. H., King, C. Y., and O'Neill, M. E., 'Source parameters of the Salmon and Sterling explosions from seismic measurements', *Journal of Geophysical Research*, vol. 76 (1971), pp. 3344–55.

[20] Sharpe, J. A., 'The production of elastic waves by explosive pressures, I, Theory and empirical field observations', *Geophysics*, vol. 7 (19042), pp. 144–54.

[21] Glenn, L. A., 'Elastic radiation from explosively-loaded axisymmetric cavities in an unbounded medium', in note 7.

[22] Heusinkveld, H. (ed.), *Lawrence Livermore National Laboratory Seismic Monitoring Research Program Annual Report*, Dec. 1985, pp. 34–40.

[23] See note 21.

[24] See note 7.

[25] Archambeau, C. B., 'Verifying a test ban: a new approach to monitoring underground nuclear tests', *Issues in Science and Technology*, Winter 1986, pp. 18–19; 'What's wrong with the Administration's arguments opposing a Test Ban Treaty—a reply to comments by J. T. Hackett', submitted to *Issues in Science and Technology*.

[26] See note 25.

[27] Horgan, J., 'Underground nuclear weapons testing', *Spectrum*, vol. 23, no. 4 (Apr. 1986), pp. 32–43.

[28] Rachlin, J., 'Cavity construction opportunities in the Soviet Union', in note 7.

[29] Merritt, J. L., 'Constraints imposed by siting conditions, construction methods, and cost on the formation and use (and possible reuse) of large cavities', in note 7.

[30] See note 27.

[31] Sykes, L. R., 'Verification of a comprehensive nuclear test ban treaty, Soviet compliance with the Threshold Test Ban Treaty, and the sizes of Soviet strategic nuclear weapons', *Modern Geology*, vol. 10, no. 4 (1986), pp. 303–301 (And as testimony to US House of Representatives, Special Panel on Arms Control and Disarmament, 25 Nov. 1985).

[32] See note 29.

[33] Hardy, H. R., Jr, 'Development of design criteria for salt cavity storage of natural gas', *Fifth Symposium on Salt*, vol. 2, eds A. H. Coogan and L. Hauber (Northern Ohio Geological Society: Cleveland, 1980), pp. 13–20.

[34] Carosello, M. E., 'The use of salt domes for the Strategic Petroleum Reserve', *Fifth Symposium on Salt*, vol. 2 (note 33); and van Fossan, N. E., 'Instrumentation and controls for solution-mined underground storage systems', *Fifth Symposium on Salt*, vol. 2 (note 33).

[35] See note 28.

[36] Potts, E. L. J., Thompson, T. W., Passaris, E. K. S. and Horseman, S. T., 'An investigation into underground gas storage in brine well cavities', *Fifth Symposium on Salt*, vol. 2 (note 33).

[37] Clerc-Renaud, A. and Dubois, D., 'Long-term operation of underground storage in salt', *Fifth Symposium on Salt*, vol. 2 (note 33).

[38] Pernette, E. and Dussaud, M., 'Underground storage at Tersanne and Etrez: prediction and simulation of cavity leaching in a slat layer charged with insoluble materials', *Sixth International Symposium on Salt*, vol. 1, eds B. C. Schreiber and H. L. Harner (The Salt Institute: Alexandria, 1983), pp. 35–48.

[39] Borg, I. Y., 'Peaceful nuclear explosions in Soviet gas condensate fields', *Energy and Technology Review*, Lawrence Livermore National Laboratory, May 1983, pp. 31–7.

[40] Borg, I. Y., 'Nuclear explosions for peaceful purposes', paper 4, this volume.

[41] Coogan, A. H. (ed.), *Fourth Symposium on Salt* (Northern Ohio Geological Society: Cleveland, 1974); Coogan, A. H. and Hauber, L. (eds), *Fifth Symposium on Salt*, vols. 1 and 2 (Northern Ohio Geological Society: Cleveland, 1980); and Schreiber, B. C. and Harner, H. L. (eds), *Sixth International Symposium on Salt*, vols. 1 and 2 (The Salt Institute: Alexandria, 1983).

[42] See notes 33 and 36; and Vouille, G. and Tassel, P., 'Stability of caverns crated on rock salt in solution mining', *Fifth Symposium on Salt*, vol. 2 (note 33).

[43] See Vouille and Tassel (note 42).

[44] See note 36, and Podio, A. L. and Saberian, A., 'Optimization of solution mining operations', *Fifth Symposium on Salt*, vol. 2 (note 33).

[45] See Podio and Saberian (note 44).

[46] Saberian, A., 'Accomplishments of Solution Mining Research Institute-sponsored salt dissolution research since the Fourth Symposium on Salt', *Fifth Symposium on Salt*, vol. 2 (note 33).

[47] See note 46.

[48] See note 33.

[49] See note 33.

[50] Urai, J. L., Spiers, C. J., Zwart, H. J. and Lister, G. S., 'Weakening of rock salt by water during long-term creep', *Nature*, vol. 324 (11 Dec. 1986), pp. 554–7.

[51] See note 33.

[52] See note 33.

[53] Serata, S. and Cundey, T. E., 'Design variables in solution cavities for storage of solids, liquids, and gases', *Fifth Symposium on Salt*, vol. 2 (note 33).

[54] See Coogan (note 41).

[55] See note 53.

[56] Fischer, F.J., 'An axisymmetric method for analyzing cavity arrays', *Sixth International Symposium on Salt*, vol. 2, eds B. C. Schreiber and H. L. Harner (The Salt Institute: Alexandria, 1983), pp. 11–26.

[57] Thoms, R. L. and Gehle, R. M., 'Borehole tests to predict cavern performance', *Sixth International Symposium on Salt*, vol. 2 (note 56).

[58] Saberian, A., 'Utilization of leaching models on the design of large crude oil storage cavities', *Sixth International Symposium on Salt*, vol. 2 (note 56).

[59] See Podio and Saberian (note 44).

[60] See note 27.

[61] See note 6.

[62] *New York Times*, 'Soviet reported acting to begin new tests', 18 Mar. 1986.

[63] See note 62.

[64] See note 62, and Adam, J. A., 'Counting the weapons', *Spectrum*, vol. 23, no. 7 (July 1986), pp. 42–56.

[65] See note 64, and Krass, A. S., *Verification: How Much is Enough?*, SIPRI (Taylor & Francis: London, 1985).

[66] See note 17, and Latter, A. L., Martinelli, E. A., Mathews, J. and McMillan, W. G., 'The effect of plasticity on decoupling of underground explosions', *Journal of Geophysical Research*, vol. 66, no. 9 (Sep. 1961), pp. 2929–36.

[67] See note 46.

[68] See note 36.

[69] van Fossan, N. E., 'Mechanisms of product leakage from solution caverns', *Fifth Symposium on Salt*, vol. 2 (note 33).

[70] Kelsall, P. C. and Nelson, J. W., 'Gas in salt domes from the Gulf', *Sixth International Symposium on Salt*, vol. 1 (note 38).

[71] Hannon, W. J. Jr., 'Seismic verification of a comprehensive test ban', *Energy and Technology Review*, Lawrence Livermore National Laboratory (May 1983), pp. 50–65.

[72] Alewine, R. W., Letter to Honourable B. B. Byron, Chairman, Special Panel on Arms Control and Disarmament, US House of Representatives, 16 Dec. 1985.

[73] Sykes, L. R., Letter to Honourable B. B. Byron, Chairman, Special Panel on Arms Control and Disarmament, US House of Representatives, 9 June 1986.

[74] Lefond, S. J., *Handbook of World Salt Resources* (Plenum Press: New York, 1969).

[75] See note 28.

[76] See note 71.

[77] See note 27.

[78] Farringdon, H., *The Strategic Geography of NATO and the Warsaw Pact* (Routledge and Kegan Paul: New York, 1986).

[79] Sykes, L. R. and Evernden, J. F., 'The verification of a comprehensive nuclear test ban', *Scientific American* vol. 247 (1982), pp. 29–37.

[80] See note 20.

[81] See notes 1, 2, 31; and Loughran, L. B. (ed.), *Final Technical Summary: NORSAR Scientific Report No. 1–85/86* (Royal Norwegian Council for Scientific and Industrial Research, 1 Apr.–30 Sep. 1985).

[82] See note 2.

[83] Alewine, R. W. III, 'Seismic sensing of Soviet tests', *Defense* (Dec. 1985), pp. 11–21.

[84] See note 83.

[85] Mykkelveit, S., in Conference on Disarmament document CD/669 (20 June 1985).

[86] See note 31.

[87] See note 31.

[88] Loughran, L. B. (ed.), *NORSAR Semiannual Technical Summary*, 1 Apr.–30 Sep. 1984.

[89] See note 85.

[90] Herrin, E., 'Studies at the Lajitas station', in *The VELA Program: A Twenty-five Year Review of Basic Research*, ed. A. U. Kerr (Defense Advanced Research Projects Agency: Washington, DC, 1985), pp. 521–5.

[91] Brune, J., Berger, J., Bodin, P., Priestley, K., Chavez, D. and Archambeau, C., 'US–Soviet co-operative arrays, the Kazak and Nevada test sites: description and preliminary results from the Kazak site', Abstract at American Geophysical Union Fall Meeting (1986).

[92] See notes 2, 25, 31, 79, 90; and Sykes, L. R., 'Advancing United States national security interests through verifiable limitations on nuclear testing', *Testimony before the Committee on Foreign Relations, US Senate* (26 June 1986).

[93] See note 31.

[94] Evernden, J. F., Written Testimony to US House of Representatives Subcommittee on Arms Control (Apr. 1985).

[95] Joint press release, Committee for National Security and the Arms Control Association (19 Feb. 1986); *New York Times* (14 Nov. 1985).

[96] See note 71.

[97] Bache, T. C., 'Seismic identification of small events', in Larson (ed.), note 7.

[98] See note 8.

[99] See note 1.

[100] Sykes, L. R., 'Comment: seismic monitoring for a nuclear test ban', *Modern Geology*, vol. 10, no. 4 (1986), pp. 293–5.

[101] Leggett, J. K., 'Comment: seismic monitoring for a nuclear test ban', *Modern Geology*, vol. 10, no. 4 (1986), pp. 297–302.

[102] Glenn, L. A., 'Verification limits for a test ban treaty', *Nature*, vol. 310 (1984), pp. 359–62.

[103] Sykes, L. R., 'Verification of nuclear test ban treaties', *Testimony before Committee on Foreign Affairs, Subcommittee on Arms Control, International Security, and Science*, US House of Representatives (8 May 1985).

[104] Goldberger, M. L. *et al.*, *Nuclear Arms Control: Background and Issues* (US National Academy of Sciences: Washington, DC, 1985).

[105] See notes 31 and 88.

[106] Batzel, R. E., Testimony to the US House of Representatives Subcommittee on Arms Control and Disarmament, Armed Services Committee.

[107] See note 31.

[108] See note 27.

[109] Leggett, J. K., Clarke, R. and Westaway, R., 'The possible role for confidence-building measures in achieving a ban on nuclear testing', Abstract, paper presented at Moscow Forum for Peace, Feb. 1987.

Chapter XI. Means of nuclear test ban verification other than seismological

Paper 13

Allan M. Din

SIPRI

Abstract

Non-seismological monitoring methods can be applied to nuclear tests under either a limited or a comprehensive test ban treaty. The effects which can be monitored include surface changes, heat releases, flashes of light and radiation, radioactive material releases, ionospheric disturbances and shock waves. The several non-seismological monitoring methods appear to be valuable complements to standard seismological verification technologies.

I. Introduction

Ever since the 1963 Partial Test Ban Treaty (PTBT), nuclear testing has been conducted underground—first by the three major nuclear weapon states, and later also by France and China. Concomitantly, the emphasis of verification technology has been on seismological detection. While seismological verification technology is and will continue to be of prime importance, there are other methods for detecting, monitoring and verifying nuclear explosions which for a number of reasons will be useful.

Systems are needed to detect endo- and exo-atmospheric nuclear explosions. The performance of standard seismological verification technologies may also be improved in conjunction with non-seismological methods. It is valuable to have a certain redundancy in monitoring methods because of possible technical shortcomings in the detection systems and other unanticipated developments.

In principle, the various test ban regimes, from the present PTB and TTB (Threshold Test Ban) Treaty regimes to a low-threshold test ban (LTTB) or a CTB, presently under discussion, may require verification systems of somewhat different degrees of sophistication. Thus, for example, under a CTB regime the problem, for the purpose of determining non-compliance, is to detect whether or not a nuclear explosion has taken place, whereas in a TTB regime information on the yield of the detected explosion would be required. In practice, however, the regimes are not very different. In fact, a CTB cannot be verified below a certain technological limit or in an explosive yield range where confusion with ordinary chemical explosions and natural events such as earthquakes is possible. Under any regime there will be a yield threshold around which compliance will be difficult to establish, so a basic requirement is that the detection systems be adapted to this threshold. However, an agreed low threshold, at whatever limit, will not necessarily induce the superpowers or other states to renounce the use of complementary methods of detection. In the foreseeable future, therefore, the spectrum of verification technologies will be both wide and state-of-the-art, rather independently of the test ban regime which is in force.

The following sections describe the most important non-seismological techniques that have been investigated or developed for the purpose of monitoring nuclear explosions. The physical effects which they can monitor include surface changes, heat releases, flashes of light and radiation, releases of radioactive materials, ionospheric disturbances and shock waves.

Some of these techniques are already in use and others have been tested and developed. The technical description in the following sections does not refer to any particular test ban regime, but in the concluding remarks the arms control relevance of the various methods is discussed.

II. Monitoring by satellite-based sensors

There are several ways in which satellites can monitor physical effects associated with nuclear explosions. This is, for example, the case for photographic reconnaissance, the quality of which has been improved steadily through the years to the present military resolution capability of around a few tens of centimetres;[1] even the LANDSAT satellites, with a resolution of only a few tens of metres, have been able to produce good pictures of surface craters created by underground nuclear explosions. The LANDSAT photograph of the Sedan event at the Nevada Test Site provides one example.[2]

Pictures from the French SPOT satellite, which are commercially available, have a resolution of around 10 metres and can even show stereographic features owing to exposure at two different angles. This means that observed earth surface depressions which are suspected of being craters associated with an underground explosion could most probably be reliably identified. However, areas with complicated topography or with older crater formations could present problems.

As a standard intelligence tool, photographic reconnaissance plays an important role in detecting activities connected with preparations for experiments at the nuclear test sites. The best known example was in 1977, when the USSR (and afterwards the USA) discovered signs of preparations for a nuclear test in South Africa. This intelligence role is of special interest for the hypothetical evasion scenarios involving decoupled underground explosions. In such scenarios, nuclear tests would take place in excavated holes, for example in salt mines; but to prepare a hole of appropriate dimensions for decoupling to take place, very large amounts of material would most likely have to be removed.[3] After being brought to the surface, this material could easily be discovered by the observance of vehicle tracks or of the deposits themselves, and any such unusual mining activity would give rise to the suspicion that preparations for a decoupling experiment were under way. However, there are pre-excavated cavities and mining districts where it is conceivable that activities associated with nuclear test experiments could be concealed from remote sensing platforms.

In principle, other types of sensors than photographic could be used to monitor relevant earth surface changes. Radar imaging techniques, for example, provide acceptable resolutions and have the advantage of being applicable independently of cloud cover. However, since the observable surface changes are of a rather permanent character, radar imaging would not seem to be particularly useful. Infra-red detectors could possibly be used to signal the underground release of a large quantity of heat from an explosion because of a slight increase in surface temperature (a fraction of a degree), but this signature would be diffuse and therefore inconclusive if it were the only evidence produced.

The most conspicuous use of satellites for nuclear explosion monitoring has been with the Vela satellite type of sensors. It came to wide attention in September 1979, when a peculiar light phenomenon was observed over the Indian Ocean, an event which has been widely suspected to be caused by a South African or a joint South African-Israeli atmospheric nuclear test. These and other nations are subject to special scrutiny as potential developers of nuclear weapons; monitoring of clandestine atmospheric tests in peacetime is therefore of importance, but an equally important use of these sensors would be in the case of a conflict involving the use of nuclear weapons.

A nuclear weapon which explodes above ground emits various types of characteristic radiation[4] which may be detected from a great distance by a satellite-based sensor. The radiation spectrum includes X- and gamma-rays which produce clear signals in, for example, scintillation counters giving a twinkling signature, but for detection of this radiation to be feasible the explosion must take place above the atmosphere since the rays would otherwise be absorbed by the air. In the earth's atmosphere, a characteristic double light pulse from the nuclear fireball may be detected by a so-called 'bhangmeter';[5] this pulse consists of a rapid 100-μsec rise in light intensity, followed by a minimum after 10 msec and a second maximum after 100 msec. Such signals, with two intensity maxima, are typical of nuclear explosions in the atmosphere. The 'bhangmeter', which is a special kind of photometer registering this peculiar succession of light peaks, is the most conclusive remote system for detecting atmospheric nuclear explosions.

The USA has (in 1987) only one old Vela-type satellite in operation, but the new navigation satellites, which are part of the Global Positioning System (GPS)[6] scheduled for full deployment in 1988, will also be nuclear (explosion) detection satellites (NDSs). They will be part of the Integrated Operational Nuclear Detection System (IONDS) which, for example, is to make damage assessment during a nuclear conflict. A total of 18 satellites will eventually be able to provide global, round-the-clock monitoring of atmospheric (and probably deep space) nuclear explosions.

III. Radar monitoring of the ionosphere

An underground explosion produces physical disturbances which propagate through the crust of the earth as standard seismic waves, but it also gives rise to an acoustic wave in the atmosphere, which may be detected by some of its secondary effects during propagation if these are sufficiently strong. What happens is simply that the explosion provokes a strong vibration in a large part of the earth surface which is transferred to the atmosphere as a sequence of over- and under-pressures, that is, as a sound wave radiating out from the ground zero (epicentre) area.

The principal secondary effect generated by the acoustic wave is a disturbance in the ionosphere which may be measured by using radar reflecting techniques,[7] if the approximate location of the test area is known. As the sound wave travels towards the upper atmosphere, its amplitude increases owing to the decreasing air density, and at ionospheric heights (90–300 km) it causes a sizeable displacement of the ambient free electrons. One result is that ordinary short-wave radio communications which depend on the reflective capacity of the ionosphere may be disrupted.

Such disruption phenomena were observed in connection with atmospheric nuclear testing in the 1950s and 1960s, when it was also noted that a horizontally moving, travelling ionospheric disturbance that circumnavigates the globe might be formed in the upper atmosphere. In fact, not only nuclear explosions but also chemical explosions, sonic booms, volcanoes, earthquakes and tsunamis may produce such effects. The problem is therefore whether technologies for monitoring the effects can be made sufficiently sophisticated to distinguish between these possible sources. It is of course also possible that the signals (for example, from a decoupled nuclear explosion) may be too weak to be detected.

Several laboratories, including the Lawrence Livermore National Laboratory, the Los Alamos National Laboratory and the Sandia Laboratory, have been developing the technique for monitoring ionospheric disturbances. In September 1981, an experiment was conducted with a chemical explosion on the earth surface, the Mill Race Event[8] at the White Sands Missile Range in New Mexico, in which vertical sounding measurements were made, allowing for calibration of models developed to describe the sound wave propagation and the ionospheric scattering of electromagnetic waves. A similar experiment had been conducted in 1964 in Canada.[9]

Although the Mill Race surface explosion, with a yield of 1 kt, produced a blast wave which was somewhat different from the acoustic wave from an underground nuclear explosion, it is reasonable to expect that the modelling of the various physical phenomena is approximately valid for a wide spectrum of situations. Experimentally, a ground radar transmitter sends radio-frequency signals, vertically or obliquely, towards the ionosphere above ground zero, and another ground receiver subsequently measures the arrival time and Doppler frequency shifts of the signals. The measurement of frequency shifts is convenient because it diminishes the effect of background noise.

It is not clear to what extent these experimental and modelling techniques allow underground nuclear explosions to be identified among the other possible sources of ionospheric disturbances. However, it is not unreasonable to assume that a detection system could be set up which singles out the signals from underground nuclear and chemical explosions (without being able to distinguish between the two) if the signals are strong enough. In any case, it is likely that the associated yield determination will be very imprecise, as will the localization of the ground zero.

Ionospheric sounding is not limited to the use of ground stations; satellites may also play a role.[10] Thus, for example, two satellites in a joint US–Canadian project, ISIS-1 and ISIS-2, were launched in 1969 and 1971, respectively, to measure ionospheric electron densities and, with a very-low-frequency receiver, to monitor radio signals produced by the movement of electrons in the ionosphere caused by the acoustic wave. Two Japanese satellites with similar capacities were launched in 1976 and 1978, respectively. However, there is no indication that development of satellite-based sounding systems has been pursued since then.

IV. Detection of airborne radioactivity

The advantages to be gained from redundancy in monitoring nuclear explosions were made rather clear by the 1979 event in the Indian Ocean. The circumstance that only one Vela-type satellite registered something unusual, and the fact that no alternative verification systems based on other physical principles were in place, gave rise to the unfortunate uncertainties about what actually happened. A global network for monitoring releases of radioactive particles into the atmosphere[11] is one alternative system which could fulfil a number of useful functions.

Atmospheric nuclear explosions produce a large number of radioactive isotopes composed of the fission products from the chain reaction and the irradiated material of the bomb casing. The radioactive particles rise high up in the atmosphere and under the effect of the wind quickly diffuse to other parts of the globe. During the days and weeks following the explosion, the particles descend to the earth surface. The radioactive isotopes can easily be detected and some of them, for example Strontium-90, may even present a global health hazard, as was strongly argued in the late 1950s and early 1960s. All radioactive fall-out effects are of course exacerbated if the explosions are surface explosions.

In principle, underground nuclear explosions do not release any radioactivity into the atmosphere, but in practice this has been the case on a substantial number of occasions. Underground testing is normally conducted at a depth of a few hundred metres (depending on the earth material) under the surface, and the bomb equipment is put in place through a vertical hole and sometimes also horizontal tunnels. When everything is in place, the drill holes are filled with magnetite, sand and rubble, and are sealed off with layers of, for example, epoxy. A complication in this filling procedure is the fact that the diagnostic system requires the emplacement of a large number of cables, running from the measuring caravans on the surface down through the hole to the nuclear device. When the filling (or 'stemming') is incorrectly designed or improperly emplaced, when the surrounding medium is faulted or when the actual explosive yield is somewhat higher than was anticipated, releases of radioactive material, or venting, may occur.

Several such cases have been reported.[12] It has, for example, been claimed that the USA has detected radioactivity near the Soviet border on about 200 different occasions over the past 23 years. In 100 of those cases, a connection with Soviet underground tests could be inferred, and US officials informally protested to the Soviet Union, on the grounds that, according to the PTBT (Article I, 1b), nuclear tests may not be conducted 'if such explosion causes radioactive debris to be present outside the territorial limits of the State under whose jurisdiction or control such explosions are conducted'.

The USSR has also complained about radioactive releases from US tests, and radioactivity from tests at the Nevada Test Site was detected in Canada on several occasions. According to the US Environmental Protection Agency, 97 weapon tests conducted between 1964 and 1970 gave rise to accidental releases of radioactive gases; on 31 of those occasions, clouds drifted outside the test area.[13] These numbers (97 and 31) amount to 39 per cent and 13 per cent, respectively, of the total US tests during the period. Even if the occurrence of such accidents may have diminished substantially since then, they do still happen. A recent example was the 'Mighty Oak' event in April 1986; a piece of containment did not work properly, with the result that radioactive Xenon was deliberately released into the atmosphere.[14]

A global network for monitoring radioactive releases from nuclear tests will of course have a detection efficiency which depends basically on the number of measuring stations. It has been estimated that a reasonably efficient system should have around 50 ground stations distributed strategically around the world.[15] Their positions can be approximately determined by taking account of the general circulation patterns of the atmosphere, but the theoretical efficiency of detection naturally depends on a number of physical assumptions concerning the diffusion of the radioactivity.

The detectors could be set to monitor various kinds of radionuclides; for above-ground explosions, Barium-140—with a half-life about 13 days—appears to be the most suitable candidate for detection; for underground explosions, radioactive noble gases may be more appropriate. Taking the example of an above-ground nuclear explosion with a 1-kt yield, it is possible to develop models for the rise and spread of radioactive aerosols in a standard large-scale wind environment, and the resulting likely deposition patterns may be estimated. Thus 50 ground stations are considered to be sufficient to detect, within 15 days, an explosion with a probability of at least 25 per cent.[16]

The detailed theoretical design of a global network must of course be made according to the particular type of nuclear tests of concern (above- or underground) and to a given level of ambition for detection efficiency. Whatever the uncertainties in such theoretical modelling, the practical experience from measurements of airborne radioactive material from atmospheric nuclear tests is encouraging for the general idea of a network.[17] Thus, for example, of 21 Chinese tests, 20 were detected in Japan within a few days of the test, at least 18 were detected in the USA within 14 days, and all of them were detected in Europe within about 20 days. The actual density of monitoring stations in the northern hemisphere is approximately as great as required by a reasonably effective global network, whereas the southern hemisphere is only poorly covered at present.

V. On-site monitoring

On-site inspection is certainly the most intrusive method of verification for determining whether a nuclear explosion has taken place and, if so, also for determining its physical characteristics. Technical methods for on-site monitoring have been discussed for a long time,[18] and some of them were developed quite extensively during the years.

The on-site inspection techniques for determining whether or not an explosion took place include seismic aftershock studies, magnetic field surveys to find ferro-magnetic material close to the explosion and studies of shock wave effects in the ground. If the site of a suspected explosion has been located within a few metres, radiochemical sampling may be feasible, leading to an absolute confirmation of the nuclear detonation. Radiochemical sampling of nuclear debris also offers a very precise method for determining the physical characteristics of the nuclear device. In fact, many underground nuclear tests are routinely assessed by sampling from a borehole which is drilled obliquely from the earth surface down to the explosion cavity.

Another interesting on-site monitoring technique is the CORRTEX method, which was developed during the past decade and came to wide public attention through a speech by President Reagan on 14 March 1986. This technique would probably be a valuable verification instrument under all the limited (high/low threshold) test ban regimes being discussed. CORRTEX is an abbreviation for Continuous Reflectometry for Radius versus Time Experiments and was developed at the Los Alamos National Laboratory.[19] In the Soviet Union a similar technique, abbreviated as MIS (Method of Impulse Sensing), has also been investigated for some time.[20]

The principle of the CORRTEX monitoring system is very simple. An underground nuclear explosion produces a shock wave which propagates radially outwards from the nuclear explosion, and the associated overpressure crushes various materials encountered on its way. Thus, a coaxial cable in the emplacement hole, or in a separate vertical hole nearby, would be gradually crushed, short-circuited and effectively shortened as the shock wave expands. A measuring instrument on the earth surface connected to the coaxial cable can easily register the rate at which the cable is short-circuited during the few tens of milliseconds it takes for the shock wave to reach the surface. Subsequently, an analysis of the shock wave expansion data permits a fairly precise estimate of the explosion yield.

More than 200 experiments with CORRTEX (not all in connection with nuclear tests) were performed in the USA during the period 1976–82. The conclusion reached is that the system is both highly efficient and easy to deploy. For nuclear tests the coaxial cable may be placed in a separate drill hole so as not to interfere with the diagnostic system; in this way only information related to the weapon yield (and not the weapon design) is retrieved. Placing a separate vertical hole at a distance of about 10–20 metres from the emplacement hole has been found to be adequate, but it may be possible to place it at even greater distances since sufficiently thin coaxial cables would be crushed at distances of up to a few hundred metres. The yield determination has been reported to be exact to within 20–30 per cent, depending on the yield. For small-yield tests, the shock wave is weaker and the CORRTEX cable must be placed closer to the nuclear device. However, there is no reason to believe that the method should not be both feasible and valuable in such situations. For the purpose of an LTTB, it would be interesting to have more precise information about the efficiency of the CORRTEX method in the yield range 1–20 kt.

VI. Conclusions

At present, the restriction on the underground nuclear testing of the superpowers is the 150-kt limit of the 1974 TTBT, even though this treaty has not been ratified. It is likely that the verification of compliance with this limit could be substantially enhanced if the provisions of the companion TTBT protocol concerning the exchange of geological data and calibration tests were respected. In this regard, the CORRTEX method described above may play an important role.

The basic problem with the TTBT is the difficulties associated with inferring the size of an explosive yield from a measured seismic magnitude; the capacity of the seismic network and knowledge about the geological structure of the test area are obviously important elements in establishing such a relation. But it is equally important to have calibration measurements where the seismic measurements can be compared directly to a known explosive yield. It is clear, however, that one side would never be certain about the exactitude of a yield reported by the other side, and this is where the possibility of an on-site use of the CORRTEX system appears to be an interesting option.

A possible scheme for calibration measurements would involve one side installing its own monitoring equipment in a prepared drill hole at the test site of the other side, and vice versa. The equipment is both portable and easy to use, and confidence in the measuring results would be as high as when applied at the proper test site. An even simpler scheme would be to allow one party to bring its own yield-certified bomb to the test site of the other party and detonate it there. In conjunction with other verification measures envisioned in the TTBT protocol, there is good reason to believe that compliance with the 150-kt limit could be assessed with a high level of confidence.

The usefulness of such measures is of course not limited to the TTBT; they could also be relevant for a low-threshold test ban.[21] The low limit to which current verification technologies could be applied rather unambiguously is at around 1–10 kt, with the discrimination threshold being somewhat higher than the detection threshold. Also, for such low-yield tests, it is likely that the CORRTEX system could play an important role in the calibration tests required to have confidence in the verification of compliance.

The above discussion may also be relevant for the purpose of a CTB. In fact, before the conclusion of a CTB a number of low-yield nuclear tests could be conducted, monitored by the full spectrum of seismological and non-seismological technologies. This would provide data that might render the detection of testing in violation of a future CTB more probable if tests were conducted above a certain threshold.

Monitoring atmospheric radioactivity associated with nuclear tests is a useful and relatively cheap complement to other verification methods. For explosions in the atmosphere, satellite monitoring using light and X-ray signals would in general appear to offer sufficient coverage, but experience shows that it is prudent, if not necessary, to use a back-up system based on a different physical principle. For underground explosions under the present TTBT or a future more restrictive regime, monitoring of atmospheric radioactivity seems useful in so far as it may provide additional information about tests detected by other means. The release of radioactivity into the atmosphere in connection with underground tests could probably be avoided if the tests were prepared with enough care; however, past experience shows that this has often not been the case. Monitoring of radioactivity could be useful under a future CTB regime in hypothetical situations where some very-low-yield tests, escaping detection by other methods, might still accidentally release radioactive gases into the atmosphere.

Radar monitoring of the ionosphere is a verification method which triggers on a secondary seismic effect: the sound wave perturbation of the upper atmosphere. It is unlikely that this effect could provide more precise information about underground nuclear tests than the primary seismic signals. Therefore, this type of monitoring should probably be seen as having only a complementary role in any test ban verification scheme.

Satellite monitoring would play a crucial role in negation (deterring violations) and confidence building under any test ban regime, including a CTB. It fulfils a general intelligence-gathering function, using photographic and other sensors, which is important for assessing whether one or the other side is taking actions which could be interpreted as a possible non-compliance with existing treaties. Photographic reconnaissance, to be effective, requires redundant satellite platforms capable of wide-area and frequent observations, as well as high resolution. Even then, surveillance will be limited to daylight and fair weather. However, in terms of area and frequency, the coverage of remote sensing platforms might very well be significantly enhanced beyond current capabilities; this is possible on both a national and an international level.

Whether or not the existing nuclear test ban treaties are ratified, it is of great importance to apply the widest possible spectrum of verification methods, including satellite-based systems, to provide a monitoring capacity for all activities related to the development and testing of nuclear weapons. In general, effective and redundant verification methods are the key to both confidence building and durable test ban treaties.

Notes and references

[1] Hafemeister, D., Romm, J. J. and Tsipis, K., 'The verification of compliance with arms control agreements', *Scientific American*, vol. 252 (1985), p. 29.

[2] Dalman, O. and Israelson, H., *Monitoring Underground Nuclear Explosions* (Elsevier: Amsterdam, 1977), fig. 14.4, p. 334.

[3] Sykes, L. R., 'Verification of nuclear test ban treaties', *Testimony before the Subcommittee on Arms Control, International Security and Science*, Committee on Foreign Affairs, United States House of Representatives, May 8, 1985, Washington, DC.

[4] Glasstone, S. and Dolan, P. J., *The Effects of Nuclear Weapons* (US DOD: Washington, DC, 1977).

[5] 'Developments in technical capabilities for detecting and identifying nuclear weapon tests', *Hearings before the Joint Committee on Atomic Energy*, US Congress (US Government Printing Office: Washington, DC, 1963), p. 415.

[6] McDonald, K. D., 'Navigation satellite systems: their characteristics, potential and military applictions', ed. B. Jasani, SIPRI, *Outer Space—A New Dimension of the Arms Race* (Taylor & Francis: London, 1982), p. 155.

[7] 'Ionospheric detection of explosions', *Energy and Technology Review* (Lawrence Livermore National Laboratory), May 1983, p. 38.

[8] Simons, D. J. *et al.*, EOS, *Transaction American Geophysical Union*, vol. 62 (1981), p. 979.

[9] Barry, G. H. *et al.*, *Journal of Geophysical Research*, vol. 71 (1966), p. 4173.

[10] Jasani, B. and Barnaby, F., *Verification Technologies* (Berg Publishers: Dover, NH, 1984).

[11] Rodhe, H. and Hamrud, M., 'On the design of a global detection system for airborne radioactivity', Report CM-68, January 1985, Department of Meteorology, University of Stockholm.

[12] See e.g. statements by various US officials reported in *Washington Post*, 9 May 1986, p. 23.

[13] Note 12.

[14] Note 12.

[15] See note 11, which was a background paper for a report submitted by the Swedish delegation to the Committee on Disarmament in August 1983.

[16] Note 11.

[17] Rangarajan, C. and Eapen, C. D., 'The global movement of radioactive debris from nuclear tests', Environmental Report EML-390, Environmental Measurements Laboratory, US Department of Energy, 1981.

[18] See e.g. George, T. A., Statement in *Hearings before the Joint Committee on Atomic Energy*, Congress of the United States, Eighty-eighth Congress, First session on developments in technical capabilities for detecting and identifying nuclear weapons tests (US Government Printing Office: Washington, DC, 1963), p. 238.

[19] See e.g. Virchow, C. F. *et al.*, *Review of Scientific Instruments*, vol. 51, no. 5 (May 1980), p. 642; and *Research Highlights* (Los Alamos National Laboratory), 1985, p. 12.

[20] Mr Petrosyants, USSR, CD document CD/P.V.353, 3 Apr. 1986, p. 12.

[21] Din, A., 'Nuclear test bans', *Journal of Peace Research*, vol. 24, no. 2 (1987), p. 105.

Chapter XII. On-site inspection to check compliance

Paper 14

Warren Heckrotte

Lawrence Livermore National Laboratory, Livermore, CA

Abstract

A seismic monitoring system and on-site inspections are the major components of a verification system for a CTBT to give parties assurance that clandestine underground nuclear weapon tests are not taking place. The primary task lies with the seismic monitoring system which must be capable of identifying most earthquakes in the magnitude range of concern, leaving at most a small number of unidentified events. If any unidentified event on the territory of one party appeared suspicious to another party, and thus potentially an explosion, an on-site inspection could be invoked to decide whether or not a nuclear explosion had taken place. Over the years, on-site inspections have been one of the most contentious issues in test ban negotiations. In the uncompleted negotiations of 1977–80 between the USA, the UK and the USSR, voluntary OSIs were established as a basis for negotiation. Voluntary OSIs would require a common interest and co-operation toward resolving suspicions if OSIs were to serve the purpose of confidence building. On the technical level, an OSI could not ensure identification of a clandestine test, but an evader would probably in any case reject any request for an OSI at the site of an evasive test, rather than run the risk of discovery. The verification system does not provide direct physical evidence of a violation. This could pose a difficult and controversial decision on compliance.

I. History of on-site inspections

Conference of Experts, 1958

In the spring of 1958, an exchange of correspondence between President Eisenhower and Premier Krushchev led to the convening of the Geneva Experts Conference, composed of experts from East and West. The conference was to study methods for detecting possible violations of an agreement on the cessation of nuclear tests. President Eisenhower had made the convening of this conference a necessary prerequisite for the start of negotiations on the cessation of nuclear weapon tests. The experts met for seven weeks in the summer of 1958. They concluded that it was 'technically feasible to set up a workable and effective control system for the detection of violations of an agreement on the world-wide cessation of nuclear weapon tests'.[1] The elements of the control system were described. A primary element was a seismic system for the detection of possible underground nuclear explosions. Another element was on-site inspections (OSIs): 'when the control posts detect an event which cannot be identified by the international control organ and which could be suspected of being a nuclear explosion, the international control organ can send an inspection group to the site of the event in order to determine whether a nuclear explosion had taken place or not'. This statement suggests that two conditions would apply for sending an inspection team to the site of the event: first, that the event was not identified, which in effect meant that it was not identified as an earthquake; and second, that it could be 'suspected' of being a nuclear explosion. What constituted a basis for suspicion was not established except for one instance—an unidentified seismic event in an aseismic region. The report also stated that a larger number of unidentified events would necessitate a larger number of on-site inspections, without, however, advancing a quantitative correlation.

The experts' report established a role for on-site inspection in the verification of a comprehensive nuclear weapon test ban, a role which persists to this day. OSIs were to be an adjunct to the seismic detection system, and their role would in effect be determined by the capabilities of the seismic system to detect and identify earthquakes. The report did not establish the procedures for the conduct of an OSI—how an OSI was to be initiated and how it was to be carried out. This latter was left to the political negotiations to develop.

Early CTB negotiations

The position of the West (the USA and the UK) in the opening stages of the political negotiations on the operation of the international control organization for OSIs was as follows. Every detected seismic event would be analysed, using agreed seismic criteria, by the control organization. Every seismic event that could not be identified as an earthquake through application of the criteria would automatically be inspected by personnel of the control organization. On-site inspections were thus mandatory, and the number would be fixed by the background of earthquakes, the capability of the seismic detection system and the character of the seismic criteria. Every unidentified seismic event was, in effect, regarded as a potential underground nuclear explosion that should be inspected in order to determine whether a nuclear explosion had taken place or not. OSIs were seen as a necessary element in the verification system to deter evasion and, failing that, to disclose an evasion attempt.

The Soviet Union had a contrary view. An unidentified seismic event about which another party was concerned should be the subject of consultation between the parties. An inspection could take place only if there was agreement between the parties. This approach to OSIs would in later years be described as 'voluntary OSIs'. For the West, this procedure constituted a veto. A party could carry out a clandestine nuclear weapon test and then, if it were detected and classified as unidentified, block an inspection. For the Soviet Union, though, the approach of the West represented unwarranted intrusion, an infringement of sovereignty, which could endanger state security by obtaining information not relevant to the purpose of verification—in short, espionage. In the Soviet view, if the consultations between the parties showed that there was a basis for suspicion, the party on whose territory the event took place would certainly agree to the inspection in order to have it demonstrated that the event was not a nuclear explosion.[2] The Soviet Union perceived OSIs not as a procedure to identify a possible nuclear explosion, but as a device—a final means—to demonstrate compliance, to show that the event, in spite of the suspicions, was an earthquake. OSIs were a confidence-building measure. Their approach rested on the view, often expressed, that when a state becomes party to an agreement it does so with the intention to observe the obligations, not to violate them.

This impasse over OSIs was partially broken when it was agreed that there should be a guaranteed yearly quota of OSIs. The eligibility of an event for inspection would be determined as before. An unidentified event in the Soviet Union could be inspected at the request of the USA and/or the UK (only, and not at the request of any other party) as long as the quota for inspections in the USSR was not exceeded. Similarly, an event in the USA (or the UK) could be inspected at the request of the Soviet Union (only, and not at the request of any other party) as long as the quota for inspections in the USA (or the UK) was not exceeded. Unidentified events on the territory of any other party to the treaty could be inspected at the request of any party as long as the quota established for the inspected party was not exceeded. Inspections, within the yearly quota, could not be rejected by the party on whose territory the event occurred.

The West took the position that the numerical value of the quota should bear a relation to the mean annual number of unidentified events on the territory of a party to the treaty. Thus the West did not change their view on the role of OSIs. The USSR, on the other hand, saw the numerical value of the quota as strictly a political matter and did not change its basic view of the matter. When numerical values were advanced the disparity was striking: for the West, 20; for the USSR, 3. The West gradually reduced the number sought, justifying the reduction on scientific and technological grounds, to a final value of 7 in 1963. About this time, the Soviet Union went from 3 to 0, holding that OSIs were not necessary for verification of a CTB.

This numerical difference over the quota came to symbolize the difference between the parties on on-site inspection and, more generally, verification. As fundamental were their differing views on the make-up of the control organization. The Soviet Union viewed the proposals of the West to be designed to ensure control by the West of the control organization. The West saw the Soviet proposals to be designed to ensure that the USSR could block actions of the control organization, and thwart the inspection of a suspicious event. There was little room for compromise.

In 1963 the USA and the UK introduced at the Eighteen-Nation Disarmament Conference (ENDC) a proposal drastically simplifying the control organization and putting verification on a largely adversarial basis.[3] Each party, and not the control organization, would have responsibility for verification of the compliance of the other parties. Each party would apply the seismic criteria and decide within the limits of the quota whether an event was eligible for inspection and the location of the inspection. By this time, the Soviet view was that OSIs were unnecessary and unacceptable, and the new proposal had no impact on negotiations. Nevertheless, this proposal marked the end of consideration of a substantive role for an international control organization for verification of a CTB.

From this time until 1977 the debate on the CTB was largely pro forma. The USA claimed that OSIs were necessary for verification of a CTB; the USSR claimed they were unnecessary. In the mid-1960s Sweden pushed the idea of challenge OSIs for verification of a CTB.[4] If a seismic event occurs on the territory of country A and the event appears suspicious to country B, and thus is possibly an explosion, country B can request permission to inspect the region surrounding the event. Country A can either accept or reject the request. If one or several requests were rejected, country B could choose to withdraw from the treaty. The Soviet Union rejected this approach—OSIs were unnecessary. The USA sharply criticized the idea, claiming that voluntary OSIs would not provide the assurance needed for adequate verification.[5]

Tripartite negotiations, 1977–80

In 1975 the USSR presented a draft CTB treaty to the UN General Assembly in which there were no provisions for OSIs. In 1976 the Soviet Union amended the text to include the possibility of voluntary inspections. They were prepared to accept voluntary OSIs in order to move the matter forward, even though they continued to believe that national technical means were adequate for verification of a CTB.

Full tripartite (USA–USSR–UK) negotiations for a CTB began in Geneva in the fall of 1977. The USSR reaffirmed its willingness to accept voluntary OSIs but was adamant that mandatory OSIs were unacceptable. In response, the USA reassessed its position in the early stages of the negotiations, switched from its long-held position that OSIs should be mandatory, and accepted voluntary OSIs. This switch was contingent on two conditions: that the rejection of an OSI request be established as a serious matter, little different from thwarting a mandatory OSI, and that effective procedures for the conduct of an OSI be established in the agreement.

The acceptance of voluntary on-site inspection by the two sides brought the issue back to the initial Soviet stance of 1958—an OSI required agreement between the requesting and the requested parties. For the USA it was a radical change. Nevertheless, the US assessment of the role of OSIs remained the same: OSIs were still seen to pose the threat of discovery, if a clandestine test were carried out. This provided the rationale for the US insistence on treaty provisions for effective procedures for the conduct of an OSI. A potential evader would be forced to minimize the chance of discovery, thus raising the cost of evasion, and none the less still face the risk of being found out. Both technical and political disincentives were posed. If, nevertheless, a clandestine test were carried out, it is unlikely that an evader presented with a request for an inspection of the actual site of a clandestine nuclear weapon test would allow the inspection to take place under either the mandatory or voluntary approach.[6] Under the mandatory approach this would be a clear breach of the agreement. In accepting the voluntary approach, the USA sought to achieve the equivalent effect by establishing that the rejection of a request would be a serious matter.

The parties agreed that any party to the treaty that had questions regarding an event on the territory of any other party could request an on-site inspection for the purpose of ascertaining whether or not the event was a nuclear explosion.[7] The requesting party must state the reason for the request, including appropriate evidence. The party receiving the request would state whether or not it was prepared to agree to the inspection. If the requested party was not prepared to accept the inspection, it would have to provide the reason for non-acceptance. The treaty also provided for any two or more parties to agree upon additional measures to facilitate verification. The three negotiating parties were negotiating such additional measures as would apply among them. The additional measures specified in greater detail the procedures under which on-site inspections would be conducted and incorporated a list of rights and functions of the personnel carrying out the inspections, as well as the role of the host party. Significant progress was made in developing these additional measures before the negotiations ended in November 1980.[8]

The negotiations were not completed, so it is not known whether terms acceptable to the parties would have been arrived at. Nevertheless, it appears that only the voluntary form of OSIs offers the basis for an agreement providing for on-site inspection in a CTB, given the Soviet position that mandatory OSIs are unacceptable.[9]

The parties to the Stockholm Conference on Confidence and Security Building Measures and Disarmament in Europe have agreed to procedures for mandatory on-site inspections with regard to certain notifiable military activities. Whether this agreement could presage a change in position of the Soviet Union regarding mandatory inspection would be only a matter of conjecture. The circumstances for inspection in the Stockholm Document are, however, very different from those for a nuclear weapon test ban. Also, the USSR has not been willing to agree to mandatory inspection in an agreement banning the production of chemical weapons for the purpose of inspecting possible or suspected undeclared storage or production sites of chemical weapons.

The UK has introduced into the chemical weapon negotiations a form of challenge inspection which retains what it calls 'a very limited right of refusal' of inspection.[10] If the requested party refuses a request for an inspection, it is bound to provide alternative measures that must satisfy the requesting party with a set time period. If the requesting party is not satisfied, the matter would go to the Executive Council (established by the agreement) for consideration.

II. Voluntary OSIs: initiation and potential problems

How would voluntary OSIs work? There are both political and technical aspects, although many of the technical aspects are independent of whether an OSI is mandatory or voluntary, since technical procedures come into play after the inspection is initiated. These will be considered later. It is in the initiation of an OSI—the request, and the acceptance or refusal—that several, primarily political, issues arise.

One scenario, compatible with the agreements of the 1977–80 negotiations, is that a party who finds an unidentified event on the territory of another party to be suspicious would raise the matter with that party. The basis of the concern would be described. Consultations could lead to a satisfactory explanation of the doubt without recourse to an OSI. If not, however, an OSI would be requested to resolve the doubt. The party upon whose territory the event occurred would surely be interested in dispelling legitimate (though incorrect) suspicions and so would agree to an OSI. This scenario requires a common interest and co-operation on the part of the parties to resolve the doubt, if the integrity of the treaty regime is to be maintained. As is discussed below, the success of the actual inspection is also dependent upon co-operation.

An argument made in the past against voluntary OSIs was that a request for an OSI was in effect an accusation of cheating, thus inherently confrontational and hardly conducive to co-operation.[11] More specific points of possible difference can be raised. Would there be a common view of an unidentified event? The historical record is full of examples of differences between the USA and the USSR over test ban seismology. Would there be a common view of what constituted a 'suspicious event', or would one party's view of suspicion be seen by the other as harassment? Could a rejection of an OSI request on the basis of legitimate protection of secrets be made convincingly acceptable to the other party, or would it be regarded as an indication of evasion (the illegitimate protection of secrets)?

These are potential problems with voluntary OSIs that could challenge good intentions of the parties. One might consider that some of these potential problems could be headed off by some measure of codification of 'unidentified' and 'suspicious'. To do so, however, would tend to move the matter back to the basis for mandatory OSIs. For, if an event by accepted criteria is unidentified and suspicious, why should there be a basis for rejection of the request of an OSI? Inherent in the structure of voluntary OSIs is some measure of flexibility in forming the basis for the justification of a request.

If there is not co-operation or good faith between the parties, then voluntary

OSIs appear to be vulnerable to misuse through either requests or rejections of requests. A party who wanted to withdraw from the agreement could refuse to accept OSIs which had a legitimate basis in the hope that the requesting party would withdraw and take the onus for ending the treaty, an argument once advanced against voluntary OSIs.[12] On the converse side, a party could make ill-founded requests for OSIs, and by such harassment use the expected rejections as a basis for withdrawal and thereby attempt to put the onus on the other party. In response to these postulated scenarios, it could be observed that, for any agreement, if one party wants to withdraw, reasons could be found for withdrawal and others would be blamed for the need to withdraw. Voluntary OSIs would not seem to be unique as a device to put blame on another party. The real concern for voluntary OSIs is not the deliberate misuse but whether, given compliance, they can stand up against the inevitable tensions that at times beset the parties—whether they will truly serve as a confidence-building procedure.

Mandatory on-site inspections as envisaged in the 1958–61 negotiations would appear to avoid the problems broached here. An event was eligible for inspection when determined to be so by the application of agreed criteria by the international control organization. Parties were obliged to accept the organization's decision. The negotiating parties, however, could not then agree on the make-up of the organization to ensure objective implementation of the rules and procedures. The approach toward mandatory OSIs proposed by the USA in 1963 left the application of the criteria for the selection of an event for inspection solely in the hands of the requesting party. This formulation could appear to be non-objective in application. Its success would certainly depend on co-operation between the parties; in effect, agreement on the application of the criteria. The actual inspection whether initiated by mandatory or voluntary procedure would be dependent, as noted, on co-operation between the parties if it was to be effective.

III. Seismic monitoring: requirements for OSIs

The experts' report established OSIs as an adjunct of a seismic monitoring system, an additional tool to assist in the identification of seismic events. The role for OSIs was dependent on the assessment of the capability of the proposed seismic monitoring system to detect and identify seismic events. Since that time there have been significant advances, scientific and technical, in seismic monitoring systems. It is not the purpose here to evaluate the capabilities of such systems. However, it is necessary to take account of these capabilities, as they are presently assessed, in so far as they have an impact on the potential role and value of OSIs.

From the US perspective that a verification system is to serve as a deterrent to evasion and failing that to have a possibility to identify an evasion attempt, the seismic monitoring system needs the capability to detect attempted clandestine nuclear explosions above some threshold yield of concern, and to identify, in so far as possible, earthquakes of comparable seismic magnitude so as to minimize false alarms. It is reasonable to assume that if a party sought to violate a CTB it would not conduct a test under present-day test practices, but would take sophisticated precautions to minimize the seismic signal or explosive-like characteristics of the test. One way would be to use decoupling—firing the explosive in a very large underground cavity[13]—by which the seismic signal from a decoupled explosion is substantially reduced so that it is equivalent to a yield about 50–100 times smaller than the actual yield.

The analyses of seismic monitoring systems that are found in the literature assume that the system should be capable of detecting a 1-kt test. This means, assuming the possibility of decoupling, that the system must be able to detect a decoupled test of 1 kt, or a seismically effective yield of about .01 kt. Seismologists appear to agree that it is possible to design a system of seismic stations within the Soviet Union that would provide this capability, although they differ as to the number and characteristics of the seismic stations required to do this.[14]

At the low seismic magnitude associated with decoupled explosions, there will be many hundreds of earthquakes annually. There is dispute among the seismologists as to whether these low-magnitude earthquakes can be distinguished from explosions. If they, or a substantial fraction of them, cannot be distinguished from explosions, there could be hundreds of ambiguous seismic events. No doubt some number could be ruled out as potential explosions because they occurred in locations that precluded a clandestine test, but a substantial number of ambiguous events would remain. If this were the case, on-site inspections do not appear to be a useful verification tool. There is the ample historical record that a large annual number of OSIs are politically unacceptable. Additionally, an OSI is a substantial endeavour in numbers of people, time, equipment and expense, and a large annual number would be an unacceptable burden. Thus a large number of ambiguous events above the threshold yield of concern would appear to pose a situation that could not be adequately verified, regardless of OSIs.

If, on the other hand, the seismic monitoring system can identify almost all of the earthquakes so that the number of unidentified events is small, then OSIs would have a role in the verification system. The main point of these considerations is that the principal burden for verification rests on the seismic monitoring system.

One complication is that a large number of chemical explosions for industrial purposes are carried out each year. Seismic monitoring might be able to distinguish some of these from potential nuclear explosions (because of the physical arrangement and firing pattern of the explosion), but not all of them. Some provision for notification and description of chemical explosions and possibly provisions for observers would probably be necessary to enable these events to be dealt with in most instances by means other than invoking a voluntary OSI.

Additionally, there are other postulated evasion schemes.[15] It is not the purpose here to evaluate them. They do not, however, lower the detection and identification threshold, as decoupling does. The burden would fall upon the seismic monitoring system to be able to pick out any such event as an unidentified or ambiguous event and thus be subject to a possible OSI.

IV. Location of an OSI: a critical element

The technical side of OSIs brings forward two basic aspects: the techniques for carrying out an OSI (the procedures and equipment), and the effectiveness of an OSI. Both aspects have complementary political issues.

The most critical element in the effectiveness of an OSI for identifying a clandestine nuclear explosion is the accurate determination of the location of the event. The reason for this is that data which could reveal the presence of a nuclear explosion can be found or detected only in the immediate vicinity of the event. The area of active search with the OSI techniques would be at most a few tens of square kilometres. To search a significantly greater area would require an inordinate number of personnel or amount of time.

The primary element in the verification system is the seismic monitoring system that detects the event. It cannot be expected, however, to determine with sufficient accuracy the location of the event, particularly for events of low magnitude—the area of uncertainty could be many hundreds of square kilometres. The accurate determination of location will depend on non-seismic national technical means and/or aerial survey. The most significant marker for determination of location within the area determined by the seismic monitoring system would be the existence of past human activity, for example, mining or drilling, which by some measure could be associated with a clandestine nuclear test. If there were no such record of human activity it would be difficult to see a basis for suspicion. In the abstract, it is probably not possible to quantify the possibility of a correct selection of the location of a clandestine test.

It was noted above that a party who carried out a clandestine test would probably not agree to an OSI if it was requested. However, this is only true if the correct location were sought for the OSI or it could be on the basis of an aerial survey. Otherwise permission could be safely given.

V. Techniques and procedures for an OSI

It is the deterrent role of OSIs which points out the apparent contradiction of requiring techniques which can identify the presence of a nuclear explosion, when permission for an OSI would be granted only if there were no explosion (or if an incorrect location were sought). Although the various techniques which can be brought to bear for OSIs do not guarantee that a clandestine explosion would be identified, they offer the possibility of identification—a possibility an evader would have to consider. There is scepticism voiced in the literature that an OSI would succeed in identifying a nuclear test; however, the scepticism is usually tempered by the observation that an evader could not rely on a negative assessment of the effectiveness of an OSI.[16]

The categories of techniques for carrying out an OSI have not changed over the years. Those put forward in the 1958–61 negotiations[17] still hold: aerial survey; visual and geological survey; seismic survey; survey for artifacts that could be associated with an explosion; and radiation survey.

Aerial survey

In the first instance the aerial survey technique could be used, as noted above, to determine the precise area for the employment of the other ground-based techniques. It could also be used to complement the ground search. A visual survey from the air would be a primary component of this activity. Features such as fractures or geological faults may be much more easily seen from the air than on the ground. Photographs would be used. Infra-red measurements can sometimes identify surface effects from ground shocks and show up areas of ground compacted by operational activities. Radiation monitoring would be employed. Electromagnetic and magnetic survey equipment could be used to look for buried metal artifacts.

Visual and geological survey

The visual and geological survey technique would entail an intensive examination of the area to look for any indications of a nuclear explosion. The survey would help locate the most appropriate sites for the seismometer, to note areas where intensive search for possible radioactivity should be undertaken. Any surface dislocations, and their pattern, would be noted. The survey would attempt to determine the sub-surface geology which would have application to the seismic survey.

Seismic survey

After-shocks follow both earthquakes and underground explosions, the rate decreasing with time. For after-shocks from an underground explosion in hard rock, the rate decreases approximately as the inverse 3/2 power of the time; six months after the explosion the rate is somewhat less than one per day.[18] For possible detection of after-shocks, the sooner the OSI takes place after the event the better. After-shocks from an explosion are very weak and would be detected only in the immediate vicinity of the explosion. The location of the after-shocks from an explosion would be expected to cluster around the cavity or the chimney produced by the explosion. It may also be possible to discriminate between explosion and earthquake after-shocks on the basis of waveform shape. The detection of a localized cluster of after-shocks at moderate depth could serve to localize further where the other inspection techniques should be employed. After-shocks located at depths of many kilometres would be an indication of an earthquake.

The local seismic network would consist of about 10–20 sensitive seismometers spread over an area of a few tens of square kilometres. The weakness of the signals from the region of a possible cavity, the requirement to accurately locate the source of signals and the size of the inspection area would establish the precise number of seismometers. The network must be set up to determine accurately the relative time of recording of an event at each of the seismometers in order to locate the place of origin of the signal. A model of the sub-surface geology would be needed. The geological survey combined with calibration by conventional geophysical techniques would provide this model. A small on-site computer would be required to process the data. The observation period should be at least 30 days in order to be able to record a significant number of events.

Survey for artifacts

One component of this survey would be the search for construction and engineering artifacts, including buried objects. Metal detectors would be used for this technique. A principal 'residue' of an underground explosion is a cavity or rubble-filled chimney. These can affect the electrical conductivity of the region. Geophysical exploration techniques can be used to search for such regions. Seismic sounding methods might also be used. While the presence of a sub-surface anomaly is not unique to a nuclear test, it could serve to localize further the application of the other techniques listed here.

Radiation survey

Radiation monitoring would be a major activity of an OSI. Radiation characteristic of a nuclear explosion would be the unique indicator of a nuclear explosion. Radiation could reach the surface through faulty containment, flow through fissures, or slow diffusion through permeable media. Portable radiation detection techniques would be used. Additionally, soil and rock samples, water supply, vegetation and small animals, and sub-surface gas samples would be obtained for laboratory analysis. Lower levels of radioactivity could be detected in this way than with the portable radiation detectors. This requires an appropriate chemical laboratory on site for the analysis of these samples.

One additional technique is that of drilling to search for radioactivity that would be in the vicinity of an explosion. The notion of drilling a large number of holes, randomly or systematically in the hope of intersecting a region of radioactivity, is hardly supportable.[19] It would probably be a hope in vain and wasteful of time and money. To justify drilling, the inspection should have uncovered some suggestive evidence of an explosion and determined a probable location. However, one could ask: If the evidence were compelling enough to justify drilling, would drilling really be necessary? Any such decision would rest on the particular evidence, but given the view that an evader would not agree to an OSI at the location of a test, drilling is unlikely to be undertaken.

General considerations

It would serve no purpose to develop a scenario of an OSI to display how these techniques would be used. The details would depend on too many particular details of a given site: the terrain, the particular character of past and present human activity, the weather, and, no doubt, unforeseen circumstances. Of more importance are some general considerations. The responsibility for carrying out the inspections, collecting the data, using the instruments and analysing the data rests with the inspection team. These are responsibilities that cannot be shared with the host party; otherwise, it could bring into question the integrity of the inspection and the conclusion to be derived from it. While there is not co-operation at this level, the OSI cannot succeed without co-operation by both parties. The inspection team will be dependent on the host party for transportation to the site, local transportation at the site, housing, subsistence, communication with the outside world, assistance, if requested, for siting equipment, and non-interference with the legitimate activities of the inspection. The inspection team will have to confine itself to legitimate activities. The data collected by the inspection team and the analysis of the data will have to be shared with the host party, although the conclusions based on the analysis would be the sole responsibility of the requesting party.

The samples and data collected will have to be analysed on site. The OSI team must be scientifically and technically self-sufficient. The necessary skills and equipment for collecting the data, analysing it on site, adjusting the programme to reflect results of analysis, and maintaining the equipment must be present with the team.[20] In 1963, an official of the US Arms Control and Disarmament Agency estimated that a team of 20 would be needed, operating in the field for 45 days.[21] However, the capability in the described techniques that would be fielded today and the self-sufficiency required would indicate a somewhat larger team than was suggested then.

Could these techniques determine the presence of a clandestine nuclear explosion? An evader would no doubt go to great length to avoid the possibility. The explosion would be set at great depths to eliminate surface effects. Large efforts would be made to ensure containment of radioactivity. No doubt some cover activity would be associated with the explosion, and artifacts could have a legitimate reason for their presence. Nevertheless, the evader could not be assured that there would not be local seismic signals from the vicinity of the explosion. The evader might seek to delay in so far as possible the inspection, to minimize this risk. On the other hand, given time, there could be a greater chance that some small amounts of radioactivity would escape to the surface. In the case of decoupling, if the cavity were to be re-used and thus opened, it could be difficult to ensure that no radioactivity escaped to the surface. Finally, a cavity or rubble-filled chimney would also exist, which might be detected. One cannot say that these techniques would succeed, but an evader could not be assured they would fail. The safest course if an evasive test were carried out would be to refuse a request for an OSI at the site of the explosion.

Finally, it should be noted that under the circumstances of compliance an OSI cannot provide proof that an explosion did not take place, nor can it be expected to prove that an earthquake took place. The only signs of a past earthquake would be surface disturbances and residual seismic activity. For a small-magnitude event, there is no assurance that such signs will be found. Under the circumstance of compliance, the OSI can only be expected to conclude that no evidence of a nuclear explosion was found.

VI. Conclusion

Seismic monitoring and on-site inspections have the purpose in the first place of providing some measure of confidence that other parties are in compliance with a CTBT, that clandestine underground nuclear tests are not taking place. The second and complementary role of the verification system is deterrence of evasion, by threat of disclosure, and failing that to disclose an evasion attempt. The principal burden for these tasks lies with the seismic monitoring system which, to be relevant to the task, should leave unidentified very few earthquakes in the magnitude range of concern. OSIs would then have the task of resolving doubt over any of these few unidentified events on the territory of one party found, for some reason, to be suspicious. Voluntary OSIs appear to be the only form of OSIs that are politically acceptable.

Assuming compliance, voluntary OSIs can only succeed in their purpose of dispelling suspicion and confidence building if there is co-operation among the parties, a mutual interest in resolving doubt. It is the presumption of these attitudes which lies at the foundation of the rationale for voluntary OSIs. Nevertheless, in times of political tension between the parties, it may be difficult to isolate the voluntary OSI procedures from these external stresses.

If one party were in time to find a motivation to resume tests, it would have three choices: to continue adherence; to test clandestinely; or to abrogate the treaty and test openly. A variety of considerations would enter into the decision, and the deterrent role of the verification system is to weigh the choice between adherence or abrogation. If deterrence failed and a clandestine test were carried out, which led to a request for an OSI at the location of the test, it seems unlikely that the evader would permit an OSI. The request would be rejected. The consequence is that evidence of violation would not be hard but would rest on indirect physical evidence (the basis for the request) and the political act of rejection (though no doubt accompanied by attempts at justification).

The verification system for a CTBT is not likely to provide unambiguous evidence of violation. Is rejection an admission of guilt? Probably yes to some, but not necessarily to others. Would it warrant strong political action, including ultimately abrogation? The assessments and actions taken would depend on the circumstances of the time, but, whatever the course of action, it would be accompanied by political controversy.

Notes and references

[1]   The experts' report can be found in *Documents on Disarmament 1945–1959* (US Department of State: Washington, DC, 1960), vol. 2, pp. 1090–11.

[2]   *Geneva Conference on the Discontinuance of Nuclear Weapon Tests, History and Analysis of Negotiations* (US Department of State: Washington, DC, 1961), p. 34. A similar exposition was put forward by Schelling, T. C. and Halperin, M. W., *Strategy and Arms Control* (Twentieth Century Fund: New York, 1961; Kraus Reprint Co: 1975), pp. 95–6.

[3]   *Documents on Disarmament 1963* (US Arms Control and Disarmament Agency: Washington, DC, 1964), pp. 141–5.

[4]   *Documents on Disarmament 1966* (US Arms Control and Disarmament Agency: Washington, DC, 1967), pp. 134–9. The term 'challenge' seems unfortunate since it appears to emphasize confrontation, which is contrary to the basis of this approach.

[5]   Note 4, pp. 194–9. *Documents on Disarmament, 1969* (US Arms Control and Disarmament Agency: Washington, DC, 1970), pp. 163–4.

[6]   Chayes, A., *Harvard Law Review*, vol. 85, no. 5 (Mar. 1972), p. 937. Chayes states that US planning proceeded on the basis that inspection of a clandestine test would not be permitted. *Nuclear Arms Control, Background and Issues* (National Academy Press: Washington, DC, 1985), pp. 220–1.

[7]   Note that this formulation poses no distinction among parties as did the formulation in the 1958–61 negotiations.

[8]   The agreed tripartite report on the status of the negotiations is in *Documents on Disarmament 1980* (US Arms Control and Disarmament Agency: Washington, DC, 1983), pp. 317–21. The additional measures also included provision for internal seismic stations on the territories of the three negotiating parties.

[9]   Also reiterated in Timerbaev, R., *Verification of Arms Limitation and Disarmament* (International Relations Publishing House: Moscow, 1983). See Heckrotte, W., 'A Soviet view of verification', *Bulletin of Atomic Scientists*, vol. 24, no. 8 (Oct. 1986), pp. 12–15.

[10]   Conference on Disarmament document CD/715, 15 July 1986.

[11]   Note 4.

[12]   Note 4.

[13]   Decoupling was introduced into the negotiations in 1959. See Seaborg, G. T., *Kennedy, Kruschev, and the Test Ban* (University of California Press: Berkeley, 1981), pp. 18–19.

[14]   Hannon, W. J., 'Seismic verification of a comprehensive test ban', *Science*, no. 227 (1985), pp. 251–61. Evernden, J. F., Archambeau, C. B. and Cranswich, E., 'An evaluation of seismic decoupling and underground nuclear test monitoring using high-frequency seismic data', *Reviews of Geophysics*, no. 24 (1986), pp. 143–215.

[15]   Some of these are: hiding the explosion in an earthquake and simulating an earthquake by a timed sequence of explosions.

[16]   Lukasik, S. F., *Hearing before the Subcommittee on Research, Development and Radiation of the Joint Committee on Atomic Energy*, 27–8 Oct. 1971 (US Government Printing Office: Washington, DC, 1971), p. 65; Giller, E., *Hearings before the Panel on the Strategic Arms Limitation Talks and the Comprehensive Test Ban Treaty . . . Committee on Armed Services, House of Representatives*, 95th Congress, 2nd Session (US Government Printing Office: Washington, DC, 1978), p. 93; Johnson, G., Hearings (as above), p. 73.

[17]   *Documents on Disarmament 1961* (US Arms Control and Disarmament Agency: Washington, DC, 1962), pp. 82–126.

[18]   Nordyke, M., 'The test ban treaties: verifying compliance', *Energy and Technology Review*, Lawrence Livermore National Laboratory, UCRL–52000–83–5, May 1983, pp. 1–9.

[19]   Krass, A. S., *Verification: How Much is Enough*, SIPRI (Taylor & Francis: London, 1985), p. 221.

[20]   The above general considerations draw upon the provision of the 1976 Treaty on Underground Nuclear Explosions for Peaceful Purposes.

[21]   Long, F. A., *Hearings before the Joint Committee on Atomic Energy, March 5, 6, 7, 8, 11 and 12, 1963* (US Government Printing Office: Washington, DC, 1963), p. 415.

Paper 15

A. A. Vasiliev
Institute of USA and Canada Studies, Moscow, USSR
I. F. Bocharov
Soviet Ministry of Defence, Moscow, USSR

Abstract

Seismological methods of detecting and identifying underground nuclear explosions are today reliable even for very low-yield explosions. On-site inspections are a useful complementary method for identifying doubtful seismic phenomena, but implementation would require a sufficient level of trust among nations. On-site inspections would also act as a confidence-building measure, enhancing national strategic stability.

I. Introduction

The problems associated with on-site inspection of a comprehensive test ban (CTB) have both political and technical dimensions. Although on-site inspection was discussed at the very outset of the CTB talks, it has still not been adequately treated in the scientific literature. Nor have studies been made of the link between the necessity for on-site inspection and the lack of adequate data from the national technical means of verification and the international exchange of data.

The talks which followed the signing of the 1963 Partial Test Ban Treaty (the Moscow Treaty) concentrated mainly on means of reliable identification of doubtful seismic phenomena. In this context, a noteworthy proposal was made by Sweden at the Eighteen-Nation Disarmament Conference (ENDC) to establish international co-operation in the field of detection and identification of underground nuclear explosions by the exchange of seismic data. According to this proposal, national observation posts were to be established and national estimates made available to all states. While the USSR reacted positively to this proposal, it was rejected by the United States.

II. The US and Soviet positions

The USA argues that insufficient measures of verification are the basis for their rejection of a CTB, while plans to develop new generations of nuclear weapons indicate that the need to test them is the real reason for the US rejection of a CTB: particularly plans to develop a large-scale anti-missile system with space-based echelons using X-ray lasers and other third-generation nuclear weapons under the US Strategic Defense Initiative (SDI) programme.

During this period, independent developments in seismology have demonstrated the achievement of reliable detection and identification of even extremely low-yield nuclear explosions and the detection of deliberately concealed tests.[1] In addition, other technologies have been developed to complement seismic means of detection and identification. However, the problem has assumed another major dimension: a CTB has acquired a special political value. It is no exaggeration to say that the political risk of destroying the understanding and confidence built up among nations would greatly surpass the negligible technical advantages of being able to conceal a single nuclear test. This may be an additional, reliable guarantee against breaches of a CTB agreement.

The Soviet position has consistently been to reach verifiable agreements, and the Soviet Union has stated its preparedness to meet the reasonable demands of its partners in reaching such a vital agreement as a CTB.

III. The need for verification

An important contradiction has emerged from the CTB talks. On the one hand, distrust has emerged among states while, on the other hand, an agreement calls for a high level of trust among nations. Regarding on-site inspection, trust is important for co-operation among states as well as to ensure that the inspecting state does not misuse its right of inspection. The procedure of on-site inspection must be implemented to contribute to strengthening the security of participating countries, increasing mutual confidence and thus consolidating strategic stability. As such, it must complement the national and possibly also bilateral or multilateral means of verification. On-site inspection must be used only in cases where available data seem to support the suspicion of a nuclear explosion but are still insufficient for unambiguous identification of such an event. Such details of inspection procedure as the place, role and techniques for carrying out on-site inspections must be considered in the context of the other technical means of detection.

The trilateral USSR–USA–UK CTB talks reached agreement on the use of the following technical means of verification: national technical means; international exchange of seismic data; trilateral exchange of seismic data from seismic stations located on the territories of the USSR, the USA and the UK; and on-site inspections of doubtful phenomena which cannot be established by the above means to be a nuclear explosion or a phenomenon associated with it.

The first three of these technical means are the means of remote control, that is, for detecting underground nuclear explosions from a distance. On-site inspection is different because its purpose is to detect possible evidence of a concealed nuclear explosion directly at the site and after it has occurred. Nevertheless, it is directly and inseparably linked to other means of control because it can be resorted to only on the basis of data which they provide.

The need for inspections will of course be reduced with a continuing process of disarmament and, accordingly, with the growth of mutual trust. Other co-operative measures will also contribute to detection and identification, such as the agreement reached between the Academy of Sciences of the USSR and the Natural Resources Defense Council (NRDC) of the USA.

Sufficient detection means can provide reliable interpretation of most seismic phenomena (which otherwise could be interpreted as nuclear explosions). It is generally recognized that one seismic method can reliably detect underground nuclear explosions, equivalent to 1 kt or less, conducted in hard rock. Other methods increase the capability to detect small underground nuclear explosions and reduce the risk of concealment. Thus, for example, data on preparations for an underground nuclear explosion cannot be taken alone as grounds for an accusation of a treaty breach but rather (*a*) are a basis for carrying out purposeful inspection of the suspected area and (*b*) combined with other means of control, can determine whether the event was a nuclear explosion or a seismic phenomenon. Unfortunately, in assessing CTB verifiability, account was not taken of the entire complex of data which could be obtained from all the remote technical means of verification. This has created a pessimistic attitude towards the ability to verify a CTB. It also increases the number of doubtful phenomena on the basis of which on-site inspection could be requested.

In 1975 the USSR put forward the principle of voluntary on-site inspection. This approach excludes carrying out inspections based on insufficient evidence: they would have to be initiated jointly by the state raising the need for inspection and the state on whose territory the dubious event occurred. And the state to be inspected could not reject the inspection without jeopardizing the whole test ban regime. This approach was agreed at the trilateral talks.

Regarding the technical–scientific and organizational modalities of on-site inspection, there is a lack of information (although certain concrete aspects of the possible techniques which may be used have been considered by Krass[2]). The present authors do not attempt to fill this gap, but the issues are discussed below.

IV. On-site inspection

The purpose of on-site inspection is the collection of data in an agreed area (approximately 100 km^2) by control personnel. Inspectors from the accusing state would on the basis of this data determine unambiguously whether the phenomenon was a nuclear explosion or not. One would have to assume that a concealed nuclear explosion would have to be completely disguised (e.g., by not releasing radioactive products).

Experiments would have to be carried out to test the practicality of such concealment measures. Irrespective of the results of the experiments, there would be a cavity, in and around which there would be observable geophysical and geochemical processes. A geophysical survey could with a certain degree of reliability detect such an underground cavity. The basic geological survey methods which could be employed are the following: (*a*) radiometric techniques, to detect on the earth's surface, in the soil, in the air above the ground, and in the surface waters the anomalies of radioactivity of artificial origin; (*b*) magnetometric techniques, to detect metallic objects originating from engineering activity in the preparation and carrying out of an explosion, as well as possible local storms in the geomagnetic field in the area of the cavity following the changes of the physical properties of the medium as a result of a nuclear explosion; and (*c*) seismic techniques to detect the local sources of seismic signals conditioned by the ongoing mechanical and geo-acoustic processes in the cavity.

Considering the political sensitivity of on-site inspections, the inspectors must obviously be highly qualified to both collect and analyse the data. If necessary, additional geophysical survey methods may also be required.

If, after an analysis of the data, there were grounds to suspect that a cavity was created by a nuclear explosion, such data could be supplemented by special radiometric analysis of rock samples obtained through drilling in the area of the cavity. This drilling should be implemented by the efforts and means of the inspected side.

Since the number of inspectors and the time they are permitted to perform the inspections are limited, they must be very efficient. They should also be assisted in their task by the use of helicopters supplied by the inspected party, in addition to effective microprocessor technology. This enables not only visual inspecton of the area but also air-radio and magnetometric research.

The organizational aspects of on-site inspection are particularly important for efficiency. The provisions of the 1976 Peaceful Nuclear Explosions Treaty (PNET) have organizational and technical aspects that may be applicable to a CTB in the resumed talks.

The 1980 Lawrence Livermore National Laboratory Roogtan experiment on the use of portable seismic stations for purposes of the PNET may be relevant to on-site inspection under a CTB. However, other aspects remain to be investigated, such as the interaction of the personnel of the inspector- and inspected-country sides.

V. Conclusion

Present developments in geophysical reconnaissance, as well as preliminary agreement on most issues of on-site inspection under a CTB, show that inspected phenomena can reliably be identified as nuclear explosions or naturally occurring phenomena.

Notes and references

[1] Vasiliev, A. A. and Kedrov, O. K., 'The problem of control of a comprehensive nuclear weapon test ban', background paper.
[2] Krass, A., SIPRI, *Verification: How Much is Enough?* (Taylor & Francis: London, 1985).

Chapter XIII. Degree of verification needed

Paper 16

Ray E. Kidder

Lawrence Livermore National Laboratory, Livermore, CA

Abstract

The military significance of nuclear explosive tests is illustrated by the 1980–84 US nuclear testing record. Nuclear tests with yields that are only a small fraction of a kiloton are militarily significant, particularly for nuclear weapon research. Very-low-yield tests could be conducted in fully decoupled, seismically quiet, reuseable cavities, and would be well below the threshold of reliable detection and identification by seismic or other means presently under consideration. It is therefore concluded that the degree of verification needed to support a CTB is not available at the present time. A threshold test ban, limiting explosive yields to 5 kt, as proposed by US Defense Secretary Harold Brown, appears to present a much more realistic near-term possibility.

I. Introduction

Let us here assume that nuclear explosive tests are not worth conducting, even if permitted, unless their yield exceeds Y_s kilotons. The yield Y_s is defined as the lowest yield of military significance, and is referred to simply as the 'significant yield'. Let us also assume that nuclear explosive tests with yields greater than Y_d kilotons can be reliably detected and identified as such; Y_d is the 'detectable yield'.

If the significant yield Y_s were greater than the detectable yield Y_d, all militarily significant tests could be detected and identified, and a comprehensive test ban (CTB) would clearly be adequately verifiable because no worthwhile cheating could be concealed. On the other hand, if Y_s were *less* than Y_d, a threshold test ban (TTB) would be verifiable because tests that are not reliably detectable would presumably not be forbidden, whereas a CTB would not be verifiable. How can a CTB be justified in these latter circumstances?

The supporter of a CTB would need to argue that even though militarily significant tests could not be reliably detected, they would not be conducted in any case. The risk of detection would never be zero, and the military advantage of testing at yield levels below the limit of reliable detection would not be worth the political cost of being caught.

The difficulty with this argument, at least from the standpoint of the United States, is that it depends on an evaluation of the state of mind of leaders in the Kremlin concerning *their* perception of the political cost of being caught, an evaluation that for the West is argumentative and speculative at best. The USSR does not always take account of world opinion where military considerations are involved.

For this reason, it is the present author's opinion that the USA will not, and should not, be willing to negotiate a CTB with the USSR unless it is convinced that tests of militarily significant yields can be reliably detected and identified. It is the need for verifiability, rather than a need to continue testing, that leads to this conclusion. Section III deals with the question of what yields are militarily significant, and why. Here there is first a consideration of the rough yield limits between which adequate detectability is thought to lie, to place consideration of militarily significant yields in perspective.

Present thinking seems to place the detectable yield Y_d at between 1 and 5 kt. For example, Professor Lynn R. Sykes has stated that: 'The lower limit of reliable identification can be reduced to about *one kiloton* with a combination of seismic listening posts within the U.S.S.R. and other national technical means such as satellite photography'.[1] (Emphasis added) Defense Secretary Harold Brown has testified: 'My own view is the United States should proceed with threshold test bans of decreasing size as verification becomes possible. I think it is possible to verify down to a few kilotons now. I would support a *five-kiloton* threshold test ban for that reason'.[2] (Emphasis added) Brown then goes on to make the significant remark that: 'I would not want, myself, to see a comprehensive test ban in the absence of *verification down to zero*. That is not in the cards'. (Emphasis added)

The question of military significance is less well defined than that of detectability, so there may be greater difficulty and disagreement in establishing a range of values for it than is the case for the detectable yield. Brown, for example, appears to believe that *any* nuclear explosion, however low its yield may be, is sufficiently significant that it must be detectable; that is, he is assigning to the significant yield Y_s the value zero, and thereby concludes that a CTB 'is not in the cards'. This is also the conclusion of this paper.

II. Distribution of US nuclear explosive yields, 1980–84[3]

Although the technical and other details of US nuclear explosive tests are classified, it is nevertheless possible to obtain a measure of perceived military significance versus yield by observing the frequency with which tests at different yields have been conducted. This is the approach of this paper, keeping in mind the important fact that the military significance of tests at a given yield will be increased if tests at any higher yield are prohibited.

Figure 16.1 shows the distribution of explosive yields of US nuclear tests conducted during the five calendar years 1980–84. All of these tests were conducted for military purposes at the Nevada Test Site (NTS). No tests were

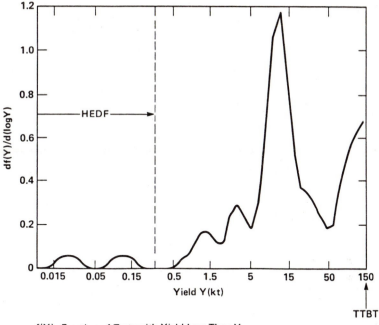

f(Y): Fraction of Tests with Yield Less Than Y
(No Yields Above 150kt)

Figure 16.1 The distribution of yields of nuclear explosions conducted at the Nevada Test Site, 1980–84

The curve shows the relative frequency of tests with yield Y versus that yield for all tests at the Nevada Test Site from 1980 through 1984. The vertical scale is designed to produce an area under the curve of one so that the relative probability of a test being of a given yield can be seen immediately. The dotted line shows the limit of yields that would be fully decoupled (i.e., be made seismically quiet) by a proposed High Energy Density Facility.

conducted with yields in excess of 150 kt, in compliance with the unratified Threshold Test Ban Treaty (TTBT).

Table 16.1 lists values of the cumulative distribution P, that is, the percentage of tests conducted with yield less than Y, versus Y.

Table 16.1. Percentage (P) of tests conducted with yield less than Y kilotons

Y (kt)	1	5	10	20	50	150
P (%)	5	18	34	62	74	100

III. Military significance of tests of various yields

If it is assumed that the number of tests performed in the neighbourhood of a given yield constitutes a measure of the military significance of tests at that yield, at least in the eyes of those responsible for deciding what was to be tested, then figure 16.1 may be interpreted as a graph of (perceived) military significance versus yield, given the constraints on testing that then existed. According to figure 16.1, in 1980–84 the military significance of US tests below 1 kt was perceived to be low, whereas that of tests in the vicinity of 10 kt and 150 was high. The accumulation of tests near 150 kt is partly the result of testing, at reduced yield, strategic weapons whose yield would otherwise exceed the TTBT limit.

From table 16.1 it can be seen that, had the TTBT yield limit been 5 kt instead of 150 kt, approximately 80 per cent of the US tests carried out during 1980–84 could not have been conducted at the yield tested. The military significance of such a yield limit was indicated in a letter dated 19 April 1977 from Harold Agnew, then director of the Los Alamos Scientific Laboratory, to Congressman Jack F. Kemp, in which he stated that:

I don't believe testing below say five or ten kilotons can do much to improve (as compared to maintaining) strategic posture, but clearly it can provide improvements at the theatre level, where yields of less than five kilotons are important. Being able to test up to a few kilotons allows a dynamic program for maintenance and development of theatre [i.e., tactical] nuclear forces.[4]

Although only about 20 per cent of US nuclear tests in 1980–84 had lower yields than 5 kt, it should not be supposed that a 5-kt TTB would result in a five-fold reduction in the testing rate. The rate of testing would most likely not be decreased at all, and quite possibly would be increased. Greater extrapolations to full weapon yield would be necessitated by a TTB, and more tests might be sought to ensure their validity. This possibility suggests that in addition to imposing a yield limit, it would also be desirable to limit the number of tests per year, to thwart any attempt to compensate for the yield limit by conducting more tests. Limiting the number of tests, however, is clearly not a verifiable treaty provision. Neither side could be sure that the other was not secretly conducting a prohibited number of fully decoupled tests with yields well below the threshold for reliable seismic detection and identification.

Alternatively, if the yield limit had been 1 kt, 95 per cent of the tests conducted during 1980–84 would not have been allowed at the yield tested. The military significance of yields in the vicinity of 1 kt was indicated in the testimony of John S. Foster, Jr, then Director, Defense Research and Engineering, DOD, before the Subcommittee on Arms Control of the Senate Foreign Relations Committee on 1 May 1973, in which he stated:

In my view, Mr Chairman, a kiloton is a very significant yield. Now, I will admit there are some cases where a half-kiloton can be very significant or a quarter of a kiloton. But certainly I know that a kiloton is a very significant yield from a military point of view. Clearly, as one raises the level above that, the number of possibilities that are included grows and so does the significance.[5]

An important element of the military significance of the sub-kiloton tests referred to by Foster is the application to nuclear weapon research discussed in the next section.

It may be pointed out that these earlier statements of Foster (1973) and Agnew (1977) concerning the military significance of nuclear tests as a function of yield are consistent with the 'military significance' interpretation of the 1980–84 US test record as presented in figure 16.1.

The testing of nuclear weapons at substantially lower yield than their full yield capability is a factor that increases the military significance of such lower-yield tests. This is particularly true in the case of two-stage thermonuclear weapons. The first stage of such weapons is designated the 'primary' and the second stage the 'secondary'. Referring to two-stage weapons now in the US stockpile, Richard L. Wagner has testified:

We can test, for example, the primary or a combination of the primary and an altered secondary, which would not exceed the threshold. The primary design is the sort of bellweather of whether it will work, and so, we can test all primary designs which are at a lower yield thereby giving us continued reasonable assurance that the weapon will work at its full yield.[6]

In the statement by Agnew quoted above, he did not rule out all possibility of maintaining (as compared to improving) the US strategic posture with testing below 5 or 10 kt, that is, maintaining a stockpile of reliable strategic nuclear weapons.

It is also possible to extrapolate to full yield the performance of single-stage nuclear weapons, or the primary of two-stage weapons, by testing them at less than their full yield. This is an important consideration in assessing the effectiveness of a TTB with a low-yield threshold. For example, while a 5-kt threshold would have permitted only 20 per cent of the US tests in 1980–84 to have been conducted at full yield, it would have permitted nearly 60 per cent of those tests to have been conducted at no less than one-third of full yield. The accuracy and reliability of such three-fold extrapolations of yield would be acceptable for many, if not most, single-stage nuclear weapons.

IV. Experiments with potential military significance: nuclear weapon research

It is not necessary to conduct nuclear tests with yields as large as 1 kt in order to create energy densities and states of matter that can be achieved (on a substantial scale) only with nuclear explosives. One need only recall that a 150-ton yield in, say, 30 lbs of fissionable material represents an energy density 10 000 times that of chemical explosives. Although such relatively low yields may have little direct military significance (except for atomic demolition munitions where a low yield is necessary), they nevertheless have considerable indirect or potential military significance in providing a unique capability for carrying out significant nuclear weapon research and tests of nuclear weapon effects. A facility in which such low-yield tests could be safely conducted has been under consideration for some time.

For example, in 1981 a study was begun at Lawrence Livermore National Laboratory of a High Energy Density Facility (HEDF), a reuseable underground facility to be located at the Nevada Test Site, in which nuclear explosions would be fully and safely contained with yields up to 300 tons at a rate of one test per week (more than double the US testing rate of late 1986). Although there are no plans to build such a facility at the present time, there is little doubt that it could be built at reasonable cost (a few hundred million dollars). It would not only allow nuclear weapon research of considerable potential military significance to be done but also provide a vehicle for maintaining the skill and interest of nuclear weapon designers.

Current interest in third-generation nuclear weapons, that is, directed-energy weapons driven by nuclear explosives, provides strong additional motivation to continue and to expand nuclear weapon research. The underlying physics and technology of these complex weapon concepts can often be profitably explored with nuclear explosive of low yield, even though the weapon itself might require a considerably higher yield.

While ICF has not been a point of contention in the negotiations on a CTB as far as is known, the US and Soviet research and development (R&D) programmes on Inertial-Confinement Fusion (ICF) will need to be considered. The initial goal of the US programme is to initiate a thermonuclear explosion in the laboratory by imploding, compressing and igniting a small capsule containing deuterium-tritium fuel. It is presently estimated that a few million joules of energy supplied in a few nanoseconds will be required and that a 100-fold gain in energy might be achieved, implying the release of 0.1 tons of nuclear explosive energy. The US ICF programme has been entirely supported by the Division of Military Applications of the Department of Energy, currently at a level of $155 million per year, suggesting that nuclear explosions with yields as low as 0.1 tons are indeed of considerable military interest.

Although the current ICF programme in the USA is primarily motivated by military applications, there is also a long-range goal of utilizing ICF for the commercial production of electric power. In this application, pellets containing deuterium-tritium would be injected into a suitable chamber, imploded and burned at a rate of a few pellets per second. The heat released would be used to generate steam to drive turbo-electric generators, and some of the released neutrons would be used to breed tritium to replace that which was burned. It is also possible, and may be economically advantageous, to use the excess neutrons that are released to breed fissile fuels such as Plutonium (from Uranium-238) or Uranium-233 (from Thorium).

V. Conclusions

Nuclear tests with yields that are but a small fraction of a kiloton are militarily significant for the reasons discussed above. The significant yield Y_s is at least as low as the quarter-kiloton referred to by Foster in 1973, and perhaps considerably lower ($Y_s < 0.25$ kt). If such low-yield explosions, fully decoupled in possibly reuseable cavities, cannot be reliably detected and identified, and it appears that they cannot, by seismic or other means proposed thus far, then a CTB is not likely to be negotiable from the point of view of the United States. The USA would need to trust the USSR not to undertake militarily significant low-yield nuclear weapon experiments that they might well be able to conceal for a long time. The possible existence in the Soviet Union of reuseable underground nuclear test facilities has been a matter of speculation for some time. For example, in 1978 Dr Harold Agnew drew congressional attention to an underground facility at Semipalatinsk that had been described in *Aviation Week & Space Technology* (2 May 1977) as a Probable Nuclear Underground Test Site (PNUTS).[7] In any case, the existence of such facilities cannot be ruled out. They could be operated under the cover of, and as part of, a legitimate mining operation. A testing rate of one 300-ton explosion per week would necessitate only 2 megawatts of additional cooling capacity to dissipate the heat generated. The test facility part of the operation could be made difficult to discover, even with on-site inspection.

Under these circumstance a threshold test ban, perhaps with yields initially limited to 5 kt, is a far more realistic possibility than a CTB. Tests would be limited to a single, well-monitored test site in each country. Given an unlimited number of tests, and a yield limit equal to that which could be reliably detected and identified, there would be no incentive to conduct secret tests outside the designated test site. As experience is gained in monitoring this TTB, and detection capabilities are improved, further reductions in the yield limit would be made. The fact that the 5-kt threshold was intended as only the first step in a sequence of further reductions in the threshold, and not an end in itself, would be explicitly stated in the TTBT.

Although a 5-kt threshold would allow much nuclear weapon testing to continue, particularly at reduced yield, it would nevertheless have important arms control value in stopping the development and testing of *new* designs of strategic weapons. A threshold of 1 kt or less would interfere with the development and testing of tactical weapons as well.

Acceptably non-intrusive means of yield measurement would need to be provided to insure that the yield threshold specified in the TTBT was not being significantly exceeded. More intrusive means are likely to be required to monitor a low threshold, such as 5 kt, than are needed to monitor the present 150-kt threshold. However, if both sides are sincere in their desire to negotiate a low-threshold test ban treaty, it seems unlikely that the degree of intrusiveness genuinely needed to ensure treaty compliance would not be agreed to.

Notes and references

[1] Lynn R. Sykes, professor of geological sciences, Lamont-Doherty Geological Observatory, Columbia University, in Statement before the Special Panel on Arms Control and Disarmament of the Procurement and Military Nuclear Systems Subcommittee of the House Armed Services Committee, 20 Nov. 1985, House Armed Services Committee, No. 99–18, p. 318.

[2] Harold Brown, US Secretary of Defense 1977–81, in *Implications of Abandoning Salt*, Hearing before the Subcommittee on Arms Control, International Security and Science of the House Foreign Affairs Committee, 15 Apr. 1986 (US Government Printing Office: Washington, DC, 1986), p. 13.

[3] Kidder, R. E., *Militarily Significant Nuclear Explosive Yields*, UCRL–93194, Lawrence Livermore National Laboratory, Aug. 1985.

[4] Harold M. Agnew, Los Alamos National Laboratory, in *Effects of a Comprehensive Test Ban Treaty on United States National Security Interests*, Hearings before the Panel on the Strategic Arms Limitation Talks and the Comprehensive Test Ban Treaty of the Intelligence and Military Application of Nuclear Energy Subcommittee of the House Armed Services Committee, 14, 15 Aug. 1978, USGPO 33–487 (US Government Printing Office: Washington, DC, 1978), pp. 192, 193.

[5] John S. Foster, Jr., Director, Defense Research and Engineering, Department of Defense, in *To Promote Negotiations for a Comprehensive Test Ban Treaty*, Hearings before the Subcommittee on Arms Control, International Law and Organization of the Senate Committee on Foreign Relations, 1 May 1973 (US Government Printing Office: Washington, DC, 1973), p. 91.

[6] Richard L. Wagner, Assistant to the Secretary of Defense for Atomic Energy, in Testimony before the Special Panel on Arms Control and Disarmament of the Procurement and Military Nuclear Systems Subcommittee of the House Armed Services Committee, 18 Sep. 1985, House Armed Services Committee, No. 99–18, p. 115.

[7] Harold M. Agnew, in *Department of Energy Authorization Legislation (National Security Programs) For Fiscal Year 1979*, Hearings before the Intelligence and Military Application of Nuclear Energy Subcommittee of the House Armed Services Committee, 15 Feb.–20 Apr. 1978, House Armed Services Committee No. 95–58 (US Government Printing Office: Washington, DC, 1979), p. 272.

Chapter XIV. Verification of a very-low-yield nuclear test ban

Paper 17

Charles B. Archambeau

The Cooperative Institute for Research into the Environment, University of Colorado

Abstract

Technical and political considerations lead to the conclusion that a time- and threshold-limited nuclear test ban is the kind of agreement between the major nuclear states that is currently possible. It would strongly limit nuclear testing for a period of one or two years and incorporate verification procedures involving seismic stations within the borders of all parties. This kind of agreement would result in the acquisition of new, in-country, seismic data required for confirmation of the capability to detect and identify underground nuclear tests anywhere within the countries involved. It would therefore provide a firm technical basis for negotiation of a verifiable permanent test ban treaty. The low-threshold limitations proposed would strongly inhibit or stop the development of new, destabilizing, nuclear weapons while negotiations proceed to affect a permanent test ban and to reduce and control current weapon systems deployment. By virtue of the time limitation, such an agreement would greatly reduce the difficulties of monitoring for compliance, since possibilities of clandestine testing are confined to areas where large underground nuclear tests have occurred. A high degree of confidence can be placed in the verification capabilities afforded by new high-performance seismic detection systems placed near 'capable' test sites in the countries involved. The conditions required to make a limited test ban agreement restrictive in terms of new weapon development, and also verifiable, are described. A major conclusion is that verification is technically possible and easy to implement.

I. Introduction

The approach that may have the most realistic chance of political success, and can settle a number of perceived technical uncertainties related to verification, is to initiate a time-limited verifiable nuclear test ban during which: some limited testing is allowed but restricted so that any new weapon development is greatly impeded or stopped; the necessary technical information can be acquired for confident design of a verification system to monitor a permanent test ban treaty; and negotiations for a permanent test ban can take place, along with other negotiations on nuclear and conventional arms control, under stabilized conditions.

This paper outlines a limited test ban agreement that may be appropriate and can be rather easily verified. The following sections discuss the necessary monitoring activity as well as the various verification procedures that can be used to ensure compliance and to provide data for design of a full monitoring system for verification. Finally, there is a brief discussion of how this largely seismic monitoring activity can be expanded to provide full continental monitoring of a permanent test ban treaty.

II. Provisions of a limited test ban and verification requirements

The following description of verification procedures for a limited nuclear test ban is based on the assumption that the test ban is of short-term duration and that it prohibits tests everywhere in the participating countries, except tests below some relatively low yield level at specific sites. It is assumed that nuclear tests in the countries involved will be limited as follows:

1. Underground nuclear tests will *not* be allowed *anywhere* except at *one designated test site*, which will be of *limited area* and, at most, near 10 km on a side.

2. An unlimited number of *tamped*[1] *underground tests below 1 kt will be allowed, but must be detonated in close proximity to high coupling media* (e.g., in strong, water-saturated rocks). Specifically, *no underground nuclear tests* of any type, at any location, are permitted in water unsaturated alluvial sediments, or similar very weak, dry or under-saturated sedimentary rocks, or in *large underground cavities*.

3. *A limited number of larger-yield tests are permitted*, but are not to exceed a *prescribed yield level*, near 10 kt, within the period of the limited test ban. All such tests must adhere to the *same restrictions*, regarding tamped emplacement in a high coupling medium, as are prescribed for the unlimited tests under 1 kt.

In order to provide assurance that the agreement is being observed by all sides and to guard against clandestine tests exceeding the limitations on yield and numbers of high-yield tests, it would be necessary to maintain both in-country seismic stations and the usual national technical means (NTM) for monitoring, with the latter including satellite surveillance and high-perform-ance external seismic stations. The requirements of these monitoring systems are that they provide high capability for detection and identification of low-yield explosions everywhere within both countries and yield estimation capa-bility in the 1- to 10-kt range, with uncertainties in yield determinations varying from at most about 50 per cent near 1 kt, to 30 per cent near 10 kt and above.[2] In addition, the in-country seismic stations must have the capability of detecting and identifying possible decoupled explosions having yields above 1 kt within test site areas in both countries where decoupling cavities may currently be in place. This means that rather small seismic events, with magnitudes as low as 2.5 to 3, must be detected and identified in these limited areas by close-in seismic stations.

Because decoupled tests with device yields near 10 kt cannot confidently be distinguished from small tamped nuclear explosions below 1 kt, which are permitted by the limited moratorium, it would be necessary to conduct a thorough inspection of the designated sites of allowed testing to ensure that no large cavities already exist within the restricted area of these sites. Assuming such inspections would be agreed to, the designated sites could probably be adequately monitored by external seismic stations provided under current NTM. However, to provide an assured and confident means of verifying that only the specified number of tests were conducted in the 1- to 10-kt range, that no tests occurred off the designated site and that no tests above 10 kt were detonated at the test site, it would be appropriate to install in-country seismic stations surrounding the designated test sites in both countries, as well as in other areas where there is reason to believe that large cavities may exist.

A key feature of the verification approach described here is the provision that only one designated site is to be used for testing and that nuclear tests elsewhere, of any size, are a violation of the agreement. Further, the site area will be small enough, and so located relative to geologic conditions, that a thorough search for large cavities can successfully be conducted using available on-site inspection methods. Finally, when tests are conducted, they will be in water-saturated strong rocks, by virtue of the uniformity of the geologic conditions at the chosen test site, so that yield estimates can be more confidently obtained.

Other important constraints that should be considered as part of such a limited test ban agreement are that:

1. Industrial explosions of large size, above about 20 tons, be banned within the 'test capable' areas being monitored by in-country stations, in order to avoid false alarms; or at least that such explosions be announced beforehand with locations, times and yields specified and with observers and on-site inspections allowed as well.

2. That complete drill cores and logs from three or four widely spaced deep drill holes, within the designated test sites, be made available and that four or five explosion tests, of independently determined yield, be conducted at each designated test site for calibration purposes, with these tests conducted after installation of the in-country seismic monitoring systems.

3. That provisions be made in the limited test ban agreement for expansion of the in-country seismic monitoring networks, or for addition of other networks, upon mutual agreement between the parties to the limited test ban.

4. A limited number (five or six) of on-site inspections be allowed, on request, at any site in either country.

Most of these verification requirements are discussed in more detail below. In addition, the distribution and types of seismic instrumentation required for such verification are described, as well as methods of detection-identification and yield estimation. It is assumed that all the provisions related to inspection of the designated test site area to determine the existence of large cavities, as well as the restrictions as to size of the area and the geologic character of the environment, are included in the agreement. Further, the restrictions on industrial explosions and the availability of geologic and seismic data at the allowed test site are also assumed to be part of the agreement.

III. Seismic verification: general considerations

Because a time-limited test ban is considered here, it would be difficult for any participant in such an agreement to construct and equip a clandestine test facility, within a short time, without discovery by the various means of surveillance currently afforded by NTM. It would be particularly difficult to do so if such a new test facility were to involve construction of a large decoupling cavity, in view of the large volume of material that would have to be excavated in order to conduct significant tests.

Therefore, in-country monitoring need be installed only at the designated test site and at sites where tests have occurred in the past, or where there exist large underground cavities suitable for large decoupled nuclear tests. Such sites can be termed 'capable test sites'. For a short-term test ban there are only a few such sites that could be employed for decoupling in the USSR and the USA. As a consequence, emplacement of a four- or five-station network surrounding each of the known 'capable' nuclear weapon test areas within the two countries would provide very high verification capability in these areas, while all other areas in each country could be monitored by the operative external seismic network which provides data that could be utilized by both countries for verification. The use of the simple seismic networks placed near 'capable' weapon test sites would provide monitoring capable of detection and identification of even a small decoupled test near 1 kt, while the existing external networks in combination with the in-country networks would be capable of monitoring other possible test areas and provide detection-identification capability for any tamped nuclear explosion test larger than about 1 kt.

The only possible tests of any significance that could be conducted without high probability of detection and identification would be decoupled explosions in large cavities at *new* testing sites, with maximum yields that could be at most of the order of 10-kt, and conventional (tamped) tests of low yield (below 1 kt), also at a *new* site. Since tests below 1 kt are of limited value in a weapon development programme and in any event could be conducted at the designated test site, it is clear that such 'off-site' tests would not be conducted under a limited test ban. On the other hand, large-cavity decoupled tests, in the 10-kt range, that might be undetected by a limited seismic network if conducted at a new site would require construction and instrumentation of a new test facility, which would take considerable time to complete and would run a high risk of discovery by other technical means. While such decoupling cavities could exist at any of the 'capable tests sites' (but not at the designated test site, in view of the inspection procedures to be used to preclude that possibility), they could not be used without detection because of the nearby in-country seismic networks surrounding these areas. Further, their identification as explosions, rather than as earthquakes, would be straightforward using spectral and depth discrimination methods.[3]

In addition to these considerations, the uncertainties related to the amplitude reduction of seismic signals from decoupling cavities are such that an attempt to test *could* result in failure to decouple at the designed level, and so might very well run a yet higher than expected risk of detection and identification by the seismic networks. In view of these risks and impediments to clandestine testing, and since some number of tests at 10 kt are allowed at a designated test site in any case, taking the risk of conducting off-site decoupled tests, which could be at most near 10 kt, would clearly not be worthwhile. Thus, not only would there be a high risk of discovery for decoupled testing but there is also little or no advantage to be achieved by such testing under the conditions of the proposed limited test ban.

Therefore, the only additional monitoring capability required for detection-identification of nuclear tests during such a limited test ban are high-performance seismic stations surrounding a few sites of limited area within the USA and the USSR. In addition, the combined capability of the external and in-country seismic stations should be more than adequate to provide the required accuracy of test yield determinations at designated test sites, particularly since signals from tests with known yields can be used to calibrate these test sites. (For example, US tests can be recorded at the Soviet test site and compared to recordings obtained elsewhere to provide a determination of the signal transmission characteristics beneath the Soviet test area, and *vice versa*. With this information, current seismic magnitude versus yield relations can be refined and adjusted, if need be, and used with confidence to obtain the required certainty in seismic yield estimation. Alternatively, or in addition, calibration explosions at each designated test site could be detonated by one side at the other's designated test site, and the seismic recordings of these tests would provide direct seismic magnitude-yield calibration relations for estimates of all future tests.)

The following sections address technical aspects of test site monitoring by regional ('close-in') seismic methods. Such in-country test site monitoring is the only aspect of compliance monitoring that need be considered in detail here, since monitoring this limited test ban need only contain this added capability, beyond that already available to the USA and the USSR. Nevertheless, while the technical aspects of monitoring using external (teleseismic) stations need not be reviewed in any detail, it is appropriate to observe that:

1. A world-wide network of high-performance teleseismic stations is cap-

able of detecting and identifying tamped explosions down to, and somewhat below, 1 kt anywhere within the USA and the USSR.

2. Such a network of external stations can provide confident yield estimates of the larger explosions, having yields from 150 kt down to about 10 kt, with an uncertainty range of about 30 per cent. At lower yields the uncertainty increases rapidly, but is probably no larger than a factor of 2 at 1 kt.

IV. The impact of new seismic verification methods

Because of recent improvements in the suppression of seismometer internal noise, particularly at high frequencies, it is now possible to record seismic data over a much wider range of frequencies and, in particular, to very high seismic frequencies, well above 10 cycles per second. (The seismometers recommended for test site monitoring are of this type.) Coupled with the more recent discovery of very low ground noise levels at high seismic frequencies in many common geologic areas in all continents, it is possible to use high-frequency seismic data to detect and identify seismic events to lower magnitude levels than was possible in the past. This high-frequency capability is being assessed and will provide enhanced capability for monitoring by external networks, as well as by in-country networks, with the precise degree of enhancement still to be fully established.

In any case, the improvement in external seismic network monitoring capability will certainly be considerable, and could be expected to take place in a year or two (during a short time period such as envisaged for the proposed ban). Because of this expectation, it is even less likely that evasion of a time-limited test ban would be attempted, or even contemplated, since national technical means of verification and in-country (regional) verification capability would be rapidly improving towards an a priori unknown upper limit on the yield that could be 'hidden' with low risk of discovery. Consequently, tests that could probably evade detection (by the time a test facility was prepared) would have to incorporate a generous 'safety factor' which would likely preclude decoupled tests in the 10-kt range at a new test site. Therefore, any sequence of low-level tests that could be conducted with 'acceptable risk' would almost certainly not be attempted, since the risk would increase with time at some unknown rate, while the advantage to be gained would decrease with time as the end of the test ban time limit approached.

V. Implications for long-term test ban verification

In addition to the sufficiency of seismic detectors deployed in the near vicinity of known and 'capable' test sites for monitoring a limited test ban, such a deployment could provide important observational data for verification of capabilities of the more comprehensive internal monitoring network required for test ban treaty verification. In this case no time limit on prohibitions for testing applies, and the necessity of monitoring of *all* possible sites for nuclear testing within the USA and the USSR would require special seismic networks, both within and outside these countries, consisting of about 25 well-distributed internal stations and 15 external stations for each country.[4]

Such numbers of internal stations are required in order to eliminate possibilities for evasion of test detection and identification by decoupling at low test yields, in the 1- to 10-kt range, assuming that the test ban precluded any tests in this yield range. Each station in these networks would consist of a very high frequency seismic recording system, with very low internal noise characteristics, and would be emplaced in a bore-hole at about 100 metres' depth in a low ground-noise environment. With such seismic systems distributed throughout the two countries, it is expected that nuclear explosions producing seismic signals as small as those from a 1-kt fully decoupled nuclear explosion (i.e., a 1-kt explosion in a large air-filled underground cavity) would be detected and identified with high probability at any site in either country. This capability would therefore provide the type of monitoring required for a verifiable (low threshold) test ban treaty (VTBT), or for a comprehensive test ban treaty (CTBT), if tests below 1 kt were not considered militarily significant.

Under a time-limited test ban, three or four widely separated sites within each country would be instrumented, with each site having several seismic stations near the test site area; each of these site networks would also function as a 'station' of an embryonic in-country seismic network of the type capable of comprehensive monitoring of the entire country. Thus, some limited capability for regional monitoring of other areas of the two countries, aside from the test site areas, would be created by emplacement of seismic instrumentation at the 'test-capable' sites in each country. In this mode of operation the seismic data from all internal sites could be used together, and jointly with data recorded outside the countries, to detect, locate and identify events in the entire country in question.

VI. Relationship to the NRDC–Soviet Academy monitoring project

The US NRDC (National Resources Defense Council)–Soviet Academy of Sciences effort was designed to monitor the Nevada Test Site (NTS) and the Soviet test site near Semipalatinsk. This limited monitoring programme, involving three high-performance seismic stations at each of the main US and Soviet test sites, is a prototype of the in-country monitoring required for the limited test ban considered here. The reproduction of networks of this type (with another station or two added) at other 'capable' US and Soviet test areas is required in order to provide verification of compliance with a limited test ban. In addition, the NRDC–Soviet Academy project has produced, and will continue to produce, seismic data bearing on calibration of the test sites for yield estimation and event detection-identification, as well as data for determinations of local seismicity (frequency and distribution of local earthquakes), signal propagation characteristics in an extended region around the test areas, and samples of noise levels at the different stations over an extended period of time. These data can be used to evaluate, in some detail, the capability of such in-country networks to detect and identify explosions. Finally, these stations can be used to assess yield levels since numerous industrial explosions as well as earthquakes in both regions are recorded and can be used to test and evaluate network capabilities. Therefore the NRDC–Soviet project can be used as a model and a 'proof test' of the networks recommended for verification.

VII. Monitoring test sites using in-country seismic stations

Since existing external seismic networks, with the capability to monitor underground nuclear tests to the level of 1 kt for tamped tests, are already functional, it is necessary only to design in-country monitoring at known or 'capable' test sites. In the USSR these would include the known weapon test sites at Novaya Zemlya and near Semipalatinsk (the Kazakh Test Site). A third area, just north of the Caspian Sea (the Azgir Test Site area), may have a

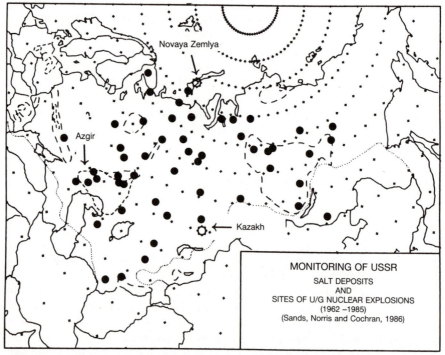

Figure 17.1. Soviet salt deposits and sites of underground nuclear explosions, 1962–85

Source: Data are taken from Sands, J. I., Norris, R. S. and Cochran, T. B., 'Known Soviet nuclear explosions, 1949–85', *Nuclear Weapons Databook* NWD–86–3 (Natural Resources Defense Council: Washington, DC, 1985).

weapon test capability since numerous, relatively large nuclear explosions have been detonated there, probably to create salt dome cavities for gas storage. Therefore, it would be appropriate to include this site as well. These sites are indicated on the map in figure 17.1, along with locations of all other known sites of underground nuclear tests in the USSR. (Most of these, except those at the two established weapon test sites, are peaceful nuclear explosions (PNEs) and are of too low a yield to have created cavities for decoupled nuclear tests.) In the USA, the sites at NTS and on Amchitka Island, in the Aleutians, should be monitored. Further, the Salmon-Sterling explosion site in Mississippi, where tests of decoupling in a salt dome were conducted, is an additional site that might be considered. Test sites in the continental USA, including sites of PNE tests, are shown in figure 17.2. In addition, there is the possibility that the participants in a ban would require monitoring at another PNE site, similar to the Azgir or Mississippi sites, in each country. Therefore, as many as four 'capable' test sites in each country might be monitored.

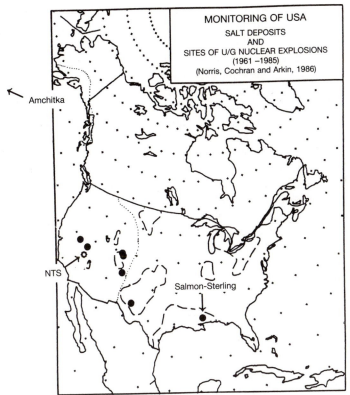

Figure 17.2. US salt deposits and sites of underground nuclear explosions, 1961–85

Source: Data are taken from Sands, J.I., Norris, R. S. and Cochran, T. B., 'Known Soviet nuclear explosions, 1949–85', *Nuclear Weapons Databook* NWD–86–3 (Natural Resources Defense Council: Washington, DC, 1985).

The seismic monitoring networks used for site monitoring would be essentially identical. These Test Site Monitoring (TSM) networks would each consist of from four to five separate stations located around the test area. Each station could consist of nine seismic detectors, or seismometers, recording three different components of ground motion, at different levels of sensitivity, and in somewhat different frequency bands. Specifically, the seismic sensors recommended would be identical to those used in the NRDC–Soviet Academy monitoring project. These include the very-high-frequency bore-hole sensors, recording three components of ground motion in the band from about 5 to 50 Hz in a 100-m bore-hole, a low-noise three-component sensor system recording at the surface in the frequency band from about 0.5 to 5 Hz, and an intermediate-period three-component system, also recording at the surface, in the frequency band from about 0.5 to 0.02 Hz. With such operative low internal noise systems, it would be possible to record the entire range of seismic signal types that can be used for detection, location and identification of seismic events, and for yield estimation when explosions are involved. In this regard, the very-high-frequency data is essential for event identification and constitutes a new, and important, feature of seismic recording systems designed for event discrimination, since this high-frequency data allows the very small events, including decoupled explosions, to be detected and identified.

The TSM network stations should be reasonably well distributed in azimuth around the centre of the area to be closely monitored, and to be in the distance range of 150–350 km from the outer boundaries of these areas. At this distance range (the 'near-regional range') the detection capability of such a TSM network is good in the high-frequency range from 10 to 40 Hz, and is certainly adequate for event detection over the areas of 'capable' test sites, which would be of the order of 100 km on a side.

Under the conditions of a limited test ban the main function of the TSM networks would be to detect,[5] locate and identify very small seismic events within and near areas of 'capable' test sites. In particular, earthquakes would have to be analysed, and identified as such, in order to eliminate them as possible underground explosions. For the capable testing areas in the USSR this would not involve a consideration of many earthquakes, since only events with seismic magnitudes above that produced by a decoupled explosion, of 5–10 kt, would be of significance. For the Soviet test areas this means that events of magnitude above about 2.5 would have to be located and identified.

The number of earthquakes that can be expected to occur in these areas per year, with magnitudes above 2.5, can be estimated, and the number is very low since none of the 'capable' test areas in the USSR is in a seismically active (tectonic) zone. In particular, figure 17.3 shows the distribution of natural seismicity in the USSR over a 15-year period, as reported by the International Seismological Centre (ISC). Earthquakes in the stable parts of the continent and in the tectonic belt along the southern border are plotted, while the large number of earthquakes occurring along the Kamchatka and the Kurile Island trench zone have been omitted. Since most of the latter are located at sea, they

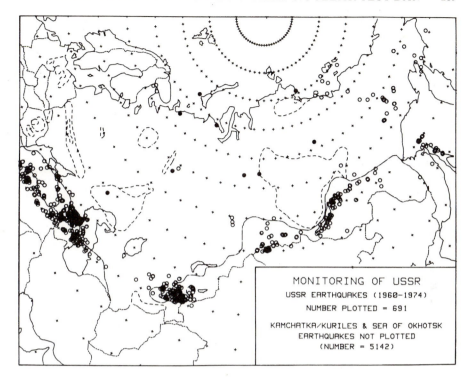

Within the map legend box:

MONITORING OF USSR

USSR EARTHQUAKES (1960–1974)

NUMBER PLOTTED = 691

KAMCHATKA/KURILES & SEA OF OKHOTSK
EARTHQUAKES NOT PLOTTED
(NUMBER = 5142)

Figure 17.3. Soviet earthquakes, 1960–74

691 earthquakes are plotted on the map. Earthquakes in the region of Kamchatka/
Kuriles and the Sea of Okhotsk (5142 events) are not plotted.

are not likely to be mistakenly identified as explosions. Further, near-surface
geology in the Kamchatka–Kuriles area consists almost entirely of water-
saturated sedimentary and volcanic formations that preclude construction of
large underground cavities that could be used for nuclear weapon tests.
Therefore, any tests in those areas would have to be tamped and would result in
seismic magnitudes above 4. The large signals produced by such events could
easily be detected and identified by high-performance seismic stations outside
the USSR, such as might be installed on the Aleutian Islands and in Japan. The
one small area where surface granite occurs, in Kamchatka, would be of
concern as a decoupling site only in the event of a permanent test ban and, in
this case, a station could be placed directly on the site to remove the possibility
that it could be used as a test location. Thus, for monitoring a limited test ban,
in-country stations in this area are not needed, and the large numbers of
earthquakes that occur there are not likely to produce difficulties of event type
identification.

Clearly, of the events plotted in figure 17.3, almost all of them are in the

USSR's southern tectonic belt. The events shown are, however, only those above about magnitude 4.5. There are, of course, more events of lower magnitude that are not represented, since they are of too small a magnitude to be detected and/or located by an international seismic network. However, the number, N, of events occurring per year with magnitudes larger than some magnitude level, m, is known to be given by a relation of the form:

$$\log N = a - b \times m$$

where a and b are constants characteristic of particular seismic regions. Using this relation, with $b \approx .65$ for stable regions of the USSR and $b \approx .8$ for tectonic regions, and with the observed numbers of events above magnitude 4.5 as shown in figure 17.3, one can expect about 1800 events per year above magnitude 2.5 in the southern tectonic belt of the USSR, and only about 60 per year throughout the entire large stable area of the Soviet Union. Thus, since the test areas being monitored by the TSM networks are a small fraction of the entire stable area of the USSR, one can expect only one or two earthquakes of magnitude equal to or above 2.5 near any of the test areas themselves and, at most, of the order of 10 per year within a radius of 1000 km from the centres of all three test sites (that is, only about 3 or so per year anywhere near any one of the test sites). The task of locating and identifying the earthquakes of importance in the test site areas should not, therefore, involve any great analysis effort. Indeed, even if one were concerned with the location and identification of *all* the expected earthquakes above magnitude 2.5, throughout the stable area of the Soviet Union *and* throughout the entire southern tectonic belt, it would only be necessary to locate and identify about half a dozen earthquakes per day. Such an analysis load is well within the capabilities of even a small staff with a mini-computer located at a central recording facility. Therefore, from an operational standpoint, monitoring of the seismic activity in the USSR for verification of a limited test ban, of the type outlined above, would not be difficult.

Similar considerations apply to monitoring of the USA, in that by far the largest number of earthquakes occur along the remote Aleutian Islands trench zone, while a smaller number occur within the western tectonic region, with most activity localized along the San Andreas fault zone in California. The earthquakes in the Aleutians are usually at considerable depth and/or located out at sea, so most of them would not be of concern as possible explosions. Further, explosion coupling and signal transmission from island locations that might be used for tests are such that strong signals are produced from small tamped explosions; in particular magnitudes above 4 for tamped 1-kt explosions would be expected. Therefore, only relatively large events would have to be located and identified, and an external network would be adequate for this purpose. A TSM network on the islands near Amchitka would further enhance detection and location of events at or above this magnitude throughout the entire island arc, as well as provide detection capability to much lower magnitude levels for the Amchitka test site. Based on the Aleutian Islands seismicity, no more than two or three events per day would require analysis, and this load could easily be accommodated, particularly because simple locations for the events are usually all that would be required.

Aside from the verification possibilities offered by seismic monitoring, the Aleutian region is so remote and has so little cultural activity that satellite monitoring would conceivably provide the necessary surveillance capability. In this case, any sustained new activity in a particular area would be suspect and could trigger an inspection. This area of high seismicity would not, consequently, present a difficult monitoring task in view of the applicable surveillance methods.

The tectonic region of the western USA is not so seismically active as to produce more than about one or two events per day that would require any careful analysis. In particular, only events with magnitudes above about 3.5 would be of any conceivable importance in this region, with the possible exception of smaller-magnitude events that could be of significance within the NTS area. Since the NTS area itself would be monitored by a close-in TSM network capable of detection of very small events, down to magnitudes of 2.5 or lower, then an external seismic network would provide adequate surveillance capability for the remaining western area. Consequently, the operational requirements for monitoring of the western USA are reasonable and could easily be accomplished with modest means. Further, since the seismicity of the eastern USA is very low, monitoring of this area is even less demanding, and at most only a few events per month might require analysis. Thus, monitoring of the entire USA for verification of a limited test ban should be straightforward and present no significant operational difficulties in terms of the numbers of events to be analysed.

VIII. Identification of seismic events

The identification of detected events is obviously important, since discrimination of earthquakes and explosions must be accomplished with high confidence and efficiency if seismic verification is to be meaningful. There are a number of seismic methods that can be used to accomplish such event identification. These methods can be divided into two groups: those that can be employed at teleseismic distances and above seismic event body wave magnitudes of about 4 (which corresponds to a tamped 1-kt explosion in a strong coupling medium), and those that are applicable at regional distances (less than about 2000 km from the source) and at all magnitudes of any significance. However, some of the methods are applicable at all distance ranges and at all magnitudes.

In this discussion one of these generally applicable methods will be emphasized, since it can be most easily applied to the TSM network data to identify possible explosions in 'capable' test areas and can as well be applied to regional and teleseismic station data that would be used to monitor other continental areas.[6] In this regard, figure 17.4a indicates locations of earthquakes and nuclear explosions in the general vicinity of the Kazakh and Azgir sites, while figure 17.4b illustrates the discrimination results that provide a means of identifying these explosion events. In this approach only the first arriving direct compressional wave from the seismic source is used; the magnitude associated with this signal is measured at two, high and low, frequencies (i.e., at the extremes of the recorded frequency band). As shown in figure 17.4b, when the values of these two magnitudes are plotted against each other, those points associated with explosions separate into a distinct 'population' in this plane and can be easily distinguished from earthquakes. As illustrated in the two figures, earthquakes and explosions from nearly the same locations are clearly more than one-half of a magnitude unit apart on such a plot. (Note that the low-frequency magnitude, at 0.55 Hz, is close to the conventional seismic magnitude usually measured and used to characterize the seismic energy released by an event.)

As noted above, it would be necessary to be able to identify explosions down to conventional magnitudes near 2.5. There is every expectation (based on theoretical predictions and limited observational data[7]) that the earthquake and explosion populations remain distinct from each other down to much lower magnitude levels; in particular at least down to a magnitude below 2.5. Further, if very-high-frequency magnitudes are used, say near the extremes of the 5–30 Hz band, then regional discrimination by this method is expected to be effective down to magnitudes near unity.[8] Since a 1-kt decoupled explosion produces a seismic magnitude near 2.5, such high-frequency discrimination is expected to provide a basis for verification to a very low threshold, below 1 kt.

The method illustrated in figure 17.4 is particularly attractive, since it is simple to implement on a computer and applies in all distance ranges and at all magnitude levels of importance when broad-band high-frequency data from high-performance seismic stations are available. Further, it provides identification results from observations at a single station and, as distinct from other methods of identification, does not require recordings and analysis of data from an entire network of stations before identification can be made. Thus, when multiple stations record first-arrival signals from an event, each station produces an independent identification of the event type, and this results in a much more confident determination of event identity.

While this particular discrimination approach is the principal method that would be used for event identification, there are others that could and should also be used in order to obtain optimal results. The simplest of these is to use the location and depth of an event as a means of identifying it. Specifically, events located in the oceans at significant distances (e.g., 25 km) from land can be confidently classed as earthquakes without further analysis. (Most earthquakes near the Kamchatka–Kuriles area are of this type.) Further, event hypocentres accurately located in depth, and with depths larger than about 5 km, can confidently be classed as earthquakes. Nearly all earthquakes are of this type, that is, deeper than 5 km, so that accurate depth determinations will discriminate almost all earthquakes (other than a few per cent) from explosions. In verification applications of the TSM stations under a limited test ban,

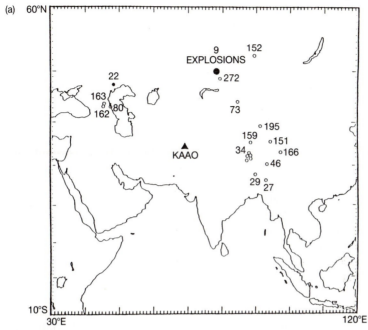

Figure 17.4(a). Earthquakes and nuclear explosions occurring in the vicinity of the Soviet Kazakh and Azgir test sites

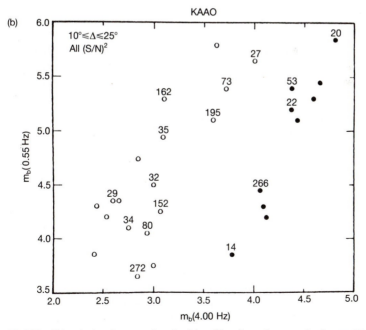

Figure 17.4(b). Discrimination results, for identification of events in figure 17.4(a)

it is certain that almost all (if not all) events within and near the 'capable' test areas can be accurately located as regards surface position and depth. Thus, it is likely that depth alone can be used as a discriminate to positively identify nearly all the earthquakes occurring in the region. If some events were of such shallow (or uncertain) depth as to be possible explosions on the basis of depth, then the previously discussed 'spectral methods' would be employed for identification, possibly along with other methods. On the other hand, for events located throughout the continental area, well outside and away from the TSM networks, one could not always achieve reliable depth determinations, and more reliance would be placed on identification using the spectral magnitude method (and other methods when appropriate) applied to both the teleseismic and in-country TSM station data.

While the identification methods involving surface location, depth and spectral character of the first arriving direct compressional wave from an event will provide considerable discrimination capability, it is important to use all the independent methods of identification that are available for any events that are questionable. In addition to those described, one can use the fact that earthquakes are predominantly quadripole sources of seismic radiation (i.e., have four lobed spatial patterns in the amplitudes of the signals emitted), while explosions are predominantly monopole sources (i.e., produce the same signal amplitude levels in all directions). Use of regional distance stations, such as TSM stations, can allow these patterns to be discerned and used to positively identify the event types. In addition, one can use the relative magnitudes of the direct compressional wave and the surface waves to discriminate earthquakes and explosions, at least at the higher magnitude levels where the low-frequency surface wave signals can be reliably measured. This approach is firmly established for larger events and should be applicable to low-magnitude levels when low-frequency noise levels are low. Thus, it can often be applied, but not always. Nevertheless, these latter two methods can serve to provide extremely definitive identification results and, particularly for events with body wave magnitudes above 4–4.5, are usually applicable.

Taken together, the available identification methods are likely to produce near-certain identification of all detected events, including any decoupled explosions of any significance, within and near the three or four capable test site areas on each continent. On a continental scale, tamped explosions above 1 kt should be similarly identifiable, since these explosions would certainly have magnitudes above about 3.5, and all the methods of identification discussed and illustrated earlier could be applied to the broad band teleseismic and regional data that would be available from such relatively large events. Since decoupling is highly unlikely to be attempted anywhere but on, or very near, the established 'capable' test areas under the conditions of a limited test ban, the identification capability of the three or four TSM networks and an external (teleseismic) network appears more than sufficient for verification of compliance with such a limited test ban. Further, since a condition of the limited test ban is the banning or prior announcement of large industrial explosions near 'capable' test areas, where such explosions could be suspected of being nuclear tests detonated in established cavities, it is unlikely that any false alarms would occur.

IX. Yield estimation

Since the proposed test ban restricts testing to yields at or below 10 kt and limits the total number allowed in the 1- to 10-kt range, it is necessary that yield estimates be available for all tests in the single allowed test area. Since seismic networks are required to ensure compliance with testing at the allowed test site, and at no other site, and also must be used to ensure that decoupled testing is not pursued in 'capable' test areas, it is appropriate to consider use of such networks for yield estimation as well.

Several seismic methods can be used to estimate explosive yields, with each employing a different type of seismic signal generated by the explosion. Specifically, the displacement amplitude of the direct compressional wave and the surface waves generated by an explosion are directly related to explosion energy or yield and so are used to estimate yields. Normally these signal amplitudes are measured in a narrow frequency band and expressed in terms of a magnitude, which is simply proportional to the logarithm of the measured displacement amplitude times the average frequency at which the measurement is made.

The most commonly used methods of yield estimation employ either the compressional wave body wave magnitude, m_b, or the fundamental mode Rayleigh-type surface wave magnitude, M_s. Figure 17.5 shows a composite plot of both m_b versus yield and M_s versus yield for NTS explosions, as well as other US and French nuclear tests.[9] Included in this figure are theoretical curves showing the expected variations of these magnitudes with yield for different material coupling at the Nevada Test Site, as well as one curve for the Aleutian Test Site. Three separate curves are shown for NTS, corresponding to high coupling explosions (labelled 'H') and two intermediate coupling explosion curves (labelled 'I_1' and 'I_2'). These lower coupling curves are appropriate when explosions are detonated in close proximity to a relatively weak and/or less than totally water-saturated material. The high coupling curves (the solid lines in the figure) are those to be expected when the explosions are detonated in strong and/or water-saturated materials. They are, therefore, those appropriate for yield estimation under the conditions imposed by the proposed limited test ban, since testing would be restricted to such high coupling ('strong and/or water-saturated') media. Also shown in figure 17.5 are observed magnitudes for US and French nuclear explosions of known yield.

There are a few points that should be made regarding the observed data and the theoretical curves. First, if differences in body wave transmission characteristics beneath the different test sites at NTS, in Mississippi (Salmon), and in the Aleutian Islands are accounted for, then all the body wave magnitudes for the high coupling explosions fit the theoretical high coupling curve very well.[10]

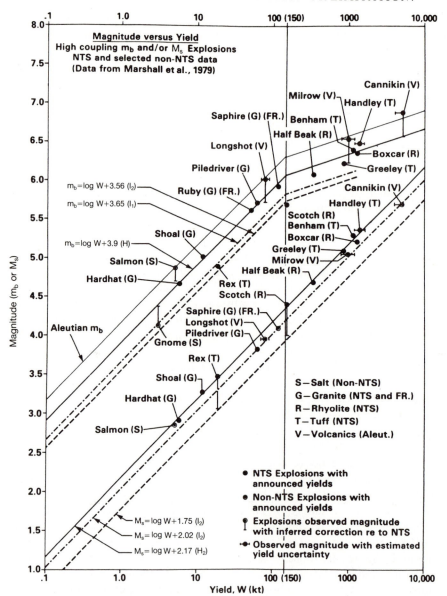

Figure 17.5. The relationship between magnitude and yield of high coupling m_b and/or M_s explosions at NTS sites, selected non-NTS US sites and French sites

Source: Data are taken from Marshall, P. D., Springer, D. L. and Rodean, H. C., 'Magnitude corrections for attenuation in the upper mantle', *Geophysical Journal of the Royal Astronomical Society* (1979), pp. 609–38.

(These are *all* the high coupling explosions with known, published yields.) Second, all the observed surface wave magnitudes lie close to the theoretical M_s versus yield line, particularly if uncertainties in the published yields for some of the explosions are taken into account. (The two explosions labelled 'Scotch' and 'Rex' are inferred to be contaminated by unusual tectonic effects, with associated 'perturbations' in the M_s values, as indicated by the bars attached to these explosion points. Therefore, these two explosions are inferred to correspond to intermediate coupled explosions.) Finally, based on these two conclusions and on knowledge of the current calibration standards for seismic stations, it can be concluded that if the high coupling theoretical curves for m_b or M_s versus yield are used to infer unknown yields from observed magnitudes, then use of either magnitude will provide yield estimates with uncertainties that are no larger than 30 per cent of the yield value, for the yield range from about 150 kt down to at least 10 kt, provided that proper network-averaged and station-corrected magnitudes are used and that any anomalous tectonic effects are accounted for. Given that calibration explosions at low yield, in the range from 1 to 10 kt, would be detonated at the designated site under a limited ban agreement, then it is likely that equally accurate yield estimates could be assured at yields as low as 1 kt.

It also follows that if sets of curves, such as these, are established for a particular test site, then it is possible to use both the body and surface wave magnitudes together to infer a single yield value for the explosion. (That is, with two or more independent observations one can ask which pair of m_b versus yield and M_s versus yield curves gives the same value of yield for that explosion.) This requirement, that both magnitudes give the same yield value, determines which pair of coupling curves are appropriated for the particular explosion and so provides estimates of both the yield and the coupling characteristics of the containing medium around the explosion. For considerations of yield under the conditions of the proposed limited ban, this procedure would allow a check to be made that only tests in a high coupling medium were being conducted.

As an example of this latter procedure, the theoretical curves inferred for the test site at Kazakh are shown in figure 17.6. The figure shows observed magnitude data from the Soviet test site, where the events selected were the *largest* detonated at this test area and the surface wave magnitudes were corrected for tectonic effects.[11] The observed body and surface magnitudes associated with a particular explosion (the numbers in the figure denote event numbers) were constrained to *both* give the same yield estimate and, as indicated above, this was accomplished by choosing a pair of 'coupling curves' that would allow both observed magnitudes to provide the same yield estimate. Based on this technique, one obtains consistent body and surface wave magnitude estimates of yield and estimates of medium coupling characteristics for these explosions. As is evident, many of these large explosions are at, or very near, 150 kt in estimated yield, with two slightly over 150 kt. Based on magnitude measurement and tectonic correction uncertainties, as well as the

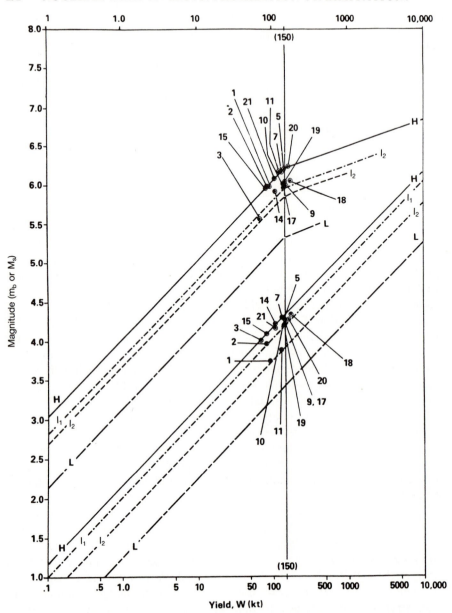

Figure 17.6. The relationship between magnitude and yield for the largest nuclear tests at eastern Kazakh

Source: Sykes, L. R. and Cifuentes, I. L., 'Yields of Soviet underground nuclear explosions from seismic surface waves: compliance with the Threshold Test Ban Treaty', *Proceedings of the National Academy of Sciences USA*, vol. 81 (Mar. 1984).

uncertainties in this process of association with a proper pair of coupling curves, it is estimated that the uncertainty in the estimated yields for these explosions are typically near 30 per cent in either direction (that is, for an estimated yield near 150 kt, the uncertainty range is 105–95 kt).

On the basis of current seismic methods for estimating explosion yields, it would appear that the yield estimates should be sufficiently accurate to detect any significant violation of a 10-kt test limitation, in particular any test above about 15 kt. In terms of providing a count of test yields in the range 1–10 kt, it is reasonable to count only those events with estimated yields above about 2 kt. In this case an accurate count should not be difficult, particularly because calibration explosions would be available and the TSM networks could be used to provide additional types of seismic magnitude measurements and, consequently, other independent yield estimates based on these 'close-in' measurements.

X. Summary

Operation of in-country low-threshold treaty networks would provide the necessary information to decide what is needed to lower a treaty threshold to a level below 1 kt and extend the treaty period indefinitely. At some point in a process of continued reduction of the testing threshold, the limit at which nuclear testing is militarily significant could be reached. At this threshold level, assuming it exists, it would be possible to impose a comprehensive ban and still maintain an effective seismic verification capability, since any lower-yield explosions that could not be detected with high probability at a large number of stations would not be nuclear weapon tests. However, even if there is no absolute limit below which nuclear tests are useless for some kind of weapon development, there are known, rather high yield limits at which many types of the most potentially destructive weapons must be tested in the course of their development. These yield limits are well above 1 kt. Consequently, a 1-kt threshold test ban treaty would be effective in halting the development of most, if not all, militarily significant nuclear weapons. Such a treaty would therefore eliminate or strongly constrain the most dangerous and destabilizing aspect of the arms race and allow meaningful negotiations for the implementation of other arms limitation measures to be carried on—with these measures designed to reduce the numbers and kinds of current nuclear weapons and their delivery systems to levels consistent with the real and rational needs of national security. In the meantime, a time-limited low-threshold treaty of the type discussed here can be implemented as an interim agreement designed to constrain new weapon developments while simultaneously providing data of the type required for design of a long-term very-low-threshold or comprehensive test ban treaty.

The discussion and evaluation of the technical issues involved in monitoring this type of limited nuclear test ban can be summarized in terms of the following conclusions and recommendations.

1. 'Assured seismic verification' will require that certain specific conditions, beyond the limits on numbers and yields of allowed tests in high-coupling media at a designated test site, be part of a limited moratorium agreement. In particular, it should be required that: (a) the designated test site be of relatively small area and in a 'hard rock' geologic environment and that inspection of the site for the existence of large cavities be allowed; (b) drill core samples and logs from as many as three or four deep holes on the designated sites be supplied, with observers present during the sampling, and with observers from one country selecting the drilling sites on the other country's test site; (c) four or five calibration explosions, of independently verified yield spanning the 1- to 10-kt range, be conducted at each designated site after installation of the in-country seismic network; (d) large industrial explosions, at or above about 20 tons, be announced beforehand (as to yield, time and place), or be banned entirely from areas that are defined as 'capable test areas'. Further, if conducted, that upon request observers be allowed to view and inspect the site immediately before and after the explosion.

2. Monitoring of a time-limited threshold nuclear test ban can be accomplished by a combination of current 'national technical means' and by the installation and operation of test site monitoring networks, with four or five seismic recording stations deployed near sites with current capability for current weapon tests. Such monitoring would provide seismic data assuring verification capability at known or 'capable' test areas and would severely restrict possibilities of testing, without discovery, at any other site within the USA and the USSR over the duration of the test ban.

3. Three to four sites in each country are probably all that need be monitored. This can be accomplished using four- or five-station networks ('TSM networks') near the boundaries of each test site area. Each seismic station would consist of three very-high-frequency seismic detectors, in a 100-metre borehole, and two sets of three seismic sensors at the surface measuring in lower-frequency bands. The recommended complement of sensors is identical to those employed in the NDRC–Soviet project in the USSR and the USA. These stations should be unmanned, with all data telemetered to 'Central Recording Facilities' in the participating countries.

4. Redeployment of high-performance seismic stations near test sites would provide data that could be used to verify predictions of event detection and identification capability at regional distances (events at distances of about 500–2000 km). Hence, 'hard data' related to verification of a permanent test ban would be obtained. Further, the TSM networks would constitute stations with partial capability for monitoring of all potential test sites in a country, and hence constitute the beginning of a deployment of comprehensive in-country networks required for verification of a long-term treaty.

5. Detection and location of all seismic events within and around the 'capable nuclear test sites', down to seismic magnitudes as low as 2.5, are highly probable using the recommended TSM networks. This capability means that no significant decoupled explosion (i.e., with a yield in the 1- to 10-kt

range) occurring within regions designated as 'capable nuclear test areas' would go undetected. Further, detection and identification of any tamped nuclear explosion above 1 kt, anywhere within either the USA or the USSR, are likewise highly probable with a combination of external stations and TSM networks. Discrimination of explosions (of any type) from earthquakes could be accomplished with high confidence using a combination of discrimination methods based on, among other possibilities: (a) depth and location of the event, (b) spectral character of the first arriving compressional wave, (c) the relative spectral amplitudes of compressional waves and surface waves from the events, and (d) the spatial patterns of radiated compressional, shear and surface waves from the events.

6. Given the requirement of a few calibration explosions of known yield at the designated test sites, yield estimates required in the 1- to 10-kt range (and possibly above) can be obtained with sufficient certainty through joint use of the regional and teleseismically recorded seismic radiation from explosions. The independent methods that may be jointly applied to obtain both the yield and values of parameters related to medium coupling characteristics for these explosions include the use of amplitudes from the following seismic signals: (a) the first arriving compressional wave, (b) regular surface waves, and (c) higher-mode, crustally guided surface waves. Joint use of such data will allow estimates of yield with about 30 per cent uncertainty near and above 10 kt. At the 1-kt yield level, the uncertainty in the determination of yield could be expected to be about 50 per cent. In addition, it will be simultaneously possible to estimate coupling characteristics for each explosion and to assess whether they have been detonated in high coupling media, as is required by the agreement.

7. Installation of encoding procedures will ensure data integrity. Telemetry, via satellite, would also provide security for the operation and greatly simplify monitoring activities.

8. The limited test ban agreement should contain provisions recognizing the right of either side, on request, to perform a fixed number of 'on-site inspections' based on evidence that a detected seismic event could be a nuclear explosion. The number of such inspections that should provide adequate deterrence is about five or six.

9. As an added feature of the agreement, it would be useful to include a provision for concurrent in-country seismic surveys designed to provide reliable high-frequency seismic data relevant to noise levels, signal propagation efficiency and levels of seismic activity in several critical areas within the countries involved, with the objective of providing the 'hard data' that are important in the design of permanent in-country seismic verification networks.

Notes and references

[1] Tamped underground explosions are those detonated in close proximity to the surrounding rock, as opposed to explosions detonated in large underground cavities containing air or any injected 'filler' material designed to absorb the explosive shock wave.

[2] Uncertainty estimates given in this paper refer to *one standard deviation* from the mean yield value, where it is assumed that the statistical distribution of values that would be obtained from repeated measurements of tests at a particular yield value would be *normally* distributed about a mean value.

[3] Evernden, J. F., Archambeau, C. B. and Cranswick, E., 'An evaluation of seismic decoupling and underground nuclear test monitoring using high-frequency seismic data', *Reviews of Geophysics*, vol. 24, no. 2 (May 1986), pp. 143–215. Evernden, J. F. and Archambeau, C. B., 'Some seismological aspects of monitoring a comprehensive test ban treaty', in *Technical Means of Verification of Compliance with Arms Control Treaties* (Pergamon-Brasseys: Washington, DC, 1986).

[4] See note 3.

[5] Detection is based on the predicted signal-to-noise ratio of the *first arrival* compressional wave at the stations. Detection of an event based on this criterion ensures that larger-amplitude, later-arriving signals will also be detected. Assured detection of multiple signals from seismic events would allow more confident location and identification of the event to be accomplished, as well as to ensure the simple detection of some of the many signals from each seismic event.

[6] See note 3 and Archambeau, C. B., *Estimates of Seismic Coupling and Nuclear Explosion Yields Using Seismic Magnitude and Moment Data*, Proceedings of Eighth Annual DARPA/AFGL Seismic Research Symposium, May 1986.

[7] Archambeau, C. B., Harkrider, D. G. and Helmberger, D. V., *Study of Multiple Seismic Events*, US Arms Control Agency Rpt. ACDA/ST–220, California Institute of Technology, 1974; Savino, J. M., Archambeau, C. B. and Masso, J. F., *Discrimination Results from a 10-Station Network*, DARPA Rpt. SSS–CR–79–4566, S-cubed (Maxwell Industries, Inc., La Jolla, CA, 1980); Evernden, J. F., 'Spectral characteristics of the P Codas of Eurasian earthquakes and explosions', *Bulletin of the Seismological Society*, vol. 67 (1977), pp. 1099–151.

[8] See note 3.

[9] Sykes, L. R. and Cifuentes, I. L., 'Yields of Soviet underground nuclear explosions from seismic surface waves: compliance with the threshold test ban treaty', *Proceedings of the National Academy of Sciences USA*, vol. 81 (Mar. 1984), pp. 1922–5.

[10] The bars on the non-NTS explosions in the figure indicate the direction and amount of the test site 'bias correction' to be applied in order to make the observations comparable to those at NTS.

[11] See note 9.

Part 5
Consequences of the prohibition or further limitation of nuclear tests

Chapter XV. Attitudes of the nuclear weapon powers

Paper 18

Carl G. Jacobsen
SIPRI

Abstract

Many issues, from technological monitoring uncertainties to the ingrained habits and biases of different politico-military cultures, affect attitudes towards a possible CTB. The single most crucial variable, however, is that of a nation's chosen or adopted strategic-doctrinal posture. A CTB is anathema to advocates of nuclear war-fighting and -winning, because it would undermine the targeting confidence that is a *sine qua non* of counterforce doctrine. For that reason, a CTB is confidence-boosting and security-enhancing to those reconciled to MAD. Years ago Soviet doctrine belonged to the former category, US doctrine to the latter, and this juxtaposition may be repeated in coming years. Today, the juxtaposition is the reverse. Soviet support for a CTB conforms to Soviet doctrine and acceptance of MAD; US opposition reflects rejection of MAD. French and Chinese postures derive from scepticism regarding CTB prospects, expectations of continued superpower pursuit of missile defence means and potential, and fear that this may emasculate the potency of lesser arsenals. The British position reflects Alliance concerns and national security predicaments. Attitudes towards SDI are indicative: SDI constitutes rejection of CTB; it necessitates a high rate of nuclear testing.

I. Introduction

Military establishments have feared that a CTB would deny opportunity or imbed disadvantage. Military concern spurred President Eisenhower's formal December 1959 abrogation of the 1958 nuclear testing moratorium. Military concern affected the Soviet decision to resume testing in 1961, after French nuclear tests.[1]

Political and ideological distrust skewered initiatives and bred further distrust. Soviet initiatives sought disarmament measures first, to negate US military advantage. The United States sought inspection and verification first, to penetrate the Soviet *maskirovka* that obscured weakness and allowed surprise.

Concessions to the concerns of the other suggested sleight-of-hand imagery. Soviet proposals for physical inspection called for national inspectors; foreign inspection was to be strictly limited, subject to host-country refusal, and was to confirm compliance, not monitor nuclear explosions.[2] US arms-cut initiatives focused on categories of Soviet strength, ignoring areas of US advantage.

The years 1963–74, and even 1977–80, saw some substantive bargaining. Negotiations on a comprehensive test ban in 1963, sparked by President Kennedy's suspension of nuclear tests and the Soviet decision to follow suit, appeared then to be close to success: the USSR accepted the principle of tamper-proof instrument monitoring stations (three, as opposed to the US demand for seven), but agreement on physical inspection remained elusive. The parties signed the Partial Test Ban Treaty that year as a first step.

Arms control efforts during the 1970s proceeded on the basis of 'national means of verification', but shifted to issues of arms balance and arms 'capping' (SALT and the ABM Treaty). However, in 1974 the Threshold Test Ban Treaty, limiting yields to 150 kt, brought testing back into the limelight. The limit was well beyond what most scientists believed could be verified, but it conceded that external verification was possible—and that on-site inspection might be a political imperative and therefore a necessary prerequisite to further restrictions, but that it may not be a strictly technical or scientific requirement.

Détente began to unravel in 1973, when the United States excluded the Soviet Union from participation in the Middle East peace process (others date the unravelling to 1974, when Congress torpedoed the US–Soviet trade agreement signed by Nixon and Brezhnev in 1972), although arms control efforts continued. The SALT II accord, outlined prior to 1974, was finally signed by President Carter, but not ratified. CTB negotiations were resumed in 1974 and made some progress. 1980, the last year of Carter's Presidency, brought Soviet agreement to the stationing on each other's territory of 10 tamper-proof seismic stations estimated to provide 90 per cent confidence down to 0.1 kt for the hard-rock conditions of Soviet test sites (0.1 kt is about one-half of 1 per cent of the Hiroshima bomb), as well as on-site physical inspection clauses.[3] But US political and perhaps military dynamics were now far more adverse than in 1963. They precluded agreement. The incoming Reagan Administration broke off the talks.

II. The Soviet position

The 1980s brought stronger statements of Soviet support for a CTB, culminating in the unilateral Soviet test moratorium announced in 1985.

The posture was no doubt designed in part to buttress Moscow's peace campaign, and to help generate Western opposition to the Reagan Administration's efforts to improve nuclear war-fighting capabilities and explore the possibility of 'prevailing' in a nuclear war. However, the Soviet posture was also in accord with the markedly changed thrust of official Soviet doctrine. Soviet doctrine had itself pursued nuclear war-fighting and the goal of victory.[4]

But General Secretary Brezhnev's 1977 Tula speech[5] and the appointment of Marshal Ogarkov as Chief of the General Staff that same year signalled a Soviet return to the (then controversial) thesis of the early- and mid-1960s that the initiation of nuclear war meant national suicide.

Marshal Ogarkov's tenure saw ever-increasing stress on the mutuality of the cataclysm that would inevitably attend the unleashing of strategic nuclear war.[6] He heaped scorn on the illusions of those who thought that such wars could be either contained or controlled. Strategic nuclear weapons could have no other purpose than to deter their use by others. They promised doomsday and had no military utility. Ogarkov instead emphasized new and 'smart' technologies which, with novel operational concepts, might circumvent the nuclear impasse. He emphasized that new non-nuclear technologies promise to achieve the military tasks assigned to nuclear weapons, without the latter's concomitant albatross of loss of control and purpose. The extreme exacerbation of East–West tensions in 1983 brought Soviet peace-time institutionalization of redefined, wartime Theatres of (strategic) Military Operations (TVDs). The essentially wartime practice of Supreme Command representatives taking direct charge of these multi-front all-arms composites was also institutionalized; Marshal Ogarkov's 1984 assignment to direct the crucial Western TVD (incorporating Soviet and Warsaw Pact forces aimed at the central front) underlined the Soviet seriousness of purpose. East–West tensions subsequently eased, but Ogarkov and like-minded officers continued to define and dominate Soviet doctrine. This entails a continued push for new technological and other options, to counter continuing US challenge and 'threat'. It also means continued adherence to the theme that nuclear-weapon use means Mutual Assured Destruction (MAD).

The new Soviet military doctrine, with its core affirmation of MAD, had immediate practical ramifications. The US Central Intelligence Agency (CIA) confirms that budgetary outlays for the Strategic Rocket Troops and Air Defence (which incorporated space defence) 'declined in absolute terms after 1977'.[7]

The Soviet doctrine compelled military support for a CTB. It dictated military support for Moscow's 1980 on-site inspection offer.

The doctrine, and apparent Soviet military acceptance of the proposition that non-explosive diagnostic methods can now ensure the viability and some limited modernization of existing nuclear arsenals, also dictated support for General Secretary Gorbachev's 1985 test moratorium.

Soviet officials continue to insist that on-site inspection is not a technical–scientific requirement: 'The United States should have become convinced of this in August 1985, when it carried out an unannounced low-yield explosion, and yet the Soviet Union was able to specify all of its characteristics . . . Modern instruments can detect tests that are under 0.5 kilotons at a distance of 4,000 to 5,000 kilometers . . . no supranational means of detection are necessary'.[8]

Nevertheless, Moscow clearly recognizes that on-site monitoring and inspection constitute a political requirement. The Soviet Union refused President Reagan's invitation to attend and monitor a US nuclear test to ascertain the accuracy of both Soviet and US yield assessment technology, not because it was superfluous but because it might be construed as acceptance of continued testing. 'The Soviet Union considers it necessary to conduct proper international on-site inspection to ensure the observance of test ban agreements, not the continuation of tests'.[9]

The USSR dramatized its position in 1986. It signed an agreement with the US (non-governmental) Natural Resources Defense Council (NRDC) to establish three seismic stations in the vicinity of the principal Soviet nuclear test site, at Semipalatinsk. It then agreed, with the US Geological Survey, to establish a broader seismic monitoring network specifically designed to assuage fears of surreptitious explosions—although this agreement has not been consummated, as it was conditioned on US participation in a testing moratorium.

The Soviet Union reaffirmed its readiness to accept on-site US and international inspection. In a noteworthy speech in Stockholm in August 1986 on security and confidence-building measures in Europe, Soviet Defence Minister Marshal S. Akhromeev indicated willingness to ease the restrictions that circumscribed earlier Soviet offers for on-site physical inspection of arms control compliance.[10] Marshal Akhromeev affirmed Soviet readiness to accept a limited number of inspections of non-designated areas and accepted the need for aerial as well as ground access. And although the readiness was limited to the agenda of the Stockholm Conference, it has clearly established a most important precedent.

US tests continued. After 24 unreciprocated test explosions, the USSR voiced frustration (we 'cannot exercise unilateral restraint forever'), and on 18 December 1986 announced that the next scheduled US test (in January 1987) would compel resumption of Soviet testing. The Soviet Union affirmed its principled stand—US abstinence would be immediately reciprocated. The USSR also softened its refusal to consider less-than-comprehensive treaties: interim stages can be agreed to, either within the context of or as a prelude to CTB negotiations. The Soviet Union is prepared to accept 'the strictest control, including on-site inspection'.[11]

III. The US position

The Reagan Administration's opposition to CTB negotiations appeared to reflect deep-seated suspicion of Soviet motives, ingrained belief in Soviet proclivity to cheat, and moral, political and strategic-doctrinal aversion to MAD.[12] The last is fundamental—the single most crucial obstacle to CTB advocacy. The former were more open to challenge, but they dominated the debate during the Administration's early years and must therefore be briefly addressed first.

Allegations that some Soviet tests had exceeded the 150-kt limit of the officially observed but still unratified Threshold Test Ban Treaty met Soviet protest. Moscow noted that full-scope information about the geological and geophysical properties of testing areas would be secured when and if the USA ratifies the TTBT; proper calibration of seismographs, taking account of test site geological conditions, guarantees against meaningful cheating.

Reagan Administration spokespersons also suggested that a CTB would cause the Allies to lose confidence in the US deterrent, that it might force nuclear weapon states to increase stockpiles and to offset lower confidence in weapon efficacy, and that it would encourage horizontal proliferation among near-nuclear weapon states hitherto deterred by the dynamism of ongoing modernization programmes; a CTB might make the economic and technological costs of emulation appear manageable. The first argument was belied by widespread Allied support for a CTB. The second found little resonance (see below). The third met a dissenting chorus from signatories to the Non-Proliferation Treaty: a CTB was, on the contrary, seen as a necessary first step for the superpowers to meet their own obligations under the treaty, and hence ultimately a prerequisite for continued adherence by others.[13]

The scepticism accorded peripheral arguments concentrated attention on the Administration's core proposition: national security demands continued testing. This proposition is in turn composed of three postulates: two controversial and the third unassailable. The first (actually a more recently elaborated variant of the second) alleges that Moscow's moratorium merely reflected the end of a testing cycle. Sharp Soviet denial is supported by Western tabulations. Soviet military tests during the preceding 18 months appear only to have exceeded US numbers if (certifiable) 'peaceful nuclear explosions' are added to the total; this is not warranted. The second US postulate concerns the asserted need to test in order to guard against weapon degradation. Yet, since 1945 only 0.4 per cent of US nuclear explosions, well under one per year, have been designed to check weapon reliability.[14] With modern diagnostic methods, the need for reliability testing is open to challenge.

It is interesting to note that the USSR, notwithstanding technological handicaps, has in fact always exhibited greater confidence as regards the ramifications of testing abstinence. The USA tested extensively underground before signing the 1963 treaty that banned other testing venues, and was prepared to implement its provisions without delay. The USSR conducted only one underground test before signing the treaty prohibiting tests in other environments and was not prepared—it took a full year before Soviet testing resumed.[15]

The unassailable US proposition concerns the need for tests in order to develop new strategic systems. Contrary allegations notwithstanding, this does not affect systems now in the pipeline. MX, Trident 2 and enhanced-radiation warheads (neutron bombs) have already been exhaustively tested. In terms of weapon deployments authorized by the US Congress, there is no clear military need for continued testing. In fact, even new weapons, incorporating evolutionary advances, can also be developed owing to advanced diagnostic methods in nuclear material testing. The development of new-generation warheads, however, would be drastically curtailed by further restrictions.[16]

Five radical new nuclear-driven weapon programmes lie at the heart of the Reagan Administration's Strategic Defense Initiative (SDI), which in turn embodies the Administration's rejection of MAD. These nuclear-generated weapon programmes are: X-ray lasers, optical lasers, particle beams, hypervelocity pellets and microwaves.[17] The X-ray laser programme, Excalibur, became the flagship of early SDI advocacies. Initial tests were not as encouraging as was first reported. Administration spokesmen now concede that 200 or more nuclear experiments (perhaps 50 actual tests) may be needed just to ascertain its viability. In fact, the development stage alone of each of the five programmes is likely to require a similar number of experiments. In other words, the task of fully evaluating the feasibility and strategic impact of currently funded, fundamentally new nuclear designs may require 200–300 nuclear explosions, and possibly more. Final evaluation furthermore necessitates atmospheric testing. Not only does pursuit of these programmes therefore preclude consideration of a CTB, but their development ultimately also entails abrogation of all treaties restricting nuclear testing environments and yields.[18]

Even if these programmes were terminated, however, whether as a result of negative evaluation or congressional fiscal restraints, the politico-military doctrine of the Reagan Administration would still dictate opposition to a CTB.

A CTB would be confidence-boosting and security-enhancing to those reconciled to MAD, because it undermines the targeting confidence that is a *sine qua non* of compellent strategy, counterforce and pre-emption; for that very same reason, it is anathema to proponents of nuclear war-fighting. The Soviet posture conforms to acceptance of MAD; the US posture conforms to rejection of MAD.

IV. The British position

Britain's posture has changed dramatically. Throughout the 1960s and 1970s, the UK was the strongest nuclear weapon state advocate of MAD and a CTB. Today, the British posture is more contortionist: acceptance of MAD, yet not rejecting rejection of MAD. Prime Minister Thatcher's Government has stressed the absolute political and military need to maintain a close alliance relationship with the USA. British testing is conducted at US test sites. British nuclear modernization programmes depend on access to US systems and US technology.[19] The British Government expresses understanding for US doctrinal predilections and supports SDI research.

While expressing support for SDI research, however, the Conservative Government remains deeply sceptical of the realizability of the larger vision. Foreign Minister Sir Geoffrey Howe spoke for majority opinion within the

Cabinet, the party and the opposition when he suggested that the ultimate ambition would be 'a Maginot line in the sky'. Britain's embrace of SDI research reflected Alliance politics, national science concerns and industrial development policy, not military doctrine.[20]

British Government opposition to a CTB, dictated by Alliance considerations and the Reagan Administration's sharp break with past attitudes, contains no renunciation of MAD. On the contrary: continued strong and unequivocal support for existing test restrictions, and for a strict interpretation of the 1972 ABM Treaty, emphatically confirm British expectations that SDI research will fall well short of the grandiose goal of population defence. British opposition to a CTB therefore focuses on the question of verifiability.

The UK concedes that, 'There now appears to be no technical obstacle to monitoring underground tests releasing as little as one kiloton or less energy'.[21] Fears that small tests 'carried out with every possible subterfuge, and at a whole host of possible places'[22] may also recede, with appreciation of the probable practical impossibility of implementing the necessary subterfuge.

Fears of verifiability *per se* do in fact appear to have receded. British spokespersons acknowledge that the question of verifiability is now one of 'political judgement'; although 'backed by technical findings', it rests 'upon a range of considerations, including the extent of political confidence of one party that others would comply with a treaty'.[23] Even 'if we are to conclude that verification provisions would be adequate we also need to be truly confident that others will abide by an agreement . . . we are far from satisfied that such confidence would be justified'.[24] The question of military risk—of whether one party's possible decision to break treaty provisions necessarily constitutes a meaningful military risk to other signatories, or whether such possible risk can be countered by preparations to respond in analogous fashion—is not addressed. The British posture is alliance-preserving.

V. The French position

French opposition to a CTB at this time ignores the issue of verification. It rests instead on a perceived strategic requirement for further tests and is not, as in the US case, to circumvent the mutual hostage implication of MAD, but rather to ensure France's ability to hold hostage.

France has conducted far fewer tests than have either the USA or the USSR; France possesses only 2 per cent as many warheads as either of the two superpowers, and has less reason for confidence. 'One cannot have weapons of which the potential efficacity . . . cannot be evaluated through tests'.[25]

The core argument may be summarized as follows:[26]

1. Nuclear tests are essential for nuclear credibility.
2. Nuclear tests confirm France's place among the 'great' nations.
3. Today's military-technological challenges mean that France must develop new-generation systems to ensure strategic viability.

The last refers to SDI and its ramifications. Official French attitudes towards SDI changed following the 1986 election. The new government declared its support, but the support was not for SDI's original MAD-negating vision. No French spokesperson considered this feasible. Rather, SDI symbolized a *de facto* intensification of military-technological competition, a parallel US–Soviet push for a defensive complement to their arsenals which was *not* likely to jeopardize the balance between the two, but which might emasculate the potency of lesser nuclear powers. France 'cannot not associate itself with this great research'; the programme is 'inevitable, irreversible and justified', because offensive weapon developments have always been followed by the search for defence.[27]

It is perhaps wrong to talk of French opposition to a CTB. More to the point: in the French view a CTB is unrealistic and unlikely—it is not how great powers behave. Great powers do not tolerate *diktat*: France long refused to sign, or even act in accordance with, the Partial Test Ban Treaty on atmospheric tests and changed its position only after the issue was brought before the International Court of Justice. France's government-sanctioned attack on the *Rainbow Warrior* in Auckland harbour, sinking the vessel and killing a crew member, dramatized French determination to defy the concerns of those who neighbour on its Pacific test site, and others, while refusing to countenance tests on its own home territory. France protests that it can in any case not be expected to adhere to a CTB without significant prior cuts in superpower arsenals.

VI. The Chinese position

China's posture is similar to the French one: China's nuclear forces are minimal, bereft of the awesome redundancy (and associated option flexibility) of superpower arsenals. The USA and the USSR 'have long since exceeded the level of "over-kill" . . . there will still be enough nuclear weapons to destroy the world more than once even if their arsenals are cut by half'. A CTB and arms reductions constitute a luxury that China cannot presently afford. It must be the responsibility of the Soviet Union and the United States to first halt the 'testing, production and deployment of all types of nuclear weapons', and to then proceed to 'drastic reductions'.[28] China shares France's concern that SDI stimulates two-superpower pursuit of a defensive edge that they will each be able to offset, but that may prove decisive *vis-à-vis* third powers.

There is a basic contradiction imbedded in the French and Chinese postures. Both feel compelled to pursue testing and force modernization to ensure the continued viability of their nuclear forces. Yet both fear that superpower testing and modernization programmes herald a military-technological environment that may negate their deterrence.

France appears to see currently unfolding missile defence dynamics as inexorable. Its response has been to intensify efforts to keep abreast of developments, to try to ensure continued penetration potential. China appears also to have taken steps to try to guard against the spectre of emasculation; cruise-missile technology has received increased developmental priority, presumably because of its potential promise as a vehicle with which to underfly and hence circumvent anti-ballistic missile installations.

But China also shows increased interest in the possibility of diverting adverse dynamics—in the possibility that economic and political pressures, perhaps reinforced by strategic ambivalence, may yet cause the superpowers to reconsider their pursuit of defence potentials. China's official posture still highlights three themes:[29]

1. China's nuclear no-first-use policy should be adopted by all.
2. Nuclear weapons must be prohibited and destroyed.
3. The USA and the USSR possess 'over 95 per cent of the world's nuclear weapons', 'bear a special responsibility', and must begin the process.

Recent years brought an addendum: if an *ad hoc* CTB committee is established within the Conference on Disarmament, 'The Chinese delegation will participate in its work'.[30] A CTB was never before a Chinese concern. Now, apparently, it is. Chinese officials have not elaborated, but the change is significant.

VII. Conclusion

A CTB presumes acceptance of the thesis that MAD is and will remain an unavoidable reality (or, at least, the lesser evil) and that absolute or sufficient verification is possible.

Today, Soviet doctrine embraces MAD; US doctrine does not. This constellation may be in flux, however. Ultimate US doctrinal ambitions, as epitomized by the grand original SDI vision, may constitute negation of MAD, but SDI as a practical near-term developmental programme looks different. Most official US spokespersons now focus on 'point defence' of offensive missile installations, on narrower defence visions that look more realizeable.[31] Ironically, what might be called SDI II in fact guarantees and imbeds MAD. SDI II is a cornerstone of US counterforce doctrine, and counterforce proclivity argues against acceptance of a CTB. But attendant test requirements are lower than those associated with rejection of MAD. The opposition is practical, not theological. The advantage sought is relative, not absolute. The suggested posture could allow consideration of a CTB or a very-low-threshold test ban treaty.

Nevertheless, notwithstanding practical funding priorities and more restrained near-term ambitions, the Reagan Administration continues to posit the original SDI vision as the final goal, and it continues to fund research directed at the attainment of that goal (see above). If this continues to be the case, then a large-scale emulative Soviet effort may be inevitable. Soviet restraint today is a function of its earlier lack of success, which forced the conclusion that MAD is *the* single inescapable determinant of the US–Soviet strategic inter-relationship (note that penetration certainty is a superpower privilege; the USSR does not concede it to France or China—the perpetuation of this imbalance has indeed long provided the main *raison d'être* behind Soviet defence research and investment). Moscow is convinced that US experience will compel the same conclusion. If the United States is not deterred, however, then Soviet re-evaluation will clearly be in order. In his Stockholm speech Marshal Akhromeev affirmed Soviet military support for a continuation of the test moratorium, because the military disadvantage that it entailed did not threaten the potency and credibility of Soviet strategic power. If that was threatened, however, or if the political cost became unacceptable, then the moratorium would end. A Soviet conclusion that stated that US ambitions might after all be realizeable would set in motion an equally grand Soviet programme. Grand Soviet programmes are not easily deflected, whether realizeable or not.

If progress is not forthcoming, we may face a reversed situation in a few years: a United States resigned to MAD, and willing to accept a CTB, versus a Soviet Union that has invested too much in pursuit of a contrary quest. There are precedents. MIRVs (multiple independently targetable re-entry vehicles) and strategic cruise missiles were both developed by the USA in the expectation that they would confer meaningful advantage; Soviet emulation led instead to less security and less stability, for both.

On the subject of verification, lingering doubts are magnified by distrust. Both parties have exploited ambiguities in previously negotiated treaty texts, and have sanctioned actions contrary to their spirit and purpose. The Soviet phased-array radar in Krasnoyarsk is one example; the US modernization of Thule and Fallingdale radars are others (as are US and Soviet periphery radars designed also to provide some inland coverage).

In the nuclear testing arena, three comments suggest themselves:

1. The scope for meaningful cheating appears negligible.
2. Moscow's concessions on verification appear real and important.
3. Soviet advocacy of a CTB conforms to Soviet military doctrine.

If meaningful cheating is not possible, then the question becomes: Is the possibility of treaty breakout militarily significant? This analyst's answer is: no, if other signatories are prepared for that eventuality, as indeed they must be.

Notes and references

[1] *Public Papers of the President of the United States, Dwight D. Eisenhower, 1959; United Nations and Disarmament, 1945–1970*, p. 214; *The Test Ban*, SIPRI Research Report, 1971, p. 5.

[2] Vigor, P.H., *The Soviet View of Disarmament* (Macmillan: London, 1986), pp. 139–66.

[3] Sykes, L. R., 'Verification of nuclear test ban treaties', *Testimony Before Subcommittee on Arms Control, International Security and Science*, Committee on Foreign Affairs, US House of Representatives (US Government Printing Office: Washington, DC, 8 May 1985), p. 16.

[4] See Fitzgerald, M., *The Soviet Union and Nuclear War*, Dalhousie University Foreign Policy Study Centre, forthcoming, for an exhaustive presentation of Soviet source documentation on the subject.

[5] *Pravda*, 19 Jan. 1977.

[6] Ogarkov, N. V., 'The defence of socialism', *Krasnaya Zvezda*, 9 May 1984; Ogarkov, N. V., *Istoria Uchit Bditelnost* (Voenizdat: Moscow, 1985), pp. 47, 48. See also *Kommunist Vooruzhiennikh Sil*, no. 21 (1984), p. 25; and Gareyev, M. A., *M. V. Frunz—Voyennyy Teoretik* (Voenizdat: Moscow, 1985), pp. 239–41 and 380–1: see also features on Soviet strategy in *International Defence Review*, Mar. and Sep. 1986.

[7] Jacobsen, C. G., 'Soviet military expenditure and the Soviet burden', in SIPRI, *World Armaments and Disarmament: SIPRI Yearbook 1986* (Oxford University Press: Oxford, 1986); CIA Deputy Director Gates, R., *The Allocation of Resources in the Soviet Union and China 1984* (GPO: Washington, DC, 21 Nov. 1984), pp. 9–20.

[8] *Stop Nuclear Weapons* (Novosti: Moscow, 30 May 1986), p. 18; 'Every nuclear explosion in Nevada (is) immediately registered in the Soviet Union': Radio Moscow, *FBIS Daily Report Soviet Union*, 10 July 1986. See also 'US detects Soviets' smallest tests', *Washington Post*, 12 Aug. 1985.

[9] *Stop Nuclear Weapons*, p. 18 (note 8).

[10] Marshal S. Akhromeev's speech, *APN release* no. 164, 1 Sep. 1986, on restrictions associated with previous Soviet no-site inspection offers; see Vigor (note 2).

[11] *Dagens Nyheter*, Stockholm, 19 Dec. 1986.

[12] Reference to relevant Reagan speeches and Defense Department documents may be found in Jacobsen, C. G., *The Nuclear Era* (Spokesman: Nottingham and Oelgeschlager, Gunn & Haig: Cambridge, MA, 1982). See also Reagan interviews in Scheer, R., *With Enough Shovels: Reagan, Bush & Nuclear War* (Random House: New York, 1982); the leaked US military strategy outline *Fiscal Year 1984–1988 Guidance*, in the *New York Times*, 30 May 1982; and follow-up comment in *International Herald Tribune*, 16 Aug. 1982; *Spectator*, 4 Sep. 1982; and *The Guardian*, 9 Jan. 1983.

[13] *Bulletin of the Atomic Scientists*, Apr. 1986, pp. 10–12.

[14] Senators Kennedy, E., Mathias, C. and Hart, G., *News Conference*, Washington, DC, 8 Apr. 1986; *Stop Nuclear Weapons*, p. 20 (note 8).

[15] Charts prepared by Bhupendra Jasani, SIPRI, Mar. 1987, for a forthcoming article on questions pertaining to a CTB.

[16] Jacobsen, C. G. (ed.), SIPRI, *The Uncertain Course: New Weapons, Strategies and Mind-sets* (Oxford University Press: Oxford, 1987).

[17] *Energy and Water Development Appropriations for 1986* (GPO: Washington, DC, Feb. 1985), p. 138; also *Christian Science Monitor*, 25 Apr. 1986.

[18] Chayes, A. and Chayes, A. H., 'The ABM Treaty and the Strategic Defense Initiative', *Harvard Law Review*, June 1986, pp. 1956–85. Note: support for SDI, by the USA and other states, *per definition* constitutes embrace of military-technological programmes that are sustainable only in the absence of a CTB; thus support for SDI clearly relegates vaguer statements of support for a CTB as a long-term goal to the realm of ritual, of political posturing. See e.g., Adelman, K., 'Nuclear test ban: a long-term goal', *NATO Review*, Apr. 1986.

[19] Sir Francis Pym, *The Future United Kingdom Strategic Nuclear Deterrent Force* (MOD: London, July 1980).

[20] Sir Geoffrey Howe, *Survey of Current Affairs*, no. 4 (1986), p. 102; see also e.g. *Flight International*, 2 July 1986.

[21] *ADIU Report*, May–June 1986, p. 14.

[22] Sir Geoffrey Howe, *Survival*, July–Aug. 1986.

[23] *Survey of Current Affairs*, Mar. 1986, p. 85.

[24] Howe (note 21).

[25] President Mitterrand, *Press Conference*, 21 Oct. 1985; *Jane's Defence Weekly*, 5 July 1986.

[26] Prime Minister Fabius, speech, *Politique de Defence*, 25 Oct. 1985.

[27] Prime Minister Chirac, *Defence Daily*, 27 May 1986; also Fabius (note 25); and Laird, R. F., 'A firm grip on independence', *Defense and Foreign Affairs*, May 1985.

[28] *China Daily*, 18 Feb. 1986; *Xinhua*, 17 Apr. 1986.

[29] Premier Zhao Ziyang, speech, 21 Mar. 1986, *Press Release*, PRC Embassy, Washington, DC, 22 Mar. 1986.

[30] *China Daily* (note 7).

[31] 'Defense in space is not Star Wars', *New York Times Magazine*, 27 June 1985; see also Lord Zuckerman's review 'The wonders of Star War', in *New York Review*, 30 Jan. 1986.

Chapter XVI. Attitudes of the nuclear threshold countries

Paper 19

Peter Lomas

SIPRI

Abstract

The present positions on a nuclear test ban of the six threshold countries are fraught with contradictions. Most pursue an official policy of favouring a comprehensive test ban in the cause of general nuclear disarmament, and only one of these countries has actually carried out a nuclear explosion. At the same time, their ambiguous nuclear status sets them apart from all other countries, both nuclear weapon and non-nuclear weapon. Moreover, their implication in regional rivalries and tensions has become a pretext for their continued attachment to the nuclear weapon option, disguised in some cases as a claim to nuclear explosions for peaceful purposes. These unresolved issues all jeopardize the realization of a universally acceptable comprehensive test ban.

I. Introduction

In any discussion of the political acceptability of a nuclear test ban, states close to the nuclear weapon 'threshold' must be considered second in importance only to the five established nuclear weapon powers. Today the attribution of threshold country is generally given to six: India, Pakistan, Argentina, Brazil, South Africa and Israel.

One suggested basis for this judgement is that these countries conduct significant nuclear activities; refuse to accept international controls over their indigenously produced nuclear material and equipment, and in most cases operate unsafeguarded plants capable of making weapon-usable material; and can provide themselves with a reasonably effective nuclear weapon delivery capability.[1] Some of these states also claim the right to carry out nuclear explosions for peaceful purposes, which require explosive assemblies essentially similar to those used in nuclear weapons. All of the six countries mentioned above are outside the 1968 Non-Proliferation Treaty (NPT). Argentina and Brazil are not full parties to the Treaty of Tlatelolco, which prohibits nuclear weapons in Latin America.

Taken together these conditions imply, at the very least, a shared desire to keep open indefinitely an option to build nuclear weapons. Such an attitude would logically extend to rejection of a ban on all nuclear explosions, or a comprehensive test ban (CTB), in so far as testing would be held necessary to prove the explosive efficacy of a patent nuclear device. For this reason the focus of this paper will be on a CTB. Reference will be made to the six threshold countries' existing commitments in respect of the 1963 Partial Test Ban Treaty (PTBT), which bans nuclear testing in all environments except underground.

In practice, the first four countries listed above are at present publicly committed to reaching a multilaterally negotiated and verified CTB treaty, as members of the informal 'Group of 21' in the Conference on Disarmament (CD), where they have submitted proposals to this effect.[2] In addition, two threshold countries have taken the issue of a test ban beyond the CD, as participants in the Six-Nation Peace Initiative.

This attempt to halt the nuclear arms race was founded at a meeting in New Delhi, in January 1985, of the political leaders of Argentina, Greece, India, Mexico, Sweden and Tanzania. Among the six leaders' first proposals was a call to the nuclear weapon states 'to immediately halt the testing of all kinds of nuclear weapons, and to conclude, at an early date, a treaty on a nuclear-weapon test ban'.[3] The focus of their second summit meetng, held in Mexico in August 1986, was on a CTB. In addition, on this occasion they made an offer of scientific personnel from their own countries to help in the verification of a CTB.

Under the terms of this offer, the United States and the Soviet Union would declare an immediate moratorium on nuclear weapon tests, while the countries of the Six-Nation Peace Initiative would establish, for an initial period of one year, temporary seismic stations at three testing sites (Nevada in the United States, and Semipalatinsk and Novaya Zemlya in the Soviet Union) and provide observers to 'internationalize' stations spaced elsewhere on US and Soviet territory. At the same time, the six countries would step up their own monitoring activities, exchanging data and publishing reports. These measures, it was argued, 'would constitute important steps towards the establishment of an adequate verification system for a comprehensive test ban treaty'.[4]

Against this background, the positions of individual countries as they have evolved to the present day are considered in the sections below.

II. India

India has a long history of opposition to nuclear weapon testing. The first proposal for a ban on such testing was put forward by Prime Minister Nehru in a letter to the United Nations in 1954. India was among the first states to ratify the Partial Test Ban Treaty in 1963.[5] Two years later its delegate to the Eighteen-Nation Disarmament Committee (ENDC) asserted that 'all tests are basically evil; they encourage evil, and the sooner the evil is dealt with the better'.[6]

By the time of the discussion of the draft NPT in 1968, however, the country's spokesmen were arguing that a distinction could be made between nuclear explosions for peaceful purposes and nuclear-weapon tests.[7] This assumption became the official rationale for India's one nuclear explosion, that of a 12-kt plutonium device in May 1974 under the Rajasthan Desert. (Since the explosion took place underground, no contravention of the PTBT would have been involved.[8]) The communiqué issued after this event described it as a 'peaceful nuclear explosion experiment' which could serve Indian progress 'in the field of mining and earth-moving operations'. At the same time it was stated that 'India had no intention of producing nuclear weapons and reiterated its strong opposition to military uses of nuclear explosions'.[9]

This remains the official position today. Prime Minister Rajiv Gandhi, while acknowledging that India has 'had the [weapon] option since 1974', persists in the claim that no Indian nuclear weapons have actually been manufactured.[10] It is fair to say that this claim still enjoys a wide acceptance outside India.

III. Pakistan

Pakistan signed the PTBT in 1963—one week after India—but has not ratified it. The Indian explosion of 1974 was unambiguously interpreted by the Pakistani authorities as that of a nuclear weapon: 'It is an incontrovertible fact, stressed by the superpowers themselves, that there is no difference between explosion of a so-called peaceful nuclear device and the detonation of a nuclear weapon'.[11] No doubt because of this position, little systematic interest has been expressed in Pakistan in nuclear explosions for peaceful purposes.

There have been Pakistani proposals since the early 1970s for the creation of a South Asian nuclear weapon-free zone, which would presumably exclude all nuclear explosive devices, regardless of their purpose, from the sub-continent. Successive Indian governments, however, have rejected these overtures.[12] At the same time, in a declared rivalry with India, a sustained effort has been under way in Pakistan to achieve nuclear weapon capability, beginning with the covert acquisition of the necessary technology from overseas and subsequently pursued in at least one major nuclear installation not subject to international control. Recently, numerous reports have spoken of intensive preparations for the manufacture of nuclear weapons, including the testing of a dummy warhead and nuclear collaboration with China, leading to the 'proxy' explosion of a Pakistani device on Chinese territory.[13] Although the accuracy of some of these accounts is open to question, they have undoubtedly contributed to a firm impression outside the country of a dedicated military nuclear programme which might at any moment be announced by a full explosive test on Pakistani soil.[14]

Pakistan's official stance on a CTB, as expressed in the CD in 1985, is broadly favourable to all existing treaty proposals. On the one hand, it upholds the view that adequate scientific and technical experience has already been accumulated for the satisfactory verification of a CTB treaty, and that such a treaty could be negotiated within the CD. On the other hand, the Pakistani position is receptive to such a treaty being initially negotiated by the nuclear-weapon states alone, possibly through the progressive yield-reducing approach suggested in the CD by Japan (with the proviso that a clear schedule be set for this procedure, envisaging the finalization of a CTB treaty by a specific date).[15]

It is, however, legitimate to doubt the substance of the official Pakistani position, not least in view of the background of suspicious nuclear activity in the country. The most likely explanation of its contradictions is that Pakistani policy on such questions is purely tactical and reactive to that of India.[16]

IV. Argentina

Argentina signed the PTBT in 1963, but did not ratify it until 23 years later. It is also signatory to the Treaty of Tlatelolco but has not ratified it. In 1967 the Argentine Government recorded its interpretation of the latter Treaty as allowing parties the right 'to carry out, by their own means or in association with third parties, explosions which involve devices similar to those used in nuclear weapons'. (This interpretation, it is worth noting, is contested by most Latin American states, as well as by the nuclear weapon powers.)

This official stance on the Tlatelolco Treaty, however, has never been connected with a practical interest in nuclear explosions for peaceful purposes. In 1984, for example, the former chairman of the Argentine Atomic Energy Commission remarked: 'We never had any concrete applications for peaceful nuclear explosives. And I don't think there will be any in the future'.[17] Similarly, in 1986 the Argentine Deputy Foreign Minister stated: 'No-one in Argentina is thinking to develop PNEs. [Their proposed uses are] not convincing enough to make them'.[18] The objections to the Tlatelolco Treaty expressed in Argentina today figure, instead, as criticism of the nuclear weapon states' military buildup (allegedly extended to the South Atlantic since the Falklands/Malvinas conflict), which the Treaty is seen as having failed to halt. Tlatelolco is thus conflated with the Non-Proliferation Treaty, as an instrument of the hegemony of the nuclear weapon states.[19]

The military government in power in Argentina from 1976 to 1983 embarked on an ambitious nuclear development plan aimed at making the country self-sufficient in nuclear energy, which left several militarily sensitive facilities built or under construction.[20] The Alfonsín Government's championing of a CTB internationally is a marked departure from the foreign policy of its predecessor. On the other hand, it has not been accompanied by such concrete steps as an extension of International Atomic Energy Agency (IAEA) safeguards over the entire nuclear programme or a change in the official position towards the NPT or the Treaty of Tlatelolco; for influential sectors of Argentine society remain strongly opposed to a definitive surrendering of the nuclear-weapon option, at least without a *quid pro quo* from Brazil.[21]

V. Brazil

Brazil has been party to the PTBT since 1964. In 1968 Brazil signed and ratified the Treaty of Tlatelolco, with an interpretation similar to Argentina's concerning the right to carry out nuclear explosions for peaceful purposes. At the same time, full adherence to the Treaty was withheld—and continues to be withheld—under a special clause.[22]

In the CD, the Brazilian policy has been to support the position of the Group of 21 on a complete test ban. In 1985 the Brazilian delegation produced its own document in favour of a CTB, describing it as 'the full implementation of the [Partial Test Ban Treaty]', which the nuclear weapon states were duty-bound to realize.[23] Notwithstanding this official policy, detailed accounts began to surface in the early 1980s of nuclear activities being pursued, independently of the safeguarded national nuclear-energy programme, in several research institutes controlled by the Brazilian Armed Forces. Following the return of civilian government in 1985, military control of these institutes has been maintained.[24]

In August 1986 investigations carried out by a São Paulo newspaper suggested that a nuclear test site had been prepared in the Serra do Cachimbo in Pará province. According to the reports, excavations had been secretly under way since 1981 within the confines of a territory of approximately 4.5 million hectares allocated to the Brazilian Armed Forces for the purposes of military experiments. A number of underground chambers had been dug out at 100 to 150 metres, and lined with concrete, lead and asbestos; and a shaft 320 metres deep and 1 metre in diameter had been bored, also lined with concrete.[25]

An official statement issued in response to these reports declared:

Brazil has no plans to manufacture nuclear weapons, nor the level of technological development to do so, nor any programme of tests with this end in view.

According to the decision made in signing the Treaty of Tlatelolco, the Brazilian Government has committed itself to using nuclear energy for solely peaceful purposes.

The Armed Forces' Cachimbo test site is at present under the control of the Air Ministry, which is carrying out works to enable the testing of material and equipment designed to develop our capability in the field of aerospace, in the interests of national security.[26]

This statement, however, leaves unresolved the question of whether 'the use of nuclear energy for solely peaceful purposes' would rule out all nuclear explosions. On this issue, given the history of nuclear rivalry between Brazil and Argentina, the positions of the two countries are—and are likely to remain—mutually influencing.[27]

VI. South Africa

South Africa ratified the PTBT in 1963. However, two major incidents have given rise to international suspicions of nuclear-weapon testing under South African auspices.

In the first incident, activities consistent with preparations for a nuclear test were reported, from satellite observations, at a location in the Kalahari Desert in the north-west of the country in August 1977. The site apparently included a large tower such as would be used to emplace a device for an atmospheric nuclear burst, and a shaft for a possible underground detonation. Intense international pressure was subsequently brought to bear on the South African authorities to interrupt the activities observed and dismantle structures already built; this was done several months later.

Following the disclosure of the site, the South African Government reportedly gave assurances in a letter to the US President that it did not possess, or intend to develop, 'nuclear explosive devices for any purpose, either peaceful or as a weapon'. The letter denied that the alleged test site was connected with plans for a nuclear explosion, and an assurance was given that 'no explosive test will be taken in South Africa now or in the future'.[28]

In the second incident, a double flash of light characteristic of that resulting from an atmospheric nuclear explosion was recorded in September 1979 by a US satellite orbiting over the southern African land-mass and the surrounding oceans. A month later the US Government, in confirming reports of the incident, set up an investigation by an *ad hoc* scientific panel. This body subsequently pronounced that, while a definitive interpretation of the event could not be reached, it was unlikely that a nuclear explosion had occurred. Some US intelligence agencies, however, disputed this finding; and the full scientific data have yet to be released. On this basis, a UN report concludes, 'the initial presumption that there had been a nuclear explosion by South Africa or any other country has not been substantiated; nor has it been fully disproved'. On this occasion the South African Foreign Minister and the President of the country's Atomic Energy Board denied all knowledge of the incident; and the latter remarked: 'We're not interested in anything [other than] the peaceful application of nuclear energy'.[29]

Given South Africa's absence from most international forums, the likely attitude of the present régime towards a CTB can only be guessed at. The high level of technical nuclear competence attained in the country may well result in no (or perhaps no more) testing of any finished nuclear weapons being considered necessary. The widespread suspicions in neighbouring states that South Africa is already a nuclear weapon power have, after all, in part been fostered by South African spokesmen. Most recently, these have included President Botha himself, who remarked on a visit to Europe that nuclear weapons could 'unquestionably' be produced in South Africa.[30]

VII. Israel

Israel has been a party to the PTBT since 1964. On the question of a CTB, Israel has lent broad support to the present US position that there can as yet be no multilateral negotiation of a treaty *per se*.[31]

The idea of a nuclear weapon-free zone in the Middle East has been on the political agenda in Israel for over a decade; the first Israeli proposal in favour of such an arrangement was introduced in the UN in 1981. The proposed zone would be 'directly negotiated among the countries of the region and based on mutual assurances', as an alternative to accession to the NPT, which was described as an inadequate assurance. Several similar proposals have followed. However, their terms have failed to find support outside Israel, not least among the Arab states of the region, which have countered in the UN with proposals of their own requiring NPT adherence and omitting any mention of direct regional negotiations.[32]

Beginning in the early 1960s, a succession of outside observers have sought to establish that Israel has manufactured nuclear weapons or is preparing to do so. Many of these allegations have focused upon the Franco–Israeli nuclear co-operation of the late 1950s and early 1960s. The possibility has been raised that this extended to nuclear testing.[33] To these allegations were added, in October 1986, detailed descriptions of a plutonium separation plant of French design and a nuclear weapon production facility at the Negev Nuclear Research Centre, near Dimona, by an Israeli citizen employed there. The technical details supplied suggested that advanced nuclear weapons were in the course of manufacture. A prominent scientific analyst, commenting on this account, said, 'there should no longer be any doubt that Israel is, and for at least a decade has been, a fully-fledged nuclear-weapon state'.[34]

The established response of Israeli governments—repeated on this occasion—to outside allegations of nuclear weapon capability is that Israel 'will not be the first' to introduce such weapons into the Middle East.[35] One must assume that the ambiguity of this response is intentional, serving the purpose of deterrence as well as that of diplomacy. In any case, Israeli sophistication in nuclear matters is now sufficiently well known for reports of manufactured but untested nuclear weapons in the country no longer to be surprising.[36]

VIII. Conclusion

Since the resurgence of the debate on a comprehensive nuclear test ban, the positions of some of the nuclear threshold states regarding such a ban have become clearer, but it would be hazardous to suggest what their final positions would be in the event of a treaty being concluded. In the first place, differing levels of technological (especially nuclear) development and differing geopolitical circumstances divide these six states from each other, while their ambiguous nuclear status divides them from all others. For this reason alone it is difficult to conceive of a common position being taken among them. In addition, their situation is complicated by regional nuclear rivalries (in Latin America and South Asia) or by military imbalances perceived as overwhelming (in the Middle East and southern Africa). Finally, there remains the question of nuclear explosions for peaceful purposes: Argentina, Brazil and India in particular would have to formally relinquish this claim in order to sign a treaty banning all nuclear explosions.

None of these issues appears about to be resolved, or can be explained away solely by reference to the arms race between the established nuclear-weapon powers. It is evident, therefore, that the very existence of nuclear threshold states is likely to prove an obstacle to a truly universal CTB.

Notes and references

[1] This definition is taken from Goldblat, J. and Lomas, P. I., 'The threshold countries and the future of the non-proliferation régime', in ed. J. Simpson, *Nuclear Non-Proliferation: An Agenda for the 1990s* (Cambridge University Press: Cambridge, forthcoming).

[2] For early formulations of their position, see Conference on Disarmament document CD/64 (27 Feb. 1980) and Conference on Disarmament document CD/72 (4 Mar. 1980).

[3] Reproduced as Conference on Disarmament document CD/549, 6 Feb. 1985.

[4] 'Verification measures: document issued at the Mexico summit of the Five-Continent Peace Initiative', reproduced as Conference on Disarmament document CD/723, 15 Aug. 1986.

[5] All references to treaty adherence and related statements are taken from Goldblat, J., *Agreements for Arms Control: A Critical Survey*, SIPRI (Taylor and Francis: London, 1982).

[6] Quoted in Jones, R., 'India', in J. Goldblat (ed.), *Non-Proliferation: The Why and the Wherefore*, SIPRI (Taylor and Francis, London, 1985), p. 102.

[7] Statement by Representative Azim Husain in the ENDC, 27 Feb. 1968, reproduced in Jain, J. P., *Nuclear India*, vol. 2 (Radiant: New Delhi, 1974), pp. 199–201.

[8] For accounts of the explosion, see Chidambaram, R. and Ramanna, R., 'Some studies on India's peaceful nuclear explosion experiment' (Bhabha Atomic Research Centre: Trombay, n.d.); and Jain (note 7), pp. 332–5.

[9] *Nuclear India*, vol. 12, no. 10 (June 1974), p. 2.

[10] *The Guardian*, 9 Oct. 1985. See also the interviews in *Le Monde*, 4 June 1985; and *International Herald Tribune*, 22 Feb. 1985.

[11] Pakistani Government statement, 19 May 1974, reproduced as Conference of the Committee on Disarmament document CCD/423, 23 May 1974.

[12] Khalilzad, Z., 'Pakistan', in Goldblat (note 6), pp. 134–6.

[13] *Nawa-E-Waqt* (Lahore), 9 Feb. 1984; *The Guardian*, 14 Aug. 1984; *International Herald Tribune*, 23 July 1984 and 5 Nov. 1986; and *Frankfurter Rundschau*, 16 Sep. 1986. Surveys of Pakistani nuclear activities may be found in Spector, L. S., *Nuclear Proliferation Today* and *The New Nuclear Nations* (Vintage Books for Carnegie Endowment for International Peace: New York, 1984 and 1985).

[14] In the summer of 1986 it was reported that both the US and the Soviet governments had issued warnings to the Pakistani authorities not to carry out a nuclear test, then apparently believed imminent. *Le Monde*, 17 and 18 July 1986; *International Herald Tribune*, 5 Nov. 1986. Under Section 670 of the US Foreign Assistance Act, US aid to Pakistan would be automatically terminated in the event of a Pakistani nuclear explosion. On this point, see Cronin, R. P., 'Prospects for nuclear proliferation in South Asia', *Middle East Journal*, vol. 37, no. 4 (autumn 1983), pp. 612–16.

[15] Conference on Disarmament document CD/PV.294, 26 Feb. 1985.

[16] For a thoughtful study of the possible outcomes of this policy, see Joeck, N., 'Pakistani security and nuclear proliferation in South Asia', *Journal of Strategic Studies*, vol. 8, no. 4 (Dec. 1985), pp. 80–98.

[17] Interview with Vice-Admiral Carlos Castro Madero in *Federation of American Scientists (FAS) Public Interest Report*, vol. 37, no. 4 (Apr. 1984), pp. 4–5.

[18] *Nucleonics Week*, 12 June 1986.

[19] Interview with Under-Secretary for Foreign Affairs Vincentes Arnaud in *FAS Public Interest Report* (note 17), p. 10.

[20] See Westercamp, J. F., 'La energía nuclear: relevancia y perspectivas para América Latina y Estados Unidos', *Cuadernos Semestrales* (CIDE, Mexico City), vol. 15, no. 1 (Apr. 1985), pp. 147–80.

[21] *Latin America Weekly Report* WR–84–23, 15 June 1984; Orsolini, M. H., 'Plan nuclear: un modelo de acción estratégica', *Estrategia* (Buenos Aires), vol. 1, no. 1 (July–Sep. 1984), pp. 44–54;

Espejo, A., 'La política nuclear: seducida y abandonada', *El Periodista de Buenos Aires*, vol. 42 (28 June–4 July 1985), pp. 12–13.

[22] Article 28 of the Treaty, setting out the conditions for its entry into force for each party, provides for a waiver of these conditions. It is this waiver which has yet to be granted on behalf of Brazil.

[23] Conference on Disarmament document CD/602, 24 June 1985; and Conference on Disarmament document CD/PV.315, 25 June 1985.

[24] The areas of research include uranium enrichment, the applications of lasers and accelerators, and the fast-breeder reactor. Space and missile research and development are carried out by the same institutes. See Manwaring, M. G., 'Nuclear power in Brazil', *Parameters*, vol. 14, no. 4 (winter 1984), pp. 40–6; Myers, D. J., 'Brazil: reluctant pursuit of the nuclear option', *Orbis*, vol. 27, no. 4 (winter 1984), pp. 881–911; *Folha de São Paulo*, 29 Apr. 1985 and 9 Aug. 1986; Pinguelli Rosa., L., 'Da genêse da bomba á política nuclear brasileira', in ed. R. Arnt, *O Armamentismo e O Brasil: A Guerra Deles* (Brasiliense: São Paulo, 1985), pp. 26–69; and *Latin American Weekly Report* WR–86–36, 18 Sep. 1986, p. 5.

[25] *Folha de São Paulo*, 8 and 9 Aug. 1986.

[26] *Folha de São Paulo*, 9 Aug. 1986 (author's translation).

[27] On Brazilian-Argentine relations, see Guglialmelli, J. E., *Argentina, Brasil y la Bomba Atómica* (Tierra Nueva: Buenos Aires, 1976); Myers (note 24); and Yriart, M. F., 'Brasil y Argentina, hacia la complementación y las salvaguardias recíprocas?', *Energéia* (Buenos Aires), vol. 5, no. 2 (Feb. 1986), pp. 14–15.

[28] *South Africa's Plan and Capability in the Nuclear Field*, Report of the UN Secretary-General, UN Document A/35/402, 1981, pp. 28–30; Jaster, R., 'Politics and the "Afrikaner Bomb"', *Orbis*, vol. 27, no. 4 (winter 1984), p. 834.

[29] Note 28. See also *Aviation Week & Space Technology*, 11 Aug. 1980, pp. 67–72.

[30] *Le Monde*, 14 Nov. 1986. See Jaster (note 28) and Spector (note 13) for earlier assertions of a South African nuclear weapon capability.

[31] See UN General Assembly Resolutions A/39/52 and A/39/53 (both 12 Dec. 1984).

[32] Freier, S., 'Israel', in Goldblat (note 6), pp. 125–30.

[33] See Pry, P., *Israel's Nuclear Arsenal* (Westview Press: Boulder, CO, 1984), pp. 46–8.

[34] *Sunday Times* (London), 5 and 12 Oct. 1986. See also *Jerusalem Post*, international edition, week ending 15 Nov. 1986.

[35] Pajark, R., 'Nuclear status and policies of the Middle East countries', *International Affairs* (London), vol. 59, no. 4 (autumn 1983), pp. 590–3; Freier, S., 'Israel' (note 32), p. 126; *Sunday Times*, 12 Oct. 1986. For analysis of Israeli policy alternatives, see Jabber, F., *Israel and Nuclear Weapons: Present Option and Future Strategies* (Chatto and Windus, for International Institute for Strategic Studies: London, 1971), part 3; and Feldman, S., *Israeli Nuclear Deterrence: A Strategy for the 1980s* (Columbia University Press: New York, 1982).

[36] Laser enrichment of uranium—a technique which can rapidly produce very pure weapon-grade material—was pioneered by Israel over a decade ago. *Science*, vol. 183, no. 4130 (22 Mar. 1974), pp. 1172–4. For an assessment of Israeli nuclear-weapon manufacturing capabilities, including miniaturization, see note 33, chapter 3.

Chapter XVII. A nuclear test ban and prevention of nuclear weapon proliferation

Paper 20

Paul C. Warnke

Former Chief US Arms Negotiator, Washington, DC

Abstract

A comprehensive test ban has become a symbol for ending the nuclear arms race. The Partial Test Ban Treaty, permitting only underground testing, satisfied the environmental objections to testing. The principal impetus behind the CTB now derives from the view that it would inhibit both potential proliferation and weapon development by present nuclear powers. Some disagree as to the beneficial impact on horizontal proliferation, citing the possibility that US allies may lose confidence in the US nuclear deterrent and contemplate acquiring their own. But most believe that superpower agreement on a CTB would marshal world opinion against testing by others. Political considerations stalled CTB negotiations in the late 1970s. The Reagan Administration has refused to negotiate, arguing that a CTB is undesirable on national security grounds. The arguments that continued testing is desirable to ensure effectiveness and to develop smaller, safer and more accurate nuclear weapons are of dubious merit.

I. Introduction

Although its practical significance is great, a comprehensive ban on nuclear weapon tests has acquired a symbolic value that transcends other considerations. It has become for many a code word for ending the nuclear arms race.

With respect to its probable impact on decisions of the present non-nuclear weapon states to develop such weapons (horizontal proliferation), opinions are widely divergent. Some see a CTB as a powerful inhibiting force, while others argue that it could lead US allies to reassess reliance on the US deterrent, and still others question whether it would have any impact on the non-proliferation regime.

However, on the question of the impact on continued development of the arsenals of the nuclear powers (vertical proliferation), there is fairly broad consensus. In agreeing that a CTB would hinder the development of new types of nuclear weapons, however, opponents cite this as a basic objection while proponents see this as a major if not the pre-eminent benefit.

II. The debate on horizontal proliferation

The drive that led to the 1963 Partial Test Ban Treaty (PTBT) was inspired by growing knowledge of the danger of radioactive fall-out. The preamble to the PTBT notes the desire 'to put an end to the contamination of man's environment by radioactive substances', but it also contains stronger language, indicating that this treaty was intended as a step towards achieving 'the discontinuance of all test explosions of nuclear weapons for all time'.

By forcing nuclear test explosions to be conducted underground, the PTBT defused much of the anti-test enthusiasm. The continued opposition to testing has largely derived from the belief that a CTB would advance the cause of non-proliferation by reducing the chances that additional countries would enter the nuclear weapon business. This view is reflected in the 1968 Non-Proliferation Treaty (NPT). The preamble contains the following phrases: 'Recalling the determination expressed by the Parties to the 1963 Treaty banning nuclear weapons tests in the atmosphere, in outer space and under-water in its Preamble to seek to achieve the discontinuance of all test explosions of nuclear weapons for all time and to continue negotiations to this end.'

Article VI specifically commits each of the parties to the NPT 'to pursue negotiations in good faith on effective measures relating to cessation of the nuclear arms race at an early date and to nuclear disarmament'. This article, declaring the intention of the nuclear powers to move away from reliance on nuclear weapons, was designed to allay concerns of the non-nuclear weapon states that they were being asked to accept second-class status.

The historical record thus documents the view that non-proliferation and nuclear arms control are complementary, and that arms reductions and the cessation of the nuclear weapon competition would lessen incentives for additional countries to test, develop and deploy their own nuclear arsenals.

Tripartite CTB negotiations, 1977–80

Logic would appear also to support this position. The three original parties to the Partial Test Ban Treaty, the United States, the United Kingdom and the Soviet Union, were engaged during the Administration of President Jimmy Carter in negotiations for a CTB. The negotiators succeeded, by the end of 1977, in reaching agreement in principle on all of the major issues—a treaty of indefinite duration, with no exception for so-called peaceful nuclear explosions, providing for on-site inspection and allowing for the installation of high-quality, tamper-proof seismic stations of agreed characteristics.

The failure to complete the treaty resulted from a lack of political will rather than negotiating difficulties. The Carter Administration feared that the pendency of a CTB treaty might interfere with the ratification of the SALT II

Treaty, particularly in view of the strong opposition from the US nuclear weapon laboratories and the top military leadership. Accordingly, the pace of the negotiations slowed in early 1978, and the US position on the term of the treaty changed first from indefinite duration to a specific period of five years and then to a limit of three years. Soviet representatives began to question the seriousness of US purpose and almost frivolous issues, such as the number of special seismic stations that would be placed in the British Isles, began to loom large. The Soviet intervention in Afghanistan contributed to suspension of the talks in 1980, and the Reagan Administration early and often has voiced its position that a CTB would be contrary to US security interests.

The exemplary value of a tripartite agreement

If the United States, the United Kingdom and the Soviet Union were to cease all nuclear weapon tests, a goal they have pledged themselves to seek in both the NPT and the PTBT, it seems certain that this would make it politically more difficult for the other present nuclear weapon states to continue or for non-nuclear weapon states to begin conducting nuclear explosions. An end to testing would generate enormous enthusiasm throughout the world, and a country continuing or initiating nuclear tests would be stigmatized as an outlaw state.

The inhibition on horizontal proliferation would, of course, be strengthened by the acceptance of a CTB by the other acknowledged nuclear weapon states—France and China. Although they were not parties to the 1977–80 negotiations, history suggests that at least their de facto acceptance would be a likelihood. Although neither has signed the PTBT, France and China gradually stopped atmospheric testing. While declining to become a signatory of the NPT, France stated that it 'would behave in the future in this field exactly as the States adhering to the Treaty'. China until recent years took the position that the superpowers were using arms control as a means to perpetuate their strategic hegemony. The changing philosophical environment in China has included a greater willingness to participate in multinational discussion of arms control issues, and China has now taken its seat at the Geneva-based Conference on Disarmament (CD).

It may be that France and China would initially refuse to adhere to a comprehensive test ban treaty. It seems far more likely than not, however, that, perhaps after a few post-treaty tests to demonstrate their independence, France and China would terminate testing. A continuation of the French nuclear testing programme after the nuclear superpowers had agreed to the permanent cessation of such tests would subject the French Government to heavy criticism, not only from the nations of the south and west Pacific. China has maintained that its nuclear force will remain a small one and would never be used first. Continued conduct of nuclear explosions would be inconsistent with this public stance. It would also leave China on one side of the issue and the USA and the USSR together on the opposite side—a development that China's leaders would want to avoid.

Impact of a CTB on allied nations

A storm of world outrage could be expected by any nation which initiated nuclear weapon testing after a CTB had been concluded by the USA, the UK and the USSR. The Soviet Union could be confidently expected to utilize its influence on those states which are in any degree dependent on Soviet favour. There would, of course, be no prospect that any East European government would get out of line.

Insofar as Western Europe is concerned, its people and its governments have tended to be ahead of the United States in supporting a test ban. The domestic dissent that would be fostered by any suggestion of embarking on nuclear weapon development would effectively prevent any contemplation of this move. There are few if any signs of pro-nuclear sentiment, and British Labour Party leaders assert their intention to eliminate both indigenous and US nuclear weapons from the United Kingdom. The Scandinavian states do not now permit any nuclear weapons on their territory.

It must be noted that, in sharp contrast to the above reasoning, the Reagan Administration has argued that a cessation of testing by the United States would compel those dependent upon its 'nuclear umbrella' to consider seriously acquiring a nuclear arsenal of their own. In a letter made public on 21 April 1986, James W. Dyer, acting Assistant Secretary of State for Legislative and Inter-governmental Affairs, wrote that a complete test ban 'would lead other countries to carefully reassess their national security calculations. In that context their adoption of nuclear options cannot be excluded.'[1] Undeniably, US allies such as the Federal Republic of Germany and Japan are acutely sensitive to any and all changes in US strategy, posture and policy. But entirely apart from such practical problems as that of where a West German or Japanese test site would be located, the political connotations of a pro-nuclear decision by countries that fought World War II against the USA and the USSR are formidable, to understate that case. As for other US allies in Western Europe or the Pacific, the possibility of horizontal nuclear weapon proliferation in the aftermath of a CTB is virtually non-existent.

Impact of a CTB in areas of regional conflict

The effect of a comprehensive test ban on countries not formally allied with the United States or with the Soviet Union may be more debatable. India set off a single explosion in 1974, but subsequent Indian governments have downplayed the possibilities of a repetition of what was officially called a test of a peaceful nuclear device. Some analysts regard India's nuclear programme as designed to offset that of China. If so, then China's response to a CTB would strongly influence India's response. More pertinent is the obvious concern in New Delhi about evidence of a Pakistani nuclear capability. Both countries might welcome a CTB. Certainly neither would want to be seen as the villain in the sub-continental rivalry.

Bitter regional relationships make difficult any confident predictions about reactions in North and South Korea (both of which are now signatories of the NPT) and the Middle East. At a minimum, however, a CTB would provide a powerful inhibition to would-be proliferators. Arab states would readily recall the Israeli strike on an Iraqi nuclear reactor. Preparation of a nuclear weapon test site could be readily detected, and any such facility could be expected to meet a similar fate. Creation of nuclear weapon facilities in Libya would be viewed as a greater provocation than that which led to the US bombing raid in 1986. For South Africa, the threat to its government lies within its own borders and cannot be eliminated by nuclear weaponry. As for the countries of South America, investment in a nuclear testing programme would not be conducive to international efforts to deal sympathetically with their mountain of debt. Well-founded fear of either military or financial reprisal would help preclude serious consideration by these nations of any move towards a nuclear weapon capability.

There would, of course, be many problems created and hackles raised by a joint US–Soviet campaign to compel conforming conduct by smaller states. No overt collaboration, however, would be necessary to alert government leaders to the unwisdom of daring the superpowers in the nuclear field by commencing the testing that the USA and the USSR had forsworn.

From the standpoint of promoting and strengthening an international non-proliferation regime, therefore, a comprehensive test ban is perhaps the single most effective step that could be taken by the nuclear powers.

III. The debate on the question of vertical proliferation

Previous US administrations can be said to have failed diligently to live up to the treaty pledge to stop 'all test explosions of nuclear weapons for all time'. The Reagan Administration has forthrightly repudiated this commitment. In its early years, President Reagan's first director of the US Arms Control and Disarmament Agency, Eugene Rostow, told the international negotiating forum in Geneva that conditions were 'not now propitious for this worthy project'. Since then, Administration officials have cited concerns about the verifiability of a total ban and about Soviet compliance with the 150-kt limit of the 1974 Threshold Test Ban Treaty.

Rationales for continued nuclear testing

Verifiability

The validity of the verification argument has been substantially discredited, as has the contention that some Soviet test explosions have exceeded the threshold. In tacit recognition of this fact, the position now taken by Administration spokesmen is that nuclear testing will continue to be required as long as the United States and its friends and allies must rely on nuclear weapons to deter aggression. Assistant Secretary of Defense Richard Perle has commented candidly that he would be opposed to a comprehensive test ban treaty, regardless of its verifiability.[2]

Need for 'improved' nuclear weapons

The argument for continued testing, therefore, is essentially that vertical proliferation serves the security interests of the United States and its allies. Those who espouse this view argue that development of new generations of nuclear weapons will ensure that they are safe, effective and survivable. Sadly, editorial writers for the *New York Times* and the *Washington Post*, usually sensible on strategic issues, uncritically accept the desirability of continued testing to 'improve' US nuclear weaponry.[3] This may be a conspicuous example of the triumph of low expectations. The evident disregard for arms control within the Reagan Administration, most recently displayed in the decision to breach the numerical limits of the SALT II Treaty, appears to have deadened journalistic sensitivity.

Supporters of a CTB for the most part accept the fact that a CTB would seriously interfere with nuclear weapon developments. Some suggest that the impact may not be as great as advertised by the opponents and that new nuclear weapons can evolve through computer simulation and other non-nuclear demonstrations. But the broadest support for a CTB derives from the belief that a ban on nuclear weapon testing will indeed hamper nuclear weapon development and lead to less reliance on such weapons. The debate about the merits or demerits of developing new types of nuclear weapons reflects a basic difference as to what constitutes sound strategic nuclear policy. The anti-CTB school of thought sees nuclear weapons as possessing military utility and versatility. If nuclear weapons can be made smaller and more accurate, for example, they can theoretically be used to fight and win a limited nuclear war.

In his book *Game Plan*,[4] former US national security adviser Zbigniew Brzezinski speaks for this school in arguing that the USA should prepare itself to employ nuclear weapons 'at levels ranging from the tactical to the strategic, selectively at a large variety of targets and over a protracted period of time'. Similarly, Secretary of State Caspar Weinberger has said that the minimum purposes of US nuclear forces include the ability 'to impose termination of a major war—on terms favorable to the United States and our allies'.[5] If the goal is a nuclear war-winning capability, then neither a test ban nor any other restriction on US nuclear weapon development is compatible with that objective.

The other school of thought accepts as doctrine the pronouncement of none other than President Reagan in his State of the Union message of January 1984.[6] In asserting then that 'the only purpose of either side having nuclear weapons is to see to it that they are never used', he voiced the conviction of those who see mutual assured deterrence as the only acceptable rationale.

Consideration of safety

The argument that further testing is required to make nuclear weapons 'smaller' and 'safer' is devoid of thought content. The only 'safe' nuclear weapon is one that will not explode, and a testing programme presumably would not be devoted to developing duds. Devices to prevent accidental nuclear detonation have been created and can be improved without themselves requiring nuclear explosion. Nuclear bombs have fallen out of aeroplanes, and nuclear warheads have been propelled out of silos as a result of accidental fuel ignition. The safety devices have proven to be adequate. Launch from miscalculation or launch in response to technical misfunction of warning systems are far graver risks—risks that further testing will aggravate rather than alleviate. If new technologies to avoid accidental detonation are discovered, their efficacy can be tested with chemical explosives. Tinkering with nuclear weapons to make them easier to use can only increase the prospect that they will in fact be used, and probably in the early stages of any hostilities.

Reliability of the stockpile

Companion to the safety argument is the contention that testing must continue in order to preserve confidence in the reliability of the nuclear stockpile. Some experts maintain that the effectiveness of nuclear weapons can be ensured by disassembly and rebuilding, without proving over and over again that enriched uranium and plutonium will blow up.[7] Moreover, deterrence may be improved if both sides lose a degree of confidence that their nuclear missiles will work. The doubt would further preclude any consideration of a pre-emptive first strike. Nor is greater accuracy an unequivocally desirable goal. Accuracy improves the capability to destroy missile silos. But putting the other's retaliatory deterrent at risk only encourages a launch-on-warning strategy and heightens the risk of nuclear war.

Arguments for an end to nuclear testing

Psychologically, the total cessation of nuclear testing would foster the healthy view that nuclear weapons are not useful for military purposes and that, indeed, their sole purpose is to prevent the use, or threatened use, of the nuclear weapons of the other side. They would be seen increasingly as irrelevant to genuine national strength. As time passed, the resumption of underground testing would tend to become as unthinkable as the concept of atmospheric testing is today.

It seems certain that a CTB would slow and could eventually stop the creation of new US nuclear weapons. But this inhibition of vertical proliferation would, obviously, restrict at least as severely the development of more advanced Soviet nuclear weapons. With technology inferior to that of the United States, designing and deploying new nuclear weaponry without testing would involve for the Soviet Union even more problems and more uncertainties than for the United States.

What is really at issue in the vertical proliferation debate is whether the United States and the Soviet Union are ready to move away from reliance on nuclear weapons or whether, despite the lip-service paid to the unwinnability of nuclear war and survivability, both countries will continue to engage in developments that make that war more likely.

IV. The low-threshold alternative

As noted above, not much remains of the verification issue as an obstacle to a comprehensive test ban. General scientific consensus exists that underground tests could be detected down to a level below that of any real military value. Former US Secretaries of Defense James Schlesinger and Harold Brown have expressed the view that a 10- or 15-kt limit would raise no problems for US security.[8]

A treaty that simply sets a new threshold, even if only a fraction of the present 150-kt limit, would be of less value than a complete test ban in blocking horizontal proliferation. The example of the nuclear superpowers going 'cold turkey' would do more to discourage potential new addicts than would any threshold. Retention of the option to test could lead to the cynical view that vertical proliferation will continue. Moreover, settling for a threshold, however low, would not meet the treaty commitments to end *all* testing.

President Reagan and his advisers are reported to have suggested at the 1986 Reykjavik summit meeting the possibility of a gradual phase-out of nuclear testing. The ostensible purpose would be to agree on further phase-in of verification measures. To the extent that this was viewed as a commitment to reach a comprehensive test ban in stages, the overall impact would approach that of an immediate, total ban. But an ambiguous undertaking that might permit indefinite testing at militarily significant levels would be of little value.

Similarly, a new treaty where the threshold was set at 10 kt or below could be regarded as almost the functional equivalent of a CTBT. There would appear to be little military purpose in continued testing at this level. The rationale that verification at a zero level could not be assured might receive some credence. Moreover, the fear of world censure would discourage others from testing at higher than the permitted threshold. It appears at least doubtful that new-comers to the nuclear game could refine their technology to the degree of sophistication required to guarantee remaining within the restrictions of a few kilotons. The high cost of preparing for and conducting tests under these constraints, and the minimal contribution to new nuclear weapon development that could be anticipated, would dampen the enthusiasm of the present nuclear powers for a continued testing programme. Sophisticated seismic detection equipment, rendered more effective by agreed measures of verification, could be expected to confirm that nuclear testing had in fact ceased. Accordingly, a single-digit kiloton threshold treaty would in itself be a worthwhile achievement and could in practice soon lead to a complete halt in testing.

Perhaps the advocates of a test ban have exaggerated its benefits. Certainly other arms control measures are required as well to put us on the path to nuclear sanity, but the benefits of a CTB in discouraging proliferation are obvious and significant. In contrast, sound arguments for continued testing are non-existent.

Notes and references

[1] Gwertzman, B., 'New US justification on nuclear tests', *New York Times*, 22 Apr. 1986.

[2] McNeil-Lehrer Show, PBS, 24 Mar. 1986.

[3] See, e.g., *New York Times*, 14 Aug. 1986; *Washington Post*, 20 Aug. 1986.

[4] Brzezinski, Z., *Game Plan: How to Conduct the US–Soviet Contest* (Atlantic Monthly Press: Boston, MA, 1986).

[5] *Annual Report to the Congress*, Fiscal Year 1983, p. I–18.

[6] *Weekly Compilation of Presidential Documents*, vol. 20, no. 2 (16 Jan. 1984).

[7] See, e.g., the letter in appendix 20A from former nuclear weapon laboratory directors and others to Dante Fascell, Chairman, Committee on Foreign Affairs of the US House of Representatives.

[8] Articles in *Baltimore Sun*, 26 Aug. 1986.

Appendix 20A. Letter to the Chairman of the House of Representatives Committee on Foreign Affairs

May 14, 1985

The Honourable Dante Fascell
Chairman
Committee on Foreign Affairs
US House of Representatives
Washington, DC 20515

Dear Mr Chairman,

Continued nuclear testing is not necessary in order to insure the reliability of the nuclear weapons in our stockpile. The best way to confirm reliability is to disassemble sample weapons and to subject the components to non-nuclear tests. Weapons can also be detonated without their nuclear components in order to insure that the complete assembly operates correctly. Nonexplosive tests are also available for determining whether the nuclear components have deteriorated during storage. If aging problems are found in some components, these components can be replaced with newly fabricated ones, using the original design specifications.

In the past these techniques have identified a number of reliability problems. In no case, however, was the discovery of a reliability problem dependent on a nuclear test to remedy the problem.

In any event, it would be completely impractical to conduct the large number of nuclear tests that would be required to establish by this method a statistically meaningful measure of the reliability of stockpiled weapons.

We hope these observations will be useful to you in considering the Comprehensive Test Ban.

Sincerely,

Hans Bethe
Nobel Laureate in Physics
former Director, Theoretical Division, Los Alamos National Laboratories

Norris Bradbury
former Director, Los Alamos National Laboratories

Richard Garwin
IBM Fellow, Thomas J. Watson Research Center
Consultant, Department of Defense, Department of Energy

Spurgeon M. Keeny, Jr
former Deputy Director, ACDA

Wolfgang Panofsky
former Director, Stanford Linear Accelerator

George Rathjens
former Deputy Director, Defense Advanced Research Projects Agency
(DARPA)

Herbert Scoville, Jr
former Deputy Director, CIA
former Technical Director, Defense Department Armed Forces Special
Weapons Project

Paul Warnke,
former Director, ACDA

Paper 21

Vitalii I. Goldanskii

Academy of Sciences of the USSR, Moscow

Abstract

A comprehensive test ban would not affect the horizontal proliferation of nuclear weapons since a state wishing to produce nuclear weapons for the first time would not need to conduct tests to do so. For vertical proliferation, a CTB would only affect a nation's programme for truly modernizing its nuclear weapons or a programme to develop third-generation nuclear weapons. Programmes to ensure the confidence in nuclear weapon stockpiles and to add to these stockpiles do not require tests and so would not be affected by a CTB.

I. Introduction

There is an important relationship between the proliferation of nuclear weapons and the need for nuclear weapon test explosions. This relationship is outlined in table 21.1 below, with regard to the three generations of nuclear weapons.

Table 21.1. Nuclear weapons and nuclear weapon testing

Generation	Political and military implications	Types	Full-scale testing
First	Horizontal proliferation	Fission (U^{235}, Pu) nuclear weapons	Unnecessary
Second	Deterrence	Thermonuclear (fission–fusion, fission–fusion–fission), strategic and tactical nuclear weapons	Unnecessary for confidence in stockpiles Necessary for modernization of second-generation and for developing third-generation nuclear weapons
Third	Race for superiority, nuclear war-fighting capability	Directed-energy (X-ray lasers for SDI); selectively enhanced (radiation, EMP, etc.); miniaturized nuclear weapons	Necessary

II. Horizontal proliferation

Full-scale nuclear explosions are not a prerequisite for the development of nuclear weapons for states which have not yet developed them. Nuclear 'newcomer' states could produce first-generation, fission nuclear bombs, with a clandestine programme.

Two types of nuclear bomb could be developed. The first, a fission Uranium-235 bomb, is the same type of bomb as that dropped over Hiroshima, which was exploded using a gun-type technique. The second type, a plutonium bomb, is the same type as that exploded over Nagasaki, using the implosion technique.

A telling proof that these early-generation bombs do not have to be tested before they are used is the case of the Hiroshima 'Little Boy' bomb, which was not tested before it was used in Japan. Nevertheless, a comprehensive nuclear test ban would be an effective *political* impediment to horizontal nuclear weapon proliferation, and would complement the non-proliferation regime.

III. Vertical proliferation

Nuclear weapon states have different requirements for testing. One requirement that is often claimed is that testing must be performed to ensure the reliability of and confidence in the existing nuclear weapon stockpiles. Again, historical evidence provides the best proof that such testing is not necessary: since 1976 neither the USA nor the USSR have conducted tests with yields above the 150-kt threshold established in the Threshold Test Ban Treaty (TTBT), even though the vast majority of the warheads in their respective stockpiles have yields above this threshold. In the United States, they are even considering stockpiling a warhead with a yield in excess of 1000 kt without ever having tested it.

Those who argue for reliability testing of stockpiled weapons frequently assert that there will be an asymmetry in the ageing of the US and Soviet arsenals since Soviet weapons are considered by them to be more robust and therefore less susceptible to serious deterioration. As a scientist from the Lawrence Livermore National Laboratory has commented:

The American weapons labs are quite concerned about a possible asymmetry in the stockpile degradation of American nuclear weapons vs. those of the Soviets. They fear that the Soviet weapons are simpler and more robust than the sophisticated American designs, so that after some years of a test ban the Soviets might be more confident of the reliability of their warheads than we are of ours. Clearly, no American government will accept a test ban until this fear is dispelled. . . . [i]t is time to ask why the weapons labs have not come up with proven designs that can be dependably manufactured in the future. If the Soviets can do it, then we can, too.[1]

Tests of the present generation of nuclear weapons are necessary only for their modernization or for transition to third-generation nuclear weapons (in particular for SDI).

IV. Threshold agreements: the arms control value

In general, any move towards a CTB, in particular such as the Soviet moratorium on tests, is preferable to a stalemate or a move in the opposite direction. However, we have also seen that the TTBT, although a positive measure, has not stopped the arms race, which has rather continued on a massive scale.

In assessing such measures as limiting the frequency or the yield of tests, one should take into account their possible impact on the programmes to develop third-generation nuclear weapons. One should also consider the dangers associated with the miniaturization of nuclear weapons, namely, the erosion of the distinction between nuclear and conventional weapons, as well as the dangers of localized conflicts with the use of tactical nuclear weapons which would inevitably escalate to a global war. In this connection, it is of interest to look at the distribution of US nuclear tests at given yields.

As shown in table 21.2, lowering the yield threshold would obviously move the 'centre of gravity' of testing towards tactical weapons. It would also, however, add new fuel to the controversy over the problems of verification. Thus, limits on the frequency and yield of tests could serve only as intermediate steps towards a CTB, but would hardly be an effective substitute for a CTB. A CTB would be the most effective measure against vertical proliferation, on the road to nuclear disarmament.

Table 21.2. US nuclear tests conducted at the Nevada Test Site, 1980–84

Yield (kt)	Percentage of tests	Percentage of nuclear devices tested	
		Tactical	Strategic
Below 1	5	28	—
1–5	13	32	—
5–20	44	21	—
20–50	12	3	26
50–150	26	8	16
150–500	—	8	31
Over 500	—	—	27

Sources: Column 2 from Kidder, R., 'Militarily significant nuclear explosive yields', paper for Cavity Decoupling Workshop, US Department of Energy, Pajaro Dunes, CA, 29–31 July 1985. Columns 3 and 4 from Cochran, T. B., Arkin, W. M. and Hoenig, M. H., *Nuclear Weapons Databook* (Ballinger: Cambridge, MA, 1984), chapter 3.

Notes and references

[1] De Witt, H. (Lawrence Livermore National Laboratory), letter in *Physics Today*, Jan. 1984, p. 111.

Chapter XVIII. Political, strategic and psychological effects of a nuclear test ban

Paper 22

Eugene J. Carroll, Jr

Deputy Director, Center for Defense Information, Washington, DC

Abstract

Arms control efforts to restrain nuclear competition have generally been conducted in a 'talk–test–build' format. Testing and building new weapons have proceeded far more rapidly than have agreements to limit or reduce nuclear weapons. A comprehensive test ban would take 'test' out of the arms control process and open the door to a series of agreements which would first freeze and then reduce nuclear arsenals. A CTB would have two immediate effects: (*a*) It would eliminate the technological push which has fuelled the nuclear arms race. (*b*) It would be the urgently needed political signal that both sides were committed to a constructive arms control process as an alternative to an expanded arms race on earth and in space. The pursuit of nuclear deterrence through new technology is actually increasing the risk of nuclear war. A CTB is the first step towards averting nuclear war.

I. Introduction

Human beings are apparently unique in the animal family in their ability to deal with abstractions. Even humans, however, are unable to deal logically with perhaps the greatest abstraction of all—nuclear war. From the reality of single atomic bombs dropped on two Japanese cities, we attempt to extrapolate the terms and conditions of war with 50 000 thermonuclear weapons. The best we can do is speculate. If war comes we may have very little opportunity to measure the validity of abstract speculation against the awful realities of nuclear war.

But speculate we do. Every effort is made to give speculation the appearance of a scientific process. Calculations are done and reported in vocabularies as obscure as they are arcane. The results (frequently predetermined by the calculator) are used to support research budgets, new weapons and expanded forces.

The same process goes on in the potential adversary's headquarters, compounded by his perception of the intentions, capabilities and latest initiatives of his adversary. In nuclear metaphysics, 'escalation dominance' is supposed to refer to one form of nuclear deterrence, but it may more accurately refer to the ability of contending theorists to dominate the escalation of nuclear budgets through their more imaginative speculation.

If we appreciate that the driving force behind nuclear competition today is nothing more than worst-case speculation, then we can understand why it is legitimate to speculate on the consequences of a best-case approach to nuclear security. Instead of always assuming that the presumed adversary is preparing to attack us with his nuclear weapons and that they will all work to maximum effect (the worst-case basis for all military planning), why is it not equally valid to make some best-case assumptions and then speculate about the consequences of actions based on these assumptions?

Specifically, what follows is based upon four assumptions:

1. Nuclear competitors have an equal commitment to survival, even in a world with 50 000 nuclear weapons.

2. The competitors understand that a nuclear war would be mutually suicidal.

3. The competitors will not permit each other to gain any advantage that would enable one to dictate the terms of their relationship.

4. Based on assumptions 1, 2 and 3, the competitors can come to mutually beneficial agreements to restrain their competition in order to reduce the risk of nuclear war.

While these assumptions are clearly additional abstractions, the principle of best-case planning should be tested by whatever means are available as a desirable alternative to simply preparing for a nuclear war. These assumptions will be useful to keep in mind while examining the potential consequences of a nuclear test ban: Would a test ban be consistent with or contradict the principle of best-case planning?

Fortunately there is evidence which seems to support some or all of these assumptions. Political statements which substantiate assumptions 1 and 2 abound. Whatever their motives at the time, the leaders of the USA and the USSR could not have been more explicit in their individual concerns about the dangers of nuclear war. President Reagan has said, 'A nuclear war cannot be won and must never be fought.'[1] General Secretary Gorbachev has said, '. . . this moment in history makes it increasingly vital to outlaw nuclear weapons, destroy them and other weapons of mass annihilation completely. . . .'[2]

The evidence supporting assumption 3 is all too prevalent. Nothing can possibly explain the existence of 50 000 nuclear weapons other than fearful over-reaction on both sides to the latest nuclear weapon system of the adversary. Not only will neither side permit the other side any advantage, but neither will tolerate any form of imbalance which creates even the perception of an advantage, military or political.

Proof for assumption 4 is less evident. The few, fragile successes of the arms control process do demonstrate that on rare occasions the two sides have fought through the obstacles of fear and distrust to come to mutually beneficial agreements that have restrained nuclear competition in important ways. The significance of the 1963 Partial Test Ban Treaty and the continuing importance of the 1972 Anti-Ballistic Missile Treaty are obvious. Soon we may recognize the foresight evident in the 1967 Outer Space Treaty which may yet serve to restrain dangerous new military programmes in space.

Despite all of its shortcomings, the world is somewhat cleaner and slightly safer because of the arms control process. Not even the most ardent arms control advocates, however, can claim that existing agreements have stopped nuclear competition from producing more destructive weapons and a less stable nuclear balance. Why do the competitors recognize the dangers of nuclear war and do less and less to prevent it? Why has the arms control process promised much and delivered little?

II. 'Talk–test–build' arms control

The history of efforts to limit or reduce nuclear weapons has been distinguished by a pattern of talking about measures to control the arms competition while simultaneously intensifying the competition through active nuclear testing and weapon production programmes. This pattern is accurately described as the 'talk–test–build' process. The consequences of this process were most evident during the 1970s when the USA and the USSR concluded 11 agreements[3] presumably intended to lessen the risk of nuclear war. In the same decade both nations approximately tripled the number of weapons aimed at each other in their strategic nuclear stockpiles.[4] Talking went on slowly and painfully for 10 years, but testing and building surged ahead much faster.

The 'talk–test–build' process results from factors which have driven the arms competition for 40 years. In the unending drive for assured deterrence, each side uses the other side's latest nuclear development to justify yet another round of weapons buildup. Pursuit of deterrence is the engine of the arms race, and the fuel to drive it is new technology advancing through nuclear testing. Thus, while the negotiators haggle interminably over details, new weapons come into the inventory. These new products are never offered up in the negotiations. In fact, they are carefully protected in treaty drafts for short-sighted reasons even though a longer-term view might well reveal the ephemeral nature of technological advantages. Everyone can agree with Henry Kissinger's retrospective wisdom when he said: 'I wish I had thought through the implications of a MIRVed world more thoughtfully in 1969 and 1970 than I did'.[5]

Although efforts to restrain the arms buildup have produced certain benefits and the world is clearly better off with the existing agreements than without them, it is also true that 'talk–test–build' negotiations have not prevented dangerous qualitative advances in nuclear weapon systems. Continued testing creates a 'moving target' for negotiators and virtually guarantees that the technological imperative will increase the destructive capacity of nuclear weapon arsenals faster than arms control measures can restrain them.

III. Possible psychological consequences of a test ban

It is this clear understanding that 'talk–test–build' negotiations cannot keep up with technological advances that compels us to examine the potential effects of stopping testing as a first step to restrain the arms competition. If what is being done is not working, simple logic requires that alternatives be evaluated with close attention to the prospective psychological and political effects of taking a first, positive step in a new direction.

The foremost, immediate benefit of a nuclear test ban would be its significance as an unambiguous signal of intentions. For more than six years nothing of any consequence has moved forward in arms control. In truth, the entire process has moved backward in floods of counterproductive rhetoric, accusations and invective. In 1986 President Reagan declared that the United States would no longer be bound by the numerical limits of SALT II.[6] Following the collapse of talks between President Reagan and General Secretary Gorbachev at Reykjavik, Iceland, in October 1986, the White House announced on 28 November the deployment of the 131st B-52 bomber modified to carry air-launched cruise missiles, thus putting the United States over the combined limit of 1320 MIRVed ballistic missiles and cruise missile-equipped intercontinental-range bombers. The Reykjavik summit meeting also ended talk of a 'grand compromise' with the Soviet Union in which the deployment of strategic defences would be 'delayed' in exchange for major reductions in existing offensive nuclear forces.

If the long-term effects of years of neglect and abuse of the arms control process are ever to be overcome, it will be through the positive effects of a clear signal from both sides that they are ready to move forward. The Soviet Union gave that unambiguous signal in its 1985–87 nuclear testing moratorium. With a similar commitment, the USA could make the same strong statement that there has been a fundamental change in policy and that progress is once again possible.

There is no way to make such a commitment in words—only actions can break down the strong and growing doubts each side has about the other's intentions and motives. Words are always suspect but constructive actions speak for themselves, establishing credibility and stimulating genuine progress.

The negative trend, of several years, in arms control can be reversed by a strong mutual effort to remove testing from the 'talk–test–build' process. Ending nuclear testing will be a real beginning in confidence building. Perhaps the best opening will be in advancing the rules and procedures for verification of a test ban.

Looking back, it is obvious that the sides have from time to time differed on procedures to verify a test ban and have used those differences as a barrier to agreement. Some progress was made on this issue in the late 1970s before the trilateral UK–USA–USSR comprehensive test ban (CTB) negotiations were terminated, but a careful reading of the Tripartite Report to the United Nations of 31 July 1980 suggests that even then verification was still a sticking point.[7]

Given that the Soviet Government permitted US scientists to set up modern seismic monitoring equipment near its nuclear test site at Semipalatinsk and expressed its willingness to accept new forms of intrusive inspection, it would seem that the verification issue can be eliminated as an obstacle to agreement. Success in working out effective verification measures during test ban negotiations would demonstrate good faith and heighten confidence on both sides that additional progress is possible on a number of chronic contentious issues.

Even one success—breaking through an old sticking point, creating confidence in the arms control process and providing positive assurance that both sides are willing to agree—will have an extremely important effect on the fear factor in US–Soviet relations. Fears on both sides concerning the intentions and objectives of the other side have always been impediments to effective arms control. But if each side agrees to restrict the push for technological advantage in nuclear weapons, one major source of fear will disappear. The current arsenals are, and will remain, frightening in the extreme, but each side understands that they cannot now be used for rational military purposes. It is acute fear of the unknown (what the other side might be creating through underground testing where precise determination of purpose or progress is impossible) that has driven much of the arms race for 20 years. Knowing that nothing new will suddenly emerge operationally will make it much easier to deal sensibly with existing problems.

In fact, reduced fears will make it possible to question the fundamental need for the excessive levels of military forces which exist today. If neither side fears that the other might soon 'break out' with some exotic new nuclear system, both will be free to take hard, critical looks at the risks and costs of maintaining the grotesque nuclear arsenals which already exist. No one argues that 50 000 nuclear weapons can be used to defend anything—they can be used only to destroy the adversary while simultaneously destroying oneself. These arsenals are being maintained and expanded today only in the belief that they might somehow be useful to address some new form of nuclear threat in the future. Halting nuclear testing and reducing fear of the unknown could eliminate that perception and make sensible political decisions much more probable in the future.

IV. Possible political consequences of a test ban

Let us turn then to the potential political consequences of an end to nuclear testing. At the present time the stated policy of the United States is that a comprehensive nuclear test ban remains a long-term goal, but that it must follow significant reductions in existing stockpiles.[8] The logic of this policy is faulty. It is not necessary to be aware of the dismal history of talk–test–build arms control efforts to doubt the feasibility of reducing nuclear arsenals while testing and producing new, more destructive weapons.

Assuming that the futility of this policy becomes obvious to the US Administration and a nuclear test ban is achieved, a number of very positive political changes can be foreseen.

The first is an entirely new climate for arms limitation and reduction negotiations at the Geneva talks. The political signal of sincere commitment to the arms control process coupled with an end to the most dangerous element of the technological competition would make it logical to give second priority to proposals for arms reductions and focus initially on additional agreements to limit the nuclear competition. It has been repeatedly demonstrated that arms cannot be reduced while both sides are building new ones faster than negotiations can restrain them. The premium arms limitation measure, a comprehensive test ban, thus would open the door to a coherent, constructive series of steps in arms control. Each measure would logically follow the one before, each would build confidence in the process, and each would encourage additional co-operative measures to replace the competition which now drives preparations for nuclear war.

The first three limitation agreements to follow a test ban are obvious, natural consequences. The first follow-on agreement is one to end all flight-testing of new, long-range strategic systems. Without new weapons to incorporate, new delivery systems might have a lower military and political justification. For example, the US Stealth bomber programme, which is already outrageously expensive, appears to require the development of new weapons to have any military utility at all because of its marginal payload and performance characteristics.[9]

Verification of long-range delivery system testing is done daily, using a wide variety of national technical means (NTM), such as early-warning and electronic intelligence satellites, and ground-based radars as well as more classic intelligence collection methods. Neither side has failed in 20 years to detect a new strategic delivery system during the testing phase and to make detailed analyses of its characteristics and performance long before it was deployed. Verification of an agreement to end flight-testing poses no problem.

With two agreements concluded, a third treaty to end the deployment of new nuclear systems would follow logically. No military commander wants untested weapons. Not only are they unsafe to use but there is no way to know how well they might work or even if they would work at all. It is virtually impossible to train people to use untested weapons or to plan effective uses for them. In short, untested weapons are useless and cannot be deployed for any practical military purpose. An agreement to end the deployment of new nuclear weapon systems would be fully verifiable using current NTM. Today the number and location of deployed weapon systems are verified with great confidence on both sides as is evident in the US annual publications *Soviet Military Power* and the corresponding Soviet series *Whence the Threat to Peace*. In these publications each side reports accurately on the numbers, deployments and characteristics of the other's strategic systems.

The first three agreements lead almost inevitably to a fourth treaty: a ban on the production of explosive nuclear materials and new strategic delivery systems. After all, if you cannot test or deploy new nuclear weapons, why build them at all? With 50 000 nuclear weapons on hand there is no need for more; and, with no way to test new technology, there is no way to make more destructive weapons even if they could be deployed. Further production would, therefore, be a pure waste of valuable resources in order to create unreliable, useless devices which would have to be hidden and guarded for no political or military purpose. Some new verification procedures would seem to be required for this fourth treaty, but both sides would have strong incentives, and the confidence, to agree to enhanced verification procedures at this point in the arms control process.

These four treaties would effectively 'freeze' the nuclear arsenals on each side. Neither side could gain any advantage over the other, and arms control negotiations would no longer be in the talk–test–build format. Testing and building would be over, and talks could proceed to produce real reductions in the excessive arsenals which exist today. Reductions could be made in an orderly, balanced way to increase the security of both sides while making it certain that neither had any intention or desire to plan the nuclear destruction of the other. First priority would be given to eliminating MIRVed missiles, both land- and sea-based.

V. The consequences of nuclear arms control

This brief, idealized vision of moving from the arms limitation phase to the arms reduction phase of arms control obviously raises significant questions about its effect on East–West relations and the possible involvement of France, Britain and China as arms reductions occur.

With respect to the nuclear balance, the effect of an orderly arms reduction programme is simply stated. The present nuclear arsenals are in a state of parity and will remain in balance if existing arms control measures are observed by both sides. In the words of Dr Herbert York, former Director of the US Lawrence Livermore National Laboratory and Chief US negotiator on the comprehensive test ban: 'There not only is parity, I would go further and say that if the ratio changed by a factor of two either way, there would still be parity'.[10] Put another way, if the US and the Soviet nuclear weapon stockpiles and delivery systems were reversed, it would have no effect on the nuclear balance; their relationship would remain mutually suicidal if either initiated nuclear war. The danger, of course, is that no one can say with any confidence what the relationship will become if current arms limitations are abandoned, testing continues and third-generation nuclear war-fighting weapons appear on earth and in space. 'Unstable' and 'unpredictable' best describe the potential relationship in a world of nuclear confrontation without effective arms control. Thus, the wisest political course is to increase arms control constraints and reduce nuclear competition. Once the fear of the unknown emerging from nuclear test tunnels is eliminated and nuclear arsenals are frozen, there is tremendous room for downward adjustment in nuclear armaments while maintaining and increasing the stability of the nuclear balance. At some point, years from now, the arms control effort could enter the 'end game' phase, and then the margin between the United States and the Soviet Union would shrink. At the same time third-nation arsenals would become critical.

To this point, this appraisal of the potential political and psychological consequences of a comprehensive nuclear test ban focuses almost entirely on US–Soviet issues. This focus is correct because these two nations possess the overwhelming majority of the world's nuclear weapons and long-range strategic delivery systems. They lead in all phases of nuclear war-fighting technology and forces. They alone can take actions which will slow, stop and reverse the march to nuclear war on a global scale. Unless, and until, they take these actions, the other nuclear weapon powers and those aspiring to nuclear weapon capability are insignificant players on the nuclear stage.

Nevertheless, it is important to appreciate that the drive for nuclear capability will continue, and be reinforced, as long as the great powers continue to expand the destructive power of their nuclear forces. Proliferation of nuclear weapons in the Third World, particularly among nations with sharp, chronic conflicts based on fundamental geographic, religious or economic issues, certainly would constitute a major threat to world peace. The best hope for preventing proliferation is mutual restraint and close co-operation by the USA and the USSR to inhibit the spread of nuclear weapons. A nuclear test ban would be the logical beginning of a co-operative programme.

The present author has received informal assurance from officials of the People's Republic of China that China is prepared to join the USA and the USSR in a test ban and in subsequent arms control arrangements when they adopt such measures. It is fair to assume that the UK would be prepared to follow US leadership in a test ban and be prepared to participate, when appropriate, in arms control and arms reduction measures. For the foreseeable future, France will continue to pursue an independent course on nuclear issues. Positive examples by the other nuclear weapon powers plus pressure from the world community will be needed to restrain their test and weapon modernization programmes, but the probability of initial French resistance should not be permitted to prevent the development of a co-operative effort to block nuclear proliferation in the Third World.

This fact explains why third-party considerations must not be permitted to interfere with initial improvements in the US–Soviet nuclear relationship. Only US and Soviet leaders can destroy the world today, and there will be no change in that fact until they act to end nuclear competition and confrontation. In the first stage of nuclear arms reductions, French, British and Chinese nuclear weapons are irrelevant. *After* the USA and the USSR have ceased testing and demonstrated a credible commitment to arms control, they will be in a much stronger position to use their political leadership to encourage third-nation participation and contributions to nuclear stability. While it is true that all nuclear states must ultimately join the arms control process, including a test ban, their premature inclusion will only complicate an already difficult process.

This same need to avoid complicating nuclear arms control applies to the problem of preventing nuclear proliferation. As long as the nuclear weapon states continue testing and expanding the destructive power of their nuclear forces, non-nuclear weapon states are going to pursue the political (if not military) advantages of joining the nuclear club. There is no argument with the proposition that more nuclear weapon states will result in less nuclear stability and will substantially increase the risk of nuclear war. A comprehensive test ban treaty is viewed by many non-nuclear weapon states as a *sine qua non* for preventing the emergence of additional nuclear weapon states and for preserving the NPT regime.

If there were no other argument for an early end to nuclear testing, the need to reduce the risks of nuclear proliferation should alone motivate the USA and the USSR to conclude the treaty. Then, with a reinforced mutual interest in preventing proliferation, they would be motivated to co-operate in expanding the test ban globally. This co-operation could result in formidable political, economic and even implied military pressure to ensure that testing and proliferation did not proceed to the detriment of global nuclear stability.

All of the political effects of a test ban would not be confined to nuclear security considerations. For example, one of the perennial justifications for increased NATO spending on conventional forces is that it is necessary to 'raise the nuclear threshold'. General Bernard Rogers, SACEUR, regularly uses this argument.[11] The commonly accepted wisdom that reduced reliance on nuclear weapons would require increases in conventional forces to maintain a credible deterrent to Soviet aggression is dubious.

What if there were genuine progress in reducing nuclear arms, not only strategic but tactical weapons as well? What if the nuclear weapon states were actively moving to raise or eliminate the nuclear threshold by reducing their capabilities to wage nuclear war on the battlefield? Without tactical nuclear weapons, the threshold between the use of conventional weapons and a strategic nuclear exchange would be much higher. In this improved international environment, pressing political (and economic) problems might produce real progress in the long, slow-moving Mutual and Balanced Force Reduction (MBFR) talks in Vienna.

Given genuine progress in reducing the risk of nuclear war and practical measures to eliminate nuclear war-fighting capabilities, would not the wisdom of maintaining a stable conventional balance in Europe at lower levels of forces on both sides be apparent? NATO and the Warsaw Pact now keep approximately 11 million people in uniform with no real reason to fear that either side is preparing to attack the other. Indeed, neither side has any credible motive to attack nor any prospect of achieving any political, military or economic objectives worth the costs and dangers of general conventional war.

With the nuclear threshold going up through constructive arms control measures, the conventional force levels could go down and still maintain a stable, secure East–West balance in Europe. Similarly, the Conference on Security and Co-operation in Europe (CSCE) could be revitalized.

VI. Conclusions

Despite the increased stability and the reduced risk of nuclear war which these arms control measures could bring, no one should regard them as a panacea. Arms control is not a magic wand which will soon or easily rid the world of nuclear danger. Instead, arms control agreements, starting with a nuclear test ban, must be parallelled with a broad attack on the many other problems of creating a 'mutual security' system based on co-operation instead of confrontation. A system which will substitute co-operation and accommodation for military force as the means of resolving differences will require foresight, wisdom and years of constructive effort if it is ever to emerge.

It is far beyond the scope of this paper to postulate what the 21st century may bring in the form of a stable, peaceful and co-operative world order. Only dim visions exist of a world in which nuclear weapons are relics, in which military–political systems such as NATO and the Warsaw Pact are part of history, and in which the use of force or threat of force are unnecessary and disputes are resolved by non-violent means under rules of international law.

The inescapable conclusion, however, is that we must soon abandon reliance on nuclear weapons to deter war because the deterrent system is failing. Pushed by the inexorable advance of military technologies, the adversaries are taking actions in the name of deterrence which make war more likely. One need look no further than the US Strategic Defense Initiative to see this dynamic moving the nuclear confrontation into a new regime in space, an action which will intensify the nuclear competition and create a relationship which is inherently unstable in time of crisis.

We must, therefore, buy time with arms control efforts which slow, stop and reverse the nuclear arms competition. The first, essential and only immediately achievable action to start this process is a nuclear test ban. While a test ban alone will do nothing about the 50 000 nuclear weapons, it would have immense psychological and political consequences that could open the door on a whole new approach to nuclear arms control.

The time we buy with successful arms control initiatives must then be used to seek the wisdom and the will to move the world order from one regulated by force to one governed by law. The choice is clear. We can either continue preparations for nuclear war with the clear knowledge that war will come, or we can acknowledge that Lord Earl Louis Mountbatten was correct when he said that preparing for nuclear war is absolute nonsense, concluding that, 'the world now stands on the brink of final abyss'.[12] We should choose the path away from that abyss while there is still time and begin with a nuclear test ban, the first essential step to avert nuclear war.

Notes and references

[1] 'Excerpts from President Reagan's speech on foreign policy and Congress', *New York Times*, 7 Apr. 1984, p. 6.

[2] United States Foreign Broadcast Information Service, *Daily Report: Soviet Union*, vol. 3, no. 038 (26 Feb. 1986), p. 1.

[3] Titles of the 11 treaties, agreements and protocols, as given in Goldblat, J., SIPRI, *Agreements for Arms Control* (Taylor & Francis: London, 1982):
   1. 1971 Treaty on the prohibition of the emplacement of nuclear weapons and other weapons of mass destruction on the seabed and the ocean floor and in the subsoil thereof
   2. 1971 Agreement between the USA and the USSR on measures to improve the direct communications link
   3. 1971 Agreement between the USA and the USSR on measures to reduce the risk of outbreak of nuclear war
   4. 1972 Treaty between the USA and the USSR on the limitation of anti-ballistic missile systems (ABM Treaty)
   5. 1972 Interim agreement between the USA and the USSR on certain measures with respect to the limitation of strategic offensive arms (SALT I Agreement)
   6. 1972 Protocol to the ABM Treaty
   7. 1973 Agreement between the USA and the USSR on the prevention of nuclear war
   8. 1974 Treaty between the USA and the USSR on the limitation of underground nuclear weapon tests (Threshold Test Ban Treaty)
   9. 1976 Treaty between the USA and the USSR on underground nuclear explosions for peaceful purposes
   10. 1979 Treaty between the USA and the USSR on the limitation of strategic offensive arms (SALT II Treaty)
   11. 1980 Convention on the physical protection of nuclear material.

[4] *MX Missile Basing System and Related Issues*, Hearing before the Committee on Armed Services, US Senate, 98th Congress (US Government Printing Office: Washington, DC, 1983), pp. 233–4.

[5] Henry Kissinger as quoted in Pranger, J. and Labrie, R. P. (eds), *Nuclear Strategy and National Security Points of View* (American Enterprise Institute for Public Policy Research: Washington, DC, 1977), p. 407.

[6] *New York Times*, 29 Nov. 1986, p. 1.

[7] *The Tripartite Report on the Progress of the Comprehensive Test Ban Negotiations*, Hearing before the Committee on Foreign Affairs, 99th Congress (US Government Printing Office: Washington, DC, 1985), pp. 167–72.

[8] *Fiscal Year 1987 Arms Control Impact Statements* (US Government Printing Office: Washington, DC, Apr. 1986), p. 7.

[9] Robinson, C. A., Jr, 'B-1/Stealth competition emerges', *Aviation Week & Space Technology*, 27 Feb. 1984, pp. 16–17; see also Congressional Research Service, *Strategic Nuclear Forces: Potential US/Soviet Trends With or Without SALT, 1985–2000* (US Library of Congress: Washington, DC, 15 July 1986), pp. 20–1.

[10] Scheer, R., *With Enough Shovels: Reagan, Bush & Nuclear War* (Random House: New York, 1982), p. 271.

[11] *DOD Authorization, Fiscal Year 1986*, Hearing before the Committee on Armed Services, US Senate, 98th Congress (US Government Printing Office: Washington, DC, 1985), part 3, p. 1369; see also Barnard, R., 'General Rogers says Europe is heedless of his arms advice', *Defence Week*, 2 July 1984, p. 5.

[12] Mountbatten, E., Address in Strasbourg, France, 11 May 1979, on the occasion of the awarding of the Cora Weiss Peace Prize to SIPRI.

Annexes

Annexe 1. Existing legal limitations on nuclear explosions

Prepared by Ragnhild Ferm

I. Major treaties

Treaty banning nuclear weapon tests in the atmosphere, in outer space and under water (PTBT)

Signed at Moscow on 5 August 1963; entered into force on 10 October 1963.

Parties: Afghanistan, Argentina, Australia, Austria, Bahamas, Bangladesh, Belgium, Benin, Bhutan, Bolivia, Botswana, Brazil, Bulgaria, Burma, Byelorussia, Canada, Cape Verde, Central African Republic, Chad, Chile, Colombia, Costa Rica, Côte d'Ivoire, Cyprus, Czechoslovakia, Denmark, Dominican Republic, Ecuador, Egypt, El Salvador, Fiji, Finland, Gabon, Gambia, German Democratic Republic, FR Germany, Ghana, Greece, Guatemala, Guinea-Bissau, Honduras, Hungary, Iceland, India, Indonesia, Iran, Iraq, Ireland, Israel, Italy, Japan, Jordan, Kenya, Republic of Korea, Kuwait, Lao People's Democratic Republic, Lebanon, Liberia, Libya, Luxembourg, Madagascar, Malawi, Malaysia, Malta, Mauritania, Mauritius, Mexico, Mongolia, Morocco, Nepal, Netherlands, New Zealand, Nicaragua, Niger, Nigeria, Norway, Panama, Papua New Guinea, Peru, Philippines, Poland, Romania, Rwanda, Samoa, San Marino, Senegal, Seychelles, Sierra Leone, Singapore, South Africa, Spain, Sri Lanka, Sudan, Swaziland, Sweden, Switzerland, Syria, Taiwan, Tanzania, Thailand, Togo, Tonga, Trinidad and Tobago, Tunisia, Turkey, Uganda, UK, Ukraine, Uruguay, USA, USSR, Venezuela, Democratic Yemen, Yugoslavia, Zaire, Zambia

The Governments of the United States of America, the United Kingdom of Great Britain and Northern Ireland, and the Union of Soviet Socialist Republics, hereinafter referred to as the 'Original Parties',

Proclaiming as their principal aim the speediest possible achievement of an agreement on general and complete disarmament under strict international control in accordance with the objectives of the United Nations which would put an end to the armaments race and eliminate the incentive to the production and testing of all kinds of weapons, including nuclear weapons,

Seeking to achieve the discontinuance of all test explosions of nuclear weapons for all time, determined to continue negotiations to this end, and desiring to put an end to the contamination of man's environment by radioactive substances,

Have agreed as follows:

Article I

1. Each of the Parties to this Treaty undertakes to prohibit, to prevent, and not to carry out any nuclear weapon test explosion, or any other nuclear explosion, at any place under its jurisdiction or control:

(*a*) in the atmosphere; beyond its limits, including outer space; or under water, including territorial waters or high seas; or

(*b*) in any other environment if such explosion causes radioactive debris to be present outside the territorial limits of the State under whose jurisdiction or control such explosion is conducted. It is understood in this connection that the provisions of this subparagraph are without prejudice to the conclusion of a treaty resulting in the permanent banning of all nuclear test explosions, including all such explosions underground, the conclusion of which, as the Parties have stated in the Preamble to this Treaty, they seek to achieve.

2. Each of the Parties to this Treaty undertakes furthermore to refrain from causing, encouraging, or in any way participating in, the carrying out of any nuclear weapon test explosion, or any other nuclear explosion, anywhere which would take place in any of the environments described, or have the effect referred to, in paragraph 1 of this Article.

Article II

1. Any Party may propose amendments to this Treaty. The text of any proposed amendment shall be submitted to the Depositary Governments which shall circulate it to all Parties to this Treaty. Thereafter, if requested to do so by one-third or more of the Parties, the Depositary Governments shall convene a conference, to which they shall invite all the Parties, to consider such amendment.

2. Any amendment to this Treaty must be approved by a majority of the votes of all the Parties to this Treaty, including the votes of all of the Original Parties. The amendment shall enter into force for all Parties upon the deposit of instruments of ratification by a majority of all the Parties, including the instruments of ratification of all of the Original Parties.

Article III

1. This Treaty shall be open to all States for signature. Any State which does not sign this Treaty before its entry into force in accordance with paragraph 3 of this Article may accede to it at any time.

2. This Treaty shall be subject to ratification by signatory States. Instruments of ratification and instruments of accession shall be deposited with the Governments of the Original Parties—the United States of America, the United Kingdom of Great Britain and Northern Ireland, and the Union of Soviet Socialist Republics—which are hereby designated the Depositary Governments.

3. This Treaty shall enter into force after its ratification by all the Original Parties and the deposit of their instruments of ratification.

4. For States whose instruments of ratification or accession are deposited subsequent to the entry into force of this Treaty, it shall enter into force on the date of the deposit of their instruments of ratification or accession.

5. The Depositary Governments shall promptly inform all signatory and acceding States of the date of each signature, the date of deposit of each instrument of ratification of and accession to this Treaty, the date of its entry into force, and the date of receipt of any requests for conferences or other notices.

6. This Treaty shall be registered by the Depositary Governments pursuant to Article 102 of the Charter of the United Nations.

Article IV

This Treaty shall be of unlimited duration.

Each Party shall in exercising its national sovereignty have the right to withdraw from the Treaty if it decides that extraordinary events, related to the subject matter of this Treaty, have jeopardized the supreme interests of its country. It shall give notice of such withdrawal to all other Parties to the Treaty three months in advance.

Article V

1. This Treaty, of which the English and Russian texts are equally authentic, shall be deposited in the archives of the Depositary Governments. Duly certified copies of this Treaty shall be transmitted by the Depositary Governments to the Governments of the signatory and acceding States.

Source: *Treaty Series*, Vol. 480 (United Nations, New York).

Treaty between the USA and the USSR on the limitation of underground nuclear weapon tests (Threshold Test Ban Treaty, TTBT)

Signed at Moscow on 3 July 1974; not in force by 1 July 1987.

The United States of America and the Union of Soviet Socialist Republics, hereinafter referred to as the Parties,

Declaring their intention to achieve at the earliest possible date the cessation of the nuclear arms race and to take effective measures towards reductions in strategic arms, nuclear disarmament, and general and complete disarmament under strict and effective international control,

Recalling the determination expressed by the Parties to the 1963 Treaty Banning Nuclear Weapon Tests in the Atmosphere, in Outer Space and Under Water in its preamble to seek to achieve the discontinuance of all test explosions of nuclear weapons for all time, and to continue negotiations to this end,

Noting that the adoption of measures for the further limitation of underground nuclear weapon tests would contribute to the achievement of these objectives and would meet the interests of strengthening peace and the further relaxation of international tension,

Reaffirming their adherence to the objectives and principles of the Treaty Banning Nuclear Weapon Tests in the Atmosphere, in Outer Space and Under Water and of the Treaty on the Non-Proliferation of Nuclear Weapons,

Have agreed as follows:

Article I

1. Each Party undertakes to prohibit, to prevent, and not to carry out any underground nuclear weapon test having a yield exceeding 150 kilotons at any place under its jurisdiction or control, beginning 31 March 1976.

2. Each Party shall limit the number of its underground nuclear weapon tests to a minimum.

3. The Parties shall continue their negotiations with a view towards achieving a solution to the problem of the cessation of all underground nuclear weapon tests.

Article II

1. For the purpose of providing assurance of compliance with the provisions of this Treaty, each Party shall use national technical means of verification at its disposal in a manner consistent with the generally recognized principles of international law.

2. Each Party undertakes not to interfere with the national technical means of verification of the other Party operating in accordance with paragraph 1 of this article.

3. To promote the objectives and implementation of the provisions of this Treaty the Parties shall, as necessary, consult with each other, make inquiries and furnish information in response to such inquiries.

Article III

The provisions of this Treaty do not extend to underground nuclear explosions carried out by the Parties for peaceful purposes. Underground nuclear explosions for peaceful purposes shall be governed by an agreement which is to be negotiated and concluded by the Parties at the earliest possible time.

Article IV

This Treaty shall be subject to ratification in accordance with the constitutional procedures of each Party. This Treaty shall enter into force on the day of the exchange of instruments of ratification.

Article V

1. This Treaty shall remain in force for a period of five years. Unless replaced earlier by an agreement in implementation of the objectives specified in paragraph 3 of article I of this Treaty, it shall be extended for successive five-year periods unless either Party notifies the other of its termination no later than six months prior to the expiration of the Treaty. Before the expiration of this period the Parties may, as necessary, hold consultations to consider the situation relevant to the substance of this Treaty and to introduce possible amendments to the text of the Treaty.

2. Each Party shall, in exercising its national sovereignty, have the right to withdraw from this Treaty if it decides that extraordinary events related to the subject matter of this Treaty have jeopardized its supreme interests. It shall give notice of its decision to the other Party six months prior to withdrawal from this Treaty. Such notice shall include a statement of the extraordinary events the notifying Party regards as having jeopardized its supreme interests.

3. This Treaty shall be registered pursuant to Article 102 of the Charter of the United Nations.

PROTOCOL TO THE THRESHOLD TEST BAN TREATY

The United States of America and the Union of Soviet Socialist Republics, hereinafter referred to as the Parties,

Having agreed to limit underground nuclear weapon tests,

Have agreed as follows:

1. For the purpose of ensuring verification of compliance with the obligations of the Parties under the Treaty by national technical means, the Parties shall, on the basis of reciprocity, exchange the following data:

(a) The geographic co-ordinates of the boundaries of each test site and of the boundaries of the geophysically distinct testing areas therein.

(b) Information on the geology of the testing areas of the sites (the rock characteristics of geological formations and the basic physical properties of the rock, i.e., density, seismic velocity, water saturation, porosity and depth of water table).

(c) The geographic co-ordinates of underground nuclear weapon tests, after they have been conducted.

(d) Yield, date, time, depth and co-ordinates for two nuclear weapon tests for calibration purposes from each geophysically distinct testing area where underground nuclear weapon tests have been and are to be conducted. In this connexion the yield of such explosions for calibration purposes should be as near as possible to the limit defined in article 1 of the Treaty and not less than one tenth of that limit. In the case of testing areas where data are not available on two tests for calibration purposes, the data pertaining to one such test shall be exchanged, if available, and the data pertaining to the second test shall be exchanged as soon as possible after a second test having a yield in the above-mentioned range. The provisions of this Protocol shall not require the Parties to conduct tests solely for calibration purposes.

2. The Parties agree that the exchange of data pursuant to subparagraphs (*a*), (*b*) and (*d*) of paragraph 1 shall be carried out simultaneously with the exchange of instruments of ratification of the Treaty, as provided in article IV of the Treaty, having in mind that the Parties shall, on the basis of reciprocity, afford each other the opportunity to familiarize themselves with these data before the exchange of instruments of ratification.

3. Should a Party specify a new test site or testing area after the entry into force of the Treaty, the data called for by subparagraphs (*a*) and (*b*) of paragraph 1 shall be transmitted to the other Party in advance of use of that site or area. The data called for by subparagraph (*d*) of paragraph 1 shall also be transmitted in advance of use of that site or area if they are available; if they are not available, they shall be transmitted as soon as possible after they have been obtained by the transmitting Party.

4. The Parties agree that the test sites of each Party shall be located at places under its jurisdiction or control and that all nuclear weapon tests shall be conducted solely within the testing areas specified in accordance with paragraph 1.

5. For the purposes of the Treaty, all underground nuclear explosions at the specified test sites shall be considered nuclear weapon tests and shall be subject to all the provisions of the Treaty relating to nuclear weapon tests. The provisions of article III of the Treaty apply to all underground nuclear explosions conducted outside of the specified test sites, and only to such explosions.

This Protocol shall be considered an integral part of the Treaty.

_____

Source: UN document A/9698, Annex I and II, 9 August 1974.

Treaty between the USA and the USSR on underground nuclear explosions for peaceful purposes (PNET)

Signed at Moscow and Washington, DC, on 28 May 1976; not in force by 1 July 1987.

The United States of America and the Union of Soviet Socialist Republics, hereinafter referred to as the Parties,

Proceeding from a desire to implement Article III of the Treaty between the United States of America and the Union of Soviet Socialist Republics on the Limitation of Underground Nuclear Weapon Tests, which calls for the earliest possible conclusion of an agreement on underground nuclear explosions for peaceful purposes,

Reaffirming their adherence to the objectives and principles of the Treaty Banning Nuclear Weapon Tests in the Atmosphere, in Outer Space and Under Water, the Treaty on the Non-Proliferation of Nuclear Weapons, and the Treaty on the Limitation of Underground Nuclear Weapon Tests, and their determination to observe strictly the provisions of these international agreements,

Desiring to assure that underground nuclear explosions for peaceful purposes shall not be used for purposes related to nuclear weapons,

Desiring that utilization of nuclear energy be directed only toward peaceful purposes,

Desiring to develop appropriately co-operation in the field of underground nuclear explosions for peaceful purposes,

Have agreed as follows:

Article I

1. The Parties enter into this Treaty to satisfy the obligations in Article III of the Treaty on the Limitation of Underground Nuclear Weapon Tests, and assume additional obligations in accordance with the provisions of this Treaty.

2. This Treaty shall govern all underground nuclear explosions for peaceful purposes conducted by the Parties after 31 March 1976.

Article II

For the purposes of this Treaty:

(*a*) 'explosion' means any individual or group underground nuclear explosion for peaceful purposes;

(*b*) 'explosive' means any device, mechanism or system for producing an individual explosion;

(*c*) 'group explosion' means two or more individual explosions for which the time interval between successive individual explosions does not exceed five seconds and for which the emplacement points of all explosives can be interconnected by straight line segments, each of which joins two emplacement points and each of which does not exceed 40 kilometres.

Article III

1. Each Party, subject to the obligations assumed under this Treaty and other international agreements, reserves the right to:

(*a*) carry out explosions at any place under its jurisdiction or control outside the geographical boundaries of test sites specified under the provisions of the Treaty on the Limitation of Underground Nuclear Weapon Tests; and

(*b*) carry out, participate or assist in carrying out explosions in the territory of another State at the request of such other State.

2. Each Party undertakes to prohibit, to prevent and not to carry out at any place under its jurisdiction or control, and further undertakes not to carry out, participate or assist in carrying out anywhere:

(*a*) any individual explosion having a yield exceeding 150 kilotons;

(*b*) any group explosion:

(1) having an aggregate yield exceeding 150 kilotons except in ways that will permit identification of each individual explosion and determination of the yield of each individual explosion in the group in accordance with the provisions of Article IV of and the Protocol to this Treaty;

(2) having an aggregate yield exceeding one and one-half megatons;

(*c*) any explosion which does not carry out a peaceful application;

(*d*) any explosion except in compliance with the provisions of the Treaty Banning Nuclear Weapon Tests in the Atmosphere, in Outer Space and Under Water, the Treaty on Non-Proliferation of Nuclear Weapons, and other international agreements entered into by that Party.

3. The question of carrying out any individual explosion having a yield exceeding the yield specified in paragraph 2(*a*) of this article will be considered by Parties at an appropriate time to be agreed.

Article IV

1. For the purpose of providing assurance of compliance with the provisions of this Treaty, each party shall:

(*a*) use national technical means of verification at its disposal in a manner consistent with generally recognized principles of international law; and

(*b*) provide to the other Party information and access to sites of explosions and furnish assistance in accordance with the provisions set forth in the Protocol to this Treaty.

2. Each Party undertakes not to interfere with the national technical means of verification of the other Party operating in accordance with paragraph 1(*a*) of this article, or with the implementation of the provisions of paragraph 1(*b*) of this article.

Article V

1. To promote the objectives and implementation of the provisions of this Treaty, the Parties shall establish promptly a Joint Consultative Commission within the framework of which they will:

(*a*) consult with each other, make inquiries and furnish information in response to such inquiries, to assure confidence in compliance with the obligations assumed;

(*b*) consider questions concerning compliance with the obligations assumed and related situations which may be considered ambiguous;

(*c*) consider questions involving unintended interference with the means for assuring compliance with the provisions of this Treaty;

(*d*) consider changes in technology or other new circumstances which have a bearing on the provisions of this Treaty; and

(*e*) consider possible amendments to provisions governing underground nuclear explosions for peaceful purposes.

2. The Parties through consultation shall establish, and may amend as appropriate, Regulations for the Joint Consultative Commission governing procedures, composition and other relevant matters.

Article VI

1. The Parties will develop co-operation on the basis of mutual benefit, equality and reciprocity in various areas related to carrying out underground nuclear explosions for peaceful purposes.

2. The Joint Consultative Commission will facilitate this co-operation by considering specific areas and forms of co-operation which shall be determined by agreement between the Parties in accordance with their constitutional procedures.

3. The Parties will appropriately inform the International Atomic Energy Agency of results of their co-operation in the field of underground nuclear explosions for peaceful purposes.

Article VII

1. Each Party shall continue to promote the development of the international agreement or agreements and procedures provided for in Article V of the Treaty on the Non-Proliferation of Nuclear Weapons, and shall provide appropriate assistance to the International Atomic Energy Agency in this regard.

2. Each Party undertakes not to carry out, participate or assist in the carrying out of any explosion in the territory of another State unless that State agrees to the implementation in its territory of the international observation and procedures contemplated by Article V of the Treaty on the Non-Proliferation of Nuclear Weapons and the provisions of Article IV of and the Protocol to this Treaty, including the provision by that State of the assistance necessary for such implementation and of the privileges and immunities specified in the Protocol.

Article VIII

1. This Treaty shall remain in force for a period of five years, and it shall be extended for successive five-year periods unless either Party notifies the other of its termination no later than six months prior to its expiration. Before the expiration of this period the Parties may, as necessary, hold consultations to consider the situation relevant to the substance of this Treaty. However, under no circumstances shall either Party be entitled to terminate this Treaty while the Treaty on the Limitation of Underground Nuclear Weapon Tests remains in force.

2. Termination of the Treaty on the Limitation of Underground Nuclear Weapon Tests shall entitle either Party to withdraw from this Treaty at any time.

3. Each Party may propose amendments to this Treaty. Amendments shall enter into force on the day of the exchange of instruments of ratification of such amendments.

Article IX

1. This Treaty including the Protocol which forms an integral part hereof, shall be subject to ratification in accordance with the constitutional procedures of each Party. This Treaty shall enter into force on the day of the exchange

of instruments of ratification which exchange shall take place simultaneously with the exchange of instruments of ratification of the Treaty on the Limitation of Underground Nuclear Weapon Tests.

2. This Treaty shall be registered pursuant to Article 102 of the Charter of the United Nations.

PROTOCOL TO THE TREATY ON UNDERGROUND NUCLEAR EXPLOSIONS FOR PEACEFUL PURPOSES

The United States of America and the Union of Soviet Socialist Republics, hereinafter referred to as the Parties,

Having agreed to the provisions in the Treaty on Underground Nuclear Explosions for Peaceful Purposes, hereinafter referred to as the Treaty,

Have agreed as follows:

Article I

1. No individual explosion shall take place at a distance, in metres, from the ground surface which is less than 30 times the 3.4 root of its planned yield in kilotons.

2. Any group explosion with a planned aggregate yield exceeding 500 kilotons shall not include more than five individual explosions, each of which has a planned yield not exceeding 50 kilotons.

Article II

1. For each explosion, the Party carrying out the explosion shall provide the other Party:

(a) not later than 90 days before the beginning of emplacement of the explosives when the planned aggregate yield of the explosion does not exceed 100 kilotons, or not later than 180 days before the beginning of emplacement of the explosives when the planned aggregate yield of the explosion exceeds 100 kilotons, with the following information to the extent and degree of precision available when it is conveyed:

(1) the purpose of the planned explosion;

(2) the location of the explosion expressed in geographical co-ordinates with a precision of four or less kilometres, planned date and aggregate yield of the explosion;

(3) the type or types of rock in which the explosion will be carried out, including the degree of liquid saturation of the rock at the point of emplacement of each explosive; and

(4) a description of specific technological

features of the project, of which the explosion is a part, that could influence the determination of its yield and confirmation of purpose; and

(b) not later than 60 days before the beginning of emplacement of the explosives the information specified in subparagraph 1(a) of this article to the full extent and with the precision indicated in that subparagraph.

2. For each explosion with a planned aggregate yield exceeding 50 kilotons, the Party carrying out the explosion shall provide the other Party, not later than 60 days before the beginning of emplacement of the explosives, with the following information:

(a) the number of explosives, the planned yield of each explosive, the location of each explosive to be used in a group explosion relative to all other explosives in the group with a precision of 100 or less metres, the depth of emplacement of each explosive with a precision of one metre and the time intervals between individual explosions in any group explosion with a precision of one-tenth second; and

(b) a description of specific features of geological structure or other local conditions that could influence the determination of the yield.

3. For each explosion with a planned aggregate yield exceeding 75 kilotons, the Party carrying out the explosion shall provide the other Party, not later than 60 days before the beginning of emplacement of the explosives, with a description of the geological and geophysical characteristics of the site of each explosion which could influence determination of the yield, which shall include: the depth of the water table; a stratigraphic column above each emplacement point; the position of each emplacement point relative to nearby geological and other features which influenced the design of the project of which the explosion is a part; and the physical parameters of the rock, including density, seismic velocity, porosity, degree and liquid saturation, and rock strength, within the sphere centred on each emplacement point and having a radius, in metres, equal to 30 times the cube root of the planned yield in kilotons of the explosive emplaced at that point.

4. For each explosion with a planned aggregate yield exceeding 100 kilotons, the party carrying out the explosion shall provide the other Party, not later than 60 days before the beginning of emplacement of the explosives, with:

(a) information on locations and purposes of facilities and installations which are associated with the conduct of the explosion;

(b) information regarding the planned date of the beginning of emplacement of each

explosive; and

(c) a topographic plan in local co-ordinates of the areas specified in paragraph 7 of Article IV, at a scale of 1:24,000 or 1:25,000 with a contour interval of 10 metres or less.

5. For application of an explosion to alleviate the consequences of an emergency situation involving an unforeseen combination of circumstances which calls for immediate action for which it would not be practicable to observe the timing requirements of paragraphs 1, 2 and 3 of this article, the following conditions shall be met:

(a) the Party deciding to carry out an explosion for such purposes shall inform the other Party of that decision immediately after it has been made and describe such circumstances;

(b) the planned aggregate yield of an explosion for such purpose shall not exceed 100 kilotons; and

(c) the Party carrying out an explosion for such purpose shall provide to the other Party the information specified in paragraph 1 of this article, and the information specified in paragraphs 2 and 3 of this article if applicable, after the decision to conduct the explosion is taken, but not later than 30 days before the beginning of emplacement of the explosives.

6. For each explosion, the Party carrying out the explosion shall inform the other Party, not later than two days before the explosion, of the planned time of detonation of each explosive with a precision of one second.

7. Prior to the explosion, the Party carrying out the explosion shall provide the other Party with timely notification of changes in the information provided in accordance with this article.

8. The explosion shall not be carried out earlier than 90 days after notification of any change in the information provided in accordance with this article which requires more extensive verification procedures than those required on the basis of the original information, unless an earlier time for carrying out the explosion is agreed between the Parties.

9. Not later than 90 days after each explosion the Party carrying out the explosion shall provide the other Party with the following information:

(a) the actual time of the explosion with a precision of one-tenth second and its aggregate yield;

(b) when the planned aggregate yield of a group explosion exceeds 50 kilotons, the actual time of the first individual explosion with a precision of one-tenth second, the time interval between individual explosions with a precision of one millisecond and the yield of each individual explosion; and

(c) confirmation of other information provided in accordance with paragraphs 1, 2, 3 and 4 of this article and explanation of any changes or corrections based on the results of the explosion.

10. At any time, but not later than one year after the explosion, the other Party may request the Party carrying out the explosion to clarify any item of the information provided in accordance with this article. Such clarification shall be provided as soon as practicable, but not later than 30 days after the request is made.

Article III

1. For the purposes of this Protocol:

(a) 'designated personnel' means those nationals of the other Party identified to the Party carrying out an explosion as the persons who will exercise the rights and functions provided for in the Treaty and this Protocol; and

(b) 'emplacement hole' means the entire interior of any drill-hole, shaft, adit or tunnel in which an explosive and associated cables and other equipment are to be installed.

2. For any explosion with a planned aggregate yield exceeding 100 kilotons but not exceeding 150 kilotons if the Parties, in consultation based on information provided in accordance with Article II and other information that may be introduced by either Party, deem it appropriate for the confirmation of the yield of the explosion, and for any explosion with a planned aggregate yield exceeding 150 kilotons, the Party carrying out the explosion shall allow designated personnel within the areas and at the locations described in Article V to exercise the following rights and functions:

(a) confirmation that the local circumstances, including facilities and installations associated with the project, are consistent with the stated peaceful purposes;

(b) confirmation of the validity of the geological and geophysical information provided in accordance with Article II through the following procedures:

(1) examination by designated personnel of research and measurement data of the Party carrying out the explosion and of rock core or rock fragments removed from each emplacement hole, and of any logs and drill core from existing exploratory holes which shall be provided to designated personnel upon their arrival at the site of the explosion;

(2) examination by designated personnel of rock core or rock fragments as they become available in accordance with the procedures specified in subparagraph 2(b)(3) of this article; and

(3) observation by designated personnel

of implementation by the Party carrying out the explosion of one of the following four procedures, unless this right is waived by the other Party:

(i) construction of that portion of each emplacement hole starting from a point nearest the entrance of the emplacement hole which is at a distance, in metres, from the nearest emplacement point equal to 30 times the cube root of the planned yield in kilotons of the explosive to be emplaced at that point and continuing to the completion of the emplacement hole; or

(ii) construction of that portion of each emplacement hole starting from a point nearest the entrance of the emplacement hole which is at a distance, in metres, from the nearest emplacement point equal to six times the cube root of the planned yield in kilotons of the explosive to be emplaced at that point and continuing to the completion of the emplacement hole as well as the removal of rock core or rock fragments from the wall of an existing exploratory hole, which is substantially parallel with and at no point more than 100 metres from the emplacement hole, at locations specified by designated personnel which lie within a distance, in metres, from the same horizon as each emplacement point of 30 times the cube root of the planned yield in kilotons of the explosive to be emplaced at that point; or

(iii) removal of rock core or rock fragments from the wall of each emplacement hole at locations specified by designated personnel which lie within a distance, in metres, from each emplacement point of 30 times the cube root of the planned yield in kilotons of the explosive to be emplaced at each such point; or

(iv) construction of one or more new exploratory holes so that for each emplacement hole there will be a new exploratory hole to the same depth as that of the emplacement of the explosive, substantially parallel with and at no point more than 100 metres from each emplacement hole, from which rock cores would be removed at locations specified by designated personnel which lie within a distance, in metres, from the same horizon as each emplacement point of 30 times the cube root of the planned yield in kilotons of the explosive to be emplaced at each such point;

(c) observation of the emplacement of each explosive, confirmation of the depth of its emplacement and observation of the stemming of each emplacement hole;

(*d*) unobstructed visual observation of the area of the entrance to each emplacement hole at any time from the time of emplacement of each explosive until all personnel have been withdrawn from the site for the detonation of the explosion; and

(*e*) observation of each explosion.

3. Designated personnel, using equipment provided in accordance with paragraph 1 of Article IV, shall have the right, for any explosion with a planned aggregate yield exceeding 150 kilotons, to determine the yield of each individual explosion in a group explosion in accordance with the provisions of Article VI.

4. Designated personnel, when using their equipment in accordance with paragraph 1 of Article IV, shall have the right, for any explosion with a planned aggregate yield exceeding 500 kilotons, to emplace, install and operate under the observation and with the assistance of personnel of the Party carrying out the explosion, if such assistance is requested by designated personnel, a local seismic network in accordance with the provisions of paragraph 7 of Article IV. Radio links may be used for the transmission of data and control signals between the seismic stations and the control centre. Frequencies, maximum power output of radio transmitters, directivity of antennas and times of operation of the local seismic network radio transmitters before the explosion shall be agreed between the Parties in accordance with Article X and time of operation after the explosion shall conform to the time specified in paragraph 7 of Article IV.

5. Designated personnel shall have the right to:

(*a*) acquire photographs under the following conditions:

(1) the Party carrying out the explosion shall identify to the other Party those personnel of the Party carrying out the explosion who shall take photographs as requested by designation personnel;

(2) photographs shall be taken by personnel of the Party carrying out the explosion in the presence of designated personnel and at the time requested by designated personnel for taking such photographs. Designated personnel shall determine whether these photogaphs are in conformity with their requests and, if not, additional photographs shall be taken immediately;

(3) photographs shall be taken with cameras provided by the other Party having built-in, rapid developing capability and a copy of each photograph shall be provided at the completion of the development process to both Parties;

(4) cameras provided by designated per-

sonnel shall be kept in agreed secure storage when not in use; and

(5) the request for photographs can be made, at any time, of the following:

(i) exterior views of facilities and installations associated with the conduct of the explosion as described in subparagraph 4(*a*) of Article II;

(ii) geological samples used for confirmation of geological and geophysical information, as provided for in subparagraph 2(*b*) of this article and the equipment utilized in the acquisition of such samples;

(iii) emplacement and installation of equipment and associated cables used by designated personnel for yield determination;

(iv) emplacement and installation of the local seismic network used by designated personnel;

(v) emplacement of the explosives and the stemming of the emplacement hole; and

(vi) containers, facilities and installations for storage and operation of equipment used by designated personnel;

(*b*) photographs of visual displays and records produced by the equipment used by designated personnel and photographs within the control centres taken by cameras which are component parts of such equipment; and

(*c*) receive at the request of designated personnel and with the agreement of the Party carrying out the explosion supplementary photographs taken by the Party carrying out the explosion.

Article IV

1. Designated personnel in exercising their rights and functions may choose to use the following equipment of either Party, of which choice the Party carrying out the explosion shall be informed not later than 150 days before the beginning of emplacement of the explosives:

(*a*) electrical equipment for yield determination and equipment for a local seismic network as described in paragraphs 3, 4 and 7 of this article; and

(*b*) geologist's field tools and kits and equipment for recording of field notes.

2. Designated personnel shall have the right in exercising their rights and functions to utilize the following additional equipment which shall be provided by the Party carrying out the explosion, under procedures to be established in accordance with Article X to ensure that the equipment meets the specifications of the other Party: portable short-range communication

equipment, field glasses, optical equipment for surveying and other items which may be specified by the other Party. A description of such equipment and operating instructions shall be provided to the other Party not later than 90 days before the beginning of emplacement of the explosives in connexion with which such equipment is to be used.

3. A complete set of electrical equipment for yield determination shall consist of:

(*a*) sensing elements and associated cables for transmission of electrical power, control signals and data;

(*b*) equipment of the control centre, electrical power supplies and cables for transmission of electrical power, control signals and data; and

(*c*) measuring and calibration instruments, maintenance equipment and spare parts necessary for ensuring the functioning of sensing elements, cables and equipment of the control centre.

4. A complete set of equipment for the local seismic network shall consist of:

(*a*) seismic stations each of which contains a seismic instrument, electrical power supply and associated cables and radio equipment for receiving and transmission of control signals and data or equipment for recording control signals and data;

(*b*) equipment of the control centre and electrical power supplies; and

(*c*) measuring and calibration instruments, maintenance equipment and spare parts necessary for ensuring the functioning of the complete network.

5. In case designated personnel, in accordance with paragraph 1 of this article, choose to use equipment of the Party carrying out the explosion for yield determination or for a local seismic network, a description of such equipment and installation and operating instructions shall be provided to the other Party not later than 90 days before the beginning of emplacement of the explosives in connexion with which such equipment is to be used. Personnel of the Party carrying out the explosion shall emplace, install and operate the equipment in the presence of designated personnel. After the explosion, designated personnel shall receive duplicate copies of the recorded data. Equipment for yield determination shall be emplaced in accordance with Article VI. Equipment for a local seismic network shall be emplaced in accordance with paragraph 7 of this article.

6. In case designated personnel, in accordance with paragraph 1 of this article, choose to use their own equipment for yield determination and their own equipment for a local seismic network, the following procedures shall apply:

(*a*) the Party carrying out the explosion shall be provided by the other Party with the equipment and information specified in subparagraphs (*a*)(1) and (*a*)(2) of this paragraph not later than 150 days prior to the beginning of emplacement of the explosives in connexion with which such equipment is to be used in order to permit the Party carrying out the explosion to familiarize itself with such equipment, if such equipment and information has not been previously provided, which equipment shall be returned to the other Party not later than 90 days before the beginning of emplacement of the explosives. The equipment and information to be provided are:

(1) one complete set of electrical equipment for yield determination as described in paragraph 3 of this article, electrical and mechanical design information, specifications and installation and operating instructions concerning this equipment; and

(2) one complete set of equipment for the local seismic network described in paragraph 4 of this article, including one seismic station, electrical and mechanical design information, specifications and installation and operating instructions concerning this equipment;

(*b*) not later than 35 days prior to the beginning of emplacement of the explosives in connexion with which the following equipment is to be used, two complete sets of electrical equipment for yield determination as described in paragraph 3 of this article and specific installation instructions for the emplacement of the sensing elements based on information provided in accordance with subparagraph 2(*a*) of Article VI and two complete sets of equipment for the local seismic network as described in paragraph 4 of this article, which sets of equipment shall have the same components and technical characteristics as the corresponding equipment specified in subparagraph 6(*a*) of this article, shall be delivered in sealed containers to the port of entry;

(*c*) the Party carrying out the explosion shall choose one of each of the two sets of equipment described above which shall be used by designated personnel in connexion with the explosion;

(*d*) the set or sets of equipment not chosen for use in connexion with the explosion shall be at the disposal of the Party carrying out the explosion for a period that may be as long as 30 days after the explosion at which time such equipment shall be returned to the other Party;

(*e*) the set or sets of equipment chosen for use shall be transported by the Party carrying out the explosion in the sealed containers in which this equipment arrived, after seals of the Party carrying out the explosion have been affixed to them, to the site of the explosion, so that this equipment is delivered to designated personnel for emplacement, installation and operation not later than 20 days before the beginning of emplacement of the explosives. This equipment shall remain in the custody of designated personnel in accordance with paragraph 7 of Article V or in agreed secure storage. Personnel of the Party carrying out the explosion shall have the right to observe the use of this equipment by designated personnel during the time the equipment is at the site of the explosion. Before the beginning of emplacement of the explosives, designated personnel shall demonstrate to personnel of the Party carrying out the explosion that this equipment is in working order;

(f) each set of equipment shall include two sets of components for recording data and associated calibration equipment. Both of these sets of components in the equipment chosen for use shall simultaneously record data. After the explosion, and after duplicate copies of all data have been obtained by designated personnel and the Party carrying out the explosion, one of each of the two sets of components for recording data and associated calibration equipment shall be selected, by an agreed process of chance, to be retained by designated personnel. Designated personnel shall pack and seal such components for recording data and associated calibration equipment which shall accompany them from the site of explosion to the port of exit; and

(g) all remaining equipment may be retained by the Party carrying out the explosion for a period that may be as long as 30 days, after which time this equipment shall be returned to the other Party.

7. For any explosion with a planned aggregate yield exceeding 500 kilotons, a local seismic network, the number of stations of which shall be determined by designated personnel but shall not exceed the number of explosives in the group plus five, shall be emplaced, installed and operated at agreed sites of emplacement within an area circumscribed by circles of 15 kilometres in radius centered on points of the surface of the earth above the points of emplacement of the explosives during a period beginning not later than 20 days before the beginning of emplacement of the explosives and continuing after the explosion not later than three days unless otherwise agreed between the Parties.

8. The Party carrying out the explosion shall have the right to examine in the presence of designated personnel all equipment, instruments and tools of designated personnel specified in subparagraph 1(b) of this article.

9. The Joint Consultative Commission will consider proposals that either Party may put forward for the joint development of standardized equipment for verification purposes.

Article V

1. Except as limited by the provisions of paragraph 5 of this article, designated personnel in the exercise of their rights and functions shall have access along agreed routes:

(a) for an explosion with a planned aggregate yield exceeding 100 kilotons in accordance with paragraph 2 of Article III:

(1) to the locations of facilities and installations associated with the conduct of the explosion provided in accordance with subparagraph 4(a) of Article II; and

(2) to the locations described in paragraph 2 of Article III; and

(b) for any explosion with a planned aggregate yield exceeding 150 kilotons, in addition to the access described in subparagraph 1(a) of this article:

(1) to other locations within the area circumscribed by circles of 10 kilometres in radius centered on points on the surface of the earth above the points of emplacement of the explosives in order to confirm that the local circumstances are consistent with the stated peaceful purposes;

(2) to the locations of the components of the electrical equipment for yield determination to be used for recording data when, by agreement between the Parties, such equipment is located outside the area described in subparagraph 1(b)(1) of this article; and

(3) to the sites of emplacement of the equipment of the local seismic network provided for in paragraph 7 of Article IV.

2. The Party carrying out the explosion shall notify the other Party of the procedure it has chosen from among those specified in subparagraph 2(b)(3) of Article III not later than 30 days before beginning the implementation of such procedure. Designated personnel shall have the right to be present at the site of the explosion to exercise their rights and functions in the areas and at the locations described in paragraph 1 of this article for a period of time beginning two days before the beginning of the implementation of the procedure and continuing for a period of three days after the completion of this procedure.

3. Except as specified in paragraph 4 of this article, designated personnel shall have the

right to be present in the areas and at the locations described in paragraph 1 of this article:

(*a*) for an explosion with a planned aggregate yield exceeding 100 kilotons but not exceeding 150 kilotons, in accordance with paragraph 2 of Article III, at any time beginning five days before the beginning of emplacement of the explosives and continuing after the explosion and after safe access to evacuated areas has been established according to standards determined by the Party carrying out the explosion for a period of two days; and

(*b*) for any explosion with a planned aggregate yield exceeding 150 kilotons, at any time beginning 20 days before the beginning of emplacement of the explosives and continuing after the explosion and after safe access to evacuated areas has been established according to standards determined by the Party carrying out the explosion for a period of:

(1) five days in the case of an explosion with a planned aggregate yield exceeding 150 kilotons but not exceeding 500 kilotons; or

(2) eight days in the case of an explosion with a planned aggregate yield exceeding 500 kilotons.

4. Designated personnel shall not have the right to be present in those areas from which all personnel have been evacuated in connexion with carrying out an explosion, but shall have the right to re-enter those areas at the same time as personnel of the Party carrying out the explosion.

5. Designated personnel shall not have or seek access by physical, visual, or technical means to the interior of the canister containing an explosive, to documentary or other information descriptive of the design of an explosive nor to equipment for control and firing of explosives. The Party carrying out the explosion shall not locate documentary or ·other information descriptive of the design of an explosive in such ways as to impede the designated personnel in the exercise of their rights and functions.

6. The number of designated personnel present at the site of an explosion shall not exceed:

(*a*) for the exercise of their rights and functions in connexion with the confirmation of the geographical and geophysical information in accordance with the provisions of subparagraph 2(*b*) and applicable provisions of paragraph 5 of Article III—the number of emplacement holes plus three;

(*b*) for the exercise of their rights and functions in connexion with confirming that the local circumstances are consistent with the information provided and with the stated peaceful purposes in accordance with the provisions in subparagraphs 2(*a*), 2(*c*), 2(*d*) and 2(*e*) and applicable provisions of paragraph 5 of Article III—the number of explosives plus two;

(*c*) for the exercise of their rights and functions in connexion with confirming that the local circumstances are consistent with the information provided and with the stated peaceful purposes in accordance with the provisions in subparagraphs 2(*a*), 2(*c*), 2(*d*) and 2(*e*) and applicable provisions of paragraph 5 of Article III and in connexion with the use of electrical equipment for determination of the yield in accordance with paragraph 3 of Article III—the number of explosives plus seven; and

(*d*) for the exercise of their rights and functions in connexion with confirming that the local circumstances are consistent with the information provided and with the stated peaceful purposes in accordance with the provisions in subparagraphs 2(*a*), 2(*c*), 2(*d*) and 2(*e*) and applicable provisions of paragraph 5 of Article III and in connexion with the use of electrical equipment for determination of the yield in accordance with paragraph 3 of Article III and with the use of the local seismic network in accordance with paragraph 4 of Article III—the number of explosives plus 10.

7. The Party carrying out the explosion shall have the right to assign its personnel to accompany designated personnel while the latter exercise their rights and functions.

8. The Party carrying out an explosion shall assure for designated personnel telecommunications with their authorities, transportation and other services appropriate to their presence and to the exercise of their rights and functions at the site of the explosion.

9. The expenses incurred for the transportation of designated personnel and their equipment to and from the site of the explosion, telecommunications provided for in paragraph 8 of this article, their living and working quarters, subsistence and all other personal expenses shall be the responsibility of the Party other than the Party carrying out the explosion.

10. Designated personnel shall consult with the Party carrying out the explosion in order to co-ordinate the planned programme and schedule of activities of designated personnel with the programme of the Party carrying out the explosion for the conduct of the project so as to ensure that designated personnel are able to conduct their activities in an orderly and timely way that is compatible with the implementation of the project. Procedures for such consultations shall be established in accordance with Article X.

Article VI

For any explosion with a planned aggregate yield exceeding 150 kilotons, determination of the yield of each explosive used shall be carried out in accordance with the following provisions:

1. Determination of the yield of each individual explosion in the group shall be based on measurements of the velocity of propagation, as a function of time, of the hydrodynamic shock wave generated by the explosion, taken by means of electrical equipment described in paragraph 3 of Article IV.

2. The Party carrying out the explosion shall provide the other Party with the following information:

(a) not later than 60 days before the beginning of emplacement of the explosives, the length of each canister in which the explosive will be contained in the corresponding emplacement hole, the dimensions of the tube or other device used to emplace the canister and the cross-sectional dimensions of the emplacement hole to a distance, in metres, from the emplacement point of 10 times the cube root of its yield in kilotons;

(b) not later than 60 days before the beginning of emplacement of the explosives, a description of materials, including their densities, to be used to stem each emplacement hole; and

(c) not later than 30 days before the beginning of emplacement of the explosives for each emplacement hole of a group explosion, the local co-ordinates of the point of emplacement of the explosive, the entrance of the emplacement hole, the point of the emplacement hole most distant from the entrance, the location of the emplacement hole at each 200 metres distance from the entrance and the configuration of any known voids larger than one cubic metre located within the distance, in metres, of 10 times the cube root of the planned yield in kilotons measured from the bottom of the canister containing the explosive. The error in these co-ordinates shall not exceed 1 per cent of the distance between the emplacement hole and the nearest other emplacement hole or 1 per cent of the distance between the point of measurement and the entrance of the emplacement hole, whichever is smaller, but in no case shall the error be required to be less than one metre.

3. The Party carrying out the explosion shall emplace for each explosive that portion of the electrical equipment for yield determination described in subparagraph 3(a) of Article IV, supplied in accordance with paragraph 1 of Article IV, in the same emplacement hole as the explosive in accordance with the installation instructions supplied under the provisions of paragraph 5 or 6 of Article IV. Such emplacement shall be carried out under the observation of designated personnel. Other equipment specified in subparagraph 3(b) of Article IV shall be emplaced and installed:

(a) by designated personnel under the observation and with the assistance of personnel of the Party carrying out the explosion, if such assistance is requested by designated personnel; or

(b) in accordance with paragraph 5 of Article IV.

4. That portion of the electrical equipment for yield determination described in subparagraph 3(a) of Article IV that is to be emplaced in each emplacement hole shall be located so that the end of the electrical equipment which is farthest from the entrance to the emplacement hole is at a distance, in metres, from the bottom of the canister, containing the explosive equal to 3.5 times the cube root of the planned yield in kilotons of the explosive when the planned yield is less than 20 kilotons and three times the cube root of the planned yield in kilotons of the explosive when the planned yield is 20 kilotons or more. Canisters longer than 10 metres containing the explosive shall only be utilized if there is prior agreement between the Parties establishing provisions for their use. The Party carrying out the explosions shall provide the other Party with data on the distribution of density inside any other canister in the emplacement hole with a transverse cross-sectional area exceeding 10 square centimetres located within a distance, in metres, of 10 times the cube root of the planned yield in kilotons of the explosion from the bottom of the canister containing the explosive. The Party carrying out the explosion shall provide the other Party with access to confirm such data on density distribution within any such canister.

5. The Party carrying out an explosion shall fill each emplacement hole, including all pipes and tubes contained therein which have at any transverse section an aggregate cross-sectional area exceeding 10 square centimetres in the region containing the electrical equipment for yield determination and to a distance, in metres, of six times the cube root of the planned yield in kilotons of the explosive from the explosive emplacement point, with material having a density not less than seven-tenths of the average density of the surrounding rock, and from that point to a distance of not less than 60 metres from the explosive emplacement point with material having a density greater than one gram per cubic centimetre.

6. Designated personnel shall have the right to:

(*a*) confirm information provided in accordance with subparagraph 2(*a*) of this article;

(*b*) confirm informtion provided in accordance with subparagraph 2(*b*) of this article and be provided, upon request, with a sample of each batch of stemming material as that material is put into the emplacement hole; and

(*c*) confirm the information provided in accordance with subparagraph 2(*c*) of this article by having access to the data acquired and by observing, upon their request, the making of measurements.

7. For those explosives which are emplaced in separate emplacement holes, the emplacement shall be such that the distance D, in metres, between any explosive and any portion of the electrical equipment for determination of the yield of any other explosive in the group shall be not less than 10 times the cube root of the planned yield in kilotons of the larger explosive of such a pair of explosives. Individual explosions shall be separated by time intervals, in milliseconds, not greater than one-sixth the amount by which the distance D, in metres, exceeds 10 times the cube root of the planned yield in kilotons of the larger explosive of such a pair of explosives.

8. For those explosives in a group which are emplaced in a common emplacement hole, the distance, in metres, between each explosive and any other explosive in that emplacement hole shall be not less than 10 times the cube root of the planned yield in kilotons of the larger explosive of such a pair of explosives, and the explosives shall be detonated in sequential order, beginning with the explosive farthest from the entrance to the emplacement hole, with the individual detonations separated by time intervals, in milliseconds, of not less than one times the cube root of the planned yield in kilotons of the largest explosive in this emplacement hole.

Article VII

1. Designated personnel with their personal baggage and their equipment as provided in Article IV shall be permitted to enter the territory of the Party carrying out the explosion at an entry port to be agreed upon by the Parties, to remain in the territory of the Party carrying out the explosion for the purpose of fulfilling their rights and functions provided for in the Treaty and this Protocol, and to depart from an exit port to be agreed upon by the Parties.

2. At all times while designated personnel are in the territory of the Party carrying out the explosion, their persons, property, personal baggage, archives and documents as well as their temporary official and living quarters shall be accorded the same privileges and immunities as provided in Articles 22, 23, 24, 29, 30, 31, 34 and 36 of the Vienna Convention on Diplomatic Relations of 1961 to the persons, property, personal baggage, archives and documents of diplomatic agents as well as to the premises of diplomatic missions and private residences of diplomatic agents.

3. Without prejudice to their privileges and immunities it shall be the duty of designated personnel to respect the laws and regulations of the State in whose territory the explosion is to be carried out insofar as they do not impede in any way whatsoever the proper exercising of their rights and functions provided for by the Treaty and this Protocol.

Article VIII

The Party carrying out an explosion shall have sole and exclusive control over and full responsibility for the conduct of the explosion.

Article IX

1. Nothing in the Treaty and this Protocol shall affect proprietary rights in information made available under the Treaty and this Protocol and in information which may be disclosed in preparation for and carrying out of explosions; however, claims to such proprietary rights shall not impede implementation of the provisions of the Treaty and this Protocol.

2. Public release of the information provided in accordance with Article II or publication of material using such information, as well as public release of the results of observation and measurements obtained by designated personnel, may take place only by agreement with the Party carrying out an explosion; however, the other Party shall have the right to issue statements after the explosion that do not divulge information in which the Party carrying out the explosion has rights which are referred to in paragraph 1 of this article.

Article X

The joint Consultative Commission shall establish procedures through which the Parties will, as appropriate, consult with each other for the purpose of ensuring efficient implementation of this Protocol.

AGREED STATEMENT

The Parties to the Treaty Between the

United States of America and the Union of Soviet Socialist Republics on Underground Nuclear Explosions for Peaceful Purposes, hereinafter referred to as the Treaty, agree that under subparagraph 2(*c*) of Article III of the Treaty:

(*a*) Development testing of nuclear explosives does not constitute a 'peaceful application' and any such development tests shall be carried out only within the boundaries of nuclear weapon test sites specified in accordance with the Treaty Between the United States of America and the Union of Soviet Socialist Republics on the Limitation of Underground Nuclear Weapon Tests;

(*b*) Associating test facilities, instrumentation or procedures related only to testing of nuclear weapons or their effects with any explosion carried out in accordance with the Treaty does not constitute a 'peaceful application'.

Source: Disarmament Conference documents CCD/496, 23 June 1976, and CCD/496/Corr. 1, 5 August 1976.

II. Other treaties

Antarctic Treaty

Signed at Washington, DC, on 1 December 1959; entered into force on 23 June 1961.

Excerpts:

. . .

Article I

1. Antarctica shall be used for peaceful purposes only. There shall be prohibited, *inter alia*, any measures of a military nature, such as the establishment of military bases and fortifications, the carrying out of military maneuvers, as well as the testing of any type of weapons.

2. The present Treaty shall not prevent the use of military personnel or equipment for scientific research or for any other peaceful purpose.

. . .

Article V

1. Any nuclear explosions in Antarctica and the disposal there of radioactive waste material shall be prohibited.

2. In the event of the conclusion of international agreements concerning the use of nuclear energy, including nuclear explosions and the disposal of radioactive waste material, to which all of the Contracting Parties whose representatives are entitled to participate in the meetings provided for under Article IX are parties, the rules established under such agreements shall apply in Antarctica.

. . .

Source: *Treaty Series*, Vol. 402 (United Nations, New York).

Treaty on principles governing the activities of states in the exploration and use of outer space, including the moon and other celestial bodies (Outer Space Treaty)

Signed at London, Moscow and Washington, DC, on 27 January 1967; entered into force on 10 October 1967.

Excerpt:

. . .

Article IV

States Parties to the Treaty undertake not to place in orbit around the earth any objects carrying nuclear weapons or any other kinds of weapons of mass destruction, install such weapons on celestial bodies, or station such weapons in outer space in any other manner.

The moon and other celestial bodies shall be used by all States Parties to the Treaty exclusively for peaceful purposes. The establishment of military bases, installations and fortifications, the testing of any type of weapons and the conduct of miiltary manoeuvres on celestial bodies shall be forbidden. The use of military personnel for scientific research or for any other peaceful purposes shall not be prohibited. The use of any equipment or facility necessary for peaceful exploration of the moon and other celestial bodies shall also not be prohibited.

. . .

———

Source: *Treaty Series*, Vol. 610 (United Nations, New York).

Treaty for the prohibition of nuclear weapons in Latin America (Treaty of Tlatelolco)

Signed at Mexico, Distrito Federal, on 14 February 1967; entered into force on 22 April 1968.

Excerpts:

. . .

Article 1. *Obligations*

1. The Contracting Parties hereby undertake to use exclusively for peaceful purposes the nuclear material and facilities which are under their jurisdiction, and to prohibit and prevent in their respective territories:

(*a*) The testing, use, manufacture, production or acquisition by any means whatsoever of any nuclear weapons, by the Parties themselves, directly or indirectly, on behalf of anyone else or in any other way, and

(*b*) The receipt, storage, installation, deployment and any form of possession of any nuclear weapons, directly or indirectly, by the Parties themselves, by anyone on their behalf or in any other way.

2. The Contracting Parties also undertake to refrain from engaging in, encouraging or authorizing, directly or indirectly, or in any way participating in the testing, use, manufacture, production, possession or control of any nuclear weapon.

. . .

Article 18. *Explosions for peaceful purposes*

1. The Contracting Parties may carry out explosions of nuclear devices for peaceful purposes—including explosions which involve devices similar to those used in nuclear weapons—or collaborate with third parties for the same purpose, provided that they do so in accordance with the provisions of this article

and the other articles of the Treaty, particularly articles 1 and 5.

2. Contracting Parties intending to carry out, or to co-operate in carrying out, such an explosion shall notify the Agency and the International Atomic Energy Agency, as far in advance as the circumstances require, of the date of the explosion and shall at the same time provide the following information:

(*a*) The nature of the nuclear device and the source from which it was obtained;

(*b*) The place and purpose of the planned explosion;

(*c*) The procedures which will be followed in order to comply with paragraph 3 of this article;

(*d*) The expected force of the device, and

(*e*) The fullest possible information on any possible radioactive fall-out that may result from the explosion or explosions, and measures which will be taken to avoid danger to the population, flora, fauna and territories of any other Party or Parties.

3. The General Secretary and the technical personnel designated by the Council and the International Atomic Energy Agency may observe all the preparations, including the explosion of the device, and shall have unrestricted access to any area in the vicinity of the site of the explosion in order to ascertain whether the device and the procedures followed during the explosion are in conformity with the information supplied under paragraph 2 of this article and the other provisions of this Treaty.

4. The Contracting Parties may accept the collaboration of third parties for the purpose set forth in paragraph 1 of the present article, in accordance with paragraphs 2 and 3 thereof.

. . .

———

Source: *Treaty Series*, Vol. 634 (United Nations, New York).

Treaty on the prohibition of the emplacement of nuclear weapons and other weapons of mass destruction on the seabed and the ocean floor and in the subsoil thereof (Seabed Treaty)

Signed at London, Moscow and Washington, DC, on 11 February 1971; entered into force on 18 May 1972.

Excerpt:

. . .

Article I

1. The States Parties to this Treaty undertake not to emplant or emplace on the seabed and the ocean floor and in the subsoil thereof beyond the outer limit of a seabed zone, as defined in article II, any nuclear weapons or any other types of weapons of mass destruction as well as structures, launching installations or any other facilities specifically designed for storing, testing or using such weapons.

2. The undertakings of paragraph 1 of this article shall also apply to the seabed zone referred to in the same paragraph, except that within such seabed zone, they shall not apply either to the coastal State or to the seabed beneath its territorial waters.

3. The States Parties to this Treaty undertake not to assist, encourage or induce any State to carry out activities referred to in paragraph 1 of this article and not to participate in any other way in such actions.

. . .

Source: *Treaties and Other International Acts, Series 7337* (US Department of State, Washington, DC, 1972).

Agreement governing the activities of states on the moon and other celestial bodies (Moon Treaty)

Opened for signature at New York on 18 December 1979; entered into force on 11 July 1984.

Excerpt:

. . .

Article 3

1. The moon shall be used by all States Parties exclusively for peaceful purposes.

2. Any threat or use of force or any other hostile act or threat of hostile act on the moon is prohibited. It is likewise prohibited to use the moon in order to commit any such act or to engage in any such threat in relation to the earth, the moon, spacecraft, the personnel of spacecraft or man-made space objects.

3. States Parties shall not place in orbit around or other trajectory to or around the moon objects carrying nuclear weapons or any other kinds of weapons of mass destruction or place or use such weapons on or in the moon.

4. The establishment of military bases, installations and fortifications, the testing of any type of weapons and the conduct of military manoeuvres on the moon shall be forbidden. The use of military personnel for scientific research or for any other peaceful purposes shall not be prohibited. The use of any equipment or facility necessary for peaceful exploration and use of the moon shall also not be prohibited.

. . .

Source: UN document, General Assembly Resolution 34/68, Annex.

South Pacific nuclear free zone treaty (Treaty of Rarotonga)

Signed at Rarotonga, Cook Islands, on 6 August 1985; entered into force on 11 December 1986.

Excerpt:

. . .

Article 6

Prevention of testing of nuclear explosive devices

Each Party undertakes:

(*a*) to prevent in its territory the testing of any nuclear explosive device;

(*b*) not to take any action to assist or encourage the testing of any nuclear explosive device by any State.

. . .

Source: Conference on Disarmament document CD/633, 16 Aug. 1985.

Annexe 2. Major proposals for a comprehensive test ban treaty

I. UK–USA–USSR: Tripartite Report to the Committee on Disarmament, 30 July 1980

1. This report on the status of the negotiations between the Union of Soviet Socialist Republics, the United Kingdom of Great Britain and Northern Ireland and the United States of America on a treaty prohibiting nuclear weapon test explosions in all environments and its protocol covering nuclear explosions for peaceful purposes has been jointly prepared by the three parties to the negotiations.

2. The three negotiating parties are well aware of the deep and long-standing commitment to the objective of this treaty that has been demonstrated by the Committee on Disarmament and its predecessor bodies. They recognize the strong and legitimate interest of the Committee on Disarmament in their activities, and they have reported to the Committee on Disarmament previously, most recently on 31 July 1979. They welcome the opportunity to do so again, just as they welcome the continued support and encouragement that their negotiations derive from the interest of the Committee on Disarmament.

3. Since the last report to the Committee on Disarmament, the three delegations have completed two rounds of negotiations. The negotiations reconvened on 16 July 1980.

4. The negotiating parties are seeking a treaty that for decades has been given one of the highest priorities in the field of arms limitation, and the Soviet Union, the United Kingdom and the United States continue to attach great importance to it. The desire to achieve an early agreement, which is so widely shared by the international community, has been repeatedly expressed at the highest level of all three governments.

5. Global interest in the cessation of nuclear weapon tests by all States has been recorded by a succession of resolutions of the United Nations General Assembly and by the Final Document of the Special Session on Disarmament of the United Nations General Assembly. It has been stated in the preambles to a number of international arms limitation treaties now in force, and its significance will again be underlined in the forthcoming second Review Conference of the Treaty on the Non-Proliferation of Nuclear Weapons.

6. The objectives which the negotiating parties seek to achieve as a result of this treaty are important to all mankind. Specifically, they seek to attain a treaty which will make a major contribution to the shared objectives of constraining the nuclear arms race, curbing the spread of nuclear weapons, and strengthening international peace and security.

7. Given the importance of these objectives, it is understandable that the international community has repeatedly called for the earliest possible conclusion of the treaty. At the same time, it is important to note that this treaty is, in many respects, a difficult one to negotiate. Many of the issues are novel, sensitive and intricate. The treaty directly affects vital national security concerns and the process of negotiation requires considerable and painstaking work.

8. In spite of these challenges, however, the Soviet Union, the United Kingdom and the United States have made considerable progress in negotiating the treaty.

9. The negotiating parties have agreed that the treaty will require each party to prohibit, prevent and not to carry out any nuclear weapon test explosion at any place under its jurisdiction or control in any environment; and to refrain from causing, encouraging or in any way participating in the carrying out of any nuclear weapon test explosion anywhere.

10. The negotiating parties have agreed that the treaty will be accompanied by a protocol on nuclear explosions for peaceful purposes, which will be an integral part of the treaty. The protocol will take into account the provisions of Article V of the Treaty on the Non-Prolifer-

ation of Nuclear Weapons. In the protocol, the parties will establish a moratorium on nuclear explosions for peaceful purposes and accordingly will refrain from causing, encouraging, permitting or in any way participating in, the carrying out of such explosions until arrangements for conducting them are worked out which would be consistent with the treaty being negotiated, the Treaty Banning Nuclear Weapon Tests in the Atmosphere, in Outer Space and Under Water and the Treaty on the Non-Proliferation of Nuclear Weapons. Without delay after entry into force of the treaty, the parties will keep under consideration the subject of arrangements for conducting nuclear explosions for peaceful purposes, including the aspect of precluding military benefits. Such arrangements, which could take the form of a special agreement or agreements, would be made effective by appropriate amendment to the protocol.

11. To ensure that the treaty does not detract from previous arms limitation agreements, there will be a provision stating that the treaty does not affect obligations compatible with it that have been assumed by parties under other international agreements. Such other agreements include the Treaty Banning Nuclear Weapon Tests in the Atmosphere, in Outer Space and Under Water and the Treaty on the Non-Proliferation of Nuclear Weapons. The three negotiating parties have agreed that the treaty will provide procedures for amendment, and that any amendments will require the approval of a majority of all parties, which majority shall include all parties that are permanent members of the Security Council of the United Nations. They have also agreed that, as in other arms limitation agreements, there will be provision for withdrawal from the treaty on the grounds of supreme national interests. They have also agreed that the treaty should enter into force upon ratification by twenty signatory governments, including those of the Soviet Union, the United Kingdom and the United States.

12. The parties are considering formulations relating to the duration of the treaty. They envisage that a conference will be held at an appropriate time to review the operation of the treaty. Decisions at the conference will require a majority of the parties to the treaty, which majority shall include all parties that are permanent members of the Security Council of the United Nations.

13. The negotiating parties, recognizing the importance of verification, have agreed that a variety of verification measures should be provided to enhance confidence that all parties to the treaty are in strict compliance with it. Such measures in the treaty itself, and the additional measures under negotiation to facilitate verification of compliance with the treaty, must first be agreed in principle, and then drafted in detail, which is of course a laborious process. It must be done with care because the implementation of these measures will have important impact not only on ensuring compliance with the treaty, but also on political relations among its parties.

14. It has been agreed that the parties will use national technical means of verification at their disposal in a manner consistent with generally recognized principles of international law to verify compliance with the treaty, and that each party will undertake not to interfere with such means of verification.

15. It has long been recognized that cooperative seismic monitoring measures can make an important contribution to verifying compliance with the treaty. The Committee on Disarmament and its predecessors have played a leading role in developing such measures. On the basis of the work done in the past few years under those auspices, the negotiating parties have agreed to provisions establishing an International Exchange of Seismic Data. Each treaty party will have the right to participate in this exchange, to contribute data from designated seismic stations on its territory, and to receive all the seismic data made available through the International Exchange. Seismic data will be transmitted through the Global Telecommunications System of the World Meteorological Organization or through other agreed communications channels. International seismic data centres will be established in agreed locations, taking into account the desirability of appropriate geographical distribution.

16. A Committee of Experts will be established to consider questions related to the International Seismic Data Exchange and all treaty parties will be entitled to appoint representatives to participate in the work of the Committee. The Committee of Experts will be responsible for developing detailed arrangements for establishing and operating the International Exchange, drawing on the recommendations of the *Ad Hoc* Group of Scientific Experts, which was established under the auspices of the Conference of the Committee on Disarmament and has continued its work under the Committee on Disarmament. Arrangements for establishing and operating the International Exchange will include the development of standards for the technical and operational characteristics of participating seismic stations and international seismic data centres, for the form in which data are transmit-

ted to the centres, and for the form and manner in which the centres make seismic data available to the participants and respond to their requests for additional seismic data regarding specified seismic events.

17. In addition to its role in setting up the International Exchange, the Committee of Experts will have ongoing responsibility for facilitating the implementation of the International Exchange, for reviewing its operation and considering improvements to it, and for considering technological developments that have a bearing on its operation. The Committee will serve as a forum in which treaty parties may exchange technical information and co-operate in promoting the effectiveness of the International Exchange. The Committee of Experts will hold its first meeting not later than 90 days after the entry into force of the treaty and will meet thereafter as it determines.

18. The negotiating parties have agreed to other co-operative measures as well. There will be provision in the treaty for direct consultations, and for the exchange of inquiries and responses among treaty parties in order to resolve questions that may arise concerning treaty compliance. If a party has questions regarding an event on the territory of any other party, it may request an on-site inspection for the purpose of ascertaining whether or not the event was a nuclear explosion. The requesting party shall state the reasons for its request, including appropriate evidence. The party which receives the request, understanding the importance of ensuring confidence among parties that treaty obligations are being fulfilled, shall state whether or not it is prepared to agree to an inspection. If the party which receives the request is not prepared to agree to an inspection on its territory, it shall provide the reasons for its decision. Tripartite agreement on these general conditions with regard to on-site inspections represents an important achievement by the negotiating parties in resolving issues regarding verification of compliance with the treaty.

19. The three negotiating parties believe that the verification measures being negotiated—particularly the provisions regarding the International Exchange of Seismic Data, the Committee of Experts, and on-site inspections—break significant new ground in international arms limitation efforts and will give all treaty parties the opportunity to participate in a substantial and constructive way in the process of verifying compliance with the treaty.

20. The treaty will also contain a provision permitting any two or more treaty parties, because of special concerns or circumstances, to agree by mutual consent upon additional measures to facilitate verification of compliance with the treaty. The three negotiating parties have agreed that it is necessary to develop such additional measures for themselves in connexion with the treaty under negotiation.

21. The additional measures to facilitate verification of compliance with the treaty, while paralleling those of the treaty itself, will specify in greater detail the procedures under which on-site inspection would be conducted, and will incorporate a list of the rights and functions of the personnel carrying out the inspection. They will also contain a description of the role to be played by the host party during an inspection.

22. In addition, the three parties are negotiating an exchange of supplemental seismic data. This would involve the installation and use by the three parties of high-quality national seismic stations of agreed characteristics.

23. Despite significant accomplishments, there are important areas where substantial work is still to be done.

24. The three negotiating parties have demonstrated their strong political commitment to completion of this treaty by achieving solutions to problems that for many years made a treaty difficult to attain. Most notable in this regard are the agreements concerning the prohibition of any nuclear weapon test explosion in any environment, the moratorium on nuclear explosions for peaceful purposes, the general conditions with regard to on-site inspections, and a number of important seismic verification issues.

25. The negotiating parties are mindful of the great value for all mankind that the prohibition of nuclear weapon test explosions in all environments will have, and they are conscious of the important responsibility placed upon them to find solutions to the remaining problems. The three negotiating parties have come far in their pursuit of a sound treaty and continue to believe that their trilateral negotiations offer the best way forward. They are determined to exert their best efforts and necessary will and persistence to bring the negotiations to an early and successful conclusion.

Source: Committee on Disarmament document CD/130, 30 July 1980.

II. Sweden: Draft treaty banning any nuclear weapon test explosion in any environment, 14 June 1983

The States Parties to this Treaty,

Declaring their intention to achieve at the earliest possible date the cessation of the nuclear arms race and to undertake effective measures towards nuclear disarmament,

Urging the co-operation of all States in the attainment of this objective,

Have agreed as follows:

Article I

1. Each Party to this Treaty undertakes not to carry out any nuclear weapon test explosion in any environment at any place under its jurisdiction or control.

2. Each Party to this Treaty undertakes, furthermore, to refrain from causing, encouraging, assisting, permitting or in *any* other way participating in the carrying out of any nuclear weapon test explosion anywhere.

3. Each Party to this Treaty undertakes to take any measures it considers necessary in accordance with its constitutional process to prohibit and prevent any activity in violation of the provisions of the Treaty anywhere under its jurisdiction or control.

Article II

1. Each Party to this Treaty undertakes not to carry out any nuclear explosion for peaceful purposes and accordingly to refrain from causing, encouraging, assisting, permitting or in any other way participating in the carrying out of any such explosion until international arrangements for conducting them are worked out which would be consistent with this Treaty and the obligations of each Party under other relevant international treaties.

2. The Parties undertake to keep under consideration the question of arrangements for conducting nuclear explosions for peaceful purposes on a non-discriminatory basis, including the aspect of precluding military benefits. Such arrangements may take the form of a special agreement or agreements constituting an integral part of this Treaty.

Article III

This Treaty does not affect obligations which have been assumed by Parties under other international agreements, including the Treaty banning nuclear weapon tests in the atmosphere, in outer space and under water.

Article IV

1. Each Party to this Treaty will use national technical means of verificaton at its disposal in a manner consistent with generally recognized principles of international law to verify compliance with the Treaty and undertakes not to interfere with such means of verification.

2. Each Party to this Treaty undertakes to co-operate in good faith in an effective international exchange of seismological data in order to facilitate the monitoring of this Treaty.

Each Party to this Treaty undertakes to co-operate in good faith in order to achieve an effective international exchange of data on atmospheric radioactivity and other measures for facilitating the monitoring of this Treaty.

The arrangements for these international co-operative measures, which are laid down in Protocol I annexed to this Treaty, shall be operative at the time of the entry into force of this Treaty.

3. The Parties to this Treaty undertake to consult one another and to co-operate in good faith for the clarification of all events pertaining to the subject matter of this Treaty. In accordance with this provision, each Party to the Treaty is entitled:

(*a*) to request and receive information from any other Party;

(*b*) to request an on-site inspection in the territory of any other Party for the purpose of ascertaining whether or not a specified event was a nuclear explosion. The requesting Party shall state the reasons for its request, including available evidence. Recognizing the importance of ensuring confidence among Parties that treaty obligations are being fulfilled, the Party which receives the request shall state whether or not it is prepared to agree to an inspection. If the Party which receives the request does not agree to an inspection in its territory, it shall state the reason for its refusal. Procedures for such inspections and the manner of their conduct, including the rights and functions of the inspecting personnel, are laid down in Protocol II annexed to this Treaty.

4. In order to avoid unfounded accusations or misinterpretations of large non-nuclear explosions the Party conducting such an explosion may invite an inspection at the site of the explosion. The rules and procedures for such inspections are laid down in Protocol II.

5. For the purpose set forth in this article a Consultative Committee shall be established to

oversee the implementation of the Treaty and of the international verification arrangements. A Technical Expert Group and a permanent Secretariat shall be established to assist the Consultative Committee. The functions and rules of procedure of the Consultative Committee, the Technical Expert Group and the Secretariat are set out in Protocol III annexed to this Treaty.

Article V

The Protocols annexed to this Treaty constitute an integral part of the Treaty.

Article VI

Any Party may propose amendments to this Treaty. Such proposals shall be submitted to the Depositary, who shall, in consultation with States Parties, take appropriate action. Amendments shall enter into force for each Party accepting them upon their acceptance by a majority of the Parties to the Treaty and thereafter for each remaining Party on the date of acceptance by it.

Article VII

Five years after the entry into force of this Treaty, a conference of Parties to the Treaty shall be held in Geneva, Switzerland, in order to review the operation of this Treaty with a view to assuring that the purposes of the preamble and the provisions of the Treaty are being realized. At intervals of five years thereafter, a majority of the Parties to the Treaty may obtain, by submitting a proposal to this effect to the Depositary, the convening of further conferences with the same objective of reviewing the operation of the Treaty.

Article VIII

1. This Treaty shall be open to all States for signature. Any State which does not sign the Treaty before its entry into force in accordance with paragraph 3 of this article may accede to it at any time.
2. This Treaty shall be subject to ratification by signatory States. Instruments of ratification and instruments of accession shall be deposited with the Secretary-General of the United Nations, who shall be the Depositary of this Treaty.
3. This Treaty shall enter into force upon the deposit with the Depositary of instruments of ratification by twenty Governments, including the Governments of the United States of America, the United Kingdom of Great Britain and Northern Ireland and the Union of Soviet Socialist Republics.
4. For those States whose instruments of ratification or accession are deposited after the entry into force of this Treaty it shall enter into force on the date of the deposit of their instruments of ratification or accession.
5. The Depositary shall promptly inform all signatory and acceding States of the date of each signature, the date of deposit of each instrument of ratification or of accession and the date of the entry into force of this Treaty and of any amendments thereto, any notice of withdrawal, as well as of the receipt of other notices. He shall also inform the Security Council of the United Nations of any notice of withdrawal.
6. This Treaty shall be registered by the Depositary in accordance with Article 102 of the Charter of the United Nations.

Article IX

This Treaty shall be of unlimited duration. Each Party shall in exercising its national sovereignty have the right to withdraw from the Treaty, if it decides that extraordinary events, related to the subject matter of this Treaty, have jeopardized the supreme interests of its country. It shall give notice of such withdrawal to the Depositary three months in advance. Such notice shall include a statement of the extraordinary events it regards as having jeopardized its supreme interests.

Article X

If this Treaty has not been adhered to by all Permanent Members of the United Nations Security Council five years after its entry into force, each Party shall by giving notice to the Depositary have the right to withdraw from the Treaty with immediate effect.

Article XI

1. This Treaty, of which the Arabic, Chinese, English, French, Russian and Spanish texts are equally authentic, shall be deposited with the Secretary-General of the United Nations who shall send certified copies thereof to the Governments of the signatory and acceding States.

PROTOCOL I

International co-operative measures to facilitate

the verification of a Treaty banning any nuclear weapon test explosion in any environment

1. Each Party to this Treaty undertakes to co-operate in good faith in an effective international exchange of seismological and other data. The purpose of these international measures is to assist the Parties in the verification of the Treaty by providing additional technical information for their national assessment. These international co-operative measures include designated seismological stations in participating countries and in other territories, efficient systems for the exchange of seismological data, and especially established International Data Centres.

2. Each Party to this Treaty shall have the right to participate in the international exchange of seismological data by contributing data from designated seismological stations and by receiving all the seismological data made available through the international exchange. To ensure that seismological stations having the necessary geographical coverage will be incorporated in the exchange, the States given in table 1 have agreed to provide data from the stations specified in the same table.

Each Party participating in the international data exchange shall provide geographical co-ordinates, geological site description and a description of the instrumentation of each designated station. Any changes in these data shall be immediately reported. Data on designated stations are collected, compiled and regularly reported by the Secretariat of the Consultative Committee.

3. Each Party participating in the international data exchange shall for this purpose designate an appropriate National Body through which it will communicate.

This body shall handle the exchange of seismological data and contacts with International Data Centres, the Consultative Committee and its Secretariat on matters related to the operation of the data exchange.

4. The seismological stations designated for participation in the international exchange shall have the basic equipment as specified in the Operational Manual for Seismological Stations. These stations shall be operated, calibrated and maintained as specified in the same manual. Information on the operation and the calibration of the stations shall regularly be sent to the Secretariat of the Consultative Committee.

5. Seismological data from each designated station shall routinely and regularly be reported through the appropriate National Body. The seismological data to be reported, the reporting format and time schedule are specified in the

Operational Manual for Data Exchange. The seismological stations shall, through the appropriate National Body, co-operate with the International Data Centres to clarify any technical question in connection with reported data.

In addition to routinely submitted data each Party participating in the international data exchange shall provide any additional seismological data from its designated stations requested through International Data Centres by any Party to the Treaty. The procedures for making such requests and the format and time schedule for responding are laid down in the Operational Manual for Data Exchange.

6. Seismological data shall be transmitted through the Global Telecommunication System of the World Meteorological Organization, WMO/GTS, or through other agreed communication channels. The detailed procedures for exchanging data are laid down in the Operational Manual on Data Exchange.

7. International Data Centres shall be established at the following locations:

. . .

Each Centre shall be under the jurisdiction of the State in whose territory it is located, and the cost of establishing and operating it shall be borne by that State. Easy and free access for representatives from all Parties to the Treaty and for Officers of the Secretariat of the Consultative Committee shall be guaranteed to all facilities of all International Data Centres.

Each International Data Centre shall receive all seismological data contributed to the international exchange by its participants, process these seismological data without interpreting the nature of seismological events, make the processed seismological data available to all participants and maintain all seismological data contributed by participants as well as the results of the processing at the Centres. The procedures to be used at International Data Centres to receive and compile reported data, to conduct necessary computation, to interact with other International Data Centres in the analysis and to transmit the results of the computations to participating States are laid down in the Operational Manual for International Data Centres.

International Data Centres shall also co-ordinate requests for additional seismological data from one Party to another and redistribute data obtained as a result of such requests.

8. In addition to the exchange of seismological data specified in paragraphs 2–7 of this Protocol, a similar exchange of data on atmospheric radioactivity shall be established. This exchange shall include equipment for collecting

atmospheric radioactivity operated by each contributing State, an exchange of collected data and International Data Centres where data are processed, compiled and redistributed as described in paragraph 7 of this Protocol. The additional rules and procedures needed to establish and operate this exchange, are laid down in an Operational Manual for the Exchange of Atmospheric Radioactivity.

9. International Co-operative Measures described in this Protocol and in the Operational Manuals annexed to it, shall be established and be operative at the time of entry into force of this Treaty.

10. The Consultative Committee and its Secretariat have the task of overseeing the over-all operation of the international data exchange as is set forth in Protocol III.

The Committee, its Technical Expert Group and Secretariat have the responsibility to maintain the efficiency of the exchange by improving and amending the equipment and the operational procedures. The Parties to the Treaty undertake to implement such changes of the data exchange which may be agreed upon.

11. With a view to improving the verification of this Treaty, negotiations on additional international measures such as the exchange of data on atmospheric radioactivity, hydro-acoustic signals in the oceans and infrasound and microbarographic signals in the atmosphere, shall be undertaken by the Parties to the Treaty. Such additional measures shall as closely as possible be integrated in the co-operative measures specified in this Protocol and an agreement on such additional measures shall be annexed to this Protocol.

TABLE I

(Text to be elaborated.)

PROTOCOL II

Procedures for International On-Site Inspection

1. The Parties to this Treaty undertake to consult one another and to co-operate in good faith for the clarification of all events pertaining to the subject-matter of this Treaty. If any Party sees the need to further clarify any event observed in the territory of another Party to the Treaty it shall seek such clarification through bilateral consultations. These consultations may include the exchange of additional technical information and other measures, such as on-site inspections, which the two Parties concerned may agree upon.

If the event cannot be satisfactorily clarified through such bilateral consultations, the Party seeking further clarification can request an international on-site inspection. Requests for such international on-site inspection shall be made through the Consultative Committee. The requesting Party shall state the reasons for its request, including appropriate technical and other evidence.

The requesting Party shall further specify the area to be inspected. This area must be continuous and not exceed 1000 km^2 or a length of 50 km in any direction.

2. If a Party receiving a request agrees to an international on-site inspection of the requested area, or part thereof, the practical arrangements for the inspection shall be worked out by the Secretariat of the Consultative Committee in co-operation with the Party to be inspected. Such arrangements shall be worked out within one month after a Party has agreed to an inspection. The inspection shall be conducted by experts chosen by the Chairman of the Consultative Committee among experts made available for this purpose by the Parties to the Treaty. The experts shall be selected taking into account available expertise and the desire to obtain equitable geographical and political representation. The International Inspection Team shall be headed by an officer from the Secretariat and contain . . . additional experts. The International Inspection Team shall further comprise necessary technicians, interpreters and secretaries provided by the Secretariat.

The total number of such support personnel shall not exceed . . . .

At all times while the inspecting personnel are in the territory of the Party to be inspected, their persons, property, personal baggage, archives and documents as well as their temporary official and living quarters shall be accorded the same privileges and immunities as provided in Articles 22, 23, 24, 29, 30, 31, 34 and 36 of the Vienna Convention on Diplomatic Relations to the persons, property, personal baggage, archives and documents of diplomatic agents as well as to the premises of diplomatic missions and private residences of diplomatic agents.

Without prejudice to their privileges and immunities it shall be the duty of the inspecting personnel to respect the laws and regulations of the State in whose territory the inspection is to be carried out, in so far as they do not impede in any way whatsoever the proper exercising of the rights and functions provided for by the Treaty and this Protocol.

3. The purpose of an international on-site inspection is purely fact-finding and the International Inspection Team shall not make any assessment as to the nature of the inspected event. The Inspection Team shall present a

factual report of the observations made during the inspection. This report shall as far as possible present the consensus view of the participating experts. In case consensus cannot be achieved, the report shall reflect the views of all the participating experts.

The report shall be made available to all Parties to the Treaty through the Consultative Committee.

4. (This paragraph should contain a specification of the techniques to be used and the procedures to be followed when conducting on-site inspections. As these issues have not been properly discussed, there is at preent no basis for preparing an appropriate text. To facilitate further discussions some more or less intrusive techniques are presented that might be considered in connection with on-site inspections. More technical data must be collected and compiled on the various inspection techniques and their potential usefulness. Rules and procedures have to be worked out for the conduct of these inspections, for the selection and the acceptance or refusal of more intrusive techniques and for the transportation of people and material.

The following inspection techniques might be useful to consider:
- —visual inspection from the air and on the ground including rules and procedures for taking photographs;
- —measurement of radioactive radiation in the atmosphere above the area, at ground level and in waters;
- —temporary seismological measurements in the area to record possible aftershocks and also events at larger distances to improve the possibilities to interpret the recordings of the event that led to the inspection;
- —seismological reflection measurements, in limited areas, to provide data for detection of possible subsurface activities;
- —measurement of temperature anomalies;
- —drilling and measurements in boreholes to obtain subsurface data at selected points.)

5. If the Party which receives the request does not agree to the inspection of the requested area or part of it, it shall provide the reasons for its decision.

6. As stated in Article IV, paragraph 4, of this Treaty, a Party conducting a large non-nuclear explosion may invite an inspection at the site of the explosion. An Inspection Team, established as in paragraph 2 of this Protocol and headed by an officer of the Secretariat of the Consultative Committee, containing . . . experts, shall be established. The privileges and immunities of members of this Inspection Team shall be the same as specified in paragraph 2 of this Protocol. The Inspection Team shall be

present before the explosion takes place and stay until the explosion has been conducted. Only visual observations shall be made. The Inspection Team shall provide a factual report of the observations during the inspection. This report shall be distributed to all Parties to the Treaty.

PROTOCOL III

The Consultative Committee, its functions and rules of procedures

1. A Consultative Committee shall be established to oversee the over-all functioning of the Treaty and its verification arrangements. The Consultative Committee shall also serve as a forum to discuss and resolve disputes concerning the Treaty and its verification arrangements which might occur between Parties to the Treaty. The Consultative Committee and its subsidiary bodies, the Technical Expert Group and the Secretariat shall be established when the Treaty enters into force.

In performing its duties the Consultative Committee shall:
- —oversee the implementation of the Treaty;
- —prepare review conferences in accordance with Article VII of this Treaty;
- —review the verification arrangements of the Treaty on the basis of material provided by the Technical Expert Group and the Secretariat;
- —decide on changes in the equipment and technical procedures used to verify compliance with the Treaty;
- —be a forum in which any Party can make inquiries and receive information as a result of such inquiries;
- —be a forum in which any Party can request an international on-site inspection and the factual results of such inspections are presented;
- —guide and oversee the work of the Technical Expert Group and the Secretariat;
- —decide on the annual budget of the Secretariat and elect the Director and the Deputy Director of the Secretariat.

2. Each Party to the Treaty shall have the right to be a member of the Consultative Committee.

3. The Depositary of the Treaty or his representative shall act as Chairman of the Consultative Committee.

4. The Committee shall meet annually and, in addition, upon the request of any Party when an extraordinary meeting is considered necessary to oversee the implementation of the Treaty or to settle disputes between Parties to the Treaty concerning its compliance.

The Consultative Committee shall work on the basis of consensus on the following matters;
—review and analysis of the over-all operation of the Treaty and its verification arrangements;
—decisions on changes in the equipment and technical procedures used to verify compliance with the Treaty.

The Consultative Committee shall take decisions by a majority of the members present and voting on the following issues:
—decisions on the annual budget of the Secretariat;
—election of the Director and the Deputy Director of the Secretariat.

5. The Consultative Committee shall establish a Technical Expert Group open to governmental experts from all Parties to the Treaty. The Technical Expert Group shall evaluate the technical performance of the international verification measures, including the techniques and procedures for on-site inspections, propose changes in the equipment and technical procedures used to verify compliance with the Treaty and to undertake any technical studies that the Consultative Committee may request. The Technical Expert Group shall further be a forum for technical discussions of events for which a Party seeks clarification through international measures.

The Technical Expert Group shall meet at least once a year. The Group shall establish its own rules of procedure and elect its own Chairman. The Group shall try to achieve consensus. In case consensus cannot be achieved, reports from the Group shall reflect the views of all the participating experts.

The Technical Expert Group shall report to the Consultative Committee on an annual basis or when requested.

6. To support the work of the Consultative Committee and the Technical Expert Group a permanent Secretariat shall be established.

The Secretariat shall:
—support the work of the Consultative Committee and the Technical Expert Group by organizing their meetings and by preparing requested background material and studies;
—supervise that the participating seismological stations are operated and data are reported as specified in paragraphs 4 and 5 of Protocol I of this Treaty;
—act as a contact with the WMO on matters of Data Exchange through its Global Telecommunications System and supervise and review, in co-operation with WMO, the data exchange specified in paragraph 6 of Protocol I of this Treaty;
—supervise the operation of the International Data Centres to ascertain that these Centres are established and operated as specified in paragraph 7 of Protocol I of this Treaty;
—supervise the exchange of data on atmospheric radioactivity to ascertain that the exchange is established and conducted as specified in paragraph 8 of Protocol I of this Treaty;
—compile and present operational statistics and reports on experiences of the International Data Exchange to the Technical Expert Group;
—organize and conduct international on-site inspections as specified in Protocol II of this Treaty, and report the result of such inspections to the Consultative Committee;
—maintain lists, in co-operation with the Parties to the Treaty, of international experts available to conduct on-site inspections and the equipment necessary for such inspections.

7. The Secretariat shall consist of a Director and a Deputy Director, elected for a period of four years by the Consultative Committee, as specified in paragraph 2 of this Protocol, and an appropriate number of officers and support personnel. The annual budget of the Secretariat shall be approved by the Consultative Committee, as specified in paragraph 2 of this Protocol. The cost shall be borne by the Parties to the Treaty in accordance with the United Nations assessment scale prorated to take into account differences between the United Nations membership and the number of Parties to this Treaty. The Secretariat shall be located at . . . .

Source: Committee on Disarmament document CD/381*, 14 June 1983.

III. Group of Socialist Countries: Basic provisions of a treaty on the complete and general prohibition of nuclear weapon tests, 8 June 1987

A. General provisions

1. The complete and general prohibition of nuclear weapon tests is in itself an important measure facilitating progress toward the limi-

tation, reduction and complete elimination of nuclear arms.

2. The prohibition of nuclear weapon tests by the Soviet Union and the United States of America, the States which possess the greatest nuclear potentials, is an important step toward general and complete prohibition of such tests. They must be joined by the other nuclear Powers if the main objective of the Treaty is to be attained and its universal nature genuinely ensured.

3. The States Parties to the Treaty are guided by a desire to complement and develop the regime established by the Treaty Banning Nuclear Weapon Tests in the Atmosphere, in Outer Space and under Water of 5 August 1963, which would be consistent with the determination expressed in that Treaty to achieve the discontinuance of all test explosions of nuclear weapons for all time, and to that end to prohibit such explosions in the only remaining environment, i.e. underground.

4. When all nuclear weapons have been completely eliminated the Treaty will serve as a safeguard against the reappearance of this kind of weapon in the future and an important element in the comprehensive system of international security.

B. Scope of the prohibition

1. Each State Party to this Treaty shall undertake to prohibit, to prevent, and not to carry out any nuclear weapon test explosions at any place under its jurisdiction or control, in all environments—in the atmosphere, in outer space, under water or underground.

2. No Party shall cause, encourage or in any way participate in the conduct of any nuclear weapon test explosions anywhere.

3. Provision should be made for the formulation of a provision preventing the ban on nuclear weapon test explosions from being circumvented by means of peaceful nuclear explosions.

C. Termination of activities at nuclear weapon test ranges

I. Declarations

Thirty days after the entry into force of the Treaty, the States Parties shall declare the locations of the test ranges for nuclear weapon test explosions in their territory or under their control, including the geographical co-ordinates of nuclear weapon test sites.

II. Termination of activities at nuclear weapon test ranges

On the day of the entry into force of the Treaty, each State Party to the Treaty shall terminate all activities related to nuclear weapon test explosions at its test ranges.

D. Ensuring compliance with the Treaty

I. General provisions on verification

Effective comprehensive verification of strict and unfailing fulfilment by the Parties of their obligations under the Treaty shall be carried out using national technical means of verification, international verification measures and on-site inspection.

II. National technical means of verification

1. For the purpose of verifying the implementation of this Treaty, each State Party to this Treaty shall use the national technical means of verification which it has at its disposal in a manner consistent with the generally recognized norms of international law, and undertakes not to interfere with such means of verification of other States Parties to this Treaty.

2. States Parties to this Treaty which possess national technical means of verification shall place the information which they obtained through those means, and which is important for the purposes of this Treaty, at the disposal of the appropriate organ established under the Treaty, and may, where necessary, place it at the disposal of other Parties.

III. International verification measures

International system of seismic verification

1. For the purpose of better assuring compliance with obligations under this Treaty, the States Parties shall establish an international system of seismic verification.

2. To this end, a network of seismic stations with standard specifications shall be established on the territory under the jurisdiction or control of the States Parties to the Treaty, to ensure the continuous international exchange of level II seismic data in accordance with agreed guidelines which will form an integral part of the Treaty.

3. These stations shall operate with the participation of observers from among the members of an international inspectorate.

The number, location, main performance characteristics and general principles of operation of such stations shall be subject to agreement.

International exchange of data on atmospheric radioactivity

1. For the purpose of better assuring compliance with obligations under the Treaty, each State Party to this Treaty undertake to co-operate in good faith in an international exchange of data on atmospheric radioactivity.

2. To this end, the States Parties to this Treaty shall establish, on the territory under their jurisdiction or control, aerosol monitoring stations to ensure the international exchange of data on atmospheric radioactivity in accordance with agreed guidelines which will form an integral part of this Treaty.

IV. Ensuring the non-functioning of nuclear weapon test ranges

Verification that no nuclear explosions are conducted at test ranges shall be carried out by national personnel with the participation of international inspectors in accordance with agreed procedures.

V. On-site inspection

1. For the purpose of clarifying and resolving questions which give rise to doubt as to compliance with the Treaty and which cannot be eliminated by means of the other verification measures provided for in the Treaty, each State Party shall have the right to request an on-site inspection in the territory of another State Party, citing appropriate grounds for the request.

2. The State so requested will be obligated to grant access to the locations specified in the request for the purpose of an inspection at the site of the event whose status is unclear, in order to clarify whether it was related to a nuclear explosion carried out in circumvention of the provisions of this Treaty.

3. Criteria and procedures for requesting such inspections, and rules for conducting them, shall be elaborated, including a list of the rights and functions of the inspecting personnel.

VI. Treaty organs

1. For the purpose of effective implementation of this Treaty, there shall be established appropriate organs, including an international inspectorate, whose functions will be specified in the annex to this Treaty.

2. A method of decision-making in the Treaty organs is to be agreed upon which will ensure that decisions are taken on a mutually acceptable basis and within a short time where necessary.

E. Concluding provisions of the Treaty

1. The Treaty shall be of unlimited duration. It shall enter into force upon ratification by . . . States, including the USSR and the United States of America.

Five years after the entry into force of the Treaty, a conference of the States Parties to the Treaty shall be convened to review the operation of the Treaty and to consider whether it should remain in effect if other nuclear Powers have not acceded thereto over the five-year period.

2. Provision should be made for a procedure for the signing and ratification of the Treaty, for the depositary, for accession by States to, and withdrawal from, the Treaty, for amendment and for review conferences.

Source: Conference on Disarmament document CD/756*, 17 June 1987.

Annexe 3. Seismological means of nuclear test ban verification: techniques and equipment

Eva Johannisson

National Defence Research Institute (FOA), Stockholm, Sweden

I. Introduction

Seismology provides an efficient tool for detecting underground nuclear explosions and distinguishing them from earthquakes. When a nuclear explosion detonates underground, this generates ground vibrations similar to those from an earthquake. These vibrations, or seismic waves, travel through the earth and can be observed by sensitive seismographs at great distances from the source.

Highly sensitive seismograph stations and several so-called array stations have been set up to improve the capability to detect and identify underground nuclear explosions. Recordings of ground vibrations caused by nuclear explosions have been carried out since the first underground nuclear test was conducted in 1957.

Research on nuclear test ban verification has significantly contributed to the understanding of seismic waves and the mechanisms of earthquakes and thus to a better understanding of the interior of the earth.

The purpose of this annexe is to provide the reader with the fundamental concepts of seismology which are relevant to the problems of verification of a test ban treaty. Seismic waves and the instruments and equipment used to observe such waves are briefly described. The fundamental seismological detection and identification techniques are also discussed.

II. Earthquakes

The occurrence of seismic activity and the properties of seismic waves are determined by the structure of the interior of the earth. The sections or layers of the earth can be divided into the crust, the mantle and the core. The crust and the solid outer parts of the mantle, down to a depth of about 100 km, form the lithosphere. Present models of the lithospheric layer, which consists of a small number of rigid plates in relative movement, explain many characteristics of earthquakes. Most earthquakes are concentrated in zones along the plate boundaries, and only a small fraction of them originate within the plates (see figure 1).

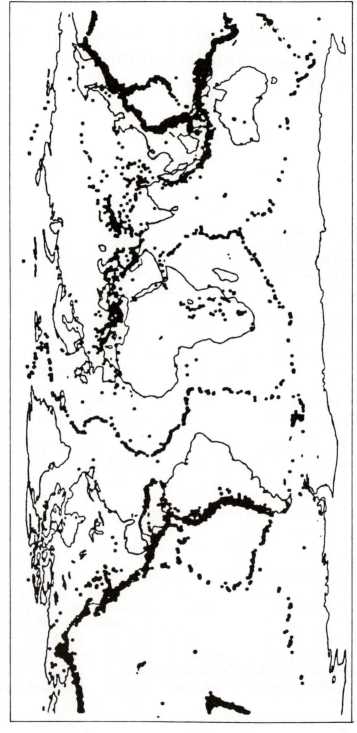

Figure 1. World seismicity for a six-year period (1969–74) with body wave magnitudes larger than 4.0 and focal depths between 0 and 100 km

Epicentres are reported by the US Geological Survey.

The source of an earthquake can be related to accumulated stress within the earth. As the elastic strength of the material in the source region is exceeded, the stored energy is released and transformed into frictional heat and into various elastic waves. The energy release occurs in a narrow zone along a pre-existing or new geological fault. The focus (or hypocentre) of an earthquake is defined as the point where the energy release originates; the epicentre is the point on the earth's surface immediately above the focus.

III. Explosions

The main test sites where nuclear explosions are conducted are the Nevada Test Site in the USA, Novaya Zemlya and Eastern Kazakhstan in the USSR, Lop Nor in China and the French test site on the Polynesian island of Mururoa. India has conducted one nuclear test claimed to be for civil application. The Soviet Union has conducted about 100 nuclear explosions outside the test areas, presumably for civil purposes. A map showing the main test sites used today is given in figure 2.

The geometry of an explosion source is usually described by the surface of an elastic sphere. As the pressure of the explosion shock wave acts on the surface of the sphere, seismic waves are generated. If the sphere is truly symmetric, only compressional waves with constant amplitude in all directions are generated. For such a model, the initial ground motion of the compressional waves recorded at the surface of the earth should be directed upwards.

Figure 2. The main test sites where nuclear explosions are currently conducted: the Nevada Test Site in the USA, Novaya Zemlya and Semipalatinsk (Eastern Kazakhstan) in the USSR, Lop Nor in China and the French test site at Mururoa

IV. Seismic waves

There are two main types of seismic wave generated from earthquakes and explosions: body waves and surface waves.

Body waves travel through the interior of the earth over large distances, and may be detected by seismograph stations up to 10 000 kilometres from the source. The principal types of body wave are compressional waves and shear waves, which differ according to the particle motion involved.

Compressional waves, or P- (primary) waves, and shear waves, or S- (secondary) waves, are characterized by different propagation velocities and by different direction of particle motion relative to the direction of wave propagation. For P-waves, the particle motion in the medium coincides with the direction of wave propagation, as is the case with ordinary sound waves. For S-waves, the particles in the medium move in a plane that is perpendicular to the direction in which the wave propagates. The S-wave travels at about 60 per cent of the velocity of a P-wave, which means that the P-waves will appear on a seismogram before the S-waves, as can be seen in figure 3.

The velocity of body waves generally increases with depth, which causes the waves to refract. The body waves therefore follow a curved path through the earth, as indicated in figure 4. These waves have relatively short periods. Waves with periods of 0.2–2 seconds with a corresponding wavelength of the order of 1–10 km, are most commonly used in detection seismology. Recently, however, waves of higher frequencies (i.e., shorter periods) have gained increasing interest.

The signals recorded at stations contain a large amount of information. To facilitate the international exchange of this information, a limited number of parameters characterizing the signal are extracted from the data. Figure 5 shows the most common parameters measured from a seismic record, that is, the period of one cycle (seconds), frequency (Hz), wavelength (km), amplitude (nm) and arrival time. The parameters extracted from the signal are sometimes referred to as Level I data, whereas the recorded signal is called Level II data.

When a large seismic event occurs, signals can be recorded at most places around the earth. However, at the boundary between the mantle and the core where a sharp change of velocity occurs, body waves undergo reflection (PcP-waves) and refraction (PKP-waves) in such a way that virtually no signal will reach the earth's surface at an angular distance from about 100–140 degrees from the event, the so-called shadow zone (see figure 4).

Of particular importance in detection seismology is the reflection of a P- and S-wave at the earth's surface immediately above the source. After reflection, the waves continue to propagate into the earth's interior and then follow a path similar to that of the direct P- or S-wave. These reflected waves, whose travel paths are outlined in figure 4, are called depth phases (pP and sP) and are important for estimating the depth of earthquakes.

Surface waves are a second important class of waves generated by a seismic

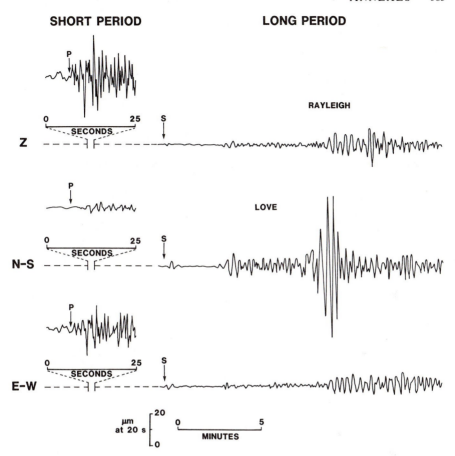

SHORT PERIOD   **LONG PERIOD**

Figure 3. Seismogram showing P-, S-, Rayleigh and Love waves recorded from an earthquake

The fastest travelling body wave is the P-wave and is the first signal recorded by a seismograph station. This may be followed by other P-waves that propagate along different and slower propagation paths and by the S-wave, which travels at about 60 per cent of the velocity of a P-wave. Surface waves travel much more slowly than body waves and are recorded several minutes after the P-waves. The upper trace is recorded by a vertical-component seismometer, and the two lower traces are recorded by horizontal-component seismometers. Because of the different particle motion involved for P- and S-waves, the vertical-component seismogram (Z) shows a larger P-wave amplitude and a smaller S-wave amplitude than the horizontal components (N-S and E-W).

event. These waves travel over large distances along the surface of the earth. The two main types of surface wave are called Rayleigh waves and Love waves. Examples of records of such waves are shown in figure 3.

Rayleigh waves propagate with a retrograde, elliptical particle motion in the direction in which the wave is propagating. As can be seen in figure 3, Rayleigh

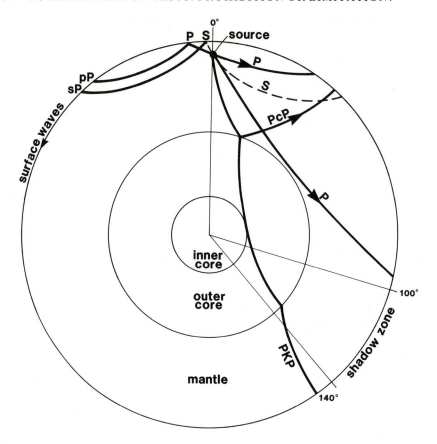

Figure 4. Seismic waves drawn as examples of some of the phases that can be found in a recording of a seismic event

P- and S-waves travel through the earth's interior, and the different propagation properties of the core and the mantle cause a shadow zone. The reflection and refraction of P-waves at the boundary between the core and the mantle give rise to the PcP and PKP phases. P- and S-waves, which first travel upwards and then are reflected downwards again by the earth's surface, give rise to the pP and sP depth phases. The time delay between the direct P and pP phases is indicative of the depth of the seismic event. Love and Rayleigh waves travel along the surface of the earth.

waves have thus both vertically and horizontally oriented motion. For Love waves, the particles move perpendicular to the direction of wave propagation, and the motion is entirely horizontally oriented.

Surface waves have relatively long periods, and Love and Rayleigh waves with periods from 10 to 100 seconds are relevant in detection seismology, but a narrow band around a period of 20 seconds is usually measured. The surface waves travel with a velocity of about 3–4 km/s, corresponding to wavelengths of

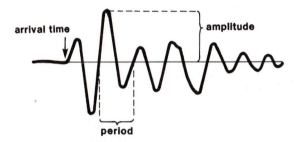

Figure 5. Arrival time, amplitude (nm) and period of one cycle (seconds), as measured from the seismogram in order to locate an event and determine its strength

The frequency (Hz) is the inverse of the period, i.e., the number of cycles per second. These parameters, extracted from a seismogram, are sometimes referred to as Level I data. The recorded wave form is called Level II data.

60–80 km. The surface waves are therefore less sensitive than P-waves to fine-scale variations in the structure through which they propagate. Owing to the relatively low velocity of the surface waves, they appear later in the seismogram than do the body waves, as can be seen in figure 3.

Travel time and travel path properties of the P-waves are determined by the structure of the earth and are equal for explosion-generated and earthquake-generated waves, whereas properties such as amplitude and period are determined both by the earth's structure and by the seismic source and thus differ for explosions and earthquakes. The present knowledge of the earth's structure and the theory of elastic waves allows very accurate prediction of the travel time and travel path of the seismic waves. The arrival time for seismic signals can be predicted within 0.1 per cent of the total travel time from the source using standard travel timetables.

The variations in amplitude and period of seismic signals, on the other hand, are less well known. Significant efforts have been devoted to theoretical calculations of such characteristics of seismic waves. These calculations have become an increasingly useful tool in the interpretation of seismic records and for discrimination between earthquakes and explosions.

V. Magnitudes and yields

As the body waves propagate, the amplitudes will be reduced with increasing travel distance owing to geometrical effects. Seismic waves are also to some extent absorbed in the interior of the earth. These effects must be taken into account when estimating the strength of an earthquake from amplitudes observed at different distances from the event.

The strength of a seismic event is usually expressed in terms of magnitudes on the so-called Richter scale, which is defined so that a magnitude increase by one unit corresponds to a factor of 10 increase in the actual strength of the event.

The body wave magnitude, m_b, can be calculated from the amplitude and period of the P-wave, measured by a seismogram, and from a correction term. The correction term, obtained empirically from a large sample of earthquake observations, depends on the distance between the recording station and the earthquake and also on the depth of the earthquake.

Other magnitude scales are calculated, for example, from surface waves (M_s) or are based on estimates of the total energy release (M_w), and local magnitudes for near distances are based on crustal waves.

The magnitude is a quantitative measure of the strength of a seismic source, but it has no direct physical relation to the seismic source. For example, the P-wave amplitude depends not only on the distance to the source but also strongly on existing lateral heterogeneities within the earth. However, the average magnitude from estimates made at a number of stations in a global network is usually a good measure of the strength of a seismic event. The Richter scale has no lower or upper boundaries, but the largest seismic magnitudes observed from an earthquake are about 9. Earthquakes with magnitudes of less than 1 can be detected by stations located within a distance of 100 km from the event.

The strength or yield, Y, of an underground explosion can be estimated approximately from recorded seismic signals, in particular from long-period Rayleigh waves. Yields are usually given in kilotons, where 1 kt corresponds to 4.2×10^{12} joules (J), which is roughly the energy released by 1000 tons of exploding trinitrotoluene (TNT). Most of the energy radiated by an underground nuclear explosion is deposited as thermal energy in the immediate vicinity of the explosion, and only a small fraction is radiated as seismic waves.

The strength of the seismic signals depends strongly on the medium in which the explosion occurs. Explosions in, for example, hard granitic rocks and salt deposits give considerably stronger signals than do explosions in unconsolidated material, like tuff (a rock composed of compacted volcanic fragments) and alluvium (see figure 6). Theoretical models also predict that signals generated from explosions conducted in hard-rock material contain higher frequencies than the signals generated from explosions conducted in material such as tuff or alluvium.

The signals recorded at a seismic station depend not only on the explosion yield and the shot medium but also on the wave transmission properties of the earth. These transmission properties vary considerably from one region to the other. The strong dependence of seismic signals on both the shot medium and the signal transmission properties from the test site to the seismological stations makes it difficult to calculate explosion yields directly from seismic signals. Yields therefore have to be estimated in relation to a nearby calibration explosion of which the yield is known from radio-chemical or close-in shock wave measurements.

If detailed information about the testing conditions, such as the explosion medium, emplacement depth and depth of static water table, is available, more

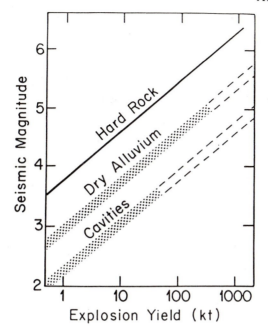

Figure 6. Seismic magnitudes as a function of explosion yield for different geological environments

One magnitude unit on the Richter scale corresponds to approximately 10 times greater explosion yield.
Source: Direction du controle des armements et du desarmement, *Seismic Verification* (Ottawa, 1986).

accurate yield estimates are possible. For a high-yield explosion the estimated yield will be rather close to the real yield, because such explosions can be contained only at depths where hard-rock conditions usually exist. For a low-yield explosion, which could be contained at shallow depth in unconsolidated alluvial material, the real yield can be up to 10 times higher than the estimated yield.

VI. Seismographs

When a seismic event occurs, the generated waves give rise to ground movements of the earth's surface. The weak vibrations of a seismic wave can be detected by an electromechanical instrument called a seismometer, as illustrated in figure 7. The entire instrument, of which the seismometer is one component, is called a seismograph.

The seismometer is usually in the form of a canister, about 20 centimetres in diameter and 30 centimetres high, lined with a coil of wire. Inside the coil and

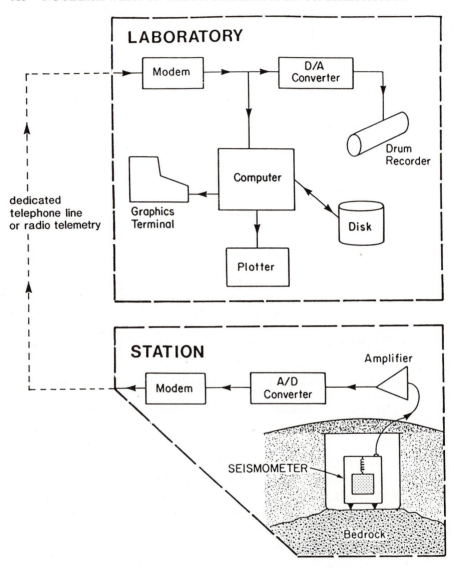

Figure 7. Outline of a typical modern digital seismograph installation

Source: Direction du controle des armements et du desarmement, *Seismic Verification* (Ottawa, 1986).

suspended from the top of the canister by a spring, a permanent magnet is free to move up and down within the coil.

The coil-lined canister is fixed to the ground on solid rock, and any vibration of the earth surface will cause it to move up and down, whereas the vibration leaves the suspended magnet virtually unaffected. These small relative motions will induce a weak electric current in the coil that can be magnified by electronic amplifiers. The electric signals generated by the motions can be recorded on paper (the classical method) or on analogue magnetic tape, or can be digitally stored on magnetic tape or disk media for immediate computer analysis.

A complication in recording seismic events is the omnipresent seismic background noise, or microseismic noise. Microseisms originate from natural sources such as storms and wind, and from human and industrial activity. Sites close to the sea are generally more noisy than mid-continental sites. In order to detect weak signals, seismographs must be designed so that they are affected as little as possible by the microseisms.

For detection of P- and S-waves, seismographs which magnify periods of about one second are used. The size of the seismometer mass and the spring constant in principle determine the capability of a seismometer to enhance different periods. The current induced in the coil will be proportional to the movement of the magnet within the coil. The natural period of vibration of the spring is that of an average P-wave, or about one second. However, by tuning the electric amplifier that records these movements, one can record seismic waves with frequencies of up to 100 cycles per second (Hz). The most sensitive short-period seismometers connected to high-quality amplifiers are capable of recording seismic waves with ground motions as weak as one-millionth of a millimetre, if they are placed at quiet sites.

To detect long-period seismic waves such as surface waves, seismographs that magnify waves with periods of about 20 seconds are commonly used.

A third type of seismograph records frequencies in a wide range of periods; these are called broadband seismographs.

A seismograph station usually operates seismometers to detect three components of ground motion. One is sensitive to the vertical motion of the ground, and the other two respond to horizontal ground motion, usually one in a north-south direction and one in an east-west direction. The vertical-component seismometer gives the best recordings of both the compressional P-waves and the Rayleigh surface waves. The horizontal component seismometer is able to record waves with transverse or shear motion, such as S- and Love waves; this is illustrated in figure 3.

VII. Detection and location of seismic events

The possibility to detect low-magnitude events is limited by earth noise. In addition to using different types of seismometer to enhance the signals, various data-processing techniques for reducing the noise are employed in order to improve the detection capability of seismic stations.

Array stations

In order to reduce the influence of ground noise and thus to increase the capability to record weak seismic signals, several seismometers can be connected in a certain configuration. Such seismic array stations with various numbers of seismometers, geometries and geographical dimensions have been tested and are now in operation in many countries. The number of seismometers tested in one array ranges from three to more than 500, and the area over which they have been located ranges from less than 1 km to 200 km.

The detection capability of an array is determined not only by the number of seismometers and their geometry but also, to a large extent, by the way data from the individual seismometers are combined.

The fundamental principle of array stations is that each element of the array receives signals that are identical in form but shifted in time. Using appropriate time delays, the signals recorded by the individual stations are put on top of each other and added in a process called beam-forming. The sum is frequently called the beam since the time delays are chosen so that the array is focused, or beamed, towards some point on the earth's surface.

This processing method is a standard technique used in present medium-sized and large arrays. The seismic noise is incoherent and the signals are coherent across the array; the noise will therefore be suppressed and the signals enhanced. The beam-forming technique could theoretically provide a gain in detection capability proportional to the square root of the number of seis-mometers in the array. In practice, however, this gain is difficult to achieve since the seismic signals are not always identical at seismometers several kilometres apart, and the noise is not always incoherent across the array.

Interest now seems to be focused on small and medium-sized arrays. For small arrays with short distances between the seismometers, beam-forming is not so efficient since the short-period seismic noise may become coherent at the seismometers. However, P-waves recorded from distant events and coherent noise have quite different propagating velocities. The utilization of this difference in propagating velocities across the array is called velocity filtering.

An important advantage of using array stations is that an estimate of the location of an event can be achieved without data from other stations. In order to locate a seismic event from the signals recorded by an array station, the distance to the event and the direction from which the signals are coming need to be determined. The distance can be estimated from the time differences between the arrival of different waves, for example P-, S- and Rayleigh waves, or by measuring the velocity at which the P-wave travels across the array. The direction to the event can be estimated either from the arrival of the incoming waves at the different seismometers or from the relative amplitudes of the horizontal components.

The location accuracy depends on the distance between the seismometers and on the accuracy in measuring the arrival time differences between signals recorded at the seismometers. The location accuracy will in general increase with the distance between seismometers. However, the signal coherency decreases with increasing seismometer spacing, which in turn decreases the accuracy of the time estimates. It is usually easier to estimate the direction from which the signals are coming than the distance to the event. An array can alone locate a seismic event with an accuracy of a few hundred kilometres, which is poor accuracy compared to what can be achieved using a network of globally distributed stations.

Station networks

One isolated seismograph station cannot adequately monitor underground nuclear explosions, no matter how advanced its equipment may be. Data from many globally distributed seismograph stations must be interpreted to give a reliable location. This has led to an extensive international exchange of seismic data, in the form of bulletins, among seismograph stations and institutes. These bulletins usually contain observed arrival times, primarily for P-waves, and to some extent also amplitude and period data as well as information on later phases. The need for accurate location of epicentres of events has also led to the establishment of institutes specialized in computation and distribution of epicentre data.

Using high-quality data from a network of seismic stations it is possible to determine the location of a seismic event with an accuracy of approximately 10–20 km. The most important factors contributing to the detection capability of a network of stations are the geographical distribution of the stations in the network, the seismic noise level at each station and the factor by which the signal amplitude must exceed the background noise level at individual stations to be recognized with confidence.

The detection threshold for a station can be estimated from observed P-waves of seismic events in different regions or by calculating the magnitude threshold for which there is a certain probability of P-wave detection, given knowledge of the local noise conditions. The threshold over which events of a certain magnitude will be detected at a station is specified as a probability; for example, a 90 per cent detection threshold means that signals from 90 per cent of all events with magnitudes equal to that threshold value will be detected.

A seismic station network may consist of both single stations and array stations. Signal detection by at least four single stations is required to define and locate an event, which involves determination of the latitude, longitude, depth and origin time of the event. A larger number of stations usually provides a more accurate location. In order to locate seismic events, P-wave arrival time data from many stations distributed around the event are most commonly used.

Both theoretical studies and full-scale experiments have shown that a network of approximately 50 globally distributed stations reaches a body wave magnitude threshold of about 4.0 in the northern hemisphere, which means that 90 per cent of all seismic events equal to magnitude 4.0 will be detected by such a network. The corresponding magnitude threshold for events in the southern hemisphere has been estimated to be about 4.5 to 5.0. There is also a similar hemispherical difference for the surface wave threshold. The reason for this greater sensitivity in the northern than in the southern hemisphere is the significantly larger number of existing stations in the northern hemisphere than in the southern hemisphere. In order to detect smaller events, stations located close to the event are normally required.

VIII. Identification

A central question in the assessment of a seismological verification system is the degree of certainty with which signals generated by underground explosions can be distinguished from those generated by earthquakes.

The most important parameters for the identification of seismic events are location and depth. Events occurring in areas where nuclear explosions cannot reasonably be carried out or at depths below those that can be reached by drilling can immediately be classified as earthquakes. The largest depth reported for a nuclear explosion is less than 3 km, and present drilling techniques do not allow penetration deeper than about 10–15 km.

About 8000 earthquakes with a body wave magnitude of 4.0 or greater (m_b 4.0 roughly corresponds to a 1-kt nuclear explosion conducted in hard rock) occur each year. The depth of earthquakes varies from 0 km (the surface of the earth) down to about 700 km, and 90 per cent of all earthquakes are deeper than 10 km. More than half of the earthquakes occur beneath the oceans.

The accuracy of the present depth estimation methods is often not sufficient for reliable discrimination between earthquakes and explosions. Other discrimination methods are therefore needed in addition to depth-estimation methods.

Depth estimation

There are two principal methods for estimating the depth of a seismic event. One is based on the surface reflection of short-period P- and S-waves, and the other method utilizes the arrival times of the short-period P-waves.

The surface reflection method is considered to be the most accurate method for depth estimation. The time delay beteen the first recorded P-wave and the surface reflected waves (pP and sP; see figure 4) can be used, since this delay is directly related to the focal depth and is nearly independent of the epicentral distance for events with depths shallower than 100 km. It is usually more difficult to detect reflected phases from shallow-focus earthquakes above 20 km than from earthquakes at depths greater than 100 km (see figure 8). The reflected waves may be either hidden in the seismic signal or severely attenuated at the source if there is a strongly absorbing geologic structure between the focus of the earthquake and the surface. There are several ways in which to facilitate detection of secondary phases, for example, by using different signal processing techniques or by utilizing wave-form data from seismic arrays or from a network of stations. When depth phases are found in the record, it is easy to estimate the focal depth of the event with an error of only a few kilometres.

In cases where no depth phases can be found, depth can be estimated along

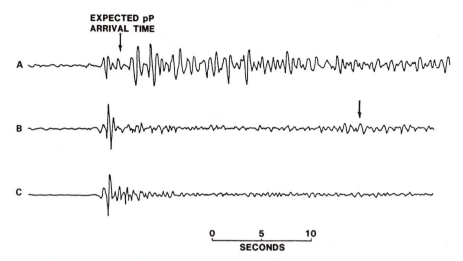

Figure 8. Examples of short-period records of a shallow (A) and a deep (B) earthquake and of a nuclear explosion (C)

The depths of these earthquakes were estimated at 30 and 120 km, respectively, whereas nuclear explosions are detonated at considerably shallower depths. Knowledge about the focal depth is important for discrimination since seismic signals from a deep earthquake frequently resemble those from an explosion. The depth of a deep earthquake can be accurately determined by identifying the pP phase in a seismogram; for a shallow earthquake, this is more difficult.

with the epicentre and origin time using the P-wave arrival times from a seismic network. The uncertainty of such an estimate can be as large as 100 km. The accuracy can, however, be increased by refining the standard travel time-tables used in the computation. Corrections to the travel times in the standard tables can, for example, be achieved from larger events that have occurred in the same region and for which the depth and location are known. The depth of such events can be estimated from depth phases or by other methods.

With a local network surrounding the event, depth can be accurately measured with an error of only 1 or 2 km. Local arrival time data in combination with P-wave arrival times recorded at far distant stations, that is, at distances greater than 2000 km, can provide quite accurate and verifiable depth estimates.

Depth can also be estimated from long-period seismic signals, since the spectrum of the Rayleigh wave is strongly dependent on the depth. For short-period body waves, the signal shape from shallow and deeper earthquakes also differs significantly. These variations in wave form with depth can therefore be utilized for depth estimation.

If an event cannot be confidently identified on the basis of its location and depth, other discrimination techniques can be used. However, seismic signals

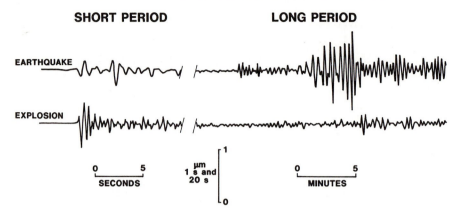

Figure 9. Short- and long-period signals recorded at the Hagfors Observatory from an underground explosion and an earthquake, both in the USSR

There is a pronounced difference between explosions and shallow earthquakes with respect to the ratio of P-wave to Rayleigh wave amplitude. The Rayleigh wave amplitude of an earthquake can be up to 10 times larger than that from an explosion if the P-wave amplitudes are of comparable size.

from a deep earthquake can frequently resemble those from an explosion, as shown by the example in figure 9. Therefore, knowledge about the focal depth is important also for these techniques.

Discrimination techniques

Theoretical models predict that explosions should radiate only P-waves and that the initial motion of the P-waves should be entirely compressional; this means that the first motion recorded in a seismogram should be directed upwards at all stations detecting the event. However, earthquakes should radiate both P- and S-waves, and the initial P-waves may be both compressional and dilatational; so the first motion recorded in the seismogram may be directed upwards or downwards, depending on the location of the seismic station relative to the direction of the fault plane.

An explosion is a simpler phenomenon than an earthquake. It lasts over a shorter time period and is limited to a smaller region compared to an earthquake of comparable strength. This implies that the waves generated by earthquakes should have a longer duration, and the observed signals should be more complex than the waves generated by explosions. These differences in signal characteristics provide the basis for several different discrimination techniques.

The m_b: M_s discriminant, which compares the short-period P-wave magnitude, m_b, with the long-period surface wave magnitude, M_s, has been the most extensively studied method for discrimination of seismic signals. There is

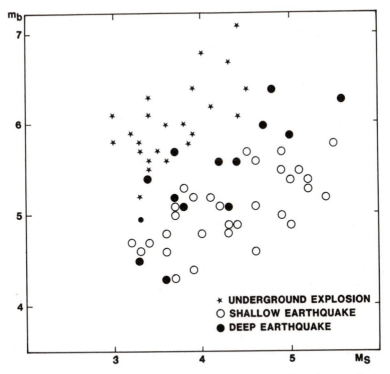

Figure 10. m_b and M_s values for a number of underground nuclear explosions and shallow and deep earthquakes located in the USSR, plotted in a m_b: M_s diagram

The focal depths of the shallow earthquakes have been estimated to be less than 30 km and for the deep earthquakes to be more than 100 km. A line can usually be drawn in the diagram which separates the earthquake and explosion populations. However, for deep earthquakes the m_b: M_s values are often close to those from explosions.

a pronounced difference between explosions and shallow earthquakes with respect to the ratio of P-wave to Rayleigh wave strengths. If P-wave amplitudes are of comparable size, the Rayleigh wave amplitude of the earthquake is usually up to 10 times as large as that from the explosion. An example of such events is shown in figure 9.

Figure 10 illustrates the difference in m_b values for explosions and earthquakes for a given M_s. The m_b: M_s values from underground explosions usually differ considerably from those of shallow earthquakes, but for deep earthquakes the m_b: M_s values are often very close to those from explosions. The larger M_s values generally observed from shallow earthquakes compared to explosions can be explained by the different source mechanisms, the large difference in time duration and the dimensions of the source regions. Strong lateral variations have been observed in the m_b: M_s and values; the m_b: M_s discriminant can be applied only to seismic events occurring in the same region.

The separation between earthquake and explosion populations has been predicted to be greatest at larger magnitudes, but it has been shown that this separation is attainable also for weak events down to and below a magnitude of 4.0. The applicability of the m_b: M_s method is limited by the surface wave detection capability and is therefore related to the surface wave detection threshold of a global network of stations.

Even though the parameters that influence the m_b: M_s relation are to some extent understood, it is not possible to predict in detail the m_b: M_s relations that are valid for new areas where no nuclear explosions have been conducted.

In addition to the m_b: M_s, a number of other discriminants have been used. The wave form complexity and the different frequency contents of the short-period signals can be used for discrimination. P-wave signals from an earthquake and an explosion are shown in figure 11. Since these methods utilize only the short-period signals, they can be applied to smaller events for which the m_b: M_s criteria cannot be used, but the success of these methods is strongly regionally dependent.

The analysis of complexity is a discrimination technique which consists in comparing the amplitudes of the initial part of the signal with those of the following part of the signal, or the so-called coda. Complexities for shallow earthquakes often increase with increasing magnitude, possibly owing to the increased dimension of the earthquake source region. Explosion complexities, however, do not change significantly with magnitude. The complexity of earthquakes also depends on the focal depth; the complexity for deep earthquakes frequently resembles that of an explosion, as can be seen in figure 11.

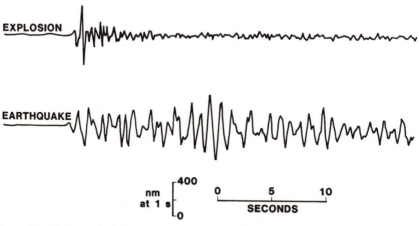

Figure 11. Short-period signals observed at the Hagfors Observatory from a shallow earthquake and an underground explosion

The earthquake signal is of much longer duration and is more complex, and the characteristic period is longer than for the explosion signal. The waveform complexity and the different frequency contents of the short-period signals can be used for discrimination between earthquakes and explosions.

The enrichment of high frequencies in the P-wave signals from an explosion has been used in a number of discriminants, so-called spectral discriminants. In one method, called the Spectral Ratio, amplitudes in a low-frequency interval are compared with amplitudes in a high-frequency interval. These intervals are different for different stations and are usually chosen by comparing the average frequency contents in signals recorded from explosions and earthquakes. The separation can be improved by using several different frequency intervals.

There are also parameters expressing the relative high-frequency content without considering the detailed amplitude information. One such parameter, which has been widely used, is the Third Moment of Frequency. This parameter usually has a larger value for explosions than for earthquakes since it gives high weights to the high-frequency components of the signal.

The spectral methods generally provide better discrimination between explosions and earthquakes than do the complexity discriminants. The success of spectral discriminants depends not only on the seismic event (explosion or earthquake) but also on several other factors such as the strength of the source. The larger the source, the smaller is the proportion of energy radiated at high frequencies. This effect is approximately the same for explosions and earthquakes and can be corrected for. The spectral discriminant values for deep earthquakes are often similar to those for explosions. This is probably partly due to the fact that P-waves from deep earthquakes traverse the crust only at the receiver end of their propagation path, that is, at the station.

Systematic large-scale regional variations in the frequency content of the P-waves have also been observed. Spectral discriminants, therefore, have to be tailored to each specific region and each seismic station to provide effective discrimination.

Most of these discriminants have not been tested systematically on representative amounts of data from different regions. However, a number of studies have demonstrated that the spectral discriminants, when applied on a regional basis, distinguish well between explosions and earthquakes.

Great interest in regional discrimination has emerged in the past decade. Discrimination based on recordings at stations located at distances from a few kilometres to about 2000 km from the event can be applied to weaker events. A large number of discriminants have with different degrees of success been tested. Regional variants of the m_b: M_s criteria, spectral ratios of P-waves, and spectral and amplitude ratios based on the short-period surface waves (Lg-phases) are a few of these techniques. Utilizing higher frequencies than was previous practice has also shown to be promising not only for improving the detection capability but also for increasing the possibility to discriminate between explosions and earthquakes.

In addition to the methods described above, other methods utilizing the physical source parameters of an event can be used for discrimination. Such parameters include, for example, the orientation of the fault plane, the motion along these planes, and the difference in stress before and after the earthquake. As the source mechanisms of earthquakes differ from those of explosions, such a physical interpretation of the observations could offer an important tool for discrimination. By combining several discriminants, and by combining discriminants obtained at seismic stations widely separated in direction and distance from the source, the discrimination capability will be improved.

However, there are a number of situations for which discrimination is very difficult. One example of this is when the explosion triggers a small earthquake. The signals from such an event will obviously be very difficult to interpret. The lateral inhomogeneities within the earth is another complicating factor. These will usually cause the signals to be more complex and thereby more difficult to interpret as long as full knowledge about the structure of the earth cannot be achieved.

IX. Conclusions

Seismology provides a number of efficient tools for detecting nuclear explosions and distinguishing them from earthquakes. However, no simple technique exists by which a single observation from a single seismometer can provide a reliable discrimination.

Instead, a variety of discrimination techniques must be used based on the different depths for earthquakes and nuclear explosions, the different complexities and durations of signals from such events and the relative magnitudes of body and surface waves. The variety of seismic waves that can be observed from a seismic event provides a large amount of information, but a global network of seismographs and arrays of seismographs plus sophisticated data processing techniques are required for reliable discrimination.

Annexe 4. Nuclear explosions, 16 July 1945–1 July 1987

Robert S. Norris

Natural Resources Defense Council, Washington, DC

Ragnhild Ferm

SIPRI

Basic to an informed debate about nuclear weapon testing is an accurate and a comprehensive list of all known or presumed nuclear explosions. Facts about how many nuclear explosions have been conducted, and by whom, where and when they have taken place, are an essential starting point for further research and debate about testing and test ban issues. The lists provided in this appendix are as accurate and as comprehensive as it is possible to make them at this time. Because a large amount of secrecy has surrounded and still surrounds nuclear testing, these lists are inevitably incomplete.

I. Sources

Basic factual information about nuclear testing comes from several sources. Each of the governments that have conducted nuclear tests (the USA, the USSR, the UK, France, China and India) has provided information, in varying degrees, about its programme. In addition those governments have occasionally reported on the testing programmes and activities of other countries. Official government data, while the most authoritative, are normally incomplete and must be supplemented by other sources.

The US Government has provided the most information about its own test programme and the programmes of other countries. The basic document is the Department of Energy's *Announced United States Nuclear Tests, July 1945 through December 1986.*[1] All US tests conducted prior to the Partial Test Ban Treaty (PTBT) of 1963 are included, though at the time many of those tests were not announced. As for the tests conducted since 1963, '[s]ome tests conducted underground since the signing of the Treaty and designed to be contained completely have not been announced. Information concerning these events is classified'. The information which has been provided includes the date (in Greenwich Mean Time), location, type, purpose and yield or yield range of the event.[2]

The United States Geological Survey (USGS), a part of the Department of the Interior, publishes a monthly listing called *Preliminary Determination of*

Epicenters, which reports global seismic activity as recorded by stations all over the world. While the USGS does not identify certain seismic events as nuclear tests, activities listed in such places as Southern Nevada, Eastern Kazakhstan, Novaya Zemlya, Tuamoto Archipelago and Sinkiang Province are likely candidates. The analyst must be knowledgable about the exact geographic co-ordinates of each nation's test site(s). Another indicator that certain seismic activity may be a test is the origin time. Explosions, unlike earthquakes, normally occur on the minute or the hour and usually during the daytime.

The USSR had, by 1987, not announced its tests. It has published some information about its peaceful nuclear explosion (PNE) programme and during a turbulent period following the 1958–61 moratorium announced a few high-yield atmospheric tests.

The UK has conducted only a few dozen tests since it started its nuclear testing programme in 1952. This could mean either that Britain has a very small number of warhead types in its stockpile or that it obtains a good deal of information from the USA, or both. The first 21 British tests were conducted in the atmosphere between October 1952 and September 1958.[3] The tests from 1962 to 1987 were conducted jointly with the United States at the Nevada Test Site and were announced by the US Government.

Keeping track of French tests is not too difficult. The French Government reported quite a lot of information about many of the tests of the 1960s and early 1970s. More recent French tests were announced by New Zealand seismologists who record the explosions at Tuamotu Archipelago from a station at Rarotonga in the Cook Islands.[4] France stopped testing in the atmosphere in 1975.

China announced almost all of its tests in 1964–77.[5] China's test on 16 October 1980 was the last conducted in the atmosphere. Premier Zhao Ziyang announced on 21 March 1986 that China would no longer conduct tests in the atmosphere.

An important source of official information is that supplied by certain non-nuclear-weapon state governments which record the testing activity of the nuclear powers. The most prominent source in this category is the Swedish National Defence Research Institute (known by its Swedish acronym as FOA). Its work on seismic discrimination, which is financed by the Swedish Foreign Office, is meant to establish an acceptable verification system for a comprehensive test ban. FOA operates the Hagfors Observatory and publishes the data; it uses data from its own seismic network and those from other observatories, comparing them and updating the lists. Several other institutions, such as those in New Zealand, Norway and the Australian Seismological Centre which opened in 1986, are co-operating in efforts to establish a world-wide seismic monitoring system. Most of the seismic data exchanged by such institutions are incomprehensible to the non-specialist, although several institutions translate these data into understandable lists of nuclear explosions or seismic events.

Newspaper accounts, books and journal articles also constitute a source of information.

II. Interpretation

With as much information accumulated about the tests as possible, certain patterns emerge which begin to indicate the more significant aspects of testing. Simple statistical summaries reveal basic and interesting facts. How many tests have been conducted by each country? How many were conducted above and below ground? How many were conducted before and after the PTBT? How many were done underwater, at very high altitudes, and so on?

Other patterns emerge by examining US and Soviet testing activity just prior to the entry into force of the PTBT and the Threshold Test Ban Treaty (TTBT). From November 1958 to September 1961, neither the USA nor the USSR tested nuclear weapons. The USSR resumed testing on 1 September 1961 and conducted approximately 50 tests by the end of the year, while the United States conducted only 10. In 1962 the USA conducted 98 tests (including 2 with the UK) and the Soviet Union 44. These more than 200 explosions in a 16-month period (one every two and one-half days) represent an intense period of testing. One cause of this fervent pace was no doubt to test the backlog of designs developed during the moratorium.

The TTBT was signed on 3 July 1974, prohibiting tests having a yield exceeding 150 kt. As stipulated in Article I, the ban would not take effect until 31 March 1976.[6] The interesting period of time is therefore the 21 months between July 1974 and March 1976: during that time the USA conducted 34 tests and the Soviet Union 29, of which 5 may have been PNEs.

In the US case, numerous officials have stated that the warhead designs for the Minuteman III (335 kt), the MX (300 kt), the Trident II (450 kt) and the B83 strategic bomb (1.2 Mt) were tested at their full yield prior to 31 March 1976. By comparing the known yields of those warheads with yield estimates of certain tests during the period, it is possible to speculate on which tests were for which warheads. It seems to be the case that no new warhead introduced into the stockpile, with the exception of the above four, has a yield greater than 150 kt, thus implying that new warheads may not be certified for the stockpile unless they have been tested at full yield.

In the Soviet case, according to one analyst, several high-yield tests (c. 2–3.5 Mt) conducted during this period were for the single-re-entry vehicle ICBM modifications (SS–17 mod. 2, SS–18 mod. 1 and SS–19 mod. 2), and a series of 500-kt tests were probably for later modifications of these MIRVed missiles (SS–17 mod. 3, SS–18 mod. 4 and SS–19 mod. 3).[7]

Notes and references

[1] DOE Nevada Operations Office, NVO–209 (Rev. 7), Jan. 1987. Announced tests are notified by the Nevada Operations Office, Las Vegas, Nevada. If a test is to be announced it is done approximately 48 hours before the scheduled time. Occasionally a test is announced after it has taken place.

[2] More detail must be obtained from other sources. It is useful to know the exact time of the explosion as well as the co-ordinates of where it took place. The purpose of the test is given in vague

terms, such as 'weapons related' or for 'weapons effects'. The exact purpose of the test is not divulged, nor in recent years is the exact yield.

[3] For valuable information about the dozen tests conducted in Australia, see *A History of British Atomic Tests in Australia*, prepared by Dr J. L. Symonds, Department of Resources and Energy (Australian Government Publishing Service: Canberra, 1985).

[4] Department of Scientific and Industrial Research, Geophysics Division, Wellington, New Zealand.

[5] Twenty of the first 23.

[6] Submission for ratification was held in abeyance until the companion Peaceful Nuclear Explosions Treaty was negotiated. That Treaty was negotiated between October 1974 and April 1976, and was signed on 28 May 1976. Both treaties were submitted to the Senate on 29 July 1976, where they still awaited ratification by July 1987.

[7] Sykes, L. R. and Davis, D. M., 'The yields of Soviet strategic weapons', *Scientific American*, Jan. 1987 p. 34. The warheads for the first group of Soviet MIRVed ICBMs deployed between 1974 and 1976 were tested earlier.

Table 1. Estimated number of nuclear explosions 16 July 1945–5 August 1963 (the signing of the Partial Test Ban Treaty)

a = atmospheric
u = underground

Year	USA a	USA u	USSR a	USSR u	UK a	UK u	France a	France u	Total
1945	3	0							3
1946	2[a]	0							2
1947	0	0							0
1948	3	0							3
1949	0	0	1	0					1
1950	0	0	0	0					0
1951	15	1	2	0					18
1952	10	0	0	0	1	0			11
1953	11	0	4	0	2	0			17
1954	6	0	7	0	0	0			13
1955	17[a]	1	5[a]	0	0	0			23
1956	18	0	9	0	6	0			33
1957	27	5	15[a]	0	7	0			54
1958	62[b]	15	29	0	5	0			111
1949–58, exact years unknown			18						18
1959	0	0	0	0	0	0			0
1960	0	0	0	0	0	0	3	0	3
1961	0	10	50[a]	1	0	0	1	1	63
1962	38[a]	58	43	1	0	2[d]	0	1	143
1 Jan.–5 Aug. 1963	4	25	0	0	0	0	0	2	31
Total	**216**	**115**	**183[c]**	**2**	**21**	**2**	**4**	**4**	**547**

[a] At least one of these tests was carried out under water.

[b] Two of these tests were carried out under water.

[c] The total figure for Soviet atmospheric tests includes the 18 additional tests conducted in the period 1949–58, for which exact years are not available.

[d] Conducted jointly with the USA at the Nevada Test Site.

Table 2. Estimated number of nuclear explosions 6 August 1963–30 March 1976

a = atmospheric
u = underground

Year	USA[a]		USSR		UK[a]		France		China		India		Total
	a	u	a	u	a	u	a	u	a	u	a	u	
6 Aug.–31 Dec. 1963	0	14	0	0	0	0	0	1					15
1964	0	29	0	6	0	1	0	3	1	0			40
1965	0	29	0	9	0	1	0	4	1	0			44
1966	0	40	0	15	0	0	5	1	3	0			64
1967	0	29	0	17	0	0	3	0	2	0			51
1968	0	39[b]	0	13	0	0	5	0	1	1			58
1969	0	29	0	16	0	0	0	0	1	0			47
1970	0	33	0	17	0	0	8	0	1	0			59
1971	0	15	0	19	0	0	5	0	1	0			40
1972	0	15	0	22	0	0	3	0	2	0			42
1973	0	12[c]	0	14	0	0	5	0	1	0			32
1974	0	12	0	19	0	0	7	0	1	1	0	1	41
1975	0	17	0	15	0	1	0	2	0	1	0	0	35
1 Jan.–30 Mar. 1976	0	9	0	1	0	0	0	0	1	0	0	0	11
Total	**0**	**322**	**0**	**183**	**0**	**3**	**41**	**11**	**16**	**2**	**0**	**1**	**579**

[a] See note a, table 5.
[b] Five devices used simultaneously in the same test are counted here as one explosion.
[c] Three devices used simultaneously in the same test are counted here as one explosion.

Table 3. Estimated number of nuclear explosions 31 March 1976 (date of the envisaged application of the 150-kt explosive yield limitation under the TTBT and the PNET)–1 July 1987. (For detailed information on dates of the tests, see table 4.)

a = atmospheric
u = underground

Year	USA[a]		USSR		UK[a]		France		China		India		Total
	a	u	a	u	a	u	a	u	a	u	a	u	
31 Mar.–31 Dec. 1976	0	6	0	16	0	1	0	1	2	1	0	0	27
1977	0	12	0	18	0	0	0	6	1	0	0	0	37
1978	0	16	0	28	0	2	0	7	2	1	0	0	56
1979	0	15	0	29	0	1	0	9	0	0	0	0	54
1980	0	14	0	21	0	3	0	11	1	0	0	0	50
1981	0	16	0	22	0	1	0	10	0	0	0	0	49
1982	0	18	0	31	0	1	0	5	0	0	0	0	55
1983	0	17	0	27	0	1	0	7	0	1	0	0	53
1984	0	17	0	28	0	2	0	8	0	2	0	0	57
1985	0	17	0	9	0	1	0	8	0	0	0	0	35
1986	0	14	0	0	0	1	0	8	0	0	0	0	23
1 Jan.–1 July 1987	0	9	0	9	0	0	0	4	0	1	0	0	23
Total	**0**	**171**	**0**	**238**	**0**	**14**	**0**	**84**	**6**	**6**	**0**	**0**	**519**

[a] See note a, table 5.

Table 4. Dates and locations of individual nuclear explosions 31 March 1976 (date of the envisaged application of the 150-kt explosive yield limitation under the TTBT and the PNET)–1 July 1987

Notes:
1. All explosions were conducted underground, with the exception of those marked with †
   which were conducted in the atmosphere.
2. Explosions which may be part of a programme for peaceful uses of nuclear energy, in view
   of its location outside the known test sites, are marked with *.
3. All explosions were under 150-kt yield.
4. The dates are all according to Greenwich Mean Time.

Date	Location	Date	Location
1976		27 Apr.	Nevada
		25 May	Nevada
USA		4 Aug.	Nevada
12 May	Nevada	19 Aug.	Nevada
27 July	Nevada	15 Sep.	Nevada
23 Nov.	Nevada	27 Sep.	Nevada
8 Dec.	Nevada	26 Oct.	Nevada
21 Dec.	Nevada	1 Nov.	Nevada
28 Dec.	Nevada	9 Nov.	Nevada
		17 Nov.	Nevada
USSR		14 Dec.	Nevada
21 Apr.	Semipalatinsk		
21 Apr.	Semipalatinsk		
19 May	Semipalatinsk	*USSR*	
9 June	Semipalatinsk	29 Mar.	Semipalatinsk
4 July	Semipalatinsk	25 Apr.	Semipalatinsk
23 July	Semipalatinsk	29 May	Semipalatinsk
29 July	N. of Caspian Sea*	29 June	Semipalatinsk
4 Aug.	Semipalatinsk	26 July	Central Siberia*
28 Aug.	Semipalatinsk	30 July	Semipalatinsk
29 Sep.	Novaya Zemlya	10 Aug.	Baykal*
20 Oct.	Novaya Zemlya	17 Aug.	Semipalatinsk
30 Oct.	Semipalatinsk	20 Aug.	Central Siberia*
5 Nov.	Central Siberia*	1 Sep.	Novaya Zemlya
23 Nov.	Semipalatinsk	5 Sep.	Semipalatinsk
7 Dec.	Semipalatinsk	10 Sep.	Baykal*
30 Dec.	Semipalatinsk	30 Sep.	N. of Caspian Sea*
		9 Oct.	Novaya Zemlya
UK		29 Oct.	Semipalatinsk
26 Aug.	Nevada	29 Oct.	Semipalatinsk
		30 Nov.	Semipalatinsk
France		26 Dec.	Semipalatinsk
11 July	Mururoa		
		France	
China		19 Feb.	Mururoa
26 Sep.	Lop Nor†	19 Mar.	Mururoa
17 Oct.	Lop Nor	6 July	Mururoa
17 Nov.	Lop Nor†	12 Nov.	Mururoa
		24 Nov.	Mururoa
		17 Dec.	Mururoa
1977			
		China	
USA		17 Sep.	Lop Nor†
5 Apr.	Nevada		

Date	Location	Date	Location
1978		*France*	
		27 Feb.	Mururoa
USA		22 Mar.	Mururoa
13 Feb.	Nevada	26 July	Mururoa
23 Feb.	Nevada	2 Nov.	Mururoa
16 Mar.	Nevada	30 Nov.	Mururoa
23 Mar.	Nevada	17 Dec.	Mururoa
11 Apr.	Nevada	19 Dec.	Mururoa
10 May	Nevada		
1 June	Nevada	*China*	
7 July	Nevada	15 Mar.	Lop Nor†
12 July	Nevada	14 Oct.	Lop Nor
31 Aug.	Nevada	14 Dec.	Lop Nor†
13 Sep.	Nevada		
27 Sep.	Nevada		
27 Sep.	Nevada	**1979**	
2 Nov.	Nevada		
1 Dec.	Nevada	*USA*	
16 Dec.	Nevada	24 Jan.	Nevada
		8 Feb.	Nevada
		15 Feb.	Nevada
USSR		14 Mar.	Nevada
19 Mar.	Semipalatinsk	11 May	Nevada
26 Mar.	Semipalatinsk	11 June	Nevada
22 Apr.	Semipalatinsk	20 June	Nevada
29 May	Semipalatinsk	28 June	Nevada
11 June	Semipalatinsk	3 Aug.	Nevada
5 July	Semipalatinsk	8 Aug.	Nevada
28 July	Semipalatinsk	6 Sep.	Nevada
9 Aug.	Central Siberia*	8 Sep.	Nevada
10 Aug.	Novaya Zemlya	26 Sep.	Nevada
24 Aug.	Central Siberia*	29 Nov.	Nevada
29 Aug.	Semipalatinsk	14 Dec.	Nevada
29 Aug.	Semipalatinsk		
15 Sep.	Semipalatinsk	*USSR*	
20 Sep.	Semipalatinsk	10 Jan.	N. of Caspian Sea*
21 Sep.	Central Siberia*	17 Jan.	N. of Caspian Sea*
27 Sep.	Novaya Zemlya	1 Feb.	Semipalatinsk
7 Oct.	Central Siberia*	16 Feb.	Semipalatinsk
8 Oct.	. .*	6 May	Semipalatinsk
15 Oct.	Semipalatinsk	24 May	Semipalatinsk
17 Oct.	Ural Mountains*	31 May	Semipalatinsk
17 Oct.	N. of Caspian Sea*	23 June	Semipalatinsk
31 Oct.	Semipalatinsk	7 July	Semipalatinsk
4 Nov.	Semipalatinsk	14 July	N. of Caspian Sea*
29 Nov.	Semipalatinsk	18 July	Semipalatinsk
29 Nov.	Semipalatinsk	4 Aug.	Semipalatinsk
14 Dec.	Semipalatinsk	12 Aug.	E. Siberia*
18 Dec.	N. of Caspian Sea*	18 Aug.	Semipalatinsk
20 Dec.	Semipalatinsk	6 Sep.	Central Siberia*
		14 Sep.	Semipalatinsk
		15 Sep.	Semipalatinsk
UK		24 Sep.	Novaya Zemlya
11 Apr.	Nevada	27 Sep.	Semipalatinsk
18 Nov.	Nevada	4 Oct.	W. Siberia*

Date	Location	Date	Location
7 Oct.	Central Siberia*	30 Sep.	Semipalatinsk
18 Oct.	Semipalatinsk	30 Sep.	Semipalatinsk
18 Oct.	Novaya Zemlya	8 Oct.	NW of Caspian Sea*
24 Oct.	N. of Caspian Sea*	11 Oct.	Novaya Zemlya
28 Oct.	Semipalatinsk	12 Oct.	Semipalatinsk
30 Nov.	Semipalatinsk	1 Nov.	Central Siberia*
2 Dec.	Semipalatinsk	10 Dec.	W. Siberia*
21 Dec.	Semipalatinsk	14 Dec.	Semipalatinsk
23 Dec.	Semipalatinsk	26 Dec.	Semipalatinsk
		27 Dec.	Semipalatinsk
UK			
29 Aug.	Nevada	*UK*	
		26 Apr.	Nevada
France		24 Oct.	Nevada
1 Mar.	Mururoa	17 Dec.	Nevada
9 Mar.	Mururoa		
24 Mar.	Mururoa	*France*	
4 Apr.	Mururoa	23 Feb.	Mururoa
18 June	Mururoa	3 Mar.	Mururoa
29 June	Mururoa	23 Mar.	Mururoa
25 July	Mururoa	1 Apr.	Mururoa
28 July	Mururoa	4 Apr.	Mururoa
22 Nov.	Mururoa	16 June	Mururoa
		21 June	Mururoa
		6 July	Mururoa
1980		19 July	Mururoa
		25 Nov.	Mururoa
USA		3 Dec.	Mururoa
28 Feb.	Nevada		
8 Mar.	Nevada	*China*	
3 Apr.	Nevada	16 Oct.	Lop Nor†
16 Apr.	Nevada		
2 May	Nevada		
22 May	Nevada	**1981**	
12 June	Nevada		
24 June	Nevada	*USA*	
25 July	Nevada	15 Jan.	Nevada
31 July	Nevada	5 Feb.	Nevada
25 Sep.	Nevada	25 Feb.	Nevada
25 Sep.	Nevada	30 Apr.	Nevada
31 Oct.	Nevada	29 May	Nevada
14 Nov.	Nevada	6 June	Nevada
		10 July	Nevada
USSR		16 July	Nevada
4 Apr.	Semipalatinsk	5 Aug.	Nevada
10 Apr.	Semipalatinsk	27 Aug.	Nevada
25 Apr.	Semipalatinsk	4 Sep.	Nevada
22 May	Semipalatinsk	24 Sep.	Nevada
12 June	Semipalatinsk	1 Oct.	Nevada
29 June	Semipalatinsk	11 Nov.	Nevada
13 July	Semipalatinsk	3 Dec.	Nevada
31 July	Semipalatinsk	16 Dec.	Nevada
14 Sep.	Semipalatinsk		
20 Sep.	Semipalatinsk	*USSR*	
25 Sep.	Semipalatinsk	29 Mar.	Semipalatinsk

Date	Location	Date	Location
31 Mar.	Semipalatinsk	23 Sep.	Nevada
22 Apr.	Semipalatinsk	29 Sep.	Nevada
25 May	N. European USSR*	12 Nov.	Nevada
27 May	Semipalatinsk	10 Dec.	Nevada
5 June	Semipalatinsk		
30 June	Semipalatinsk		
5 July	Semipalatinsk	*USSR*	
17 July	Semipalatinsk	19 Feb.	Semipalatinsk
14 Aug.	Semipalatinsk	25 Apr.	Semipalatinsk
2 Sep.	Ural Mountains*	11 June	Semipalatinsk
13 Sep.	Semipalatinsk	25 June	Semipalatinsk
26 Sep.	N. of Caspian Sea*	4 July	Semipalatinsk
26 Sep.	N. of Caspian Sea*	12 July	Semipalatinsk
30 Sep.	Semipalatinsk	30 July	Baykal*
1 Oct.	Novaya Zemlya	31 July	N. of Caspian Sea*
18 Oct.	Semipalatinsk	23 Aug.	Semipalatinsk
22 Oct.	Central Siberia*	28 Aug.	N. of Caspian Sea*
20 Nov.	Semipalatinsk	31 Aug.	Semipalatinsk
29 Nov.	Semipalatinsk	31 Aug.	N. of Caspian Sea*
22 Dec.	Semipalatinsk	4 Sep.	NW Siberia*
27 Dec.	Semipalatinsk	4 Sep.	Semipalatinsk
		15 Sep.	Semipalatinsk
UK		21 Sep.	Semipalatinsk
12 Nov.	Nevada	25 Sep.	Central Siberia*
		1 Oct.	N. of Caspian Sea*
France		10 Oct.	Central Siberia*
27 Feb.	Mururoa	11 Oct.	Novaya Zemlya
28 Mar.	Mururoa	16 Oct.	N. of Caspian Sea*
10 Apr.	Mururoa	16 Oct.	N. of Caspian Sea*
8 July	Mururoa	16 Oct.	N. of Caspian Sea*
11 July	Mururoa	16 Oct.	N. of Caspian Sea*
18 July	Mururoa	27 Oct.	N. of Caspian Sea*
3 Aug.	Mururoa	21 Nov.	S. Ural Mountains*
11 Nov.	Mururoa	29 Nov.	S. Ural Mountains*
5 Dec.	Mururoa	30 Nov.	N. of Caspian Sea*
8 Dec.	Mururoa	5 Dec.	Semipalatinsk
		25 Dec.	Semipalatinsk
1982		26 Dec.	Semipalatinsk
USA		*UK*	
28 Jan.	Nevada	25 Apr.	Nevada
12 Feb.	Nevada		
12 Feb.	Nevada	*France*	
17 Apr.	Nevada	20 Mar.	Mururoa
6 May	Nevada	27 June	Mururoa
7 May	Nevada	1 July	Mururoa
16 June	Nevada	21 July	Mururoa
24 June	Nevada	25 July	Mururoa
29 July	Nevada		
5 Aug.	Nevada	**1983**	
11 Aug.	Nevada		
2 Sep.	Nevada	*USA*	
23 Sep.	Nevada	11 Feb.	Nevada
23 Sep.	Nevada	17 Feb.	Nevada
		26 Mar.	Nevada

Date	Location	Date	Location
14 Apr.	Nevada	*China*	
5 May	Nevada	6 Oct.	Lop Nor
26 May	Nevada		
26 May	Nevada		
9 June	Nevada	**1984**	
3 Aug.	Nevada		
11 Aug.	Nevada	*USA*	
27 Aug.	Nevada	31 Jan.	Nevada
1 Sep.	Nevada	15 Feb.	Nevada
21 Sep.	Nevada	1 Mar.	Nevada
21 Sep.	Nevada	31 Mar.	Nevada
22 Sep.	Nevada	2 May	Nevada
9 Dec.	Nevada	16 May	Nevada
16 Dec.	Nevada	31 May	Nevada
		20 June	Nevada
		12 July	Nevada
USSR		25 July	Nevada
1 Feb.	N. of Caspian Sea*	2 Aug.	Nevada
24 Feb.	N. of Caspian Sea*	30 Aug.	Nevada
25 Feb.	N. of Caspian Sea*	13 Sep.	Nevada
2 Mar.	N. of Caspian Sea*	2 Oct.	Nevada
30 Mar.	Semipalatinsk	10 Nov.	Nevada
12 Apr.	Semipalatinsk	15 Dec.	Nevada
30 May	Semipalatinsk	20 Dec.	Nevada
12 June	Semipalatinsk		
24 June	Semipalatinsk		
10 July	S. Ural Mountains*	*USSR*	
10 July	S. Ural Mountains*	19 Feb.	Semipalatinsk
10 July	S. Ural Mountains*	7 Mar.	Semipalatinsk
28 July	Semipalatinsk	29 Mar.	Semipalatinsk
18 Aug.	Novaya Zemlya	15 Apr.	Semipalatinsk
11 Sep.	Semipalatinsk	25 Apr.	Semipalatinsk
24 Sep.	N. of Caspian Sea*	26 May	Semipalatinsk
24 Sep.	N. of Caspian Sea*	23 June	Semipalatinsk
24 Sep.	N. of Caspian Sea*	14 July	Semipalatinsk
24 Sep.	N. of Caspian Sea*	21 July	N. of Caspian Sea*
24 Sep.	N. of Caspian Sea*	21 July	N. of Caspian Sea*
24 Sep.	N. of Caspian Sea*	21 July	N. of Caspian Sea*
25 Sep.	Novaya Zemlya ·	21 July	N. of Caspian Sea*
6 Oct.	Semipalatinsk	11 Aug.	Ural Mountains*
26 Oct.	Semipalatinsk	25 Aug.	W. Siberia*
20 Nov.	Semipalatinsk	28 Aug.	Ural Mountains*
29 Nov.	Semipalatinsk	28 Aug.	Ural Mountains*
26 Dec.	Semipalatinsk	9 Sep.	Semipalatinsk
		15 Sep.	Semipalatinsk
UK		17 Sep.	SW Siberia*
22 Apr.	Nevada	18 Oct.	Semipalatinsk
		25 Oct.	Novaya Zemlya
France		27 Oct.	N. of Caspian Sea*
19 Apr.	Mururoa	27 Oct.	N. of Caspian Sea*
25 May	Mururoa	27 Oct.	Semipalatinsk
28 June	Mururoa	23 Nov.	Semipalatinsk
20 July	Mururoa	2 Dec.	Semipalatinsk
4 Aug.	Mururoa	16 Dec.	Semipalatinsk
3 Dec.	Mururoa	28 Dec.	Semipalatinsk
7 Dec.	Mururoa		

Date	Location	Date	Location
UK		*France*	
1 May	Nevada	30 Apr.	Mururoa
9 Dec.	Nevada	8 May	Mururoa
		3 June	Mururoa
France		7 June	Mururoa
8 May	Mururoa	24 Oct.	Mururoa
12 May	Mururoa	26 Oct.	Mururoa
12 June	Mururoa	24 Nov.	Mururoa
16 June	Mururoa	26 Nov.	Mururoa
27 Oct.	Mururoa		
2 Nov.	Mururoa		
1 Dec.	Mururoa		
6 Dec.	Mururoa	**1986**	
China		*USA*	
3 Oct.	Lop Nor	22 Mar.	Nevada
19 Dec.	Lop Nor	10 Apr.	Nevada
		20 Apr.	Nevada
		22 Apr.	Nevada
1985		21 May	Nevada
		5 June	Nevada
USA		17 July	Nevada
15 Mar.	Nevada	24 July	Nevada
23 Mar.	Nevada	4 Sep.	Nevada
2 Apr.	Nevada	11 Sep.	Nevada
6 Apr.	Nevada	30 Sep.	Nevada
2 May	Nevada	16 Oct.	Nevada
12 June	Nevada	14 Nov.	Nevada
12 June	Nevada	13 Dec.	Nevada
26 June	Nevada		
25 July	Nevada	*UK*	
14 Aug.	Nevada	25 June	Nevada
17 Aug.	Nevada		
27 Sep.	Nevada	*France*	
9 Oct.	Nevada	26 Apr.	Mururoa
9 Oct.	Nevada	6 May	Mururoa
12 Oct.	Nevada	27 May	Mururoa
16 Oct.	Nevada	30 May	Mururoa
28 Dec.	Nevada	10 Nov.	Mururoa
		12 Nov.	Mururoa
USSR		6 Dec.	Mururoa
10 Feb.	Semipalatinsk	10 Dec.	Mururoa
19 Apr.	. .*		
25 Apr.	Semipalatinsk		
15 June	Semipalatinsk		
30 June	Semipalatinsk	**1 Jan.–1 July 1987**	
11 July	Semipalatinsk		
18 July	N. European USSR*	*USA*	
20 July	Semipalatinsk	3 Feb.	Nevada
25 July	Semipalatinsk	11 Feb.	Nevada
		18 Mar.	Nevada
		18 Apr.	Nevada
UK		22 Apr.	Nevada
5 Dec.	Nevada	30 Apr.	Nevada

Date	Location	Date	Location
18 June	Nevada	*France*	
20 June	Nevada	5 May	Mururoa
30 June	Nevada	20 May	Mururoa
		6 June	Mururoa
USSR		21 June	Mururoa
26 Feb.	Semipalatinsk		
12 Mar.	Semipalatinsk	*China*	
3 Apr.	Semipalatinsk	5 June	Lop Nor
17 Apr.	Semipalatinsk		
19 Apr.	Ural Mountains*		
19 Apr.	Ural Mountains*		
6 May	Semipalatinsk		
6 June	Semipalatinsk		
20 June	Semipalatinsk		

Table 5. Estimated aggregate number of nuclear explosions 16 July 1945–1 July 1987

USA[a]	USSR	UK[a]	France	China	India	Total
824	606	40	144	30	1	1645

[a] All British tests from 1962 have been conducted jointly with the United States at the Nevada Test Site. Therefore, the number of US tests is actually higher than indicated here.

Sources used for the tables:

Swedish National Defence Research Institute (FOA), various estimates; Norris, R. S., Cochran, T. B. and Arkin, W. M., 'Known US nuclear tests July 1945 to 16 October 1986', *Nuclear Weapons Databook*, Working Paper no. 86–2 (Rev. 1) (Natural Resources Defense Council: Washington, DC, Oct. 1986); Sands, J. I., Norris, R. S. and Cochran, T. B., 'Known Soviet nuclear explosions, 1949–1985', *Nuclear Weapons Databook*, Working Paper no. 86–3 (Rev. 2 June 1986) (Natural Resources Defense Council: Washington, DC, Feb. 1986); Department of Scientific and Industrial Research (DSIR), Geophysics Division, New Zealand, various estimates; and US Geological Survey.

Select bibliography

Abarenkov, V., Semeiko, L. and Timerbayev, R. M., *Problems of Nuclear Disarmament* (Nauka: Moscow, 1983).

Beauchamp, K. G. (ed.), *Exploitation of Seismograph Networks*, NATO Advanced Study Institutes Series (Noordhoff: Leiden, 1975).

Blackaby, F. and Ferm, R., 'A comprehensive test ban and nuclear explosions in 1985', SIPRI, *World Armaments and Disarmament: SIPRI Yearbook 1986* (Oxford University Press: Oxford, 1986), pp. 115–29.

Bolt, B. A., *Nuclear Explosions and Earthquakes: The Parted Veil* (Freeman: San Francisco, 1976).

Bolt, B. A., 'Earthquake studies in the People's Republic of China', *Eos. Transactions of the American Geophysical Union*, vol. 55 (1974), pp. 108–17.

Campbell, B., Diven, B., McDonald, J., Ogle, B. and Scolman, T., 'Field testing—the physical proof of design principles', *Los Alamos Science*, Winter/Spring 1983, pp. 164–79.

Chidambaram, R. and Ramanna, R., *Some Studies on India's Peaceful Nuclear Explosion Experiment* (Bhabha Atomic Research Centre: Trombay, n.d.).

Cochran, T. B., Arkin, W. M. and Hoenig, M. M., *Nuclear Weapons Databook. Vol. I. US Nuclear Forces and Capabilities* (Ballinger, for Natural Resources Defense Council: Cambridge, 1984).

Cochran, T. B., Arkin, W. M., Norris, R. S. and Hoenig, M. M., *Nuclear Weapons Databook. Vol. II. US Nuclear Warhead Production* (Ballinger, for Natural Resources Defense Council: Cambridge, 1986).

Dahlman, O. and Israelson, H., *Monitoring Underground Nuclear Explosions* (Elsevier: Amsterdam, 1977).

Danielsson, B. and M.-T., *Poisoned Reign: French Nuclear Colonialism in the Pacific* (Penguin Books Australia: Victoria, 1986).

Davies, D., 'Peaceful applications of nuclear explosions', *Nuclear Energy and Nuclear Weapon Proliferation*, eds F. Barnaby, J. Goldblat, B. Jasani and J. Rotblat, SIPRI (Taylor and Francis: London, 1979), pp. 293–305.

Disarmament: Who Is Against? (Voenizdat: Moscow, 1983).

Emelyanov, V. S., 'On the peaceful use of nuclear explosions', *Nuclear Proliferation Problems*, ed. B. Jasani, SIPRI (Taylor and Francis: London, 1974), pp. 215–24.

Geneva Conference on the Discontinuance of Nuclear Weapon Tests. History and Analysis of Negotiations (Department of State, United States Disarmament Administration: Washington, DC, 1961).

Goldblat, J., 'The nuclear test ban debate', SIPRI, *World Armaments and Disarmament: SIPRI Yearbook 1972* (Almqvist & Wiksell, Stockholm, 1972), pp. 523–32.

Goldblat, J., *Ten Years of the Partial Test Ban Treaty, 1963–1973*, SIPRI Research Report No. 11, August 1973.

Goldblat, J., *French Nuclear Tests in the Atmosphere: The Question of Legality*, SIPRI, 1974.

Goldblat, J. (ed.), *Non-Proliferation: The Why and the Wherefore*, SIPRI (Taylor and Francis: London, 1985).

Goldblat, J., 'Multilateral arms control efforts', SIPRI, *SIPRI Yearbook 1987: World Armaments and Disarmament* (Oxford University Press, Oxford, 1987), pp. 389–94.

Heckrotte, W., 'A Soviet view of verification', *Bulletin of the Atomic Scientists*, vol. 43, no. 2 (Oct. 1986), pp. 12–15.

Husebye, E. S. and Mykkeltveit, S. (eds), *Identification of Seismic Sources—Earthquake or Underground Explosion*, NATO Advanced Study Institutes Series (D. Reidel Publishing Company: Dordrecht, 1981).

International Atomic Energy Agency, *Basic material for a further study of legal aspects of nuclear explosions for peaceful purposes*, IAEA Gov/COM.23/13, 30 June 1976, Vienna.

Jacobson, H. K. and Stein, E., *Diplomats, Scientists, and Politicians: The United States and the Nuclear Negotiations* (University of Michigan Law School: Ann Arbor, 1966).

Jönsson, C., *Soviet Bargaining Behavior: The Nuclear Test Ban Case* (Columbia University Press: New York, 1979).

Kalkstein, M., *International Arrangements and Control for the Peaceful Applications of Nuclear Explosives*, Stockholm Paper 4, SIPRI, 1970.

Kalyadin, A., Bogdanov, G. and Vorontsov, G., *Prevention of Nuclear War: Soviet Scientists' Viewpoints* (UNITAR, United Nations: New York, 1983).

Kalyadin, A., *The Problem of a Nuclear Weapon Test Ban and Proliferation* (Nauka: Moscow, 1976).

Kapitza, M. and Ivanenko, V., *Good Beginning* (Moscow, 1963).

Karkoszka, A., 'The comprehensive test ban', SIPRI, *World Armaments and Disarmaments: SIPRI Yearbook 1978* (Taylor & Francis, London, 1979), pp. 317–59.

Klein, J., 'Désarmement ou "arms control": la position française sous la Ve République', *Etudes Internationales*, vol. 3, no. 3 (1972), pp. 356–89.

Krass, A. S., *Verification: How Much is Enough?*, SIPRI (Taylor & Francis: London, 1985).

Lebedinsky, A. (ed.), *Soviet Scientists on the Danger of Nuclear Weapons Tests* (Moscow, 1959).

Leitenberg, M., 'Non-seismic detection of underground nuclear tests', SIPRI, *World Armaments and Disarmament: SIPRI Yearbook 1972* (Almqvist & Wiksell, Stockholm, 1972), pp. 437–60.

Meyer, S. M., *The Dynamics of Nuclear Proliferation* (University of Chicago Press: Chicago, 1984).

Morozov, I. (ed.), *Atomic Explosions for Peaceful Purposes* (in Russian) (Moscow, 1970).

Myrdal, A., *The Right to Conduct Nuclear Explosions: Political Aspects and Policy Proposals*, Stockholm Paper 6, SIPRI, 1975.

Neild, R., 'The test ban', SIPRI, *World Armaments and Disarmament: SIPRI Yearbook 1972* (Almqvist & Wiksell, Stockholm, 1972), pp. 389–436.

Pomeroy, P. W., Best, W. J. and McEvilly, T. V., 'Test ban treaty verification with regional data—a review', *Bulletin of the Seismological Society of America*, vol. 72 (1982).

Potter, W. C. (ed.), *Verification and Arms Control* (Lexington Books: Lexington, 1985).

Report of a New Zealand, Australian, and Papua New Guinea Scientific Mission to Mururoa Atoll (Ministry of Foreign Affairs: Wellington, 1984).

Seaborg, G., *Kennedy, Khrushchev and the Test Ban* (University of California Press: Berkeley, 1981).

Schelling, T. C. and Halperin, M. W., *Strategy and Arms Control* (Twentieth Century Fund: New York, 1961).

Shustov, V., *The Soviet Union and Problems of the Cessation of Nuclear Weapons Tests* (Atomizdat: Moscow, 1977).

Simpson, J., *The Independent Nuclear State* (Macmillan: London, 1984).

Simpson, J. (ed.), *Nuclear Proliferation: An Agenda for the 1990s* (Cambridge University Press: Cambridge, 1987).

SIPRI Seismic Study Group, *Seismic Methods for Monitoring Underground Explosions*, Stockholm Paper 2, SIPRI, 1969.

Spector, L. S., *The New Nuclear Nations* (Vintage Books, for Carnegie Endowment for International Peace: New York, 1985).

Spector, L. S., *Going Nuclear* (Ballinger, for Carnegie Endowment for International Peace: Cambridge, 1986).

Sykes, L. R. and Davis, D. M., 'The yields of Soviet strategic weapons', *Scientific American*, vol. 256, no. 1 (Jan. 1987), pp. 29–37.

Sykes, L. R. and Evernden, J. F., 'Seismic methods for verifying nuclear test bans', *Physics, Technology and the Nuclear Arms Race*, eds. D. W. Hafmeister and D. Schroeer (American Institute of Physics: New York, 1983).

Sykes, L. R. and Evernden, J. F., 'Verification of a comprehensive nuclear test ban', *Scientific American*, vol. 247, no. 4 (Oct. 1982), pp. 29–37.

Symonides, J., 'Mocarstwa nuklearne wobec problemu zakazu doświadczeń jadrowych', *Sprawy Miedzynarodowe* (Warsaw), no. 6 (1986), pp. 7–18.

Timerbayev, R. M., *Complete Prohibition on Nuclear Weapons Tests* (Nauka: Moscow, 1987).

Towpik, A., *Bezpieczeństwo miedzynarodowe a rozbrojenie* (Biblioteka Spraw Miedzynarodowych, PISM: Warsaw, 1970).

Tsipis, K., Hafemeister, D. W. and Janeway, P. (eds), *Arms Control Verification: The Technologies that Make it Possible* (Pergamon-Brassey's International Defense Publishers: Washington, DC, 1986).

United Nations, *Comprehensive Nuclear Test Ban, Report of the Secretary-General*, UN Document A/35/257, 23 May 1980.

Wieczorek, W., *Rozbrojenie—Teorİa i Praktyka* (Ksiazka i Wiedza: Warsaw, 1968).

Wright, M., *Disarm and Verify: An Explanation of the Central Difficulties and of National Policies* (Chatto and Windus: London, 1964).

Yorysh, A. and Lazarev, M., *Treaty Improving the Atmosphere* (Moscow, 1983).

Index